Lecture Notes in Computer Science   11933

More information about this series at http://www.springer.com/series/7410

Feng Liu · Jia Xu · Shouhuai Xu ·
Moti Yung (Eds.)

Science of Cyber Security

Second International Conference, SciSec 2019
Nanjing, China, August 9–11, 2019
Revised Selected Papers

 Springer

Editors
Feng Liu
Institute of Information Engineering
and School of Cybersecurity
University of Chinese Academy of Sciences
Beijing, China

Shouhuai Xu
Department of Computer Science
The University of Texas at San Antonio
San Antonio, TX, USA

Jia Xu
Nanjing University of Posts
and Telecommunications
Nanning, China

Moti Yung
Google and Columbia University
New York, NY, USA

ISSN 0302-9743   ISSN 1611-3349   (electronic)
Lecture Notes in Computer Science
ISBN 978-3-030-34636-2   ISBN 978-3-030-34637-9   (eBook)
https://doi.org/10.1007/978-3-030-34637-9

LNCS Sublibrary: SL4 – Security and Cryptology

This Springer imprint is published by the registered company Springer Nature Switzerland AG
The registered company address is: Gewerbestrasse 11, 6330 Cham, Switzerland

Preface

The second annual International Conference on Science of Cyber Security (SciSec 2019) took place in August 2019 in Nanjing, China. The mission of SciSec is to catalyze the research collaborations between the relevant scientific communities and disciplines that should work together in exploring the foundational aspects of Cybersecurity. We believe that this collaboration is needed in order to deepen our understanding of, and build a firm foundation for, the emerging Science of Cybersecurity discipline. SciSec is unique in appreciating the importance of multidisciplinary and interdisciplinary broad research efforts towards the ultimate goal of a sound Science of Cybersecurity, which attempts to deeply understand and systematize knowledge in the field of security.

To understand the goals of the conference, note that SciSec 2019 solicited high-quality, original research papers that can justifiably help achieve the ultimate goal of Science of Cybersecurity. Topics of interest included, but were not limited to:

- Cybersecurity Dynamics
- Cybersecurity Metrics and Their Measurements
- First-principle Cybersecurity Modeling and Analysis (e.g., Dynamical Systems, Control-Theoretic, Game-Theoretic Modeling, Logical and Verification methodologies)
- Cybersecurity Data Analytics
- Quantitative Risk Management for Cybersecurity
- Big Data for Cybersecurity
- Artificial Intelligence for Cybersecurity
- Machine Learning for Cybersecurity
- Economics Approaches for Cybersecurity
- Social Sciences Approaches for Cybersecurity
- Statistical Physics Approaches for Cybersecurity
- Complexity Sciences Approaches for Cybersecurity
- Experimental Cybersecurity
- Macroscopic Cybersecurity
- Statistics Approaches for Cybersecurity
- Human Factors for Cybersecurity
- Compositional Security
- Biology-inspired Approaches for Cybersecurity
- Synergistic Approaches for Cybersecurity
- Mechanisms for Solving Actual Cybersecurity Problems (like: Cryptographic Mechanisms, Formal Methods techniques)

SciSec 2019 was hosted by the Nanjing University of Posts and Telecommunications, Nanjing, China, August 9–11, 2019. The contributed works at the conference were selected from 62 submissions, from which the Program Committee selected 28 papers (20 full papers and 8 short papers) for presentation. These papers cover the following subjects: Artificial Intelligence for Cybersecurity, Machine Learning for Cybersecurity, and Mechanisms for Solving Actual Cybersecurity Problems (e.g., Blockchain, Attack, and Defense; Encryptions with Cybersecurity Applications). We anticipate that the topics covered by the program in the future will be more systematic and further diversified.

The committee further selected the paper titled "HoneyGadget: A Deception based ROP Detection Scheme" by Xin Huang, Fei Yan, Liqiang Zhang, and Kai Wang for the Student Distinguished Paper Award. The conference program also included three invited keynote talks: the first keynote titled "Layers of Abstraction and Layers of Obstruction: how what makes computing successful makes security hard" was delivered by Prof. Moti Yung, Google and Columbia University, USA; the second keynote titled "VRASED: Verifiable Remote Attestation for Simple Embedded Devices" was delivered by Prof. Gene Tsudik, University of California, USA; while the third keynote was titled "Advanced Threat Detection and Automated Response Using Machine Learning" and was delivered by Dr. Bo Liu, Anheng Information Technology Co., Ltd, China. The conference program presented a panel discussion on "Future Research Directions towards Science of Cyber Security."

We would like to thank all of the authors of the submitted papers for their interest in SciSec 2019. We also would like to thank the reviewers, keynote speakers, and participants for their contributions to the success of SciSec 2019. Our sincere gratitude further goes to the Program Committee, the Publicity Committee, the Journal Special Issue Chairs, the external reviewers, and the Organizing Committee, for their hard work and great efforts throughout the entire process of preparing and managing the event. Furthermore, we are grateful for the generous financial support from the Nanjing University of Posts and Telecommunications.

We hope that you will find the conference proceedings inspiring and that it will further help you in finding opportunities for your future research.

September 2019

Feng Liu
Jia Xu
Shouhuai Xu
Moti Yung

Organization

General Chair

Guo-Ping Jiang   Nanjing University of Posts and Telecommunications, China

PC Co-chairs

Feng Liu   Institute of Information Engineering, Chinese Academy of Sciences, China
Jia Xu   Nanjing University of Posts and Telecommunications, China
Shouhuai Xu   The University of Texas at San Antonio, USA
Moti Yung   Google and Columbia University, USA

Organization Committee Chair

Geng Yang   Nanjing University of Posts and Telecommunications, China

Publicity Co-chairs

Habtamu Abie   Norwegian Computing Center, Norway
Guen Chen   The University of Texas at San Antonio, USA
Wenlian Lu   Fudan University, China
Sheng Wen   Swinburne University of Technology, Australia
Xiaofan Yang   Chongqing University, China

Web Chair

Yaqin Zhang   Institute of Information Engineering, Chinese Academy of Sciences, China

Guest Editors for Systems Frontiers Special Issue Program Committee Members

Jingguo Wang   The University of Texas at Arlington, USA
Shouhuai Xu   The University of Texas at San Antonio, USA
Moti Yung   Google and Columbia University, USA

Program Committee Members Organizing Committee Members

Habtamu Abie	Norwegian Computing Centre, Norway
Luca Allodi	Eindhoven University of Technology, The Netherlands
Richard R. Brooks	Clemson University, USA
Qian Chen	The University of Texas at San Antonio, USA
Bruno Crispo	University of Trento, Italy
JianXi Gao	Rensselaer Polytechnic Institute, USA
Dieter Gollmann	Hamburg University of Technology, Germany
Arash Habibi Lashkari	University of Bruswick, Germany
Chenglu Jin	University of Conneticut, USA
Zbigniew Kalbarczyk	University of Illinois at Urbana-Champaign, USA
Wenlian Lu	Fudan University, China
Zhuo Lu	University of South Florida, USA
Sam Malek	University of California, Irvine, USA
Pratyusa K. Manadhata	Hewlett-Packard Labs, USA
Thomas Moyer	University of North Carolina at Charlotte, USA
Andrew Odlyzko	University of Minnesota, USA
Kouichi Sakurai	Kyushu University, Japan
M. Angela Sasse	University College London, UK
Nitesh Saxena	University of Alabama at Birmingham, USA
Lipeng Song	North University of China, China
Kun Sun	George Mason University, USA
Jingguo Wang	The University of Texas at Arlington, USA
Lingyu Wang	Concordia University, Canada
Zhi Wang	Nankai University, China
Sheng Wen	Swinburne University of Technology, Australia
Yang Xiang	Deakin University, Australia
Min Xiao	Nanjing University of Posts and Telecommunications, China
Jie Xu	University of Miami, USA
Maochao Xu	Illinois State University, USA
Fei Yan	Wuhan University, China
Guanhua Yan	Binghamton University and State University of New York, USA
Xiaofan Yang	Chongqing University, China
Yanfang Ye	West Virginia University, USA
Bo Zeng	University of Pittsburgh, USA
Yuan Zhang	Nanjing University, China
Jun Zhao	Carnegie Mellon University, USA
Sencun Zhu	Penn State University, USA
Cliff Zou	University of Central Florida, USA
Deqing Zou	Huazhong University of Science and Technology, China

Organizing Committee Members

Wei Zhang	Nanjing University of Posts and Telecommunications, China
Yun Li	Nanjing University of Posts and Telecommunications, China
Guozi Sun	Nanjing University of Posts and Telecommunications, China
Yurong Song	Nanjing University of Posts and Telecommunications, China
Min Xiao	Nanjing University of Posts and Telecommunications, China
Fengyu Xu	Nanjing University of Posts and Telecommunications, China

Sponsors

Contents

Blockchain, Attack and Defense

Encryption and Application

Artificial Intelligence for Cybersecurity

Cross-Domain Recommendation System Based on Tensor Decomposition for Cybersecurity Data Analytics

Yuan Wang[1,2], Jinzhi Wang[1], Jianhong Gao[1,2], Shengsheng Hu[1,2], Huacheng Sun[3], and Yongli Wang[3(✉)]

[1] State Grid Electric Power Research Institute Co., Ltd., Nanjing 211100, China
[2] China Realtime Database Co., Ltd., Nanjing 211100, China
[3] School of Computer Science and Technology, Nanjing University of Science and Technology, Nanjing 210094, China
305118154@qq.com, yongliwang@njust.edu.cn

Abstract. In the context of personalization e-commerce cyberspace based on massive data, the traditional single-domain recommendation algorithm is difficult to adapt to cross-domain information recommendation service. Collaborative filtering is a simple and common recommendation algorithm, but when the target domain is very sparse, the performance of collaborative filtering algorithm will seriously degrade. Cross domain recommendation is an effective way to solve this problem because it is made by means of the auxiliary data domain associated with the target data domain. Most of the existing cross-domain recommendation models are based on two-dimensional rating matrix, and much other dimension information is lost, which leads to a decrease in recommended accuracy. In this paper, we propose a cross-domain recommendation method based on tensor decomposition, which can reduce the sparseness of data and improve the diversity and accuracy. It extracts the scoring patterns in different fields to fill the vacancy value in the target domain by transfer learning method. Many experiments on three public real data sets show that the proposed model's recommendation accuracy is superior to some of the most advanced recommendation models. It can be applied to large-scale cross-domain information recommendation service and cybersecurity data analytics.

Keywords: Cloud recommendation service · Collaborative filter · Cross-domain

1 Introduction

Recommender systems are becoming more and more popular because it can help users find items that they interest in (such as movies, books, music, etc.), and it can relieve the problem of information overload. In recent decades, many researchers have developed some recommendation systems [1, 2], such as Amazon, LastFm, Movie-Lens, but there are still some challenges, such as cold start [3–5] and data sparsity problems [6].

© Springer Nature Switzerland AG 2019
F. Liu et al. (Eds.): SciSec 2019, LNCS 11933, pp. 3–19, 2019.
https://doi.org/10.1007/978-3-030-34637-9_1

The recommendation results from a large number of recommender systems are only single-domain, and in fact, there is a lot of dependency and correlation between different domains. The information in one domain can be improved by combining by other domains rather than just thinking about it independently. For example, if some users like the singer's song (music as the source domain), then some movies (as target domains) can be recommended to the users which are performed by the singer. This method can solve the cold-start problem [7], and data sparsity problems [8] in target domains. Therefore, cross domain recommendation has become a hot topic in recommender systems recently.

Currently, cross domain recommendations usually require that the rating information from different domains shares users and items, but it rarely exist in real-world scenarios. This paper focuses on cross domain recommender systems without shared users and items. In this paper, a method of cross domain recommendation is proposed, which can be used to construct association between users in different domains. Firstly, the redundant information is extracted from the auxiliary domain, then the tensor is constructed by using the information after clustering, after that we can construct the rating model. The next step is to transfer the rating model obtained from the source domain to the target domain to fill the target domain's vacancy value.

The main contributions of this paper are as follows:

(1) Extract the rating model with tensor decomposition on the clustering level.
(2) A recommended approach is proposed to transfer the rating model of auxiliary domain to target domains.

The structure of this paper is as follows, Sect. 2 discusses the related work of tensor decomposition and cross-domain systems. Section 3 discusses the definition of problem about tensor and cross-domain. Section 4 describes the details of the proposed method. Section 5 presents the experiments and analysis, and uses relevant experiments to validate the feasibility of the proposed method. Finally, we conclude in Sect. 6.

2 Related Work

Cross-domain recommendations have become an important means of resolving cold start and alleviate sparsity problems. Some researchers have studied cross-domain related work as defined in [9], where there are two cross-domain recommended tasks.

The first task is to use the knowledge of the source domain to improve the quality of the target domain recommendation. Li et al. [10] proposed a cross-domain collaborative filter method to alleviate sparsity. They extract the rating model between the user items on the cluster level, and then they transferred the knowledge of auxiliary domain to the target domain in the form of codebook. Kumar [11, 12] and others proposed a cross-domain topic model to alleviate the sparsity of data. They assume that each domain has N different topics, each user in these topics subject to a distribution. Using topic matching for cross-domain collaborative recommendation rather than traditional matching by shared authors. Karatzoglou et al. [13] proposed a method of using machine learning to transfer dense source domain knowledge to sparse target areas to solve data sparsity problems. They have developed a transfer learning technique to extract knowledge from multiple domains that contain rich data, and then generate recommendations for sparse target domains. This technique studies the relevance and linear integration of all the source domain rating models into one model that makes it possible to predict the rating model that is unknown to the target domain. Enrich et al. [14] proposed the use of user tags as a bridge between different domains, from which they learn the user's rating model (for example, how the user rating in the source domain, in other words, the relationship between these tags and rating) to improve the performance of target domain.

The second task is recommending items in different domains jointly. Li et al. [15] proposed a method of sharing knowledge by pooling multidisciplinary rating data. They created a rating matrix which is the multidisciplinary shared latent factor, and then the shared rating matrix was extended to a general cluster rating model called rating matrix generation model. The rating matrix of any relevant user can be generated or predicted by this generation model and user-item joint mixed model. Shi et al. [16] proposed a label-induced collaborative cross-domain recommendation. They use user-generated tags as a cross-domain link. These tags can be used to calculate the similarity between cross-domain users and the similarity between items, and then the similarity is integrated into a matrix decomposition model to improve the recommended effect. Gao et al. [17] proposed a clustering latent factor model (CLFM) based on a joint non-negative matrix framework. Unlike [10], they use CLFM not only to learn multi-domain shared rating models, but also to learn specific domain clustering rating models from each domain that contains important information. Hu [18] proposed modeling the user-item-domain as a third-order tensor. Then, they use the standard CANDECOMP/ PARAFAC (CP) tensor decomposition model to extract the relationship between user factors and items factors from different domains, so that we can predict the rating in each domain.

This paper focuses on the first cross-domain recommendation task. By transferring the cross-domain multi-dimensional rating model to solve the first task.

3 Problems and Definitions

The main problem of cross-domain recommendation is that there is no shared coverage information, as in [19]. In this paper, we use the tensor decomposition to extract the rating models of the two domains and then make use of the cross-domain approach of the transferring model to solve the sparsity problem and cold-start problem [20]. This section focuses on the definition of tensor decomposition and cross-domain transfer learning [21–23] (Table 1).

Table 1. Notations

Symbol	Description
$\mathcal{X}_{\text{aux}}$	auxiliary domain
$\mathcal{X}_{\text{tgt}}$	target domain
$\mathcal{X}_{\text{tgt}_{ijk}}$	element of tensor $\mathcal{X}_{\text{tgt}}$
S	rating model
U	factors of user matrix
I	factors of item matrix
T	factors of tag matrix
$\mathcal{X}_{(n)}$	n-mode unfolded version of $\mathcal{X}$
$U^{(n)}$	the n-th factor of N-th order tensor
$\times_n$	n-mode product of a tensor by matrix
$\mathcal{W}_{ijk}$	binary weights tensor

3.1　The Concept of Tensor

Formally, the tensor is a multidimensional matrix. The order of a tensor is the number of dimensions, also called the mode. The tensor in this paper is represented by bold script letters, such as $\mathcal{X}$. The matrix is represented in bold letters, such as X. The vector is represented in bold lowercase letters, for example x. Elements are represented by lowercase letters, for example $x_{i,j,k}$. The i-th row of the matrix X is expressed as $X_{i,*}$, the j-th column is expressed as $X_{*,j}$, the element (i,j) is expressed as $X_{i,j}$.

Definition 1 (matrix unfolding). The mode expansion operation of the tensor is to map the tensor into a matrix form, such as $X_{(2)}$ is a representation of $\mathcal{X}^{I \times J \times K} \rightarrow X^{J \times (IK)}$. An N-order tensor $\mathcal{A}$ as $\mathcal{A} \in \mathbb{R}^{I_1 \cdots I_N}$, have the elements $a_{i_1,\ldots,i_N}$. Expanding the third order tensor in three directions to get $A_{(1)} \in \mathbb{R}^{I_1 \times (I_2 I_3)}$, $A_{(2)} \in \mathbb{R}^{I_2 \times (I_2 I_3)}$, $A_{(3)} \in \mathbb{R}^{(I_1 I_2) \times I_3}$, here $A_{(1)}, A_{(2)}, A_{(3)}$ is the *mode-1, mode-2, mode-3* expansion of the $\mathcal{A}$.

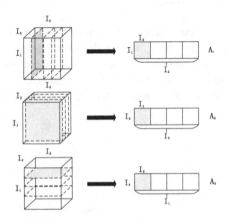

Fig. 1. Tensor mode-n matrix expansion

Definition 2 (mode product). The product's result of the n-mode is the tensor $\mathcal{A} \in \mathbb{R}^{I_1 \times I_2 \times \dots \times I_N}$ multiplied by the matrix $U \in \mathbb{R}^{J_n \times I_n}$ in the n-th mode, represent as $\mathcal{A} \times_n U$, the size of the result is $\mathbb{R}^{I_1 \times \dots \times J_n \times \dots \times I_N}$. And the mode product satisfies the exchange law and the union law [23]:

$$\mathcal{A} \times_n A \times_m B = (\mathcal{A} \times_n A) \times_m B = \mathcal{A} \times_m B \times_n A \tag{1}$$

3.2 Tensor Decomposition

There are many ways to decompose tensor. In this paper, we use the HOSVD. Higher order singular value decomposition (HOSVD) is an extension of the concept of matrix singular value decomposition (SVD). For a mode-n expansion, the singular value decomposition on two dimensions can be rewritten as follows:

$$U = S \times_1 U^{(1)} \times_2 U^{(2)} \tag{2}$$

By extension, the third order tensor HOSVD can be written as follows:

$$\mathcal{A} = \mathcal{S} \times_1 U^{(1)} \times_2 U^{(2)} \times_3 U^{(3)} \tag{3}$$

HOSVD decomposition can decompose a N-order tensor into a core tensor and N factor matrixes product in the form of Fig. 1. Figure 1 is a third-order tensor decomposition of a tensor kernel and three factor matrixes, the tensor core $\mathcal{S}$ can be seen as the compression of the original tensor $\mathcal{A}$ (Fig. 2).

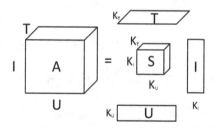

Fig. 2. HOSVD decomposition of third - order tensor

When the factor matrix is determined, the core tensor can be calculated by tensor and factor matrix:

$$\hat{S} = \mathcal{A} \times_1 U^{(1)^T} \times_2 U^{(2)^T} \times_3 U^{(3)^T} \tag{4}$$

Then use the formula (1) can get the low rank tensor approximation, fill the vacancy value and compress the data.

3.3   Recommendation with HOSVD

For a rating system that contains tags, it can be defined as a relational structure $\mathbb{F} := (U, I, T, Y)$, where,

U, I, T are Non-empty finite set, elements are users, items, tags,

Y is an observable relationship of triples, $Y \subseteq U \times I \times T$,

$(u, i, T_{u,i})$ is a user's tag for a item i, $u \in U, i \in I$ and non-empty set $T_{u,i} := \{t \in T | (u, i, t) \in Y\}$,

Y represents the ternary relationship among user, item and tags, expressed with a binary tensor $\mathcal{A} = (a_{u,i,t}) \in \mathbb{R}^{|U| \times |I| \times |T|}$, where with a tag is 1, others 0.

$$a_{u,i,t} := \begin{cases} 1, (u, i, t) \in Y \\ 0, else \end{cases} \tag{5}$$

At this point, the tensor decomposition is expressed as:

$$\hat{\mathcal{A}} := \hat{S} \times_u \hat{U} \times_i \hat{I} \times_t \hat{T} \tag{6}$$

$\hat{U}, \hat{I}, \hat{T}$ are the user, item, label low rank feature matrix factors, their latent factor dimensions are k_U, k_I, k_T, and the tensor kernel $\hat{S} \in \mathbb{R}^{k_U \times k_I \times k_T}$ represents the relationship between these latent factors.

The optimization function of this model is $\hat{\theta} := (\hat{S}, \hat{U}, \hat{I}, \hat{T})$.

The basic idea of HOSVD [22] is to minimize the estimation error, we can use the mean square error as an optimization function

$$\arg \min_{\hat{\theta}} \sum_{(u,i,t) \in Y} (\hat{a}_{u,i,t} - a_{u,i,t})^2 \tag{7}$$

When the parameters are optimized, the following formula can be used to predict:

$$\hat{a}(u, i, t) := \sum_{\tilde{u}=1}^{k_U} \sum_{\tilde{i}=1}^{k_I} \sum_{\tilde{t}=1}^{k_t} \hat{s}_{\tilde{u}, \tilde{i}, \tilde{t}} \cdot \hat{u}_{u, \tilde{u}} \cdot \hat{i}_{i, \tilde{i}} \cdot \hat{t}_{t, \tilde{t}} \tag{8}$$

where $\hat{U} = [\hat{u}_{u, \tilde{u}}]_{u=1,...,k_U}^{u=1,...,U}, \hat{I} = [\hat{i}_{i, \tilde{i}}]_{i=1,...,k_I}^{i=1,...,I}, \hat{T} = [\hat{t}_{t, \tilde{t}}]_{t=1,...,k_T}^{t=1,...,T}$. The feature dimension of the feature matrix is denoted by $\sim$, and the element of the characteristic matrix is denoted by $\wedge$.

3.4 Cross-Domain Recommendation

Table 2. Notations

Symbol	Description
D_S	source domain
D_T	target domain
U_S	set of users in source domain
U_T	set of users in target domain
I_S	set of users in source domain
I_T	set of items in target domain
I_{ST}	overlap of items between source and target domain
U_{ST}	overlap of users between source and target domain
R_S	rating matrix of source domain
R_T	rating matrix of target domain

There exists four different cross- domain scenarios, these are illustrated in Fig. 3 (Table 2):

(a) User overlap. There are some common users across different domains and these users have ratings in both domains, i.e., $U_{ST} \neq \varnothing$.
(b) Item overlap. There are some common items across different domains and these items have been rated by some users in two domains, i.e., $I_{ST} \neq \varnothing$.
(c) Full overlap. The two domains have overlap both among users and items, i.e. $U_{ST} \neq \varnothing$ and $I_{ST} \neq \varnothing$
(d) No overlap. There is no overlap of both users and items between two domains, i.e. $U_{ST} = \varnothing$ and $I_{ST} = \varnothing$

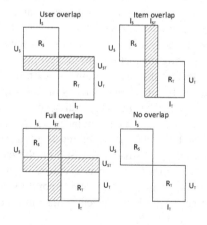

Fig. 3. Cross-domain scenarios

Most collaborative filtering algorithm can be applied in the first three scenarios to solve the cross-domain recommendation problem. However, the last scenario is seldom solved due to the lack of any overlap of users or items in two different domains. In this paper, we mainly focus on cross-domain recommendation in the last scenario. As is shown in Fig. 4, it mainly consists of the following two types:

(1) Integrate knowledge. Knowledge is integrated from multiple source domains into the target domain.
(2) Knowledge transfer. Knowledge is recommended by association or migration.

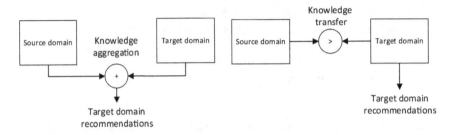

Fig. 4. Cross-domain recommendation classification

Shared latent factors or transferring rating model are usually combined with matrix decomposition or tensor decomposition.

3.5 Transfer Learning

The latent factor model is a popular method for collaborative filtering (CF). The users' preferences and items attributes in these models are usually very sparse and can be represented by the latent factors in the data. In the collaborative filtering system based on latent factor analysis, the potential user preferences and items attributes can be captured and matched well. There are two approaches of latent factor transfer learning: adaptation models and union models. The former is using the source domain to learn the latent factors, then integrating the factors into the recommended model of the target domain. The latter is to integrate the two domains to learn the latent factor.

In addition to sharing the latent factors of users or items there is another popular way for knowledge transfer learning. In many real scenes, even if the users and the items is different, similar domain still have similar users' preferences and popularity. The potential association can be a set of user preferences for a set of items, called rating models. The method proposed in this paper is based on the method of extracting the rating model from the source domain to the target domain. As shown in Fig. 6, the source and target domain shown in the figure correspond to the rating matrix of the user-item. The mode extraction is done by tensor decomposition, with more information can improve accuracy (Fig. 5).

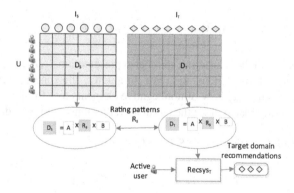

Fig. 5. Shared rating model cross-domain recommendation

4 Cross-Domain with Tensor Decomposition

The method proposed in this paper is divided into two stages, the first stage extracts the post-clustering rating model from the auxiliary domain, and then, the second stage transfers the rating mode of the first stage to the target domain to fill the target domain's vacancy value.

4.1 Extract Rating Mode

In a collaborative filtering system, the same preference users and the items with similar attributes behaves similarly. Therefore, the users and the items can be clustered, and the clustered rating tensor only contains the cluster information of the users and the items which can remove the redundant information of the original rating tensor. On this basis, to represent the original rating tensor only need to retain the clustered ID without considering other information.

Definition 3 (Rating mode, RatingKernel). RatingKernel is a tensor and its size is $k_U \times k_I \times k_T$, which compresses the original score tensor with k_U user clusters and k_I item clusters and k_T tag clusters. Analog codebook in [10], but with difference, the mode in this paper is that the rating model based on the tensor kernel, which retains more information, and the method of mode extraction and migration has a wider range of applications.

Ideally, if user, item, tag are the same in the same cluster, you only need to select a pair from the cluster user, item, tag to build the RatingKernel. However, the elements in the same cluster can not be exactly the same. It is common practice to select the cluster center for each cluster to represent the cluster. In this case, it is necessary to simultaneously cluster the users, the items and the tags. For the construction of RatingKernel, only need to retain the user and item cluster ID, in which case you can choose any clustering algorithm. The auxiliary rating tensor can be decomposed as follows:

$$\min\left\|\mathcal{X}_{aux} - \mathcal{S} \times_u \widehat{U} \times_i \widehat{I} \times_t \widehat{T}\right\|_F^2 \qquad (9)$$

The current users, items clustering number representation U, I, T, can not express the literal meaning of user, item, tag. For simplicity, this paper uses binary data representation by setting each row of nonnegative elements to 1 for the remainder of 0. These binary clustering matrix from the auxiliary rating tensor are recorded as U_{aux}, I_{aux} and T_{aux}.

The way to build a rating mode $\mathcal{S}$ is as follows:

$$\mathcal{S} = \mathcal{X} \times_1 U_{aux}^{(1)^T} \times_2 I_{aux}^{(2)^T} \times_3 T_{aux}^{(3)^T} \qquad (10)$$

Algorithm 1 Extract rating mode

Input: The initial tensor $\mathcal{X}_{aux} \in \mathbb{R}^{I_1 \times I_2 \times I_3}$ with user, tag, and item dimensions. k_U, k_I and k_T : The approximate tensor $\widehat{\mathcal{X}}_{aux}$ left leading eigenvectors of each dimension, respectively.

Output: $\mathcal{S}$

1: Initialize core tensor $\mathcal{S}$ and left singular vectors $U_{k_U}^{(1)}, I_{k_I}^{(2)}, T_{k_T}^{(3)}$ of A_1, A_2 and A_3, respectively.

2: **repeat**

3: $\mathcal{S} = \mathcal{X}_{aux} \times_1 U_{k_U}^{(1)^T} \times_2 I_{k_I}^{(2)^T} \times_3 T_{k_T}^{(3)^T}$

4: $\widehat{\mathcal{X}}_{aux} = \mathcal{S} \times_1 U_{k_U}^{(1)} \times_2 I_{k_I}^{(2)} \times_3 T_{k_T}^{(3)}$

5: $U_{k_U}^{(1)} \leftarrow k_U$ leading left singular vectors of A_1

6: $I_{k_I}^{(2)} \leftarrow k_I$ leading left singular vectors of A_2

7: $T_{k_T}^{(3)} \leftarrow k_T$ leading left singular vectors of A_3

8: **until** $\left\|\mathcal{X}_{aux} - \widehat{\mathcal{X}}_{aux}\right\|^2$ ceases to improve **OR** maximum iterations reached

9: **return** $\mathcal{S}$

In Algorithm 1, the complexity of calculating tensor core on line 3 is the same as the complexity of calculating the approximate tensor on line 4 $O\left(\Pi_{i=1}^3 I_i\right)$. Line 5, 6, 7 are the process of each loop SVD expansion, and the complexity is $O\left(I_1 k_U^2 + I_2 k_I^2 + I_3 k_T^2\right)$, so the overall complexity is $O\left(T(2\Pi_{i=1}^3 I_i + I_1 k_U^2 + I_2 k_I^2 + I_3 k_T^2)\right)$, T is that the number of iterations, several iterations can be convergence. So you can automatically initialize multiple times to obtain better local minimum. Since the tensor dimension is much larger than the dimension of the shared pattern, the approximation is given $O\left(T\Pi_{i=1}^3 I_i\right)$, depending on the tensor dimension.

The remaining task is choosing the number k_U, k_I and k_T of clusters user, item, tag. The number of clusters, that is, the number of latent factors. The higher feature dimension will increase the computational complexity. When the number of clusters is too small, the construction data is insufficient, resulting in the algorithm losing too much effective information. Therefore, the choice of the appropriate RatingKernel size not only need to be fully compressed so that the calculation can also fully represent most of the original information, the experimental part of the experimental scene will verify the number of clusters.

4.2   Transfer Rating Model

After gaining the rating model S, the rating model can be transferred from X_{aux} to X_{tgt}. The clusters of *user, item, tag* in the auxiliary domain task are implicitly related to these in the target domain task. X_{tgt} can be reconstructed by the extended rating model, for example, we can use the 3-dimensional matrix factor in the rating model as base to combine. In the rating mode, the combination behavior of *user, item, tag* in the representation is similar to these in X_{aux}.

The reconstruction process of X_{tgt} is to extend the RatingKernel because it reduces the difference between the observation rating tensor X_{tgt} and the reconstruction rating tensor on the loss function (the square loss function used in this paper). Here, we apply the binary weight matrix W whose size equivalent to X_{tgt} to cover the unobserved elements. When $[X_{tgt}]_{ijk}$ has been rated $W_{ijk} = 1$ others $W_{ijk} = 0$. Finally, the objective function only includes the squared difference of the observed elements.

The MF (Matrix Factorization) method defines the loss function as follows:

$$\text{L}\left(\widehat{X}_{\text{tgt}}, X_{\text{tgt}}\right) := \min_{\widehat{U}_{tgt},\widehat{I}_{tgt},\widehat{T}_{tgt}} \left|\left|\left[X_{tgt} - S \times_u \widehat{U}_{tgt} \times_i \widehat{I}_{tgt} \times_t \widehat{T}_{tgt}\right] \circ W\right|\right|_F^2 \qquad (11)$$

The direct minimization of the loss function leads to overfitting, so the addition of a regular term to the objective function is considered, and the F norm regular term for a given matrix factor $U_{tgt}, I_{tgt}, T_{tgt}$ is expressed as follows:

$$\Omega\left[U_{tgt}, I_{tgt}, T_{tgt}\right] := \frac{1}{2}\left[\lambda_U ||U_{tgt}||_F^2 + \lambda_I ||I_{tgt}||_F^2 + \lambda_I ||I_{tgt}||_F^2\right] \qquad (12)$$

The objective function after adding the regular term is:

$$\min_{\widehat{X}_{\text{tgt}}} \text{L}\left(\widehat{X}_{\text{tgt}}, X_{\text{tgt}}\right) + \Omega\left[U_{tgt}, I_{tgt}, T_{tgt}\right] \qquad (13)$$

Algorithm 2 Transfer rating mode

Input $\mathcal{X}_{tgt} \in \mathbb{R}^{p \times q \times r}, k_U, k_I, k_T, \mathcal{S}$
Output $\widetilde{\mathcal{X}}_{tgt}$

1: Initialize $U_{tgt} \in \mathbb{R}^{p \times k_U}, I_{tgt} \in \mathbb{R}^{q \times k_I}, T_{tgt} \in \mathbb{R}^{r \times k_T}$ with small random values.
2: Set $t = t_0$
3: **While** (i, j, k) in $\mathcal{X}_{tgt}$ do
4: $\qquad\qquad\qquad \eta \leftarrow \frac{1}{\sqrt{t}} \ and \ t \leftarrow t+1$
5: $\qquad\qquad\qquad \widehat{\mathcal{X}}_{tgt} = \mathcal{S} \times_U U_{tgt_{i\bullet}} \times_I I_{tgt_{j\bullet}} \times_T T_{tgt_{k\bullet}}$
6: $\qquad\qquad\qquad U_{tgt_{i\bullet}} \leftarrow U_{tgt_{i\bullet}} - \eta \lambda_U U_{tgt_{i\bullet}} - \eta \partial_{U_{tgt_{i\bullet}}} L(\widehat{\mathcal{X}}_{tgt}, \mathcal{X}_{tgt})$
7: $\qquad\qquad\qquad I_{tgt_{j\bullet}} \leftarrow I_{tgt_{j\bullet}} - \eta \lambda_I I_{tgt_{j\bullet}} - \eta \partial_{I_{tgt_{j\bullet}}} L(\widehat{\mathcal{X}}_{tgt}, \mathcal{X}_{tgt})$
8: $\qquad\qquad\qquad T_{tgt_{k\bullet}} \leftarrow T_{tgt_{k\bullet}} - \eta \lambda_T T_{tgt_{k\bullet}} - \eta \partial_{T_{tgt_{k\bullet}}} L(\widehat{\mathcal{X}}_{tgt}, \mathcal{X}_{tgt})$
9: **End while**
10: Calculate the filled-in rating matrix $\widetilde{\mathcal{X}}_{tgt}$ using
$\widetilde{\mathcal{X}}_{tgt} = \mathcal{W} \circ \mathcal{X}_{tgt} + [1 - \mathcal{W}] \circ [\mathcal{S} \times_u \widehat{U}_{tgt} \times_i \widehat{I}_{tgt} \times_t \widehat{T}_{tgt}]$

For the optimization of the objective function, the random gradient reduction (SGD) can be used to optimize as soon as possible in order to face the ever-increasing data set.

In line 2 of Algorithm 2, the approximate tensor complexity is approximated $O(pqr)$. Line 6, 7, 8 use the random gradient descent method. In each loop an element is updated once, it can be done in the process of one element traversal and the complicity is $O(pk_U + qk_I + rk_T)$. Therefore, the overall computational complexity is $O(pqr(pqr + pk_U + qk_I + rk_T))$, because the algorithm can be done within one traversal, so we can do multiple experiments to take the mean.

The value of the objective function represents the correlation of the target domain and the source domain. The smaller the value, the more relevant the rating model. In contrast, larger values suggest that weak correlations lead to negative transitions. We can make recommendations after filling the vacancy value.

5   Experiments

In order to validate the efficiency of the tensor decomposition model proposed in this paper, a lot of experiments will be performed to verify the performance on three data sets and to compare with several advanced recommendation methods. This experiment evaluates the performance of the algorithm with MAE (mean absolute error) as a measure. We use matlab to program this algorithm, the experimental environment is shown in Table 3.

Table 3. Linux cluster experimental environment

Nodes	Amount	CPU	RAM	Hard-Disk
manage node	1	Xeon2.0 GHz*64*8	128 GB	512 GB*2
compute node	6	Xeon2.3 GHz*64*6	64 GB	512 GB
storage node	6	Xeon2.4 GHz*64*6	31 GB	512 GB

5.1 Dataset

We tested based on the following three common real data sets: MovieLens [24] data set, containing 943 users, 1682 movies and more than 1 million scoring data (range 1 to 5); EachMovie dataset, containing 72916 users, 6214 movies and more than 2 million scoring data (range 1 to 6, this paper will be mapped to 1 to 5); Book-Crossing data set [25], containing 278858 users, 271379 books and more than 100 million Score data (range 0 to 9, this map will be mapped to 1 to 5). In the experiment, 70% of the users in the above data and their rating were used as training data samples, and the remaining part was used as the test sample. For cross-domain experiments, EachMovie was set as the source domain, MovieLens and Book-Crossing as the test environment for the target domain. The experiment was repeated 10 times in each test environment and the average value was calculated as the experimental result.

This paper chooses the other 3 related algorithms to compare with the algorithm:

UPCC. Recommending items for similar users by the Pearson correlation coefficient;

RMGM (rating-matrix generative model). As the current best cross-domain rec-ommended algorithm to test cross-domain recommended performance.

CBT (codebook transfer). An advanced cross-domain collaborative filtering model, assuming that a rating model is shared between domains and uses a post-clustering codebook to describe a shared rating model and then transfer the information with the codebook.

TKT (Tensor kernel transfer). The method proposed in this paper, using the clustering level of the tensor kernel as model for cross-domain migration.

All experimental tests use MAE (mean absolute error) as a measure, the smaller the value of MAE, the better the performance of the algorithm. MAE is calculated as follows:

$$\mathrm{MAE} = \frac{\sum_{i \in T_E} \left| r_i - r_i^* \right|}{|T_E|} \tag{19}$$

5.2 Experimental Results

In this paper, we verified the effect of this algorithm in cross-domain recommendation. Randomly we select 300 users and ratings from each data set as training set (ML300 means 300 from the MovieLens data set, BC300 means 300 from Book-Crossing), and 200 more as test set. For each test user, we consider the number of different scores, such as 5, 10, 15 scores recorded as (Given5, Given10, Given15), the other scores used to assess. Since that waRMGM, CBT and other experimental latent factor space (also the number of clusters) set to 50, in this paper in order to simplify the experimental process, the experimental clustering latent factor space are set to the same $R = k_U = k_I = k_T = 50$. Followed by the experimental analysis of is the analysis of the value R.

Table 4. Average MAE of 10 experiments

Training set	Method	Given5	Given10	Given15
ML300	UPCC	0.9347	0.8752	0.8631
	RMGM	0.8387	0.7933	0.7827
	CBT	0.8715	0.8571	0.8413
	TKT	**0.8352**	**0.7738**	**0.7693**
BC300	UPCC	0.6931	0.7172	0.6975
	RMGM	0.6423	0.6214	0.6012
	CBT	0.6179	0.6038	0.5881
	TKT	**0.6087**	**0.5975**	**0.5793**

It can be seen from the results in Table 4 that the effect of the method in this paper is better than that of other comparison methods on all test sets. By CBT, RMGM is better than UPCC, we can know that cross-domain can improve the recommendation accuracy. RMGM and CBT extract the two-dimensional matrix scoring modes in different fields. TKT makes full use of the ternary relationship between tag information and user items, and learns from the source domain to learn in the target domain to adapt to the specificity of the target domain. From the test results we can see that by adding the latent factor dimensions of the shared model, we can improve the recommendation accuracy and alleviate the sparsity of the target area.

The effect of the algorithm is different from the value of R. In this paper, the results of different latent factor space selection are as follows:

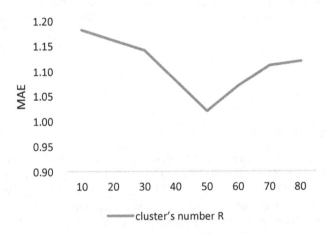

Fig. 6. Effects of the cluster's number

It can be seen from Fig. 7 that the average absolute error MAE of the recommended result increases with the number of latent factors increasing and the optimal effect is achieved at the factor is about 50, and as the number of factors increases, the MAE rise that may because of the overfitting leading to a decrease in recommended accuracy.

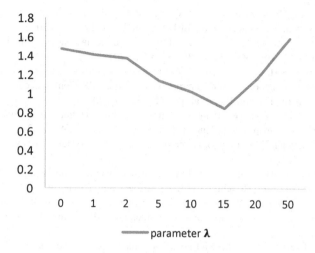

Fig. 7. Effects of parameter λ

λ reflects the specificity of the target domain, so we need to select the appropriate λ to avoid over-fitting or under-fitting. Figure 7 is based on EachMovie as the source domain MovieLens as the target domain, R = 50, we select the experimental results of Given10. From the figure we can see that the larger λ which will weaken of the source domain of the model, the smaller λ will produce a greater error. Under this experiment set, when it takes 15 can get good experimental results.

6 Conclusions

In this paper, we propose a novel cross-domain collaborative filtering method, which can be used to disseminate useful knowledge from the auxiliary rating tensor to supplement other sparse target domains by sharing the tensor rating model. The knowledge is transferred in the form of a rating model, and the rating mode is compressed into a rich and compact representation by learning the clustered user scoring mode from the auxiliary domain. Thus, sparse target domains can be reconstructed by extending the rating model. Experimental results show that rating mode transferring can be significantly better than many of the most advanced methods. Therefore, it is possible to obtain additional useful information from the source domain to help the target domain.

In the future work can use a variety of optimization techniques to optimize the process of clustering and tensor decomposition process. We can try to use different similarity measures to improve recommendation for cybersecurity data analytics.

References

1. Wang, Y., Yin, G., Cai, Z., et al.: A trust-based probabilistic recommendation model for social networks. J. Netw. Comput. Appl. **55**, 59–67 (2015)

2. Liu, H., Xia, F., Chen, Z., et al.: TruCom: exploiting domain-specific trust networks for multicategory item recommendation. IEEE Syst. J. **11**(1), 295–304 (2015)
3. Qiu, T., Chen, G., Zhang, Z.K., et al.: An item-oriented recommendation algorithm on cold-start problem. EPL (Europhys. Lett.) **95**(5), 58–63 (2011)
4. Zhou, K., Yang, S.H., Zha, H.: Functional matrix factorizations for cold-start recommendation. In: Proceedings of the 34th International ACM SIGIR Conference on Research and Development in Information Retrieval, pp. 315–324. ACM (2011)
5. Bobadilla, J.S., Ortega, F., Hernando, A., et al.: A collaborative filtering approach to mitigate the new user cold start problem. Knowl. Based Syst. **26**, 225–238 (2012)
6. Bobadilla, J., Ortega, F., Hernando, A., et al.: Recommender systems survey. Knowl. Based Syst. **46**, 109–132 (2013)
7. Abel, F., Herder, E., Houben, G.J., et al.: Cross-system user modeling and personalization on the social web. In: User Modeling and User-Adapted Interaction, pp. 1–41 (2013)
8. Robillard, M.P., Maalej, W., Walker, R.J., Zimmermann, T. (eds.): Recommendation Systems in Software Engineering. Springer, Heidelberg (2014). https://doi.org/10.1007/978-3-642-45135-5
9. Cantador, I., Cremonesi, P.: Tutorial on cross-domain recommender systems. In: Proceedings of the 8th ACM Conference on Recommender Systems, pp. 401–402. ACM (2014)
10. Li, B., Yang, Q., Xue, X.: Can movies and books collaborate? Cross-domain collaborative filtering for sparsity reduction. In: IJCAI 2009, vol. 9, pp. 2052–2057 (2009)
11. Kumar, A., Kumar, N., Hussain, M., et al.: Semantic clustering-based cross-domain recommendation. In: 2014 IEEE Symposium on Computational Intelligence and Data Mining (CIDM), pp. 137–141. IEEE (2014)
12. Tang, J., Wu, S., Sun, J., et al.: Cross-domain collaboration recommendation. In: Proceedings of the 18th ACM SIGKDD International Conference on Knowledge Discovery and Data Mining, pp. 1285–1293. ACM (2012)
13. Karatzoglou, A., Amatriain, X., Baltrunas, L., et al.: Multiverse recommendation: n-dimensional tensor factorization for context-aware collaborative filtering. In: Proceedings of the Fourth ACM Conference on Recommender Systems, pp. 79–86. ACM (2010)
14. Enrich, M., Braunhofer, M., Ricci, F.: Cold-start management with cross-domain collaborative filtering and tags. In: Huemer, C., Lops, P. (eds.) EC-Web 2013. LNBIP, vol. 152, pp. 101–112. Springer, Heidelberg (2013). https://doi.org/10.1007/978-3-642-39878-0_10
15. Li, B., Yang, Q., Xue, X.: Transfer learning for collaborative filtering via a rating-matrix generative model. In: Proceedings of the 26th Annual International Conference on Machine Learning, pp. 617–624. ACM (2009)
16. Shi, Y., Larson, M., Hanjalic, A.: Tags as bridges between domains: improving recommendation with tag-induced cross-domain collaborative filtering. In: Konstan, J.A., Conejo, R., Marzo, J.L., Oliver, N. (eds.) UMAP 2011. LNCS, vol. 6787, pp. 305–316. Springer, Heidelberg (2011). https://doi.org/10.1007/978-3-642-22362-4_26
17. Gao, S., Luo, H., Chen, D., Li, S., Gallinari, P., Guo, J.: Cross-domain recommendation via cluster-level latent factor model. In: Blockeel, H., Kersting, K., Nijssen, S., Železný, F. (eds.) ECML PKDD 2013, Part II. LNCS (LNAI), vol. 8189, pp. 161–176. Springer, Heidelberg (2013). https://doi.org/10.1007/978-3-642-40991-2_11
18. Hu, L., Cao, J., Xu, G., et al.: Personalized recommendation via cross-domain triadic factorization. In: Proceedings of the 22nd International Conference on World Wide Web, pp. 595–606. ACM (2013)
19. Iwata, T., Koh, T.: Cross-domain recommendation without shared users or items by sharing latent vector distributions. In: Artificial Intelligence and Statistics, pp. 379–387 (2015)

20. Fernández-Tobías, I.: Matrix factorization models for cross-domain recommendation: Addressing the cold start in collaborative filtering (2017)
21. Symeonidis, P., Zioupos, A.: Matrix and Tensor Factorization Techniques for Recommender Systems, pp. 3–102. Springer Briefs in Computer Science. Springer, Cham (2016)
22. Cantador, I., Fernández-Tobías, I., Berkovsky, S., Cremonesi, P.: Cross-domain recommender systems. In: Ricci, F., Rokach, L., Shapira, B. (eds.) Recommender Systems Handbook, pp. 919–959. Springer, Boston (2015). https://doi.org/10.1007/978-1-4899-7637-6_27
23. Cichocki, A., Zdunek, R., Phan, A.H., et al.: Nonnegative Matrix and Tensor Factorizations: Applications to Exploratory Multi-Way Data Analysis and Blind Source Separation. Wiley, Chichester (2009)
24. [EB/OL] (2019). http://files.grouplens.org/datasets/movielens/ml-latest.zip
25. [EB/OL] (2019). http://www2.informatik.uni-freiburg.de/~cziegler/BX/

Density Peak Clustering Algorithm Based on Differential Privacy Preserving

Yun Chen[1], Yunlan Du[2], and Xiaomei Cao[1(✉)]

[1] School of Computer Science, Nanjing University of Posts
and Telecommunications, Nanjing 210046, China
caoxm@njupt.edu.cn
[2] Department of Computer Science and Technology, Nanjing University,
Nanjing 210046, China

Abstract. Clustering by fast search and find of density peaks (CFSFDP) is an efficient algorithm for density-based clustering. However, such algorithm inevitably results in privacy leakage. In this paper, we propose DP-CFSFDP to address this problem with differential privacy, which adds random noise in order to distort the data but preserve its statistical properties. Besides, due to the poor performance of CFSFDP on evenly distributed data, we further optimize the clustering process with reachable-centers and propose DP-rcCFSFDP. The experimental results show that, under the same privacy budget, DP-rcCFSFDP can improve the clustering effectiveness while preserving data privacy compared with DP-CFSFDP.

Keywords: Differential privacy · Clustering · Density peak · Privacy preserving

1 Introduction

In the era of big data, the launches of services and products are relying more on the user data (i.e. privacy) and information mined from it. As data privacy is inevitably exposed in the process of data collection, analysis and publication, privacy protection technology is developed to address these privacy threats. Recently, many privacy protection methods based on k-anonymity [1, 2] and partition [3, 4] have emerged. Although these methods can protect more details of data, they all under special attack assumptions.

Differential privacy is an innovative conception demonstrated by Dwork [5–7] for privacy leakage of statistical databases. With random noise, it distorts the sensitive data and preserves the privacy from the malicious attackers. This technique inspires researchers to introduce appropriate noise to data and arm clustering analyses with differential privacy correspondingly.

For example, Blum et al. [8] first introduced differential privacy into clustering analysis. They improved a k-means clustering algorithm and perturbed the query response to protect each database entry. Wu et al. [9] then applied differential privacy technique to density-based clustering algorithm for the first time and proposed DP-DBSCAN algorithm. Though the clustering methods with differential privacy are

F. Liu et al. (Eds.): SciSec 2019, LNCS 11933, pp. 20–32, 2019.
https://doi.org/10.1007/978-3-030-34637-9_2

improving year by year, the algorithms are still limited by the unsuitability of clusters with complex shapes [8, 10, 11] and the sensitiveness to input parameters [9, 12–14].

In this paper, we leverage a more efficient density peak clustering algorithm, clustering by fast search and find of density peaks (CFSFDP) [20], which clusters data by connecting points to the nearest and denser points, and propose an improved DP-CFSFDP by introducing differential privacy protection to it, aiming at solving privacy leakage problem. We add Laplacian noise depending on the differential privacy mechanism when the Gaussian kernel function is called during the density calculation. Due to the poor performance of CFSFDP on data with uniform distribution, an improved algorithm with reachable-centers (DP-rcCFSFDP) is proposed to optimize the clustering process. We allow the lower-density center points to cluster with the reachable and higher-density center points, thus DP-rcCFSFDP can improve the effectiveness of clustering while satisfying the requirement of security.

2 Background and Related Work

2.1 Differential Privacy

Differential privacy preserving is a technique to protect private data by adding random noise to sensitive data while maintaining the data attributes or their statistical properties [5]. We suppose the attacker has obtained all data except the target data. With differential privacy preserving, he still cannot obtain the target. The definitions of differential privacy are as follows.

Definition 1. Suppose D and D' are any pair of neighboring datasets that differ by at most one piece of data, M is a randomized algorithm, $Pr[X]$ is the disclosure risk of event X, and $S \subseteq Range(M)$ is the output of algorithm M. If the algorithm M satisfies:

$$Pr[M(D) \in S] \le e^{\varepsilon} \times Pr[M(D') \in S] \tag{1}$$

Then the algorithm M is said to be ε-differentially private [5]. ε denotes the privacy protection parameter, also known as the privacy budget. The smaller the ε is, the more noise is added, and the more privacy protection is provided.

Definition 2. For the query function $f\colon D \to D^d$, its sensitivity [6] Δf is defined as:

$$\Delta f = \max_{D, D'} \|f(D) - f(D')\|_1 \tag{2}$$

where $\|\cdot\|_1$ denotes the first-order norm distance.

Differential privacy works by adding noise perturbations. There are two common noise addition mechanisms: Laplace mechanism [7] for numerical data and Exponential mechanism [15] for non-numeric data. The amount of noise depends on sensitivity and privacy budget. In this paper, we implement differential privacy with Laplace mechanism.

Definition 3. Given a dataset D, a function f with sensitivity Δf, and privacy budget ε, thus the randomized algorithm $M(D)$:

$$M(D) = f(D) + Lap\left(\frac{\Delta f}{\varepsilon}\right) \tag{3}$$

provides ε-differential privacy preserving [7]. The Lap $(\Delta f/\varepsilon)$ is a random noise of Laplace distribution.

Let b denote the scale parameter $\Delta f/\varepsilon$, the probability density function of the Laplace distribution is:

$$p(x) = \frac{1}{2b} exp\left(-\frac{|x|}{b}\right) \tag{4}$$

2.2   CFSFDP Algorithm

The main idea of CFSFDP is that each class has a maximum density point as the center point which attracts and connects the lower density points around it, while different class centers are far away from each other. The algorithm defines two quantities: local density ρ_i and distance δ_i.

Definition 4. ρ_i denotes the local density, and there are two calculation methods: based on the cutoff kernel and based on the Gaussian kernel. The local density of x_i calculated by cutoff kernel is defined as:

$$\rho_i = \sum_j \chi(d_{ij} - d_c) \tag{5}$$

where d_{ij} denotes the Euclidean distance between x_i and x_j, d_c denotes the cutoff distance, and ρ_i denotes the number of all remaining points contained in the circle with point x_i as the center and d_c as the radius.

When the data distribution of the dataset is uniform, Eq. (5) may make different points with the same local density, which affects the subsequent cluster calculation. For this reason, another method is proposed for calculating the local density ρ_i with Gaussian kernel function:

$$\rho_i = \sum_j e^{-\left(\frac{d_{ij}}{d_c}\right)^2} \tag{6}$$

In this paper, Gauss kernel function is used to calculate local density.

Definition 5. Distance δ_i denotes the minimum distance between point x_i and other points with higher density, and the equation is as follows:

$$\delta_i = \begin{cases} \min\limits_{j:\rho_j > \rho_i} \{d_{ij}\} \\ \max\limits_{j} \{d_{ij}\}, otherwise \end{cases} \tag{7}$$

When point x_i has the maximum local density, δ_i denotes the distance between x_i and the point with the maximum distance from x_i.

The CFSFDP selects cluster centers by the decision graph. The decision graph takes ρ as the abscissa and δ as the ordinate. When the point has both larger values of ρ and δ, it is considered as the cluster center. An instructive measurement for choosing the number of centers is provided by the plot of $\gamma_i = \rho_i \cdot \delta_i$ sorted in decreasing order [20]. The remaining points are connected to the nearest point corresponding to their δ_i for clustering.

3   CFSFDP Algorithm Based on Differential Privacy

3.1   DP-CFSFDP

CFSFDP algorithm selects k cluster centers according to the decision graph. The rest points are arranged in descending order of local density and gradually connected to the nearest point with higher density until to a center point. The algorithm performs well on datasets with different shapes or uneven density distribution. However, the density of points may expose the distribution of dataset. The density peak clustering algorithm based on differential privacy preserving (DP-CFSFDP) introduces Laplacian noise to the function of local density calculation, in order to accord with the ε-differentially private and avoid the risk of privacy leakage caused by local density.

The steps of DP-CFSFDP are as follows:

First, initialize the quantities of each point - ρ_i' and δ_i. Calculate the Euclidean distance between points and local density ρ_i. Based on sensitivity and privacy budget, we generate random noise corresponding to Laplace distribution and add it to the density ρ_i. The new densities ρ_i' are arranged in descending order. Thus, we calculate δ_i which indicates the distance from point i to its nearest point with a larger local density.

Second, generate the decision graph based on density ρ_i' and distance δ_i, thereby determine the class centers.

Finally, cluster non-central points. We traverse the rest points in descending order of density, and classify each point and its nearest point with distance δ_i into a class.

The pseudo code of the DP-CFSFDP algorithm is presented in the Algorithm 1.

Algorithm 1 DP-CFSFDP

Input: data set D, cutoff distance d_c, privacy budget ε
Output: clustering results with differential privacy
1: Calculate ρ_i from Eq.(6) on D,
   and generate its descending-order subscript q_i
2: $b = \Delta f / \varepsilon$, Generate random noise $Lap(b)$
3: $\rho_i' = \rho_i + Lap(b)$
4: Calculate δ_i from Eq.(7), and generate
   its corresponding subscript n_i
5: Draw the decision graph based on ρ_i' and δ_i
6: Select the appropriate class centers m_j,
   initialize the clustering label $C_i = -1$
7: **for** $i = 1:j$ **do**
8:     $C_{mj} = i$
9: **end for**
10:**for** $i = 1:N$ **do**
11:     **if** point q_i is not classified
12:         $C_{qi} = C_{nqi}$
13:     **end if**
14:**end for**

3.2 DP-CFSFDP with Reachable-Centers

DP-CFSFDP algorithm protects data privacy by introducing noise into local density. However, the arrangement order of local density may change due to the added Laplacian noise, and then interfere with the calculation of the distance δ resulting in the change in the distribution of the decision graph. Since the center points is generated from the decision graph, the parameters with noise may lead to the deviation between the new center point and the correct one. Besides, points are likely to be misclassified under the influence of noise during the clustering.

In addition, CFSFDP algorithm supposes that each class must be a maximum density point as the class center. If the density distribution of a class is uniform, or there are multiple distant points with high density, an entire class will be divided into several subclasses. CFSFDP algorithm selects k centers based on the decision graph. However, the inappropriate number of centers may have a great impact on the clustering results.

In this paper, DP-CFSFDP algorithm with reachable-centers (DP-rcCFSFDP) is proposed to reduce the influence of Laplacian noise on clustering results, optimize the selection of centers and make up for the inapplicability of CFSFDP algorithm to uniformly distributed data. The improved algorithm refers to some ideas of DBSCAN [21] and defines *reachable*, and applies it to the classification of the center points. The definitions used in DP-rcCFSFDP are as follows:

Neighbors. The neighbors of x_i are all points in the neighborhood with x_i as the center and *eps* as the radius. In our algorithm, the cutoff distance d_c is used as *eps* to represent the radius of neighborhood.

Reachable. There is a series of points $p_1, p_2, p_3 \ldots p_m$, p_m is said to be reachable from p_i if each p_{i+1} lies in the neighborhood of p_i.

The specific steps of DP-rcCFSFDP are as follows:

First, initialize the quantities ρ_i' and δ_i, and generate the decision graph. This process is the same as the beginning of DP-CFSFDPs.

Second, we select k_init points as the initial centers according to the decision graph. We then calculate the delta-density value of gamma by $\gamma_i = \rho_i' \cdot \delta_i$, and arrange them in descending order. The k_init points with the largest gamma are selected as initial cluster centers points.

Third, the initial centers are arranged in descending order of density for traversal processing. If the center point with higher density is reachable from a point with lower density with respect to d_c, the lower one will be classified into the cluster of the higher one. We will obtain the accurate number of centers k after the traversal.

Finally, the remaining points are traversed in descending order of density, and classified to the cluster of the nearest point with higher density until each of them is connected to a class center. The clustering results will be printed at last.

The cluster process of DP-rcCFSFDP algorithm is presented in the Algorithm 2.

Algorithm 2 DP-rcCFSFDP

Input: data set D, cutoff distance d_c, privacy budget ε
Output: clustering results with differential privacy
1: Calculate ρ_i from Eq.(6) on D,
    and generate its descending-order subscript q_i
2: $b = \Delta f / \varepsilon$, Generate random noise $Lap(b)$
3: $\rho_i' = \rho_i + Lap(b)$
4: Calculate δ_i from Eq.(7), and generate
    its corresponding subscript n_i
5: Draw the decision graph based on ρ_i' and δ_i,
    and calculate $\gamma_i = \rho_i' \cdot \delta_i$ in descending order
6: Calculate the neighbors of each point based on d_c
7: Select k_init points with the largest γ
    as the initial cluster centers
8: Initialize class count $nc=1$
9: The initial centers are sorted in descending order
    of density $Clist_m$, and $Clist_1$ is the nc class
10: **for** $i = 1:m$ **do**
11:     **for** $j = 1:i$ **do**
12:         **if** $Clist_j$ is reachable from $Clist_i$ w.r.t. d_c
13:             $Clist_i$ is classified to $Clist_j$
14:             **break**
15:         **end if**
16:     **end for**
17:     **if** $Clist_i$ is not classified
18:         $nc=nc+1$
19:         $Clist_i$ is the nc class
20:     **end if**
21: **end for**
22: Non-central points are arranged according to q_i,
    and classified to the class of n_i

DP-CFSFDP algorithm is sensitive to the selection of centers. Though the number of center points meets the actual clustering requirements, the selection of centers will still be interfered with Laplacian noise, resulting in biased centers or even multiple centers in one class. While DP-rcCFSFDP selects k_init points as initial centers (k_init is greater than or equal to the number of actual centers number), it classifies the reachable centers into one class, which finally corrects the biased center points generated by noise to connect to the right one. The algorithm reduces the dependence on the number of centers, reduces the interference of noise on clustering, and improves the stability.

3.3   Privacy Analysis

According to Eq. (6) of local density and Definition 2 of sensitivity, the sensitivity of the local density function is 1 when a point is added or deleted in the normalized space $[0, 1]^d$.

Suppose that two datasets $D1$ and $D2$ differ by at most one record, $M(D1)$ and $M(D2)$ denote the output of CFSFDP algorithm with Laplacian noise on $D1$ and $D2$, S denotes the arbitrary output, $f(D1)$ and $f(D2)$ denote the true clustering results on these datasets, and $s(x)$ denotes a certain clustering result. According to Eqs. (2) and (4), the security proof of DP-CFSFDP and DP-rcCFSFDP is as follows:

$$\frac{Pr[M(D1) \in S]}{Pr[M(D2) \in S]} = \frac{exp\left(-\frac{\varepsilon|f(D1)-s(x)|}{\Delta f}\right)}{exp\left(-\frac{\varepsilon|f(D2)-s(x)|}{\Delta f}\right)}$$

$$= exp\left(\frac{\varepsilon(|f(D2)-s(x)| - |f(D1)-s(x)|)}{\Delta f}\right)$$

$$\leq exp\left(\frac{\varepsilon|f(D2)-f(D1)|}{\Delta f}\right)$$

$$= exp\left(\frac{\varepsilon\|f(D2)-f(D1)\|_1}{\Delta f}\right)$$

$$\leq exp(\varepsilon)$$

The first inequality follows from the triangle inequality which indicates the difference between any two sides is less than the third. According to Definition 1, it is proved that DP-CFSFDP and DP-rcCFSFDP are ε-differentially private.

4   Experiments

4.1   Experiment Setup

The proposed algorithms are implemented in the Python language. The experiments are conducted on a computer with win10 x64 system, Intel i7-6700HQ @2.60 GHz CPU and 8 GB RAM. The datasets used are from the artificial datasets [22] and UCI Knowledge Discovery Archive database [23].

The specific information of the datasets is shown in Table 1.

Table 1. Datasets information

Datasets	Instances	Dimensions	Clusters
Jain	373	2	2
Wine	178	13	2
Aggregation	788	2	7
Iris	150	4	3

4.2   Evaluation Criteria

F-measure [24] and adjusted Rand index (ARI) [25] are used to compare the similarity between the clustering results of proposed algorithms and the ground truth class assignment to evaluate the clustering effectiveness. F-measure is the harmonic average of the precision and recall. ARI is to measure the similarity of the two assignments.

Suppose that T_j is the class in the real clustering results, and D_i the clustering results output from the algorithm proposed in the paper. N is the total number of points in the dataset. $|T_j|$ and $|D_i|$ denote the number of points in the class. The rate of precision, recall and the value of F-measure of T_j and D_i are defined as follows:

$$P(T_j, D_i) = \frac{|T_j \cap D_i|}{|D_i|} \tag{8}$$

$$R(T_j, D_i) = \frac{|T_j \cap D_i|}{|T_j|} \tag{9}$$

$$F(T_j, D_i) = \frac{2 \cdot P(T_j, D_i) \cdot R(T_j, D_i)}{P(T_j, D_i) + R(T_j, D_i)} \tag{10}$$

F-measure of the clustering results is the weighted average of F-measure for all clusters:

$$F\text{-measure} = \sum_j \frac{|T_j|}{N} \max_i F(T_j, D_i) \tag{11}$$

ARI is the improvement of Rand index (RI). Variations of the ARI account for different models of random clustering [26]. Suppose that T is the actual clustering results, D is the clustering results obtained by the improved algorithm, a is the number of pairs of elements that are in the same set in T and D, and b be the number of pairs of elements that are in different sets in T and D. $E[RI]$ denotes the expectation of RI, then RI and ARI are defined:

$$RI = \frac{a+b}{C_N^2} \tag{12}$$

$$ARI = \frac{RI - E[RI]}{\max(RI) - E[RI]} \tag{13}$$

The range of F-measure is [0, 1] and ARI is [−1,1]. The higher the value is, the more similar the outputs of clustering algorithm are to the real clustering results and the less the impact of Laplacian noise on clustering effectiveness.

4.3   Results and Discussion

In the experiment, the datasets are normalized so that each attribute value is limited to [0, 1]. To achieve the best clustering effect, appropriate parameters should be selected before we add the noise. DP-CFSFDP and DP-rcCFSFDP are applied on four datasets.

For each privacy budget and each metric, we apply the algorithms on each dataset for 30 times and compute their average performances. When the privacy budget ε changes, the F-measure and ARI values of the clustering results are shown in the figure.

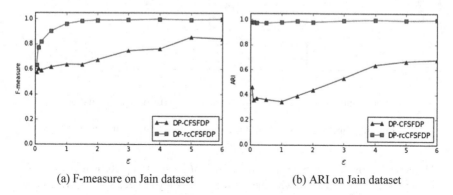

(a) F-measure on Jain dataset   (b) ARI on Jain dataset

Fig. 1. F-measure and ARI comparison of algorithms on Jain dataset

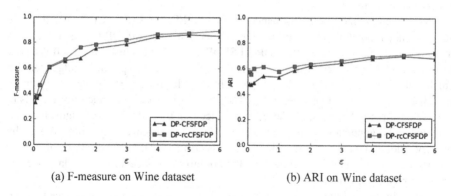

(a) F-measure on Wine dataset   (b) ARI on Wine dataset

Fig. 2. F-measure and ARI comparison of algorithms on Wine dataset

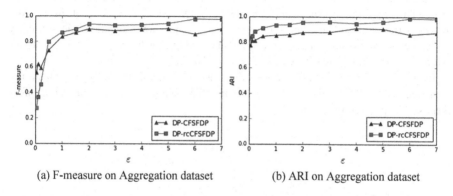

(a) F-measure on Aggregation dataset   (b) ARI on Aggregation dataset

Fig. 3. F-measure and ARI comparison of algorithms on Aggregation dataset

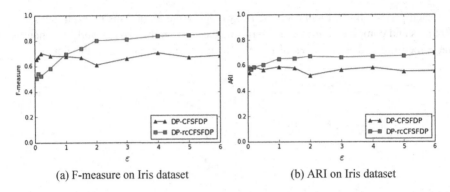

(a) F-measure on Iris dataset   (b) ARI on Iris dataset

Fig. 4. F-measure and ARI comparison of algorithms on Iris dataset

The left side of the figures (Figs. 1(a), 2(a), 3(a), 4(a)) depicts **F-measure** of the clustering results. As is shown, with the growth of privacy budget, F-measure gradually increases and tends to be stable. Since the privacy budget is inversely proportional to the size of the Laplacian noise, the higher the privacy budget, the less the noise and the better the clustering results.

When we compare the performance of DP-CFSFDP and DP-rcCFSFDP under the same privacy budget, it is easy to find that in Figs. 1(a) and 2(a), DP-rcCFSFDP always has a higher F-measure value than DP-CFSFDP, and that the clustering result is closer to the real result. However, in Figs. 3(a) and 4(a), when the privacy budget takes a small value, the F-measure value of DP-CFSFDP becomes higher but seems more unstable. The reason is that when the privacy budget is small, too much noise leads to the increasing randomness of the centers selection by DP-CFSFDP algorithm and coincidentally generates even better centers than the original algorithm. When the privacy budget takes a larger value, the clustering of DP-rcCFSFDP is of higher accuracy and more stable, resulting from the optimization of center points classification with the reachable centers.

The right side of the figures (Figs. 1(b), 2(b), 3(b) and 4(b)) depicts **ARI** of the clustering results. As we can see, ARI gradually increases and then flattens with the increase of privacy budget. Under the same privacy budget, the ARI value of DP-rcCFSFDP is generally superior than DP-CFSFDP, since the calculation of ARI ignores permutations. Thus, under the same level of privacy protection, the similarity between clustering results of DP-rcCFSFDP and real ones is higher, indicating that DP-rcCFSFDP algorithm clusters with higher effectiveness.

In general, DP-rcCFSFDP reduces the impact of Laplacian noise on clustering compared with DP-CFSFDP and achieves a better balance between clustering effectiveness and privacy preserving.

5   Conclusion

In this paper, a density peak clustering algorithm based on differential privacy preserving (DP-CFSFDP) is proposed to protect private data. Meanwhile, an improved DP-CFSFDP algorithm with reachable-centers (DP-rcCFSFDP) is proposed for the poor performance on data with uniform distribution and the bad clustering with Laplacian noise by CFSFDP. The experiments show that the improved algorithm can meet the requirement of privacy preserving while ensuring the effectiveness of clustering. In the future, we are going to optimize the allocation of input parameters and privacy budget in DP-rcCFSFDP, and further improve the clustering performance.

References

1. Sweeney, L.: k-anonymity: a model for protecting privacy. Int. J. Uncertain. Fuzziness Knowl. Based Syst. **10**(5), 557–570 (2002)
2. Karakasidis, A., Verykios, V.: Reference table based k-anonymous private blocking. In: Proceedings of the 27th Annual ACM Symposium on Applied Computing, pp. 859–864. ACM (2012)
3. Machanavajjhala, A., Gehrke, J., Kifer, D., Venkitasubramaniam, M.: l-diversity: privacy beyond k-anonymity. In: 22nd IEEE International Conference on Data Engineering, p. 24. IEEE (2006)
4. Li, N., Li, T., Venkatasubramanian, S.: t-Closeness: privacy beyond k-anonymity and l-diversity. In: IEEE 23rd International Conference on Data Engineering, pp. 106–115. IEEE (2007)
5. Dwork, C.: Differential privacy. In: Bugliesi, M., Preneel, B., Sassone, V., Wegener, I. (eds.) ICALP 2006. LNCS, vol. 4052, pp. 1–12. Springer, Heidelberg (2006). https://doi.org/10.1007/11787006_1
6. Dwork, C., Roth, A.: The algorithmic foundations of differential privacy. Found. Trends Theor. Comput. Sci. **9**(3–4), 211–407 (2014)
7. Dwork, C., McSherry, F., Nissim, K., Smith, A.: Calibrating noise to sensitivity in private data analysis. In: Halevi, S., Rabin, T. (eds.) TCC 2006. LNCS, vol. 3876, pp. 265–284. Springer, Heidelberg (2006). https://doi.org/10.1007/11681878_14
8. Blum, A., Dwork, C., McSherry, F., Nissim, K.: Practical privacy: the SuLQ framework. In: PODS, pp. 128–138. ACM (2005)
9. Wu, W., Huang, H.: A DP-DBScan clustering algorithm based on differential privacy preserving. Comput. Eng. Sci. **37**(4), 830–834 (2015)
10. Nissim, K., Raskhodnikova, S., Smith, A.: Smooth sensitivity and sampling in private data analysis. In: STOC, pp. 75–84. ACM (2007)
11. Ren, J., Xiong, J., Yao, Z., Ma, R., Lin, M.: DPLK-means: a novel differential privacy K-means Mechanism. In: IEEE Second International Conference on Data Science in Cyberspace, DSC 2017, pp. 133–139. IEEE (2017)
12. Dwork, C.: A firm foundation for private data analysis. Commun. ACM **54**(1), 86–95 (2011)
13. Wang, H., Ge, L., Wang, S., et al.: Improvement of differential privacy protection algorithm based on OPTICS clustering. J. Comput. Appl. **38**(1), 73–78 (2018)
14. Chen, L., Yu, T., Chirkova, R.: Wavecluster with differential privacy. In: CIKM, pp. 1011–1020. ACM (2015)

15. McSherry, F., Talwar, K.: Mechanism design via differential privacy. In: Proceedings of 48th Annual IEEE Symposium on Foundations of Computer Science, Providence, RI, pp. 94–103 (2007)
16. Dwork, C.: Differential privacy: a survey of results. In: Agrawal, M., Du, D., Duan, Z., Li, A. (eds.) TAMC 2008. LNCS, vol. 4978, pp. 1–19. Springer, Heidelberg (2008). https://doi.org/10.1007/978-3-540-79228-4_1
17. Dwork, C., Lei, J.: Differential privacy and robust statistics. In: STOC, pp. 371–380 (2009)
18. Dwork, C., Naor, M., Reingold, O., Rothblum, G.N., Vadhan, S.: On the complexity of differentially private data release: efficient algorithms and hardness results. In: STOC 2009: Proceedings of the 41st Annual ACM Symposium on Theory of Computing, pp. 381–390. ACM, New York (2009)
19. Dwork, C.: The differential privacy frontier (Extended Abstract). In: Reingold, O. (ed.) TCC 2009. LNCS, vol. 5444, pp. 496–502. Springer, Heidelberg (2009). https://doi.org/10.1007/978-3-642-00457-5_29
20. Rodriguez, A., Laio, A.: Clustering by fast search and find of density peaks. Science **344** (6191), 1492–1496 (2014)
21. Ester, M., Kriegel, H., Sander, J., Xu, X.: A density-based algorithm for discovering clusters in large spatial databases with noise. In: Proceedings of the Second ACM SIGKDD International Conference on Knowledge Discovery and Data Mining, pp. 226–231 (1996)
22. Clustering datasets. http://cs.joensuu.fi/sipu/datasets/
23. UCI Machine Learning Repository. https://archive.ics.uci.edu/ml/datasets.html
24. Chinchor, N.: MUC-4 evaluation metrics. In: Proceedings of the Fourth Message Understanding Conference, pp. 22–29 (1992)
25. Hubert, L., Arabie, P.: Comparing partitions. J. Classif. **2**(1), 193–218 (1985)
26. Gates, A., Ahn, Y.: The impact of random models on clustering similarity. J. Mach. Learn. Res. **18**(1), 3049–3076 (2017)
27. Zhang, Y., Wei, J., Zhang, X., et al.: A two-phase algorithm for generating synthetic graph under local differential privacy. In: ICCNS 2018: Proceedings of the 8th International Conference on Communication and Network Security, pp. 84–89. ACM, New York (2018)
28. André, L., Brito, F., et al.: DiPCoDing: a differentially private approach for correlated data with clustering. In: IDEAS 2017: Proceedings of the 21st International Database Engineering & Applications Symposium, pp. 291–297. ACM (2017)
29. Huang, Z., Liu, J.: Optimal differentially private algorithms for k-Means clustering. In: Proceedings of the 37th ACM SIGMOD-SIGACT-SIGAI Symposium on Principles of Database Systems, pp. 395–408. ACM, New York (2018)

An Automated Online Spam Detector Based on Deep Cascade Forest

Kangyang Chen[1], Xinyi Zou[1], Xingguo Chen[1,2(✉)], and Huihui Wang[3,4]

[1] Jiangsu Key Laboratory of Big Data Security and Intelligent Processing, Nanjing University of Posts and Telecommunications, Nanjing, People's Republic of China
chenxg@njupt.edu.cn
[2] National Engineering Laboratory for Agri-product Quality Traceability, Beijing Technology and Business University, Beijing, People's Republic of China
[3] PCA Lab, Key Lab of Intelligent Perception and Systems for High-Dimensional Information of Ministry of Education, Nanjing, People's Republic of China
[4] Jiangsu Key Lab of Image and Video Understanding for Social Security, School of Computer Science and Engineering, Nanjing University of Science and Technology, Nanjing, People's Republic of China

Abstract. With the development of internet communication, spam is quite ubiquitous in our daily life. It not only disturbs users, but also cms. Although there exists many methods of spam detection in both the area of cyber security and natural language processing, their performance is still not capable to satisfy requirements. In this paper, we implemented deep cascade forest for spam detection, a deep model without using backpropagation. With less hyperparameters, the training cost can be easily controlled and declines compared with that in neutral network methods. Furthermore, the proposed deep cascade forest outperforms other machine learning models in the F1 Score of detection. Therefore, considering the lower training cost, it can be considered as a useful online tool for spam detection.

Keywords: Spam detection · Deep forest · Deep learning · Machine learning · Ensemble methods

1 Introduction

In the era of information explosion, communication through digital media becomes prevalent in peoples' daily life. There is a lot of complicated information in our daily life. However, among these messages, there exists a large amount of information that is false, violent, or illegal. These messages not only affect user's product experience, but may also lead to cyber security issues such as financial fraud and personal privacy leaks [20]. According to the report presented by Kaspersky, an independent cybersecurity company, spammers continuously exploit new methods to propogate malicious messages to their "audience", including instant messengers and social networks [13].

© Springer Nature Switzerland AG 2019
F. Liu et al. (Eds.): SciSec 2019, LNCS 11933, pp. 33–46, 2019.
https://doi.org/10.1007/978-3-030-34637-9_3

Owing to the fact that spam is too multitudinous to be recognized and filtered in advance manually, spam detection is of great significance. There are two major difficulties in spam detection. One is how to convert text information into numerical information, especially those conveys less information such as word abbreviations, expressions, and symbols. The other is how to build an online tool that can recognize spam in time.

Spam detection plays a predominant way in cyber security. Early in 1999, Harris Drucker et al. applied Support Vector Machines (SVM) to email spam detection [7]. In order to encode texts into computer-readable mathematical features, he combined Term Frequency-Inverse Document Frequency (TF-IDF) representation method with binary representation method. According to his research, compared with boosting decision tree, SVM is considered as the most suitable model at that time. In 2011, McCord used a variety of traditional machine learning methods to detect spam on twitter. In his work, several classic classification algorithms such as random forest (RF), naive bayes (NB), support vector machine (SVM), and k nearest neighbors (KNN) are compared. Among them, RF shows the best performance as an ensemble learning method [14]. When combining with multiple base classifiers, ensemble classifier provides a more accurate prediction than single classifier. In 2013, Cailing Dong developed an ensemble learning framework for online web spam detection, and their experimental results reflect the effectiveness of integrated learning [6].

In around 2006, the idea of Deep Learning started to take shape. Hinton believes that neural networks can be used to reduce dimensions of data so as to contribute to feature extraction [8]. Its true in many areas such as speech recognition [5], image recognition [11]. Deep learning is also widely used in natural language processing (NLP) [12,19], Long Short-Term Memory (LSTM) is one of its best-known models. Hochreiter discusses [9] how LSTM is trained to store information over a period of time. Recent years, some researchers began to use deep learning models to detect spam. In 2017, Wu et al. compared multilayer perception with RF, decision tree (DT) and NB [22]. Later, Ren empirically explored a neural network model to learn document-level representation for detecting deceptive opinion spam [15]. They compared gated recurrent neural network (GRNN) with convolutional neural network (CNN) and recurrent neural network (RNN), finding that GRNN outperforms others on datasets which consist of truthful and deceptive reviews in three domains. Furthermore, Gauri Jain et al. firstly used LSTM to categorize SMS spam and Twitter spam [10] in 2019. The results show that LSTM is superior to traditional machine learning methods in SMS and Twitter spam datasets. Due to the fact that some datasets contain not only texts but also images, Yang et al. used CNN for image extraction and LSTM for text extraction respectively [23].

When dealing with text information, a traditional approach is vector space model [17]. It is designed to encode each word respectively. Therefore, it washes away semantic information and generates high dimensional and sparse features that are not suitable for neural networks. Another mainstream approach is semantic-based textual representation, which translates textual information into continuous dense features to learn the distributed representation of words [4].

This method is also called word embedding, which has high autocorrelation and is suitable for use in neural networks.

Our goal is to find promising methods and settings that can recognize spam in social networks. Many developers have developed anti-spam tools for spam detection, but they are not efficient. Most of these spam detection methods are based on traditional machine learning methods. In recent years, with the development of NLP, deep learning methods emerged in spam detection, which have achieved satisfying results in accuracy. Nevertheless, the deeper the network is, the higher training cost and complexity the model will be.

In summary, this article uses the gcForest method, the deep ensemble method proposed by Zhou et al. in 2017 [24], and its structure has been improved to adapt to spam detection problems. It is a highly-ensemble learning model with fewer hyperparameters than deep neural network. Furthermore, its model complexity can be determined in a data-dependent way which makes our model less time-consuming. Compared with previous machine learning methods, our model shows a higher accuracy and efficiency and solves training overhead problems simultaneously.

The rest of the paper is organized as follows: Sect. 2 offers the description of the cascade structure of gcForest approach (Deep Cascade Forest, DCF) that is the core of our method. Section 3 briefly describes the text processing methods. In Sect. 4, we illustrate models elaborately including datasets we use and parameter settings in experiments. After that, we compare the accuracy, F1 Score, training time, etc. of models. Finally, Sect. 5 describes the main conclusion and offers guidelines for future work.

2   Deep Cascade Forest

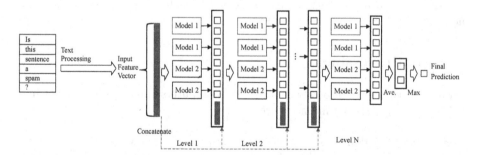

Fig. 1. Example of the cascade structure of gcForest (DCF) for spam detection. Suppose each level of the cascade consists of two kinds of base models. There are two classes to predict (spam or ham), thus, each model will output a two-dimensional class vector, which is then concatenated for re-representation of original input.

In 2017, Zhou et al. proposed an ensemble approach with a deep cascade structure, named gcForest [24]. The basic form of gcForest contains 2 parts:

Multi-Grained Scanning and Cascade Forest. The former is used for feature preprocessing, and for spam detection tasks, we replace it with text preprocessing method. In order to train the model, we only use the cascade structure and call the model the deep cascade forest (DCF).

As is elaborately illustrated in Fig. 1, first, it is necessary to split the input document into words, and then carried out the text processing procedure that extracting the textual information as a feature vector. Inspired by the well-known recognition that representation learning in deep neural network mostly relies on the layer-by-layer processing of raw features, DCF then feed the feature vector into the layer-by-layer cascade structure. After training various base models on the feature vector, the output predictions will then be concentrated with raw features and fed to the next layer together. In each layer, different types of base models can be selected to encourage the ensemble diversity. Base model can even be an ensemble model, e.g. random forest and this constitutes an "ensemble of ensembles". The output of each base model is a class vector, indicating the probability of predicting a sentence as a class. In the spam detection task, there are two classes (spam and ham), that is, each model outputs a two-dimensional probability class vector. To reduce the risk of overfitting, which is common in deep learning models, class vectors are generated by k-fold cross validation. In detail, each instance will be trained k-1 times to generate k-1 class vectors, and then averaged to get the final class vector. Before generating a new layer, the performance of the entire cascade structure is estimated on validation data, and if the performance does not improve, the training process terminates. So that the number of cascade levels is automatically determined.

DCF can achieve good results in different dimensions of input data. However neural networks are difficult to get good results on high dimensional and sparse text features. Comparing with deep neural networks, DCF has much fewer hyper-parameters and lower training cost, and it opens the door of deep learning based on non-NN (Neural Network) styles, or deep models based on non-differentiable modules.

3   Text Processing

In order to turn text into information that computers can recognize, following different text processing methods are used:

Remove the Stop Words. A stop word is a commonly used word (such as "the", "a", "an", "in") that a search engine has been programmed to ignore, both when indexing entries for searching and when retrieving them as the result of a search query. We can remove them easily, by storing a list of words that considered as stop words.

Build Word Count Vector. To build the word count vector for each sample, we firstly create a dictionary of words and their frequency. Once the dictionary is ready, we can extract word count vectors from training set. A sample corresponds to a word count vector. The dimension of the word count vector is the total number of words in the training set. If the sample contains a word in the training set, the value in the vector is the frequency of the word in the training set. If not, the value is zero. All word count vectors are combined into a word count matrix, rows represent each sample, and columns represent each word.

Term Frequency-Inverse Document Frequency (TF-IDF). TF-IDF stands for term frequency-inverse document frequency, and the TF-IDF weight is a weight often used in information retrieval and text mining, to produce a composite weight for each term in each document. [16].

TF determines a terms (a word or a combination) relative frequency within a document. The $TF(w_i)$ is the number of times that word w_i appears in a document.

TF-IDF uses the above TF multiplied by the IDF, the inverse document frequency (IDF) is defined as:

$$IDF(w_i) = \log(\frac{|D|}{DF(w_i)}) \tag{1}$$

Where $|D|$ is the number of documents, and the document frequency $DF(w_i)$ is the number of times that word w_i appears in all documents.

Texts to Sequences. This approach will create a vector for each sample, converting words to their index in the word count dictionary. An example of texts to sequences is shown in Fig. 2.

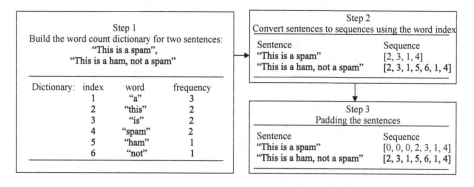

Fig. 2. An example of texts to sequences method

4   Experiments and Results

The experiments use two public data sets to train the model. In order to compare models performance on detecting spam and their training cost, we used F1 Score to evaluate the model and calculated the training and testing time of each model. Our experiments use a PC with Intel Core i5 7260u CPUs (2 cores), and the performance and running efficiency of DCF is good.

4.1   Datasets and Evaluation Measures

The experiments are performed on SMS spam dataset and YouTube comments spam dataset. All the information is available in UCI repository [1,21]. The SMS spam dataset is a public set of SMS labeled messages that are collected for mobile phone spam research. It has one collection composed by 5,574 English, real and non-encoded messages, tagged in legitimate (ham) or spam [2]. The YouTube comments spam dataset was collected using the YouTube Data API v3. The samples were extracted from the comments section of five videos that were among the 10 most viewed on YouTube during the collection period [3]. For these two datasets, each is divided into 70% training sets and 30% test sets. The training set is used to train the model, and the test set is used to assess the effectiveness of models. The overview of these datasets is reported in Table 1.

Table 1. Datasets overview

Dataset	No. of instances	No. of ham	No. of spam
SMS spam	5574	4825	747
YouTube spam	1956	951	1005

The experiments were performed on four processed datasets, shown in Table 2, where Count in the first row denotes the approach of building word count vector, Sequence denotes the approach of texts to sequences.

Table 2. Number of features in four processed datasets

Dataset	TF-IDF	Count	Sequence
SMS spam	8710	8710	200
YouTube spam	4454	4454	500
SMS spam (stop)	9403	9403	200
YouTube spam (stop)	4185	4185	500

In order to assess the effectiveness of proposed methods, this paper uses different evaluation indicators, including accuracy, recall, precision and F1 score, which are defined as follows:

$$Accuracy = \frac{TP + TN}{TP + TN + FP + FN} \tag{2}$$

$$precision = \frac{TP}{TP + FP} \tag{3}$$

$$recall = \frac{TP}{TP + FN} \tag{4}$$

$$F1 = 2 \cdot \frac{precision \cdot recall}{precision + recall} \tag{5}$$

Where true positive (TP) means the number of spam that are correctly classified, false positive (FP) means the number of legitimate emails (ham) that are misclassified, true negative (TN) means the number of legitimate emails (Ham) that are correctly classified and false negative (FN) is the number of misclassified spam.

4.2 Parameter Settings

The grid search method is used to select hyperparameters of models [18]. Both machine learning methods and deep learning methods are the benchmark, including support vector machine (SVM), k nearest neighbors (KNN), Naive Bayes (NB), decision tree (DT), logistic regression (LR), random forest (RF), adaptive boosting (Adaboost), Bagging, extra-trees classifier (ETC, standing for extremely randomized trees), and long short-term memory (LSTM).

For SMS spam detection, SVM uses a sigmoid kernel with gamma set to 1.0. KNN uses 49 neighbors. NB uses a multinomial kernel with alpha set to 0.2. The minimum of DT samples in each split is 7, and the best *gini* value is used to measure the quality of a split. LR uses the L1 penalty, random forest contains 31 decision trees. The Adaboost classifier contains 62 decision trees. The Bagging classifier contains 9 decision trees. ETC contains 9 decision trees.

For YouTube spam detection, SVM uses a sigmoid kernel with gamma set to 1.0. KNN uses 5 neighbors. NB uses a multinomial kernel with alpha set to 1. The minimum of DT samples in each split is 2, and the best *gini* value is used to measure the quality of a split. LR uses the L2 penalty, and random forest contains 10 decision trees. The Adaboost classifier contains 50 decision trees. The Bagging classifier contains 10 decision trees. ETC contains 10 decision trees.

For SMS spam detection, each layer of DCF contains 1 RF with 31 decision trees, and an NB classifier with a multinomial kernel. For YouTube spam detection, each layer of DCF contains 1 DT, an NB classifier with a multinomial kernel and a LR classifier. There are many hyperparameters used by LSTM. The specific structure and settings refer to Appendix B. It can be seen that the complexity of DCF is much smaller than that of LSTM.

4.3 Results and Analysis

Datasets shown in Table 2 are split into 70% training data and 30% test data. All models use two text processing approaches: building word count vectors and TF-IDF. In addition, given that LSTM is better suited to use semantic-based text processing methods, the texts to sequences approach is used and compared with other approaches. In order to further validate the performance of those models, we compared their training time which is an important factor in building an online detector.

Figures 3 and 4 show the accuracy and F1 score of different models on the SMS dataset and YouTube dataset, respectively. More details of precision, recall, training and testing time are shown in Tables 3 and 4.

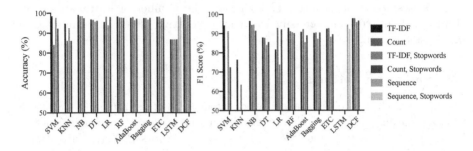

Fig. 3. Accuracy and F1 Score of different models on the test dataset of SMS spam

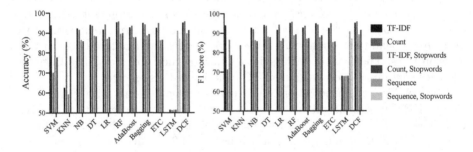

Fig. 4. Accuracy and F1 Score of different models on the test dataset of YouTube spam

From Fig. 3, we can conclude that DCF outperforms others in both the accuracy and F1 Score on the SMS spam dataset. After building word count vectors, DCF achieves the highest accuracy of 99.40% and highest F1 Score of 97.84% which can be found in Table 3. Simultaneously, DCF gets the highest accuracy of 99.40% after using TF-IDF method. The DCF's performance is better on datasets without removing stop words. The training time of DCF is much less than LSTM after building word count vectors and using TF-IDF method. LSTM performs poorly after using the building word vector and using the TF-IDF method, because high dimensional and sparse samples produced by these two methods are not well handled by LSTM. However, after using the texts to sequences method, LSTM performance has been greatly improved but still does not exceed DCF Among many machine learning models, NB not only has a short training time, but also has an accuracy of 99.04%. In addition, since TP is equal to zero, the accuracy, recall, and F1 score of some models are zero in Table 3, which means that all spam is incorrectly classified.

It can be inferred from Fig. 4 and Table 4, as for YouTube spam dataset, DCF also achieved the highest accuracy (95.74%) and F1 Score (95.87%). LSTM performs worst on the dataset after building word count vector and using TF-IDF method, with the lowest accuracy and F1 Score, as well as the longest training time, which denotes that it is less likely to be applied in this field. Regardless of the text processing method used, KNN works very poorly.

Overall, DCF shows the highest accuracy and F1 Score in the spam detection mission. This model not only has quite robust performance to different datasets, but also has lower training cost than the deep neural network due to its automatically determined complexity. The LSTM model is much suitable to use the texts to sequences processing approach, but when facing high-dimension and sparse data (e.g. the YouTube spam dataset), the model not only performs worse, but also has a long training time.

Among other machine learning and ensemble learning methods, NB seems more suitable for spam detection on account of its relatively higher accuracy and lower training cost.

5   Conclusion

In this paper, differing from other researches who use machine learning methods and deep learning methods to carry out spam detection, we attempted deep forest, a non-NN style deep model based on non-differentiable modules. We concluded that deep forest shows the highest accuracy and F1 Score on both SMS spam datasets and YouTube spam datasets. Deep forests are suitable for input data of different kinds of dimensions, however neural networks are difficult to produce good results on high dimensional and sparse samples. Owing to the fact that deep forest has fewer hyperparameters and lower training cost than LSTM, it can be considered as a more suitable model for building an online detector.

In the future, we hope to use new techniques to solve problems with more datasets that include both images and texts. We also aim to explore more text processing methods to further improve performance of classifiers. As an alternative towards deep neural networks, we intend to apply deep forest to other tasks that can not be well handled by deep neural networks. With regard to online tools, we plan to develop web browser and mobile phone plugins to filter spam directly.

Acknowlededgment. This work was supported by the National Natural Science Foundation, China (Nos. 61806096, 61872190, 61403208).

A   Performance Comparison Between Deep Cascade Forest and Other Classifiers

Tables 3 and 4 shows the precision, recall, precision, accuracy and training/testing time of different models by different kinds of text processing methods on SMS datasets and YouTube datasets, respectively.

Table 3. Performance comparison between deep cascade forest and other classifiers on SMS spam dataset

Classifier	Text processing	Precision (%)	Recall (%)	Accuracy (%)	F1 (%)	Training time (s)	Testing time (s)
SVM	TF-IDF	99.05	89.66	98.45	94.12	0 m 0.4593 s	0 m 0.1385 s
	Count	40.82	34.48	83.97	37.38	0 m 0.4723 s	0 m 0.1495 s
	TF-IDF, Stopwords	98.02	85.34	97.73	91.24	0 m 0.3706 s	0 m 0.4958 s
	Count, Stopwords	71.91	72.84	92.28	72.38	0 m 0.1763 s	0 m 0.1140 s
KNN	TF-IDF	100.00	61.64	94.68	76.27	0 m 0.0041 s	0 m 0.2161 s
	Count	0.00	0.00	86.12	0.00	0 m 0.0010 s	0 m 0.3007 s
	TF-IDF, Stopwords	99.08	46.55	92.52	63.34	0 m 0.0014 s	0 m 0.9363 s
	Count, Stopwords	0.00	0.00	86.12	0.00	0 m 0.0010 s	0 m 0.3494 s
NB	TF-IDF	98.21	94.83	99.04	96.49	0 m 0.0018 s	0 m 0.0003 s
	Count	91.50	97.41	98.39	94.36	0 m 0.0019 s	0 m 0.0004 s
	TF-IDF, Stopwords	95.20	93.97	98.50	94.58	0 m 0.0017 s	0 m 0.0005 s
	Count, Stopwords	87.11	96.12	97.49	91.39	0 m 0.0022 s	0 m 0.0016 s
DT	TF-IDF	90.05	85.78	96.71	87.86	0 m 0.2270 s	0 m 0.0006 s
	Count	88.21	87.07	96.59	87.64	0 m 0.1238 s	0 m 0.0008 s
	TF-IDF, Stopwords	86.70	81.47	95.69	84.00	0 m 0.1950 s	0 m 0.0104 s
	Count, Stopwords	87.39	83.62	96.05	85.46	0 m 0.1386 s	0 m 0.0026 s
LR	TF-IDF	93.33	72.41	95.45	81.55	0 m 0.0107 s	0 m 0.0002 s
	Count	96.73	89.22	98.09	92.83	0 m 0.0153 s	0 m 0.0015 s
	TF-IDF, Stopwords	90.06	62.50	93.84	73.79	0 m 0.0085 s	0 m 0.0005 s
	Count, Stopwords	97.13	87.50	97.91	92.06	0 m 0.0104 s	0 m 0.0022 s
RF	TF-IDF	100.00	86.64	98.15	92.84	0 m 0.9180 s	0 m 0.0150 s
	Count	100.00	83.62	97.73	91.08	0 m 0.9301 s	0 m 0.0290 s
	TF-IDF, Stopwords	100.00	82.76	97.61	90.57	0 m 1.2973 s	0 m 0.0437 s
	Count, Stopwords	100.00	81.90	97.49	90.05	0 m 1.3429 s	0 m 0.0448 s
AdaBoost	TF-IDF	95.26	86.64	97.55	90.74	0 m 2.4091 s	0 m 0.0185 s
	Count	96.24	88.36	97.91	92.13	0 m 2.1926 s	0 m 0.0189 s
	TF-IDF, Stopwords	96.72	76.29	96.35	85.30	0 m 2.5404 s	0 m 0.0370 s
	Count, Stopwords	93.78	84.48	97.07	88.89	0 m 2.4455 s	0 m 0.0234 s
Bagging	TF-IDF	93.52	87.07	97.37	90.18	0 m 1.1530 s	0 m 0.0579 s
	Count	91.59	89.22	97.37	90.39	0 m 0.7393 s	0 m 0.0214 s
	TF-IDF, Stopwords	91.08	83.62	96.59	87.19	0 m 1.0032 s	0 m 0.0284 s
	Count, Stopwords	95.67	85.78	97.49	90.45	0 m 0.8343 s	0 m 0.0408 s
ETC	TF-IDF	99.50	86.21	98.03	92.38	0 m 0.6672 s	0 m 0.0115 s
	Count	99.02	87.07	98.09	92.66	0 m 0.6012 s	0 m 0.0131 s
	TF-IDF, Stopwords	100.00	78.88	97.07	88.19	0 m 0.9153 s	0 m 0.0454 s
	Count, Stopwords	100.00	81.03	97.37	89.52	0 m 0.7918 s	0 m 0.0201 s
LSTM	TF-IDF	0.00	0.00	86.60	0.00	14 m 54.3540 s	0 m 35.1124 s
	Count	0.00	0.00	86.60	0.00	20 m 19.1406 s	0 m 32.3467 s
	TF-IDF, Stopwords	0.00	0.00	86.60	0.00	9 m 49.5561 s	0 m 28.2616 s
	Count, Stopwords	0.00	0.00	86.60	0.00	15 m 53.9231 s	0 m 30.3698 s
	Sequence	98.08	91.07	98.56	94.44	0 m 32.2483 s	0 m 3.2479 s
	Sequence, Stopwords	91.27	93.30	97.91	92.27	0 m 45.1065 s	0 m 1.2113 s
DCF	TF-IDF	98.68	96.98	**99.40**	97.83	1 m 41.7678 s	0 m 9.7851 s
	Count	98.26	97.41	**99.40**	97.84	0 m 46.6826 s	0 m 4.6078 s
	TF-IDF, Stopwords	98.63	93.10	98.86	95.79	1 m 54.8653 s	0 m 2.4483 s
	Count, Stopwords	97.79	95.26	99.04	96.51	1m 6.5370 s	0 m 1.3066 s

Table 4. Performance comparison between deep cascade forest and other classifiers on YouTube spam dataset

Classifier	Text processing	Precision (%)	Recall (%)	Accuracy (%)	F1(%)	Training time (s)	Testing time (s)
SVM	TF-IDF	95.86	92.05	93.87	93.92	0 m 0.1041 s	0 m 0.0281 s
	Count	70.68	71.85	70.19	71.26	0 m 0.1014 s	0 m 0.0229 s
	TF-IDF, Stopwords	96.36	78.81	87.56	86.70	0 m 0.0908 s	0 m 0.0288 s
	Count, Stopwords	77.67	79.47	77.68	78.56	0 m 0.0521 s	0 m 0.0117 s
KNN	TF-IDF	98.81	27.48	62.52	43.01	0 m 0.0017 s	0 m 0.0258 s
	Count	98.65	72.85	85.52	83.81	0 m 0.0011 s	0 m 0.0202 s
	TF-IDF, Stopwords	98.46	21.19	59.28	34.88	0 m 0.0008 s	0 m 0.0279 s
	Count, Stopwords	98.34	58.94	78.36	73.71	0 m 0.0007 s	0 m 0.0243 s
NB	TF-IDF	90.79	94.70	92.33	92.71	0 m 0.0018 s	0 m 0.0004 s
	Count	90.42	93.71	91.65	92.03	0 m 0.0009 s	0 m 0.0001 s
	TF-IDF, Stopwords	89.68	83.44	86.54	86.45	0 m 0.0010 s	0 m 0.0001 s
	Count, Stopwords	88.69	83.11	85.86	85.81	0 m 0.0011 s	0 m 0.0013 s
DT	TF-IDF	95.88	92.38	94.04	94.10	0 m 0.0450 s	0 m 0.0003 s
	Count	93.71	93.71	93.53	93.71	0 m 0.0247 s	0 m 0.0004 s
	TF-IDF, Stopwords	95.02	82.12	88.59	88.10	0 m 0.0481 s	0 m 0.0003 s
	Count, Stopwords	93.63	82.78	88.25	87.87	0 m 0.0348 s	0 m 0.0007 s
LR	TF-IDF	95.34	88.08	91.65	91.57	0 m 0.0081 s	0 m 0.0001 s
	Count	95.27	93.38	94.21	94.31	0 m 0.0045s	0 m 0.0001s
	TF-IDF, Stopwords	96.69	77.48	87.05	86.03	0 m 0.0030 s	0 m 0.0001 s
	Count, Stopwords	95.65	80.13	87.90	87.21	0 m 0.0034 s	0 m 0.0001 s
RF	TF-IDF	97.90	92.72	95.23	95.24	0 m 3.5051 s	0 m 0.1002 s
	Count	97.92	93.71	95.74	95.77	0 m 3.3739 s	0 m 0.1228 s
	TF-IDF, Stopwords	97.62	81.46	89.44	88.81	0 m 4.3453 s	0 m 0.0874 s
	Count, Stopwords	97.27	82.45	89.78	89.25	0 m 4.5593 s	0 m 0.1163 s
AdaBoost	TF-IDF	94.20	91.39	92.67	92.77	0 m 0.4922 s	0 m 0.0071 s
	Count	94.30	93.05	93.53	93.67	0 m 0.4322 s	0 m 0.0068 s
	TF-IDF, Stopwords	94.92	80.46	87.73	87.10	0 m 0.4404 s	0 m 0.0071 s
	Count, Stopwords	95.29	80.46	87.90	87.25	0 m 0.4357 s	0 m 0.0071 s
Bagging	TF-IDF	97.22	92.72	94.89	94.92	0 m 0.2403 s	0 m 0.0085 s
	Count	95.89	92.72	94.21	94.28	0 m 0.2488 s	0 m 0.0081 s
	TF-IDF, Stopwords	97.57	79.80	88.59	87.80	0 m 0.2903 s	0 m 0.0083 s
	Count, Stopwords	96.14	82.45	89.27	88.77	0 m 0.2522 s	0 m 0.0082 s
ETC	TF-IDF	94.48	90.73	92.50	92.57	0 m 0.1329 s	0 m 0.0024 s
	Count	96.90	93.05	94.89	94.93	0 m 0.1476 s	0 m 0.0035 s
	TF-IDF, Stopwords	94.02	78.15	86.20	85.35	0 m 0.1577 s	0 m 0.0025 s
	Count, Stopwords	95.14	77.81	86.54	85.61	0 m 0.1473 s	0 m 0.0030 s
LSTM	TF-IDF	51.45	100.00	51.45	67.94	2 m 56.7070 s	0 m 8.4437 s
	Count	51.37	99.67	51.28	67.79	3 m 20.1492 s	0 m 7.8555 s
	TF-IDF, Stopwords	51.45	100.00	51.45	67.94	2 m 7.2586 s	0 m 9.3072 s
	Count, Stopwords	51.45	100.00	51.45	67.94	2 m 7.2586 s	0 m 8.1658 s
	Sequence	94.95	87.09	90.97	90.85	0 m 47.4032 s	0 m 1.1193 s
	Sequence, Stopwords	88.97	85.43	87.05	87.16	1 m 10.3903 s	0 m 1.0290 s
DCF	TF-IDF	95.65	94.70	95.06	95.17	0 m 8.7054 s	0 m 0.2663 s
	Count	95.71	96.03	**95.74**	**95.87**	0 m 8.6446 s	0 m 0.2523 s
	TF-IDF, Stopwords	95.82	83.44	89.61	89.20	0 m 10.4687 s	0 m 0.0996 s
	Count, Stopwords	92.54	90.40	91.31	91.46	0 m 11.8891 s	0 m 0.3085 s

B   Parameters of LSTM in our Experiment

The LSTM layer contains 64 units for SMS spam detection and 100 units for YouTube spam detection. On both datasets, the batch size is set to 128 In addition, an embedding layer is used to convert each word in the sequence into a dense vector in advance. The embedding layer follows the LSTM layer, a fully connected layer with 256 units, an activation layer using ReLu function, a dropout layer with a dropout rate of 0.1, a fully connected layer with 1 unit, and an activation layer using sigmoid function.

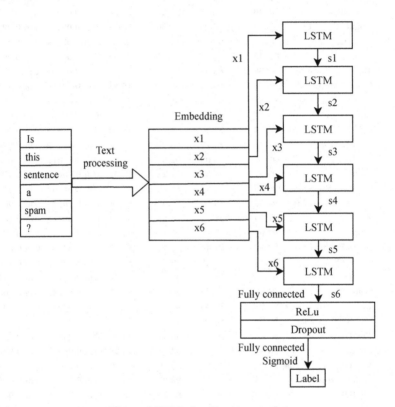

Fig. 5. LSTM classification model

The structure of LSTM is shown in Fig. 5, suppose the texts to sequences processing approach is used, then the output integer sequence is fed to the LSTM model. After embedding each token in the sequence into a 50-dimension word vector x, it is then fed to the LSTM layer with 100 hidden units. Overall, the output 100-dimension vector is processed through a 256 units fully connected layer, a 256 units ReLu layer, a fully connected layer with 1 unit in turn, and finally gets the predicted label through the sigmoid mapping.

References

1. Almeida, T.A.: Sms spam collection data set. https://archive.ics.uci.edu/ml/datasets/SMS+Spam+Collection. Accessed 25 Apr 2019
2. Almeida, T.A.: SMS spam collection data set from Tiago A. Almeida's homepage. http://www.dt.fee.unicamp.br/~tiago/smsspamcollection/. Accessed 25 Apr 2019
3. Almeida, T.A.: Youtube spam collection data set from Tiago A. Almeida's homepage. http://www.dt.fee.unicamp.br/~tiago//youtubespamcollection/. Accessed 25 Apr 2019
4. Bengio, Y., Ducharme, R., Vincent, P., Jauvin, C.: A neural probabilistic language model. J. Mach. Learn. Res. **3**, 1137–1155 (2003)
5. Dahl, G.E., Yu, D., Deng, L., Acero, A.: Context-dependent pre-trained deep neural networks for large-vocabulary speech recognition. IEEE Trans. Audio Speech Lang. Process. **20**(1), 30–42 (2012)
6. Dong, C., Zhou, B.: An ensemble learning framework for online web spam detection. In: 2013 12th International Conference on Machine Learning and Applications, vol. 1, pp. 40–45. IEEE (2013)
7. Drucker, H., Wu, D., Vapnik, V.N.: Support vector machines for spam categorization. IEEE Trans. Neural Netw. **10**(5), 1048–1054 (1999)
8. Hinton, G.E., Salakhutdinov, R.R.: Reducing the dimensionality of data with neural networks. Science **313**(5786), 504–507 (2006)
9. Hochreiter, S., Schmidhuber, J.: Long short-term memory. Neural Comput. **9**(8), 1735–1780 (1997)
10. Jain, G., Sharma, M., Agarwal, B.: Optimizing semantic LSTM for spam detection. Int. J. Inf. Technol. **11**(2), 239–250 (2019)
11. Krizhevsky, A., Sutskever, I., Hinton, G.E.: ImageNet classification with deep convolutional neural networks. In: Advances in Neural Information Processing Systems, pp. 1097–1105 (2012)
12. Le, Q., Mikolov, T.: Distributed representations of sentences and documents. In: International Conference on Machine Learning, pp. 1188–1196 (2014)
13. Vergelis, M., Shcherbakova, T., Sidorina, T.: Spam and phishing in 2018. https://securelist.com/spam-and-phishing-in-2018/89701/. Accessed 25 Apr 2019
14. McCord, M., Chuah, M.: Spam detection on twitter using traditional classifiers. In: Calero, J.M.A., Yang, L.T., Mármol, F.G., García Villalba, L.J., Li, A.X., Wang, Y. (eds.) ATC 2011. LNCS, vol. 6906, pp. 175–186. Springer, Heidelberg (2011). https://doi.org/10.1007/978-3-642-23496-5_13
15. Ren, Y., Ji, D.: Neural networks for deceptive opinion spam detection: an empirical study. Inf. Sci. **385**, 213–224 (2017)
16. Salton, G.: Developments in automatic text retrieval. Science **253**(5023), 974–980 (1991)
17. Salton, G., Wong, A., Yang, C.S.: A vector space model for automatic indexing. Commun. ACM **18**(11), 613–620 (1975)
18. Sanville, E., Kenny, S.D., Smith, R., Henkelman, G.: Improved grid-based algorithm for bader charge allocation. J. Comput. Chem. **28**(5), 899–908 (2007)
19. Tang, D., Qin, B., Liu, T.: Document modeling with gated recurrent neural network for sentiment classification. In: Proceedings of the 2015 Conference on Empirical Methods in Natural Language Processing, pp. 1422–1432 (2015)
20. Tracy, M., Jansen, W., Bisker, S.: Guidelines on electronic mail security. NIST Special Publication (2002)

21. Alberto, T.C., Lochter, J.V., Almeida, T.A.: Youtube spam collection data set. http://archive.ics.uci.edu/ml/datasets/YouTube+Spam+Collection. Accessed 25 Apr 2019
22. Wu, T., Liu, S., Zhang, J., Xiang, Y.: Twitter spam detection based on deep learning. In: Proceedings of the Australasian Computer Science Week Multiconference, pp. 3:1–3:8. ACM (2017)
23. Yang, H., Liu, Q., Zhou, S., Luo, Y.: A spam filtering method based on multi-modal fusion. Appl. Sci. **9**(6), 1152 (2019)
24. Zhou, Z.H., Feng, J.: Deep forest: towards an alternative to deep neural networks. In: Proceedings of the 26th International Joint Conference on Artificial Intelligence, pp. 3553–3559. AAAI Press (2017)

Multiplex PageRank in Multilayer Networks Considering Shunt

Xiao Tu[1], Guo-Ping Jiang[2(✉)], and Yurong Song[2]

[1] School of Computer Science and Technology (School of Software,
School of Cyberspace Security), Nanjing University of Posts
and Telecommunications, Nanjing 210003, China
[2] College of Automation, Nanjing University of Posts and Telecommunications,
Nanjing 210003, China
jianggp@njupt.edu.cn

Abstract. Recently it has been recognized that many complex biological, technological and social networks have a multilayer nature and can be described by multilayer networks. Multilayer networks are formed by a set of nodes connected by links having different connotations forming the different layers of the multilayer. Illustrating the centrality of the nodes in a multilayer network is an interesting task since the centrality of the node organically depends on the importance associated to links of a certain type. Here we propose to assign to each node of a multilayer network a centrality called Coupling Multiplex PageRank that is a modification of the coupling given to every distinct pattern of connections (multi-links) existent in the multilayer network between any two nodes. Since multi-links differentiate all the possible ways where the links in distinct layers can overlap, the Coupling Multiplex PageRank can describe the coupling effects during the multi-links. Here we apply the Coupling Page Rank to a multilayer artificial network and to a multiplex traffic network. Findings indicate that considering the network with multilayers helps uncover the rankings of nodes, which are different from the rankings in a monotonous network.

Keywords: Multilayer networks · Multiplex PageRank · Shunt

1 Introduction

Networks become more and more representative in complex systems [1–3]. Although many achievements have been achieved in traditional network research, many researches, expectation, interpretation and control of the dynamic fields of various systems still remain to be studied, as traditional networks support limited representation of complex systems. There are interdependent interconnections among various systems, which produce various interacting systems. Various types of interrelated nodes comprise many complex systems of interaction that form multilayer networks [4–7]. Multilayer networks can be used to model large numbers of complex systems, examples include financial [8, 9], ecological [10], information system [11], transportation [12] and numerous other areas. The potential characteristics of multilayer networks describe the complex systems more accurately than before, which has led to the upsurge of research.

© Springer Nature Switzerland AG 2019
F. Liu et al. (Eds.): SciSec 2019, LNCS 11933, pp. 47–58, 2019.
https://doi.org/10.1007/978-3-030-34637-9_4

Centrality has promoted the interest of sociologists for decades [13, 14]. Centrality is usually used to measure the relative importance of nodes in the network, which is important for identifying influential diffusers [15], engineering optima topologies for network traffic congestion with local search [16], exploring efficient ways in which to construct the network structure [17], identifying proteins crucial for the cell survival [18], and other applications. Various methods are used to evaluate centrality, such as Betweenness centrality [19], Degree centrality [20], Eigenvector centrality [21], Closeness centrality [13], PageRank centrality [22], etc. In these methods, the PageRank centrality may be the earliest and most frequently used measure, originally running behind Google's general search engine and then applied to a large number of scenarios.

Recently, researchers are concerning about measuring the centrality of multiplex networks. The Eigenvector multiplex centrality assumed that the centrality of nodes in a layer is influenced by the centrality of other layers [23]. The Versatility of nodes highlights the relevance of the related nodes in different layers and is applicable to multilayer networks, in which the corresponding nodes in different layers are connected through interconnections [24]. The Multiplex PageRank centrality utilizes the correlation between node degrees in different layers by random walk of transmission [25–29].

In these centrality measures, the Versatility of nodes is the only measure of interconnection, while both the Multiplex PageRank and the Eigenvector multiplex centrality stipulate one-to-one links in the nodes of different levels, which will be called inner links in the rest of the paper. The major problem when identifying a centrality of the nodes in a multiplex network with inner links is that the centrality depends on the relationship associated to the distinct types of connection that may exist between the nodes in the same layer. However, as important as the impact of connections, the influence of any two nodes in different layers depends on the coupling relationship in the internal links. This paper intends to solve this problem by considering the coupling relationship of a generalization of PageRank.

Adopting with the model of random-walk, PageRank is depicted as a random surfer that constrained by two rules: the suffer skip to one of any nodes chosen within the same probabilities; the suffer walk randomly to one of his or her neighbors. The time for a random walker to pass a node is a measure of the importance of the node, and it can also be identified by the assigned score. In order to extend the measurement of PageRank center to an instance of multilayer networks, Multiplex PageRank is originally proposed in a double layer network composed of small world networks and fully connected networks, in which the same users send instant messages and publish information to a forum. In addition, it is assumed that the PageRank centrality of a node in a layer may affect the node can be obtained in another layer, and Multiplex PageRank obtains the affected centrality of the latter node [29]. However, the influence of the latter node on the former leads to the feedback effect of the former on the latter, and the latter is ignored. In order to identify the interactions between corresponding nodes in different layers, we introduce coupling terms to illustrate their relationships.

Coupling is originally a physical concept. It describes the phenomenon that two or more than two systems or motions interact through various interactions [30, 31]. The coupling coefficient describes the degree of system or motion interaction. As a complex system, there is a coupling relationship between nodes and connections in the network.

The properties of distribution, amplification [30] and reduction [31] caused by couplers and dividers in physical systems is also applicable to networks. Here, we propose a new centrality measure called Coupling Multiplex PageRank, which takes the feedback influence into account, collects the centrality of the corresponding nodes in different layers, and distributes the total centrality back to each node according to the coupling coefficient caused by the two specifications. In this way, we can surpass the influence model in each layer.

The remainder of this paper is organized as follows. In Sect. 2 we briefly describe the basic notation of PageRank and devote to, in detail, analysis the centrality of nodes in multilayer networks in considering of the coupling effect. In Sect. 3, several numerical computations are presented in this section. Finally, we summarize our findings and some prospects in Sect. 4.

2 Discussion

In order to evaluate the importance of web pages, the PageRank s_i of a node i in a network with N nodes is defined as Eq. (1) [22]:

$$s_i(t+1) = \alpha \sum_{j=1}^{N} A_{ji} \frac{s_j(t)}{h_j} + (1 - \alpha) \frac{1}{N}, \tag{1}$$

where h_j means the out-neighbors of j that meet $h_j = \max(1, k_j^{out}) = \max(1, \sum_{r=1}^{N} A_{rj})$ in directed networks and $h_j = \max(1, k_j)$ in undirected networks. The node without any neighbor is considered to be pointing at itself. In addition, A_{ji} is an adjacency matrix. If there is a connection from node j to node i, its element is equal to 1 and otherwise to 0, and α is called the damping factor satisfying $0 < \alpha < 1$. PageRank can be interpreted as a centrality contribution, and each node transfers its centrality to other nodes. A node j uniformly transfers the α of its total centrality equally to the out-neighbors of j, while the total scores of $(1 - \alpha)$ points to each node in the network averagely. The sorting process starts at the same centrality of each node and continues to the steady state. The PageRank of a node is associated with the other nodes pointing to it. Thus, the PageRank of a node is predicted to vary as a function of the node's in-degree. If nodes in a network are assembled into classes relying on their expanded degrees $k = (k^{in}, k^{out})$, the average PageRank for nodes' class with k degree presents as:

$$\bar{x}(k) = \alpha \frac{k^{in}}{<k^{in}> N} + \frac{1 - \alpha}{N}, \tag{2}$$

where the symbol $<\dots>$ indicates the average over the N nodes of the network.

Contrasted with normal networks, nodes in multilayer networks can be connected to each other through more than one type of link, thus providing a more detailed model that can evaluate the location of the nodes. According to the various attributes of nodes, each node can be divided into multiple subordinate nodes, which are regarded as corresponding nodes, such as in Fig. 1(a). The multilayer network in Fig. 1(a) is converted to a single layer network, and the result is shown in Fig. 1(b). Figure 1 shows that the connectivity of nodes in multilayer networks is more obvious than that of normal, because there are various types of relationships, especially overlapping relations. Therefore, the generation of PageRank to the multilayer network will adopt a novel way to measure the importance of nodes associated with their multiple interrelated connections. Therefore, new sorting of nodes can be obtained that can be easily exported with nodes in a single-layer network.

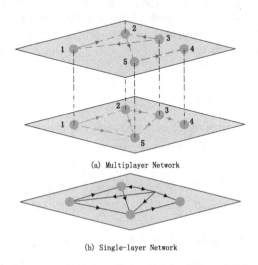

(a) Multiplayer Network

(b) Single-layer Network

Fig. 1. Example of how the multiplex offers more detailed model than the monotonous

Here, we define an extended and generalization PageRank measurement called Coupling Multiplex PageRank centrality, which takes the effect of feedback into account and can be applied to any multilayer network dataset. First, the basic symbols used are introduced. In order to adapt to any network different from PageRank, we define a multilayer network $G = (G_1, G_2, \ldots, G_M)$ composed of M layers, each with N nodes, and $g_{ij}^{(L)}$ with $L = 1, 2, \ldots, M$ represent the connection between node i and node j in the L layer. It should be noted that in this definition, multilayer network include only normal connections between each unrelated N node in the same layer, as well as the internal links between each M corresponding node in the different layers.

This centrality measure depends on the set of parameters c and α_L, which represents the coupling and dividing coefficient, L means the number of layers. In multilayer networks two irrelevance nodes may connect simultaneously in no less than two layers that we nominate overlap connections in the above. The overlap connections of any two irrelevance nodes exists a coupling amplifier or attenuator that can amplify or reduce the contribution through by each connection with a coupling coefficient. In the model of contributions of centralities, each node at each time step obtains its centrality by accepting the contributions of its in-neighbors. The centrality of corresponding nodes in different layers will aggregate to a comprehensive centrality by a coupling relation caused by the inner links between the corresponding nodes. The comprehensive centrality subsequently assigns to the corresponding nodes by the coupling coefficient α_L. The redistributed centrality will then divide to its out-neighbors and repeat the above process. Considering of the significance of this measure in physical systems, we will adopt an urban multiplex traffic network that contains various transportation to explicate the Coupling PageRank centrality measure.

Supposing a model of population migration in an urban multiplex traffic network that in purpose to obtain the rankings of hub cities of transportation. An urban multiplex traffic network includes numerous ways of transportation that can be deemed as several monotonous networks. To clarify our measure simply, we firstly consider the urban multiplex traffic network to a double layer network including N nodes in each layer that comprises of a flight network G_1 including the status of each airline $g_{ij}^{(1)}$ and a railway network G_2 including the status of each railway $g_{ij}^{(2)}$, where $i,j = 1,2,\ldots,N$ depicting the airports and train stations. A city contains a train station or an airport or both the two is considered as a global node in our urban multiplex traffic network, while the train station or airport in a city is regard as a local node, which will be called node for short. In additional, we call the nodes coexisting in a global node corresponding to each other and nominated as the corresponding nodes. A link between two corresponding nodes is nominated as an inner link. It is important to note each node i adopt one-to-one connection to i's corresponding nodes in other layers that all belong to the global node i. As we are aiming on obtaining the rankings of hub cities of transportation, the train stations or airports in a same city can be deemed as one train station or airport. The connections between irrelevant nodes in the same layer are identified by the existence of railway or airline between cities. A directed link exists as there is a railway or an airline from one city to another city. A coupler will occur when a railway and an airline existing simultaneously, and impact the transmission ability of the railway and the airline by a coupling coefficient c that meets the condition $c > 0$. The transmission ability amplifies as $c > 1$ or reduces as $0 < c < 1$, while $c = 1$ represents a standard mode. For instance, a railway and an airline existing with the same beginning point and ending point enrich the optional transmission ways that discount the number of passengers in both the airline and railway to c times. Corresponding nodes in different layers exist inner links that couple the centrality of the nodes to a comprehensive centrality and redistributing the comprehensive centrality to these nodes respectively by a distribute coefficient α_L that meets $0 < \sum_L \alpha_L < 1$. Thus, in our urban multiplex traffic network model we record the association probability of airport network as α_1 and train station network as α_2. Aiming on depicting our centrality measure in a convenient way, we define the comprehensive Coupling Multiplex PageRank centrality of each M corresponds nodes as S_i, while the distributed centrality of the node i in L layer expresses as $s_i^{(L)}$. In the urban multiplex traffic network model, we adopt the distributed centrality of an airport in city i as $s_i^{(1)}$ and a train station in city i as $s_i^{(2)}$. Therefore, the relation of a comprehensive centrality S_i to each distributed centrality $s_i^{(L)}$ presents as Eq. (3):

$$s_i^{(1)}(t) + s_i^{(2)}(t) \xrightarrow{\Delta} S_i(t), \tag{3}$$

In which Δ is a modifying coefficient that will be illustrated later. The parameter t represents the time step of a process that at here describe the coupling aggregation occurring between each two corresponding nodes in different layers to be considered as an inner interaction of the global node i that without occupying time step. A comprehensive centrality S_i mixes the centrality of each node i in all layers, and then delivers back to these nodes that will contribute to their out-neighbors in each layer at next time step. Defining the redistributed centrality of a node i in network G_L as $\tilde{s}_i^{(L)}$, a dividing process of the comprehensive centrality for each two corresponding nodes presents as Eq. (4):

$$\begin{aligned} \tilde{s}_i^{(1)}(t) &= \alpha_1 S_i(t) \\ \tilde{s}_i^{(2)}(t) &= \alpha_2 S_i(t). \end{aligned} \tag{4}$$

It should be noted that the parameters α_1 and α_2 are the decompose coefficient that meet the condition $\alpha_1 \geq 0$, $\alpha_2 \geq 0$ and $\alpha_1 + \alpha_2 < 1$. The adjacent matrix of each monotonous network of a multilayer network writes as G_L, in which contains the element of the linkage status record as $g_{ji}^{(L)}$ that equal to 1 if there exists a link form node j to node i, otherwise 0.

Refer to Eq. (1) we can discover that the PageRank centrality of a node distributes to all the node's out-neighbors at each step time by the method of average. The Coupling Multiplex PageRank centrality measure, however, differ from the classical PageRank centrality measure, can be described as a model of population migration that the centrality of a node distributes to its out-neighbors with considering of overlap connections. Assuming a single railway or a single airline that through from one city to another city, Humans move by the monotonous way with a normal probability. Nevertheless, the number of humans who travel by the existed single mode of transportation will reduce when the second mode occurs, for the increasing of optional way, which is reflected by c. An opposite instance refers to virus spreading model that the transmission ability may increase when two or more than two transmission ways coexist. Depending on these views, we define a distributed Coupling Multiplex PageRank centrality of a node i in an airport network G_1 presents in Eq. (5):

$$s_i^{(1)}(t+1) = \sum_j g_{ji}^{(1)} c^{g_{ji}^{(2)}} \frac{\tilde{s}_j^{(1)}(t)}{H_j^{(1)}}, \tag{5}$$

where $H_j^{(1)} = \sum_r g_{jr}^{(1)} c^{g_{jr}^{(2)}} + \delta(0, \sum_r g_{jr}^{(1)} c^{g_{jr}^{(2)}})$, $\delta(x, y)$ is the Kronecker delta which equals to one as $x = y$ and zero as $x \neq y$ that exploited to control a node j without any out-neighbor delivers j's contribution to itself. This equation refers to the contribution to the centrality of node i in network G_1. Like with the classical PageRank measure, this contribution is inversely proportional to the out-degree of the in-neighbors of node i.

However, unlike the classical measure, Eq. (5) enable this contribution to be also impacted by the process of transmission by the link that both from node j to node i in network G_1 have in network G_2, and also affected by the centrality of node i with its in-neighbors in network G_1. This interaction between the two networks has a two-fold influence on the centrality of a node. Firstly, a link from node j to node i in network G_1 amplifies or reduces with a parameter c if the link from node j to node i in network G_2 exists. The distributed centrality for node i depends on the in-neighbors of i that amplifies or reduces with the c. Secondly, the contribution of each in-neighbor j to i's centrality is discounted by dividing j's centrality by the number of j's out-neighbors in network G_1. Similarly, a distributed centrality of a train station node i in a directed train station network G_2 can present as Eq. (6):

$$
s_i^{(2)}(t+1) = \sum_j g_{ji}^{(2)} c^{g_{ji}^{(1)}} \frac{\tilde{s}_j^{(2)}(t)}{H_j^{(2)}},
\tag{6}
$$

where $H_j^{(2)} = \sum_r g_{jr}^{(2)} c^{g_{jr}^{(1)}} + \delta(0, \sum_r g_{jr}^{(2)} c^{g_{jr}^{(1)}})$. This equation refers to the contribution to the centrality of a node i in network G_2 and the link from i's in-neighbors to i in network G_2.

Equations (5, 6) can describe as a process of population migrate from a city to its out-neighbors in an airport or a train station network with uncertain probabilities that associate with the links from the city to its out-neighbors in another network. This process, which is distinct from the inner process of a global node, occurs between irrelevant nodes in same layers that occupies a time step and obtains the centrality of a node in each layer at time step $(t+1)$. The centrality of the node in each layer then continue to aggregate at time step $(t+1)$. To acquire the rankings of the comprehensive centralities of nodes in an urban multiplex traffic network, we refine Eq. (3) to Eq. (7) presents as:

$$
S_i(t+1) = \sum_j g_{ji}^{(1)} c^{g_{ji}^{(2)}} \frac{\alpha_1 S_j(t)}{H_j^{(1)}} + \sum_j g_{ji}^{(2)} c^{g_{ji}^{(1)}} \frac{\alpha_2 S_j(t)}{H_j^{(2)}} + (1 - \alpha_1 - \alpha_2)v_i,
\tag{7}
$$

where $H_j^{(1)} = \sum_r g_{jr}^{(1)} c^{g_{jr}^{(2)}} + \delta(0, \sum_r g_{jr}^{(1)} c^{g_{jr}^{(2)}})$, and $H_j^{(2)} = \sum_r g_{jr}^{(2)} c^{g_{jr}^{(1)}} + \delta(0, \sum_r g_{jr}^{(2)} c^{g_{jr}^{(1)}})$.
The first term in Eq. (7) describes the number of passengers who tend to move by an airplane. It concerns with the contribution to node i's centrality that delivered from the centrality of the nodes pointing to i in network G_1. This contribution associate with the out-degree of node i's in-neighbors in network G_1 that also affected by the links from i's in-neighbors to i in network G_1 have in network G_2. Each i's in-neighbor j in network G_1 is assigned α_1 of the comprehensive centrality S_j and divide into $H_j^{(1)}$ parts that will deliver to all of j's out-neighbors in network G_1. The contribution from j to i in network G_1 accounts for $g_{ji}^{(1)} c^{g_{ji}^{(2)}}$ of $H_j^{(1)}$ parts. The status of a link from j to i in network G_1 expresses as $g_{ji}^{(1)}$ that identifies if j is i's in-neighbor or not and will be retained or discarded. The contribution from j to i equals to zero if the link from j to i

without existing in network G_1. Otherwise, the contribution occupies a standard part if the link from j to i is non-exist in network G_2, or occupies a part modified by a coupling coefficient c if the link from j to i exists in G_2. In other words, the contributions from node i's in-neighbors to i in network G_1 concern with the link from i's in-neighbors to i in network G_2.

The second term is similar with the first term that describe the number of passengers who tend to move by a train. Each node i's in-neighbor j in network G_2 is assigned α_2 of the comprehensive centrality S_j that divide into $H_j^{(2)}$ parts and deliver proportionally to j's out-neighbors in network G_2. The contribution from j to i in network G_2 similarly associates with the link from j to i in network G_1. This contribution tend to be zero as if the link from j to i is deficient in network G_2, otherwise accounts for a portion of j's entire contribution. The entire contribution of j in network G_2 divides into $H_j^{(2)}$ parts that one of these parts will be delivered to i if the link from j to i without existing in network G_1, or one of the parts changing with c will be delivered to i if the link from j to i exists in network G_1.

The third term nominated the modifying coefficient that describe as the people who reluctant to migrate and incline to stay back. According to the above, a global node j distributes α_1 of the comprehensive centrality S_j to the node j in network G_1 and α_2 of S_j to the node j in network G_2. It can describe as the passengers originally from a city migrate randomly in a multiplex network that α_1 of them prefer migrating by air, and α_2 of them prefer migrating by train. Simultaneously, the people accounting for $(1 - \alpha_1 - \alpha_2)$ decline to migrate and tend to stay back with a personalized element v_i belonging to a personalized vector $V = (v_1, v_2, \ldots, v_N)$ in which contains the average interestingness of staying back in each city for majority people and meets $\sum_i v_i = 1$.

As a result, we can obtain the rankings of the comprehensive centrality of global nodes i by S_i, and the centrality of nodes i with considering of feedback influence in each layer L by $s_i^{(L)}$. The only thing should be noted is the nodes in each layer of a multilayer network adopt one-to-one connect. For instance, if there exists a train station in our urban multiplex traffic network without an airport in the same city, it should be represented by a virtual node that dangling in the airport network.

3 Simulations

To testify the validity of our method, we generated a duplex network that consists of network G_1 and network G_2. Both the two layers were considered as a BA network, constructed primarily by a fully connected network of m nodes that introducing a new node with m_0 links to the existed nodes until there are totally N nodes. We adopted $m = 20$, $m_0 = 12$ and $N = 2000$ in G_1, while $m = 30$, $m_0 = 15$ and $N = 2000$ in G_2 and then obtained the duplex network. Imposing the original centrality of each node i as $S_i(t = 0) = \frac{1}{N}$, the coupling distribution coefficient $c = 0.2$, $\alpha_1 = 0.5$, $\alpha_2 = 0.35$, and the personalized vector of each node i as $v_i = \frac{1}{N}$. The distribution of Multiplex PageRank S on in-degree is shown in Fig. 2. Furthermore, the data of our Multiplex PageRank comparing with the classical PageRank on the monotonous network converted from the multiplex network by combined the overlapped edges is shown in Fig. 3. For large values of PageRank, the Multiplex PageRank is larger than the monotonous PageRank that due to the position of nodes in both the two layers and the role of each layer. A node which is important in both two layers positively possesses a large value of PageRank, while the values of nodes with high importance in only one layer is similarly rely on other factors.

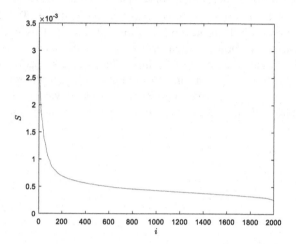

Fig. 2. Results of Multiplex PageRank in a artificial double-layer network, i is the number of rankings of nodes, while S depicts the centrality of the node, both of the two layers are BA networks.

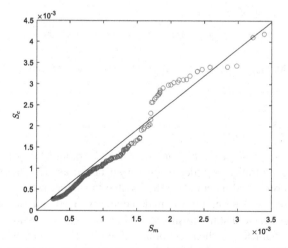

Fig. 3. Coupling Multiplex PageRank S_c versus Monotonous PageRank S_m in Artificial Network

To testify the validity of our method, we adopt the real Air-Train network [32]. The multilayer networks data will be combined to classical single-layer networks. The comparison of the data of the multilayer networks and the corresponding classical networks will show. For the multilayer networks, the original centrality of each node i is set as $S_i(t = 0) = \frac{1}{N}$, the coupling distribution coefficients as $c = 0.2$, $\alpha_1 = 0.5$, $\alpha_2 = 0.35$, and the personalized vector of each node i as $v_i = \frac{1}{N}$. For the corresponding classical networks, the original centrality of each node i is also set as $S_i(t = 0) = \frac{1}{N}$, and the damping factor as $\alpha = 0.85$. A comparison of the Multiplex PageRank and the classical PageRank of Air-Train network is shown in Fig. 4. This figure reveals the centrality difference between the multilayer network and the single-layer network. For large values of PageRank, the Coupling Multiplex PageRank is smaller than the single-layer PageRank due to the positions of nodes in both layers and the role of each layer. A node that is important in both layers corresponds to a large value of PageRank, while the values of nodes with high importance in only one layer depend on other factors.

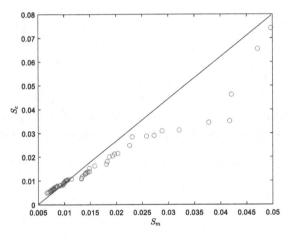

Fig. 4. Coupling Multiplex PageRank S_c versus Monotonous PageRank S_m in real Air-Train Network

4   Conclusions

In conclusion we have proposed here to study the Coupling Multiplex PageRank for characterizing the centrality of nodes in multilayer networks. This measure associates to a node a function called its coupling that is able to capture the role of the different type of connections in determining the node centrality. Two generic nodes of a multilayer network can have distinct positions leading to their success, and here we propose a way to characterize their coupling. From this measure we can extract a comprehensive Multiplex PageRank which provides a comprehensive rank between the nodes of the multiplex. We have applied this measure to an artificial multiplex networks, and to airport multilayer networks. The Coupling Multiplex PageRank can be efficiently measured on duplex multiplex networks, and when suitably simplified, it can be applied to multiplex networks with arbitrary number of layers M.

References

1. Newman, M.E.J.: Networks: An Introduction, vol. 327, no. 8. Oxford Univ Press, New York (2010)
2. Boccaletti, S., Latora, V., Moreno, Y., Chavezf, M., Hwang, D.-U.: Complex networks: structure and dynamics. Complex Syst. Complex. Sci. **424**(4–5), 175–308 (2006)
3. Barrat, A.: Dynamical Processes on Complex Networks. Cambridge University Press, New York (2008)
4. Boccaletti, S., et al.: The structure and dynamics of multilayer networks. Physics reports, vol. 544, no. 1 (2014)
5. Kivelä, M., Arenas, A., Barthelemy, M., Gleeson, J.P., Moreno, Y., Porter, M.A.: Multilayer networks. J. Complex Netw. **2**(3), 203–271 (2014)
6. D'agostino, G., Scala, A.: Networks of Networks: The Last Frontier of Complexity, 340 pages. Springer, Cham (2014). https://doi.org/10.1007/978-3-319-03518-5
7. Bianconi, G.: Interdisciplinary and physics challenges of network theory. Eur. Lett. **111**(5), 56001 (2015)
8. Caccioli, F., Shrestha, M., Moore, C., Farmer, J.D.: Stability analysis of financial contagion due to overlapping portfolios. J. Bank. Finance **46**, 233–245 (2014)
9. Huang, X., Vodenska, I., Havlin, S., Stanley, H.: Cascading failures in bi-partite graphs: model for systemic risk propagation. Scientific reports, vol. 3 (2013)
10. Pocock, M.J.O., Evans, D.M., Memmott, J.: The robustness and restoration of a network of ecological networks. Science **335**(6071), 973–977 (2012)
11. Iacovacci, J., Bianconi, G.: Extracting information from multiplex networks. Chaos **26**(6), 065306 (2016)
12. Gallotti, R., Barthelemy, M.: Anatomy and efficiency of urban multimodal mobility. arXiv preprint arXiv:1411(1274) (2014)
13. Sabidussi, G.: The centrality index of a graph. Psychometrika **31**(4), 581–603 (1966)
14. Katz, L.: A new status index derived from sociometric analysis. Psychometrika **18**(1), 39–43 (1953)
15. Kitsak, M., et al.: Identification of influential spreaders in complex networks. Nat. Phys. **6**(11), 888–893 (2010)
16. Guimerà, R., Díaz-Guilera, A., Vega-Redondo, F., Cabrales, A., Arenas, A.: Optimal network topologies for local search with congestion. Phys. Rev. Lett. **89**(24), 248701 (2002)
17. Guimera, R., Mossa, S., Turtschi, A., Amaral, L.N.: The worldwide air transportation network: anomalous centrality, community structure, and cities' global roles. Proc. Natl. Acad. Sci. **102**(22), 7794–7799 (2005)
18. Jeong, H., Mason, S.P., Barabási, A.-L., Oltvai, Z.N.: Lethality and centrality in protein networks. Nature **411**(6833), 41–42 (2001)
19. Freeman, L.: A set of measures of centrality based on betweenness. Sociometry **40**(1), 35–41 (1977)
20. Freeman, L.: Centrality in social networks conceptual clarification. Soc. Netw. **1**(3), 215–239 (1978)
21. Bonacich, P., Lloyd, P.: Eigenvector-like measures of centrality for asymmetric relations. Soc. Netw. **23**(3), 191–201 (2001)

22. Page, L., Brin, S., Motwani, R., Winograd, T.: The PageRank citation ranking: Bringing order to the web. Stanford InfoLab (1999)

23. Solá, L., Romance, M., Criado, R.: Eigenvector centrality of nodes in multiplex networks. Chaos **23**(3), 033131 (2013)

24. Domenico, M.D., Solé-Ribalta, A., Omodei, E., Gómez, S., Arenas, A.: Ranking in interconnected multilayer networks reveals versatile nodes. Nature Commun. **6**, 6868 (2015)

25. Solé-Ribalta, A., Domenico, M., Gómez, S., Arenas, A.: Centrality rankings in multiplex networks, vol. 9. ACM (2014)

26. Pedroche, F., Romance, M., Criado, R.: A biplex approach to PageRank centrality: from classic to multiplex networks. Chaos **26**(6), 065301 (2016)

27. Jiang, B., Kloster, K., Gleich, D.F., Gribskov, M.: AptRank: An Adaptive PageRank Model for Protein Function Prediction on Bi-relational Graphs. arXiv preprint arXiv:160105506 (2016)

28. Iacovacci, J., Rahmede, C., Arenas, A., Bianconi, G.: Functional multiplex PageRank. Eur. Lett. **116**(2), 28004 (2016)

29. Halu, A., Mondragón, R.J., Panzarasa, P., Bianconi, G.: Multiplex PageRank. PLoS ONE **8** (10), e78293 (2013)

30. Ayasli, Y., Miller, S.W., Mozzi, R., Hanes, L.K. (eds.) Capacitively Coupled Traveling-Wave Power Amplifier. Microwave and Millimeter-Wave Monolithic Circuits (1984)

31. Huang, W.P., Haus, H.A.: Power exchange in grating-assisted couplers. J. Lightwave Technol. **7**(6), 920–924 (1989)

32. Kleineberg, K.K., Buzna, L., Papadopoulos, F., et al.: Geometric correlations mitigate the extreme vulnerability of multiplex networks against targeted attacks. Phys. Rev. Lett. **118** (21), 218301 (2017)

Machine Learning for Cybersecurity

LogGAN: A Sequence-Based Generative Adversarial Network for Anomaly Detection Based on System Logs

Bin Xia[1], Junjie Yin[1], Jian Xu[2], and Yun Li[1(✉)]

[1] Jiangsu Key Laboratory of Big Data Security and Intelligent Processing,
Nanjing University of Posts and Telecommunications, Nanjing, China
{bxia,liyun}@njupt.edu.cn
[2] School of Computer Science and Engineering,
Nanjing University of Science and Technology, Nanjing, China
dolphin.xu@njust.edu.cn

Abstract. System logs which trace system states and record valuable events comprise a significant component of any computer system in our daily life. There exist abundant information (i.e., normal and abnormal instances) involved in logs which assist administrators in diagnosing and maintaining the operation of the system. If diverse and complex anomalies (i.e., bugs and failures) cannot be detected and eliminated efficiently, the running workflows and transactions, even the system, would break down. Therefore, anomaly detection has become increasingly significant and attracted a lot of research attention. However, current approaches concentrate on the anomaly detection in a high-level granularity of logs (i.e., session) instead of detecting log-level anomalies which weakens the efficiency of responding anomalies and the diagnosis of system failures. To overcome the limitation, we propose a sequence-based generative adversarial network for anomaly detection based on system logs named LogGAN which detects log-level anomalies based on the patterns (i.e., the combination of latest logs). In addition, the generative adversarial network-based model relieves the effect of imbalance between normal and abnormal instances to improve the performance of capturing anomalies. To evaluate LogGAN, we conduct extensive experiments on two real-world datasets, and the experimental results show the effectiveness of our proposed approach to log-level anomaly detection.

Keywords: Anomaly detection · Generative adversarial network · Log-level anomaly · Negative sampling

1 Introduction

Anomaly detection is an important task in protecting our daily life from those intended or unintended malicious attacks such as the network intrusion, mobile fraud, industrial damage, and abnormal condition of system [3]. However, with

© Springer Nature Switzerland AG 2019
F. Liu et al. (Eds.): SciSec 2019, LNCS 11933, pp. 61–76, 2019.
https://doi.org/10.1007/978-3-030-34637-9_5

the rapid development of computer science, systems and applications become increasingly complex which makes anomalies diverse and non-trivial to be detected even by human beings. Except for the intended malicious attacks, unknown bugs and errors which are seemingly controllable but caused by non-artificial reason in online systems damage the secure and reliable operating environment. Therefore, the effectiveness and efficiency of anomaly detection have become a big challenge for the further development of information-based society.

Currently, the automated generation of logs is an indispensable component of any large scale system. System logs trace every status of the system and record each critical event in detail to assist administrators in diagnosing bugs, failures, and errors of systems. Therefore, the density of arrival logs and the description of logs directly determine the value of the quantity of knowledge for improving the performance of running systems [9,15]. For example, if arrival logs are extremely dense, it is a challenge to analyze the dependency between events due to the concurrency of logs. Likewise, if the description of logs is colloquial and obscure to represent the state of a system, it is non-trivial to trace the workflows. Figure 1 illustrates the arrival frequency of system logs in practical scenarios, where Fig. 1a shows the logs generated by 203 nodes during 2 days in HDFS and Fig. 1b illustrates the logs generated by 1 node during 215 days in BlusGene/L. Observed from Fig. 1, the peak frequency of arrival logs is 198,878/min and 152,929/hour for HDFS and BGL, respectively. In addition, the number of normal instances is much more than that of anomalies, and generally, anomalies are unlabeled. Therefore, such an extremely frequent arrive of unlabeled logs results in a significant challenge to the prompt response and the precise diagnosis.

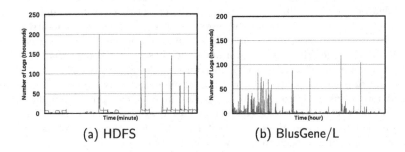

(a) HDFS   (b) BlusGene/L

Fig. 1. Arrival frequency of system logs in the real-world datasets

To overcome the challenges mentioned above, researchers take a lot of efforts on the anomaly detection based on system logs. The proposed approaches are mainly categorized into the supervised, semi-supervised, and unsupervised strategy based on the availability of labeled data (i.e., normal and abnormal instances). Most of these approaches have good performance in detecting anomalies based on diverse system logs. However, there exist two problems in restricting the further development of system diagnosis [1,11–13]. First, these approaches detect session-level anomalies where a session contains many logs and is divided base on some rules (e.g., period, transaction, and node). In other words, the session including abnormal logs will be detected, however, the abnormal logs cannot be located in the session. Therefore, administrators need to diagnose the workflows in the session which is a non-trivial task. Second, the anomaly is not alerted until the logs are traversed in the session. In other words, the anomaly cannot be detected and responded efficiently when the abnormal log is appearing. This two problems significantly limit the effectiveness and efficiency of system diagnosis.

In this paper, we cast the task of anomaly detection as a pattern-based sequential prediction and propose an LSTM-based generative adversarial network to distinguishing upcoming abnormal events named LogGAN based on temporal system logs. First, we exploit a customized log parser to extracting the structured information (i.e., timestamps, signature, and parameters) and transforming each log into an event. Second, the combinations of events (i.e., pattern) and the corresponding upcoming event are collected from temporal system logs using the sliding window. The collected pairs of patterns and events are utilized to construct real training dataset. LogGAN consists of two major components: (1) generator and (2) discriminator. The generator tries to capture the distribution of real training dataset and synthesizes plausible instances (i.e., normal and abnormal data), while the discriminator aims to distinguish the fake ones from the dataset which is built using the real and synthetic data. Finally, the fully-trained generator is applied to detect whether the upcoming log is normal or abnormal based on the latest events. According to the game setting of anomaly detection, the problem of the imbalance between normal and abnormal instances can be relieved by generating 'real' anomalies to supply the real anomalies in the training set. In addition, the LSTM-based generator identifies whether each upcoming log is normal or abnormal, which efficiently responds alerts of anomalies and effectively assists administrators to diagnose workflows, instead of detecting abnormal sessions including anomalies. To the best our knowledge, this is the first attempt to apply a game setting (i.e., adversarial learning) for the anomaly detection based on system logs. Our contribution can be summarized as below:

- A generative adversarial network is proposed to relieve the problem of imbalance between normal and abnormal instances while improving the performance of anomaly detection.
- An LSTM-based detector promotes the efficiency of responding anomalies and marks anomalies of logs instead of detecting session-level anomalies.
- Extensive experiments are conducted to evaluate the effectiveness of LogGAN based on two real-world datasets.

2 Related Work

Generally, the techniques of anomaly detection (i.e., outlier detection) are categorized as supervised, semi-supervised, and unsupervised anomaly detections.

In this section, we will briefly introduce some popular anomaly detections in each category of techniques.

2.1 Supervised Anomaly Detection

Supervised anomaly detections operate under two general assumptions: (1) the labels of normal and abnormal instances are available; (2) the normal and abnormal instances are distinguishable given the feature space. Chen et al. proposed a decision tree-based approach to detecting the actual failures from large Internet sites (i.e., eBay) based on the temporal request traces [5]. The decision trees simultaneously handle the varying types of runtime properties (i.e., continuous and discrete variables). Therefore, the proposed approach was widely used in many practical scenarios. Bodik et al. proposed a fingerprint (i.e., vector) to effectively demonstrate the performance state of systems and implemented a regularized logistic regression-based method for selecting the relevant metrics to build the appropriate fingerprints [1]. The anomalies can be precisely identified using the fingerprints which summarize the properties of the whole data center (e.g., CPU utilization). Liang et al. employed several classifiers (e.g., SVM and nearest neighbor) to detecting the failures in the massive event logs which were collected from the supercomputer IBM BlueGene/L [10]. Similar to Bodik et al., they also derived the specific combination of features to effectively describe each event log for improving the performance of classification tasks, which demonstrates that the representation of normal and abnormal logs is significant. The supervised methods have a quick test phase for the online detections, however, the extreme dependency on the quality of labels limits the application scenarios [18].

2.2 Semi-supervised Anomaly Detection

The semi-supervised anomaly detection operates under the assumption: given the feature space, the normal samples are located closely while the anomalies are far from the clusters of normal ones [3]. The representative of the semi-supervised model is the nearest neighbor-based techniques which can be categorized as (1) distance-based neighbors, and (2) density-based neighbors. To address the problem of the high-dimensional feature space, Zhang et al. proposed a High-Dimension Outlying subspace Detection (HighDOD) to searching for the optimal subset of features to represent outliers [20]. Due to the subset of features (i.e., low-dimensional data), the Euclidean distance is capable of describing the actual distance between normal and abnormal instances. Besides distance-based approaches, the density-based method is also useful to distinguish anomalies. To improve Local Outlier Factor (i.e., a type of popular measure to calculating the density given the instance), Chawla et al. proposed a new measure called Spatial Local Outlier Measure (SLOM) [4,14]. Du et al. proposed LSTM-based anomaly detection and diagnosis framework named DeepLog based on unstructured system logs [6]. DeepLog analyzes and detects anomalies using the log key and the parameter value vector to help administrators for diagnosing the system errors based on workflows. DeepLog is trained based on the normal patterns in system logs and provides a way to be incrementally updated using upcoming logs; therefore, DeepLog is categorized as semi-supervised anomaly detection. Tuor et al. also proposed a recurrent neural network-based approach to detecting abnormal instances where the proposed model considered system logs as sentences in language models [16]. Compared to the supervised anomaly detections, semi-supervised techniques do not extremely rely on the labeled data and the distribution of observed instances and outperform the unsupervised approaches generally. However, the selection of measuring distance is significant for the performance of semi-supervised anomaly detections.

2.3   Unsupervised Anomaly Detection

The unsupervised technique is the most popular approach in the domain of anomaly detection because this technique still works even if the label of data is unknown. This characteristic of the unsupervised technique satisfies the assumption that anomalies are generally rare and unknown in practical scenarios. Lin et al. proposed a cluster-based approach (i.e., LogCluster) to addressing the log-based anomalies detection problem based on the data from Microsoft service product teams [11]. LogCluster aims to cluster the historical and upcoming logs using the knowledge base, and engineers only need to distinguish several logs (i.e., events) in each cluster that can identify the type of anomalies which is located in the same cluster. Therefore, it is not necessary to obtain the label of logs, and the similarity between logs is more essential to operate LogCluster. Lou et al. proposed a novel anomaly detection approach to identifying program invariants based on the unstructured console logs [13]. The proposed approach concentrates on structuring the free form description in console logs and mining the meaningful anomalies after grouping the structured logs with parameters. Different from the traditional anomaly detections which construct models fitting normal instances and distinguish instances that do not conform to the constructed model, Liu et al. proposed a novel concept that explicitly isolates abnormal instances [12]. The proposed isolation forest (iForest) is capable of addressing the high-dimensional problems using an attribute selector (i.e., the characteristic of the decision tree). In addition, iForest achieves good performance even if there are no anomalies occurred in the training set. Xu et al. proposed a PCA-based anomaly detection and visualized the promising results using a decision tree [19]. The main contribution of this work is that the source code is considered as a reference to parse console logs for improving the quality of structured data and the quality data will improve the representation of console logs (i.e., extracted distinguishable features). The advantage of unsupervised techniques is that the approaches are independent with the label information of the training set. The disadvantage of unsupervised techniques is that expert knowledge is still needed to utilize unsupervised approaches for detecting anomalies in practical scenarios, although the techniques reduce the massive workloads.

3   Method

In this paper, we propose a generative adversarial network-based anomaly detection approach named LogGAN which improves the performance of identifying anomalies in an adversarial setting. Figure 2 illustrates the overview of LogGAN. The main modules of LogGAN are categorized into three parts:

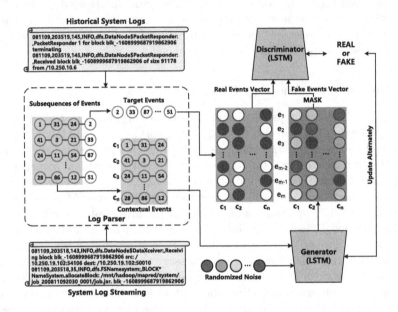

Fig. 2. The framework of anomaly detection generative adversarial network

- *Log Parser:* is the module to parsing unstructured logs into structured logs (or events) which are considered as the minimum units for the following machine learning-based techniques.
- *Adversarial Learning:* is the module to training the LSTM-based anomaly detection model based on the timestamps, signatures, and attributes extracted from structured log.
- *Anomaly Detection:* is the module to detecting and diagnosing anomalies using the LSTM-based model and incrementally update the model based on the upcoming logs and users' feedbacks.

In the following parts of this section, we will introduce each part of LogGAN in detail.

3.1   Log Parser

In the module of log parser, the original unstructured logs are converted into the structured logs. The log parsing, which is considered as the common preprocessing of unstructured logs, is the significant part in the majority of log analysis tasks. Many approaches were proposed to generate events, which are extracted and summarized based on raw logs, for automated performance analysis of system [8,15]. These template-free methods are capable of parsing logs using statistical approaches. However, the performance of these methods is not convincing, because the formations of logs from different systems are chaotic and that is nontrivial to be captured. Therefore, in this paper, we first divide the unstructured logs into several parts (e.g., datetime and content) using the corresponding template, then further extract meaningful information (i.e., event) from these parts [21]. Generally, the event consists of three major components: (1) timestamps, (2) signature and (3) parameters. To make readers fully understand the process of log parser, Fig. 3 illustrates the examples of parsing unstructured logs from two real-world systems (i.e., HDFS and BlusGene/L), respectively.

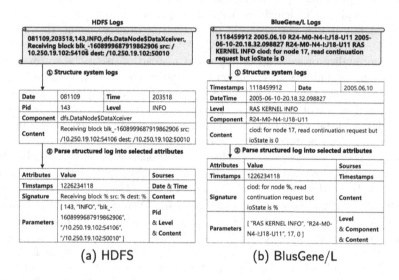

Fig. 3. Example of log parser to converting from logs to structured entities

Note that, HDFS and BlusGene/L are different in the system structures and workflows, hence the parsed structures from the first step are also different. Observed from Fig. 3a, the timestamps, signature, and parameters are extracted exactly where the signature is a static content that presents a type of logs and the parameters record dynamic parts in each log. The three-tuple representation (i.e., timestamps, signature, and parameters) effectively describes the status of each event which provides administrators with sufficient references to diagnose the broken-down system.

3.2 Adversarial Learning

In this paper, we cast the task of anomaly detection as a set of adversarial learning and propose an LSTM-base generative adversarial network named LogGAN to improve the performance of identifying anomalies. The concept of the generative adversarial network (GAN) was proposed by Goodfellow et al. where GAN considers a machine learning problem as a game between two models (i.e., generator and discriminator) [7]. The generator (G) captures the distribution of real samples and generates plausible samples which are similar with real samples in the representation of features, while the discriminator (D) tries to identify whether the upcoming sample is real or synthetic one for improving the quality of samples generated by G. The iteration repeats until both G and D converge, then G is capable of generating 'real' samples. This game setting of machine learning exactly addresses a significant problem in anomaly detection: the overwhelming ratio of normal and abnormal instances. The fully-trained G can capture the distribution of anomalies which further improves the performance of detecting whether the upcoming log is normal or abnormal.

The original GAN, which is utilized to generate continuous variables of images, do not match the scenario of predicting discrete event ID (i.e., signature) [7]. Therefore, we propose LogGAN to independently generate the continuous probability of each upcoming event instead of using the softmax layer to output the probability distribution of overall events [2,17]. In details, given an observed set of temporal events $\mathbf{S} = \{e_{(1)}, e_{(2)}, ..., e_{(s)}\}$ from parsed system logs and a set of event $\mathbf{E} = \{e_1, e_2, ..., e_m\}$ where e_j presents a signature of the j_{th} event, the task of LogGAN is to predict whether the upcoming event (i.e., log) is normal or abnormal based on the context combinations from the set $\mathbf{C} = \{c_1, c_2, ..., c_n\}$ where c_i demonstrates the i_{th} combination $(e_{(k-2)}, e_{(k-1)}, e_{(k)})$ within a 3-size sliding window. As a game setting, we exploit Long Short Term Memory network (LSTM) for both G and D where G aims to generate fake normal and abnormal instances and D tries to distinguish whether the instance is real or fake. For G, we utilize a random noise $\mathbf{z}$ and a combination c_i as the input of LSTM[1] while the output is an $m-$dimensional vector representing the independent occurring probability of each event in $\mathbf{E}$. For D, we utilize a combination c_i as the input and an $m-$dimensional vector of the independent occurring probability as the parameter[2] of LSTM while the output is whether the $m-$dimensional vector is real or fake sample under the contextual combination c_i. Therefore, the objective function of G and D is defined as follows, respectively:

$$J^G = \min_{\theta} \sum_{i=1}^{n} (\mathbb{E}_{\hat{\mathbf{e}} \sim P_\theta}[\log(1 - D(\hat{\mathbf{e}}|\mathbf{c}))] + \sum_{j=1}^{m} (\hat{e_j} - e_j)^2)$$
$$= \min_{\theta} \sum_{i=1}^{n} (\log(1 - D(\hat{\mathbf{e_{c_i}}}|\mathbf{c_i})) + \frac{1}{m} \sum_{j=1}^{m} (\hat{e_{c_ij}} - e_{c_ij})^2)), \tag{1}$$

---

[1] Learned event embedding is used to demonstrate each event.

[2] In D, we cast the combination c_i as the input of LSTM and LSTM directly outputs the hidden layer without any manipulation. Then, we concatenate the $m-$dimensional vector with the hidden layer as an input of a two-layer full Connected neural network which outputs whether the $m-$dimensional vector is real or fake as a binary classification.

$$J^D = \min_\phi - \sum_{i=1}^n (\mathbb{E}_{\mathbf{e} \sim P_{true}}[\log D(\mathbf{e}|\mathbf{c})] + \mathbb{E}_{\hat{\mathbf{e}} \sim P_\theta}[\log(1 - D(\hat{\mathbf{e}}|\mathbf{c}))])$$

$$= \min_\phi - \sum_{i=1}^n (\log D(\mathbf{e}_{\mathbf{c_i}}|\mathbf{c_i}) + \log(1 - D(\hat{\mathbf{e}_{\mathbf{c_i}}}|\mathbf{c_i}))), \tag{2}$$

where θ and ϕ is the parameter of G and D, respectively. Note that, $\hat{\mathbf{e}_{\mathbf{c_i}}} = \mathbf{e}'_{\mathbf{c_i}} \odot \mathbf{o}_{\mathbf{c_i}}$ is an $m-$dimensional vector representing the independent occurring probability of each event in $\mathbf{E}$ (i.e., input of D), where $\mathbf{e}'_{\mathbf{c_i}}$ is the output of G and $\odot$ is the element-wise mask multiplication. $\mathbf{o}_{\mathbf{c_i}}$, which is an $m-$dimensional observed vector (i.e., $o_{c_i j}$ stands for the observation of e_j where $o_j \in \{1, 0\}$ represents whether e_j is an upcoming event next to $\mathbf{c_i}$ or not), is used to filter the occurring probability of unobserved events in $\mathbf{e}'_{\mathbf{c_i}}$. This setting assists LogGAN to only update the gradients based on the loss of observed events (i.e., both normal and abnormal instances) and avoid the disturbance generated by the unobserved one. In addition, during the process of updating G, we apply a reconstruction error (i.e., $\sum_{j=1}^m (\hat{e_{c_i j}} - e_{c_i j})^2$) to help G capture the actual distribution of training data for further improving the performance. Algorithm 1 shows the overall algorithm of LogGAN in detail.

Algorithm 1. The algorithm of LogGAN

Input:
    G_θ: the generator G,
    D_ϕ: the discriminator D,
    B: the size of minibatch,
    N: the number of maximum iteration.
Output:
    G_{θ^*}: converged generator G.
 1: Initialize G_θ and D_ϕ with random weights θ and ϕ.
 2: Set $t \leftarrow 0$
 3: **repeat**
 4:     **for** G-steps **do**
 5:         Sample B combinations of events as a minibatch M_G
 6:         Generate corresponding fake instances using generator G_θ and train G_θ
 7:         Update G_θ by $\theta^* \leftarrow \theta - \frac{1}{B}\nabla_\theta J^G$
 8:     **end for**
 9:     **for** D-steps **do**
10:         Sample B combinations of events as a minibatch M_D
11:         Generate corresponding fake instances using generator G_θ
12:         Combine the generated instances with sampled real instances and train D_ϕ
13:         Update D_ϕ by $\phi^* \leftarrow \phi - \frac{1}{B}\nabla_\phi J^D$
14:     **end for**
15:     Update $t \leftarrow t + 1$
16: **until** LogGAN converges OR $t >= N$
17: **return** G_{θ^*}.

Negative Sampling: In practical scenarios, given a combination of events, the possible upcoming events are sparse. In other words, the real event vector (i.e., $\mathbf{e}_{\mathbf{c_i}}$) is more like a one-hot or multi-hot encoding vector which causes the overfitting problem. Therefore, we exploit a negative sampling strategy to avoid the overfitting problem [2]. During the G-steps, we randomly sample the unobserved instances according to a specific ratio and set the corresponding position of mask o_{c_i} as 1 for retaining the gradients.

3.3 Anomaly Detection

After completing the training LogGAN, generator G is applied to detect anomalies based on the streaming events from system logs. During the stage of anomaly detection: (1) the historical and upcoming system logs are transformed into structured data (i.e., event) via the log parser; (2) the input of G is the combination of several latest events (i.e., several one-hot encoding vectors) and G generates a corresponding $m-$dimensional vector representing the independent occurring probability of each event; (3) a set of normal events is built based on the generated $m-$dimensional vector filtered using a predefined threshold of normal probability in the step 2; (4) the upcoming event is considered as a normal instance if the event has an intersection with the set of normal events, otherwise, the event will be alerted as an anomaly.

4   Experiment

In this section, we propose the experiments to evaluate the effectiveness of Log-GAN on two real-world datasets, and mainly concentrate on the following issues:

- *Parameter:* We analyze the effect of different parameters on the performance of LogGAN.
- *Session-level Anomaly Detection:* The performance of LogGAN on the task of session-level anomaly detection is compared to that of baselines.
- *Log-level Anomaly Detection:* The performance of LogGAN on the task of log-level anomaly detection is compared to the performance of DeepLog.

4.1   Experimental Setup

Datasets: Generally, up-to-date system logs are rarely published and are sensitive data that describe the detailed information (i.e., business and transaction) about the deployed large scale system, however, the data collected from own small scale system hardly show the actual anomalies in practical scenarios. Therefore, we exploit two real-world datasets (i.e., HDFD and BGL) collected several years ago which is published for research [21]. HDFS is collected from Amazon EC2 platform where 11,197,705 system logs are divided into 575,139 sessions and generated by 203 nodes during two days while BGL contains 4,747,963 logs collected from the BlueGene/L supercomputer system during 215 days. The detailed information of datasets is shown in Table 1.

Baselines: In the experiments, to evaluate the performance of our proposed approach, we compare LogGAN with several selected baselines:

Table 1. The overview of two real-world datasets

System	Start date	Days	Size (GB)	Rate (log/sec)	Messages	Alerts	Signatures
HDFS	2008-11-09	2	1.490G	64.802	11,197,705	16,916/575,139	29
BGL	2005-06-03	215	0.708G	0.256	4,747,963	348,698	394

- iForest [12]: is an *unsupervised* tree-based isolation forest which tries to isolate anomalies from other normal instances, especially for the imbalanced training set.
- PCA [19]: is an *unsupervised* principal component analysis-based anomaly detection technique which improves the parser of unstructured systems and visualizes the promising diagnosis of abnormal instances.
- Invariants Mining [13]: is an *unsupervised* anomaly detection technique applied to build the structured logs based on the unstructured description in console logs.
- LogCluster [11]: is an *unsupervised* cluster-based approach to clustering events extracted from the historical and upcoming logs based on the knowledge base.
- DeepLog [6]: is a *supervised* LSTM-based deep learning framework which utilizes LSTM to fit the distribution of normal instances using the log key and the performance value vector extracted from each log.

In the experiments, we exploit the first 30% of dataset as the training set while the remaining data as the test set based on time series. In addition, we will briefly introduce the key parameters of LogGAN for the reproduction of our model. The size of sliding window determines the capacity of contextual events to the upcoming log. The larger size demonstrates the more specific contextual patterns are used to identify anomalies while the smaller size means upcoming anomalies are determined by the latest events (i.e., the more regular contextual patterns). The event embedding is used to represent events in the continuous space. In this paper, we utilize the 3-size sliding window to extracting contextual pattern of upcoming logs. To distinguish normal and abnormal events from the output of generator (i.e., an $m-$dimensional vector), we define a threshold to filtering normal logs. When the occurring probability of a event is below the predefined threshold, the event is considered as an anomaly based on the contextual pattern. In addition, we define the threshold as 0.90 which means the upcoming log is normal if the appearing probability of the log is 90% based on the output of generator. The ratio of negative sampling is set as 0.1. The 2-layer LSTM is applied as the basic model of generator and discriminator in LogGAN. The dimension of event embedding is set as 200. To keep the correspondence with DeepLog, in the experiments, we define the accurate identification of true anomalies as the true positive. Therefore, the metrics (e.g., precision and recall) demonstrate the performance of detecting anomalies.

4.2 Result and Discussion

Parameters: Figure 4 illustrates the performance of LogGAN within different settings of parameters including the size of sliding window, the threshold to filtering normal logs, and the layer of LSTM. In this section, we concentrate on the task of log-level anomaly detection. First, Fig. 4a shows the performance (i.e., Precision, Recall, and F1-measure) of LogGAN on different sizes of sliding window (i.e., size 1 to 5). Observed from Fig. 4a, abnormal logs are correlated with the appropriate context of events (i.e., 3-size sliding window). Neither the concurrence of pair-wise events (i.e., 1-size sliding window) nor the extremely specific contextual pattern (i.e., 5-size sliding window) is beneficial to identity log-level anomalies. Second, Fig. 4b illustrates the performance on different settings of threshold to filtering normal logs. Note that, LogGAN has the similar performance on the threshold from 0.90 to 0.30 while the performance becomes worse when the threshold is 0.10. In other word, the appearing probability of normal and abnormal logs largely depends on whether the combination of contextual events and logs occurs in the training set. Finally, Fig. 4c shows the performance of LogGAN using different layers of LSTM in the generator and discriminator. The experimental results demonstrate that appropriately using deep features (i.e., 2-layer LSTM) is capable of improving the performance of detecting anomalies.

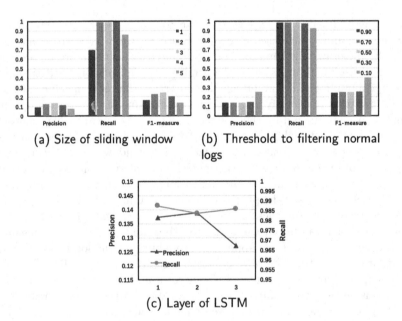

(a) Size of sliding window

(b) Threshold to filtering normal logs

(c) Layer of LSTM

Fig. 4. The performance of LogGAN within different settings of parameters

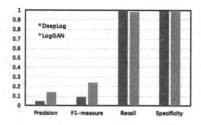

Fig. 5. The comparison between DeepLog and LogGAN on log-level anomaly detection

Log-level Anomaly Detection: Figure 5 illustrates the comparison between DeepLog and LogGAN on the log-level anomaly detection on BGL. The characteristic of DeepLog is to utilize feedbacks (i.e., false positive samples) from administrators to update the model incrementally. In other words, DeepLog aims to learn the whole normal instances including the upcoming ones to detect anomalies without considering the correlation between normal and abnormal logs. Any method, which has the strategy of incremental learning, has the benefit of this setting including LogGAN. In this experiment, we concern more about the generalization ability of model based on the limited training set. Observed from Fig. 5, LogGAN outperforms DeepLog on the task of anomaly detection based on the same size of training set (i.e., 30%). However, the overall performance of DeepLog and LogGAN is not satisfactory. To further improve the performance of anomaly detection, we need to extract more meaningful feature from logs instead of only using the sequential information.

Table 2. The comparison between baselines and LogGAN on session-level anomaly detection on HDFS

Method	Recall	Precision	F1-score
Invariants miner	**1.000**	0.084	0.154
PCA	0.346	0.707	0.465
DeepLog	0.016	0.939	0.032
iForest	0.318	**1.000**	0.482
LogClustering	0.362	**1.000**	**0.532**
LogGAN-sess	0.356	**1.000**	**0.525**

Session-level Anomaly Detection: Table 2 shows the performance of baselines and LogGAN on HDFS dataset. Different from the version of LogGAN used in the log-level anomaly detection, we propose a session-level version of LogGAN (LogGAN-sess) in the session-level task. The generator of LogGAN-sess aims to match a 30−dimensional vector where the first 29 dimensions record the number of corresponding events appeared in the current session, and the last one represents the abnormal score instead of fitting an m−dimensional vector. The experimental results show that LogGAN-sess outperform other baselines except for LogClustering. The limitation of current LogGAN-sess is the model only exploits the statistics of independent event that occurred in the session. However, the traditional anomaly detection methods concentrate on the concurrence of several events in the temporal sequence. In addition, the structure of workflows is also significant information which describes the normal and integrated transactions in the system. Therefore, the performance of LogGAN-sess could be further improved using the statistics of specific patterns (i.e., the combination of temporal logs).

5   Conclusion

To overcome the limitation of diagnosing log-level anomaly detection, in this paper, we propose a sequence-based generative adversarial network to detecting abnormal events among system logs named LogGAN. In practical scenarios, we consider that the occurring anomalies depend on specific patterns which comprise the latest logs and regard specific patterns as the contextual information of upcoming logs. Due to the benefit of the generative adversarial network, the problem of the imbalance between normal and abnormal logs is relieved where LogGAN is capable of generating 'real' anomalies for supplying the lack of abnormal logs in system logs. In addition, LogGAN can be transformed into the session version only to changing the representation of samples without reforming the overall structure of LogGAN. The experimental results show the effectiveness of LogGAN on both the tasks of session-level and log-level anomaly detection.

The current LogGAN still has some problems that need to be solved for further improvement, and there exist several ideas to extend our work in the future. First, the current LogGAN has similar structures of discriminator and generator, and we exploit the generator to distinguish anomalies from system logs. Can the combination of outputs from discriminator and generator be used to identify anomalies? Second, only the signature and the temporal information of system logs are used to train LogGAN in this paper. The parameter of each event and other meaningful feature need to be considered to precisely describe anomalies. Third, the diagnosis of anomalies is also an important task which helps administrators solve anomalies efficiently. Therefore, the root cause analysis (RCA) should be considered in the process of detecting anomalies.

Acknowledgment. This work was supported by the National Natural Science Foundation of China under Grant No. 61802205, 61872186, and 61772284, the Natural Science Research Project of Jiangsu Province under Grant 18KJB520037, and the research funds of NJUPT under Grant NY218116.

References

1. Bodik, P., Goldszmidt, M., Fox, A., Woodard, D.B., Andersen, H.: Fingerprinting the datacenter: automated classification of performance crises. In: Proceedings of the 5th European Conference on Computer Systems, pp. 111–124. ACM (2010)

2. Chae, D.K., Kang, J.S., Kim, S.W., Lee, J.T.: CFGAN: a generic collaborative filtering framework based on generative adversarial networks. In: Proceedings of the 27th ACM International Conference on Information and Knowledge Management, pp. 137–146. ACM (2018)

3. Chandola, V., Banerjee, A., Kumar, V.: Anomaly detection: a survey. ACM Comput. Surv. (CSUR) 41(3), 15 (2009)

4. Chawla, S., Sun, P.: SLOM: a new measure for local spatial outliers. Knowl. Inf. Syst. 9(4), 412–429 (2006)

5. Chen, M., Zheng, A.X., Lloyd, J., Jordan, M.I., Brewer, E.: Failure diagnosis using decision trees. In: International Conference on Autonomic Computing. Proceedings, pp. 36–43. IEEE (2004)

6. Du, M., Li, F., Zheng, G., Srikumar, V.: DeepLog: anomaly detection and diagnosis from system logs through deep learning. In: Proceedings of the 2017 ACM SIGSAC Conference on Computer and Communications Security, pp. 1285–1298. ACM (2017)

7. Goodfellow, I.J., et al.: Generative adversarial nets. In: Advances in Neural Information Processing Systems 27: Annual Conference on Neural Information Processing Systems 2014, Montreal, Quebec, Canada, 8–13 December 2014, pp. 2672–2680 (2014). http://papers.nips.cc/paper/5423-generative-adversarial-nets

8. Guo, S., Liu, Z., Chen, W., Li, T.: Event extraction from streaming system logs. In: Information Science and Applications 2018 - ICISA 2018, Hong Kong, China, 25–27th June 2018, pp. 465–474 (2018). https://doi.org/10.1007/978-981-13-1056-0_47

9. Li, T., et al.: FIU-Miner (a fast, integrated, and user-friendly system for data mining) and its applications. Knowl. Inf. Syst. 52(2), 411–443 (2017)

10. Liang, Y., Zhang, Y., Xiong, H., Sahoo, R.: Failure prediction in IBM BlueGene/L event logs. In: Seventh IEEE International Conference on Data Mining (ICDM 2007), pp. 583–588. IEEE (2007)

11. Lin, Q., Zhang, H., Lou, J.G., Zhang, Y., Chen, X.: Log clustering based problem identification for online service systems. In: Proceedings of the 38th International Conference on Software Engineering Companion, pp. 102–111. ACM (2016)

12. Liu, F.T., Ting, K.M., Zhou, Z.H.: Isolation forest. In: 2008 Eighth IEEE International Conference on Data Mining, pp. 413–422. IEEE (2008)

13. Lou, J.G., Fu, Q., Yang, S., Xu, Y., Li, J.: Mining invariants from console logs for system problem detection. In: USENIX Annual Technical Conference, pp. 1–14 (2010)

14. Sun, P., Chawla, S.: On local spatial outliers. In: Fourth IEEE International Conference on Data Mining (ICDM 2004), pp. 209–216. IEEE (2004)

15. Tang, L., Li, T., Perng, C.S.: LogSig: generating system events from raw textual logs. In: Proceedings of the 20th ACM International Conference on Information and Knowledge Management, pp. 785–794. ACM (2011)

16. Tuor, A.R., Baerwolf, R., Knowles, N., Hutchinson, B., Nichols, N., Jasper, R.: Recurrent neural network language models for open vocabulary event-level cyber anomaly detection. In: Workshops at the Thirty-Second AAAI Conference on Artificial Intelligence (2018)

17. Wang, J., et al.: IRGAN: a minimax game for unifying generative and discriminative information retrieval models. In: Proceedings of the 40th International ACM SIGIR Conference on Research and Development in Information Retrieval, pp. 515–524. ACM (2017)

18. Xia, B., Li, T., Zhou, Q.F., Li, Q., Zhang, H.: An effective classification-based framework for predicting cloud capacity demand in cloud services. IEEE Trans. Serv. Comput. (2018)
19. Xu, W., Huang, L., Fox, A., Patterson, D., Jordan, M.I.: Detecting large-scale system problems by mining console logs. In: Proceedings of the ACM SIGOPS 22nd Symposium on Operating Systems Principles, pp. 117–132. ACM (2009)
20. Zhang, J., Wang, H.: Detecting outlying subspaces for high-dimensional data: the new task, algorithms, and performance. Knowl. Inf. Syst. **10**(3), 333–355 (2006)
21. Zhu, J., et al.: Tools and benchmarks for automated log parsing. CoRR abs/1811.03509 (2018). http://arxiv.org/abs/1811.03509

Security Comparison of Machine Learning Models Facing Different Attack Targets

Zhaofeng Liu[1]([✉]), Zhen Jia[1], and Wenlian Lu[1,2,3,4]

[1] School of Mathematical Sciences, Fudan University, Shanghai 200433, China
zhaofengliu@hotmail.com
[2] Shanghai Center for Mathematical Sciences, Fudan University,
Shanghai 200433, China
[3] Shanghai Key Laboratory for Contemporary Applied Mathematics,
Shanghai 200433, China
[4] State Key Laboratory of Information Security,
Institute of Information Engineering, Chinese Academy of Sciences,
Beijing 100093, China

Abstract. Machine Learning has exhibited great performance in several practical application domains such as computer vision, natural language processing, automatic pilot and so on. As it becomes more and more widely used in practice, its security issues attracted more and more attentions. Previous research shows that machine learning models are very vulnerable when facing different kinds of adversarial attacks. Therefore, we need to evaluate the security of different machine learning models under different attacks. In this paper, we aim to provide a security comparison method for different machine learning models. We firstly classify the adversarial attacks into three classes by their attack targets, respectively attack on test data, attack on train data and attack on model parameters, and give subclasses under different assumptions. Then we consider support vector machine (SVM), neural networks with one hidden layer (NN), and convolution neural networks (CNN) as examples and launch different kinds of attacks on them for evaluating and comparing model securities. Additionally, our experiments illustrate the effects of concealing actions launched by the adversary.

Keywords: Machine learning · Adversarial attack · Security
evaluation · Support vector machine · Neural network

1 Introduction

Machine Learning has been a hot topic for a long while both in research area and application area. It contains several different kinds of subfields, and for each the models and technologies exhibit great performance in corresponding practical domains or tasks such as computer vision, natural language processing, automatic pilot and so on. As it becomes more and more widely used in practice, its security issues have attracted more and more attentions.

© Springer Nature Switzerland AG 2019
F. Liu et al. (Eds.): SciSec 2019, LNCS 11933, pp. 77–91, 2019.
https://doi.org/10.1007/978-3-030-34637-9_6

Machine learning models could be exposed to various kinds of security risks. Firstly, previous studies [1,2] showed that machine learning models are vulnerable. For example, a machine learning classifier could make terrible mistakes when facing specific adversarial examples while humans would not be fooled by them. That means a rather small perturbation could fool the models [3]. They can be intentionally crafted by an adversary if he has access to the models or has the capability to obtain information to some extent. Secondly, based on the assumptions on modelling the adversary given by the security evaluation framework in [4,5], the train data and model parameters could also be attacked in some specific situations. This means the machine learning models could be manipulated by an adversary, which appears huge risks both for correctness and effectiveness.

Because some practical tasks could be done by several different machine learning models, we may wonder which models should we choose in practice when considering effectiveness, efficiency and security. This paper aims to provide a quantified comparison framework between different machine learning models. We can make our choices by referring to the evaluation results of this comparison framework when dealing with security-effectiveness trade-off dilemma.

We perform our experiments in the case of MNIST two-class (3 and 7) classification problem, as MNIST classification is one of the fundamental problems of machine learning, on which there are several models performing well [6]. We compare three models including linear support vector machine, neural networks with one hidden layer, and convolution neural networks. While the three models all have rather good performance, their complexities are hugely different. We compare these models under the situation of facing three different attack targets, which are test data, train data, and model parameters. These three adversarial settings are under different adversary capability assumptions. Besides, we perform experiments under the situation that adversaries try not to make the changing too obvious on the attack targets. For attacks on model parameters, we limit the capability of the adversary by only enabling attacks on one layer of the model, or one parameter of the model. For attacks on train data or model parameters, we control the attacks strength by limiting the changing range of the attack target. And for attacks on test data, we measure the mimicry behavior initiated by [2]. This action is initiated for leading the adversarial examples to an adversarial area with high density in the whole parameter space. From another perspective, it has an effect of concealing the attack actions launched by the adversary.

This paper is organized as follows: Sect. 1 gives an introduction of this paper. Section 2 gives a review of previous related works. Section 3 introduces the relevant machine learning models including support vector machine, multilayer perceptron and convolutional neural networks. And we also give a review of the concept of adversarial attack and how to model the adversary based on several assumptions for evaluating the model security. Section 4 presents the comparison experiments between these machine learning models which the adversary attacks on the test data (i.e. Evasion Attack). This experiment is based on the idea given by [2]. Section 5 presents the comparison experiments between these machine learning models which adversary attacks on the train data. We focus on a simple attack method called *Label Reversal Poisoning*. It's a subclass of poisoning attack. Section 6 presents the comparison experiments between these machine learning models which the adversary directly attacks on the model, which means that the adversary can directly change the parameters of the models to some extent based on our assumptions. Section 7 gives our conclusion on the comparison experiments and some further thoughts.

2   Related Work

Research on adversarial environment of machine learning has lasted for many years. [9] initiated the adversarial attacks against machine learning and gave a framework of modelling the adversary strategy. [10] analyzed the capability of adversary on getting information and launching attacks based on several assumptions. [11,12] classified the adversarial attacks into several categories and provided several defense strategies. [20] explored the space of adversarial images and explained the existence of adversarial images which cannot trick human beings.

Quantified security evaluation of machine learning models has also been studied during recent years. [2] defined an adversarial attack model based on the capability and knowledge of the adversary. They also provided a general security evaluation framework in [13] considering the machine learning models under adversarial environments. [14] provided a forward derivative algorithm to effectively craft adversarial examples without the need of existing samples. [3] argued that instead of non-linearity, the linear nature of neural networks is the primary cause of neural networks vulnerability to adversarial perturbation. [19] evaluated the robustness of models while considering different layers modified.

As to the different attack targets, [15] utilized the poisoning attacks to evaluate the security of SVM model, while [2] evaluated the security of SVM model under evasion attacks. There are also attack method takes effect when adversary couldn't get perfect knowledge or capability, which called transferable adversarial attack [16]. There are also several papers elaborate on how to launch adversarial attacks on machine learning tasks in practice, especially the models using in security domain. For example, the spam email filters [7] and malicious control of automobile [8].

3   Preliminary

3.1   Relevant Machine Learning Models

We define a two-class classifier $g(x)$, classifying x as a positive (negative) sample when $g(x) > 0 (g(x) < 0)$. We compare different models as follows:

Support Vector Machine (SVM) [17] is a classification algorithm which mainly applied on two-class classification tasks. It's aimed to find a hyperplane to well separate the data of different classes with maximized margin. As a classic and representative algorithm of machine learning, it appears good learning ability and has been applied widely in different tasks such as data mining, image processing and pattern recognition. And besides, it has a relatively strong robustness compare to neural networks. In our experiment here in this paper, we use the basic linear SVM model trained with Hinge Lost. Noticing that the parameters of SVM model only depend on a small number of train samples, so the model appears good robustness.

Multilayer Perceptron also known as Neural Network, has been widely used in lots of application field of real world. It and its several variations appear great power and effectiveness in computer vision, natural language processing and many other artificial intelligence scenarios. In our experiment here in this paper, we use an one-hidden-layer neural network model with 20 hidden nodes and adopt ReLU as activation function, denoted by NN.

Convolutional Neural Network has been the most remarkable machine learning technique since it came out. Almost every state of the art model in computer vision field takes advantage of the convolutional structure. It shows amazing power on picture classification, object detection and many other tasks. And also it's the most advanced model with respect to the MNIST classification problem. In our experiment here in this paper, we use the classic LeNet with two convolutional layers and two full-connected layers and adopt ReLU as activation function [18].

3.2   Adversarial Attack

Adversarial learning refers to a learning environment in which an adversary attacks the defender's machine learning models, resulting in a confrontation between the adversary and the defender. Generally, the adversary has a purpose, mostly wants to disable the model to reach his goal. Under the assumptions of given capability and knowledge of the adversary, he may launch different attack type based on different attack targets. For a spam filter, for example, if the adversary has the perfect knowledge of this filter model, he could craft a spam email which can evade the filter by avoiding the illegitimate keywords defined by the filter. And furthermore, if he could get the authority to manipulate the train data or model parameters, he can launch attacks by manipulating the train data or model parameters to crack the models.

Besides launching attacks on the three models in our experiments, we also consider a more realistic situation in which the adversary should restrict his movement size. Because in some cases, the defender may set up additional defense such as another filter in different model or even human monitoring. If your attack appears too obvious, for example, changing all the model parameters to zero or crafting a totally unrecognizable handwriting number picture, the defender may soon detect the attack and launch a new defense immediately. This will make the attack fail very quickly. So the adversary often launches attacks along with some kinds of concealing techniques, such as mimicry the original data or limit the action size at each time step. We will expound on the corresponding method in each following experiment.

3.3   Security Evaluation

Based on the security evaluation framework proposed by [4], we believe that simulating different kinds of potential attack scenarios is the key step for evaluating the security of machine learning models. More specifically, we can empirically evaluate the security by following three steps. Firstly, identify possible attack scenarios. Secondly, design corresponding attacks. Thirdly, systematically assess the impact of the attacks. Noticing that the final step must be done in a specific way for every unique model. Also noticing that our proposed attack model is based on some specific assumptions on the adversary, including purpose, knowledge obtained of the model, and capability with regard to the data or model.

4   Attack on Test Data

Attack on Test Data is also called *Evasion Attack*, which means modifying the test samples to evade the filter models. In this section, we consider SVM, NN and CNN under evasion attack and try to find out how to modify the test samples according to our purpose such as evading the filter with limited range of movement. Then we simulate several attack scenarios and compare the results.

4.1   Background and Settings

We use a gradient descent algorithm to evade different filter models. This algorithm is to calculate the derivative of $g(x)$ to x, and then subtract the unitized derivative from the original sample x. It is similar to the classical gradient descent training algorithm of neural networks, only with a difference that here we calculate the derivative of the input, not the weights. We can express one attack step into formula as:

$$x_{new} = x_{old} - \frac{\frac{\partial g(x)}{\partial x}\big|_{x=x_{old}}}{\left\|\frac{\partial g(x)}{\partial x}\big|_{x=x_{old}}\right\|} \tag{1}$$

where x_{new} is the newly generated adversarial example.

Although the adversary aims to make the model more likely to wrongly classify the test data (classify a positive sample into negative class), an overlarge movement range could make the attack action rather easily to be detected by the defender. Therefore, the adversary may limit his movement range when attacking. Besides, he may also conduct a mimicry action proposed in [2] to imitate real positive samples, so that the adversarial examples seem not to be modified too far from a real picture from the perspective of human. For example, many noise points may indicate that the picture has been intentionally modified, and this usually happens under gradient attacks. Noticing that in [2], it is initiated for avoiding local minimum of the gradient descent algorithm. However, from another perspective, it has an effect of concealing the attack actions launched by the adversary.

We describe the problem as an optimization problem. Under above assumptions, for any positive (negative) test sample x_0, the optimal attack strategy is trying to find a modified adversarial example x^* minimizing (maximizing) the output of corresponding two-class classifier $g(x)$, while limiting the distance between x^* and x_0 smaller than given d_{max}. But this may lead the adversarial example appears far too different from a real number picture, which may result in being detected by additional defense process launched by the defender. For overcoming this shortage, we add an additional term into our attack objective function to launch a mimicry action. Then we get the following modified optimization problem:

$$\arg \min_x f(x) = g(x) - c \sum_{i|y_i=-1} K(x - x_i), d(x, x_0) \leq d_{max} \qquad (2)$$

where y_i is the label of x_i, and K is the kernel density estimator (KDE) function. Here we use Gauss Kernel as KDE in our experiment.

4.2　Experiments and Results

We conduct two experiments in this section. In the fist one, we use the evasion attack algorithm mentioned above to attack SVM, NN and CNN model. We compare the results and analyze their security positions under this attack.

In the second experiment, we take the linear SVM algorithm as an example to visually demonstrate how the mimicry action takes effect. And we also compare the results between original SVM and mimicry SVM.

Comparison Between Models. We compare the performances of SVM, NN and CNN models under evasion attack. We launch attack on every positive samples (i.e. number 3 in MNIST) of test set by different attack strength (i.e. the distance between original sample and adversarial sample), and calculate the average accuracy. Then we get three accuracy curves as shown in Fig. 1.

From Fig. 1 we can find that CNN model has the highest accuracy, followed by NN model and SVM model when there is no attack. This meets our common sense. But comparing these three models on security, we can find that the accuracy of CNN reduces rapidly as the evasion attack intensifies. This vulnerable security position is caused by the relatively high irregularity (non-linearity) of the classification bound of neural network. Because when a picture facing gradient attacks, the non-linearity of neural network leads the samples changing toward different directions respectively to achieve the classification bound

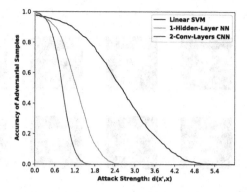

Fig. 1. Accuracy changing under gradient descent attack ($\lambda = 0$)

through a quicker route, while SVM model appears stable because the linearity leads all the samples changing toward the same direction. So we can infer that the irregularity of the classification bound of neural network causes model's vulnerable when facing gradient attack. On the other side, this characteristic enhances the fitting capability of a model. So there is a security-effectiveness trade-off dilemma when facing this kind of attacks.

It is worthy noting that in [3], the authors argued that the vulnerability of neural network isn't caused by the non-linearity, but its linearity nature. And they showed that the non-linear RBF based classification models can resist the attacks to some degree while sacrifice the classification accuracy. So they claim that neural network is not non-linear enough to resist the perturbation. This conclusion is not incompatible with our result, because the non-linearity here we talk about in this paper refers to the bending or irregularity characteristics of the classification bound. This can be supported by [20]. But this bound is to some extent warped from a hyperplane which appears intrinsic linearity nature because of the linear mappings and activation function within neural networks. That means, the non-linearity concept used here can be used to explain the comparative vulnerability of neural networks to SVM while holding the accuracy, but it's too coarse to explain all the adversarial characteristics of a model. So more specific concepts and theories beyond non-linearity may need to be proposed in the future to clarify this intricate problem.

Mimicry Attack. We take linear SVM model as an example to illustrate the effect of mimicry action mentioned above. We exhibit the samples generated by the attack algorithm. Figure 2 is the visual comparison of common attack (first line) and mimicry attack (second line). We can see from the figure that the mimicry action truly is more confusable to us. So the adversary may take advantage of this action to conceal his attack.

Furthermore, the gradient descent attack follows the shortest descent path when there is no mimicry action. After adding the mimicry action, the adversary

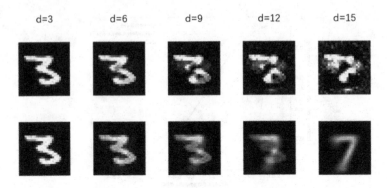

Fig. 2. Adversarial examples generated by different attack strengths and styles

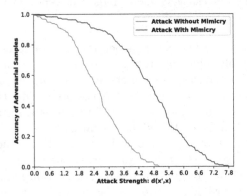

Fig. 3. Accuracy changing under gradient attack with/without mimicry

needs more attack steps to achieve the same adversarial effect, as shown in Fig. 3. Therefore, this behavior can be a trade-off dilemma for the adversary. As for us, we may launch other filter models to assist in defending the attack. This may take effect when facing no mimicry adversarial actions.

5   Attack on Train Data

Attack on Train Data is also called *Poisoning Attack*, which means the adversary manipulates the training set of a model before the training process begins. This kind of attacks could easily disable the machine learning model because the model even cannot be properly trained. This section based on a simple attack method called *Label Reverse Attack* and compare the security positions of SVM, NN, CNN under this kind of attacks.

5.1   Background and Settings

We experiment on a simple attack method called label reverse attack, which means to reverse the label (0 or 1) of samples in train data. It can deal with two-category problems such as positive sample filter. Noticing that this kind of attacks only need limited knowledge of the model and do not need the knowledge of model structure and parameters. The attack can be launched very easily if the adversary gets the knowledge and authority of the training set, and can be destructive to the model. Because the machine learning models usually learn the distribution of train data, while the poisoning attacks change the distribution to some extent.

In our experiments, we use random label reversing method to attack. That means to randomly select some training samples in the training set at a certain percentage and reverse their labels. Then we train the model with contaminated train data and finally test the model with the same test data. As the percentage of poisoned data (i.e. the attack strength) increases, we analyze and compare the security positions of SVM, NN and CNN models.

5.2 Experiments and Results

We still experiment on the MNIST dataset. Firstly, we train the three models (i.e. SVM, NN and CNN) and calculate the average model output and the classification accuracy for each model. Then we randomly select 1% of the training samples in the train set and reverse their labels. After newly training these models, we can newly calculate the values of the two indexes under the poisoning attack. Continuing intensify the attack at a step of 1%, we finally obtain Fig. 4.

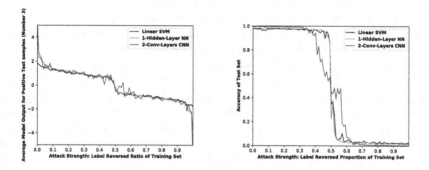

Fig. 4. Model output (Left) and accuracy (Right) changing under label reverse attack

From Fig. 4 we can find that CNN is the most unstable model, so we need to keep a balance between classification accuracy and security position when using CNN as a classifier. Besides, we can see in the right figure that when the attack strength reaches 50%, the classification accuracy on test set exhibits a cliff-like fall from 0.9 to 0.1. We can explain this phenomenon through the left figure which depicts the model output. Because when the model output declines to zero, the classification results of the test samples remain unchanged. But the classification confidence indicated by the model output has declined either, so we can see a cliff-like fall of accuracy near the percentage of 50%.

Comparing to the evasion attack, the poisoning attack brings down the classification accuracy rather slowly. One possible reason is that the poisoning attack only takes advantage of limited knowledge, while evasion attack uses the perfect knowledge of underlying model to launch gradient attack.

6 Attack on Model Parameters

We first define three concepts for this sections. *Authority* means the adversary's authority on changing corresponding attack target, which is the model parameter in this section. *Knowledge* means the adversary's knowledge on model parameters, determining whether the model is a black box or white box to him. *Attack Time Window* means the period when model's vulnerability exposing to the adversary, so the adversary must conduct attack quickly for seizing the opportunity.

Now we imagine an attack scenario as follows. If the adversary has perfect knowledge and capability of the model, which means that he has obtained the complete authority of directly manipulating the model. He may modify the model parameters to disable the model under this scenario. We call this kind of adversarial movement *Attacks on Model Parameters*. This scenario presents an extreme case that may seldom appear in practice because of the complete authority. Besides, when it happens, the adversary could launch far more vicious attacks on the models than manipulating the model parameters, such as directly attack the defender's system to shut down the defense.

But it's still worthy to analyze the impact of manipulating parameters directly. Because the complete authority is hardly obtained, so how about part of the authority? If the adversary gets the authority to manipulate some of the parameters to some extent, the analysis on model parameter attack may become valuable. Besides, an adversary may need to conceal his action by limiting his own movement range. Obviously, shutting down the defense of the system directly is far more easily to be detected by the defender than just changing the values of few parameters. We consider this situation as adversary with part of the authority. Following gives some discussions on this kind of attacks based on different assumptions made. Noticing that the intercept of a weight layer is regarded as one weight parameter of corresponding layer, which multiplies one all the time.

6.1 With Complete Authority

Noticing that the complete authority brings perfect knowledge. Under this situation, the most effective attack method under this situation is to calculate the derivative of $g(x)$ to the parameters w and then train w towards the direction given by derivative. This is a kind of adversarial training process and is all the same as the regular training process of a classifier model, except they are just trained toward opposite directions. So we can know that the attack result share the same ranking list with the classification accuracy of the models. Besides, if we consider limited attack time window, then the training speed of corresponding model should be taken into consideration. Still considering SVM, NN and CNN here, we can easily know that the training speed of a model has a negative correlation with the complexity of the model, which means the number of parameters and number of layers. So by contrast, CNN appears the most difficult to train (even if it's adversarial training) which could be the most secure position when attack time window is limited.

6.2   With Part of Authority and Perfect Knowledge

Assume that the adversary has perfect knowledge of the model but he can only launch attacks on one layer of parameters, noted w. As discussed in complete authority situation, the most effective attack method is still calculating the gradients of parameters and launch a gradient attack. Noticing that one layer of parameters means entirely different on SVM, NN and CNN. For NN it's 50% of all the parameters, and for CNN it's 25%, but 100% for SVM which equivalent to complete authority. This means the adversarial training authority of the original model is limited. Besides, if we consider a limited attack time window, the convolution operation is the most complicated one with regard to calculating gradients. This means the SVM exhibiting worst security position here.

6.3   With Part of Authority and Limited Knowledge

But if the adversary only gets limited knowledge, he could not launch gradients attack on the models. That is to say, he can only modify the parameters touchable for him. We assume that the adversary can only launch attacks on one layer or one parameter of the model. With regard to the robustness of models while considering one layer, [19] conducted several experiments and concludes that this analysis is better performed respecting the network architectures due to the heterogeneous behaviors of different layers. And with regard to one parameter, we conduct experiments as follows. Comparing to take his chance on modifying the parameter randomly and get unpredictable adversarial effect, he may utilize simple attack methods. In our experiment, with regard to a given parameter within a layer, the adversary multiplies this parameter by a constant number. We call it *Single Parameter Multiplying Attack*. Noted that this kind of attacks can be done very easily and quickly regardless of the attack time window. We conduct two experiments under this assumption. The first experiment demonstrates different impacts when different layers of a multilayer model facing this kind of attacks. We use the first convolutional layer and the second fully connected layer of a CNN model to illustrate. Noticing that these two layers are the first and the last layer of the model. We traverse all the parameters of these two layers respectively (noticing that we ignore the intercepts and focus on the weights), and execute single parameter multiplying attack on each of the parameters at different attack strengths (choosing multiplier constant from -40 to 50 at a step of 10). We calculate the average output and the average classification accuracy. Results are shown in Fig. 5.

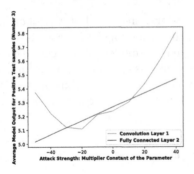
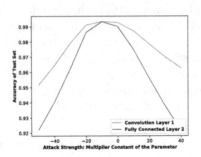

Fig. 5. Model Output (Left) and Accuracy (Right) Changing under Single Parameter Multiplying Attack on First/Last Layer of CNN. The figures are drawn from scatter points at a step of 10.

The figures indicate that the attacks on last layer is more destructive. This is in line with the intuition that the absolute values of gradients of last layer are usually bigger than those of front layers. Besides, from the figure we can infer that the attacks on front layers may appear unpredictability in the results, due to the non-linearity provided by the deep structure of neural networks.

The second experiment demonstrates the correlation between the attack effect and the complexity of model. The experiment method is same as before. First, we conduct attacks only aiming at one random parameter of SVM, NN and CNN respectively (still ignore the intercepts and focus on the weights). It turns out that CNN suffers the least as we expect, and NN follows. Then we conduct attacks aiming at the last layer of SVM, NN and CNN respectively and compare the results. Besides, we newly train a NN model with a hidden layer of 10 cells, compared to the original NN model with 20 hidden cells. Results are shown in Fig. 6.

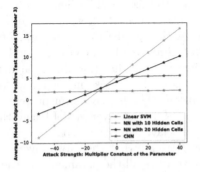
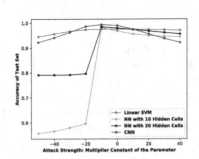

Fig. 6. Model Output(Left) and Accuracy(Right) Changing under Single Parameter Multiplying Attack on Last Layer of SVM/NN/CNN. The figures are drawn from scatter points at a step of 10. Noted that the results of NN are unstable, in another word, they could be affected more by the trained parameter distribution of the last layer. The reason could be that the number of neurons in last layer of NN is relatively small.

In this experiment, the SVM model has 784 weight parameters, the last layer of CNN model has 1024 weight parameters, and the last layer of NN merely has 10 or 20 weight parameters. We can infer from the figures that a higher complexity (i.e. the numbers of parameters within a layer) of the layer under attack can improve the robustness of the model, resulting in less damage as the attack intensifies. This presents an opposite result on model complexity, compared to the result of evasion attack. The main reason is that a higher complexity becomes a sort of protection when the adversary only got very limited authority like this experiment, as he can only influence the model on a small scale.

7   Conclusion

In this paper, we firstly summarize the security issues faced by machine learning, describe the current research status of machine learning security under adversarial environment, classify the adversarial attacks that machine learning models might encounter by their different attack targets. Then We simulate different kinds of attacks on SVM, NN and CNN models based on a evaluation framework and compare their security positions.

In the evasion attack (i.e. attack on test data) experiments, we show that machine learning model with high complexity appears poor security position, due to a large number of parameters could be manipulated under adversarial environment. Additionally, we conduct an experiment on the mimicry attack of adversary to illustrate the impact of concealing action on machine learning models. In the poisoning attack (i.e. attack on train data) experiments, we show that even the simplest *Label Reversal Poisoning* attack can significantly affect the test accuracy of the classifier. The SVM, NN and CNN models all exhibit a cliff-like fall of accuracy when train data has changed by 50%, while CNN model exhibits the most unstable fluctuation. For model parameter attacks, we classify the attacks into several scenarios through making different assumptions on the authority of adversary. The models show different security positions under different scenario due to their intrinsic properties, especially complexity and linearity. Brief results on robustness ranking (security position) under three main attacks are listed in following table, while *1* represents the strongest one. Noted that *Authority* means the adversary's authority on changing corresponding attack target, and *Knowledge* means the adversary's minimum requirement of knowledge on model parameters.

This paper shows that different attack scenarios make different security results with respect to these three kinds of models. We could not summarize the correlations between complexity, non-linearity and vulnerability of different models simply into positive or negative. Because the correlations could be quite different in specific situations as mentioned above. So when facing a real attack, we need to analyze the authority, the knowledge, the attack goal, the attack target and the movement range of the adversary in detail. Further research could focus on more complicated and advanced attack methods, and may take other machine learning models into consideration.

Attack target	Authority & Knowledge	Attack type	SVM	NN	CNN
Test data	Complete & Perfect	Evasion attack	1	2	3
Train data	Complete & None	Label reversal poisoning attack	1	2	3
Model parameter	Part & Limited	Single parameter multiplying attack on all layers	3	2	1
Model parameter	Part & Limited	Single parameter multiplying attack on last layer	Related to the number of neurons in last layer		

References

1. Szegedy, C., Zaremba, W., Sutskever, I., et al.: Intriguing properties of neural networks. arXiv preprint arXiv:1312.6199 (2013)
2. Biggio, B., et al.: Evasion attacks against machine learning at test time. In: Blockeel, H., Kersting, K., Nijssen, S., Železný, F. (eds.) ECML PKDD 2013. LNCS (LNAI), vol. 8190, pp. 387–402. Springer, Heidelberg (2013). https://doi.org/10.1007/978-3-642-40994-3_25
3. Goodfellow, I.J., Shlens, J., Szegedy, C.: Explaining and harnessing adversarial examples. arXiv preprint arXiv:1412.6572 (2014)
4. Biggio, B., et al.: Security evaluation of support vector machines in adversarial environments. In: Ma, Y., Guo, G. (eds.) Support Vector Machines Applications, pp. 105–153. Springer, Cham (2014). https://doi.org/10.1007/978-3-319-02300-7_4
5. Biggio, B., Nelson, B., Laskov, P.: Poisoning attacks against support vector machines. In: Proceedings of the 29th International Conference on International Conference on Machine Learning, pp. 1467–1474. Omnipress (2012)
6. LeCun, Y., Jackel, L.D., Bottou, L., et al.: Comparison of learning algorithms for handwritten digit recognition. In: International Conference on Artificial Neural Networks, vol. 60, pp. 53–60 (1995)
7. Wittel, G.L., Wu, S.F.: On attacking statistical spam filters. In: Proceedings of the Conference on E-mail and Anti-Spam (CEAS) (2004)
8. Papernot, N., McDaniel, P., Goodfellow, I., et al.: Practical black-box attacks against deep learning systems using adversarial examples. arXiv preprint arXiv:1602.02697 (2016). 1(2): 3
9. Dalvi, N., Domingos, P., Sanghai, S., et al.: Adversarial classification. In: Proceedings of the Tenth ACM SIGKDD International Conference on Knowledge Discovery and Data Mining, pp. 99–108. ACM (2004)
10. Lowd, D., Meek, C.: Adversarial learning. In: Proceedings of the Eleventh ACM SIGKDD International Conference on Knowledge Discovery in Data Mining, pp. 641–647. ACM (2005)
11. Barreno, M., Nelson, B., Sears, R., et al.: Can machine learning be secure? Proceedings of the 2006 ACM Symposium on Information, Computer and Communications Security, pp. 16–25. ACM (2006)
12. Barreno, M., Nelson, B., Joseph, A.D., et al.: The security of machine learning. Mach. Learn. 81(2), 121–148 (2010)

13. Biggio, B., Fumera, G., Roli, F.: Security evaluation of pattern classifiers under attack. IEEE Trans. Knowl. Data Eng. **26**(4), 984–996 (2014)
14. Papernot, N., McDaniel, P., Jha, S., et al.: The limitations of deep learning in adversarial settings. In: 2016 IEEE European Symposium on Security and Privacy (EuroS&P), pp. 372–387. IEEE (2016)
15. Srndic, N., Laskov, P.: Detection of malicious PDF files based on hierarchical document structure. In: Proceedings of the 20th Annual Network & Distributed System Security Symposium, pp. 1–16 (2013)
16. Papernot, N., McDaniel, P., Goodfellow, I.: Transferability in machine learning: from phenomena to black-box attacks using adversarial samples. arXiv preprint arXiv:1605.07277 (2016)
17. Cortes, C., Vapnik, V.: Support-vector networks. Mach. Learn. **20**(3), 273–297 (1995)
18. LeCun, Y., Bottou, L., Bengio, Y., et al.: Gradient-based learning applied to document recognition. Proc. IEEE **86**(11), 2278–2324 (1998)
19. Zhang, C., Bengio, S., Singer, Y.: Are All Layers Created Equal? arXiv preprint arXiv:1902.01996 (2019)
20. Tabacof, P., Valle, E.: Exploring the space of adversarial images. In: 2016 International Joint Conference on Neural Networks (IJCNN), pp. 426–433. IEEE (2016)

Adversarial Training Based Feature Selection

Binghui Liu, Keji Han, Jie Hang, and Yun Li$^{(\boxtimes)}$

School of Computer Science, Nanjing University of Post
and Telecommunications, Nanjing, China
liyun@njupt.edu.cn

Abstract. Feature selection is one of key problems in machine learning and data mining. It has been widely accepted that adversarial training is an effective strategy to improve the accuracy and robustness of classifiers. In this paper, in order to improve the performance of feature selection, adversarial training is also adopted, and an adversarial training based feature selection framework is proposed. To validate the effectiveness of the proposed feature selection framework, three classical feature selection algorithms, i.e. Relief-F, Fisher Score and minimum Redundancy and maximum Relevance (mRMR) are chosen and two methods are used to generate adversarial examples in experiments. The experimental results on benchmark datasets containing low-dimension and high-dimension datasets demonstrate show that adversarial training is able to improve the performance of classical feature selection methods in most cases.

Keywords: Machine learning · Data mining · Adversarial training · Feature selection

1 Introduction

Feature selection is an important and frequently used technique for dimension reduction by removing irrelevant and redundant features from the dataset to obtain an optimal feature subset. Feature selection is a knowledge discovery tool for providing insights into the problem through the interpretation of the most relevant features. Feature selection is also widely used in information security fields such as intrusion detection, malware detection, and spam detection. There exist two key problems for feature selection: evaluation criterion and search strategy. According to evaluation criteria, feature selection algorithms are categorized into filter, wrapper and hybrid (embedded) models. Feature selection algorithms under filter model rely on analyzing the general characteristics of data and evaluating features without involving any learning algorithm. Wrapper model utilizes a predefined learning algorithm instead of an independent measure for subset evaluation. A typical hybrid algorithm makes use of both an independent measure and a learning algorithm to evaluate feature subsets. Search strategies for feature selection can be divided into exhaustive, heuristic, and stochastic methods. Based on the output type, the feature selection algorithms can also be classified as feature weighting (ranking) and feature subset [1].

To improve the performance of feature selection, previous works focus on designing new evaluation criterion or new search strategy for different learning

© Springer Nature Switzerland AG 2019
F. Liu et al. (Eds.): SciSec 2019, LNCS 11933, pp. 92–105, 2019.
https://doi.org/10.1007/978-3-030-34637-9_7

scenario, however, in this paper, we would like to enhance feature selection via augmenting the training data by adversarial training [5]. Jeff Donahue use BiGANs as a mean to learn the feature representation and the result is useful for auxiliary supervised discrimination tasks [17].

The adversarial training is usually used to against the adversarial examples, Weilin Xu et al. proposed two method of feature squeezing to make DNN more sensitive to adversarial examples [18]. However, it has been proved that adversarial training not only improve the robustness but also improve the classification performance of classifier. Generally, adversarial training is used to generate many adversarial examples for training a robust classifier. Miyato et al. [2] conducted experiments to demonstrate that adversarial training has good regularization performance on text classification tasks with a LSTM based neural network [3], on the other hand, adversarial training and virtual adversarial training [4] can improve classification performance.

However, there are few studies about the combination of adversarial training and feature selection. In this paper, the adversarial training is applied into feature selection, and some adversarial examples are generated according to appropriate algorithms, then feature selection will be performed on the datasets mixed with the adversarial examples and the original examples. The main contribution of this paper is to put forward a new feature selection framework based on adversarial training, which can enhance the performance of original feature selection in many cases.

The paper is organized as follows. Section 2 presents the way to generate adversarial examples in adversarial training and the adversarial training based feature selection framework. The experiments are introduced in Sect. 3. And the paper ends up with conclusion and discussion in Sect. 4.

2 Framework of Adversarial Training-Based Feature Selection

Adversarial training is first proposed to make model robust under attack scenario. [5]. Its main idea is to generate some adversarial examples, and then train model with both original examples and adversarial examples, aiming to make the model more robust to adversarial examples and enhance the performance of the learning model. The key problem for adversarial training is how to generate the adversarial examples. Usually, the process to generate an adversarial example is an optimization problem, which includes objective function and optimization algorithm.

2.1 Objective Functions in Adversarial Training

Szegedy et al. have proposed a method to generate adversarial examples for deep neural networks [6]. Given an example $x \in \Re^m$ and its corresponding label y, an adversarial example x' is generated by adding a small perturbation r to x, i.e. $x' = x + r$, which will be miss-classified by the classifier $f: \Re^m \rightarrow \{1, \ldots, h\}$, h is the number of labels. The processes of finding an adversarial example can be formulated as Eq. (1).

$$\begin{cases} \min c\|r\|_2 + loss_f(x+r,l) \\ \qquad x+r \in [0,1]^m \end{cases} \tag{1}$$

The objective function above consists of two terms, the first is the magnitude of perturbation r, the other term is the classification loss. l is the target label, which is different from original label y. To get the valid data, each dimension of the data should be limited to [0,1], i.e. $x+r \in [0,1]^m$. c is a balance parameter and needs to be adjusted to generate effective adversarial examples. The c is higher, the bias (pertubation r) is larger and it is easier to get a miss-classified example. In this paper, Hinge loss [7] is chosen as the loss function in Eq. (1). Hinge loss is often used for "maximum margin classification", especially for Support Vector Machines(SVM) [8]. Hinge loss can be expressed as Eq. (2).

$$loss(y) = \max(0, 1 - \hat{y} \cdot y) \tag{2}$$

where $\hat{y}$ is the predicted label of an example x, y is its true label.

2.2 Optimization Method

In this paper, two optimization methods are adopted to minimize the Eq. (1), i.e., gradient descent (GD) algorithm and the ADAM algorithm.

Gradient Descent Algorithm. GD [9] is one of the simplest and the most popular iterative optimization algorithms which calculates a gradient direction in each iteration. The negative gradient direction of the objective function is the direction where the function value is reduced at the fastest speed. The basic idea of GD is to gradually approach the minimum point along the descent direction of the objective function instead of the negative gradient direction. Concretely, an appropriate initial example x_0 is chosen firstly, then iterate and update the value of x along the descent direction until convergence and obtain the corresponding adversarial example of x. The iteration formulation is shown in Eq. (3).

$$x_{j+1} = x_j - \alpha g(x_j) \tag{3}$$

Where x_j is the example obtained at j-iteration, α is the learning rate and $g(x_j)$ is the gradient at x_j.

ADAM Algorithm. ADAM optimization algorithm [10] is the extension of stochastic gradient descent algorithm (SGD) [9]. The SGD keeps the single learning rate updated with all weights, and the learning rate does not change during training. However, ADAM computes independent adaptive learning rate for different parameters by calculating first-order Momentum estimation and second-order Momentum estimation of gradient. Compared with SGD, ADAM requires less memory resources and the model converges faster.

2.3 Adversarial Training Based Feature Selection

For feature selection with adversarial training, given an original data set $D = \{x_i, y_i\}$, $i = 1,\ldots,n$, the adversarial examples (x_i', y_i) are generated by GD or ADAM algorithm, these adversarial examples are added to the original dataset to obtain a mixed adversarial dataset D_{mix}. Then feature selection is performed on this mixed adversarial dataset. The pseudo code for adversarial training based feature selection framework is shown in Algorithm 1. Of course, in the proposed framework, any feature selection algorithm can be used, and the number of adversarial examples to be added to original data depends on the application.

Algorithm 1: Feature Selection With Adversarial Training

Input: Original data set D

Output: Feature subset T ;

    1. **Initialize** $D_{adv} = \Phi$;

    2. **FOR** $i = 1$ to n

    3.   Generate adversarial example (x_i', y_i) for (x_i, y_i) by GD or ADAM algorithm;

    4.   Add adversarial example (x_i', y_i) to D_{adv} ;

    5. **END FOR**

    6. $D_{mix} = D + D_{adv}$;

    7. T=**Feature Selection** (D_{mix});

---

3 Experiment Results and Analysis

3.1 Datasets

In experiments, seven datasets are employed to evaluate performance of proposed feature selection framework, i.e., the Breast Cancer Wisconsin dataset [11] (Breast), the Spambase dataset (Spam), the Parkinson dataset [12] (Parkinson), the Sonar dataset (Sonar) from the UCI Machine Learning Repository site, sklearn's Breast Cancer dataset (Scikit_Breast), Arcene dataset and Madelon dataset from NIPS 2003 (http://clopinet. com/isabelle/Projects/NIPS2003/). Details of these datasets are shown in Table 1.

Table 1. The information of datasets

Data Set	Number of examples	Number of features
Breast	699	9
Spam	4601	57
Parkinson	195	23
Sonar	208	60
Scikit_Breast	569	30
Arcene	200	10000
Madelon	2000	500

3.2 The Experiment Setup

Three classical feature selection algorithms, i.e. Relief-F [13], Fisher Score [14] and mRMR [15], are chosen to validate the performance of adversarial training for feature selection.

The Relief algorithm is considered as one of the most successful feature selection algorithms due to its simplicity and effectiveness. The Relief-F is an extension of Relief to deal with multiple class problems. Relief-F algorithm needs to choose an example x_i randomly, then select k nearest examples H (nearest-hit) in the examples with the same label of x_i, and select k nearest examples M (nearest-miss) from the examples with different labels.

Fisher Score is also one of the most widely used feature selection methods. The key idea of the Fisher score is to find a subset of features so that the distance between the data points in the different classes is as large as possible in the data space spanned by the selected features, and the distance between the data points in the same class is as small as possible.

The mRMR is an effective method to preprocess high-dimension data. It takes into account not only the correlation between features and labels to identify the relevant features, but also the correlation between features and features to find the redundant ones. Mutual information is always used to measure the correlation.

The GD and ADAM optimization algorithms introduced in Sect. 2 are employed to generate adversarial examples, and these adversarial examples are mixed with original training examples to obtain new training datasets respectively. Based on the cross-validation experiments, the best mix ratio of adversarial examples and original examples in training set is set as 0.7 for low-dimension datasets (Breast, Spam, Parkinson, Sonar and Scikit_Breast), and it is set as 0.5 for high dimension datasets (Arcene and Madelon). The value of parameter c in Eq. (1) is set according to cross-validation. In experiments, the c values of the various data sets are shown in the Table 2. SVM and KNN classifiers are utilized to evaluate the accuracy of feature selection results with or without adversarial training. Ten-cross validation is adopted in the experiments.

Table 2. The parameter c value for different datasets

	Breast	Scikit_Breast	Spam	Parkinson	Sonar	Arcene	Madelon
c	9	25	35	6	15	25	30

3.3 Experiment Result on Feature Selection

We would like to compare the performance of feature selection with and without adversarial training on seven data sets. The feature selection algorithms with adversarial training are ReliefF+GD, ReliefF+ADAM, Fisher+GD, Fisher+ADAM, mRMR +GD and mRMR+ADAM. "GD" means adversarial examples are generated by GD optimizer and "ADAM" means adversarial examples generated by ADAM optimizer. For example, the ReliefF+GD means using Relief-F algorithm to select features on the mixed dataset which consists of original dataset and the adversarial dataset generated by the GD algorithm. The meanings of other legends are similar. The performance of feature selection with and without adversarial training are shown in Figs. 1, 2, 3, 4, 5, 6 and 7 for seven datasets. X-axis is the number of selected features, and Y-axis is the classification accuracy of SVM or KNN classifiers.

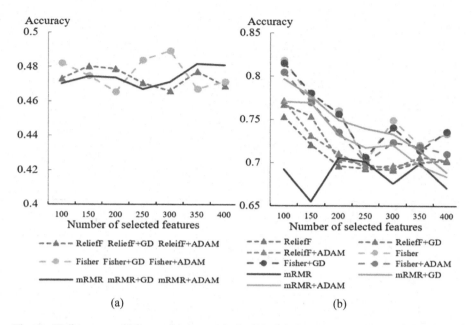

Fig. 1. The accuracy of feature selection methods with and without adversarial training for SVM and KNN on Madelon. (a) SVM; (b) KNN.

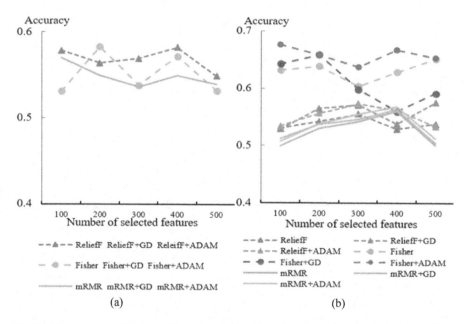

Fig. 2. The accuracy of feature selection methods with and without adversarial training for SVM and KNN on Arcene (a) SVM; (b) KNN.

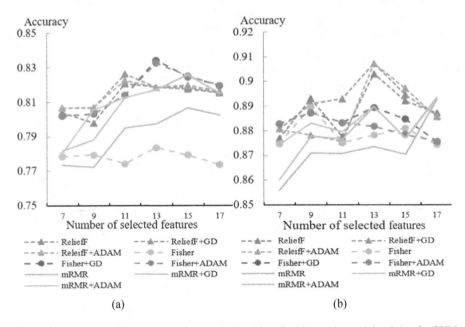

(a)   (b)

Fig. 3. The accuracy of feature selection methods with and without adversarial training for SVM and KNN on Parkinson. (a) SVM; (b) KNN.

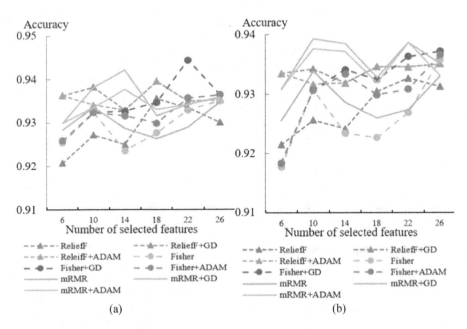

(a)   (b)

Fig. 4. The accuracy of feature selection methods with and without adversarial training for SVM and KNN on Scikit_Breast. (a) SVM; (b) KNN.

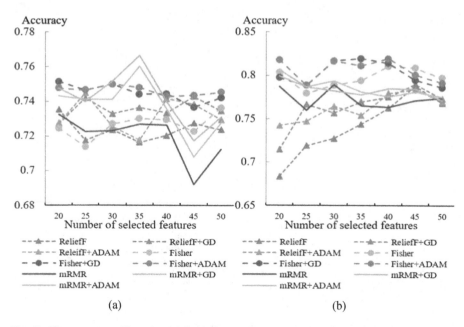

Fig. 5. The accuracy of feature selection methods with and without adversarial training for SVM and KNN on Sonar. (a) SVM; (b) KNN.

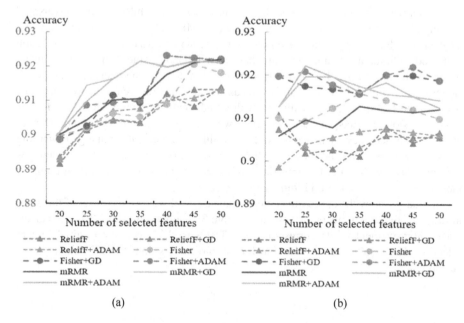

Fig. 6. The accuracy of feature selection methods with and without adversarial training for SVM and KNN on Spam. (a) SVM; (b) KNN.

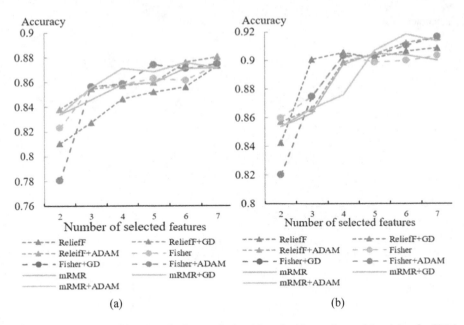

Fig. 7. The accuracy of feature selection methods with and without adversarial training for SVM and KNN on Breast. (a) SVM; (b) KNN.

As shown in figures and Table 3, we can observe that mRMR with adversarial training always obtains better performance than mRMR without adversarial training for all data sets. For the high-dimension datasets, Arcene and Madelon, feature selection with and without adversarial training has the similar classification accuracy using SVM, as shown in Figs. 1(a) and 2(a). For Madelon and Arcene data sets, their small sample size with high dimensionality leads to the little difference on performance between the feature selection with and without adversarial training. However, for the low-dimension datasets, feature selection with adversarial training obtains higher classification accuracy than feature selection without adversarial training. Regarding the KNN classifier, the performance of feature selection with adversarial training is obviously higher than the feature selection algorithms without adversarial training in most cases, especially the high-dimension dataset.

In order to show the approximate performance effect, we take the mean of the cases in different feature numbers, as shown in Table 3. The data in Table 3 is the performance improvement of its corresponding ATBFS method over the original feature selection. The results demonstrate that for the most cases, the ATBFS obtains better performance.

Table 3. The average of comparison between classical feature selections and ATBFS

	RF (GD)	RF (ADAM)	FS (GD)	FS (ADAM)	mRMR (GD)	mRMR (ADAM)
Arcene(SVM)	0	0	0	0	0	0
Arcene(KNN)	1.6%	1.3%	−2.1%	2.7%	0.6%	0.9%
Madelon(SVM)	0	0	0	0	0	0
Madelon(KNN)	0.9%	0.7%	−0.1%	−1.3%	5.7%	4.1%
Parkinson(SVM)	0.3%	0.3%	3.8%	3.7%	1.6%	1.8%
Parkinson(KNN)	0.4%	0	0.5%	−0.3%	0.7%	1.0%
Sklearn(SVM)	0.6%	0.6%	0.5%	0.3%	0.7%	0.6%
Sklearn(KNN)	0.8%	0.7%	0.5%	0.2%	0.5%	0.3%
Sonar(SVM)	1.2%	0.8%	1.9%	2.0%	2.2%	1.7%
Sonar(KNN)	2.2%	2.1%	0.5%	0.9%	1.2%	0
Spam(SVM)	0	0.1%	0.4%	0.5%	0.3%	0.4%
Spam(KNN)	0	0	0.6%	0.7%	0.6%	0.6%
Breast(SVM)	1.7%	1.7%	−0.3%	−0.3%	0	0
Breast(KNN)	−0.2%	−0.2%	−0.2%	−0.2%	0.2%	0.2%

Table 4. Variance for experiment results (SVM)

	Breast	Scikit_Breast	Spam	Parkinson	Sonar	Arcene	Madelon
RF	0.0041	0.0177	0.0012	0.0064	0.0236	0.0237	0.0031
RF+GD	0.0067	0.0142	0.0013	0.0065	0.0393	0.0330	0.0022
RF+ADAM	0.0067	0.0154	0.0013	0.0060	0.0264	0.0338	0.0028
Fisher	0.0048	0.0036	0.0017	0.0205	0.1105	0.0173	0.0050
Fisher+GD	0.0047	0.0063	0.0014	0.0196	0.0779	0.0337	0.0049
Fisher+ADAM	0.0047	0.0065	0.0013	0.0197	0.1000	0.0361	0.0053
mRMR	0.0038	0.0039	0.0017	0.0533	0.0423	0.0473	0.0028
mRMR+GD	0.0031	0.0022	0.0014	0.0356	0.0345	0.0435	0.0016
mRMR+ADAM	0.0031	0.0027	0.0014	0.0410	0.0215	0.0347	0.0016

Moreover, we also calculate the variance and conducts statistical tests on the classification accuracy results for different feature selection algorithms. Since the ten-cross validation is adopted by experiments, the variance is used to verify the fluctuation of classification accuracy results among ten crosses. The smaller the fluctuation, the more reliable the classification results. The variance is shown in Tables 4 and 5, each variance result corresponds to a line on Figs. 1, 2, 3, 4, 5, 6 and 7.

Table 5. Variance for experiment results (KNN)

	Breast	Scikit_Breast	Spam	Parkinson	Sonar	Arcene	Madelon
RF	0.0054	0.0025	0.0009	0.0595	0.0752	0.0682	0.0058
RF+GD	0.0034	0.0026	0.0011	0.0526	0.0575	0.0682	0.0060
RF+ADAM	0.0034	0.0022	0.0011	0.0584	0.0889	0.0682	0.0062
Fisher	0.0057	0.0027	0.0010	0.0825	0.1440	0.0551	0.0017
Fisher+GD	0.0054	0.0027	0.0009	0.0782	0.1453	0.0551	0.0017
Fisher+ADAM	0.0054	0.0015	0.0009	0.0822	0.1450	0.0551	0.0017
mRMR	0.0092	0.0068	0.0006	0.1106	0.0530	0.0680	0.0011
mRMR+GD	0.0059	0.0075	0.0005	0.1027	0.0394	0.0674	0.0011
mRMR+ADAM	0.0059	0.0081	0.0005	0.1067	0.0364	0.0669	0.0011

As shown in Tables 4 and 5, the ten-cross classification accuracy results using SVM classifier are more stable than using KNN. Most of the classification accuracy results of adversarial training-based feature selection are reliable in terms of variance.

To furtherly show the reliability of the classification accuracy results, we conduct a statistic test, namely the method of cross-validation t-test [16]. For two learning models A (i.e., feature selection with adversarial training) and B (i.e., feature selection without adversarial training), the two models' classification accuracy got through k-cross validation are $\varepsilon_1^A, \varepsilon_2^A, \ldots, \varepsilon_i^A, \ldots, \varepsilon_k^A$ and $\varepsilon_1^B, \varepsilon_2^B, \ldots, \varepsilon_i^B, \ldots, \varepsilon_k^B$, so the paired t-test could be used for comparative test. The basic idea here is that if the performance of the two learning models is same, then the test accuracy obtained by using the same test set should be same.

A hypothesis "the performance of feature selection with and without adversarial training is same" is made. And the difference on performance are calculated, i.e., $\Delta_1, \Delta_2, \ldots, \Delta_i, \ldots, \Delta_k$, $\Delta_i = \varepsilon_i^A - \varepsilon_i^B$. Then, cross-validation t-test is applied on the sets of difference sets as shown in Eq. (4).

$$\tau_t = \left| \frac{\sqrt{k}\mu}{\sigma} \right| \qquad (4)$$

where μ and σ are the mean value and standard deviation of $\Delta_1, \Delta_2, \ldots, \Delta_i, \ldots, \Delta_k$, respectively.

According to the experiment setups, we takes $t_{0.5/2,10-1}$ *(1.8331)* as the threshold, if the value of t-test is less than the threshold, the hypothesis is valid, i.e., the performance of feature selection with and without adversarial training is same. If the value of t-test is larger than the threshold, significant difference on performance appears in methods with and without adversarial training, and the method obtaining better performance would be adopted. Due to the limitations of space, this article only shows three data sets' t-test results (Parkinson, Sonar and Arcene) whose variance are greater than other data sets. The results of t-test are shown in Table 6, 7 and 8 for datasets Parkinson, Sonar and Arcene respectively.

Table 6. t-test on the performance of feature selection on Parkinson

	7	9	11	13	15	17
ReliefF+GD(SVM)	–	2.8942	1.2594	2.0453	–	–
ReliefF+ADAM(SVM)	–	2.8408	0.8347	2.0453	–	0.7477
Fisher+GD(SVM)	2.3237	2.3914	2.3914	2.3914	3.3360	3.0560
Fisher+ADAM(SVM)	2.3237	2.3914	2.3914	3.3360	2.9006	3.0560
mRMR+GD(SVM)	2.5381	1.4519	1.2196	1.2196	2.5352	2.0135
mRMR+ADAM(SVM)	2.5381	2.6736	1.2196	1.2196	2.5352	2.0135
ReliefF+GD(KNN)	2.6150	1.4417	1.1490	2.5493	1.1019	1.5768
ReliefF+ADAM(KNN)	2.6150	1.8120	0.2017	2.5493	0.1757	0.2556
Fisher+GD(KNN)	0.6511	2.3374	0.3554	0.3554	0.0329	0.0329
Fisher+ADAM(KNN)	0.6511	2.3374	0.3554	0.1794	0.5717	0.0329
mRMR+GD(KNN)	1.2063	1.0043	1.3191	1.2570	1.9352	1.4496
mRMR+ADAM(KNN)	0.4917	0.5438	0.8855	1.2570	1.9352	1.4496

In tables, the first column (from left to right) is the feature selection algorithm with adversarial sample generation method and the adopted classifier. The elements in the table is credibility of performance difference between the original algorithm and feature selection algorithm with adversarial training. For example, the element in the row 7 and column 1 is 0.0308, which means credibility of performance difference between the Relief-F algorithm and Relief-F algorithm with adversarial training (GD algorithm) on KNN classifier. The '–' in the table means that the performance of feature selection with and without adversarial training is same which corresponds to the points in lines of ReliefF and ReliefF + GD overlap together in Fig. 1(a). As shown in Table 8, the t-test results of KNN are better and we can draw a conclusion that KNN is more suitable for high-dimension data in the proposed framework. Half of the t-test values exceed threshold, which indicates that the experiment results are reliable enough and the feature selection with adversarial training can obtain better performance in most cases.

In a word, adversarial training is effective for feature selection and it can improve the feature selection performance in most cases.

Table 7. t-test on the performance of feature selection on Sonar

	20	25	30	35	40	45	50
ReliefF+GD(SVM)	5.8953	2.0654	0.4567	0.4243	2.8604	4.5511	1.0974
ReliefF+ADAM(SVM)	1.6905	1.1928	1.7695	7.1349	3.4125	3.3514	1.2444
Fisher+GD(SVM)	0.7481	0.4179	2.6907	3.2733	7.4684	2.8922	7.2008
Fisher+ADAM(SVM)	0.7481	8.4751	1.1742	5.9998	7.4684	2.8922	4.1905
mRMR+GD(SVM)	1.2206	0.4482	2.1919	3.5214	2.2354	0.4269	0.6124
mRMR+ADAM(SVM)	1.2206	2.8365	2.1919	3.6589	1.8381	0.4269	1.6906
ReliefF+GD(KNN)	0.0770	4.3763	1.0821	0.3570	2.4599	1.0310	0.5412
ReliefF+ADAM(KNN)	3.1453	2.6151	0.2704	1.5147	1.6723	0.9717	0.3433
Fisher+GD(KNN)	4.3830	6.5801	3.0319	0.7051	1.9574	3.9675	3.0102
Fisher+ADAM(KNN)	4.3830	4.7840	2.8664	0.4863	1.9574	3.9675	3.2501
mRMR+GD(KNN)	1.9910	1.9125	3.0066	5.2172	1.1473	3.5227	0.1683
mRMR+ADAM(KNN)	1.9910	3.5117	3.0066	4.3793	0.1302	3.5227	0.1764

Table 8. t-test on the performance of feature selection on Arcene

	100	200	300	400	500
ReliefF+GD(SVM)	–	–	–	–	–
ReliefF+ADAM(SVM)	–	–	–	–	–
Fisher+GD(SVM)	–	–	–	–	–
Fisher+ADAM(SVM)	–	–	–	–	–
mRMR+GD(SVM)	–	–	–	–	–
mRMR+ADAM(SVM)	–	–	–	–	–
ReliefF+GD(KNN)	0.0308	1.0713	0.7393	0.8371	2.5034
ReliefF+ADAM(KNN)	0.1246	1.5079	3.4182	1.9243	0.9119
Fisher+GD(KNN)	1.2186	2.0500	1.6805	0.3937	0.3411
Fisher+ADAM(KNN)	1.3306	3.0289	4.1002	2.7406	1.3327
mRMR+GD(KNN)	0.0024	2.1008	1.0654	2.2871	–
mRMR+ADAM(KNN)	0.2726	0.9897	1.4896	0.3742	–

4   Conclusion and Discussion

In this paper, a novel feature selection framework based on adversarial training is proposed. In detail, the GD and ADAM algorithms are implemented to generate the adversarial examples. And feature selection algorithms with adversarial training are performed on the datasets mixed with adversarial examples. Three popular feature selection algorithms (Relief-F, Fisher Score and mRMR) are used to validate the effectiveness of adversarial training. And seven benchmark datasets are utilized in experiments to evaluate the performance of feature selection with adversarial training. The experimental results show that adversarial training is effective to enhance the feature selection performance in most cases. This experiment results have been statistically tested (t-test) to prove the confidence of this conclusion.

In the proposed framework, adversarial examples are generated by GD and ADAM algorithms. Other methods to produce adversarial examples, such as generative adversarial network (GAN), will be explored in the future work.

Acknowledgement. This work was partially supported by the National Key Research and Development Program of China 2018YFB1003702 and Natural Science Foundation of China (No. 61603197, 61772284, 41571389).

References

1. Li, Y., Li, T., Liu, H.: Recent advances in feature selection and its applications. Knowl. Inf. Syst. **53**(3), 551–577 (2017)
2. Miyato, T., Dai, A.M., Goodfellow, I.: Adversarial training methods for semi-supervised text classification. In: International Conference on Learning Representations (2017)
3. Graves, A., Schmidhuber, J.: Framewise phoneme classification with bidirectional LSTM and other neural network architectures. Neural Netw. **18**(5–6), 602–610 (2005)
4. Miyato, T., Maeda, S., Koyama, M.: Distributional smoothing with virtual adversarial training. In: International Conference on Learning Representations (2016)
5. Chivukula, A.S., Liu, W.: Adversarial learning games with deep learning models. In: 2017 International Joint Conference on Neural Networks (IJCNN), pp: 2758–2767. IEEE (2017)
6. Szegedy, C., Zaremba, W., Sutskever, I.: Intriguing properties of neural networks. Computer Science (2013)
7. Bartlett, P.L., Wegkamp, M.H.: Classification with a reject option using a hinge loss. J. Mach. Learn. Res. **2008**, 1823–1840 (2008)
8. Cortes, C., Vladimir, V.: Support-vector networks. Mach. Learn. **20**(3), 273–297 (1995)
9. Ruder, S.: An overview of gradient descent optimization algorithms. arXiv preprint (2016). arXiv:1609.04747
10. Kingma, D.P., Ba, J.: Adam: a method for stochastic optimization. In: International Conference on Learning Representations (2015)
11. Olvi, M.L.: Cancer diagnosis via linear programming. SIAM News **23**(5), 1–18 (1990)
12. Little, M.A., McSharry, P.E., Roberts, S.J.: Exploiting nonlinear recurrence and fractal scaling properties for voice disorder detection. Biomed. Eng. Online **6**(1), 23 (2007)
13. Kononenko, I., Edvard, S.: Induction of decision trees using RELIEFF. In: Proceedings of the ISSEK94 workshop on mathematical and statistical methods in artificial intelligence. Springer, Vienna (1995)
14. Gu, Q., Li, Z., Han, J.: Generalized fisher score for feature selection. In: Proceedings of the Twenty-Seventh Conference on Uncertainty in Artificial Intelligence (2011)
15. Peng, H., Long, F., Ding, C.: Feature selection based on mutual information criteria of max-dependency, max-relevance, and min-redundancy. IEEE Trans. Pattern Anal. Mach. Intell. **27**(8), 1226–1238 (2005)
16. Dietterich, T.G.: Approximate statistical tests for comparing supervised classification learning algorithms. Neural Comput. **10**(7), 1895–1923 (1998)
17. Donahue, J., Philipp, K., Trevor, D.: Adversarial feature learning. In: International Conference on Learning Representations (2017)
18. Xu, W., David, E., Yan, Q.: Feature squeezing: detecting adversarial examples in deep neural networks. In: Network and Distributed Systems Security Symposium (NDSS) (2018)

Application of DeepWalk Based on Hyperbolic Coordinates on Unsupervised Clustering

Shikang Yu[1], Yang Wu[1], Yurong Song[2,3(✉)], Guoping Jiang[2,3], and Xiaoping Su[4]

[1] School of Computer Science, Nanjing University of Posts and Telecommunications, Nanjing 210003, China
[2] School of Automation, Nanjing University of Posts and Telecommunications, Nanjing 210003, China
songyr@njupt.edu.cn
[3] Jiangsu Engineering Lab for IOT Intelligent Robots (IOTRobot), Nanjing 210023, China
[4] School of Computer and Software Engineering, Nanjing Institute of Industry Technology, Nanjing 210046, China

Abstract. In the real world, various information can be represented by graph structure data. For example, interpersonal relationships and protein structure. In recent years, with the development of artificial intelligence, graph embedding has become a popular method of network analysis. It can reduce the dimension of network structure data, so that network structure data can be applied to various machine learning and deep learning tasks. At the same time, many studies of network geometry show that the hidden metric of many complex networks is hyperbolic. After hyperbolic space mapping, nodes in the original network data structure can be represented by hyperbolic coordinates. Hyperbolic coordinates contain information about the popularity and similarity of nodes which is very important for unsupervised clustering tasks. However, the random walk strategy in the native DeepWalk algorithm cannot effectively extract this information. So we propose an improvement of the DeepWalk algorithm based on hyperbolic coordinates and achieved good results on many datasets.

Keywords: DeepWalk · Graph embedding · Hyperbolic coordinates · Unsupervised clustering

1 Introduction

In the real world, network structure data is of great significance, which can effectively represent some realistic relationships. Since many years ago, scholars have begun to study graph data. In the traditional analysis method, the graph data is stored in the form of an adjacency matrix. Therefore, the graph data of

F. Liu et al. (Eds.): SciSec 2019, LNCS 11933, pp. 106–118, 2019.
https://doi.org/10.1007/978-3-030-34637-9_8

hundreds of millions of nodes requires a very large storage cost, not to mention the computational cost during the analysis process. This is the so-called curse of dimensionality.

With the development of artificial intelligence, machine learning and deep learning methods have achieved remarkable results in many tasks. For example, image recognition [2] and natural language processing [3]. However, graph data stored by traditional adjacency matrix is not suitable for machine learning models, but also leads to curse of dimensionality. Therefore, methods of graph embedding are getting more and more attention from scholars. First, it can save most of the information of the graph data. Second, it reduces the dimension of the graph structure data, so reduce the storage and computational costs. Finally, the vector representation of a node is more suitable as an input to machine learning and deep learning models than an adjacency matrix [4,5]. Therefore, the graph embedding method has achieved good results in many fields, such as product recommendations [6], item categorisation [7], link prediction [8], community discovery [9], customer value prediction [10,11] and network classification [12,13].

Over the years, scholars have proposed a number of graph embedding methods. In 2014, Perozzi et al. proposed the DeepWalk [14] algorithm which applies the SkipGram [15] model in the natural language processing (nlp) domain to social networks, so that it can use the deep learning method to not only represent nodes, but also to represent the topological relationship between nodes. The LINE algorithm [16] (Large-scale Information Network Embedding) constructs an objective function using the existing edges in the graph. The objective function explicitly depicts the first-order and second-order neighbor relationships. Node2vec [8] optimizes the sequence extraction strategy for random walks on the DeepWalk architecture. This strategy has some hyperparameters, and different choices of parameters can be suitable for different kinds of network data. HyBed [17] does graph embedding in hyperbolic space, rather than in European space.

In practical applications, the data set we can generally get are only the adjacency matrixes of networks. If there is no other extra information, how can we improve the graph embedding method to make it save more similarity information of the node? Fortunately, scholars in the field of network geometry give us a solution to this problem. Krioukov, Papadopoulos et al. found the negative curvature and metric property in the hyperbolic space can correspond well to heterogeneous degree distributions and strong clustering in complex networks [18]. And The PSO (popularity-similarity-optimization)algorithm suggests that the hyperbolic coordinates of the hyperbolic coordinates of the network nodes contain the similarity and popularity information of the nodes [19]. Based on the PSO model, Papadopoulos et al. proposed a hyperbolic mapping algorithm called HyperMap [20]. The input of the HyperMap algorithm is the graph data of the adjacency matrix format, and the output is the hyperbolic coordinates of each node of the network. This solves a problem that without any additional information, how can we only use the adjacency matrix to embed the graph to preserve more useful information of the graph data?

2   DeepWalk

DeepWalk takes a certain point as the starting point, obtains the sequence of points by random walk, and then the obtained sequence is regarded as a sentence, combined with the SkipGram algorithm in NLP to obtain the representation vector of the point. Essentially, random walks are used to capture the local context information of the points in the graph. The learned representation vector reflects the local structure of the point in the graph, and the adjacent points (or higher-order neighbors) shared by the two points in the graph. The more, the shorter the distance between the corresponding two vectors. So two main parts of the DeepWalk algorithm are random walk and the SkipGram model.

2.1   RandomWalk

Given a network structure data, a node is randomly selected as the starting point, and then we randomly select a point in the neighbor of this starting point as the next point. And move to this point and repeat the above steps. Know that we stop moving. This is called a random walk on the graph structure. [21] In the DeepWalk algorithm, the length of random walks is fixed. Random walk randomly and uniformly selects network nodes and generates a fixed-length random walk sequence, which is analogized to sentences in natural language (node sequence as a sentence, nodes in the sequence as words in a sentence) The input and output of the SkipGram model are the one-hot encoding of the network node, and the hidden layer is the vector representation of the nodes we need to learn (Fig. 1).

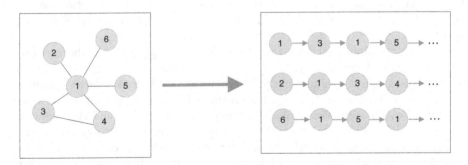

Fig. 1. The left side is the original graph structure data, On the right is the node sequence generated by random walk. The two adjacent nodes in the node sequence, in the original graph structure data, there must be a joint between them.

2.2   SkipGram Model

The input and output of the SkipGram model are the one-hot encoding of the network node, and the hidden layer is the vector representation of the nodes we

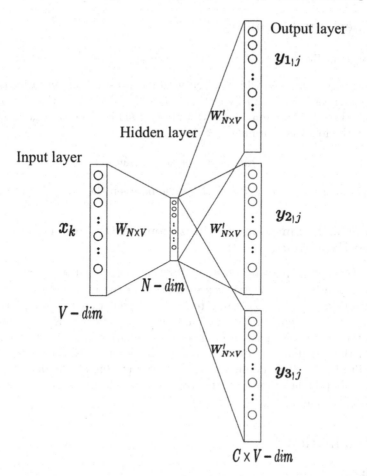

Fig. 2. SkipGram architecture. The model predicts context vertices from a single input vertex. Final embedding is a collection of learned weights $W_{N \times V}$ in the hidden layer x_k represents the one-hot code of a single node, y_{1j}, y_{2j}, y_{3j} represents the one-hot code of context node of x_k.

need to learn. If in the random walk, the two nodes have very many common neighbors, that is, the context node, then their vector representations will be very similar through the SkipGram model. This preserves the structural information of the network. The input and output of the SkipGram model are the one-hot encoding of the network node, and the hidden layer is the vector representation of the nodes we need to learn (Fig. 2).

3   Hyperbolic Geometry

3.1   Hyperbolic Space

In mathematics, a space in which the curvature is constant and negative is called a hyperbolic space. Points in hyperbolic space are $x = (r, \theta)$, the approximate hyperbolic distance between $A(r_a, \theta_a)$ and $B(r_b, \theta_b)$ can be calculated approximately by the following formula:

$$Distance_{ab} \approx r_a + r_b + \ln(\Delta\theta_{ab}2). \tag{1}$$

where $\Delta\theta_{ab} = \pi - |\pi - |\theta_a - \theta_b||$ is the angle between the point A and B.

3.2   Popularity Similarity Optimization (PSO) Model and HyperMap

The popularity similarity optimization (PSO) model indicates that the real network has a consistent geometric representation in the hyperbolic space, where each network node maps according to the angle and radial coordinates of the polar coordinate system. On the one hand, the node similarity is the angular distance in the hyperbolic space: the higher the similarity between the two nodes, the closer their angular coordinates are. On the other hand, the degree of node is related to the intrinsic popularity of the node: the higher the degree of node, the higher its popularity in the network, and the lower its radial coordinate in the hyperbolic space.

4   Combination

4.1   Disadvantage

In network clustering problems, such as commodity networks, many nodes represent unpopular goods, and subgraphs composed of some popular commodities are the focus that needs to be sampled. Since the random walk is randomly sampled, it does not distinguish between popular and unpopular items. Therefore, the sampled node sequence does not have a high confidence level, that is, the similarity and popularity information of the nodes is not considered. Moreover, without additional information, we can not obtain the similarity and popularity information of the nodes through the adjacency matrix. This also leads to the fact that the node vector obtained by DeepWalk using random walk does not perform well in clustering tasks. Because the general clustering task utilizes the distance between the vector representations of the two nodes, such as the Euclidean distance. The vector between the unpopular node and the hot node indicates that if there is no discrimination, that is, the distance is not far enough, then the clustering effect is not good.

4.2 Improvement

In the case where only the adjacency matrix is given, and there is no additional information, how to obtain more useful information of the node?

The coordinates of the nodes proposed by the PSO model in the hyperbolic space contain the similarity and popularity information of the nodes. And the hyperbolic coordinates can only be obtained by adjacency matrix. In the PSO model, r, which is the polar path, is related to the popularity of the node. Theta, which is the angle, is related to the similarity of the nodes. So we need to set a metric that measures the similarity and popularity of the two nodes based on the hyperbolic coordinates. Then convert the original unweighted undirected graph obtained from the adjacency matrix into a full undirected graph and convert the random walk into a weighted walk. That is, according to the weight of the edge, the next node is selected with probability.

4.3 Weighted Walk

In hyperbolic space, the distance between two nodes is called the hyperbolic distance. However, we do not directly use this formula (1), because for different kinds of networks, the popularity of network nodes and the similarity between nodes have different impressions on the effect of classification of network nodes. For example, in an Internet network, two nodes with high popularity, that is, nodes with higher degrees, have a high probability of belonging to the same kind. In the interpersonal relationship network, the similarity information of two nodes, that is, structural similarity information, the distance between nodes, etc., is very important in the clustering task. So we set up two extra global hyperparameters for different types of networks, then we propose the following formula based on formula 1:

$$W_{ij} = \alpha * r_{ij} + \beta * \theta_{ij}. \tag{2}$$

Where W_{ij} represents the weight of the edge between node i and node j, $j \subseteq N(i)$, $N(i)$ represents the one step neighbors of node i, r_{ij} represents the similarity information between node i and node j obtained from the polar diameter of the hyperbolic coordinates, θ_{ij} represents the popularity information between node i and node j obtained from the angle of hyperbolic coordinates. α and β can change the proportion of similarity and popularity in the W_{ij}. r_{ij} is calculated by formula (3) and formula (4):

$$pro_{ij} = \frac{\Sigma_m |r_m + r_i|}{|r_j + r_i|}, m \in N(i). \tag{3}$$

$$r_{ij} = \frac{pro_{ij}}{\Sigma_m pro_{im}}, m \in N(i). \tag{4}$$

θ_{ij} is calculated by formula (5):

$$\theta_{ij} = \frac{\cos(\theta_i - \theta_j) + 1}{\Sigma_m (\cos(\theta_i - \theta_m) + 1)}, m \in N(i). \tag{5}$$

Based on these formulas, each edge has its W calculated by formula (1). Then we can use W to convert the random walk into a weighted walk.

Tables Data charts which are typically black and white, but sometimes include color.

Algorithm 1. Imporved DeepWalk($G, w, d, r, t, \alpha, \beta$)

Input:graph $G(V, E)$
      window size w
      embedding size d
      walks per vertex γ
      walk length t
      Hyperparameters of WeightedWalk α and β
Output:matrix of vertex representations$\Phi \in \mathbb{R}^{(|V| \times d)}$
1. Initialization
2. Build a binary Tree T from V
3. Get hyperbolic coordinates by HyperMap,$H(G)$
4. for $i = 0$ to γ do
5. O=Shuffle(V)
6.   for each $v_i \in O$ do
7. $W_{(v_i)}$ =WeightedWalk($G, v_i, t, H(G), \alpha, \beta$)
8.   SkipGram($\Phi, W_{(v_i)}, \omega$)
9.   end for
10. end for

Algorithm 2. WeightedWalk($G, v_i, t, H(G), \alpha, \beta$)

---

1. Initialization $SUM_w = 0, \alpha, \beta$
2. for each $v_j \in N(v_i)$ do
3.   get $W_{(v_i, v_j)}$ by formula (2) with $H(G)$
4. $SUM_w + = W_{v_i v_j}$
5. end for
6. choose next node v_x with the probability $\frac{W_{v_i v_x}}{SUM_w}$

---

5   Experiment

In the experiment, we selected the following network for unsupervised clustering (Table 1).

Network vector representation using native DeepWalk and improved Deep-Walk for k-means algorithm for unsupervised clustering.

Table 1. $|V|$ represents the number of nodes, $|E|$ represents the number of edges, $|y|$ represents the number of clusters. All data comes from MEJ Newman [23]

Name	$|V|$	$|E|$	$|y|$
karate	34	77	2
polbooks	105	441	3
football	115	613	12
adjnoun	112	425	2
polblogs	1224	16781	2

5.1   K-Means

The k-means algorithm is an indirect clustering method based on the measure of similarity between samples, which belongs to the unsupervised learning method. This algorithm takes k as a parameter and divides n objects into k clusters so that the clusters have higher similarity. The calculation of the similarity is performed based on the average value of the objects in a cluster (considered as the center of gravity of the cluster). This algorithm first randomly selects k objects, each object representing the centroid of a cluster. For each of the remaining objects, according to the distance between the object and the centroid of each cluster, it is assigned to the cluster most similar to it. Then, calculate the new centroid of each cluster. Repeat the above process until the criterion function converges.

5.2   Metric for Clustering Task

In order to compare the native DeepWalk with the improved DeepWalk, we selected six commonly used clustering algorithm evaluation indicators, as follows:

Adjusted Rand Index (ARI): Bounded range $[-1, 1]$, negative values are bad, similar clusterings have a positive ARI, 1.0 is the perfect match score

Adjusted Mutual Information (AMI): Bounded range $[-1, 1]$, 1.0 is the perfect match score as ARI. Homogeneity: Each cluster contains only members of a single class. Bounded range $[0, 1]$, 0.0 is as bad as it can be, 1.0 is a perfect score.

Completeness: All members of a given class are assigned to the same cluster. Bounded range $[0, 1]$, 0.0 is as bad as it can be, 1.0 is a perfect score.

V-measure: Bounded range $[0, 1]$, 0.0 is as bad as it can be, 1.0 is a perfect score.

Fowlkes-Mallows scores (FMI): Bounded range $[0, 1]$, 0.0 is as bad as it can be, 1.0 is a perfect score.

The specific meaning of the above indicators can be found in the document of scikit-learn v0.20.2 [24].

6   Qualitative Assessment

We use the default parameters of native DeepWalk to embed the dataset, i.e. number-walks = 10, representation-size = 64, walk-length = 40, window-size = 5. For the improved DeepWalk, we make αchange from 0.1 to 0.9, the step size is 0.1, and β also changes with α, from 0.9 to 0.1, then we use HyperMap and Weighted Walk to get the sequence of the node, and then get the vector representation of the node through the SkipGram model as described in the pseudo code. Since the result of the k-means algorithm has some randomness, in the experiment, we call the k-means api in sklearn and perform 500 k-means algorithms for each network. The results of all indicators are the average of five hundred results. This avoids the randomness of the results and shows the pros and cons of the two algorithms on different indicators. The figure below is the experimental result. We show the result of the original DeepWalk algorithm as a red dotted line. The abscissa is the value of the hyperparameter α, and the ordinate is the index of the different clustering tasks.

As can be seen from figures [3–7], for different types of networks, the improved DeepWalk algorithm using weightedwalk has a certain improvement over the native DeepWalk algorithm in different indicators. The selection of hyperparameters will also have an impact on the effectiveness of the improved DeepWalk algorithm. The change in hyperparameters sometimes makes the effect of the

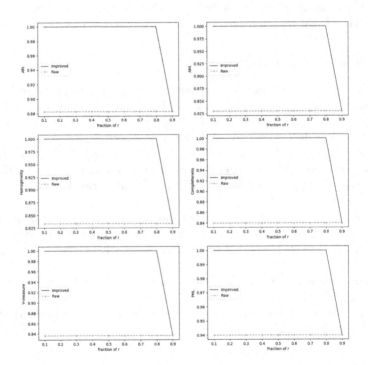

Fig. 3. karate (Color figure online)

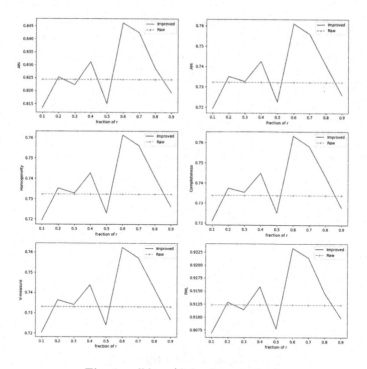

Fig. 4. polblogs (Color figure online)

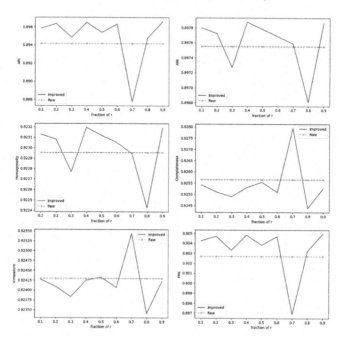

Fig. 5. football (Color figure online)

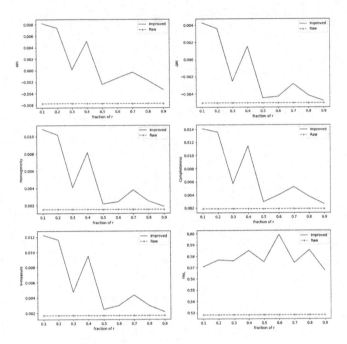

Fig. 6. adjnoun (Color figure online)

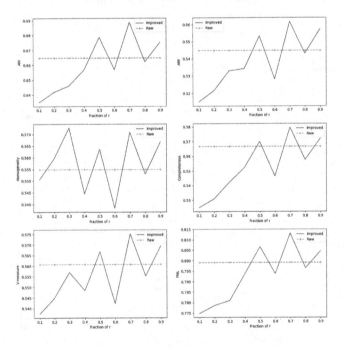

Fig. 7. polbooks (Color figure online)

improved DeepWalk algorithm better than the native DeepWalk algorithm, but overall, for different networks, the appropriate hyperparameters can increase the algorithm index and be superior to the native DeepWalk algorithm. In the experiment, the types of networks are different and the nature is different. Therefore, the hyperparameter enables the weighted walk to better extract the information in the original data that is more conducive to the classification task, thereby improving the generalization ability of the algorithm (Figs. 3, 4, 5, 6 and 7).

7   Conclusion

We propose a method to convert the random walk module in the native Deep-Walk algorithm into a Weighted Walk by hyperbolic coordinates. The hyperbolic coordinates of the nodes in the network are obtained by the HyperMap algorithm, and the weights of the connected edges in the network are determined by the hyperbolic coordinates. Then combine the PSO model to convert the weight into the probability of selecting the node during the weighted walk. In the weight conversion part, in order to improve the generalization ability of the algorithm for different kinds of networks, we also set the proportion of the popular information and the similarity information extracted by the hyperparametric control algorithm with two linear relationships. Finally, in the unsupervised classification task of network nodes using k-means algorithm, our proposed algorithm has significantly improved on many indicators compared with the native DeepWalk algorithm.

References

1. Keogh, E., Mueen, A.: Curse of dimensionality. In: Gass, S.I., Fu, M.C. (eds.) Encyclopedia of Machine Learning, pp. 257–258. Springer, Boston (2011). https://doi.org/10.1007/978-1-4419-1153-7_200110
2. He, K., Zhang, X., Ren, S., Sun, J.: Deep residual learning for image recognition. In: Proceedings of the IEEE Conference on Computer Vision and Pattern Recognition, pp. 770–778 (2016)
3. Cambria, E., White, B.: Jumping NLP curves: a review of natural language processing research. IEEE Comput. Intell. Mag. 9(2), 48–57 (2014)
4. Cai, H., Zheng, V.W., Chang, K.: A comprehensive survey of graph embedding: problems, techniques and applications. IEEE Trans. Knowl. Data Eng. 30, 1616–1637 (2018)
5. Goyal, P., Ferrara, E.: Graph embedding techniques, applications, and performance: a survey. Knowl. Based Syst. 151, 78–94 (2018)
6. Grbovic, M., et al.: E-commerce in your inbox: product recommendations at scale. In: Proceedings of the 21st ACM SIGKDD International Conference on Knowledge Discovery and Data Mining, pp. 1809–1818. ACM, August 2015
7. Barkan, O., Koenigstein, N.: Item2Vec: neural item embedding for collaborative filtering. In: 2016 IEEE 26th International Workshop on Machine Learning for Signal Processing (MLSP), pp. 1–6. IEEE, September 2016

8. Grover, A., Leskovec, J.: node2vec: scalable feature learning for networks. In: Proceedings of the 22nd ACM SIGKDD International Conference on Knowledge Discovery and Data Mining, pp. 855–864. ACM, August 2016

9. Ding, W., Lin, C., Ishwar, P.: Node embedding via word embedding for network community discovery. IEEE Trans. Signal Inf. Process. Netw. **3**(3), 539–552 (2017)

10. Kooti, F., Grbovic, M., Aiello, L.M., Bax, E., Lerman, K.: iPhone's digital marketplace: characterizing the big spenders. In Proceedings of the Tenth ACM International Conference on Web Search and Data Mining, pp. 13–21. ACM, February 2017

11. Chamberlain, B.P., Cardoso, A., Liu, C.H., Pagliari, R., Deisenroth, M.P.: Customer lifetime value prediction using embeddings. In: Proceedings of the 23rd ACM SIGKDD International Conference on Knowledge Discovery and Data Mining, pp. 1753–1762. ACM, August 2017

12. Perozzi, B., Kulkarni, V., Skiena, S.: Walklets: multiscale graph embeddings for interpretable network classification. arXiv preprint arXiv:1605.02115 (2016)

13. Li, J., Zhu, J., Zhang, B.: Discriminative deep random walk for network classification. In: Proceedings of the 54th Annual Meeting of the Association for Computational Linguistics (Volume 1: Long Papers), vol. 1, pp. 1004–1013 (2016)

14. Perozzi, B., Al-Rfou, R., Skiena, S.: DeepWalk: online learning of social representations. In: Proceedings of the 20th ACM SIGKDD International Conference on Knowledge Discovery and Data Mining, pp. 701–710. ACM, August 2014

15. Cheng, W., Greaves, C., Warren, M.: From n-gram to SkipGram to concgram. Int. J. Corpus Linguist. **11**(4), 411–433 (2006)

16. Tang, J., Qu, M., Wang, M., Zhang, M., Yan, J., Mei, Q.: Line: large-scale information network embedding. In: Proceedings of the 24th International Conference on World Wide Web, pp. 1067–1077. International World Wide Web Conferences Steering Committee, May 2015

17. Chamberlain, B.P., Clough, J., Deisenroth, M.P.: Neural embeddings of graphs in hyperbolic space. arXiv preprint arXiv:1705.10359 (2017)

18. Krioukov, D., Papadopoulos, F., Kitsak, M., Vahdat, A., Boguná, M.: Hyperbolic geometry of complex networks. Phys. Rev. E **82**(3), 036106 (2010)

19. Papadopoulos, F., Kitsak, M., Serrano, M.Á., Boguná, M., Krioukov, D.: Popularity versus similarity in growing networks. Nature **489**(7417), 537 (2012)

20. Papadopoulos, F., Psomas, C., Krioukov, D.: Network mapping by replaying hyperbolic growth. IEEE/ACM Trans. Netw. (TON) **23**(1), 198–211 (2015)

21. Lovász, L.: Random walks on graphs: a survey. In: Combinatorics, Paul Erdos Is Eighty, vol. 2(1), pp. 1–46 (1993)

22. Duc, D.M., van Hieu, N.: Graphs with prescribed mean curvature on Poincaré disk. Bull. Lond. Math. Soc. **27**(4), 353–358 (1995)

23. Newman, M.E.: Finding community structure in networks using the eigenvectors of matrices. Phys. Rev. E **74**(3), 036104 (2006)

24. Scikit-learn developers. Custering. https://scikit-learn.org/stable/modules/clustering.html#clustering-performance-evaluation. Accessed 24 Feb 2019

Attack and Defense

HoneyGadget: A Deception Based ROP Detection Scheme

Xin Huang, Fei Yan$^{(\boxtimes)}$, Liqiang Zhang, and Kai Wang

Key Laboratory of Aerospace Information Security and Trusted Computing,
Ministry of Education, School of Cyber Science and Engineering,
Wuhan University, Wuhan 430072, China
yanfei@whu.edu.cn

Abstract. Return-Oriented Programming (ROP) is a robust attack which has been proven to be Turing-complete. ROP reuses code segments named gadget in vulnerable applications and modifies control flow to achieve malicious attacks. Existing defense techniques for code reuse attacks attempt to restrict the policy of control flow transfer (e.g. CFI) or make locating gadgets a hard work (e.g. ASLR). However, decades of the arm race proved the ability to detect up-to-date attacks remains the Achille's heel. In honeypot, a general pattern for operators is spreading honeytokens and hunting spammers by capturing their malicious behavior. In order to capture the attack pattern of code reuse attacks, we present a novel deception based ROP detection model named Honey-Gadget. HoneyGadget inserts various types of honey gadgets as tokens to some specific points of binary files where normal control flow would not reach and record their places once the application is loaded. During the execution, HoneyGadget uses Last Branch Record (LBR) to trace execution records. On performing a sensitive function call, HoneyGadget compares LBR records with the maintained address list, and terminates the program immediately if some records match. Since these honey gadgets will not be executed by normal control flow, there must be a ROP attack. We have developed a fully functioning prototype of HoneyGadget. Our evaluation results show that HoneyGadget can (1) capture ROP attacks actively and (2) incurs an acceptable overhead of 7.61%.

Keywords: Return-Oriented Programming · Gadget insertion · Deception · Control flow · Last Branch Record

1 Introduction

Code injection attack was a tricky problem for software security practitioners before non-executable memory was introduced. With the widely deployment of DEP [2] and $W \oplus X$, attackers are forced to reuse existing code segments in binary. Over time, the state-of-art code reuse attacks have dramatically evolved from reusing sensitive system functions in related libraries of victim application (e.g. return-to-libc [33]) to chaining small code segments named gadgets into a

© Springer Nature Switzerland AG 2019
F. Liu et al. (Eds.): SciSec 2019, LNCS 11933, pp. 121–135, 2019.
https://doi.org/10.1007/978-3-030-34637-9_9

gadget chain (e.g. Return-Oriented Programming [5,30]). Triggered by a simple buffer overflow vulnerability, code reuse attack proved that it can perform arbitrary Turing-complete computation without injecting any malicious code [8]. In addition, there are several automated tools or methods available to help attackers to mount ROP attacks [28,29].

On the other hand, attempts to defense ROP attacks never stop. Existing defense techniques can be classified into two categories [24,26], which are randomization and control flow transfer checks respectively. A general purpose of Address Space Layout Randomization (ASLR) is to make data segments of the target application and the exact memory address of gadgets unpredictable. Control Flow Integrity (CFI) introduced by Abadi et al. [1] calls for validation checks for each control flow transfer. By constructing Control Flow Graph (CFG) statically and applying integrity checks at execution, CFI-based defense schemes restrict policies of control flow transfer.

However, existing defense methods are either one-time effort or detecting malicious behavior according to pre-defined policies, the ability to detect up-to-date attacks is outdated. Code reuse attacks via remote code execution is considered the most frequently used attack technique [4,31] in modern application scenarios. The remote adversary manipulates a code pointer to create memory disclosure and locates available gadgets for ROP attack. Equipped with weapons to exploit 0-day vulnerability, these advanced attacks are able to break existing defenses [4,6,7,15,31].

In order to capture these code reuse attacks, we propose HoneyGadget, a deception based defense scheme just like Honey-Patches [3]. HoneyGadget inserts honey gadgets as honeytokens to binary files of the target application and its related libraries, then we can detect attacks at runtime if inserted gadgets are executed. We have implemented a prototype of HoneyGadget on x86-based Linux platform. The experiment results show that the HoneyGadget incurs a modest overhead of 7.61% on average.

In summary, our main contributions of this paper include:

1. We propose HoneyGadget, a deception based ROP detection scheme, which provides a new method to capture ROP attacks.
2. We propose novel techniques combining constructing gadgets, inserting gadgets automatically and runtime ROP gadget chain detection method to achieve a ROP detection scheme.
3. We have implemented a prototype of HoneyGadget, and our evaluation shows that HoneyGadget achieves high accuracy with low overhead, proving our scheme practical.

The rest of this paper is organized as follows. We begin in Sect. 2 by introducing background knowledge on existing ROP attack methods and relative defenses. In Sect. 3, we detail our threat model and assumptions. The basic idea of HoneyGadget and the concrete implementation are illustrated in Sects. 4 and 5 respectively. We evaluate our system in Sect. 6. Related works are given in Sect. 7, and conclude in Sect. 8.

2   Background

2.1   Return-Oriented Programming

Return-Oriented Programming (ROP) is a typical code reuse attack. The main idea of ROP is chaining gadgets in the binary files of the target application as attack payload. Gadgets chosen for gadget chain are usually short with no more than 6 instructions [10] to avoid unplanned adjustment to pointers or registers. Each gadget in the attack payload is responsible for performing one or several steps of computation, such as loading argument from a specific register or performing arithmetic operations [8]. Triggered by an inconspicuous vulnerability, stack buffer overflow for example, control flow of the target application is hijacked. Together with the deployment of ROP defense schemes in modern system, ROP based attack techniques update correspondingly [6,7,15]. These attack techniques utilize flaws in control flow transfer policies, and bring defense schemes false negatives. Flexible and powerful, these features make ROP a state-of-art attack technique.

In modern application situations, except from software on the local host, applications and services provided by remote servers become a growing trend [3, 13,27]. Correspondingly, attacks on those remote hosts based on remote code execution and code reuse techniques appear [4]. Based on the feature that servers do not rerandomize the address space layout after a crash under particular circumstances, BROP rewrites every single byte of stack canary after several attempts, and this corrupts stack integrity protection. The adversary then invokes write to dump more available gadgets in process memory. BROP enriches the arsenal of remote attackers and expand the attack surface of code reuse attacks.

2.2   Last Branch Record

Last Branch Record (LBR) provides a way to trace the execution control flow of a program, as it can log the branch information executed in a looped buffer at real-time. CPU can record the execution pace parallel at execution, and it incurs no slowdown. The length of the looped buffer is limited. For an Intel Haswell CPU, the length is set to 16, indicating that LBR can record the past 16 instruction branches executed. For an Intel Skylake CPU, LBR can record the last 32 executed instruction. While the looped buffer of LBR is filled, the newly recorded branches overwrite the old ones [16]. The functionality of LBR is enabled/disabled by certain model-specific registers (MSRs). The access to MSRs requires kernel privilege, which makes the status of LBR transparent to programs running in user space.

3   Threat Model and Assumptions

HoneyGadget aims to capture attack patterns of ROP attacks from both local-host and remote attackers. To ensure that our scheme is practical, we define our threat model based on strong yet realistic attack assumption. With attack models in previous literature [4,6,7,15] and application scenarios of HoneyGadget, we generate the threat model as follows.

We assume the target application has at least buffer overflow vulnerability and the adversary has ready knowledge to exploit the vulnerability. The adversary is allowed to exploit the vulnerability repeatedly and can use automatic gadget generating tools to locate available gadgets and construct attack payload.

For remote side, we assume servers restart their worker processes after a crash and do not change their address space layout. Currently, servers such as Nginx and Apache are compatible with this feature. We further assume that the adversary is allowed to overwrite a variable length of bytes including a return instruction pointer [4]. These assumptions mean that the adversary can mount BROP attack successfully.

We assume the operating system enables standard defense mechanisms such as $W \oplus X$ and ASLR by default. However, as HoneyGadget focuses on capturing the malicious behavior of adversaries, methods aim to stop unintended control flow transfer such as CFI are disabled.

4   HoneyGadget

In this section, we describe the architecture of HoneyGadget. We first introduce the overview of our scheme, then we give out the detail of each component of HoneyGadget.

4.1   Overview

HoneyGadget owns two main components: *static processing module* and *runtime checking module* (see Fig. 1). The static processing module is responsible for (1) source code iteration and locating places to insert honey gadget as honeytokens; (2) generating gadgets that meet the requirement of potential code reuse attacks and (3) gadget insertion. After processed by the static processing module, the input file together with secured libraries are then taken over by runtime checking module. The runtime checking module of HoneyGadget (1) maintains address list of inserted gadgets and a pre-defined sensitive function list, and (2) performs runtime monitoring of execution. At last the output file is provided to local users and remote users. The output file has no interference on normal operations. However, those inserted honey gadgets are tempting but dangerous traps for attackers.

4.2   Static Processing Module

As we mentioned, the key idea of HoneyGadget is deception. Based on the observation of attack principle of code reuse attacks, we draw a conclusion that those attacks assemble gadgets into attack payload and hijack the control flow of victim

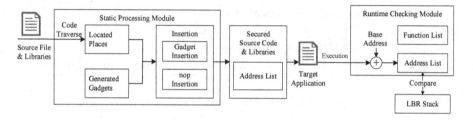

Fig. 1. Overview of HoneyGadget.

program no matter attack trick transforms. Thus, we can insert honey gadgets that meet the requirement of code reuse attacks as honeytokens. In order to avoid potential altering of execution flow caused by our gadgets, HoneyGadget inserts them to places where benign control flow would never reach.

In general, we summarize these places into two categories, which are opaque instructions [23] and function outlet.

Type I: Opaque Instruction: Opaque instructions have been used in software protection extensively. By setting predicates according to the value of invariant, context or execution result, opaque instruction is designed to clutter the control flow graph and it can redirect execution flow to a certain path.

Type II: Function Outlet: Code spaces right after function outlets is another case. The outlet of a function can be identified with the *ret* instruction and normal execution flow would never reach code segments right after *ret* instruction. However, inserting honey gadgets right after *ret* will grant the function with multiple outlets. Automatic gadget generating tool such as ROPEME [21] and ROPgadget [28] will regard the second function outlet as a fake one and discard it. In order to separate honey gadgets from existing function outlets, the static processing module selects instruction *nop* to complete this task. Those inserted *nop* sequences form interspaces between original outlet and the inserted gadget, and it confuses the automatic gadget generating tool.

Due to the poor alignment on x86 platform, unintended gadgets enrich attackers' options on their way to construct gadget chains. In order to eliminate potential unintended gadgets, HoneyGadget randomizes source code layout by randomly inserting *nop* instructions (0x90) before each assembly instruction. Shown in Fig. 2, by inserting a *nop* sequence between instruction "*mov [ecx], edx*" and "*add ebx, ebx*", the unintended gadget disappears. We will introduce the detailed implementation of inserting *nop* instructions and gadgets in Sect. 5.

For each honey gadget inserted, the static processing module records the offset to the start of the source code file in a formulation of address list. The address list is then maintained by runtime checking module during executions. Finally, the static processing module gives out a sensitive function list. The list contains function calls that can elevate privilege or perform arbitrary execution such as *execve()* and *setreuid()*.

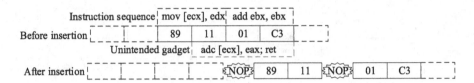

Fig. 2. The layout of instruction sequence after *nop* insertion.

4.3 Runtime Checking Module

Gadgets inserted are independent from existing code segments in source code, and there is no legal control flow transferred to them. Thus, it is most likely triggered by malicious attackers once the inserted gadgets are executed. Runtime checking module is designed to check whether there are inserted gadgets in execution branches of CPU. When loading application, ASLR randomizes the space layout of the application. Thus, in order to have an accurate record of honey gadgets inserted, the runtime checking module updates the saved address list. This module adds the base address of code segments with offsets of each honey gadget when the application is loaded. This maintenance procedure is done in kernel space, which is also transparent to user level applications.

Based on the observation that malicious executing code will eventually need to perform system calls to achieve something meaningful, the static processing module pre-defines a sensitive function call list and saves it in the kernel module together with the address list. While the target application is about to perform a sensitive function call, the runtime checking module pauses the execution of the target application and reads from the looped buffer of LBR. Then the runtime checking module compares the recorded instruction addresses with maintained address list. If one or more record matches, HoneyGadget confirms a ROP attack.

5 Implementation

In this section, we detail the implementation of our HoneyGadget, and give algorithms on gadget insertion and *nop* insertion.

5.1 Honey Gadget Insertion

Since HoneyGadget is a deception based defense scheme trying to confuse the ROP attacker by inserting honey gadgets. It turns out that the place where the gadgets are inserted, the number of inserted honey gadgets and types of those gadgets are the main factors that affects the effectiveness of HoneyGadget.

Places of Honey Gadget. The place to insert gadgets should be carefully arranged. Inserting gadgets inside normal instruction sequences may conflict with benign execution. For example, the gadget which modifies register *eax* may change the return address of benign execution flow. Consequently, the gadgets should be placed to unreachable execution paths. However, the diversification of unreachable execution path should be guaranteed to avoid those honey gadgets from identification. We generate those places in two types: opaque instructions and code spaces right after function outlet.

Function Outlet: As mentioned in Sect. 4, inserting gadgets directly after ret instruction will grant a function with multiple outlets. In this case, automatic gadget generating tool will recognize the fake gadget discard it. In HoneyGadget, we insert *nop* instructions to space out the two outlets as a disguise. After analyzing several frequently used dynamic libraries including *glibc* and *ld*, we noticed that there are several *nop* instructions between basic blocks. The number of *nop* instruction is between 5 to 40. Thus, we disguise those inserted gadgets as normal code segments by inserting 5 to 40 *nop* instructions after *ret*.

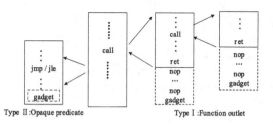

Fig. 3. Layout of code segment after inserting honey gadget.

Opaque Instruction: For opaque instructions, there exists three different types, which are invariant opaque predicates, contextual opaque predicates and dynamic opaque predicates [23]. In HoneyGadget, we focus on locating invariant opaque predicates in the source code. Due to its easy deployment, it is the most frequently leveraged opaque predicate [23]. HoneyGadget uses KLEE [32] to perform symbolic execution. KLEE is built on top of LLVM compiler infrastructure with a symbolic virtual machine engine. During this procedure, KLEE engine is responsible for locating the unreachable path and iterate to the end of this path. Following the end of the path, a gadget is inserted. The layout of code segment after inserting gadgets and *nop* instructions is shown in Fig. 3.

Insertion Algorithm. The honey gadget insertion algorithm is given in Algorithm 1. HoneyGadget randomly inserts *nop* instructions and gadgets after functions in source code at the probability of *pGadget*. For each insertion place, static processing module generates a random number *pRand*. If requirements are met, static processing module first inserts several *nop* instructions, then it randomly chooses a set of operation instructions such as *call*, *mov* or *sub* and an ending instruction to construct a gadget. To be noticed, HoneyGadget is able to generate all types of gadgets. This makes those honey gadgets inserted applicable for constructing a gadget chain. The length of generated honey gadget is no more than 6 instructions.

Algorithm 1. Honey gadget insertion

Input:
    (1) The list of functions and opaque instructions, FList;
    (2) The probability of insertion, pGadget;
    (3) List of candidate operation instruction, operationTypeTable;
Output:
    The list with deception gadgets inserted, FList.
     1: numOperationTypes ← operationTypeTable
     2: **for** F ∈ FList **do**
     3:    pRand = random (0,1)
     4:    **if** pRand ¡ pGadget **then**
     5:       i = the ret instruction of F
     6:       numNOP = random (5,40)
     7:       insertAfter (i, nop, numNOP)
     8:       i ← i.next (numNOP)
     9:       nOpt = random (1,5)
    10:       **for** index **from** 1 **to** nOpt **do**
    11:          *optIndex* = random (0, numOperationTypes)
    12:          insertAfter (i, operationTypeTable [optIndex])
    13:          i ← i.next
    14:       **end for**
    15:       insertAfter (i, endRet)
    16:    **end if**
    17: **end for**
    18: **return** FList

5.2   Insert nop

As presented in Sect. 4, HoneyGadget randomizes code layout by randomly inserting *nop* before each instruction, this procedure can eliminate potential unintended gadgets.

Similar with gadget insertion procedure, during *nop* insertion procedure, static processing module traverses each instruction from the first line in source code. For each instruction traversed, the module generates a random number *pInsert*. If *pInsert* is less than *pNop* defined previously, static processing module inserts a *nop* ahead of the instruction.

5.3   Trigger Detection

Runtime detection module of HoneyGadget leverages LBR to monitor execution states of instruction branches. Runtime detection module reads LBR buffer by using privilege instruction *rdmsr* and *wrmsr*. For an Intel Skylake CPU, the buffer of LBR can record last 32 executed instructions.

HoneyGadget pre-defines a sensitive function list containing function calls that can elevate privilege or perform arbitrary execution such as *execve*() and *setreuid()* during static processing procedure. It will trigger runtime detection mechanism if one of the sensitive functions is called. While the detection mechanism is invoked, HoneyGadget pauses the execution of the target application. Then runtime checking module sends the privilege instruction *rdmsr* to kernel to read LBR buffer. After reading the 32 recorded instructions, the module leverages binary search algorithm to search if there exist one or more recorded instructions match with items in the address list. Since only malicious execution flow can reach inserted gadgets, those addresses in the address list shall never appear in LBR record during normal execution.

6   Evaluation

In this paper, we evaluate the space cost of inserting *nop* instructions and gadgets, effectiveness and performance of HoneyGadget. We implement HoneyGadget on Ubuntu 12.04 with 4 GB available memory. The machine equips an Intel Skylake i5-6500 CPU. And the deployed LLVM and Clang version are both 3.5.2.

6.1   Effectiveness

In order to evaluate the effectiveness of our scheme, we verify HoneyGadget with real ROP attacks under two real world vulnerabilities. During these tests, *pNop* and *pGadget* are both set to 50%. Results of these tests indicate that HoneyGadget can prevent ROP attacks effectively.

Proof of Concept. In the first test, we test HoneyGadget on a small program containing a stack buffer overflow vulnerability. By inputting long parameters, the vulnerability is triggered and can be then utilized to launch a ROP attack. We use the automatic ROP gadget generating tool ROPGadget [28] to search available gadgets and randomly choose them to construct a ROP gadget chain. We repeat this test 50 times and report the final results. Among the 50 repeated tests, 49 of them used at least one of the inserted gadgets to construct the ROP gadget chain. HoneyGadget captured all the gadget chains containing inserted gadget with no false positive.

No-IP DUC. We also choose No-IP Dynamic Update Client (DUC) version 2.1.9 to conduct the test. The application fails to perform a boundary check while invoke vulnerable function *strcpy()*. The exploit database Exploit-db gives a ROP gadget chain example. We substitute gadgets in the gadget chain with gadgets generated by automatic gadget generating tool. Similar to the first test, we generate 50 gadget chains as ROP payload using different gadgets and 48 out of them contains at least one inserted gadget.

Nginx Web Server. HoneyGadget performs a deception based defense on remote code execution. Nginx web server is one of the most popular web servers in real world application situations. However, the weak security enforcement makes it vulnerable to a couple of attacks [4,14]. We exploit a simple stack vulnerability on Nginx 1.4.0 (64-bit) to launch a BROP attack. We apply HoneyGadget on

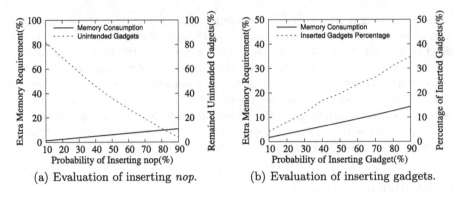

(a) Evaluation of inserting *nop*.   (b) Evaluation of inserting gadgets.

Fig. 4. Space cost and effectiveness evaluation.

Nginx server, and the scheme inserted honey gadgets that meets the requirement of BROP attack automatically. We repeat BROP attack attempt 50 times, 46 out of them leveraged at least one inserted gadgets during stage 2 or 3 in attack payload. As expected, our HoneyGadget can detect those attacks with no false positive.

6.2 Memory Cost Evaluation

On loading the application, those inserted gadgets and *nop* instructions are loaded into the memory together with the application. Consequently, memory requirement of the target application inevitably increases. In our experiment, we evaluate the extra memory requirement of *nop* insertion and gadget insertion respectively. The insertion procedure increases the program binary size. We set *pNop* and *pGadget* 50% as benchmark, the average increase in binary size is 8.41%. Increasement on binary file size has a positive relationship with insertion probability.

Space Cost and Effectiveness Evaluation of Inserting nop. We use HoneyGadget to process different applications and evaluate the space cost and effectiveness of *nop* insertion. In this test, we set *pGadget* 50%. Inserting *nop* instructions into source code of the target application inevitably increases its size, and the extra memory requirement has a linear positive relationship with nop insertion probability. Figure 4(a) shows that it takes 1.31% extra memory space while *pNop* is set to 0.1, and 10.84% extra memory cost while *pNop* is set to 0.9. On the other hand, along with the increase of *pNop*, the possibility of corrupting an unintended gadget raises. The dashed line in Fig. 4(a) gives the remained unintended gadgets percentage. The percentage of remained unintended gadgets drops from 82.13% to 3.72%.

Space Cost and Effectiveness Evaluation of Inserting Gadgets. Similar to the evaluation on *nop* insertion, in this evaluation procedure, we leverage same applications to perform the evaluation, and *pNop* is set to 50% as benchmark. It then takes about 1.71% extra memory when *pGagdet* is set 0.1, and the memory consumption raises to 14.33% while *pGadget* is 0.9. Together with the increment of *pGadget*, the scale of inserted gadget increases. The results of the experiment show that with *pGadget* of 0.1, only 4.61% of gadgets are inserted. The ratio increases to 19.74% for *pGadget* of 0.5, and to 34.82% for *pGagdet* of 0.9. Figure 4(b) shows the results.

6.3   Performance Overhead

To evaluate the overhead brought by HoneyGadget, we divide the evaluation into 2 phases. Corresponding to the architecture of HoneyGadget, the first phase is static processing, and another one is runtime checking.

We set *pGadget* and *pNop* to 50% and evaluate performance overhead of static processing phase by adding *-time-passes* argument. During the traverse procedure, the module identifies all instructions, basic blocks and functions. Thus, the larger the library size is, the longer time for static processing is needed. Time for processing frequently-used libraries are shown in Fig. 5(a). The experiment results meet this idea. As the results show, except from some huge libraries, it takes about 30 s to process a dynamic library. For example, it takes 35.96 s to process ld-2.23.so and 36.86 s to process liblzma.so. As for libraries with a huge quantity of basic blocks and functions, processing these libraries requires much time. Taking the library libc-2.23.so for an example, the time consumption increases to 468 s. Although it does take some time to do the static processing work, fortunately, operations in static processing phase is mostly a one-time effort, for libraries can be shared by different applications.

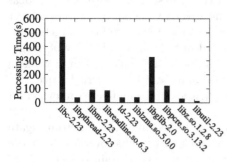

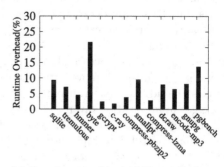

(a) Time consumption for processing different libraries.

(b) Runtime overhead of HoneyGadget.

Fig. 5. Performance overhead of HoneyGadget.

For runtime checking phase, we evaluate the performance overhead by running a benchmark test using *phoronix test suite* [20] with optimization level *-O2*. As we have introduced, those inserted gadgets are unreachable for benign control flow, and they introduce no runtime overhead during execution. The main performance overhead incured by honeygadget is to compare LBR records when handling sensitive system calls. On the other hand, the *nop* instructions we inserted will be executed. With more *nop* instructions inserted, the normalized runtime overhead increases accordingly. In our experiment, we set *pNop* 50%, the evaluation results are shown in Fig. 5(b). HoneyGadget introduces an average overhead of 7.61% which is less than Readactor++ (8.4%) and other fine-grained CFI solutions.

7   Related Work

Address Space Layout Randomization (ASLR) is a representative mechanism to defend ROP attacks. By re-allocating the space layout, ASLR changes the base address of the application and its related libraries. However, a single memory leakage vulnerability is enough to de-randomize the whole memory space.

Enhancement on ASLR is mainly on re-randomization and applying fine granularity. For example, ASLP [19] randomizes the target application at the function level, Remix [9] randomizes the address space at basic block level, and ILR [17] realizes randomization at instruction level. Bigelow et al. promoted a timely randomization scheme to re-randomizes address layout during execution [21]. Although these fine-grained ASLR significantly increase the difficulty for attackers to locate useful information in memory, it also brings extra time consumption and memory allocation.

Inserting some instructions in the program that do not affect the execution of the program can also increase the difficulty for the attacker to obtain internal information of the program. kGuard [18] uses a *nop* sled to change address locations, but they only do this to protect and diversify the kernel. HoneyGadget randomly inserts *nop* instructions and gadgets to source code of the target application and its related libraries. As mentioned in Sect. 5, the diversity of gadget types and inserted places makes attackers hard to distinguish inserted gadgets from original ones. Moreover, the maintained address list is in kernel space, this makes the address list transparent to adversaries and immune to information leakages in application layer.

Though the strict control flow transfer check mechanism is able to mitigate potential control flow hijacking, CFI poses an unacceptable overhead of more than 20%. In order to make CFI practical, a few coarse-grained mechanisms based on CFI are proposed. Coarse-grained CFI mechanisms relax the limitation of legal indirect control flow transfers, and simplify the checking method. Compared with fine-grained CFI, coarse-grained CFI mechanisms such as CCFIR [34] and binCFI [35] loose the indirect control flow checking policy and reduce overhead to an acceptable level. However, the loose checking policy brings potential vulnerabilities.

Another way to reduce overhead of checking the validity of control flow transfer is based on hardware. Liu et al. introduced a CFI enforcement using Intel Processor Trace [22]. Compared to using IPT to trace the execution path, CPU is able to read LBR registers parallel at execution. This feature makes LBR a more efficient way to log instruction branches of the application. Kbouncer [25] uses LBR to detect ROP attacks. ROPecker [10] also leverages LBR to optimize performance overhead. During offline processing procedure, ROPecker identifies potential gadgets and saves them in Instruction & Gadget database (IG). ROPecker reads LBR buffer and analysis executed gadgets in IG, then it indicates following instructions by simulating execution. If the number of gadgets reaches the limit, ROPecker warns user of ROP attack. HoneyGadget also uses LBR to record execution branch of the target application. However, different from these two approaches, the main idea of HoneyGadget is tempting adversaries to launch attacks by inserting gadgets to binary code. The behavior of the attacker is then captured and logged by host.

Booby trap [11] is a mechanism to actively detect and respond to attacks against a target application proposed by Crane et al. The main idea of booby traps is as follows: in a diversified application, code sequences (the actual booby traps) are added that trigger an active response, such as terminating the program or generating an alert. Readactor++ [12] inserts booby traps in both PLT and vtables to mitigate blind probing of table entries. HoneyGadget inserts *nop* instructions and honey gadgets to confuses adversary with traps. Compare to Readactor++, our HaneyGadget is more active and has a greater chance of getting attackers into the traps.

8 Conclusion

In this paper, we present a deception based ROP defense scheme named HoneyGadget. By inserting *nop* instructions and honey gadgets, our HoneyGadget confuses adversary with traps. HoneyGadget maintains an address list recording addresses of inserted gadgets in kernel space and defines a set of sensitive function calls. Once executing the sensitive function call, HoneyGadget pauses execution of the target application and reads LBR buffer to check if recorded instruction branches match with addresses in address list. If the record matches, HoneyGadget alarms a potential ROP attack. Our evaluation shows that Honey-Gadget incurs an acceptable runtime overhead of about 7%. Compared to other ROP defense mechanisms, the key idea of HoneyGadget is deception, which is a brand-new method to detect code reuse attacks.

Acknowledgement. This work was supported in part by the National Natural Science Foundation of China under Grant No. 61272452 and the National Basic Research Program of China (973 Program) under Grant No. 2014CB340601.

References

1. Abadi, M., Budiu, M., Erlingsson, U., Ligatti, J.: Control-flow integrity. In: Proceedings of the 12th ACM Conference on Computer and Communications Security, pp. 340–353. ACM (2005)
2. Andersen, S., Abella, V.: Data execution prevention. Changes to functionality in Microsoft Windows XP Service Pack 2, Part 3: memory protection technologies (2004)
3. Araujo, F., Hamlen, K.W., Biedermann, S., Katzenbeisser, S.: From patches to honey-patches: lightweight attacker misdirection, deception, and disinformation. In: Proceedings of the 2014 ACM SIGSAC Conference on Computer and Communications Security, pp. 942–953. ACM (2014)
4. Bittau, A., Belay, A., Mashtizadeh, A., Mazières, D., Boneh, D.: Hacking blind. In: 2014 IEEE Symposium on Security and Privacy (SP), pp. 227–242. IEEE (2014)
5. Buchanan, E., Roemer, R., Shacham, H., Savage, S.: When good instructions go bad: generalizing return-oriented programming to RISC. In: Proceedings of the 15th ACM Conference on Computer and Communications Security, pp. 27–38. ACM (2008)
6. Carlini, N., Barresi, A., Payer, M., Wagner, D., Gross, T.R.: Control-flow bending: on the effectiveness of control-flow integrity. In: USENIX Security Symposium, pp. 161–176 (2015)
7. Carlini, N., Wagner, D.: ROP is still dangerous: breaking modern defenses. In: USENIX Security Symposium, pp. 385–399 (2014)
8. Checkoway, S., Davi, L., Dmitrienko, A., Sadeghi, A.R., Shacham, H., Winandy, M.: Return-oriented programming without returns. In: Proceedings of the 17th ACM Conference on Computer and Communications Security, pp. 559–572. ACM (2010)
9. Chen, Y., Wang, Z., Whalley, D., Lu, L.: Remix: on-demand live randomization. In: Proceedings of the Sixth ACM Conference on Data and Application Security and Privacy, pp. 50–61. ACM (2016)
10. Cheng, Y., Zhou, Z., Miao, Y., Ding, X., Deng, H., et al.: ROPecker: a generic and practical approach for defending against ROP attack (2014)
11. Crane, S., Larsen, P., Brunthaler, S., Franz, M.: Booby trapping software. In: Proceedings of the 2013 New Security Paradigms Workshop, pp. 95–106. ACM (2013)
12. Crane, S.J., et al.: It's a trap: table randomization and protection against function-reuse attacks. In: Proceedings of the 22nd ACM SIGSAC Conference on Computer and Communications Security. pp. 243–255. ACM (2015)
13. Durumeric, Z., Bailey, M., Halderman, J.A.: An internet-wide view of internet-wide scanning. In: USENIX Security Symposium, pp. 65–78 (2014)
14. Evans, I., et al.: Missing the point (ER): On the effectiveness of code pointer integrity. In: 2015 IEEE Symposium on Security and Privacy (SP), pp. 781–796. IEEE (2015)
15. Göktas, E., Athanasopoulos, E., Bos, H., Portokalidis, G.: Out of control: overcoming control-flow integrity. In: 2014 IEEE Symposium on Security and Privacy (SP), pp. 575–589. IEEE (2014)
16. Guide, P.: Intel® 64 and ia-32 architectures software developer's manual. Volume 3B: System programming Guide, Part 2 (2011)
17. Hiser, J., Nguyen-Tuong, A. Co, M., Hall, M., Davidson, J.W.: ILR: where'd my gadgets go? In: 2012 IEEE Symposium on Security and Privacy (SP), pp. 571–585. IEEE (2012)

18. Kemerlis, V.P., Portokalidis, G., Keromytis, A.D.: kGuard: lightweight kernel protection against return-to-user attacks. In: Presented as part of the 21st USENIX Security Symposium (USENIX Security 2012), pp. 459–474 (2012)
19. Kil, C., Jun, J., Bookholt, C., Xu, J., Ning, P.: Address space layout permutation (ASLP): towards fine-grained randomization of commodity software. In: 22nd Annual Computer Security Applications Conference, ACSAC 2006, pp. 339–348. IEEE (2006)
20. Larabel, M., Tippett, M.: Phoronix test suite. Phoronix Media (2011). http://www.phoronix-test-suite.com/. Accessed June 2018
21. Le, L.: Payload already inside: datafire-use for ROP exploits. Black Hat USA (2010)
22. Liu, Y., Shi, P., Wang, X., Chen, H., Zang, B., Guan, H.: Transparent and efficient CFI enforcement with Intel processor trace. In: 2017 IEEE International Symposium on High Performance Computer Architecture (HPCA), pp. 529–540. IEEE (2017)
23. Ming, J., Xu, D., Wang, L., Wu, D.: Loop: logic-oriented opaque predicate detection in obfuscated binary code. In: Proceedings of the 22nd ACM SIGSAC Conference on Computer and Communications Security, pp. 757–768. ACM (2015)
24. Pappas, V.: Defending against return-oriented programming. Columbia University (2015)
25. Pappas, V.: kBouncer: efficient and transparent ROP mitigation, pp. 1–2, 1 April 2012 (2012)
26. Pappas, V., Polychronakis, M., Keromytis, A.D.: Transparent ROP exploit mitigation using indirect branch tracing. In: USENIX Security Symposium, pp. 447–462 (2013)
27. Riden, J., McGeehan, R., Engert, B., Mueter, M.: Know your enemy: web application threats, using honeypots to learn about http-based attacks (2007)
28. Salwan, J.: ROPgadget-Gadgets finder and auto-roper (2011)
29. Schwartz, E.J., Avgerinos, T., Brumley, D.: Q: Exploit hardening made easy. In: USENIX Security Symposium, pp. 25–41 (2011)
30. Shacham, H.: The geometry of innocent flesh on the bone: return-into-libc without function calls (on the X86). In: Proceedings of the 14th ACM Conference on Computer and Communications Security, pp. 552–561. ACM (2007)
31. Snow, K.Z., Monrose, F., Davi, L., Dmitrienko, A., Liebchen, C., Sadeghi, A.R.: Just-in-time code reuse: on the effectiveness of fine-grained address space layout randomization. In: 2013 IEEE Symposium on Security and Privacy (SP), pp. 574–588. IEEE (2013)
32. Team, K.: KLEE LLVM execution engine. http://klee.github.io/
33. Tran, M., Etheridge, M., Bletsch, T., Jiang, X., Freeh, V., Ning, P.: On the expressiveness of return-into-libc attacks. In: Sommer, R., Balzarotti, D., Maier, G. (eds.) RAID 2011. LNCS, vol. 6961, pp. 121–141. Springer, Heidelberg (2011). https://doi.org/10.1007/978-3-642-23644-0_7
34. Zhang, C., et al.: Practical control flow integrity and randomization for binary executables. In: 2013 IEEE Symposium on Security and Privacy (SP), pp. 559–573. IEEE (2013)
35. Zhang, M., Sekar, R.: Control flow integrity for COTS binaries. In: USENIX Security Symposium, pp. 337–352 (2013)

LET-Attack: Latent Encodings of Normal-Data Manifold Transferring to Adversarial Examples

Jie Zhang[(✉)] and Zhihao Zhang

Nanjing University of Posts and Telecommunications, Nanjing, China
zhangjie@njupt.edu.cn

Abstract. Recent studies have highlighted the vulnerability and low robustness of deep learning model against adversarial examples. This issue limits their deployability on ubiquitous applications requiring a high level of security such as driverless system, unmanned aerial vehicle and intrusion detection. In this paper, we propose latent encodings transferring attack (LET-attack) to generate target natural adversarial examples to fool well-trained classifiers. In order to perturb in latent space, we train WGAN-variants on various datasets to achieve feature extraction, image reconstruction and image discrimination against counterfeit with good performance. Thanks to our two-stage procedure of mapping transformation, the adversary performs precise and semantic perturbations on source data referring to target data in latent space. By using the critic in WGAN-variant and the well-trained classifier, the adversary crafts more verisimilar and effective adversarial examples. As shown in the experimental results on MNIST, FashionMNIST, CIFAR-10 and LSUN, LET-attack can yield a distinct set of adversarial examples with partly data manifold targeted transfer and attains similar attack performance against state-of-the-art models in different attack scenarios. What is more, we evaluate LET-attack on the characteristic of transferability in different classifiers on MNIST and CIFAR-10 respectively, and find that the adversarial examples are easy to transfer with high confidence.

Keywords: Adversarial example · Mapping transformation · Black-box attack · Transferability

1 Introduction

In recent years, deep learning has made great progress in the fields of computer vision and natural language processing. With its advantages of no need to manually extract features from raw datasets, deep learning is widely used in many high secure-requirements scenarios such as driverless system, unmanned aerial vehicle, robotics, and intrusion detection. At the same time, the security problems of deep learning based on adversarial examples is gradually becoming a research hotspot [1–3]. Although deep

This study was supported by the National Key R&D Program of China (2018YFB1500902) and NUPTSF (Grant No.NY219122).

F. Liu et al. (Eds.): SciSec 2019, LNCS 11933, pp. 136–150, 2019.
https://doi.org/10.1007/978-3-030-34637-9_10

learning has achieved phenomenal success in dealing with complex problems, recent studies have highlighted the vulnerability of various deep learning models to adversarial examples, targeted crafted by adversary to fool a well-trained model to misclassify with high confidence, which putting the applications with high security-requirements into a colossal security bungle [4–6].

The low robustness of deep learning models against adversarial examples is confirmed in physical world [7]. For instance, the perturbations is added to the input against autopilot and face recognition system. Most attacks occur in the inference process by contaminating input data with no effect on human judgment, such as posting malicious stickers on road signs to mislead the driverless system to identify the stop sign as a speed limit sign with great confidence [8]. In face recognition system, when the invisible but malicious perturbation is added to the input data, such as wearing lipstick [9], the accuracy of face recognition has dropped dramatically.

The methods of generating adversarial examples are known as the attacks against deep learning models. Attacks are generally classified into untargeted attacks and targeted attacks [3]. Untargeted attacks generally refer to an attack in which the original label changes after adding a well-crafted perturbation to the input. By contrast, targeted attacks need targeted label change. After being compromised by adversarial examples, poorly interpretable deep learning models are unable to explain the cause of the problem and the characteristic of adversarial subspace because of its end-to-end property. So reference [10] improves the robustness and interpretability by regularizing their input gradients. Meanwhile, many attempts have been to design a secure defense against adversarial examples to achieve high robustness and resistance against adversarial examples. General defense algorithms focus on modifications to the parameters of target model [11, 12] and attachment for target model with additional adversarial example detection modules [13–16]. Up to now, even a great many of detection algorithms have been implemented [13, 15, 16], the intrinsic characteristics of adversarial examples against normal data are still ambiguous. So there is still a great limitation on adversarial detection.

All of the above algorithms of attacks and defenses are based on imperceptible and unnatural adversarial examples. Limited by L_1, L_2-norm, most of the existing attacks are performed in input space with the access of target model, and lack of interpretation of their intrinsic properties. The perturbations crafted with the help of internal information looks like unnatural and lack of unambiguous semantics. So the search in latent space for adversaries is to generate natural adversarial examples without internal information of target model [17]. But it still exists large limitation on the target-direction search for adversaries due to the semi-random noise attached to the latent encodings of source data. What is more, the adversarial examples they craft are still of low quality.

In this paper, we introduce a framework of WGAN-variant referring to WGAN [18, 19] to achieve mapping transformation by using different reconstruction metrics, and our LET-attack generating targeted adversarial examples with more precise and natural perturbations by using the components of the pre-trained WGAN-variant. The algorithm is based on black-box attack to craft targeted semantic adversarial examples. Figure 1 provides an example performed in MNIST dataset to fool LeNet-5.

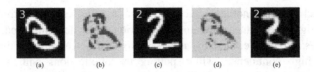

Fig. 1. (b) is the subtraction between source data(a) and target data(c). After the process of our attack finished, (e) is the target adversarial example we craft, and (d) is the subtraction between (a) and (e). By (d) we can find that the targeted perturbation is more natural and prone to mislead pre-trained LeNet-5 on MNIST, but still remaining positive identification by human.

Equipped with this perspective, we make the following contributions.

- We introduce a two-stage training process of generator to achieve mapping transformation between input space and latent space by using different distance metrics. We use an Encoder-Decoder block and a Decoder-Encoder block to perform image reconstruction and feature extraction. The Reconstruction error of $R(x, x^{'})$ uses L_2-distance and $R(z, z^{'})$ uses L_1-distance. By using L_2-distance, the reconstructed image looks like real image. By using L_1-distance, it contributes to the feature disentangle in latent space.
- We use the given pre-trained classifier and the critics to generate targeted and natural adversarial examples. Whether the process of data manifold transfer makes the label change from origin to target is determined by the given classifier. Whether the generated adversarial example looks like real is determined by the pre-trained critic. The above two sub-nets ensure the great quality of the targeted natural adversarial examples.
- The adversarial examples crafted by our attack mislead target models with high confidence and they are easy to perform black-box attack to fool other well-trained classifiers with great transferability.

The rest of this paper is organized as follows. In the following section, we provide a survey of related works that we analyze their advantages and disadvantages to lead to our LET-attack. In Sect. 3, we provide a framework of WGAN-variant to achieve mapping transformation, and our targeted LET-attack. We present the process of data manifold transfer and our experimental evaluation on various datasets in Sect. 4. In Sect. 5, we show the great transferability of our adversarial examples in various pre-trained classifiers. Finally, we conclude with a discussion and future studies in Sect. 6.

2   Related Work

In this section, we introduce four categories of recent studies on adversarial attacks: gradient-based attacks, score-based attacks, transfer-based attacks, decision-based attacks and FCN attack.

2.1   Gradient-Based Attack

By accessing the gradient of target model to inversely increase loss function, Gradient-based attacks are completely easy to craft non-targeted and targeted adversarial examples. Common gradient-based attack algorithms are as follows: fast gradient sign method (FGSM) [2] is based on the hypothesis about linear interpretation to craft adversarial examples via one-step operation. Basic iterative method (BIM) [7] uses iterative steps to craft more exquisite adversarial examples. Jacobian-based saliency map attack (JSMA) calculates the significant point scores of each pixel to find the pixels affecting the accuracy of classification most, by setting limitation about the norm of perturbation [20]. Up to now, Carlini and Wagner attack becomes one of the most effective attack algorithms by using modified objective function to generate adversarial examples in different levels of confidence [21].

2.2   Score-Based Attack

Score-based attacks belong to black-box attack. Whether the model is sensitive to the change of pixel value is determined by replacing the pixel value of input image with maximum or minimum, which is based on the change of output probability of label prediction [22, 23].

2.3   Transfer-Based Attack

In transfer-based attacks, the adversary feeds local data to the target model to obtain information feedback, such as the data similar to the training set with high correlation, and crafts a substitute model to generate adversarial example. It only depends on the data, not on the target model instead [24].

2.4   Decision-Based Attack

Decision-based attacks belong to black-box attack. Relying only on the final output of the model and minimizing the norm-based adversarial examples, decision-based attacks implement a kind of more effective and imperceptible attacks [25].

2.5   FCN Attack

FCN attack is based on the adversarial transformation networks [26] to generate adversarial examples that minimally perturb the original input to fool the classifiers. FCN attack uses multi-target training, multi-task training and gradient hints to perform the attack. By using the models they pre-trained, they craft target adversarial examples fast and precisely.

With the continuous evolution of the attack algorithms, it requires less information of target model and its perturbation is becoming more exquisite and imperceptible [25]. The above-mentioned attack algorithms achieve the destruction against accuracy of the target model to a certain extent. However, there are still large limitation in practice. First of all, the white-box attacks need to obtain internal information of target model to generate adversarial examples by using the gradient of target model, mining the "blind spot" in deep learning models [1]. By adding the adversarial examples of blind spots to adversarial training, target models are fitting the decision boundary better. Adversarial training provides additional regularization benefits for target model, and improves the robustness of adversarial examples. However, the adversary generally has no access to internal information to perform this kind of attack. Therefore, the white-box attack is only effective on the adversarial examples crafted by using internal information on laboratory setting, not impressively practical in actual scenarios. Secondly, the black-box attacks mentioned above require a large number of times to access target models to indirectly acquire model information, such as model structure or training data [24]. This kind of attack is limited by the times of access, so it also has large limitation on the mentioned black-box attacks. Last but not least, there is a similar problem exiting in all of the above attack algorithms. Although the influence of the malicious perturbation on target model is obviously great, the perturbation added to the input is unnatural. In other words, the pixel-uncorrelated perturbation is not semantic in human observation. Therefore, the uninterpretable adversarial subspace the adversary revealing is not clear and sufficient. Besides, most of the attacks do not work when the model is deployed to real scenes. The attacks with obviously semantic perturbation are more common in practice, such as slight image rotation and image saturation adjustment, causing the target model to make different decisions [1].

There is an obvious defect that the present various deep learning models only extract black-box features from input data, and fail to understand the input in a deeper way. It leads to the malicious perturbations with imperceptibility in human to destruct the accuracy of target model. But it does not exist such a kind of perturbations in reality. Therefore, the study focusing on how to generate natural adversarial examples with semantic perturbation is becoming gradually meaningful [24, 27]. Reference [17] using latent encodings iteration or recursively tightening search to find natural adversarial examples makes great progress, but fails to generate targeted adversarial examples with reference to targeted data. What is more, the quality of the adversarial example generation is not stable enough.

3   Latent Encodings Targeted Transferring

In this section we describe the framework of WGAN-variant and latent encodings targeted transferring algorithm (LET-attack). Based on the idea of Wasserstein GAN, we combine an encoder with a decoder as a generator in WGAN, and introduce a critic to determine whether the image generated by generator is real. The pre-trained generator is capable of mapping between input space and latent space. Finally, we introduce the LET-attack to perform a targeted semantic adversarial attack without the access of internal information in target model.

3.1   Generative Adversarial Networks

Generative Adversarial Networks (GAN) is an emerging kind of generation model, consisting of generator model $G(\cdot)$ and critic model $C(\cdot)$. Given a large number of unlabeled data from training set and a prior distribution of latent encodings z, the GAN model learns to represent z in input space through the Max-min game training. Whether the image generated by generator is real is determined by the critic. The training process continues to alternately optimize $G(\cdot)$ model and $C(\cdot)$ model until reaching the Nash equilibrium. At this point, the critic can hardly discriminate whether the data is generated from generator or sampled from training set. The objective function can be described as:

$$W(P_{data}, P_G) \approx \min_G \max_C V(C, G) = E_{x \sim P_x}[C_w] - E_{z \sim P_z}[C_w(G(z))] \qquad (1)$$

C_w is the critic to determine whether the image generated by G is real. After training the G and the D iteratively, P_G is almost close to real data distribution P_{data}.

In this paper, we use the framework of WGAN to provide a stable training process with the replacement of objective function and some tricks in WGAN [18, 19].

3.2   Mapping Transformation WGAN-Variant

To perform an effective adversarial attack in latent space, it is necessary to map between input space x and latent space z. During the process of feature extraction and image reconstruction, it is required that we retain original information of source data as much as possible. Therefore, we introduce generative adversarial networks to meet this requirement. We refine the framework of WGAN as WGAN-variant in Fig. 2:

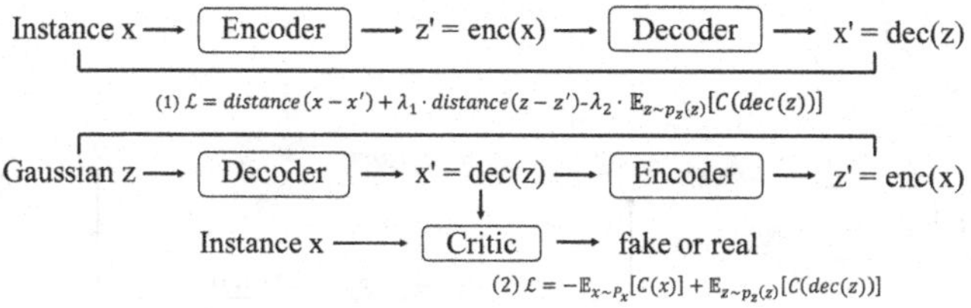

Instance x $\longrightarrow$ [Encoder] $\longrightarrow$ z' = enc(x) $\longrightarrow$ [Decoder] $\longrightarrow$ x' = dec(z)

(1) $\mathcal{L} = distance\,(x - x') + \lambda_1 \cdot distance\,(z - z') - \lambda_2 \cdot \mathbb{E}_{z \sim p_z(z)}[C\,(dec\,(z))]$

Gaussian z $\longrightarrow$ [Decoder] $\longrightarrow$ x' = dec(z) $\longrightarrow$ [Encoder] $\longrightarrow$ z' = enc(x)

Instance x $\longrightarrow$ [Critic] $\longrightarrow$ fake or real

(2) $\mathcal{L} = -\mathbb{E}_{x \sim P_x}[C(x)] + \mathbb{E}_{z \sim p_z(z)}[C(dec(z))]$

Fig. 2. The process of generating verisimilar data includes two parts. One is image reconstruction from x to x', another is feature extraction from z to z'. (1) combines the distances between x and x', z and z' in L_2 and L_1 metrics. The critic tries to discriminate generated data from the whole dataset by minimizing (2).

The WGAN-variant consists of two parts, one is the generative model combined with an Encoder and a Decoder, and the other is the discriminator model named Critic. Firstly, we feed instance x from training set into an Encoder-Decoder block, calculating the reconstruction error between x and x'. And then we feed z from Gaussian distribution into a Decoder-Encoder block, calculating the L_1-distance between z and z'. Finally, we minimize (1) by different weights on the distances in generator-training step to fool the critic. In critic-training step, we use x' from the prior z to determine whether the image generated by Decoder is real. By reasonably setting representation dimensions, we obtained well-performed WGAN-variants to perform feature extraction and image reconstruction on various datasets.

3.3   LET-Attack

We hypothesis that there is little overlap between source and target data manifold in original high-dimension input space, but a part in latent space. When increasing the overlaps or decreasing the distance between source and target manifold in given latent space, we try to search adversaries with normal-data manifold targeted transferring to adversarial targets. After the partly transferring latent encodings mapping into input space, we enlarge the overlaps between source and target data manifold. The concrete process is as follows.

After the training process of WGAN-variant, we perform LET-attack on different datasets. Given a local image pre-trained classifier on the dataset with high classification accuracy, we select a group of source and target data with their correct labels in training dataset. The source data x_{source} and target data x_{target} are mapped into the fixed latent space from input space by the Encoder to get their latent encodings:

$$z_{source} = Enc(x_{source}) = [a\_1, \ldots, a\_i, a\_n] \tag{2}$$

$$z_{target} = Enc(x_{target}) = [b\_1, \ldots, b\_i, b\_n] \tag{3}$$

Giving a transferring step size R, we iteratively search the decision boundary in latent encodings of source data transferring to target data until the label of source data changes to targeted label:

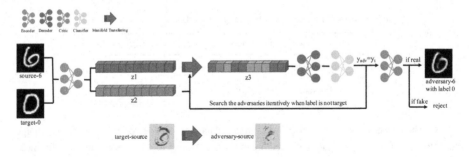

Fig. 3. The process of LET-attack. The subtraction between source and adversary is much smaller than the original subtraction after the process of transfer.

$$z_{adv(i)} = z_{adv(i-1)} + R \times distance\left(z_{adv(i-1)} - z_{target}\right) \tag{4}$$

$$x_{adv} = Dec\left(z_{adv(i)}\right), \ when \ y_{adv} \ is \ y_{target} \tag{5}$$

$z_{adv(i)}$ is the intermediate product of the process of manifold transferring. Every transferring step needs decoding the $z_{adv(i)}$ to determine whether the attack is completed.

The process is shown in Fig. 3.

When targeted latent-space transfer in each iteration is performed and the adversarial latent encodings are mapped back to the input space, the adversary is classified by the given classifier. The adversary returns to the process of transfer when it fails to change its label to target. After the label of adversarial example calculated by the given classifier target changes and it looks like real judged by the critic, the process of search iterations is finished. The adversarial examples generated in this way is partly changed in some semantic local features, but with its original identification maintained in human perspective. In other words, it changes slightly without misleading the perception of human, but a lot in deep learning models.

The process of targeted latent-space transfer dynamically reduces the distance between latent encodings mapped from source data and target data step by step to generate targeted semantic adversarial examples. Here is the pseudo-code of our LET-attack:

Algorithm: Minimal version of the LET-attack

Require: a dataset X of image classification, a classifier f pre-trained on the dataset

Hyperparameter: representation dimension z, transferring step size R, maximum transferring steps n

Input: x_{source}, x_{target}, y_{source}, y_{target}

1. Use Mapping transformation WGAN-variant in 3.2 to train an Encoder enc, a Decoder dec and a Critic c on target dataset.

2. select a corpus of x_{source}, a corpus of x_{target} with different label

3. initialize z_{adv} with z_{source}, $z_{source} = z_{adv(0)} = enc(x_{source})$, $z_{target} = enc(x_{target})$, $\Delta z = z_{source} - z_{target}$, $i = 0$.

4. **while** $\tilde{y} \neq y_{target}$, do

5.   partial transferring, $z_{adv(i+1)} = z_{adv(i)} + \Delta z \times R$

6. $\tilde{x} = dec(z_{adv(i+1)})$, $\tilde{y} = f(\tilde{x})$

7. $i = i + 1$

8.   **if** reach maximum iteration n, then

9.   break

10. $z_{source} = z_{adv(i+1)}$, update Δz

11. **if** x_{adv} looks like real judged by the critic, then

12.   return $x_{adv} = \tilde{x}$, where $\tilde{y} = y_{target}$

13. else reject the adversary, return *None*

4   Experiment

We apply the algorithm we proposed in sect. 3 into various datasets including MNIST, Fashion-MNIST, CIFAR-10 and LSUN. The given classifiers are pre-trained on various datasets with high accuracy. The results of our attack performed on various datasets are as follows.

4.1   Process of Data Manifold Transfer

As is shown in Fig. 4, the process of data manifold transfer is demonstrated and explained on MNIST, which process of transferring is obviously clear. Taking the number 3 as the source data and the number 7 as the target data, it can be seen that the process of data manifold transferring is gradually closer to target data manifold without dropping its original identification in human perception. During the process, the label is not directly changed from 3 to 7 while via 3, 2, 8 and 7. Furthermore, there are some similarities between 2, 3 and 8, such as a length of arc in the same position. In contrast, the process of data manifold transferring from 9 to 4 is directly changed.

Based on the above examples we demonstrated, we make following explanations:

(1) The decision boundary of target model in high-dimension input space is not sufficiently regular.
(2) The distance between classes with local semantic similarity is not large enough.
(3) The given classifier exits clearly under-fitting or over-fitting adversarial subspace between the classes with local semantic similarity.

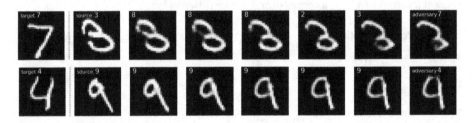

Fig. 4. The first row shows the process of **indirect** transfer via 3, 8, 2, 3 to 7 while the second row shows the **direct** transfer from 9 to 4.

In the process of data manifold transfer, there is another special phenomenon aroused our interest that the value of hyper-parameter R has a great impact on the process. As is mentioned in the process of 3 to 7 manifold transfer, the latent manifold in the first 10 dimensions in Fig. 5 is almost like the data after only 20 iterations when $R = 0.1$. But when the step size R is adjusted to 0.01, we find tighter adversarial subspace such as 2 and 8. Therefore, we can search for tighter adversarial subspaces by using smaller step size R to find under-fitting or over-fitting decision boundaries. But it also causes an increase in the computational cost due to the increased number of iterations.

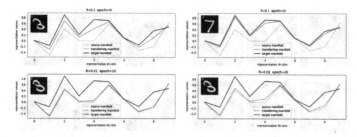

Fig. 5. The visualization of latent manifold transfer from 3 to 7 in first 10 dimensions on different R.

The success rates of our attack on LeNet-5 trained on MNIST in different R are as follows. A success attack means the adversarial example keeping its original identification in human observation makes a given classifier targeted misled.

Table 1. Success rate and iteration steps in different R

R	0.1	0.05	0.01	0.005	0.001
Success rate	17%	46%	**93%**	95%	96%
Iteration steps	18	41	**87**	150	280

Above Table 1 we find that the success rate of attack reaches 93% when $R = 0.01$, which is little different in success rate with the result of $R = 0.005$ and $R = 0.001$. But they need more iterations steps to reach the decision boundary with much more times of access to the given classifier.

4.2 Experiments on Various Datasets

After training classifiers and WGAN-variants on MNIST, FashionMNIST, CIFAR-10 and LSUN, we obtain four sets of pre-trained classifiers, encoders, decoders and critics, each of the encoders and decoder perform feature extraction and image reconstruction well on target dataset. Given all the preparations above, we apply our attack on various datasets to take a look.

(1) MNIST & FashionMNIST

The accuracies of pre-trained LeNet-5 classifiers on the datasets are 98% and 85% respectively. Handwritten digits have relatively clear and simple semantic information, so the effect of our attack performed on MNIST is obvious. Figure 6 shows that under the given target data manifold, the process of data manifold transfer is less unexpected on MNIST and the effect on it is relatively intuitive.

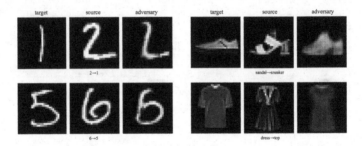

Fig. 6. The attack on MNIST from 2 to 1 and 6 to 5, on FashionMNIST from sandal to sneaker and dress to top.

FashionMNIST is an enhancement of MNIST with the same size but more local features. When it performs well on MNIST, it is necessary to apply the same algorithm into FashionMNIST. As a result, the source data targetedly changes its label with changes its manifold partly and slightly. Moreover, there are some local similarities between source and target data that are prone to perform our attack easily. For instance, the transfer from sandal to sneaker and dress to top.

(2) CIFAR-10 & LSUN

After performing our attack on gray-scale image, we also apply it to the images with RGB channels. As a consequence, the adversarial examples we craft only need slightly semantic perturbation to targeted change its label, such as color saturation shift, color change, and slight shape change.

In addition, we attack the open-source pre-trained classifier on LSUN with our attack in Fig. 7. Limited by the larger size of image and computer power, we select bedroom and dining room as our two categories to perform our attack. It can be seen from the results that it exits broader adversarial subspace in the higher-dimension input space.

Fig. 7. The attack on CIFAR-10 and LSUN subsets. The attack on LSUN is only performed on the subset of bedroom and dining room due to the limitation of our computational power.

4.3   Comparisons with Present Attacks

Comparing the adversarial examples generated by different attacks, we find that the perturbations of excellent attacks at present focus on the region of main features. But most of the attacks are merely search adversarial example in pixel-scale so that the perturbations have no characteristic of semantics. Without the correlation of pixels, most attacks at present are incapable to craft more effective perturbations that misleading target model at the same time. In this paper, it turns out that the encoder is capable of reasonably mapping the modified latent encodings into original space. And the critic rejecting the unnatural adversarial examples in the end ensures that the adversarial examples crafted by our attack is real and reliable with high-confidence deception.

Our attack is an excellent targeted black-box attack algorithm without the access to target model for internal information by using target data manifold to search the decision boundary to reduce computational cost. We can give a large R to evaluate the image reconstruction at first. According to the feedback of the classifier, we can dynamically adjust the transfer step R to a reasonable value. For instance, when the label changes targetedly, we reduce step size R to perform a tighter search for more precise decision boundary. Compared with latent space search attack, our attack using target data manifold and R can reduce the times of access to target model largely to find targeted adversarial examples in latent space with similar perturbation size and higher-quality of reconstruction.

We also evaluate the confidence level of adversarial examples crafted by pixel-scale attack such as FGSM and Carlini and Wagner attack (L_2), and feature-scale attack such as latent space semi-random search and our attack. We use standard model and distilled model with temperature-augmented softmax of the type:

$$softmax(x, T)_i = \frac{e^{x_i/T}}{\sum_j e^{x_j/T}} \tag{6}$$

We use the defensive distillation [14] to train a teacher network with temperature T. And then, on the softmax outputs of the teacher we train a distilled network which is same with the teacher. We use the temperature T = 1 at test time to evaluate the distilled network.

Table 2. The confidence of adversarial examples crafted by different attacks on standard and distilled networks

AttackType	MNIST		CIFAR-10	
	Standard	Distilled	Standard	Distilled
FGSM	94.7%	Fails	96.3%	Fails
Carlini and Wagner (L_2)	98.5%	96.3%	98.2%	97.1%
Latent space search	87.0%	71.5%	78.2%	70.8%
Our attack (targeted)	**99.3%**	**98.8%**	**98.4%**	**98.5%**

From Table 2 we can find that adversarial examples have high confidence to mislead the standard model both on MNIST and CIFAR-10. But when the attack is performed on the latent space search [17], the confidence is obviously lower than other attacks including our attack. Besides, our attack remains at the same level of high confidence as the FGSM and Carlini and Wagner attack. But when the distilled networks mask their gradient of the cross-entropy loss [28]: we decrease the temperature of the softmax at test time in order to make gradients of the cross-entropy loss vanish, on which FGSM relies. So the adversarial examples crafted by FGSM fails on distilled networks. We also find that the distilled networks have a great influence on latent space search attack but slight influence on our attack. Our adversarial examples still remain 93.8% on MNIST and 93.3% on CIFAR-10 adversarial confidence on average. It demonstrates that defensive distillation fails to robust our adversarial examples

5 Transferability of Adversarial Examples

The characteristic of transferability is another concerned aspect of the target adversarial examples crafted by our attack. We randomly select 400 images in the training set of each dataset to probe into the transferability between different classifiers. We use the pre-trained local classifiers on MNIST and CIFAR-10 as our source classifiers to generate adversarial examples. After performing our attack on the selected images, we find that a great decrease is occurred in the accuracy of other pre-trained classifiers without any additional changes in the adversarial examples we craft.

As the transfer rate shown in Fig. 8, it can be seen that the adversarial examples generated by our attack have a great impact on various pre-trained target models. Given a source classifier LeNet-5 with 99.25% accuracy on the gray-scale image dataset MNIST, the adversarial examples generated by it also have a great destruction on other kinds of traditional machine learning models, such as random forest, SVM, and kNN. We consider that deep learning models are capable of fitting better the dataset with much more linear and nonlinear properties. So the adversarial examples generated by our attack based on LeNet-5 discover the adversarial subspaces, which are also applicable in traditional ML models. But it also remains considerable transfer rate when we use other kinds of source models to generate adversarial examples. As the dimensions of input space becomes larger, the process of training on CIFAR-10 is much more difficult, so the accuracies are all below 94%. However, the transfer rate of our attack still stays above 65%. It shows that with great transferability, LET-attack is an effective black-box targeted attack against various well-performed traditional ML models and deep learning models due to the large but semantic distortions.

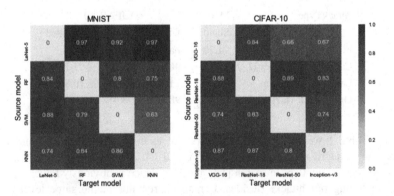

Fig. 8. The transfer rate of targeted adversarial examples generated using LET-attack appproach. *Cell*(i,j) indicates that the transfer rate of targetd adversarial examples generated for source model $i(row)$ when evaluated on target model $j(column)$. In order to demonstrate the transferability clearly, the transfer rates of *Cell*(i, i) are set to zero.

6 Conclusion and Future Work

Generally speaking, the categories of target datasets in the high-dimension space are divided into clusters, which means a cluster is a class. We hypothesis that the distance of inter-clusters is much larger than the inner-clusters. In other words, the data manifold in a cluster is a dense and continuous manifold in the subspace of input space while the manifolds between clusters is far away from each other. Due to the above characteristics, there is little overlap between inter-clusters manifolds in input space. Most previous attacks based on the internal information of target model only perform semi-random search for the adversarial subspace caused by under-fitting or over-fitting. The perturbations lack of interpretation of their formation and make it hard to perform more precise and effective attack. Besides, most kinds of attacks are performed in pixel scale, and their computational cost significantly increases accompanied by the requirement of more sophisticated search for adversarial subspace.

In this paper, we introduce a feature-scale targeted adversarial attack named LET-attack by using mapping transformation WGAN-variant. To reasonably map between original input space and latent space, we pre-train a WGAN-variant including an encoder, a decoder and a critic to perform our attack. Utilizing the pre-trained classifier and the critic, we add extra semantic perturbation by using LET-attack we mentioned in Sect. 3. The attack is based on fully black-box attack by perturbing the latent encodings in latent space to reconstruct the targeted adversarial examples, which mislead the target model in high confidence and high success rate. We also find that the adversarial examples we craft are easy to transfer between various well-performed classifiers.

In addition, the previous adversarial training is based on gradient-based attack. This kind of data re-training is effective to robust the adversarial examples generated by FGSM and BIM, and provides an additional regularization on target model. But it cannot robust other kinds of adversarial examples and generalize well. Up to now, there is not a more generalized re-training process to perform better. It means the generalization of the re-trained model is not good enough to classify the unlabeled data and other kinds of adversarial examples into correct classes. In the future, we consider to introduce the idea in this paper to perform a more generalized re-training in order to improve the robustness of unlabeled data and more kinds of adversarial examples in target model. We are also supposed to use our model to build more robust verification-code system in order to prevent black market from batch-cracking the digit code automatically.

Finally, we are supposed to get a WGAN-variant to perform better. For instance, the process of feature extraction and image reconstruction needs to be improved because it exists some unnatural distortions in some details.

Acknowledgment. This work was supported by the National Key R&D Program of China (2018YFB1500902) and NUPTSF (Grant No. NY219122).

References

1. Szegedy, C., Zaremba, W., Sutskever, I., et al.: Intriguing properties of neural networks. Comput. Sci. (2013)
2. Goodfellow, I.J., Shlens, J., Szegedy, C.: Explaining and harnessing adversarial examples. Comput. Sci. (2014)
3. Tramèr, F., Papernot, N., Goodfellow, I., et al.: The space of transferable adversarial examples (2017)
4. Nguyen, A., Yosinski, J., Clune, J.: Deep neural networks are easily fooled: high confidence predictions for unrecognizable images (2014)
5. Fawzi, A., Fawzi, O., Frossard, P.: Analysis of classifiers' robustness to adversarial perturbations. Mach. Learn. 107(3), 481–508 (2015)
6. Rauber, J., Brendel, W., Bethge, M.: Foolbox: a python toolbox to benchmark the robustness of machine learning models (2017)
7. Kurakin, A., Goodfellow, I., Bengio, S.: Adversarial examples in the physical world (2016)
8. Evtimov, I., Eykholt, K., Fernandes, E., et al.: Robust physical-world attacks on deep learning models (2018)
9. Rozsa, A., Günther, M., Rudd, E.M., et al.: Facial attributes: accuracy and adversarial robustness. Pattern Recognit. Lett., S0167865517303926 (2018)
10. Ross, A.S., Doshi-Velez, F.: Improving the adversarial robustness and interpretability of deep neural networks by regularizing their input gradients (2017)
11. Sinha, A., Namkoong, H., Duchi, J.: Certifying some distributional robustness with principled adversarial training (2017)
12. Tramèr, F., Kurakin, A., Papernot, N., et al.: Ensemble adversarial training: attacks and defenses (2017)
13. Ma, X., Li, B., Wang, Y., et al.: Characterizing adversarial subspaces using local intrinsic dimensionality (2018)
14. Papernot, N., Mcdaniel, P.: On the effectiveness of defensive distillation (2016)
15. Metzen, J.H., Genewein, T., Fischer, V., et al.: On detecting adversarial perturbations (2017)
16. Meng, D., Chen, H.: MagNet: a two-pronged defense against adversarial examples (2017)
17. Zhao, Z., Dua, D., Singh, S.: Generating natural adversarial examples (2017)
18. Arjovsky, M., Chintala, S., Bottou, L.: Wasserstein GAN (2017)
19. Gulrajani, I., Ahmed, F., Arjovsky, M., et al.: Improved Training of Wasserstein GANs (2017)
20. Papernot, N., Mcdaniel, P., Jha, S., et al.: The limitations of deep learning in adversarial settings (2015)
21. Carlini, N., Wagner, D.: Towards evaluating the robustness of neural networks (2016)
22. Narodytska, N., Kasiviswanathan, S.P.: Simple black-box adversarial perturbations for deep networks (2016)
23. Hayes, J., Danezis, G.: Machine learning as an adversarial service: learning black-box adversarial examples (2017)
24. Papernot, N., Mcdaniel, P., Goodfellow, I., et al.: Practical black-box attacks against machine learning (2017)
25. Brendel, W., Rauber, J., Bethge, M.: Decision-based adversarial attacks: reliable attacks against black-box machine learning models (2017)
26. Baluja, S., Fischer, I.: Adversarial transformation networks: learning to generate adversarial examples (2017)
27. Ebrahimi, J., Lowd, D., Dou, D.: On adversarial examples for character-level neural machine translation (2018)
28. Carlini, N., Wagner, D.: Defensive distillation is not robust to adversarial examples (2016)

New Robustness Measures of Communication Networks Against Virus Attacks

Yinwei Li[1], Bo Song[1], Xu Zhang[1], Guo-Ping Jiang[2,3],
and Yurong Song[2,3(✉)]

[1] School of Computer Science, Nanjing University of Posts
and Telecommunications, Nanjing 210003, China
[2] School of Automation, Nanjing University of Posts and Telecommunications,
Nanjing 210003, China
songyr@njupt.edu.cn
[3] Jiangsu Engineering Lab for IOT Intelligent Robots (IOTRobot),
Nanjing 210023, China

Abstract. The robustness of the communication network is an important measurement of network connectivity after some attacks, such as virus and failure. To evaluate the network robustness, many robustness measures have been presented depending on the type of attacks. These measures mainly concentrate on the relation between the robustness of the network and the number of deleted nodes, and seldom consider the robustness of the network in the scenarios that the network is attacked by the virus. The existing measures can not completely evaluate the robustness of the network against virus attacks and can not accurately reveal the relation between network robustness and the transmissibility of the virus. So, it is necessary to study the relation between the robustness of the network and the effective spreading rate of the virus, especially important for communication networks. In this paper, we first introduce three new measures based on the effective spreading rate to evaluate the robustness. Then, we further study the relation between network topology and the three measures. Our results are helpful in designing robust communication networks according to the new robustness measures.

Keywords: Communication network · Robustness measures · Virus attacks · Network topology

1 Introduction

With the rapid development of information and communication technology, human society has stepped into the era of network [1, 2]. As one of the most important networks, communication networks, e.g., computer networks [3], optical communication networks [4], ad-hoc networks [5], and wireless sensor networks [6], are gradually changing people's work and lifestyle. Communication networks are widely used in both military and civil fields. They bring great convenience to the production and life of human society and improve the production efficiency and living standards. Meanwhile, the security of communication networks is more challenging. More and more malicious attacks have caused huge losses to people's production and life.

© Springer Nature Switzerland AG 2019
F. Liu et al. (Eds.): SciSec 2019, LNCS 11933, pp. 151–162, 2019.
https://doi.org/10.1007/978-3-030-34637-9_11

To prevent these losses, it is necessary to design robust networks to combat these malicious attacks.

The robustness of the network is an important property that the network maintains its functionality after being attacked, which causes nodes or links to be removed from the network [7, 8]. In general, most of the research about the network robustness has focused on two main types of attacks: random attacks and targeted attacks [9–11]. For random attacks, each node or link is removed with the same probability from the network. While in targeted attacks, the more important the nodes or links for the network robustness is, the larger the probability that they will be removed. In order to evaluate the network robustness and explore the robust network topology, some robustness measures have been presented depending on the two types of attacks [9, 11–15]. Albert et al. [9] studied the changes of maximal connected component (*MCC*) that the size of the largest connected subgraph in the remaining network after a small fraction of the nodes are removed for the exponential network and scale-free network under random attacks and targeted attacks respectively. They found that scale-free networks display a surprisingly resilient against random attacks but extremely vulnerable to targeted attacks, while the exponential networks don't show this property. Schneider et al. [11] introduced a new measure (*R*) for robustness and used it to devise a method to reconstruct networks against malicious attacks. Their results showed that networks with an "onion-like" structure have significantly high robustness against malicious targeted attacks. Louzada et al. [15] proposed a new measure based on communication efficiency and outlined a procedure that one can modify any given network to enhance its robustness by an optimization approach using simulated annealing. Their results showed that high assortativity and the onion-like structure are the characteristics of the robust networks.

The main difference between communication networks and other networks is that it will not only suffer physical attacks but also be attacked more easily by viruses through information interaction. Attackers usually control a non-critical node in the network at a low cost and then implant the virus. So, it is not appropriate to use the measures of robustness based on random attacks and targeted attacks only to evaluate the robustness of communication networks. When the virus spread over the network and infect more and more nodes, it will result in the decline or even loss of network functions. Many scholars measure the network robustness against virus attacks by three criteria, namely, the epidemic threshold [16], the fraction of infected nodes at steady state [17] and the epidemic velocity [18]. For communication networks, their function must be supported by a connected network composed of a certain number of nodes and links to keep the communication networks as operative as possible. Therefore, we are more concerned about the size of the connected components after some nodes removed from the network by virus attacks. So, the above three criteria cannot evaluate the connectivity of the networks which had been destroyed by the virus. If a large number of nodes and links are removed from the communication networks, it will disintegrate into many isolated connected components, and its functionality will decline dramatically. For an attacked communication network, each connected component can maintain the basic functionality for the area where the connected component is located. The larger the size of the connected component is, the greater functionality is. Therefore, we can use the *MCC* and the average size of the other connected components (*ACC*) in the attacked network to represent the functionality to some extent. Moreover, the number of links in the connected component also indicates the level of functionality. With the same size of the connected component, the more links in the connected component are, the greater the functionality is.

When the communication network is attacked by viruses with different infection rates, the larger the connected network composed of the remaining nodes and links is, the better the robustness of the communication network is. At present, there are few studies on the relation between the robustness of the network and the effective spreading rate of the virus. Therefore, in this paper, we first propose three new measures to measure the network robustness against virus attacks. Existing researches have shown that communication networks generally have scale-free properties [19], so we mainly use three new measures to measure the robustness of scale-free networks in which degree distribution follow power-law distribution and have scale-free properties. We further use the degree-preserving rewiring algorithm [20] to generate a large number of networks with different topology parameters, and then use susceptible-infected-removed (SIR) propagation model [21] to study the impact of network topology on these three measures.

The rest of the paper is arranged as follows: In Sect. 2, we briefly review the existing robustness measures. In Sect. 3, we propose three new anti-virus robustness measures. In Sect. 4, we use Monte Carlo simulations to analyze the network robustness based on the effective spreading rate of virus, and study the relation between network robustness and the network topology in detail. The conclusions are given in Sect. 5.

2   Review of Robustness Measures

In 2000, Albert et al. [9] investigated the robustness of the ER and scale-free models. They used the size of MCC (S) and the average size of the ACC ($<S>$) to evaluate network robustness. They found that scale-free networks display a surprisingly resilient against random attacks but extremely vulnerable to targeted attacks, while the exponential networks don't show this property. They confirmed that error tolerance and attack vulnerability are generic properties of communication networks which rooted in their inhomogeneous connectivity distribution, namely, scale-free property.

Schneider et al. [11] introduced a new measure R for network robustness according to the MCC. The measure is shown as follow,

$$R = \frac{1}{N} \sum_{Q=1}^{N} S(Q) \tag{1}$$

where $S(Q)$ is the fraction of nodes of the MCC after removing Q largest degree nodes and N denotes the size of the initial network. It is proper to compare the network robustness with different sizes by the normalization factor $1/N$ which makes sure that the value of R is in the range of 0 and 1. The larger the value of R is, the more robust the network is.

Louzada et al. [15] proposed a new measure integral efficiency based on communication efficiency. The measure is shown as follow,

$$IntE = \frac{1}{N} \sum_{Q=1}^{N} E(Q) \tag{2}$$

where $E(Q)$ is the efficiency of the network after the removal of Q nodes and N denotes the size of the initial network. They outlined a procedure that modifies any given network to enhance its robustness by an optimization approach using simulated annealing. Their results showed that high assortativity and an onion-like structure are the characteristics of the robust networks.

As the number of nodes removed from the network by the virus attacks is closely related to the effective spreading rate and these removal nodes are often interconnected, it is not appropriate to use R to evaluate the network robustness against virus attacks. In Sect. 3, we propose three robustness measures to study the relation between network robustness and the effective spreading rate of the virus.

3   The New Anti-virus Robustness Measures: R_τ^S, R_τ^L, and $R_\tau^{\langle S \rangle}$

The core nodes in communication networks may be protected by the network managers. So, it is difficult to remove them from the communication networks by physical targeted attacks. However, attackers may easily control the non-critical nodes. For communication networks, nodes forward information through links in the network. Some viruses can easily spread in the networks by means of this forwarding mechanism. So, attackers can implant viruses into the network by the non-critical nodes which can be easily controlled. Viruses spread in the network depending on this forwarding mechanism, and ultimately cause the damage of the network. According to the character of virus attacks, we need to formulate some measures of network robustness. Figure 1 shows the different scenarios of a network under virus attacks. The component in blue dotted lines denote the MCC of the network and the component in green dotted lines denotes the ACC after the nodes (red solid nodes) removed from the network. We can see that Fig. 1(b) has the largest MCC. Comparing Fig. 1(b) and (c), we can see that the MCC of Fig. 1(b) is larger than that of Fig. 1(c), but the ACC of Fig. 1(c) is larger than that of Fig. 1(b). The MCC of Fig. 1(d) has the same size as the MCC of Fig. 1(c), but the number of links in MCC from Fig. 1(d) less than that the number of links in MCC from Fig. 1(c).

Based on the analysis above, we will propose three new anti-virus robustness measures R_τ^S, R_τ^L and $R_\tau^{\langle S \rangle}$. When the network is attacked by a virus, it will disintegrate into many isolated connected components. Among them, the MCC may maintain the main functions of the attacked network. Therefore, we can use R_τ^S to evaluate the network robustness. It is shown as follows,

$$R_\tau^S = \int_0^1 S(\tau)d\tau \qquad (3)$$

where $S(\tau)$ is the fraction of nodes of the *MCC* when the network is attacked by a virus with the effective spreading rate τ.

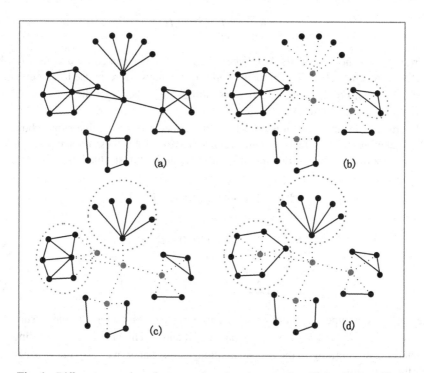

Fig. 1. Different scenarios of a network under virus attacks. (Color figure online)

This measure captures the network response to any effective spreading rate τ. For the same effective spreading rate τ, the larger the value of R_τ^S is, the more robust the network is. The number of links in the connected component also indicates the level of the functionality. With the same size of connected component, the more links in the network, the more transmission paths in the network. This means that the communication efficiency of the network will be higher. So, we can also use R_τ^L to evaluate the network robustness. R_τ^L is shown as follows:

$$R_\tau^L = \int_0^1 L(\tau)d\tau \qquad (4)$$

where $L(\tau)$ is the fraction of links of the *MCC* when the network is attacked by a virus with the effective spreading rate τ. This measure captures the network response to any effective spreading rate τ. For the same effective spreading rate τ, the larger the value of R_τ^L is, the more robust the network is. Besides MCC, the size of other connected components is also an appropriate criterion to assess the functionality of remained networks. For simplicity, we use the size of ACC to evaluate the network robustness. $R_\tau^{\langle S \rangle}$ is shown as follow:

$$R_\tau^{\langle S \rangle} = \int_0^1 \langle S \rangle(\tau) d\tau \tag{5}$$

where $\langle S \rangle(\tau)$ is the size of the ACC when the network is attacked by a virus with the effective spreading rate τ. This measure captures the network response to any effective spreading rate τ. For the same effective spreading rate τ, the larger the value of $R_\tau^{\langle S \rangle}$ is, the more robust the network is.

In practical experiments, it is unrealistic and unnecessary to evaluate the robustness with all continuous τ. In fact, we can evaluate network robustness by sampling only a certain proportion of τ. So, Eqs. (4), (5) and (6) can be transformed as follows:

$$R_\tau^S = \frac{1}{n} \sum_{i=1}^n S(\tau(i)), 0 < \tau(i) \leq 1 \tag{6}$$

$$R_\tau^L = \frac{1}{n} \sum_{i=1}^n L(\tau(i)), 0 < \tau(i) \leq 1 \tag{7}$$

$$R_\tau^{\langle S \rangle} = \frac{1}{n} \sum_{i=1}^n \langle S \rangle(\tau(i)), 0 < \tau(i) \leq 1 \tag{8}$$

where n is the number of sampling of τ. The normalization factor $1/n$ makes sure that the value of R_τ^S, R_τ^L and $R_\tau^{\langle S \rangle}$ are in the range of 0 and 1. The principle of sampling can be determined according to the actual situation. In this paper, we carry out experiments with the uniformly-spaced sampling.

4   Experimental Data and Simulations

In this section, we will use SIR model to study and analyze the relation between network robustness and the effective spreading rate of virus by Monte Carlo simulation. We generate some networks with different topology properties. For each network, the simulations are performed by starting from a randomly chosen initial spreader, and the corresponding simulation results are averaged over 1000 runs. Through the comparative analysis of the Monte Carlo simulation results, we can obtain some conclusions about the influence of network topology on network robustness against virus attacks.

4.1   Experimental Data

Inspired by the Ref. [9], we start by generating a homogeneous network and a heterogeneous network based on WS [22] and BA [23] models, respectively. The size of two models is $N = 1000$, and the average degree is $<k> = 6$. With the help of the two models, we study the effects of degree distribution on the new robustness measures. Different from the Ref. [12], we define that isolated nodes do not belong to the connected components in the communication networks. Since most communication networks have scale-free characteristics, it is important to study the influence of the network topology characteristics on network robustness under the condition that the network degree distribution remains unchanged. In this paper, we mainly study the effects of average clustering coefficient and the maximum eigenvalue of adjacency matrix. Firstly, we take the two network topology properties as objective functions and use degree protection reconnection algorithm to generate two kinds of network sets with identical degree distribution. Then, we select 8 networks from each network set to create C set (see Table 1) and λ_1 set (see Table 2). Each set comprises 8 networks with $N = 1000$, average degree $\langle k \rangle = 6$, C denotes average clustering coefficient, λ_1 denotes the maximum eigenvalue of the adjacency matrix.

Table 1. The characteristic parameters of the C set.

	1	2	3	4	5	6	7	8
N	1000	1000	1000	1000	1000	1000	1000	1000
$\langle k \rangle$	6	6	6	6	6	6	6	6
C	0.1183	0.2000	0.2817	0.3635	0.4450	0.5269	0.6086	0.6903

Table 2. The characteristic parameters of the λ_1 set.

	1	2	3	4	5	6	7	8
N	1000	1000	1000	1000	1000	1000	1000	1000
$\langle k \rangle$	6	6	6	6	6	6	6	6
λ_1	10.9542	13.7154	16.4971	19.2602	22.0213	24.8049	27.5769	30.3443

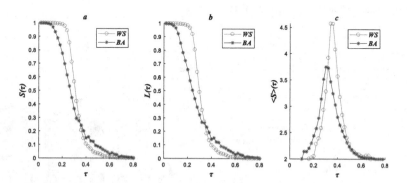

Fig. 2. $S(\tau)$, $L(\tau)$ and $\langle S \rangle(\tau)$ as the functions of effective spreading rate τ for WS and BA networks, respectively.

4.2 Simulations

In this section, we use Monte Carlo simulations to study the relation between network topology and the robustness according to the new measures. Figure 2a shows that $S(\tau)$ of *WS* network is larger than that of *BA* network when the effective spreading rate τ is below 0.34. Similar conclusions about $L(\tau)$ are shown in Fig. 2b. When the effective spreading rate τ is above 0.34, $S(\tau)$ and $L(\tau)$ of *WS* network are lower than those of *BA* network. As shown in Fig. 2c, $\langle S \rangle(\tau)$ of *WS* network is smaller than that of *BA* network when the effective spreading rate τ is below 0.34. We note that the results of robustness comparison between *WS* and *BA* networks have a transition at $\tau = 0.34$. Therefore, we need to compare network robustness in a certain range of effective spreading rate according to the actual situation. When the effective spreading rate is high, the influence of network structure on robustness will be reduced. In addition, too small effective spreading rate is not enough to cause the virus spread in the network. So, we evaluate network robustness by sampling a certain proportion of $\tau \in [0.1, 0.3]$ in the next simulations.

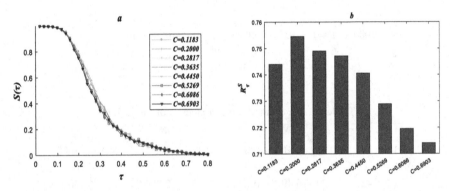

Fig. 3. *a*: $S(\tau)$ as the function of effective spreading rate τ for C set. *b*: R_{τ}^{S} as the function of effective spreading rate $\tau \in [0.1, 0.3]$ for C set.

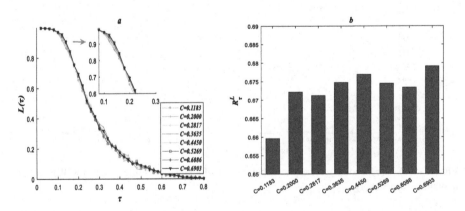

Fig. 4. *a*: $L(\tau)$ as the function of effective spreading rate τ for C set. *b*: R_{τ}^{L} as the function of effective spreading rate $\tau \in [0.1, 0.3]$ for C set.

Figure 3*a* shows that C has little influence on $S(\tau)$ of C set. From Fig. 3*b*, we can see that R^S_τ become smaller with increase of C, but the value of change is very limited. We can also obtain that the C have little influence on $L(\tau)$ of C set form Fig. 4*a*. In Fig. 4*b*, we can see that R^L_τ become non-monotony increase with increase of C, but the value of change is very limited. Figure 5*a* shows that $\langle S \rangle(\tau)$ become larger with increase of C when the effective spreading rate τ is below 0.3. When the effective spreading rate τ is above 0.36, $\langle S \rangle(\tau)$ becomes smaller with increase of C. From Fig. 5*b*, we can see that $R^{\langle S \rangle}_\tau$ becomes larger with increase of C.

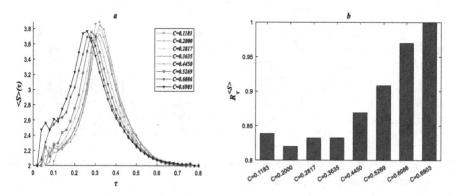

Fig. 5. *a*: $\langle S \rangle(\tau)$ as the function of effective spreading rate τ for C set. *b*: $R^{\langle S \rangle}_\tau$ as the function of effective spreading rate $\tau \in [0.1, 0.3]$ for C set. In order to facilitate comparison, the numerical values are normalized by virtue of maximum value.

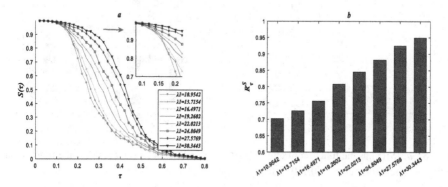

Fig. 6. *a*: $S(\tau)$ as the function of effective spreading rate τ for λ_1 set. *b*: R^S_τ as the function of effective spreading rate $\tau \in [0.1, 0.3]$ for λ_1 set.

Figure 6*a* shows that the λ_1 have much influence on $S(\tau)$. We can see that $S(\tau)$ becomes larger with the increase of λ_1 when the effective spreading rate τ is above 0.14. From Fig. 6*b*, we can see that R^S_τ becomes larger with increase of λ_1. We can also obtain that the λ_1 has much influence on $L(\tau)$ of λ_1 set form Fig. 7*a*. We note that $L(\tau)$ of λ_1 set has a transition at $\tau = 0.15$. In Fig. 7*b*, we can see that R_τ^L becomes monotonously increase with increase of λ_1. Figure 8*a* shows that $\langle S \rangle(\tau)$ becomes smaller with increase of λ_1 when the effective spreading rate τ is below 0.3. When the effective spreading rate τ is above 0.5, $\langle S \rangle(\tau)$ becomes larger with increase of λ_1. From Fig. 8*b*, we can see that $R_\tau^{\langle S \rangle}$ becomes smaller with increase of λ_1.

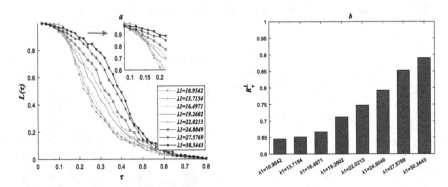

Fig. 7. *a*: $L(\tau)$ as the function of effective spreading rate τ for λ_1 set. *b*: R_τ^L as function of effective spreading rate $\tau \in [0.1, 0.3]$ for λ_1 set.

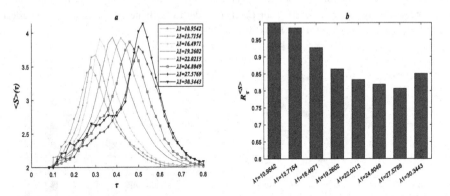

Fig. 8. *a*: $\langle S \rangle(\tau)$ as the function of effective spreading rate τ for λ_1 set. *b*: $R_\tau^{\langle S \rangle}$ as the function of effective spreading rate $\tau \in [0.1, 0.3]$ for λ_1 set.

5   Conclusion

According to the characteristics of communication networks, three new anti-virus robustness measures have been proposed in this paper. These new measures can reveal the relation between network robustness and virus infection rate. We have used degree protection reconnection algorithm to swap the underlying network which is generated by *BA* model, and have obtained two set of networks with different C and λ_1. We have also used generated networks to study the influence of network topology on network robustness. Our results show that average clustering coefficient of network has little effect on R_τ^S and R_τ^L. For $R_\tau^{\langle S \rangle}$, the networks with high clustering coefficients are more robust against low infection virus attacks, but they become less robust against virus attacks with high infection. R_τ^S and R_τ^L of the network can be effectively improved by increasing the maximum eigenvalue of the network under the condition that the degree distribution of the network remains unchanged. $R_\tau^{\langle S \rangle}$ becomes smaller with increase of λ_1 when the network is attacked by low infection virus. While $R_\tau^{\langle S \rangle}$ becomes larger with increase of λ_1 when the network is attacked by high infection virus. Our results are useful for the robust communication networks designing according to the new robustness measures.

Acknowledgments. This research has been supported by the National Natural Science Foundation of China (Grant Nos. 61672298, 61873326, 61373136, 61802155), the Philosophy Social Science Research Key Project Fund of Jiangsu University (Grant No. 2018SJZDI142) and the Research Foundation for Humanities and Social Sciences of Ministry of Education of China (Grant Nos. 17YJAZH071).

References

1. Mendes, J.F.F.: Evolution of Networks. Oxford University Press, Oxford (2003)
2. Newman, M.: Networks: An Introduction. Oxford University Press, Oxford (2010)
3. Comer, D.E., Droms, R.E.: Computer Networks and Internets, 2nd edn. Prentice-Hall Inc., Upper Saddle River (2003)
4. Ramaswami, R., Sivarajan, K., Sasaki, G.: Optical Networks: A Practical Perspective, 3rd edn. Morgan Kaufmann Publisher Inc., San Francisco (2009)
5. Conti, M., Giordano, S.: Mobile ad hoc networking: milestones, challenges, and new research directions. IEEE Commun. Mag. **52**(1), 85–96 (2014)
6. Chen, X., Makki, K., Yen, K., et al.: Sensor network security: a survey. IEEE Commun. Surv. Tutor. **11**(2), 52–73 (2009)
7. Liu, J., Zhou, M., Wang, S., et al.: A comparative study of network robustness measures. Front. Comput. Sci. **11**(4), 568–584 (2017)
8. Wu, J., Tan, S.Y., Liu, Z., et al.: Enhancing structural robustness of scale-free networks by information disturbance. Sci. Rep. **7**(1), 7559 (2017)
9. Albert, R., Jeong, H., Barabasi, A.L.: Error and attack tolerance of complex networks. Nature **406**(6794), 378–382 (2000)
10. Paul, G., Sreenivasan, S., Stanley, H.E.: Resilience of complex networks to random breakdown. Phys. Rev. E **72**(5), 056130 (2005)
11. Schneider, C.M., Moreira, A.A., Andrade, J.S., et al.: Mitigation of malicious attacks on networks. Proc. Natl. Acad. Sci. **108**(10), 3838–3841 (2011)
12. Gallos, L.K., Cohen, R., Argyrakis, P., et al.: Stability and topology of scale-free networks under attack and defense strategies. Phys. Rev. Lett. **94**(18), 188701 (2005)
13. Qin, J., Wu, H., Tong, X., et al.: A quantitative method for determining the robustness of complex networks. Phys. D Nonlinear Phenom. **253**, 85–90 (2013)

14. Tang, X., Liu, J., Zhou, M.: Enhancing network robustness against targeted and random attacks using a memetic algorithm. EPL **111**(3), 38005 (2015)
15. Louzada, V.H.P., Daolio, F., Herrmann, H.J., et al.: Generating robust and efficient networks under targeted attacks. SSRN Electron. J. **85**, 215–224 (2012)
16. Wang, Y., Chakrabarti, D., Wang, C., et al.: Epidemic spreading in real networks: an eigenvalue viewpoint. In: 22nd International Symposium on Reliable Distributed Systems, Florence, pp. 25–34. IEEE (2003)
17. Youssef, M., Kooij, R., Scoglio, C.: Viral conductance: quantifying the network robustness with respect to spread of epidemics. J. Comput. Sci. **2**(3), 286–298 (2011)
18. Barthélemy, M., Barrat, A., Pastor-Satorras, R., et al.: Velocity and hierarchical spread of epidemic outbreaks in scale-free networks. Phys. Rev. Lett. **92**(17), 178701 (2004)
19. Cohen, R., Havlin, S.: Complex Networks: Structure, Robustness and Function. Cambridge University Press, Cambridge (2010)
20. Van Mieghem, P., Wang, H., Ge, X., et al.: Influence of assortativity and degree-preserving rewiring on the spectra of networks. Eur. Phys. J. B **76**(4), 643–652 (2010)
21. Moreno, Y., Pastor-Satorras, R., Vespignani, A.: Epidemic outbreaks in complex heterogeneous networks. Eur. Phys. J. B **26**(4), 521–529 (2002)
22. Watts, D.J., Strogatz, S.H: Collective dynamics of 'small-world' networks. Nature **393** (6684), 440 (1998)
23. Barabási, A.L., Albert, R: Emergence of scaling in random networks. Science **286**(5439), 509–512 (1999)

Application and Performance Analysis of Data Preprocessing for Intrusion Detection System

Shuai Jiang and Xiaolong Xu$^{(\boxtimes)}$ ⓘ

Nanjing University of Posts and Telecommunications, Nanjing 210023, China
xuxl@njupt.edu.cn

Abstract. In the era of network and big data, network information security has become a major issue. Intrusion Detection System (IDS) is an essential component of network security facilities, which utilizes network traffic data to detect attacks. IDS can adopt data analysis and data mining technologies to detect attacks to network systems. However, the computational overhead of IDS is too large to serve for real-time detection due to the redundancy and irrelevant features in the network traffic dataset. We hence analyze seven classification algorithms for intrusion detection, where we separately perform data preprocessing with two kinds of dimensionality reduction techniques, Principal Component Analysis (PCA) and Singular Value Decomposition (SVD), to improve the performance of IDS. The experimental results on the NSL-KDD dataset indicate that the classification algorithms with dimensionality reduction outstands in detection rate and detection speed. Meanwhile, SVD demonstrate its superiority to PCA in boosting these algorithms.

Keywords: Intrusion Detection System · Principal Component Analysis · Dimensionality reduction · Singular Value Decomposition

1 Introduction

Intrusion Detection System (IDS) is a network security device that monitors network data in real time and takes proactive measures when it detects suspicious transmissions. Due to frequent malicious network activity and network policy violations, IDS is widely implemented in different types of networks (e.g., education and financial organizations) [1]. The main problem of current IDS is that there are too many attributes of network data, and there may be a high correlation between some attributes, which makes the classifier unable to accurately and quickly distinguish the normal and abnormal behavior of the system [2]. In addition, when IDS selects a subset of samples, it takes a lot of time to exhaustively search and test each subset due to the dimension of the samples. Compressing data into relatively low-dimensional subspace is thus of

This work was jointly supported by the National Key Research and Development Program of China under Grant 2018YFB1003702, the Scientific and Technological Support Project of Jiangsu Province under Grant BE2016776, the "333" project of Jiangsu Province under Grant BRA2017228 and the Talent Project in Six Fields of Jiangsu Province under Grant 2015-JNHB-012.

© Springer Nature Switzerland AG 2019
F. Liu et al. (Eds.): SciSec 2019, LNCS 11933, pp. 163–177, 2019.
https://doi.org/10.1007/978-3-030-34637-9_12

great help. Data dimensionality reduction not only reduces the demands of storage space, but also accelerates the classification algorithms.

As a common technique for data preprocessing, dimensionality reduction, is utilized to clear the noise, and compress the data into a subspace of smaller dimension while retaining the relevant information to the greatest extent. But it may also reduce the accuracy of algorithms. Multiple highly correlated features, which are referred to as redundant features, along with features that have a small effect on sample classification, which are referred to as irrelevant features, causes a long-term problem in network traffic classification. These features not only slow down the process of classification and increase computational overhead, but also prevent a classifier from making accurate decisions, especially when coping with big data [3]. Removal of redundant and irrelevant feature is the main goal in any feature selection algorithm. In terms of high-dimensional network traffic data, feature selection can reduce the training time of the classification algorithm, minimize the computational overhead of IDS, and thereby improving the performance.

A relatively high detection rate and a relatively high detection speed are both required for intrusion detection. Finding the best intrusion classification algorithm is not easy due to the lack of ideal preprocessing and classification techniques for detecting anomalies. Recent advances in information technology have produced a wide variety of machine learning methods, which can be integrated into an IDS [4]. Many supervised and unsupervised learning methods from the field of machine learning and pattern recognition have been used to increase the efficacy of IDS [5]. A good classification algorithm achieves imposing and adequate result of detecting attacks [6]. There are many classic classifiers, such as Naïve Bayes (NB), BP neural network, Decision Tree (DT), Logistic Regression (LR), Support Vector Machine (SVM), etc. However, these classifiers have different classification effects for different datasets. Classifiers without preprocessing have problems such as high computational overhead and low detection rate.

Therefore, we analyze seven classification techniques: NB, LR, K-Nearest Neighbor (KNN), SVM, DT, AdaBoost (AB), Random Forest (RF) in this paper. Principal Component Analysis (PCA) and Singular Value Decomposition (SVD) are adopted to reduce computational overhead. Our work can be summarized as follows: reducing the computational overhead with SVD and PCA; comparing seven different classification algorithms on indicators such as accuracy, recall, precision, etc.; analyzing the respective effects of adopting PCA and SVD in the above algorithms; analyzing the effect of adopting dimension reduction.

The rest of the paper is organized as follows: Sect. 2 provides a brief overview of the current work on data preprocessing and classification algorithms. Section 3 introduces intrusion detection system. Section 4 covers experimental setup and results analysis. Conclusion and future work are provided in Sect. 5.

2 Related Work

Thaseen et al. [7] proposed an intrusion detection model using Linear Discriminant Analysis (LDA), chi-square feature selection and modified NB classification. Their hybrid model produces better accuracy and lower false alarm rate than in comparison to the traditional approaches. However, LDA cannot perform dimensionality reduction for the two-class problem, and the model used is not compared with other machine learning models.

Subba et al. [8] proposed a model that uses PCA dimensionality reduction techniques to reduce computational overhead. The dimensionally reduced dataset obtained after PCA is analyzed by Naïve Bayes, C4.5 decision tree, SVM and Multilayer Perceptron (MLP). Application PCA can significantly reduce the dimensionality of data processed by anomaly-based IDS, thereby minimizing its computational overhead without adversely affecting its performance. However, they only use a data dimension reduction method, which takes a long time to detect. For the classification model parameters, no optimal parameters are given.

Salo et al. [9] proposed a novel hybrid dimensionality reduction technique that combines the approaches of Information Gain (IG) and PCA with an ensemble classifier based on instance-based learning algorithms (IBK), SVM, and MLP. The performance of the IG-PCA-Ensemble method was evaluated based on three well-known datasets, namely ISCX 2012, NSL-KDD and Kyoto 2006+. Experimental results show that the proposed hybrid dimensionality reduction method with the ensemble of the base learners contributes more critical features and significantly outperforms individual approaches, achieving high accuracy and low false alarm rates. However, their proposed model cannot handle large amounts of data streams in real time.

Shahbaz et al. [10] proposed an effective feature selection algorithm to solve the problem of high dimensionality. The algorithm considers the correlation between feature subsets and behavioral class labels. Correlation-based Feature Selection (CFS) and Symmetrical Uncertainty (SU) are two correlation metrics used to measure the dependency level between features and class labels, and among features. Experimental results on NSL-KDD dataset shows that the proposed approach with fewer features, significantly outperforms the existing schemes in terms of the training time, time taken to build the model, while it preserves or increases the system accuracy. In addition, they tested the efficiency of the proposed feature selection technique on different classification algorithms. The results show that the proposed algorithm has high accuracy. However, they have no further dimensional reduction to reduce detection time.

Raman et al. [11] proposed a novel feature selection technique based on Rough Sets (RS) and few interesting properties of Hyper-graph (RSHGT), such as minimal transversal and vertex linearity for the identification of the optimal feature subset. Experiments were carried out using the KDD cup 1999 intrusion dataset. The results show the dominance of RSHGT over the existing feature selection techniques with respect to the reduct size, classifier accuracy and time complexity. RSHGT was found to be flexible, accommodative and computationally attractive for high dimensional datasets. However, due to the long detection time of the model, it cannot be applied to real-time detection.

Umbarkar et al. [12] proposed a smart heuristic-based approach for feature reduction. Three feature reduction techniques, IG, Gain Ratio (GR) and CFS, are used to calculate the reduced feature set. The number of features is reduced without degrading the performance of the system and demonstrate the nature of each feature reduction technique with respect to number of features. The results show that CFS is superior as compared to other methods. With feature subset of 15 accuracies increased to 92.65% which is better than the accuracy of the normal dataset having 41 features.

Miao et al. [13] mainly studied the preprocessing stage of network traffic data, using PCA to compare six machine learning algorithms. Accuracy and F-measure are two metrics to be analyzed to find the best classifier, and computational time is also considered in analyzing the performance. KNN and RF are the top 2 algorithms among all the 6 regarding the 2 metrics mentioned above. However, they only compared the six classifiers, did not use the advanced techniques of the combining classifiers to improve the classification accuracy.

Tengl et al. [14] proposed a collaborative and robust intrusion detection model using a novel optimal weight strategy based on Genetic Algorithm (GA) for ensemble classifier. PCA is used for dimension reduction and attribute extraction, GA is used to optimize the weight of each basic classifier of ensemble classifier. However, although the proposed method has high precision and generalized performance, it takes a lot of time to adjust the weight, and has a low detection rate for data with less training samples.

3   Intrusion Detection System

3.1   Basic Theory

Intrusion detection is the detection of intrusion behavior. It collects and analyzes network behavior, security logs, audit data, information available on other networks, and information on several key points in a computer system to check for violations of security policies and signs of attacks in the network or system. As a proactive security protection technology, intrusion detection provides real-time protection against internal attacks, external attacks, and misuse, intercepting and responding to intrusions before being compromised. Therefore, it is considered as the second security gate behind the firewall, which can monitor the network without affecting network performance. Network Intrusion Detection System (NIDS) is a tool for dynamically detecting and classifying network vulnerabilities in Information and Communication Technology (ICT) systems. The original network packet is used as the data source, and the network card of the detection host in the network data is set to the promiscuous mode, and the NIDS receives and analyzes the data packets flowing in the network in real time to detect whether there is an intrusion behavior. The intrusion detection system is shown in Fig. 1.

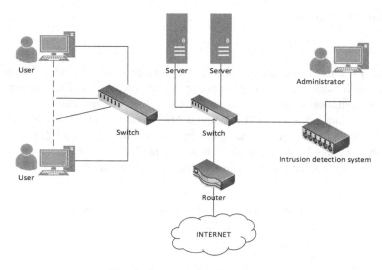

Fig. 1. Intrusion detection system

In this paper, we have tried two data reduction algorithms, PCA and SVD. The dimensionality reduction can compress the data to a subspace with a smaller dimension while retaining the relevant information to the greatest extent, but it may also reduce the performance of some algorithms in terms of accuracy. However, in view of the correlation often existing in the actual data, we try to reduce the loss of information as much as possible while reducing the dimension. Then we used the more classic seven classifiers for classification: Naïve Bayes, Logistic Regression, KNN, SVM, Decision Tree, AdaBoost, Random Forest. The architectural model of the overall algorithm is shown in Fig. 2. The algorithm is used as a detection engine in IDS to receive event information and analyze it to determine whether it is an intrusion or anomaly.

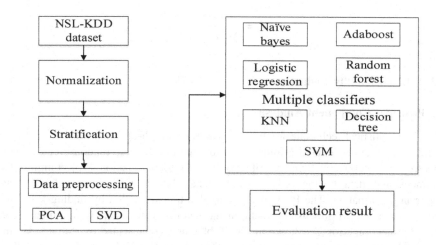

Fig. 2. Algorithm framework

3.2 Data Preprocessing

(1) Data Mapping

Since many features in the sample data are composed of letters, in order to eliminate its influence on the algorithm, we need to convert the characteristics of the corresponding letters into numerical values. For example, for the protocol_type feature, it consists of three types of data, namely TCP, UDP, and ICMP. Since distance calculation cannot be performed on such data, we replace them one by one with 0, 1, and 2, so that these unavailable features become available, as shown in Table 1. The conversion rule for the tag type of the sample data is: normal record is 0, and abnormal record is 1.

Table 1. Data mapping of protocol_type feature

Original eigenvalue	Converted eigenvalue
TCP	0
UDP	1
ICMP	2

(2) Maximum and Minimum Normalization

Since the minimum value of some features in the data is less than 1, the maximum value is hundreds of thousands, which affects the use of distance-based classification algorithms, so we need to normalize the continuous data. Here, min-max normalization is used for normalization which is given in (1). Each column feature is subtracted from the minimum value of the column, and then divided by the difference between the maximum value and the minimum value of the column feature. Where x_j^* represents the normalized data, x_j represents raw data, Min represents the minimum value of each column feature, Max represents the maximum value of each column feature.

$$x_j^* = \frac{x_j - \text{Min}}{\text{Max} - \text{Min}} \tag{1}$$

3.3 Dimensionality Reduction

A. Principal Component Analysis

PCA is a statistical technique for finding patterns in high-dimensional data. It transforms component-correlated original random vectors into new random vectors with uncorrelated components by means of an orthogonal transformation. Project high-order n-dimensional data to low-order k-dimensional data (n > k) without losing any important information. The PCA implements this transformation by finding k feature vectors, projecting n-dimensional data on the feature vector, thereby minimizing the overall projection error. As shown in Fig. 3, blue dots (represented by features X_1 and X_2) can be projected onto any of the two lines (Line 1 and Line 2). However, PCA chooses Line 1 over Line 2 for projection, since the overall orthogonal projection error for projecting the data points onto Line 1 is much smaller compared to orthogonal projection error for projecting the same data points onto Line 2 [8].

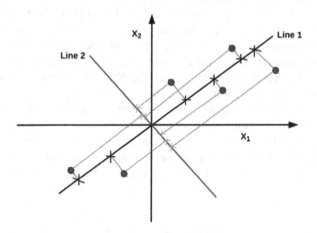

Fig. 3. Projection of two-dimensional data points onto a one dimensional line (Color figure online)

B. Singular Value Decomposition

Singular Value Decomposition [15] is a generalization of feature decomposition on arbitrary matrices. Assuming that our matrix A is m × n matrix, then we define the SVD of matrix A as:

$$A = U\Sigma V^T \tag{2}$$

Where U is a matrix of m × m and V is an n × n matrix. Σ is an m × n matrix whose elements outside the main diagonal are all 0, and each element on the main diagonal is called a singular value. Both U and V are unitary matrices, $U^T U = I$, $V^T V = I$. For singular values, it is similar to the eigenvalues in our feature decomposition. It is also arranged in the singular value matrix from large to small, and the singular value is reduced especially fast. In many cases, the sum of the singular values of the first 10% or even 1% accounts for more than 99% of the sum of all singular values. That is to say, we can also approximate the description matrix with the largest k singular values and the corresponding left and right singular vectors.

$$A_{m\times n} = U_{m\times m} \sum\nolimits_{m\times n} V^T_{n\times n} \approx U_{m\times k} \sum\nolimits_{k\times k} V^T_{k\times n} \tag{3}$$

Where k is much smaller than n, a large matrix A can be represented by three small matrices $U_{m\times k}$, $\sum_{k\times k}$ and $V^T_{k\times n}$.

4 Experiments

4.1 Experimental Setup

The dataset used in this experiment is the NSL-KDD public dataset [16, 17], which solves the inherent problems in the KDD CUP 99 dataset [18]. The training set of the NSL-KDD dataset does not contain redundant records, so the classifier does not bias towards more frequent records. Since the record number setting is reasonable, this makes the experiment running on the entire set of experiments inexpensive. Deshmukh et al. [19] have experimentally verified that NSL-KDD is the best intrusion detection dataset for classification algorithms. Although the NSL-KDD dataset has a small number of samples, it can still be used as a valid baseline dataset, which can help researchers compare different intrusion detection methods. The dataset used in this experiment is "KDDTrain+.txt", as shown in Table 2. The training set randomly samples 80% of the samples from the dataset, and the test set randomly extracts 20% of the samples from the dataset, which can prevent the model from over-fitting and under-fitting.

Table 2. KDDTrain+.txt

KDDTrain+ Attribute:42	
Label	Count
Normal	67343
Anomaly	58630
Total	125973

In order to facilitate the comparison of subsequent performance, the following indicators are defined in advance. Classifier performance is evaluated by calculating performance metrics such as Accuracy, Error rate, Detection rate, Precision, F-measure, AUC, and Detection time. Equations (4) to (8), where TP represents the number of true positives, TN represents the number of true negatives, FP represents the number of false positives, and FN represents the number of false negatives. Accuracy: the proportion of correctly classified instance; Error rate: the proportion of incorrectly classified instance; Recall/Detection rate: the proportion of elements correctly classified as positive out of all positive elements; Precision: the proportion of elements correctly classified as true alarms out of all the elements the intrusion detection model classified as positive; F-measure: the average of the sum of the detection rate and the recall rate; AUC: the size of the area under the ROC curve; Detection time: the time taken for the test sample to complete the test.

$$Accuracy = \frac{TP + TN}{TP + TN + FP + FN} \tag{4}$$

$$Error\ rate\ = \frac{FP + FN}{TP + TN + FP + FN} \tag{5}$$

$$Recall/Detection\ rate = \frac{TP}{TP + FN} \tag{6}$$

$$Precision = \frac{TP}{TP + FP} \tag{7}$$

$$F - measure\ = \frac{2\ *\ Precision\ *\ Recall}{Precision\ + Recall} \tag{8}$$

4.2 Experimental Results and Analysis

In this section, we evaluate the models' performance. All experiments were performed on a Windows 10 PC with Intel Core i7 CPU @ 3.70 GHz and 16 GB RAM. In order to show the necessity of data preprocessing, we conducted three experiments respectively: experiment 1 did not perform data preprocessing, and directly used seven classification algorithms for classification; experiment 2 after PCA processing, using seven classification algorithms for classification; experiment 3 after SVD processing, seven classification algorithms are used for classification. Experiment 1 was carried out on 41 features of the original dataset, and Experiment 2 and Experiment 3 were performed on the first 23 features after dimensionality reduction. Table 3 is Logistic Regression (LR), KNN, SVM, Naïve Bayes (NB), Decision Tree (DT), AdaBoost (AB), Random Forest (RF) seven algorithms in the accuracy, error rate, recall rate, precision, F-measure, AUC and detection time comparison. Tables 4 and 5 show the comparison of the indicators of the seven machine learning algorithms after PCA and SVD.

Table 3. Comparison of various indicators of seven machine learning algorithms

	Accuracy	Recall	Precision	F-measure	AUC	Error rate	Time (ms)
LR	0.95388	0.941036	0.958899	0.949884	0.953027	0.04612	31
KNN	0.997539	0.997607	0.997096	0.997352	0.997544	0.002461	71000
SVM	0.942965	0.896599	0.978823	0.935908	0.939888	0.057035	28
NB	0.898512	0.899932	0.883696	0.89174	0.898606	0.101488	174
DT	0.997619	0.998205	0.996672	0.997438	0.997658	0.002381	31
AB	0.980353	0.974022	0.983519	0.978747	0.979933	0.019647	800
RF	0.998412	0.997265	0.999315	0.998289	0.998336	0.001588	217

Table 4. Comparison of the indicators of seven machine learning algorithms after PCA

	Accuracy	Recall	Precision	F-measure	AUC	Error rate	Time(ms)
PCA-LR	0.952054	0.938472	0.957454	0.947868	0.951153	0.047946	7
PCA-KNN	0.996706	0.996753	0.996157	0.996455	0.996709	0.003294	4000
PCA-SVM	0.953126	0.940694	0.957634	0.949088	0.952301	0.046874	10
PCA-NB	0.900695	0.896257	0.890625	0.893432	0.9004	0.099305	70
PCA-DT	0.994999	0.994787	0.994447	0.994617	0.994985	0.005001	21
PCA-AB	0.977773	0.971629	0.980341	0.975966	0.977366	0.022227	641
PCA-RF	0.996507	0.994702	0.997771	0.996234	0.996387	0.003493	166

Table 5. Comparison of the indicators of seven machine learning algorithms after SVD

	Accuracy	Recall	Precision	F-measure	AUC	Error rate	Time(ms)
SVD-LR	0.95253	0.939498	0.957499	0.948413	0.951665	0.04747	8
SVD-KNN	0.996864	0.996838	0.996412	0.996625	0.996863	0.003136	4000
SVD-SVM	0.949355	0.922919	0.966529	0.944221	0.947601	0.050645	7
SVD-NB	0.882397	0.880619	0.868082	0.874305	0.882279	0.117603	89
SVD-DT	0.994086	0.994274	0.993002	0.993638	0.994099	0.005914	21
SVD-AB	0.969637	0.965647	0.968876	0.967259	0.969372	0.030363	702
SVD-RF	0.99611	0.994018	0.997599	0.995805	0.995971	0.00389	164

By analyzing Tables 3, 4 and 5, we conclude that:

(1) When using seven algorithms for classifying data without dimensionality reduction, RF, KNN, and DT are superior to other algorithms in Accuracy, Detection rate, Precision, F-measure, AUC, and Error rate. SVM, LR, DT have less detection time than the other four algorithms. Especially in terms of computational overhead, the overhead of KNN and AdaBoost is too large, and KNN is about 2500 times that of SVM. The NB classifier has low indicators, and it is impossible to accurately perform intrusion detection for the current dataset.

(2) After the data of PCA or SVD dimensionality reduction is classified, the parameters of the seven algorithms before and after the dimension reduction are not very different, and the time has been significantly improved. It can be seen that after data dimensionality reduction processing, although the data characteristics are reduced, it does not have an excessive negative impact on the accuracy of the classification and other indicators. In addition, after the data preprocessing, the running time of the classifier is greatly reduced, and the average time consumption of KNN in PCA and SVD is 94.37%.

(3) The reason why the seven algorithms are greatly improved in time performance is that the feature dimension reduction greatly simplifies the dimension of the data and reduces the amount of data calculation during the detection process. Some algorithms have a slight improvement in each index because when the proposed model is applied, the obtained dataset cannot fully represent the original record, but the selected principal component contribution rate is over 95%. The redundancy has been cleared and the indicators have been improved.

(4) After the seven algorithms are subjected to feature dimensionality reduction by SVD or PCA, the accuracy and other indicators remain at a high level compared to the use of all features. This means that the features are not as good as possible. Some features in the original feature set do not work for anomaly detection. The existence of these features will not only become a burden of anomaly detection, but also increase the false alarm rate. The seven KNN algorithms have longer training time and larger computational cost, while the SVD and PCA methods have the advantages of fast calculation speed and high operational efficiency, which can greatly reduce the computational overhead. By using the PCA or SVD dimensionality reduction method, both high detection rate and computation time can be greatly reduced.

(5) As shown in Figs. 4, 5, 6, 7 and 8, SVD-DT is generally superior to other algorithms. To demonstrate the performance of the SVD-DT algorithm, we performed experiments using approximately 500,000 samples of "kddcup.-data_10_percent" in the KDD CUP 99 dataset [18], as shown in Fig. 9. The algorithm can maintain high accuracy with less detection time.

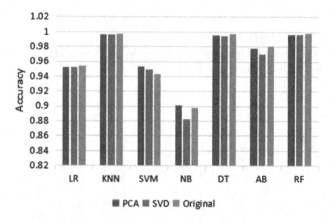

Fig. 4. Comparison of Accuracy of 7 classifiers with PCA versus SVD

Figure 4 depicts the accuracy of 7 classifiers with respect to PCA and SVD. The interpretations from Fig. 4 are:

- Seven algorithms are reduced in size by PCA, and their accuracy is higher than SVD.
- KNN has the highest accuracy through seven algorithms processed by PCA and SVD.
- Naïve Bayes has lower accuracy and KNN, DT, and RF have higher accuracy.

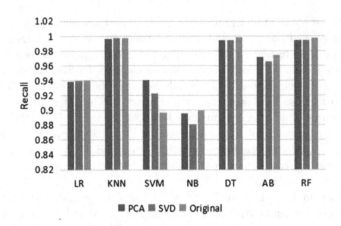

Fig. 5. Comparison of Recall of 7 classifiers with PCA versus SVD

Figure 5 depicts the recall of 7 classifiers with respect to PCA and SVD. The interpretations from Fig. 5 are:

- SVD-KNN has the highest recall.
- The KNN, DT, and RF algorithms processed by PCA or SVD have a high recall.
- SVD-NB and PCA-NB have the lowest recall.

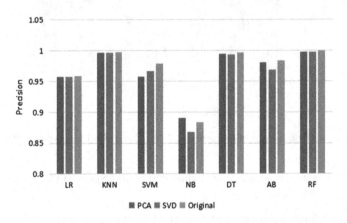

Fig. 6. Comparison of Precision of 7 classifiers with PCA versus SVD

Figure 6 depicts the precision of 7 classifiers with respect to PCA and SVD. The interpretations from Fig. 6 are:

- PCA-RF has the highest precision.
- KNN, DT, and RF algorithms processed by PCA or SVD have higher precision.
- SVD-NB and PCA-NB have the lowest precision.

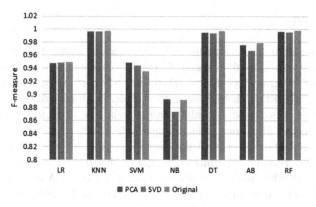

Fig. 7. Comparison of F-measure of 7 classifiers with PCA versus SVD

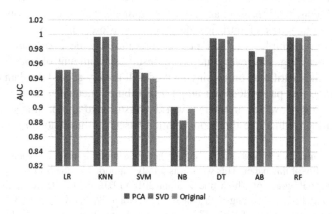

Fig. 8. Comparison of AUC of 7 classifiers with PCA versus SVD

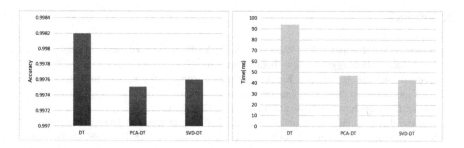

Fig. 9. Comparison of Accuracy and Time of 3 algorithms in KDD CUP 99

5   Conclusion

In this paper, we study the performance of seven machine learning algorithms through PCA and SVD. In addition to the recall, SVD performance analysis is always superior to PCA feature selection technology. Therefore, SVD is the best feature selection technique for NSL-KDD dataset because it reduces dimensionality by selecting important feature vectors and discarding unimportant feature vectors. SVD and PCA can achieve effective dimension reduction and redundancy removal of data based on the maximum extraction of original data features, and solve the high computational overhead of IDS. Through experiments, we found that the DT method processed by SVD is superior to other methods in detection rate and time. PCA and SVD reduce the computational cost and improve the efficiency of IDS while ensuring high detection rate. It has a certain meaning for real-time deployment in high-speed networks.

Although PCA provides better performance analysis in terms of Accuracy, Error rate, Recall, Precision, F-measure and AUC, it requires a lot of computation time due to its complexity. In terms of intrusion detection, there are still improvements in this experiment. For example, you can put the program on the Spark architecture for distributed processing. However, due to the insufficient amount of data in the NSL-KDD dataset, the distributed processing method will greatly exceed the data processing time. Therefore, this paper does not adopt a distributed method to further reduce the time consumption. However, in the real world, a distributed approach is still desirable, which can further reduce the time consumption based on dimensionality reduction.

Acknowledgement. We would like to thank the reviewers for their comments to help us improve the quality of this paper. This work was jointly supported by the National Key Research and Development Program of China under Grant 2018YFB1003702, the Scientific and Technological Support Project of Jiangsu Province under Grant BE2016776, the "333" project of Jiangsu Province under Grant BRA2017228 and the Talent Project in Six Fields of Jiangsu Province under Grant 2015-JNHB-012.

References

1. Meng, W., Tischhauser, E.W., Wang, Q., Wang, Y., Han, J.: When intrusion detection meets blockchain technology: a review. IEEE Access **6**, 10179–10188 (2018)
2. Kaur, R., Kumar, G., Kumar, K.: A comparative study of feature selection techniques for intrusion detection. In: 2015 2nd International Conference on Computing for Sustainable Global Development (INDIACom), pp. 2120–2124. IEEE (2015)
3. Ambusaidi, M.A., He, X., Nanda, P., Tan, Z.: Building an intrusion detection system using a filter-based feature selection algorithm. IEEE Trans. Comput. **65**(10), 2986–2998 (2016)
4. Aburomman, A.A., Reaz, M.B.I.: A survey of intrusion detection systems based on ensemble and hybrid classifiers. Comput. Secur. **65**, 135–152 (2017)
5. Ashfaq, R.A.R., Wang, X.Z., Huang, J.Z., Abbas, H., He, Y.L.: Fuzziness based semi-supervised learning approach for intrusion detection system. Inf. Sci. **378**, 484–497 (2017)
6. Anbar, M., Abdullah, R., Hasbullah, I.H., Chong, Y.W., Elejla, O.E.: Comparative performance analysis of classification algorithms for intrusion detection system. In: 2016 14th Annual Conference on Privacy, Security and Trust (PST), pp. 282–288. IEEE (2016)

7. Thaseen, I.S., Kumar, C.A.: Intrusion detection model using chi square feature selection and modified Naïve Bayes classifier. In: Vijayakumar, V., Neelanarayanan, V. (eds.) Proceedings of the 3rd International Symposium on Big Data and Cloud Computing Challenges (ISBCC – 16'). SIST, vol. 49, pp. 81–91. Springer, Cham (2016). https://doi.org/10.1007/978-3-319-30348-2_7

8. Subba, B., Biswas, S., Karmakar, S.: Enhancing performance of anomaly based intrusion detection systems through dimensionality reduction using principal component analysis. In: 2016 IEEE International Conference on Advanced Networks and Telecommunications Systems (ANTS), pp. 1–6. IEEE (2016)

9. Salo, F., Nassif, A.B., Essex, A.: Dimensionality reduction with IG-PCA and ensemble classifier for network intrusion detection. Comput. Netw. **148**, 164–175 (2019)

10. Shahbaz, M.B., Wang, X., Behnad, A., Samarabandu, J.: On efficiency enhancement of the correlation-based feature selection for intrusion detection systems. In: 2016 IEEE 7th Annual Information Technology, Electronics and Mobile Communication Conference (IEMCON), pp. 1–7. IEEE (2016)

11. Raman, M.G., Kirthivasan, K., Sriram, V.S.: Development of rough set–hypergraph technique for key feature identification in intrusion detection systems. Comput. Electr. Eng. **59**, 189–200 (2017)

12. Umbarkar, S., Shukla, S.: Analysis of heuristic based feature reduction method in intrusion detection system. In: 2018 5th International Conference on Signal Processing and Integrated Networks (SPIN), pp. 717–720. IEEE (2018)

13. Miao, Y., Ruan, Z., Pan, L., Zhang, J., Xiang, Y.: Comprehensive analysis of network traffic data. Concurr. Comput. Pract. Exp. **30**(5), e4181 (2018)

14. Tengl, S., et al.: A collaborative intrusion detection model using a novel optimal weight strategy based on genetic algorithm for ensemble classifier. In: 2018 IEEE 22nd International Conference on Computer Supported Cooperative Work in Design (CSCWD), pp. 761–766. IEEE (2018)

15. Golub, G.H., Van Loan, C.F.: Matrix Computations, vol. 3. JHU Press, Baltimore (2012)

16. Tavallaee, M., Bagheri, E., Lu, W., Ghorbani, A.A.: A detailed analysis of the KDD CUP 99 data set. In: 2009 IEEE Symposium on Computational Intelligence for Security and Defense Applications, pp. 1–6. IEEE (2009)

17. The NSL-KDD dataset. https://www.unb.ca/cic/datasets/nsl.html

18. The KDD CUP 99 Data. http://kdd.ics.uci.edu/databases/kddcup99/kddcup99

19. Deshmukh, D.H., Ghorpade, T., Padiya, P.: Improving classification using preprocessing and machine learning algorithms on NSL-KDD dataset. In: 2015 International Conference on Communication, Information & Computing Technology (ICCICT), pp. 1–6. IEEE (2015)

Blockchain, Attack and Defense

Anonymous IoT Data Storage and Transaction Protocol Based on Blockchain and Edge Computing

Zhi Qiao[1,2,4]([✉]), Congcong Zhu[1,2,4], Zhiwei Wang[1,2,4],
and Nianhua Yang[3,4]

[1] School of Computer, Nanjing University of Posts and Telecommunications,
Nanjing, China
qiaozhi0831@126.com
[2] Guangxi Key Laboratory of Cryptography and Information Security,
Guilin, China
[3] Jiangsu Key Laboratory of Big Data Security and Intelligence Processing,
Nanjing, China
[4] School of Statistics and Information, Shanghai University of International
Business and Economics, Shanghai, China

Abstract. This paper proposes a distributed data anonymous storage and transaction protocol that discards the centralized architecture and distributes the computational pressure to each edge device through blockchain and edge computing. In addition, a pseudo-identity-based data anonymous storage scheme is designed based on ElGamal cryptosystem, and the anonymous transaction scheme based on ECDLP and blinding signature allows sellers and buyers to directly trade through the blockchain. The protocol proposed in this paper effectively guarantees the security of data storage and the anonymity of data transactions.

Keywords: Blockchain · Edge computing · Pseudo identity · Anonymous transaction

1 Introduction

The blockchain was first proposed by Nakamoto in [1] describing Bitcoin. He pointed out that blockchain is a data structure used to record bitcoin transaction history. There are no third parties in the blockchain, so the blockchain is decentralized, which greatly reduces security threats from third parties, and all transactions in the blockchain are traceable, which provides assurance for the verification and arbitration of the transaction.

The Internet of Things is a huge network formed by combining various sensing devices with the Internet, such as temperature sensors and infrared sensors [2]. The number and scale of the IoT is rapidly expanding. As the number of IoT devices grows, a large amount of data is generated at the edge of the network. These data need to be processed in time rather than sent back to the cloud server, so processing data at the edge of the network is more effective [3]. Edge computing has the characteristics of

© Springer Nature Switzerland AG 2019
F. Liu et al. (Eds.): SciSec 2019, LNCS 11933, pp. 181–189, 2019.
https://doi.org/10.1007/978-3-030-34637-9_13

high real-time and close to the edge. The basic principle of edge computing is that computing should be near the data source, not in the remote cloud [4], and it is proposed as an intermediate architecture that supports blockchain and interact with IoT devices [5].

With the increasing number of IoT devices and the ever-increasing amount of data generated, how to store these data securely and securely trade these data has become the focus of attention. Xu et al. [6] proposed a blockchain-based storage system for data analytics applications in the Internet of Things. Li et al. [7] proposed a distributed data storage scheme employing blockchain and certificateless cryptography. Wang et al. [8] proposed a new architecture for data synchronization based on fog computing. Liu et al. [9] proposed a new blockchain-based decentralization DNS data storage method. Kogan et al. Yang et al. [10] proposed to use a credit-based payment for fast computing resource trading in edge-assisted blockchain-enabled IoT. Nagato et al. [11] provided a data framework for edge computing where developers can easily attain efficient data transfer between devices or users.

The contributions of this paper are listed as follows:

First, based on the ElGamal cryptosystem [12], we design an anonymous storage scheme for data that can generate pseudo identities, protect the correspondence between real identities and data. Second, we propose a data anonymous transaction scheme based on blinding signature and ECDLP [13], which realized the complete anonymity of the transaction.

This paper is organized as follows. We introduce the preliminary setting of the protocol in Sect. 2. We propose our anonymous storage and transaction protocol for IoT data based on blockchain and edge computing in Sect. 3. We analyze the security of our protocol in Sect. 4. Finally, we conclude our paper in Sect. 5.

2 Preliminary

The blockchain is the core supporting technology of the digital cryptocurrency system represented by bitcoin. The core advantage of blockchain technology is decentralization, which can be achieved through the use of data encryption, time stamping, distributed consensus and economic incentives. Nodes do not need to trust each other in distributed systems to achieve peer-to-peer-based transaction, coordination and collaboration, thus providing solutions to solve the problems of high cost, low efficiency and insecure data storage that are common in centralized architecture.

In the blockchain network, there is a role called miner, which can also be called a work node. The role of the miner is to package the transaction into blocks and solve the proof-of-work problem when a user posts a transaction to the Bitcoin network, blocks that successfully solve the problem will be broadcast throughout the network. A block consists of a block header and a block body. The block body mainly contains transaction counts and transaction details. That is, the Merkel tree [14] is stored in the block body except the root node, the block header is composed of the following parts:

$$block\ header: (Prehash, MerkelRoot, Nonce, Ts, Currenthash)$$

Where *Prehash* is the hash value of the previous block; *MerkelRoot* is the root of Merkel tree, which is a transaction tree; *Nonce* is a random number found by solving proof-of-work problem; *Ts* is the timestamp and *Currenthash* is the hash of current block, Fig. 1 shows the structure of the blockchain.

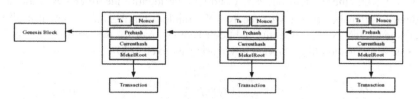

Fig. 1. Blockchain structure

3 Data Anonymous Storage and Transaction Protocol Based on Blockchain and Internet of Things

Our protocol is divided into two parts, the first part is the data anonymous storage protocol and the second part is the data anonymous transaction protocol.

3.1 Data Anonymous Storage Protocol

In this section, the edge device encrypts the received data which collected from the IoT device, including generating a pseudo identity for the IoT device and generating a symmetric key for encrypting the original data. Pseudo-identity protects the correspondence between real identity and data. Figure 2 shows the architecture diagram of the protocol.

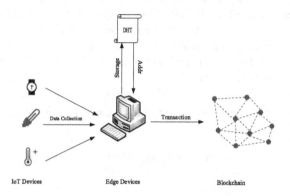

Fig. 2. Data anonymous storage architecture

Pseudo Identity Generation

The pseudo-identity generation is based on ElGamal cryptosystem, which is a kind of public key cryptosystem based on discrete logarithm problem, we assume that the reader is familiar with the discrete logarithm problem and the ElGamal cryptosystem.

1. A trusted third party *TA* distributes a unique identity Tid_i, $(1 \leq i \leq n)$ for each IoT device, where n means number of IoT devices.
2. The edge device randomly selects a large prime number p that satisfies the security requirements, and generates a generator g of Z_p, $g \in Z_p^*$.
3. The edge device sends a random number T to the terminal device; the terminal device sends the random number R and its own identity identifier Tid_i to the edge device. After the edge device receives the random number R, it computes $g^{H(T) \cdot R}$ and generates a pseudo-identity public-private key pair for the terminal device. The expression of the public private key pairing is given below:

$$PK_{pse} = g^{H(Tid)} \cdot g^{H(g^{H(T) \cdot R})} (\bmod\ p) \equiv g^{H(Tid) + H(g^{H(T) \cdot R})} (modp) \tag{1}$$

$$SK_{pse} = H(Tid) + H\left(g^{H(T) \cdot R}\right) \tag{2}$$

4. Divide the identity *Tid* into t groups, each group has L length, where $Tid = Tid_1 Tid_2 \ldots Tid_n$, select a random number r_i for Tid_i, $1 < i < n$, $1 < r_i < p - 1$, and computing $\left(c_i, c_i'\right)$, so that the pseudo identity is:

$$c_i \equiv g^{r_i} (mod\ p), \quad c_i' \equiv Tid_i \cdot PK_{pse}^{r_i} (mod\ p), PseID = (c_1, c_1')(c_2, c_2') \ldots (c_n, c_n') \tag{3}$$

Data Encryption

Since the amount of IoT device data is too large, a symmetric cryptographic algorithm is used when encrypting the IoT device data, and symmetric encryption algorithm has higher encryption efficiency.

Selecting a part of the private key as the symmetrically encrypted key has the advantage of reducing the computational complexity of the edge device to generate the symmetric encryption key again. And more importantly, in the subsequent data transaction process, the IoT device delegates the edge device to trade data, If the IoT device questions the data sold by the edge device during the transaction, that is, whether the edge device sells the correct data belonging to the IoT device instead of the forged data, the IoT device can use the symmetric key to verify whether the data generated by itself is correctly sold.

The symmetric key is $K = H(g^{H(T) \cdot R})$, use this key to generate ciphertext C, the generated ciphertext is tagged, in order to indicate which type of data is being traded during the data transaction.

$$C = En_K(M, PseID, Ts) \tag{4}$$

Where M is the data of the IoT device, $PseID$ is the pseudo identity of the corresponding device and Ts is the current timestamp. En is a symmetric encryption algorithm. It can be AES or other symmetric encryption algorithms. Store the data pairing $<label, C>$ ($label$ is the tag) to the distributed hash table (DHT) [15], and return the address of the data $Addr$ in the DHT to the edge device.

The mapping relationship $Mapping = <PseID, Tid>$ between the real identity and the pseudo identity is also saved and stored in the DHT. If the buyer suspects that the data he purchased is forged by the edge device during the data transaction, the edge device presents the $Mapping$ for verification.

3.2   Data Anonymous Transaction Protocol

In this section, we present a data anonymous transaction protocol. The details of this part are given below, including edge device registration and data anonymous transaction.

Edge Device Registration

Since the data transactions are based on the blockchain, the edge device needs to register with the blockchain before the data transaction. The registration process is as follows:

1. The edge device generates a random number R_e and uses the public key of the blockchain PK_C to encrypt the random number to generate the ciphertext Z_e, where $Z_e = En_{PK_c}(R_e)$ and sends it to the blockchain, Similarly, the blockchain generates R_c and generate the ciphertext Z_c, where $Z_c = En_{PK_e}(R_c)$ and send it to the edge device.
2. After each party decrypts the random number sent by the other party, both of them combine two random numbers into one number N by using an XOR operation, where $N = R_e \oplus R_c$, the blockchain stores the random number in its own access control list.

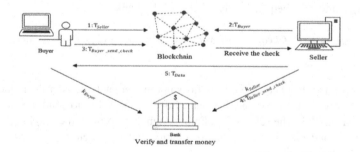

Fig. 3. Data anonymous transaction

Data Anonymous Transaction

In the process of data transaction, the edge device is actually the *Seller* who owns the data, and the user who purchases the data is the *Buyer*. In this section, all transactions are signed with the sender's private key and verified using the sender's public key. Figure 3 is the diagram of anonymous transaction protocol:

1. The buyer posted a transaction in the blockchain indicating that the buyer wanted to purchase the data:

$$T_{Buyer} = \left(val, label_B, PK_{Buyer}, ECC_{Buyer}, H\left(T_{Buyer}\right)\right) \tag{5}$$

   Where *val* indicates the price of the data, $label_B$ indicates which type of data the buyer wants to purchase, PK_{Buyer} is the buyer's public key, ECC_{Buyer} is an elliptic curve equation $Q = kP$, $Q, P \in E_p(a, b)$ and $k < p$, but in this step, only the value of Q_{Buyer}, P_{Buyer} are given. $H\left(T_{Buyer}\right)$ is the hash function of this transaction.

2. When the seller in the blockchain receives a suitable transaction request and the seller is willing to trade data with the buyer, the seller sends a transaction to the buyer:

$$T_{Seller} = (label_S, ECC_{Seller}, PK_{Seller}, H(T_{Seller})) \tag{6}$$

3. After the buyer receives the transaction sent from the seller, the buyer generates a cheque and send it to the seller, The cheque is used to transfer money between the buyer and the seller's bank account. In order to prove the identity of himself, the buyer needs to give the secret value k_{Buyer} and his account, the specific structure of the cheque is:

$$T_{Seller\_send\_Cheque} = \left(Cheque: < SN, val, ECC_{Buyer}, acc\_no_{Buyer} >, k_{Buyer}\right). \tag{7}$$

4. The seller receivers the cheque sent from the buyer, firstly uses the secret value k_{Buyer} to verify the buy's identity, and then add his bank account acc_no_{Seller} and ECC_{Seller} into the cheque, finally send it to the bank.

$$T_{Seller\_send\_Cheque} = Cheque: < SN, val, ECC_{Buyer}, acc\_no_{Buyer}, ECC_{Seller}, acc\_no_{Seller} > \tag{8}$$

5. After receiving the cheque, the bank does not immediately transfer the money in the buyer's account to the seller, the bank informs the seller to send the data to the buyer. Meanwhile, the seller uses blinding signature to blind the *Mapping*, which is the correspondence between pseudo identity and real identity, here we give the detail of blinding signature:

   Firstly, the seller generates a random number *r* named blinding factor, and then uses buyer's public key to encrypt the blinding factor, then computes *Mapping'*. Secondly, the seller stores $H(r)$ on the blockchain, and then add the *Mapping'*, the data's address, the secret value k_{Seller} and the symmetric key that decrypts the data into a transaction:

$$T_{data} = \left(Mapping' = Mapping \cdot PK_{Buyer}(r), Addr, k_{Seller}, H\left(g^{H(T) \cdot R}\right)\right) \quad (9)$$

6. After the buyer receives the transaction, the identity of the seller is authenticated, and then the data is obtained and decrypted in the DHT. Then the buyer and seller send their secret value k_{Buyer} and k_{Seller} to the bank. The bank verifies the identity of the seller and the buyer, and after the verification is successful, transfers the money in the buyer's account to the seller's account.

4   Security Analysis

4.1   Security of the Protocol

In the part of pseudo-identity generation algorithm, the security of the algorithm is based on the security of the ElGamal encryption algorithm, and the security of the ElGamal algorithm is based on the mathematical problem of computing the discrete logarithm is complex on a finite field. The security of data anonymous transaction protocols is based on the security of blockchain and the hardness of the elliptic curve discrete logarithm problem.

The security of the blockchain means that once the transaction on the blockchain is broadcast, it is visible to all other nodes in the entire network and cannot be modified. The miners on the blockchain find a nonce by computing the proof-of-work, who first calculated the nonce is given the right to write the block which containing the transaction to the blockchain. The advantage of this mechanism is that it can prevent double spending attack.

The anonymous transaction means that in the equation $Q = kP$, only know Q and P are difficult to compute k, When the identity needs to be presented, the identity information is replaced by presenting k, there is no identity-related information throughout the transaction, thereby realizing anonymous transactions.

4.2   Traceability

When encrypting data using a symmetric key, use $K = H\left(g^{H(T) \cdot R}\right)$ as the symmetric key. The advantage of using $K = H\left(g^{H(T) \cdot R}\right)$ as a symmetric key when encrypting data is that if the data sold by the seller (edge devices) is not generated by the IoT device but is forged, the IoT device can verify the generated pseudo-identity to ensure that the data the seller sells is generated by himself.

When selling data, the buyer blinds the *Mapping* by using blinding signature. The advantage of this is that if the buyer questions the authenticity of the data sold by the seller, the value is revealed to prove whether he sold the data the buyer needs, rather than the seller's forged data. Meanwhile, the blinding factor generated in the blinding signature, the seller will store $H(r)$ on the blockchain, and when necessary, present the value so that the buyer can obtain the true mapping value.

When the buyer obtains the blinding factor r, he computes:

$$SK_{Buyer}\left(Mapping'\right) = SK_{Buyer}(Mapping) \cdot r \cdot r^{-1} = SK_{Buyer}(Mapping) \qquad (10)$$

$$PK_{Buyer}\left(SK_{Buyer}(Mapping)\right) = Mapping \qquad (11)$$

Now the buyer gets the knowledge of *Mapping*.

5 Conclusion

In this paper, we present an anonymous data storage and transaction protocol based on blockchain and edge computing. In the data anonymous storage section, the edge device generates a pseudo identity for the terminal device to protect the correspondence between the real identity and the data. In the data anonymous transaction section, we designed a structure of an electronic cheque. Through the blockchain, the buyer signs the cheque to the seller, the seller sells the data to the buyer, and the seller then entrusts the bank to use the cheque to transfer the money.

This research is partially supported by the National Natural Science Foundation of China under Grant No. 61672016, Guangxi Key Laboratory of Cryptography and Information Security (No. GCIS201815).

Funding. The funding that Humanities and Social Science Research Planning Fund of the Education Ministry of China under grant No. 15YJCZH201.

References

1. Nakamoto, S.: Bitcoin: A peer-to-peer electronic cash system (2008)
2. Gubbi, J., Buyya, R., Marusic, S., Palaniswami, M.: Internet of Things (IoT): a vision, architectural elements, and future directions. Future Gener. Comput. Syst. 29(7), 1645–1660 (2013)
3. Fernández-Caramés, T.M., Fraga-Lamas, P.: A review on the use of blockchain for the Internet of Things. IEEE Access 6, 32979–33001 (2018)
4. Bonomi, F., Milito, R., Zhu, J., Addepalli, S.: Fog computing and its role in the internet of things. In: Proceedings of the First Edition of the MCC Workshop on Mobile Cloud Computing, pp. 13–16. ACM (2012)
5. Yeow, K., Gani, A., Ahmad, R.W., Rodrigues, J.J., Ko, K.: Decentralized consensus for edge-centric internet of things: A review, taxonomy, and research issues. IEEE Access 6, 1513–1524 (2017)
6. Xu, Q., Aung, K.M.M., Zhu, Y., Yong, K.L.: A blockchain-based storage system for data analytics in the internet of things. In: Yager, R., Pascual Espada, J. (eds.) New Advances in the Internet of Things. SCI, vol. 715, pp. 119–138. Springer, Cham (2018)
7. Li, R., Song, T., Mei, B., Li, H., Cheng, X., Sun, L.: Blockchain for large-scale internet of things data storage and protection. IEEE Trans. Serv. Comput. (2018)
8. Wang, T., Zhou, J., Liu, A., Bhuiyan, M.Z.A., Wang, G., Jia, W.: Fog-based computing and storage offloading for data synchronization in IoT. IEEE Internet Things J. (2018)

9. Liu, J., Li, B., Chen, L., Hou, M., Xiang, F., Wang, P.: A data storage method based on blockchain for decentralization DNS. In: 2018 IEEE Third International Conference on Data Science in Cyberspace (DSC), pp. 189–196. IEEE (2018)

10. Li, Z., Yang, Z., Xie, S., Chen, W., Liu, K.: Credit-based payments for fast computing resource trading in edge-assisted internet of things. IEEE Internet Things J. (2019)

11. Nagato, T., Tsutano, T., Kamada, T., Takaki, Y., Ohta, C.: Distributed key-value storage for edge computing and its explicit data distribution method. In: 2019 International Conference on Information Networking (ICOIN), pp. 147–152. IEEE (2019)

12. Tsiounis, Y., Yung, M.: On the security of ElGamal based encryption. In: Imai, H., Zheng, Y. (eds.) PKC 1998. LNCS, vol. 1431, pp. 117–134. Springer, Heidelberg (1998). https://doi.org/10.1007/BFb0054019

13. Johnson, D., Menezes, A., Vanstone, S.: The elliptic curve digital signature algorithm (ECDSA). Int. J. Inform. Secur. 1, 36–63 (2001)

14. Merkle, R.C.: Protocols for public key cryptosystems. In: 1980 IEEE Symposium on Security and Privacy, p. 122. IEEE (1980)

15. Kaashoek, M.F., Karger, D.R.: Koorde: a simple degree-optimal distributed hash table. In: Kaashoek, M.F., Stoica, I. (eds.) IPTPS 2003. LNCS, vol. 2735, pp. 98–107. Springer, Heidelberg (2003). https://doi.org/10.1007/978-3-540-45172-3_9

Incentive Mechanism for Bitcoin Mining Pool Based on Stackelberg Game

Gang Xue, Jia Xu$^{(\boxtimes)}$, Hanwen Wu, Weifeng Lu, and Lijie Xu

Jiangsu Key Laboratory of Big Data Security and Intelligent Processing, Nanjing University of Posts and Telecommunications, Nanjing, Jiangsu 210023, China
xujia@njupt.edu.cn

Abstract. Bitcoin is the most popular cryptocurrency all over the world. Existing mining pool systems do not consider the cost of miners. In this paper, we propose a novel pool mining mechanism based on Stackelberg game to incentivize the rational miners in Bitcoin mining pool. Through both theoretical analysis and simulations, we demonstrate that the proposed mechanism achieve computational efficiency, individual rationality, and profitability. Moreover, we show that the Stackelberg game has a unique Equilibrium.

Keywords: Bitcoin · Mining pool · Incentive mechanism · Nash equilibrium

1 Introduction

Bitcoin is the world's first decentralized digital currency, which relies on the network of computers that synchronize transactions with a process called mining to find valid blocks. In this way, miners repeatedly compute hashes until one finds a numerical value, which is low enough, and thus get the reward from the block. Small miners participate in the mining pool to achieve large computing power in total, and divide the reward from blocks in order to receive a smaller but steadier stream of income.

Incentive mechanisms are important for many human-involved cooperative systems, such as computation offloading [1], and crowdsourcing [2, 3]. Some research efforts [4–6] focus on designing incentive mechanisms to entice miners to participate in mining pools. However, none of them considers the cost of each miner. Designing an efficient mechanism to incentive the rational miners within the mining pool is a challenging issue.

This paper considers the rational miners with different cost. For example, people living in areas with high electricity bills will have higher mining cost than others. Their mining strategies will be influenced by their cost. To solve this problem, we design an incentive mechanism to motivate the miners to participate in the mining pool. In our incentive mechanism, the mining pool platform has the absolute control over the total payment to the miners affiliated, and miners can determine the mining actions based on the total payment decided by mining pool platform and their cost.

There are two noteworthy properties of our mechanism which are distinguished with most mining mechanisms. First, our mechanism satisfies the property of individual rationality, which can guarantee nonnegative utility for both side of miner and

F. Liu et al. (Eds.): SciSec 2019, LNCS 11933, pp. 190–198, 2019.
https://doi.org/10.1007/978-3-030-34637-9_14

platform. Second, the platform has the absolute control of the pool, and takes all risk of the miners. This means that the platform needs to pay to the miners no matter whether the pool finds a valid block, and the miners always have steady income.

2 System Model and Problem Formulation

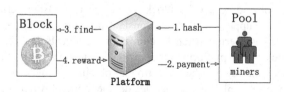

Fig. 1. A mining pool system

We use Fig. 1 to illustrate the mining pool system. The system consists of a mining pool platform and a mining pool which contains a set $M = \{1, 2, \ldots, n\}$ of rational miners, where $n \geq 2$. The Miners provide hash quantity by consuming their computing power with different unit cost. Therefore, these rational miners expect the payment to compensate for their cost. Each miner makes its own mining strategy, which is the hash quantity, and then submits it to the platform. After collecting the mining strategies from miners, the platform sends the payments to the miners. The miners with positive hash quantity send the hash to the platform. If they are lucky enough, through the integrated efforts of the miners in the pool, the mining pool will find a valid block and receive the reward from the block. On the other side, if any miner outside the pool finds a valid block, the platform can't get reward. Overall, the platform absorbs all the variance for the miners in the pool.

The platform is only interested in maximizing its own utility. Since computing power is owned by different individuals, it is reasonable to assume that miners are selfish and rational. Hence each miner only wants to maximize its own utility and won't participate in mining pool unless there is sufficient incentive.

For mining a block, the platform announces a total payment $P > 0$, motivating miners to participate in the mining pool. Each miner decides its mining strategy of participation based on the payment. The mining strategy of any miner $i \in M$ is represented by h_i, $h_i \geq 0$, the hash quantity he is willing to provide. Specifically, if $h_i = 0$, miner i indicates that he will not participate in the mining pool. The mining cost of miner i is $k_i h_i$, where $k_i > 0$ is its unit cost. Assume that the payment received by miner i is proportional to h_i. Then the utility of miner i can be defined as the difference between payment and cost:

$$u_i = \frac{h_i}{\sum_{j \in M} h_j} P - h_i k_i \tag{2.1}$$

For the reason that the mining process is subject to Poisson process [4], we can get the utility of the platform in expectation:

$$u_0 = \frac{\sum_{j \in M} h_j}{A + \sum_{j \in M} h_j} R - P \tag{2.2}$$

where $A = \frac{D \times 2^{32}}{10min}$ is the total hash power in Bitcoin network. We can estimate it easily from the difficulty of finding a valid block, D, which is adjusted periodically by the Bitcoin network. We suppose that A is a constant because it is almost stable for two weeks (the approximate period when Bitcoin network adjusts D). The probability of finding a valid block by the platform is proportional to its total computing power in the whole network. R is the reward the platform can obtain if it finds a valid block.

The objective of the platform is to decide the optimal value of P such as to maximize (2.2), while each miner $i \in M$ decides its hash quantity h_i to maximize (2.1) for the given value of P. Since no rational user is willing to mine with negative utility, user i will set $h_i = 0$ when $P \le k_i \sum_{j \ne i \cap j \in M} h_j$.

Our objective is to design an incentive mechanism for mining pool satisfying the following four desirable properties:

- Computational Efficiency: A mechanism is computationally efficient if the outcome can be computed in polynomial time.
- Individual Rationality: Each participating miner will have a non-negative utility.
- Profitability: The value brought by the miners should be at least as large as the total payment paid to the miners. Note that profitability here is profitability in expectation because of the randomness of Bitcoin mining.
- Uniqueness: The combination of strategies is called *Nash Equilibrium*, where each player's equilibrium strategy is to maximize his/her expected utility, while all other players follow the equilibrium strategy. Uniqueness requires that there exists only one *Nash Equilibrium*. Being uniqueness, we can predict and compute the equilibrium strategies of all players exactly.

3   Incentive Mechanism

We model the mining process as *Stackelberg* game, which can be called *Mining* game. There are two phases in this mechanism: In the first phase (called payment determination), the platform announces its payment P; in the second phase (called hash determination), each miner strategizes its mining plan to maximize its own utility. Therefore, the platform is the leader and the miners are the followers in our *Mining* game. The strategy of the platform is its payment P. The strategy of any miner i is its hash amount h_i. Let $\boldsymbol{h} = (h_1, h_2, \dots, h_n)$ denote the strategy profile of all miners' strategies. Let h_{-i} denote the strategy profile excluding h_i. As a notational convention, we write $\boldsymbol{h} = (h_i, h_{-i})$.

Note that the second process of the *Mining* game itself can be considered as a non-cooperative game, which we call the *Hash Determination (HD)* game. Given *Stackelberg* game formulation, we introduce the following two definitions:

Definition 1 (Nash Equilibrium, NE). *A set of strategies ($h_1^{ne}, h_2^{ne}, \ldots, h_n^{ne}$) is a Nash Equilibrium of the HD game if for any user i,*

$$u_i(h_i^{ne}, h_{-i}^{ne}) \geq \bar{u}_i(h_i, h_{-i}^{ne})$$

for any $h_i \geq 0$, where u_i is defined in (2.1).

Definition 2 (Subgame Perfect Nash equilibrium). *The Stackelberg game can be solved by finding the Subgame Perfect Nash Equilibrium (SPNE), i.e. the strategy profile serves best for each player, given the strategies of the other player, and entails every player playing in a Nash Equilibrium in every subgame.*

3.1   Hash Determination

We first introduce the concept of best response strategy.

Definition 3 (Best Response Strategy). *Given h_{-i}, the strategy is miner i's best response strategy, denoted by $\beta_i(h_{-i})$, if it maximizes $u_i(h_i, h_{-i})$ over all $h_i \geq 0$.*

Based on the definition of *NE*, every player is playing its best response strategy in a *NE*. From (2.1), we know that $h_i \leq \frac{P}{k_i}$ because u_i will be negative otherwise. To study the best response strategy of miner i, we compute the derivatives of u_i with respect to h_i:

$$\frac{\partial u_i}{\partial h_i} = \frac{1}{\sum_{j \in M} h_j} P - \frac{h_i}{\left(\sum_{j \in M} h_j\right)^2} P - k_i \tag{3.1}$$

$$\frac{\partial^2 u_i}{\partial h_i^2} = -\frac{2p \sum_{j \in M \setminus \{i\}} h_j}{\sum_{j \in M} h_j} < 0 \tag{3.2}$$

Since the second-order derivative of u_i is negative, the utility u_i is a strictly concave function with h_i. Therefore, given any $P > 0$ and any strategy profile h_{-i} of the other miners, the best response strategy $\beta_i(h_{-i})$ of user i is unique, if it exists. If the strategy of all other miners $j \neq i$ is $h_j = 0$, then miner i does not have a best response strategy, as it can have a utility arbitrarily close to P, by setting h_i to a sufficiently small positive number. Therefore, we are only interested in the best response for miner i when $\sum_{j \in M \setminus \{i\}} h_j > 0$. Setting the first derivative of u_i to 0, we have

$$\frac{1}{\sum_{j \in M} h_j} P - \frac{h_i}{\left(\sum_{j \in M} h_j\right)^2} P - k_i = 0 \tag{3.3}$$

Solving for h_i in (3.3), we obtain

$$h_i = \sqrt{\frac{P \sum_{j \in M \setminus \{i\}} h_j}{k_i}} - \sum_{j \in M \setminus \{i\}} h_j \tag{3.4}$$

Remark: h_i is the total hash that can make i achieve maximum utility in the current mining pool. Of course, i can put the remaining hash power to any other pools.

If the right-hand side of (3.4) is positive, it is also the best response strategy of miner i, due to the concavity of u_i. If the right-hand side of (3.4) is less than or equal to 0, then miner i does not participate in the mining task by setting $h_i = 0$ (to avoid a deficit). Hence we have

$$\beta(h_i) = \begin{cases} 0 & \text{if } P \leq k_i \sum_{j \neq i \cap j \in M} h_j \\ \sqrt{\frac{P \sum_{j \in M \setminus \{i\}} h_j}{K_i}} - \sum_{j \in M \setminus \{i\}} h_j & \text{otherwise} \end{cases} \tag{3.5}$$

These analyses lead to Algorithm 1 for computing an *NE* of the *HD* game.

Algorithm 1: Computation of the NE

1 Sort miners according to their unit costs,
   $k_1 \leq k_2 \leq \ldots \leq k_n$;
2 $S \leftarrow \{1,2\}$, $i \leftarrow 3$;
3 **while** $i \leq n$ and $k_i < \frac{k_i + \sum_{j \in S} k_j}{|S|}$ **do**
4 $\quad\big|\ S \leftarrow S \cup \{i\}, i \leftarrow i + 1$;
5 **end**
6 **for each** $i \in M$ **do**
7 $\quad\big|\ $ **if** $i \in S$ **then** $h_i^{ne} = \frac{(|S|-1)P}{\sum_{j \in S} k_j} \left(1 - \frac{(|S|-1)k_i}{\sum_{j \in S} k_j} \right)$;
8 $\quad\big|\ $ **else** $h_i^{ne} = 0$;
9 **end**
10 **return** $h^{ne} = (h_1^{ne}, h_2^{ne}, \ldots, h_n^{ne})$;

Theorem 1. *The strategy profile* $h^{ne} = (h_1^{ne}, h_2^{ne}, \ldots, h_n^{ne})$ *computed by Algorithm 1 is a NE of the HD game.*

PROOF 1: From Algorithm 1, we get:

(1) for $i \notin S$, $k_i \geq \dfrac{\sum_{j \in S} k_j}{n_0 - 1}$

(2) $\sum_{j \in S} h_j^{ne} = \dfrac{(|S|-1)P}{\sum_{j \in S} k_j}$

(3) for $i \in S$, $\sum_{j \in S \setminus \{i\}} h_j^{ne} = \dfrac{(|S|-1)^2 P k_i}{\left(\sum_{j \in S} k_j \right)^2}$

There are two cases:

① For $i \notin S$: It is obvious that $k_i \sum_{j \in S \setminus \{i\}} h_j^{ne} = k_i \sum_{j \in S} h_j^{ne}$. Using (1) and (2), we get $k_i \sum_{j \in S \setminus \{i\}} h_j^{ne} \geq P$. According to (3.5), we have $\beta(h_{-i}^{ne}) = 0$. So, it is the best response strategy given h_{-i}^{ne} for $\notin S$.

② For $i \in S$: From the Line 3 of Algorithm 1, we get $(i-1) k_i < \sum_{j=1}^{i} k_j$. Then

$$(n_0 - 1)k_i = (i-1)k_i + (n_0 - i)k_i$$
$$< \sum_{j=1}^{i} k_j + \sum_{j=i}^{n} k_j = \sum_{j=1}^{n} k_j$$

Thus, $k_i < \frac{\sum_{j=1}^{n} k_j}{n_0 - 1}$. Furthermore, using (3) we have

$$k_i \sum_{j \in M \setminus \{i\}} h_j^{ne} = k_i \sum_{j \in S \setminus \{i\}} h_j^{ne} = k_i \frac{(n_0 - 1)^2 P k_i}{\left(\sum_{j \in S} k_j \right)^2} = P \frac{(n_0 - 1)^2 k_i^2}{\left(\sum_{j \in S} k_j \right)^2}$$
$$< P \frac{(n_0 - 1)^2 \left(\frac{\sum_{j \in S} k_j}{n_0 - 1} \right)^2}{\left(\sum_{j \in S} k_j \right)^2} = P$$

Thus, $k_i < \frac{P}{\sum_{j \in M \setminus \{i\}} h_j^{ne}}$. According to (3.5), we have

$$\beta(h_{-i}^{ne}) = \sqrt{\frac{P \sum_{j \in M \setminus \{i\}} h_j}{k_i}} - \sum_{j \in M \setminus \{i\}} h_j = \frac{(n_0 - 1)P}{\sum_{j \in S} h_j} - \frac{(n_0 - 1)^2 P h_i}{\left(\sum_{j \in S} h_j \right)^2} = h_i^{ne}$$

In summary of ① and ②, h^{ne} is an *NE* of *HD* game. ∎

Theorem 2. *The NE in Theorem 1 is unique.*

PROOF 2: First, we assume that there exists one miner $i \in M$ whose $h_i' \neq h_i^{ne}$, but it also satisfies $u_i(h_i', h_{-i}^{ne}) \geq u_i(h_i, h_{-i}^{ne})$ for any $h_i > 0$.

① If $i \notin S$, There must have $h_i' > 0$ for the reason that $h_i' \neq h_i^{ne}$ and $h_i^{ne} = 0$. However, it cannot change the truth that $k_i < \frac{k_i + \sum_{j \in S} k_j}{|S|}$, which means that $k_i \sum_{j \in S \setminus \{i\}} h_j^{ne} \geq P$ (In proof 1). So, its h_i' have to be 0 in order to avoid a deficit. $h_i' = 0$ is contradict with $h_i' > 0$.

② If $i \in S$, reminding that (2.1) is a concave function and it reaches the maximum when $h_i = h_i^{ne}$. So, $u_i(h_i', h_{-i}^{ne}) < u_i(h_i^{ne}, h_{-i}^{ne})$. Which is contradict with $u_i(h_i', h_{-i}^{ne}) \geq u_i(h_i, h_{-i}^{ne})$ for any $h_i > 0$.

In summary of ① and ②, there is no any miner $i \in M$ whose $h_i' \neq h_i^{ne}$, and it still satisfies $u_i(h_i', h_{-i}^{ne}) \geq u_i(h_i, h_{-i}^{ne})$ for any $h_i > 0$.   ∎

3.2 Platform Utility Maximization

According to the above analysis, the platform, which is the leader in the *Stackelberg* game, knows that there exists a unique NE for the miner for any given value of P. Hence the platform can maximize its utility by setting the optimal value of P. Substituting h^{ne} into (2.2), we have

$$u_0 = \frac{X}{A+X} - P \tag{3.6}$$

where $X = \sum_{j \in S} \frac{(|S|-1)P}{\sum_{j \in S} k_j} \left(1 - \frac{(|S|-1)k_i}{\sum_{j \in S} k_j}\right)$, and $X' = \frac{\partial X}{\partial P} = \sum_{j \in S} \frac{(|S|-1)}{\sum_{j \in S} k_j} \left(1 - \frac{(|S|-1)k_i}{\sum_{j \in S} k_j}\right)$.
Obviously, X' is a constant. We use Y to represent X'.

Theorem 3. There exists a unique *Stackelberg* Equilibrium (P^*, h^{ne}) in the Mining game, where P^* is the unique value of P to maximize the platform utility in (3.6) over $P \in [0, \infty)$.

PROOF 3: We have

$$\frac{\partial u_0}{\partial P} = \frac{AY}{(A+X)^2} - 1 \tag{3.7}$$

$$\frac{\partial^2 u_0}{\partial P^2} = -\frac{2AY^2}{(A+X)^3} < 0 \tag{3.8}$$

Therefore the utility u_0 defined in (3.6) is a strictly concave function of P, for any $P \in [0, \infty)$. Since the value of u_0 in (3.6) is 0 if $P = 0$, and goes to $-\infty$ when P goes to ∞, it has a unique maximum value P^* that can be effectively computed using either bisection or Newton's method.   ∎

In the following, we present the analysis, demonstrating that *Mining* game can achieve the desired properties.

Theorem 4. *Mining game is computationally efficient, individually rational, profitable, and has unique Equilibrium.*

PROOF 4: The Sorting in Line 1 can be done in $O(n \log n)$ time. The while-loop (Lines 3–5) requires a total time of $O(n)$. The for-loop (Lines 6–9) requires a total time of $O(n)$. Hence the time complexity of Algorithm 1 is $O(n \log n)$.

The property of individually rational is obvious from (3.3). The property of profitability is also obvious because the pool can always set $P = 0$ in (2.2) to get $u_0 = 0$ (In this case, all miners should set $h_i = 0$ according to (3.5)). This means that u_0 can be at least 0 because the u_0 defined in (3.6) is a strictly concave function of P. The uniqueness of Equilibrium has been proved in Theorem 3.   ∎

4 Performance Evaluation

We consider that the block reward R is 100. The default number of miners in the pool is 100. We assume the cost of each miner subjects to normal distribution or uniform distribution with $\mu = 4.0788 \times 10^{-12}$, which can be estimated from the miners in [7].

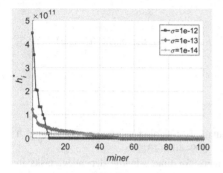

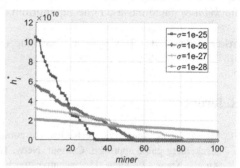

Fig. 2. Hash amount provided by each miner under normal distribution

Fig. 3. Hash amount provided by each miner under uniform distribution

To explore the influence of σ further, we pick some meaningful value of σ and plot Figs. 2 and 3. We find that when σ is not large enough, there is only part of the miners provide hash to the pool, which means that other miners set $h_i = 0$. Second, we find that the larger σ is, the steeper the curve. Extremely, the curve can be a horizontal line when $\sigma = 0$. Third, notice that the unit cost of miners is sorted by $k_1 \leq k_2 \leq \ldots \leq k_n$. We find that miners with lower cost are willing to provide more hash to the pool since the NE computed by Algorithm 1 is a decreasing function with the unit cost. Accordingly, from Fig. 2 we find the miners, who contribute more hash, will be paid more.

5 Related Work

Since launched in 2009, Bitcoin has received lots of attention in the research community. Eyal et al. [8], and Kiayias et al. [9] all focus on the problem called selfish mining in Bitcoin network. Rosenfeld et al. [4], Schrijvers et al. [5], and Lewenberg et al. [6] focus on profit distribution in a mining pool. Eyal et al. [10] focus on improving the protocol of the Bitcoin network. However, there isn't much work taking the cost into consideration.

6 Conclusion

We have proposed a novel pool mining mechanism based on *Stackelberg* game to incentive the rational miners in Bitcoin mining pool. Through both theoretical analysis and simulations, we demonstrate that the proposed mechanism achieves computational efficiency, individual rationality, and profitability. Moreover, we show that the *Stackelberg* game has a unique Equilibrium.

Acknowledgements. This work has been supported in part by the NSFC (No. 61872193, 61872191, 61872197).

References

1. Liu, Y., et al.: Incentive mechanism for computation offloading using edge computing: a Stackelberg game approach. Comput. Netw. **129**, 399–409 (2017)
2. Xu, J., Xiang, J., Yang, D.: Incentive mechanisms for time window dependent tasks in mobile crowdsensing. IEEE Trans. Wireless Commun. **14**(11), 6353–6364 (2015)
3. Xu, J., Rao, Z., Xu, L., et al.: Incentive mechanism for multiple cooperative tasks with compatible users in mobile crowd sensing via online communities. In: IEEE Transactions on Mobile Computing, (2019)
4. Rosenfeld, M.: Analysis of bitcoin pooled mining reward systems. arXiv preprint arXiv: 1112.4980 (2011)
5. Schrijvers, O., Bonneau, J., Boneh, D., Roughgarden, T.: Incentive compatibility of bitcoin mining pool reward functions. In: Grossklags, J., Preneel, B. (eds.) FC 2016. LNCS, vol. 9603, pp. 477–498. Springer, Heidelberg (2017). https://doi.org/10.1007/978-3-662-54970-4_28
6. Lewenberg, Y., et al.: Bitcoin mining pools: a cooperative game theoretic analysis. In: Proceedings of the 2015 International Conference on Autonomous Agents and Multiagent Systems (2015)
7. Btcfans Homepage. http://mining.btcfans.com/. Last accessed 21 Apr 2019
8. Eyal, I., Sirer, E.G.: Majority is not enough: bitcoin mining is vulnerable. Commun. ACM **61**(7), 95–102 (2018)
9. Kiayias, A., Koutsoupias, E., Kyropoulou, M., et al.: Blockchain mining games. In: Proceedings of the 2016 ACM Conference on Economics and Computation, pp. 365–382. ACM (2016)
10. Eyal, I., Gencer, A.E., Sirer, E.G., et al.: Bitcoin-ng: a scalable blockchain protocol. In: 13th Symposium on Networked Systems Design and Implementation, pp. 45–59 (2016)

Automated Ransomware Behavior Analysis: Pattern Extraction and Early Detection

Qian Chen[1(✉)], Sheikh Rabiul Islam[2], Henry Haswell[1], and Robert A. Bridges[3]

[1] Electrical and Computer Engineering Department,
University of Texas at San Antonio, San Antonio, TX, USA
`guenevereqian.chen@utsa.edu, henry.haswell@my.utsa.edu`
[2] Computer Science Department, Tennessee Technological University,
Cookeville, TN, USA
`sislam42@students.tntech.edu`
[3] Computational Sciences and Engineering Division,
Oak Ridge National Laboratory, Oak Ridge, TN, USA
`bridgesra@ornl.gov`

Abstract. Security operation centers (SOCs) typically use a variety of tools to collect large volumes of host logs for detection and forensic of intrusions. Our experience, supported by recent user studies on SOC operators, indicates that operators spend ample time (e.g., hundreds of man hours) on investigations into logs seeking adversarial actions. Similarly, reconfiguration of tools to adapt detectors for future similar attacks is commonplace upon gaining novel insights (e.g., through internal investigation or shared indicators). This paper presents an automated malware pattern-extraction and early detection tool, testing three machine learning approaches: *TF-IDF* (term frequency–inverse document frequency), *Fisher's LDA* (linear discriminant analysis) and *ET* (extra trees/extremely randomized trees) that can (1) analyze freshly discovered malware samples in sandboxes and generate dynamic analysis reports (host logs); (2) automatically extract the sequence of events induced by malware given a large volume of ambient (un-attacked) host logs, and the relatively few logs from hosts that are infected with potentially polymorphic malware; (3) rank the most discriminating features (unique patterns) of malware and from the behavior learned detect malicious activity, and (4) allows operators to visualize the discriminating features and their correlations to facilitate malware forensic efforts.

This manuscript has been authored by UT-Battelle, LLC, under contract DE-AC05-00OR22725 with the US Department of Energy (DOE). The US government retains and the publisher, by accepting the article for publication, acknowledges that the US government retains a nonexclusive, paid-up, irrevocable, worldwide license to publish or reproduce the published form of this manuscript, or allow others to do so, for US government purposes. DOE will provide public access to these results of federally sponsored research in accordance with the DOE Public Access Plan (http://energy.gov/downloads/doe-public-access-plan).".

© Springer Nature Switzerland AG 2019
F. Liu et al. (Eds.): SciSec 2019, LNCS 11933, pp. 199–214, 2019.
https://doi.org/10.1007/978-3-030-34637-9_15

To validate the accuracy and efficiency of our tool, we design three experiments and test seven ransomware attacks (i.e., WannaCry, DBGer, Cerber, Defray, GandCrab, Locky, and nRansom). The experimental results show that *TF-IDF* is the best of the three methods to identify discriminating features, and *ET* is the most time-efficient and robust approach.

1   Introduction

Ransomware, a class of self-propagating malware, uses encryption to hold victim's data and has experienced a 750% increase in frequency in 2018 [1]. Recently, the majority of these ransomware attacks target local governments and small business [2]. For example, the 2018 SamSam ransomware hit the city of Atlanta, encrypted at least one third of users' applications, disrupted the city's vital services [3], and resulted in $17M of remediation to rebuild its computer network [4]. Unlike large multinational businesses, small cities and businesses usually face stricter financial constraints than larger enterprises and struggle to establish or keep pace with cyber defensive technology and adversary/malware advancements. Consequently, they are less capable to defend against cyber threats. More generally, SOC's resource constraints and the shortage of cybersecurity talent [5–7] motivate us to develop an automated tools for SOCs.

Currently, manual investigation of logs is commonplace in SOCs and extremely tedious. E.g., our interaction with SOC operators revealed a 160 man-hour forensic effort to manually analyze a few CryptoWall 3.0 infected hosts' logs [8] with the goal of (a) identifying the adversary/malware actions from user actions in their logs and (b) leveraging learned information to reconfigure tools for timely detection. This motivates our target use case—from SOC-collected logs from an attacked host (esp. a ransomware infection) and non-attack host logs, we seek to automated the (currently manual) process of identifying the attack's actions. In the ransomware case, this should be used to provides a pre-encryption ransomware detector. For testing in a controlled environment, we use "artificial logs", that is, logs obtained by running malware and ambient (emulated user) activities in a sandbox.

Note that this mirrors classical dynamic analysis—(a) performing dynamic malware analysis to (b) extract indicators or signatures—and, hence, dynamic analysis is a second use case. Malware analysis takes considerable time and requires an individual or a team with extensive domain knowledge or reverse engineering expertise. Therefore, malware analysts usually collaborate across industry, university and government to analyze the ransomware attacks that caused disruptive global attacks (e.g., WannaCry). However, the security community has insufficient resources to manually analyze less destructive attacks such as Defray, nRansom and certain versions of Gandcrab. Therefore, manual analysis reports of such malware do not provide enough information for early detection [9–16]. Our approach, regardless of the malware's real-world impacts and potential damages, efficiently help to automate tedious manual analysis by accurately extracting the most discriminating features from large amount of host logs and identifying malicious behavior induced by malware.

While our approach holds promise for more general malware and other attacks, we focus on ransomware. Note that upon the first infection identified in an enterprise, the logs from the affected host can be automatically turned into a detector via our tool. The tool applies three machine learning algorithms, (1) Term Frequency-Inverse Document Frequency (*TF-IDF*), (2) Fisher's Linear Discriminant Analysis (*Fisher's LDA*) and (3) Extra Trees/Extremely Randomized Trees (*ET*) to (a) automatically identify discriminating features of an attack from system logs (generated by an automatic analysis system, namely, Cuckoo Sandbox [17]), and (b) detect future attacks from the same log streams. Using Cuckoo and set scripts for running ransomware and emulated user activity provides source data for experimentation with ground truth. We test the tool using infected system logs of seven disruptive ransomware attacks (i.e., WannaCry, DBGer, Cerber, Defray, GandCrab, Locky, and nRansom) and non-attack logs from emulated user activities, and present experiments varying log quality and quantity to test robustness. These system logs include files, folders, memory, network traffic, processes and API call activities.

Contributions of the pattern-extraction and early detection tool are

1. analyzing ransomware (esp. initial infection) using Cuckoo Sandbox logs (more generally, ambient collected host logs) and generating features from the host behavior reports.
2. extracting the sequence of events (features) induced by ransomware given logs from (a few) hosts that are infected and (a potentially large amount of) ambient logs from presumably uninfected hosts;
3. ranking the most discriminating features (unique patterns) of malware and identifying malicious activity before data is encrypted by the ransomware.
4. creating graph visualizations of ET models to facilitate malware forensic efforts, and allowing operators to visualize discriminating features and their correlations.

We compare outputs with ransomware intelligence reports, and validate that our tool is robust to variations of input data. *TF-IDF* is the best method to identify discriminating features, and *ET* is the most time-efficient approach that achieves an average of 98% accuracy rate to detect the seven ransomware. This work builds on preliminary results of our workshop paper [8], which only considered feature extraction, only used TF-IDF, and only tested with one ransomware.

2 Background and Related Work

Ransomware. In contrast to the 2017 ransomware WannaCry that infected 300K machines across the globe, the majority of ransomware attacks in 2018 and 2019 have been targeting small businesses. These crypto-ransomware attacks usually use Windows API function calls to read, encrypt and delete files. Ransom messages are displayed on the screen after the ransomware infecting the host. This paper selects and analyzes seven recently disruptive ransomware attacks.

1. **WannaCry** *(2017)*, a ransomware with historic world-wide effect, was launched on May 12, 2017 [18]. The WannaCry dropper is a self-contained program consists of three components, an application encrypting and decrypting data; an encryption key file; and a copy of Tor. WannaCry exploits vulnerabilities in Windows Server Message Block (SMB) and propagates malicious code to infect other vulnerable machines on connected networks.

2. **DBGer** *(2018)*, a new variant of the *Satan* ransomware [19], scans the victim local network for vulnerable computers with outdated SMB services. DBGer incorporates a new open-source password-dumping utility, *Mimikatz*, to store credential of vulnearble computers [20]. The dropped Satan file is then executed to encrypt files of the infected computers with AES encryption algorithm. A text file ⎽How⎽to⎽decrypt⎽files.txt containing a note of demands from the attackers is displayed on victim's screen.

3. **Defray** *(2017)*, a ransomware attack targets healthcare, education, manufacturing and technology industries [16]. Defray propagates via phishing emails with an attached *Word* document embedding an *OLE* package object. Once the victim executes the OLE file, the Defray payload is dropped in the %TMP% folder and disguises itself as an legitimate executable (e.g., `taskmgr.exe` or `explorer.exe`). Defray encrypts the file system but does not change file names or extensions. Finally, it deletes volume shadow copies of the encrypted files [15]. Defray developers encourage victims to contact them and negotiate the payment to get the encrypted files back [14].

4. **Locky** *(2016, 2017)* has more than 15 variants. It first appeared in February 2016 to infect Hollywood Presbyterian Medical Center in Los Angeles, California. The ransomware attackers send millions of phishing emails containing attachments of malicious code that can be activated via *Microsoft Word Macros* [11]. Locky encrypts data using RSA-2048 and AES-128 cipher that only the developers can decrypt data. In this research, we analyze the malicious behavior of a new variant of Locky ransomware called *Asasin*, which encrypts and renames the files with a `.asasin` extension.

5. **Cerber** *(2016–2018)* infected 150K Windows computers in July 2016 alone. Several Cerber variants appeared in the following two years have gained widespread distribution globally. Once the Cerber ransonware is deployed in the victim computer, it drops and runs an executable copy with a random name from the hidden folder created in %APPDATA%. The ransomware also creates a link to the malware, changes two Windows Registry keys, and encrypts files and databases offline with `.cerber` extensions [21, 22].

6. **GandCrab** *(2018, 2019)*, a Ransomware-as-a-Service (RaaS) attack has rapidly spread across the globe since January, 2018. GandCrab RaaS online portal was finally shut down in June, 2019. During these 15 months, GandCrab creators regularly updated its code and sold the malicious code, facilitating attackers without the knowledge to write their own ransomware [23]. Attackers then distribute GandCrab ransomware through compromised websites that are built with *WordPress*. The newer versions of GandCrab use *Salsa20* stream cipher to encrypt files offline instead of applying RSA-2048 encryption technique connecting to the C2 server [24]. GandCrab scans

logical drives from A: to Z:, and encrypts files by appending a random Salsa20 key and a random initialization vector (IV) (8 bytes) to the contents of the file. The private key is encrypted in the registry using another Salsa20 key and the IV is encrypted with an RSA public key embedded in the malware. This new encryption method makes GandCrab a very strong ransomware, and the encrypted files can be decrypted by GandCrab creators only [25].

7. **nRansom** *(2017)* blocks the access to the infected computer rather than encrypting victim's data [13]. It demands ten nude photos of the victim instead of digital currency to unlock the computer. As recovery from nRansom is relatively easy, it is not a sophisticated malware but a "test" or a "joke".

Ransomware Pattern Extraction and Detection Works. Homayoun et al. [26] apply sequential pattern mining to find maximal frequency patterns (MSP) of malicious activities of four ransomware attacks. Unlike generating behavioral features directly from host logs, their approach summarizes activity using types of MSPs. Using four machine learning classifiers, the team found that atomic Registry MSPs are the most important sequence of events to detect ransomware attacks with 99% accuracy.

Verma et al. [27] embed host logs into a semantically meaningful metric space. The representation is used to build behavioral signatures of ransomware from host logs exhibiting pre-encryption detection, among other interesting use cases.

Morato et al. introduces REDFISH [28], a ransomware detection algorithm that identifies ransomware actions when it tries to encrypt shared files. RED-FISH is based on the analysis of passively monitored SMB traffic, and uses three parameters of traffic statistics to detect malicious activity. The authors use 19 different ransomware families to test REDFISH, which can detect malicious activity in less than 20 seconds. REDFISH achieves a high detection rate but cannot detect ransomware before it starts to encrypt data. Our approach, discovering ransomware's pre-encryption footprint, promises a more accurate and in-time detection.

The Related Work section our preliminary work [8] includes works published previously to those above. As the more general topic of dynamic analysis is large and diverse, a comprehensive survey is out of scope, but many exist, e.g. [29].

3   Methodology

The proposed approach requires a set of normal (presumably uninfected) system logs and at least one log stream containing ransomware behavior. In this study, the seven ransomware executables introduced in Sect. 2 are deployed inside a realistic but isolated environment with a sandbox tool, Cuckoo [17], for harvesting reproducible and shareable host logs. The Cuckoo host logs are dynamic analysis reports outlining behavior (i.e., API calls, files, registry keys, mutexes), network traffic and dropped files

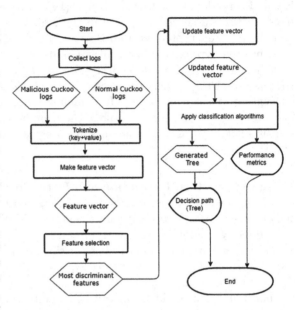

Fig. 1. Flowchart of research methodology

Meanwhile, Cuckoo also captures logs from scripted, emulated normal user activity such as reading and writing of executables, deleting files, opening websites, watching YouTube videos, sending and receiving emails, searching flight tickets, and posting and deleting tweets on Twitter (see [8]). The normal user and the ransomware events/behavior in the raw host logs produced by Cuckoo are then converted to features, and the three machine learning techniques are used to automatically obtain the most discriminating features from normal and ransomware-including logs. Afterwards, we discard the features that have little or no influence, and update the feature vector to reduce the search space of ET decision tree models. The decision tree graphs are created to present the most discriminating features of ransomware attacks. See flowchart in Fig. 1.

3.1   Feature Generation

To build features we only use the *enhanced* category and part of the *behavior* category of Cuckoo-captured logging output. The details of the feature building can be found in our previous work [8]. As malware often uses random names to create files, modules and folders, in this study, we augment paths of specific files to emphasize their names only. For example, C:\\Windows\\system32\\rsaenh.dll is converted to a string "c:..rsaenh.dll". Here, ".." is used as a wild-card to avoid generating duplicated features that represent similar host behavior.

3.2   Discriminating Feature Extraction with Machine Learning

TF-IDF, Fisher's LDA and ET are algorithms used in this research to automatically extract the most discriminating features of ransomware from host logs.

TF-IDF, was defined to identify the relative importance of a word in a particular document out of a collection of documents [30]. Our TF-IDF application follow our previous work for accurate comparison. Given two sets of documents let $f(t, d)$ denote the frequency of term t in document d, and N the size of the corpus. The TF-IDF weight is the product of the Term Frequency, $\mathrm{tf}(t, d) = f_{t,d} / \sum_{t' \in d} f_{t',d}$ (giving the likelihood of t in d) and the Inverse Document Frequency, $\mathrm{idf}(t, D) = \log[N/(1 + |\{d \in D : t \in d\}|)]$ (giving the Shannon's information of the document containing t). Intuitively, given a document, those terms that are uncommonly high frequency in that document are the only terms receive high scores. We use log streams from infected hosts as one set of documents and a set of normal log streams as the other to apply TF-IDF; hence, highly ranked features occur often in (and are guaranteed to occur at least once in) the "infected" document, but infrequently anywhere else [8].

Fisher's LDA is a supervised learning classification algorithm that operates by projecting the input feature vectors to a line that (roughly speaking) maximizes the separation between the two classes [31]. For our application we consider a binary classification where one class (C_1) is comprised of the feature vectors $\{x_i\}_i \subseteq \mathbb{R}^m$ representing host logs that included ransomware, and the second class (C_2) are those vectors of ambient logs. We use this classifier for identifying the discriminating features between the classes. Consider the set $\{v^t x_i : x_i \in C_1 \cup C_2\} \subset \mathbb{R}$, which is the projection of all feature vectors to a line in $\mathbb{R}^m$ defined by unit vector v. Fisher's LDA identifies the unit vector v that maximizes $S(v) := [v^t(\mu_1 - \mu_2)]^2 / [v^t(\Sigma_1 + \Sigma_2)v]$ with μ_j, Σ_j the mean and covariance of $C_j, j = 1, 2$, respectively. $S(v)$ is the squared difference of the projected classes' means divided by the sum of the projected classes' variances. It is an exercise in linear algebra to see the optimal $v \propto (\Sigma_1 + \Sigma_2)^{-1}(\mu_1 - \mu_2)$. Geometrically, v can be thought of as a unit vector pointing from C_1 to C_2; hence, ranking the components of v by absolute values sorts the features that most discriminate the ransomware and normal activity.

Extremely Randomized Trees (ET) is a tree-based ensemble algorithm for supervised classification and regression. "It consists of randomizing strongly both attribute and cut point choice while splitting the tree node" [32]. In the extreme case, the algorithm provides "totally randomized trees whose structures are independent of the output values of the learning sample" [32,33]. The randomization introduces increased bias and variance of individual trees. However, the effect on variance can be ignored when the results are averaged over a large ensemble of trees. This approach is tolerant with respect to over-smoothed (biased) class probability estimates [32]. See the cited works for details.

4 Experimental Results

Experiment One: Extracting Discriminating Features from Host Logs.
This experiment applies the machine learning approaches to extract the most discriminating features/behavior of each ransomware attack. In addition to obtaining a Cuckoo analysis report (raw behavior log) for each ransomware sample, Python scripts immitating various users' normal activities (such as reading, writing and deleting files, opening websites, etc.) are submitted to the Cuckoo sandbox to generate a large volume of normal reports.

Table 1 illustrates the most discriminating features of the seven ransomware attacks. The first column of the table (#) lists the name of seven ransomware. The second column (*Pattern*) presents the pre-encryption patterns (activities) of each ransomware attack obtained from the detailed ransomware technical (static) analysis produced by cybersecurity companies (e.g., FireEye [34]), security help websites (e.g., Bleeping Computer [35, 36]) and malware research teams (e.g., The Cylance Threat Research [16]). The third column (*Feature*) presents the features extracted from the host logs using the proposed approaches that match the unique patterns of rasomware attacks. The last column (*Rank*) lists the TF-IDF, Fisher's LDA and ET rankings of the features that represent the unique patterns of the seven ransomware attacks. The features that have the largest TF-IDF and Fisher's LDA scores, or the non-leaf nodes (features) of the Extremely Randomized Trees that have smallest levels, are top-ranked discriminating features. For the ET algorithm, the features that are at the top of the tree contribute more to correctly classifying a larger portion of input logs. E.g., a feature with rank = 1 is one of the most indicative feature of the malware according to that algorithm. Ties are possible as the scores may be the same between multiple features. We use the rankings of these features to evaluate the efficiency of the proposed three machine learning methods. The methods that provide higher rankings of the selected features are more efficient than the approaches that yield a lower rank of the same feature.

We set a large `class_weight` parameter for the target class in *ExtraTreesClassifier* of Python's *Scikit-Learn* library to make the ET classifier biased to learn the pattern of malicious logs more meticulously. Therefore, some features representing the ransomware patterns are not selected as the nodes to compose the tree. In this scenario, we use "NA" to present the rankings of the feature that are not nodes in the tree. Details are elaborated by ransomware:

1. **WannaCry:** The six patterns of WannaCry before the attack encrypting data are presented in Table 1. All of these patterns can find WannaCry-generated features from the host logs. A total of 1, 207 unique features have been extracted from host logs containing both normal and abnormal behavior, while only a small portion are resulting from WannaCry actions. The experimental results indicate that TF-IDF is better than the other two methods for identifying WannaCry's behaviors. The rankings generated by the ET classifier are slightly lower than the TF-IDF's. However, ET is more time efficient for extracting the most discriminating features from large volume of host logs,

Table 1. The most discriminating features of the seven ransomware attacks

#	Pre-Encryption Pattern	Feature	Rank		
			TF-IDF	LDA	ET
1. WannaCry	1. Import CryptoAPI from advpi32.dll	data_file+'advapi32.dll'+event+'load'+object+'library'	3	294	6
	2. Unzips itself to .wrny files	*.wrny	1	176	1
	3. Creates a registry, HKEY_LOCAL_MACHINE\ Software\WanaCrypt0r\wd	api+'regcreatekeyexw'+arguments_1_value+'33554432' +category+'registry' (subkey="Software\\WanaCrypt0r")	6	177	NA
	4. Run 'attrib +h', to set the current directory as a hidden folder	data_file+'attrib +h .'+event+'execute'+object+'file'	6	298	11
	5. Run 'icacls . /grant Everyone:F /T /C /Q' to grant user permissions to the current directory	data_file+'icacls . . .q'+event+'execute'+object+'file'	6	298	11
	6. Import public and private RSA AES keys (000.pky, 000.eky) from t.wrny	data_file+'c:..00000000.pky'+event+'write'+object+'file'	6	298	11
2. DBGer	1. Drop ExternalBlue files at 'C:\Users\All Users\'	data_file+'c:..users'+event+'create'+object+'dir', data_file+'c:..allusers'+event+'create'+object+'dir', data_file+'c:..blue.exe'+event+'write'+object+'file', ... **22 various dropped file features...** data_file+'c:.. satan.exe' +event+'write'+object+'file', data_file+'c:..mmkt.exe'+event+'write'+object+'file'	9	125	11, 12
	2. Drop satan.exe on C drive and execute the file for encryption	data_file+'c:..satan.exe'+event+'write'+object+'file', data_file+'c:..satan.exe'+event+'execute'+object+'file'	9	125	11, 12
	3. Drop "KSession" file at %Temp%	data_file+'c:..ksession'+event+'write'+object+'file'	9	125	11
3. Defray	1. Import/Load Microsoft OLE from "ole32.dll"	data_file+'ole32.dll'+event+'load'+object+'library'	9	10	9
	2. Drop and execute "explorer.exe"	data_file+'explorer.exe'+event+'load'+object+'library'	17	93	NA
	3. Call ShellExecute to run as more privileged user to disable startup recovery and delete volume shadow copies	data_file+'c:..-hibernate-timeout-dc0'+event+'execute' +object+'file'	17	121	NA
4. Locky	1. Read and write 'PIPE\\wkssvc' and 'PIPE\lsarpc'	data_file+'pipe..wkssvc'+event+'write'('read')+object+'file', data_file+'pipe..lsarpc'+event+'write'('read')+object+'file'	2 7	72 408	2 7
	2. Read network provider name	data_regkey+'hkey_local_machine.. networkprovidername'+event+'read'+object+'registry'	3	186	3
	3. Read the path to the network provider .dll file	data_regkey+'hkey_local_machine.. systworkproviderproviderpath'+event+'read'+object+'registry'	4	171	4
	4. Load the network provider 'ntlanman.dll' file	data_file+'c:..ntlanman.dll'+event+'load'+object+'library'	4	130	4
	5. Obtain the name ty Identifier	data_regkey+'hkey_users..s-1-5-21-1966058-1343024091 -1003name'+event+'read'+object+'registry'	5	408	5
5. Cerber	1. Create two .tmp files under a random folder	- ent+'write'+object+'file' c. data_file+'c:..5572.tmp'+event+'write'+object+'file'	10	a.105 b.230 c.230	a.10 b.10 c.11
	2. Find users profiles and read the	- rofilesdirectory'+event+'read'+object+'registry' b.data_regkey+'hkey_local_machine.. softlelistdefaultuserprofile'+even - - hine.. softs-1-5-18profileimagepath' +event+'read'+ob	a.5 b.5 c.7 d.7	a.111 b.111 c.150 d.150	a.5 b.5 c.7 d.7
	3. Read and load "rsaenh.dll"	- fileimagepath +event+'read'+object+'registry' a. data_regkey+'hkey_local_machine.. softaphic provid t+'read'+object+'registry' b. data_file+'c:..rsaenh.dll' +event+'write'+object+'file' c. data_file+'c:..rsaenh.dll'+event+'load'+object+'file'	a.3 b.1 c.6	a.79 b.15 c.119	a.3 b.1 c.6
	4. Obtain M	data_regkey+'hkey_local_machine.. cryptographymachineguid'+event+'read'+ob			
7. nRansomware	nformation a. computer name b. session manager name c. domain name d. processor typ	name'+event+'read'+object+'registry' b.data_regkey+'hkey_local_machine..sessionmanagername' +event+'read'+object+'registry' c. data_regkey+'hkey_local_machine..parametersdomain' +event+'read'+object+'registry' d.1 data_regkey+'hkey_local_ t+'read'+object+'registry' d.2 data_regkey+'hkey_local_machine..0identifier' +event+'read'+object+'registry' d.3 data_regkey+'hkey_local_machine.. systgersafeprocessearc d'+object+'registry'	a.1 b.6 c.7 d.7	a.276 b.430 c.431 d.431	a.1 b.8 c.10 d.9
	2. Copy the ransomware .exe file to %APPDATA%/Microsoft and ad unOnce key	a. data_file+'c:..lrcjty.exe'+event+'write'+object+'file' b. data_content+'..x00'+data_object+'n - +event+'write'+object+'registry'	7	431	a. 9 b.10
	1. Create temprary directory in \%TEMP%\1.tmp\ tools\	data_file+'c:..tools'+event+'**create**'+object+'**dir**'	5	32	5
	2. Download and write following files: a ransom.exe) b. a media control file (i.e.,interop.wmplib. le (i.e., your-mom-gay.mp3)	a.data_file+'c:..**nransom.exe**'+event+'**write**'+object+'file' b.data_file+'c:..**interop.wmplib.dll**'+event+'**write**'+object+'file' c. -			a.4 b.4 c.4
	3. Execute the executable (i.e., nransom.exe) using comma	- '**execute**'+object+'file' b. data_file+'c:..**cmd**'+event+'**execute**'+object+'file'	a.6 b.6	a.60 b.60	a.7 b.6
	4. Play the looped song using the downloaded audio file (i.e., your-mom-g				
	orary folders with the downloaded files	data_file+'c:..**1.tmp**'+event+'**delete**'+object+'dir' +object+'file'	6	60	6

which requires only 215 features (nodes) to make decisions (i.e., WannaCry or Normal). Therefore, the results suggest using TF-IDF to analyze the few infected hosts' logs in an attempt to produce shareable threat intelligence reports and using the ET algorithm to obtain pre-encryption detection capabilities. This experiment also illustrates that the top-ranked features generated by Fisher's LDA are quite different from the other two techniques. Most of the top-ranked features are normal activities. Features representing WannaCry's patterns are listed as low as #200. Additionally, we notice that the loading and reading events of the *rsaenh.dll* module are ranked highly (i.e., #2 and #4 for TF-IDF and #3 and #8 for ET). The module implements the Microsoft enhanced cryptographic service provider for WannaCry to encrypt the victim's data with 128-bit RSA encryption. These two top ranked features are not listed in our table, as they are not discriminating features to identify WannaCry attacks from other crypto-ransomware attacks.

2. **DBGer:** The three unique patterns of DBGer ransomware reported by [37] are presented in Table 1. `dbger.exe`, the mother file of DBGer, first creates the `C:\Users\AllUsers` folder, drops *EternalBlue* and *Mimikatz* executables in the new folder, and then saves *satan.exe* into the *C* drive. A file named `KSession` is dropped to `C:\Windows\Temp\` for storing the host ID. TF-IDF and Fisher's LDA rank $1,104$ features generated from normal and DBGer Cuckoo reports. The ET classifier builds the decision tree using 216 of the 1104 features. The three DBGer features are ranked highly. TF-IDF yields a highest ranking of the three features, which is better than the other two methods. ET is more time efficient. However, there are many features ranked higher than the ranking of the three features, but they are normal activity. E.g., dynamic link library (DLL) files `kernel32.dll` and `advapi.dll` are on the top of the three rankings, but are not discriminating features for DBGer.

3. **Defray:** The three unique patterns of Defray are loading the *ole32.dll* file, dropping and executing the ransomware executable file *explorer.exe*, and executing a shell command. The three machine algorithms rank the first feature "loading the ole32.dll file" #9 among the total $1,243$ features. As Defray's executable file is disguised as a Windows Internet Explorer, all of the three methods struggle to distinguish it from the normal activities. The second feature therefore is not selected to build the ET model, and its TF-IDF and Fisher's LDA weights are much lower than the first feature's. The three machine learning approaches rank another three features (as shown in Table 2) highest among the 1243 features. These features represent unique malicious activities performed by Defray, thus, they are discriminating features to distinguish Defray from other ransomware. However, none of these three patterns are discussed in Defray manual analysis reports [14–16].

4. **Locky:** We execute *Asasin Locky*, a 2017 variant of Locky ransomware in the Cuckoo sandbox, collect and analyze its behavior using our tool. The static analysis reports [9,11] indicate that after being deployed, Locky's executable file disappears. Its dropped copy `svchost.exe` is executed from the `%TEMP%` folder. However, our tool generates features from the behavior logs and presents that Asasin Locky does not drop the executable file.

Instead, the attack modifies the workstation services \PIPE\wkssvc launched by the svchost.exe process. As a member of the Cryptowall family, Asasin Locky also modifies PIPE\lsarpc, a file communicates with the Local Security Authority subsystem [38]. The attack then reads network provider name and the path to the Network Provider DLL file from registry by loading the network provider ntlanman.dll. Registry is retrieved by Asasin Locky to obtain the name of the Security Identifier. TF-IDF and ET provides the same and higher rankings for these five features from a total 1,047 normal and ransomware features. These two methods both rank rsaenh.dll as the top feature; however, this feature is not a unique pattern for Asasin Locky.

5. **Cerber:** This ransomware copies itself as cerber.exe to the hidden %APPDATA% folder, creates a directory with a random name, and drops two .tmp files [10]. Cerber also escalates its privilege to admin level and reads profiles from the users' profile image paths. Afterwards, Cerber finds the image path of rsaenh.dll, reads and loads the DLL file to encrypt data. Cerber obtains the Machine GUID (globally unique identifier) and uses its fourth part as the encrypted files' extension. The Cerber sample tested has an extension of 93ff. The three methods rank the total 1,137 features. ET selects 145 features to composes the decision tree. TF-IDF and ET provides similar and higher rankings of the discriminating features than Fisher's LDA's.

6. **GandCrab:** This experiment uses Gandcrab V2.3.1, a variant that scans the victim machine and collects information of user name, domain name, computer name, session manager name and processor type [12]. The execution is terminated if the ransomware finds the system language is Russian or the victim machine installed specific anti-virus (AV) software. Otherwise, it copies the executable file into %APPDATA%/Microsoft and adds an entry of the copied executable file path to the RunOnce key as a one-time persistence mechanism. GandCrab then decrypts the ransom notes and generate RSA keys for encryption. After encrypting data, the malware uses Windows' NSLOOKUP tool to (1) find IP address of the GandCrab's C2 (command and control) server; and (2) communicate with the C2 server (i.e., sending information collected from the victim's machines to the C2 server and/or receiving commands from the C2 server). Table 1 presents two unique pre-encryption patterns of Gand-Crab V2.3.1. TF-IDF and ET rank them highly among 1,017 features. The rankings of these features are much lower by Fisher's LDA.

7. **nRansom:** This attack first creates a subfolder in %TEMP% with a random name ended with .tmp. In our experiment, the subfolder is named 1.tmp. nRansom drops an executable file (i.e., nransom.exe) and two Windows Media Player control library files (i.e., Interop.WMPLib.dll and AxInterop.WMPLib.dll) in 1.tmp. An audio file your-mom-gay.mp3 is dropped in 1.tmp Tools. Then nransom.exe is executed through the command prompt cmd.exe. After locking the victim's computer screen, nRansom plays a looped song from the dropped mp3 file, and deletes the subfolders and dropped files. TF-IDF and ET both rank the five discriminating features of nRansom highly among 1046 features. 55 features are used for composing ET.

Table 2. Static analysis missed unique patterns and their behavioral features

#	Pattern	Feature
Defray	1. Read *CliEgAliases.mof* and *Cli.mof* from C:\WINDOWS\System32\Wbem	data_file+'c:..cliegaliases.mof' +event+'read'+object+'file' data_file+'c:..cliegaliases.mfl'+event+'read'+object+'file'
	2. Read/write temporary files (tmp1-tmp3.tmp) in %TMP% folder	data_file+'c:..tmp2.tmp'+event+'write'+object+'file' data_file+'c:..tmp2.tmp'+event+'read'+object+'file'
	3. Read registries to obtain the infected host's host name, domain and active computer name	data_regkey+'hkey_local_machine..parametershostname'+event+'read'+object+'registry' data_regkey+'hkey_local_machine..parametersdomain'+event+'read'+object+'registry' data_regkey+'activecomputernamecomputername'+event+'read'+object+'registry'
Locky	Embedding object created in one application into another application (e.g., embedding an excel file inside a word)	data_file+'ole32.dll'+event+'load'+object+'library'
Cerber	Embedding object created in one application into another application (e.g., embedding an excel file inside a word file).	data_file+'ole32.dll'+event+'load'+object+'library'
Gandcrab	1. Import CryptoAPI from advpi32.dll	data_file+'advapi32.dll'+event+'load'+object+'library'
	2. Control certain API functions of windows shell	data_file+'shell32.dll'+event+'load'+object+'library'
	3. Implements certificate and cryptographic messaging functions	data_file+'crypt32.dll'+event+'load'+object+'library'
nRansom	1. Read the batch file that executes commands with windows command prompt (i.e., cmd.exe)	data_file+'c:..2.bat'+event+'read'+object+'file'
	2. Control Windows Media Player	data_file+'c:..axinterop.wmplib.dll'+event+'write'+object+'file'
	3. Load the "uxtheme.dll" library	data_file+'uxtheme.dll'+event+'load'+object+'library'

Ransomware Unique Patterns Missed from Manual Analysis. As discussed above, besides the patterns obtained from Defray's threat intelligence reports, the three features shown in Table 2 are also unique behavior to distinguish Defray attacks. From the dynamic analysis provided by our methodology, we also found that many ransomware attacks have similar patterns. For example, Defray, Locky and Cerber all conduct an event to load the ole32.dll file. However, neither Locky nor Cerber's static analysis have mentioned this pattern. Similarly, manual analysis of GandCrab does not discuss the malware sample has imported CryptoAPI from advapi32.dll, which is also a discriminating feature of WannaCry attacks. Thus, our tool provides automated—more efficient and without reliance on security experts—and better quality malware behavior analysis.

Table 3. WannaCry discriminating feature ranking with varying normal data

TF-IDF				LDA				ET			
Feature	Rank			Feature	Rank			Feature	Rank		
	C1	C2	C3		C1	C2	C3		C1	C2	C3
*.wnry	1	1	1	api+'ntreadfile'+arguments_1_value+ '0x0000018c'+category+'filesystem'	1	1	1	*.wnry	1	1	1
data_file+'c:..rsaenh.dll'+event+'read'+object+'file'	2	2	2	api+'regclosekey'+category+'registry'	2	5	5	api+'ntwritefile'+arguments_1_valu e+'0x00000080'+category+..	2	2	2
data_file+'advapi32.dll'+event+'load'+object+'library'	3	3	3	api+'findfirstfileexw'+category+'files ystem'	3	2	2	data_file+'c:..rsaenh.dll'+event+'re ad'+object+'file'	3	3	3
data_file+'kernel32.dll'+event+'load'+object+'library'	4	4	4	api+'ntqueryinformationfile'+argume nts_1_value+'..x00'+..	4	6	6	api+'ntreadfile'+arguments_1_value +'0x00000090'+category+'filesystem'	4	4	4
data_regkey+'hkey_users..+event+'read'+object+'registry'	5	5	5	api+'ntreadfile'+arguments_1_value+ '0x0000009c'+category+'filesystem'	5	7	7	api+'ntreadfile'+arguments_1..+cate gory+'filesystem'	5	5	5
data_regkey+'hkey_local_machine ..softer (prototype)image path'+event+'read'+object+'registry	6	6	6	api+'ntreadfile'+arguments_1_value+ '0x00000188'+category+'filesystem'	6	16	15	api+'ntdeviceiocontrolfile'+argumen ts_1_value+'0x00000090'+category +'filesystem'	6	6	6
data_file+'rsaenh.dll'+event+'load'+object+'library'	7	7	7	api+'ntreadfile'+arguments_1_value+ '0x00000178'+category+'filesystem'	7	15	16	data_regkey+'hkey_users..+event+'read'+object+'registry'	7	7	7
data_regkey+'activecomputername computername'+event+'read'+object+'registry'	8	12	12	api+'ntreadfile'+arguments_1_value+ '0x0000017c'+category+'filesystem'	8	18	18	data_regkey+'hkey_local_machine.. softer (prototype)image path'+event+'read'+object+'registry'	8	8	8
data_file+'c:..taskdl.exe'+event+'write'+object+'file'	9	9	9	api+'regqueryvalueexw'+arguments_ 1_value+'0'+category+'registry'	9	14	14	data_file+'kernel32.dll'+event+'load'+object+'library'	9	9	9
data_file+'c:..taskse.exe'+event+'write'+object+'file'	10	10	10	api+'regopenkeyexa'+arguments1_va lue+'0x000000a4'+category+'registry	10	19	19	data_file+'advapi32.dll'+event+'load'+object+'library'	10	10	10

Experiment Two: Ransomware Feature Rankings with Varying Normal Activities. This experiment aims to validate that the rankings of the seven ransomware discriminating features are not influenced by varying the number of normal logs. To validate the hypothesis, we calculate the TF-IDF, Fisher's LDA and ET weights of the ransomware features in the following three scenarios.

- Case 1 (C1): Using Experiment One's normal logs as the baseline.
- Case 2 (C2): Adding 30% additional new normal host logs into training data.
- Case 3 (C3): Adding 60% more new normal host logs into training data.

Table 3 presents the top ten features of WannaCry that are calculated by the three machine learning methods when the ambient logging data are different. The experimental results present that the ET method is robust to provide the same rankings of the top ten features under the three tested scenarios. TF-IDF is less robust than ET, but Fisher's LDA provides completely different rankings of the top ten features in three different scenarios. Similar results were found when analyzing the top-ranked features of the other six ransomware attacks. Therefore, the ET algorithm is more robust to varying training data containing different quality and quantity of normal activity.

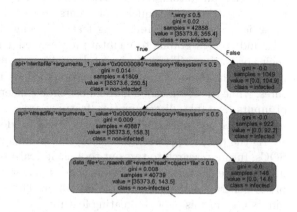

Fig. 2. Decision path based on the training logs showing how the most discriminating features are correlated in the decision making process.

Experiment Three: Ransomware Early Detection. The ET decision tree classifier is applied to detect the seven ransomware before encryption from a large majority of non-malicious activity. Table 4 presents the detection rate of the seven ransomware attacks. Note that while recall varies, meaning the method

Table 4. ET early detection results

Ransomware	Accuracy	Precision	Recall	F-Score
WannaCry	0.918	1	0.717	0.835
DBGer	0.987	1	0.308	0.471
Defray	0.994	1	0.992	0.996
Locky	0.997	1	0.806	0.893
Cerber	0.987	1	0.505	0.671
GandCrab	0.999	1	0.997	0.999
nRansom	0.994	1	0.382	0.553

produces false negatives, precision is always perfect, meaning there are no false positives. In terms of overall performance metrics, the detection model Gandcrab performs the best and DBGer performs the worst. We also create graphs of each decision tree to better interpret and visualize the detection results. Using WannaCry attack as an example, Fig. 2 displays first three levels of the decision tree. The brown non-leaf nodes (rectangular boxes) represent the features of normal activity and the blue non-leaf nodes represent features induced by WannaCry.

By retrieving the blue nodes on the top of the decision tree, we can identify WannaCry's discriminating features. The correlation coefficients of these features are provided in non-leaf boxes. The graphs facilitate malware forensics analysis and allow operators to visualize disruptive activity and determine the damages induced by the malware for proposing an optimal protection and response plan.

5   Conclusion

We develop an automated ransomware pattern-extraction and early detection tool that extracts the sequence of events induced by seven ransomware attacks, identifies the most discriminating features using three machine learning methods, and creates graphs to facilitate forensic efforts by visualizing features and their correlations. The experimental results present that TF-IDF feature ranking yields the most accurate identification of the ransomware-discriminating features, while the ET method is the most time efficient and robust to the variation of inputs. Notable, discriminating features are automatically promoted by this method that malware analysis reports failed to identify.

As the target application is using this to analyze real host logs collected by SOCs, future research to test our tool using real-world host-based data captured in enterprise networks to determine conditions for success. Moreover, large enterprises generate large volumes of host data. The offline machine learning techniques used in this paper—creating features from host logs, determining malware discriminating features and detecting attacks—may not scale. Future research using online machine learning technique (e.g., incremental decision tree) and deep learning methods (e.g., LSTMs) can enhance the tool.

Acknowledgements. Special thanks to the reviewers that helped polish this document, including Michael Iannacone. Research sponsored by the Laboratory Directed Research and Development Program of Oak Ridge National Laboratory, managed by UT-Battelle, LLC, for the U. S. Department of Energy, and by the National Science Foundation under Grant No.1812599. Any opinions, findings, and conclusions or recommendations expressed in this material are those of the authors and do not necessarily reflect the views of the National Science Foundation.

References

1. Davis, J.: 71% of ransomware attacks targeted small businesses in 2018, March 2019.   https://healthitsecurity.com/news/71-of-ransomware-attacks-targeted-small-businesses-in-2018
2. Dobran, B.: Definitive guide for preventing and detecting ransomware (2019). https://phoenixnap.com/blog/preventing-detecting-ransomware-attacks
3. Freed, B.: One year after atlanta's ransomware attack, the city says it's transforming its technology (2019). https://statescoop.com/one-year-after-atlantas-ransomware-attack-the-city-says-its-transforming-its-technology/
4. Olenick, D.: Atlanta ransomware recovery cost now at $17 million, reports say (2018). https://www.scmagazine.com/home/security-news/ransomware/atlanta-ransomware-recovery-cost-now-at-17-million-reports-say/

5. Bridges, R.A., Iannacone, M.D., Goodall, J.R., Beaver, J.M.: How do information security workers use host data? A summary of interviews with security analysts. arXiv preprint 1812.02867 (2018)

6. Goodall, J., Lutters, W., Komlodi, A.: The work of intrusion detection: rethinking the role of security analysts. In: AMCIS 2004 Proceedings, p. 179 (2004)

7. Werlinger, R., Muldner, K., Hawkey, K., Beznosov, K.: Preparation, detection, and analysis: the diagnostic work of it security incident response. Inf. Manag. Comput. Secur. **18**(1), 26–42 (2010)

8. Chen, Q., Bridges, R.A.: Automated behavioral analysis of malware: a case study of WannaCry ransomware. In: 2017 16th IEEE International Conference on Machine Learning and Applications (ICMLA), pp. 454–460, December 2017

9. Malwarebytes LABS: Look into locky ransomware, July 2016. https://blog.malwarebytes.com/threat-analysis/2016/03/look-into-locky/

10. Gao, W.: Dissecting Cerber ransomware, July 2017. https://www.ixiacom.com/company/blog/dissecting-cerber-ransomware

11. Doevan, J.: Locky virus, how to remove (2018). https://www.2-spyware.com/remove-locky-virus.html

12. Cisco's Talos Intelligence Group Blog: Gandcrab Ransomware Walks its Way onto Compromised Sites (2018). https://blog.talosintelligence.com/2018/05/gandcrab-compromised-sites.html. Accessed 25 Aug 2018

13. This Ransomware Demands Nude instead of Bitcoin - Motherboard (2017). https://motherboard.vice.com/en_us/article/yw3w47/this-ransomware-demands-nudes-instead-of-bitcoin. Accessed 24 Aug 2018

14. Defray ransomware sets sights on healthcare and other industries, August 2017. https://www.trendmicro.com/vinfo/us/security/news/cyber-attacks/defray-ransomware-sets-sights-on-healthcare-and-other-industries

15. Crowe, J.: Alert: Defray ransomware launching extremely personalized attacks, August 2017. https://blog.barkly.com/defray-ransomware-highly-targeted-campaigns

16. Threat Spotlight: Defray Ransomeware Hits Healthcare and Education (2017). https://threatvector.cylance.com/en_us/home/threat-spotlight-defray-ransomware-hits-healthcare-and-education.html. Accessed 16 Aug 2018

17. Cuckoo Sandbox - Automated Malware Analysis. https://cuckoosandbox.org/. Accessed 26 Aug 2018

18. Perlroth, N.: Boeing possibly hit by 'WannaCry' malware attack, March 2018. https://www.nytimes.com/2018/03/28/technology/boeing-wannacry-malware.html

19. Lemos, R.: Satan ransomware adds more evil tricks, May 2019. www.darkreading.com/vulnerabilities---threats/satan-ransomware-adds-more-evil-tricks/d/d-id/1334779

20. Cimpanu, C.: DBGer ransomware uses EternalBlue and Mimikatz to spread across networks (2018). https://www.bleepingcomputer.com/news/security/dbger-ransomware-uses-eternalblue-and-mimikatz-to-spread-across-networks/

21. Barkly Research: Cerber ransomware: everything you need to know, March 2017. https://blog.barkly.com/cerber-ransomware-statistics-2017

22. Malwarebytes LABS: Cerber ransomware: new, but mature, June 2018. https://blog.malwarebytes.com/threat-analysis/2016/03/cerber-ransomware-new-but-mature/

23. Tiwari, R.: Evolution of GandCrab ransomware, April 2018. https://www.acronis.com/en-us/articles/gandcrab/

24. Salvio, J.: GandCrab V4.0 analysis: new shell, same old menace (2018). https://www.fortinet.com/blog/threat-research/gandcrab-v4-0-analysis-new-shell-same-old-menace.html

25. Mundo, A.: GandCrab ransomware puts the pinch on victims, July 2018. https://securingtomorrow.mcafee.com/mcafee-labs/gandcrab-ransomware-puts-the-pinch-on-victims/

26. Homayoun, S., Dehghantanha, A., Ahmadzadeh, M., Hashemi, S., Khayami, R.: Know abnormal, find evil: frequent pattern mining for ransomware threat hunting and intelligence. IEEE Trans. Emerg. Top. Comput. (2019)

27. Verma, M.E., Bridges, R.A.: Defining a metric space of host logs and operational use cases. In: 2018 IEEE International Conference on Big Data (Big Data), pp. 5068–5077, December 2018

28. Morato, D., Berrueta, E., Magaña, E., Izal, M.: Ransomware early detection by the analysis of file sharing traffic. J. Netw. Comput. Appl. **124**, 14–32 (2018)

29. Egele, M., et al.: A survey on automated dynamic malware-analysis techniques and tools. ACM Comput. Surv. (CSUR) **44**(2), 6 (2012)

30. Salton, G., Buckley, C.: Term-weighting approaches in automatic text retrieval. Inf. Process. Manag. **24**(5), 513–523 (1988)

31. Welling, M.: Fisher linear discriminant analysis. Department of Computer Science, University of Toronto, vol. 3, no. 1 (2005)

32. Geurts, P., Ernst, D., Wehenkel, L.: Extremely randomized trees. Mach. Learn. **63**(1), 3–42 (2006)

33. Islam, S.R., Eberle, W., Ghafoor, S.K.: Credit default mining using combined machine learning and heuristic approach. In: Proceedings of the 2018 International Conference on Data Science (ICDATA), pp. 16–22. ACSE (2018)

34. Wannacry Malware Profile - FireEye (2017). https://www.fireeye.com/blog/threat-research/2017/05/wannacry-malware-profile.html. Accessed 10 Aug 2018

35. DBGer Ransomware Uses EternalBlue and Mimikatz to Spread Across Networks (2017). https://www.bleepingcomputer.com/news/security/dbger-ransomware-uses-eternalblue-and-mimikatz-to-spread-across-networks/. Accessed 10 Aug 2018

36. Locky Ransomware Switches to the Asasin Extension via Broken Spam Campaign (2017). https://www.bleepingcomputer.com/news/security/locky-ransomware-switches-to-the-asasin-extension-via-broken-spam-campaigns/. Accessed 21 Aug 2018

37. Munde, S.: Satan ransomware raises its head again! June 2018. https://blogs.quickheal.com/satan-ransomware-raises-head/

38. Monika, Zavarsky, P., Lindskog, D.: Experimental analysis of ransomware on Windows and Android platforms: evolution and characterization. Procedia Comput. Sci. **94**, 465–472 (2016)

Behavior Flow Graph Construction from System Logs for Anomaly Analysis

Hang Ling[1], Jing Han[2], Jiayi Pang[1], Jianwei Liu[2], Jia Xu[1],
and Zheng Liu[1(✉)]

[1] Nanjing University of Posts and Telecommunications, Nanjing, China
{1217043023,b16041505,xujia,zliu}@njupt.edu.cn
[2] ZTE Corporation, Shenzhen, China
{han.jing28,liu.jianweizp}@zte.com.cn

Abstract. Anomaly analysis plays a significant role in building a secure and reliable system. Raw system logs contain important system information, such as execution paths and execution time. People often use system logs for fault diagnosis and root cause localization. However, due to the complexity of raw system logs, these tasks can be arduous and ineffective. To solve this problem, we propose ETGC (Event Topology Graph Construction), a method for mining event topology graph of the normal execution status of systems. ETGC mines the dependency relationship between events and generates the event topology graph based on the maximum spanning tree. We evaluate the proposed method on data sets of real systems to demonstrate the effectiveness of our approach.

Keywords: Event topology graph · System logs · Anomaly detection · Maximum spanning tree

1 Introduction

Systems in business giants such as Google and Amazon generate tens of billions of logs every day. Numerous system logs are of great value in various application fields, and one application domain is to extract valuable knowledge from these system logs for building secure systems [4]. System logs reveal various event characteristics at critical moments, and they contain essential information concerning the operating status of the system, such as the execution traces [9]. Such system logs are the universally available resource among almost all computer systems, which is essential for understanding the overview system status.

Anomaly analysis is indispensable to establish a secure and reliable system. With the rapid iteration of the system version, the system is suffering from cyber-attacks increasingly. However, relying solely on the experience of engineers and domain experts is undoubtedly inefficient and inaccurate. Therefore, log analysis has always been a hot topic in the field of system operation and maintenance, especially in the detection of anomaly events [2,8].

Existing approaches that leverage system logs for anomaly detection can be grouped into two categories: feature-based and workflow-based. Feature-based

© Springer Nature Switzerland AG 2019
F. Liu et al. (Eds.): SciSec 2019, LNCS 11933, pp. 215–223, 2019.
https://doi.org/10.1007/978-3-030-34637-9_16

methods construct feature vectors from system logs and employ Principal Component Analysis (PCA) for anomaly detection [6,11]. Workflow-based approaches build the execution flow graphs based on system logs from normal executions [3,5,12]. Cloudseer [12] models workflow automata by repeating executions of one single task, which analyzes dependencies between events. Tong et al. propose an approach called Logsed [3], which mines the control flow graphs with time weights from operational logs and transaction logs. However, it is a critical task to extract workflow graphs from massive logs.

By carefully considering the characteristics of system logs, we have the following observations: (1) The log format varies with different system platforms, which is usually unstructured. Therefore, it is a challenging task to parse a considerable amount system log accurately and convert them into events. (2) The sequential information of log messages is essential for problem diagnosis. Modern cloud computing platforms execute tasks in parallel and system logs printed by the terminal are often intertwined. Even a single task can perform asynchronous operations which could cause interleaved logs.

The main contributions of this paper are summarized below:

- In this paper, we propose ETGC (Event Topology Graph Construction), an effective approach to mine event topology graph based on the maximum spanning tree from interleaved system logs. Compared with existing anomaly detection approaches, our method can detect more anomalies with high accuracy.
- We evaluate the effectiveness of ETGC mining algorithm on OpenStack data set and BGL data set. The experimental results prove that our method has higher accuracy and interpretability than other algorithms.

The remainder of this paper is organized as follows. In Sect. 2, we explain in detail how to construct event topology graphs, followed anomaly diagnosis in Sect. 3. We conducted extensive experiments and report the results in Sect. 4. Finally, we conclude the paper in Sect. 5.

2 Event Topology Graph Construction for Anomaly Analysis

Our approach consists of an offline phase and an online phase. In the offline phase, we adopt some simple but effective cluster approaches such as BSG [1] to generate log templates of high quality. Then we use these log templates to generate the event topology graphs, which represents the normal execution trace of the system. In the online phase, by comparing the newly arrived execution log sequence and the event topology graphs, we can find their deviation and detect anomaly events.

2.1 Parsing the Logs

Log parsing [1] converts raw and free form system logs into structured log templates with specific formats. A piece of raw system log can be divided into two parts: the constant part and the variable part. The constant part is the constant string from original texts printed by the source codes. The variable part usually carries various status information of the system. Log templates are extracted from raw system logs. For example, if the raw log is "initialize prop version req-f3eaa3dd-321d-44db-b705-937a1c26a01b", then the extracted log template will be "initialize prop version *". Compared with present works mainly based on the templates, we have fully considered the log timestamp information in addition, which significantly improves the accuracy of detecting anomalies.

2.2 Finding Candidate Successor Group

The Computation of the candidate successor group contains two steps: (1) Successor group generation. (2) Noise event filtering. Mining the candidate successor group aims at finding all the possible successor events of reference templates. First, we record all the distinct events in two closest events with the same reference template and then add them to the candidate successor group of the reference template. The noise event filtering aims to keep meaningful but rare events. We use an adaptive correlation probability to filter out noise while retaining normal rare events. Let us denote the probability of occurrence of predecessor template A as P_A, the probability of occurrence of successor template B as P_B, and the occurrence times of template B in the successor group of A as $N_{(A|B)}$. We compute the correlation possibility between event A and event B in the successor group.

$$SUP_{(A|B)} = \frac{N_{(A|B)}}{min(P_A, P_B)} * sigmoid(min(P_A, P_B)). \tag{1}$$

The threshold for SUP should be small enough to filter noise event and retain rare and meaningful events. After we set a filtering threshold, if the correlation probability is larger than the threshold, then event B is added to the final successor group of A.

2.3 Mining Dependent Event Pair

The existing method usually uses a time window mechanism to retain the subsequent events of the reference templates in a statistical manner. The items in the same sliding window are considered to be subsequent events of the same reference template. However, it is difficult to estimate the length of the time window accurately.

Li and Ma [10] proposed to use several statistics for detecting dependent event pairs and filtering candidate event pairs. The sequence of points of event type A is denoted as $P_A = < a_1, a_2, ..., a_m >$, and a_i is the specific timestamp of one log entry of event type A. Assume that the time range of the point sequence P_A is $[0, T]$, given a point z, the minimum positive distance between the z and sequence P_A is defined as

$$d(z, P_A) = min||x - z||, x \in P_A, x \geq z. \tag{2}$$

The unconditional distribution of waiting time of event B is

$$F_B(r) = P(d(z, P_B)) \leq r, \tag{3}$$

where r is a real number. The conditional distribution of waiting time of event B with respect to event A is

$$F_{B|A}(r) = P(d(z, P_B)) \leq r, z \in P_A, \tag{4}$$

where r is a real number, z is a point of P_A in the point sequence, and $F_{B|A}$ describes the conditional probability in the case of event A at time z. Then we have the following definition [10].

Definition 1. *[10] Given two corresponding sequence of points for event types A and B, if $F_B(r)$ and $F_{B|A}$ are significantly different, then statistically, event B is considered to be dependent on event A. Specifically, the dependency test between events A and B can be compared by $F_{B|A}$ and $F_B(r)$. Assuming that A and B are independent of each other, according to the central limit theorem*

$$Z = \frac{M_B - M_{B|A}}{\sqrt{\frac{var(F_B(r))}{m}}} \sim N(0,1), \tag{5}$$

where $var(F_B(r))$ represents the variance of $F_B(r)$, M_B and $M_{B|A}$ represent the first moment of $F_B(r)$ and $F_{B|A}(r)$ respectively.

2.4   Discovering Transition Time Lag

Existing methods tend to use a fixed time weight for edges in the event topology graph, which indicates the transition time period between adjacent events. However, in real world systems, fixed time lags are not practical due to noise interference, unsynchronized clocks, and so forth. Time lags usually fluctuate within a range.

For each dependent event pair $< T_i, T_j >$, we look into two adjacent template T_i and T_j in the log stream and record all the time period as $< t_1, t_2, ..., t_m >$. We use a time distribution $f(t)$ to describe the transition time of event pair $< T_i, T_j >$. Since the time distribution represents the time lag sequence of event pair, we propose a cluster-based method to get rid of redundant event pairs. In this method, we divide the time-delay sequence into multiple time lag clusters. Then the maximum and minimum values of the clusters are considered as the boundary values of the transition time interval. Intuitively, we perform the chi-square test on these time lag clusters. If they pass the chi-square test, then the event pairs are considered to have the dependency relationship, and the time delay interval is used as the time lag interval of the event pair.

2.5   Generating Maximum Spanning Tree

In the graph theory, a spanning tree of a graph is a subgraph that contains all the vertices and the maximum spanning tree [7] is the minimum connected graph with maximum weight. In a maximum spanning tree, each node represents a single distinct event, and weights of connected edges represent the transition probability between predecessor and successor events. Successor events are not always immediately follow reference events, so that some structures like loop structures and detour structures may be missing from the event topology. However, the spanning tree represents the backbone of the entire workflow. Even if some meaningful structures are missing, we can still retrieve them through the original dependency relationship between events. We employ the attenuation factor to control the possibility of the existence of the detour structure. We first define the step size as the distance from the starting node to the terminal node in the maximum spanning tree structure. Next, we define the probability of the existence of the detour structure between the starting node and the terminal node as:

$$d(E_1, E_2) = log(1 + path(E_1, E_2)), \tag{6}$$

where the $path(E_1, E_2)$ refers to the step size between E_1 and E_2 in maximum spanning tree. Then we could set a suitable threshold to preserve the edge between $E1$ and $E2$.

3   Anomaly Diagnosis

There are two kinds of anomalies: event anomalies and time anomalies. An event anomaly is raised when an unexpected log entry occurs, which cannot match to any node in the event topology graph. Unexpected log entry indicates an abnormal event that cannot be matched with any log template or a redundant occurrence of a log template.

A time anomaly is raised when a child node of a parent node occurs, but the interval time is not within the time lag interval. The time lag interval records the maximum transition time and minimum transition time of the event. Any transition time that occurs within this time lag interval is considered as a normal event. Hence, this type of anomaly is more instantaneous and could be captured easily.

4   Experimental Evaluation

4.1   The Datasets

We evaluate our approach ETGC through two real log datasets. Detailed information about the two datasets is as followed:

1. OpenStack cloud platform log dataset: OpenStack, a cloud computing platform based on PaaS, provides cloud service for millions of people all over the world and its logs are accessible to users. This data includes 30 normal deployments and 3 abnormal deployments, each of which is related to the deployment of the cluster. We collected the data from the two components: cf-pdman and pdm-cli.

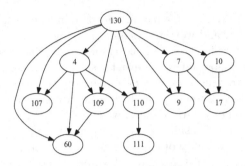

Fig. 1. An event topology graph from the OpenStack dataset

2. BGL log dataset: Blue Gene/L supercomputer system log dataset contains 4,747,963 logs, where 348,460 entries are labeled as anomalies. We choose this dataset because it contains many log templates which only appear during a certain time period.

4.2   A Case Study

To illustrate our method of anomaly diagnosis, we take an event topology graph for example. Figure 1 is a part of the event topology graph generated from OpenStack dataset. In this figure, each node represents a distinct event, and the weight of each edge represents the transition probability of an event pair. Moreover, Table 1 provides further information about these log templates. For example, path (130, 7, 17) in the transaction flow diagram in Fig. 1 represents the configuration of attributes on the server node.

4.3   Anomaly Diagnosis Evaluation

Figures 2 and 3 demonstrate the Error Event Pair Percent and the Average Error Event Percent in normal deployments and abnormal deployments results, respectively. Whether in abnormal deployments such as 514, 17, 60 or normal deployments, ETGC can detect more Error Event Pair than Logsed. The left side and right side of Fig. 4 show the proportion of event pairs on BGL data set detected by ETGC and Logsed, respectively. The result demonstrates that ETGC can detect more normal and abnormal event pairs than Logsed, which proves that our approach is feasible.

Table 1. Event IDs and the corresponding events

Event IDs	Events
130	sqlalchemy.orm.relationships.RelationshipProperty Node.servers local/remote pairs [(nodes.server_id/servers.id)] *
4	sqlalchemy.orm.mapper.Mapper (Server—servers)_configure_property(node_list, RelationshipProperty) *
107	sqlalchemy.orm.relationships.RelationshipProperty Node.servers secondary synchronize pairs *
109	sqlalchemy.orm.relationships.RelationshipProperty Server.Node secondary synchronize pairs *
60	sqlalchemy.orm.mapper.Mapper (Node—nodes) initialize prop created_at *
110	sqlalchemy.orm.mapper.Mapper (Node—nodes) initialize prop timestamp *
111	sqlalchemy.orm.relationships.RelationshipProperty Server.node_list secondary synchronize pairs *
7	sqlalchemy.orm.mapper.Mapper (Node—nodes) _configure_property(servers, RelationshipProperty) *
9	sqlalchemy.orm.mapper.Mapper (CtrlSwitch—ctrl_switch)_configure_property(created_at, Column) *
10	sqlalchemy.orm.mapper.Mapper (Lock—locks) _configure_property(state, Column) *
17	sqlalchemy.orm.mapper.Mapper (PsmRole—psmroles) _configure_property(id, Column) *

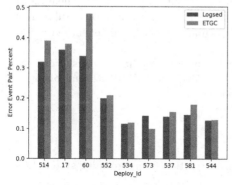 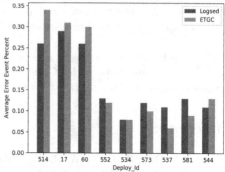

Fig. 2. The OpenStack deployments error event pair percent

Fig. 3. OpenStack deployments average error event percent

4.4   The Execution Time

At the first stage, we study the time it takes to generate candidate event pairs. At the second stage, we pay attention to the time it costs for our algorithm to filter these candidate event pairs and generate the event topology graph. In Fig. 5, the solid line and dotted line refer to the time spent at the first and second stage. It shows that the time taken to generate candidate event pairs

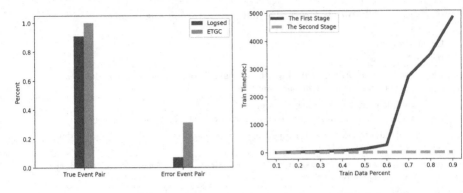

Fig. 4. The BGL validation result   **Fig. 5.** Execution time on BGL dataset

grows exponentially as the number of data increases. To solve this problem, we can use the multi-thread program to reduce the time spent at the first stage of our approach.

5   Conclusion

In this paper, we proposed ETGC (Event Topology Graph Construction), an effective approach to diagnose the abnormal events based on system logs. By using the maximum spanning tree generation, ETGC constructs the meaningful event topology graphs based on dependent event pairs. Evaluation results show that our approach can achieve superior performances in anomaly event detection.

Acknowledgments. This work is supported in part by Nanjing University of Posts and Telecommunications under Grant No. NY215045 and NY219084, and Shanghai Sailing Program under Grant No. 18YF1423300.

References

1. Guo, S., Liu, Z., Chen, W., Li, T.: Event extraction from streaming system logs. Inf. Sci. Appl. **2018**, 465–474 (2019)
2. He, S., Zhu, J., He, P., Lyu, M.R.: Experience report: system log analysis for anomaly detection. In: 2016 IEEE 27th International Symposium on Software Reliability Engineering (ISSRE), pp. 207–218, October 2016
3. Jia, T., Yang, L., Chen, P., Li, Y., Meng, F., Xu, J.: LogSed: anomaly diagnosis through mining time-weighted control flow graph in logs. In: 2017 IEEE 10th International Conference on Cloud Computing (CLOUD), pp. 447–455 (2017)
4. Li, T., Liu, Z., Zhou, Q.: Application-driven big data mining. ZTE Technol. J. **22**(2), 49–52 (2016)
5. Lin, Q., Zhang, H., Lou, J., Zhang, Y., Chen, X.: Log clustering based problem identification for online service systems. In: 2016 IEEE/ACM 38th International Conference on Software Engineering Companion (ICSE-C), pp. 102–111 (2016)

6. Lou, J.G., Fu, Q., Yang, S., Xu, Y., Li, J.: Mining invariants from console logs for system problem detection. In: USENIX Annual Technical Conference, pp. 1–14 (2010)
7. McDonald, R., Pereira, F., Ribarov, K., Hajič, J.: Non-projective dependency parsing using spanning tree algorithms. In: Proceedings of the conference on Human Language Technology and Empirical Methods in Natural Language Processing, pp. 523–530 (2005)
8. Nagaraj, K., Killian, C., Neville, J.: Structured comparative analysis of systems logs to diagnose performance problems. In: Proceedings of the 9th USENIX Conference on Networked Systems Design and Implementation, p. 26 (2012)
9. Tak, B.C., Tao, S., Yang, L., Zhu, C., Ruan, Y.: Logan: problem diagnosis in the cloud using log-based reference models. In: 2016 IEEE International Conference on Cloud Engineering (IC2E), pp. 62–67, April 2016
10. Li, T., Ma, S.: Mining temporal patterns without predefined time windows. In: Fourth IEEE International Conference on Data Mining (ICDM 2004), pp. 451–454, November 2004
11. Xu, W., Huang, L., Fox, A., Patterson, D., Jordan, M.I.: Detecting large-scale system problems by mining console logs. In: Proceedings of the ACM SIGOPS 22Nd Symposium on Operating Systems Principles, pp. 117–132 (2009)
12. Yu, X., Joshi, P., Xu, J., Jin, G., Zhang, H., Jiang, G.: Cloudseer: workflow monitoring of cloud infrastructures via interleaved logs. ACM SIGPLAN Not. 51(4), 489–502 (2016)

Knowledge Graph Based Semi-automatic Code Auditing System

Yin Hongji$^{(\boxtimes)}$ and Chen Wei$^{(\boxtimes)}$

Nanjing University of Posts and Telecommunications,
Nanjing 210023, Jiangsu, China
734970655@qq.com, chenwei@njupt.edu.cn

Abstract. Aiming at detecting various vulnerabilities in Web application system based on PHP language, a semi-automatic code auditing system based on knowledge graph is proposed. Firstly, the abstract syntax tree of each file in the Web application system is constructed to extract the taint variables and function information from the abstract syntax tree and construct the global variable information. Secondly, the data flow information of each taint variable is analyzed accurately. Finally, the knowledge graph and code auditing technology are combined to construct and display the vulnerability information of the Web application system in the form of graph. Experiments and analysis results show that this detection method can well construct and display the data flow information of each taint variable and help auditors find common vulnerabilities in Web application systems more quickly.

Keywords: Abstract syntax tree · Code auditing · Knowledge graph · Taint analysis

1 Introduction

With the rapid development of the Internet, Web technology has been widely used in science, education, transportation, finance and other important fields. According to the latest statistics of w3tech [1], 83.5% of websites use PHP as their website language, and this proportion has remained high since 2018. However, the vulnerability of PHP language makes these Web application systems vulnerable. According to OWASP TOP 10 released in 2017 [2], eight of the top 10 vulnerabilities in the list are due to the taint variable of Web applications.

In order to improve the detection speed and accuracy of taint analysis, this paper proposes a semi-automatic code auditing system based on knowledge graph. First, by constructing the abstract syntax tree of each PHP file, variable information and function information of each file can be extracted. Second, the tracking of taint variables can be carried out to check whether some sensitive sinks will be passed through in data flow of each taint variable. Third, with the help of knowledge graph, the variables and functions of each file can be regarded as entity vectors, the sensitive sinks can be regarded as entity attributes, and the variables and their passing functions are regarded as relational corpus. Finally, the knowledge graph are output by visual interface, and the

F. Liu et al. (Eds.): SciSec 2019, LNCS 11933, pp. 224–231, 2019.
https://doi.org/10.1007/978-3-030-34637-9_17

sensitive sinks are marked to help code auditors better analyze the security problems of Web application systems.

2 Review of Research

Since 1970s, static analysis technology has been applied to source code auditing. In the following decades, experts and scholars at home and abroad have done a lot of research on the detection technology of taint analysis.

Huo proposes a static detection method based on the Facebook HHVM. By using flow-sensitive, context sensitive and inter-procedural data flow analysis, it realize the taint analysis in order to improve the precision of automate-based string analysis. It also proposes a method to define rules including sensitive source, sensitive sink and vulnerability pattern [3]. Miachael and Rieck proposed a highly scalable and flexible approach for analyzing PHP applications. By leveraging the concept of code property graph which constitute a canonical representation of code incorporating a program's syntax, control flow, and data dependencies in a single graph structure, an analyst can write traversals to query the database to find various kinds of vulnerabilities [4]. Yan put forward a new detection model and static stain data analysis method, which collects and constructs contextual information by dividing the program into blocks, and then traces and analyses the variables of the fixed module and different modules, so as to effectively detect the vulnerabilities [5].

However, static detection technology has some limitations where it cannot verify whether the vulnerabilities really exist, so more and more researchers pay their attention to dynamic detection technology. Alhuzali and Birhanu combined dynamic detection with static auditing, proposed a contamination analysis model which can automatically generate attack vectors. Through the analysis of taint variables, combined with the characteristics of database back-end architecture and other modules, it may accurately generate data flow, in order to achieve high-quality vulnerability generation [6]. Gong proposed a new method of combining static detection with dynamic detection. Static detection is based on HHVM to track tainted data and dynamic fuzz technology is based on arrangement of reorganization for the parameter of url. With dynamic test results it helps static detection streamlining the process, and static analysis results are used as input to help the dynamic test by generating new more logical permutation links which can achieve higher dynamic detection coverage [7].

3 Architecture and Algorithms

3.1 Abstract Syntax Tree

Our approach is based on static analysis technology, so it is necessary to process the source code and compile it into an intermediate form which can be easily analyzed. PHP-Parser is an open source tool based on the token stream acquired by the built-in function of PHP to construct an abstract syntax tree according to context information [8].

In the source code processing step, the source code of the program is identified and the PHP code is extracted. In the grammar analysis step, because of the different types of node in abstract syntax tree, different analysis and processing can be done according to the type of node in the syntax tree to improve the compilation speed. Our system has configured common rules of node type analysis, such as file inclusion, variable definition, function call, etc.

3.2 Taint Analysis

According to the results of abstract syntax tree, when constructing data flow information of each file, it will be recorded when the sink is PHP built-in function. If it is not PHP built-in function, the definition position of variable and function name is recorded.

For example, in query "test($data1)", here we record the function name "test", the variable name $data1 and the location of the variable in the function. When the external variable refers to the function of "test", it is necessary to judge which parameter of the function corresponds to the external variable, and then continue to extend the data flow information according to the parameters.

When searching the data flow of built-in functions of PHP in files, the function name is extracted first and once the function name matches, the data stream is extracted according to the mapping relationship of the variables. When extracting file information, because of the characteristics of PHP language, the files that has been included can invoke the function call and variable value of each required files. Therefore, when extracting other file information, our system needs to inherit the included filenames.

3.3 Graph Construction

3.3.1 Entity Extraction

Entity extraction, also known as named entity recognition, refers to the automatic recognition of named entities from text data set, which is the most basic and key part of information extraction. The traditional data of knowledge graph mostly come from structured data in Encyclopedia sites and vertical sites. Attribute-value of related entities is obtained from various semi-structured data to expand the description of attributes [9]. Entities are the basis of knowledge graph construction, it is necessary to choose representative information as far as possible [10].

According to our code auditing requirements and output results, it will be slightly different from the traditional knowledge graph construction. Our paper is to detect the stained vulnerabilities, the taint variables will be automatically identified and screened according to the type of variables in this step, and the file names of the web application system will be extracted as entities into the knowledge graph.

3.3.2 Relationship Extraction

After obtaining a series of discrete named entities, in order to obtain semantic information, it is necessary to extract the relationship between entities from corpus, and link the entities through the relationship to form a network of knowledge structure [11].

Since the entities in this paper are extracted from the abstract syntax tree of web application systems, the relationships between entities will also belong to the superior and subordinate relationships like tree structures. For the entity named before, our system will automatically locate the entry position of taint variable, judge the file name where it is located, extract the inclusion relationship between filename and stain variable.

3.3.3 Attribute Extraction

The work mentioned in this paper is from the perspective of improving the efficiency of code auditing, so the selection of entity attributes should also consider whether it will help code auditing.

The entity that extracts the attribute here is the file name and the taint variable. The entity attribute of the file name is the size of the file, the latest modification time of the file, and the hash value of the file. In the real environment, it is likely that some important files of the Web application system will be maliciously changed. So when the knowledge graph of each version of the Web application system is retained, the latest modified file information can be found quickly to help auditors focus on checking the changing files. The attributes extracted from the taint variables are data flow information obtained in Sect. 3.2. Therefore, the taint variable are taken as entities and their passing functions are stored as their attributes.

3.3.4 Entity Disambiguation

Entity disambiguation is a technology specially used to solve ambiguity problem of the same-name entity. In real language environment, it often encounters the problem that an entity reference item corresponds to multiple named entity objects. For example, the term "Li Na" can correspond to the entity of Li Na as a singer or tennis player. Through entity disambiguation, we can establish entity links accurately according to the current context [12].

In our paper, it is found that different taint variables can be assigned to the same variable name in multiple program segments, and the data flow of each program segment is different. Therefore, when tracing and extending the data flow information of different variables, the data flow with the same variable name but in different program segments will be spliced into each other, resulting in false alarm.

The problem that arises here is that an entity reference corresponds to many named entity objects, which leads to the confusion of the final data flow. Therefore, it is necessary to distinguish these named entity objects. The method here is to add random numbers to the duplicate variables, and replace the duplicate variables in the data flow, so the problem has actually been transformed from entity disambiguation into how to define the range of the variables in the data flow. In the abstract syntax tree information extracted previously, there are corresponding function processing for each operation, such as file extraction, function call, variable definition, etc. Therefore, we need to start from variable definition to determine whether the assigned variable will be renamed. If renamed, then we need to define the boundary of each data flow.

Because the focus of our paper is on the taint variable and its sink function, the variable name is only the transmission media of data flow. It will not affect the original parameter's data stream when changing its variable name, so we can eliminate entity disambiguation by changing the duplicate variable name.

3.3.5   Knowledge Reasoning

Semantic relations commonly used in knowledge graph include inheritance relationship between concepts, whole-part relationship and domain-specific semantic relationship [13]. According to the relationship between entities and entities established previously, this paper makes knowledge reasoning based on the relationship between the whole and the part in the knowledge graph, and excavates the knowledge in it.

In this paper, we start from the entity of taint variable and check the function information in its entity attributes by blacklist. The blacklist here is actually the corresponding relation table of the vulnerability type and the sensitive sinks listed according to the security knowledge. If there is a sensitive sink in the data flow, but there is no filtering function of the corresponding vulnerability type, then auditors can generally determine that this is a vulnerability and our system will built the entity for sensitive sink and relationship between the function entity and taint variable entity whose relationship attribute is file name information. The greatest advantage of this method is that it can trace the source of the vulnerability and display the corresponding relationship between the sensitive sink and the stain variable directly.

4   Evaluation

4.1   Dataset

We evaluated our system on DVWA (Damn Vulnerable Web Application) and ssVote voting system [14]. DVWA is a Web application system which aims to provide a legal environment for security researchers to test their professional skills and tools and help Web developers better understand the process of Web application security prevention. DVWA also provides many vulnerability environments with different levels, such as SQL injection, cross-site scripting attacks, command execution and so on.

Since we focus on semi-automatic code auditing and display the taint variable and sensitive sinks to auditors, there are two main reasons for choosing DVWA: one is to simulate the real environment through different vulnerability levels, the other is to display the function information of taint variable through different levels of vulnerability. As an open source voting system, we also choose ssVote as a demonstration.

4.2   Measurements

The graph database used here is Neo4j [15]. This is a high-performance NOSQL graph database, which stores structured data on the network rather than in tables. Flask [16], which is a lightweight Web application framework written in Python, is used for visual output. The reason why it becomes lightweight is that its core is very simple and has strong extendibility.

Fig. 1. Knowledge graph of DVWA

Figure 1 is the knowledge graph information of DVWA, which contains the basic information of DVWA files, such as modification time, the hash value of files. For example, in the file of "dvwa/xss_s/source/high.php", the number of taint variables is two and the number of sensitive sinks is three. This kind of information mainly helps auditors find vulnerabilities faster and improve the accuracy and efficiency of auditing.

Figure 2 shows the specific file information of all injection vulnerabilities in DVWA. Since it is divided into four levels, the inconsistency of data flow can be clearly found by comparing the data flow of four files. There is no protection for the taint variable in the "low" level. The data flow of the taint variables in the "medium" level adds a "mysql_real_escape_string()" function, which is mainly used to escape special characters in SQL statements, such as single quotation, double quotation and so on. The taint variables in the "high" level are passed in through "session" type which cannot be controlled by users easily. In the "Impossible" level, the "db_bindParam" function and "is_numeric" function appear in the data flow of taint variable. The former function is a prepared function of SQL, and the latter function checks the taint variable to determine whether it is a digital type, which can prevent SQL injection. Therefore, three potential injection vulnerabilities can be inferred from the graph.

Fig. 2. SQL injection of DVWA graph

Figure 3 is the traceability graph of DVWA. Since there are four main code-level vulnerabilities in DVWA: SQL injection, cross-site scripting, file inclusion, and command execution, we can see that the graph can be divided into four categories. According to the attribute information of edges, we can trace to specific file names and specific taint variables. Through graph, we can directly infer that there may be four kinds of common vulnerabilities in the web application. With the help of the data flow of the taint variables, auditors can quickly find out the common problems.

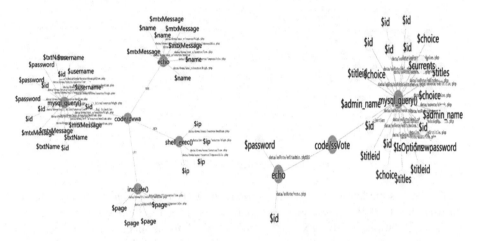

Fig. 3. Sensitive sinks of DVWA graph   **Fig. 4.** Sensitive sinks of ssVote graph

Figure 4 is the traceability graph of ssVote. From the graph, we can see that the taint variables are mainly distributed around the "mysql_query()" function and "echo" function. Therefore, auditors need to focus on the analysis of the database operation of the program to find the common vulnerabilities.

5   Conclusions

Aiming at the vulnerability detection in Web applications, a semi-automatic code auditing system based on knowledge graph is proposed. According to the type characteristics of abstract syntax tree, this paper constructs data flow information of web application system, and achieves the goal of semi-automatic detection by constructing and displaying knowledge graph. The experimental results show that the system is faster than the traditional static code auditing system in constructing data flow information and more intuitive in displaying data flow information. At the same time, multiple vulnerabilities and common problems in web application system can be found. In future work, this study considers further enriching the node types of abstract syntax tree to extend the data flow information and improve detection accuracy.

References

1. W3Techs: Usage of server-side programming languages for websites. https://w3techs.com/technologies/overview/programming_language/all
2. OWASP: OWASP Top 10 Most Critical Web Application Security Risks. https://www.owasp.org/index.php/Category:OWASP_Top_Ten_Project
3. Huo, Z.P.: PHP Code Vulnerabilities Detection Based on Static Analysis. Beijing University of Posts and Telecommunications (2015)
4. Backes, M., Rieck, K., Skoruppa, M., Stock, B., Yamaguchi, F.: Efficient and flexible discovery of PHP application vulnerabilities. In: IEEE European Symposium on Security & Privacy (2017)
5. Yan, X.X., Ma, H.T., Wang, Q.A.: A static backward taint data analysis method for detecting web application vulnerabilities. In: ICCSN 2017 (2017)
6. Alhuzali, A., Eshete, B., Gjomemo, R., Venkatakrishnan, V.N.: Chainsaw: chained automated workflow-based exploit generation. In: 2016 ACM SIGSAC Conference (2016)
7. Gong, R.L.: Research and implementation of PHP Web Application Code Defect Detection. Beijing University of Posts and Telecommunications (2016)
8. PHP-Parser: A PHP parser written in PHP. https://github.com/nikic/PHP-Parser
9. Lin, Z.Q., Xie, B., Zou, Y.Z., Zhao, J.F., Li, X.D., Wei, J.: Intelligent development environment and software knowledge graph. J. Comput. Sci. Technol. 32(2), 242–249 (2017)
10. Liu, Q., Li, Y., Duan, H.: Knowledge graph construction techniques. J. Comput. Res. Dev. 32(2), 242–249 (2017)
11. Zhang, X., Liu, X.: MMKG: an approach to generate metallic materials knowledge graph based on DBpedia and Wikipedia. Comput. Phys. Commun. 211(February), 98–112 (2016)
12. Sun, X.B., Wang, L., Wang, J.W., et al.: Construct knowledge graph for exploratory bug issue searching. Acta Electron. Sin. 46(7), 1578–1583 (2018)
13. Lin, X., Liang, Y., Giunchiglia, F., et al.: Relation path embedding in knowledge graphs. Neural Comput. Appl. 31(9), 5629–5639 (2018)
14. DVWA: A PHP/MySQL web application that is damn vulnerable. http://www.dvwa.co.uk
15. Neo4j: A graph database platform. https://neo4j.com
16. Flask: A Python Micro-framework. http://flask.pocoo.org

Encryption and Application

Effective Matrix Factorization for Recommendation with Local Differential Privacy

Hao Zhou[1,2(✉)], Geng Yang[1,2], Yahong Xu[1,2], and Weiya Wang[1,2]

[1] College of Computer Science and Software, Nanjing University of Posts
and Telecommunications, Nanjing 210023, Jiangsu, China
disintroduct@gmail.com
[2] Big Data Security and Intelligent Processing Lab, Nanjing 210003, China

Abstract. With the continuous upgrading of smart devices, people are using smartphones more and more frequently. People not only browse the information they need on the Internet, but also more and more people get daily necessities through online shopping. Faced with a variety of recommendation systems, it becomes more and more difficult for people to keep their privacy from being collected while using them. Therefore, ensuring the privacy security of users when they use the recommendation system is increasingly becoming the focus of people. This paper summarizes the related technologies. A recommendation algorithm based on collaborative filtering, matrix factorization as well as the randomized response is proposed, which satisfies local differential privacy (LDP). Besides, this paper also discusses the key technologies used in privacy protection in the recommendation system. Besides, This paper includes the algorithm flow of the recommendation system. Finally, the experiment proves that our algorithm has higher accuracy while guaranteeing user privacy.

Keywords: Local differential privacy · Matrix factorization · Recommender system · Randomized response

1 Introduction

Faced with a huge amount of item information, it is more and more difficult for people to find what they are interested in and need. The advent of the recommendation system reduces the difficulty for users to choose. Recommendation system can not only locate items with high correlation quickly according to the

The National Natural Science Foundation of China (61572263, 61502251, 61602263, 61872197), the Postgraduate Research & Practice Innovation Program of Jiangsu Province (KYCX18 0891), the Natural Science Foundation of Jiangsu Province (BK20161516, BK20160916), the Postdoctoral Science Foundation Project of China (2016M601859), the Natural Research Foundation of Nanjing University of Posts and Telecommunications (NY217119).

© Springer Nature Switzerland AG 2019
F. Liu et al. (Eds.): SciSec 2019, LNCS 11933, pp. 235–249, 2019.
https://doi.org/10.1007/978-3-030-34637-9_18

information provided by users but also make an additional recommendation in other aspects. To provide better user experience, the recommendation system usually collects relevant information of users actively and get users' profiles by mining relevant information [18]. This kind of collecting and analyzing behavior has the potential risk of privacy leakage. On the one hand, the recommendation system may actively make use of user information for profit; on the other hand, the user data maintained by the recommendation system also has the risk of being attacked and leaked.

When people use the recommendation system, the recommendation system can accurately predict users' privacy information by mining users' relevant information [19]. Many existing studies have found that recommendation systems can obtain users' relevant privacy information by mining user information. For example, the location-based recommendation system can judge the user's residence, company, travel frequency, and even the user's travel purpose by locating the user's location and the time spent in each location. Although there are already methods for protecting all the items and scoring information for each user, this method requires the user to implement large matrix multiplication locally, so that the space complexity and time complexity of the implementation will increase with the total items linearly. As a result, it is difficult for users to achieve in their local equipment. Our goal is to improve the accuracy and speed of recommendation while reducing time and space consumption to improve the practicability of the recommendation system based on protecting users' privacy information.

The purpose of this paper is to ensure the recommendation quality of recommendation while satisfying the LDP and reducing the space and time cost. In this paper, a new gradient descent matrix factorization algorithm that satisfies differential privacy is proposed. We use the LDP solution proposed by Nguyen to protect the private data of each user [6]. We also use the LDP solution proposed by Qin et al. [3] to reduce the number of related items, which greatly reduces the disturbance error caused by a large number of items.

Our main contributions of this paper are as follows. First, we proposed a new algorithm that protects all user items and scoring data. Secondly, we have greatly reduced the number of items related to users, and thus significantly reduce the relevant dimensions. As a result, space and time consumption of the algorithm is significantly reduced. Thirdly, by adding a new gradient correction parameter, the quality of the recommendation system has been significantly improved. To sum up, our algorithm guarantees high recommendation quality and needs less space and time costs while protecting items and ratings.

2   Preliminary

2.1   LDP

Local differential privacy is a popular privacy protection method based on ϵ-differential privacy. This means that before sending personal privacy data to the data collector, the user first disturbs the data locally to satisfy

the ϵ-differential privacy [15], and then uploads the disturbing information to the data collector. Generally, if a randomized algorithm f satisfies
ϵ-differential privacy, f satisfies the following inequalities for any two neighboring datasets D And D' and any possible output o:

$$Pr[f(D) \in o] \leq e^{\epsilon} \times Pr[f(D') \in S] \tag{1}$$

Generally, it is difficult for an opponent to be confident that the output
o obtained by using algorithm f comes from either D or D' [8]. So, for the
individual user, using this way to process the data, when the data is abused, he
can plausibly deny. Among them, ϵ is also called the privacy budget [7], which
is mainly used to control the strength of privacy protection. When the privacy
budget is very small, it means stronger privacy protection. In this paper, we
consider two data sets, in which each recorded information is a pair of items
that the user has scored. However, Shin et al. [1], Hua et al. [2], and Shen
et al. [8] all consider that both neighboring data sets D and D' contain all item
information, even if the user has not scored the corresponding item [3]. Different
definitions of adjacent data sets will lead to different time and space costs and
affect the final accuracy. Our algorithm is more realistic for it only considers the
related items and has lower space, time consumption as well as higher accuracy
while satisfying the privacy protection for each user.

One of the important concepts of differential privacy is sequential combin-
ability [3], that is, for all algorithm f_i of a series of randomized algorithms,
they satisfy ϵ_i-differential privacy, then for the whole sequence of f_i, it satisfies
$\sum_{i=1} \epsilon_i$- differential privacy. Early studies [3] have shown that for a given privacy budget ϵ, users can divide ϵ into several parts, and each part can release
perturbation information [6], the overall process is to satisfy the ϵ-differential
privacy.

2.2   Existing LDP Solution

Because LDP only requires locally perturbed of privacy data to satisfy the
ϵ-differential privacy. Therefore, theoretically, every user can apply LDP to their
private information. However, in reality, it is often the data collector who can
obtain the user's real data, and only disturbs the user's private information when
it is released. If the user uses LDP to disturb his information locally and then
publishes the proceed information, the recommendation system cannot get the
real exact data of the user, therefore the final information released by the system
can only be the data set of all users disturbed information [13]. This ensures privacy protection for user data. The following is a summary of the existing LDP
methods, which have received extensive attention recently.

RandomizedResponse. The randomized response algorithm (RR) is based
on LDP. Generally, RR refers to whether or not a user answers a judgmental
question, such as 'have you eaten today?'. He can reasonably deny the answer.
RR controls the intensity of privacy protection by adjusting the probability of
real and false answers. That is to say, if the probability of true answers is set

to be smaller, the intensity of privacy protection will be higher. To use RR in LDP, we set the probability of getting the true value to p [14]. According to the existing works, when p satisfies the following values, the RR satisfies the ϵ-differential privacy:

$$p = \frac{e^\epsilon}{1 + e^\epsilon} \tag{2}$$

RR can only be used to answer questions with binary answers. But it is the cornerstone of solving more complex problems.

RAPPOR. RAPPOR can deal with more complex questions, especially when the answer is non-binary. RAPPOR is mainly used to estimate the frequency of items. Generally, suppose there are n users and m item categories, and each user u_i has an item v_j. The purpose of the data collector is to collect the occurrence frequency of each item category. In RAPPOR, user u_i represents the ownership of the item v_j by uploading a vector of m bit length. In this m bit vector, all the bits except v_j-th are zero. Then, the user uses RR independently for each bit in the m-bit vector [3]. The specific values will be described below. Data collectors collect vectors sent by all users to calculate unbiased estimates of the occurrence of each item in m item categories.

To get the value of p, the concept of sensitivity in differential privacy needs to be used in RAPPOR. Generally speaking, for any function F, sensitivity Δ_f can be defined as

$$\Delta_f = max_{DD'} \|F(D) - f(D')\|_1 \tag{3}$$

D' and D are adjacent data sets, and $\|\bullet\|$ denotes ζ_1 of a vector. Since there is only 1 bit which value is one and all the others are zero, the maximum value of $\|F(D) - f(D')\|_1$ is 2. Therefore, the sensitivity is 2. According to the existing papers, when p satisfies the following values, RAPPOR can satisfy ϵ-differential privacy:

$$p = \frac{e^{\frac{\epsilon}{2l}}}{e^{\frac{\epsilon}{2l}} + 1} \tag{4}$$

Generally, l is much smaller than m. In the existing recommendation system, the gradient matrix of all items is uploaded. As a result, the maximum ζ_1 is $2m$ for the vector subtraction of two m bits and the sensitivity is $2m$. This paper assumes that users own l items. By using the RAPPOR method for l items owned by users, we can protect the related items owned by users to satisfy ϵ-differential privacy, while greatly reducing the sensitivity. Besides, the space complexity and time complexity of the algorithm are significantly reduced.

2.3   Matrix Factorization

This paper is based on the standard collaborative filtering recommendation algorithm. We assume that there are n users scoring m items (movies, etc.). We assume that the matrix is $R^{n \times m}$, and the element r_{ij} whose value is not zero indicates that the user i scored the item j [9]. Let the set of valid scoring subscripts $D \subset \{1, ..., n\} \times \{1, ..., m\}$, which represents the user/item pair. Then the total number of valid scores M can be expressed by $|D|$ [10]. The scoring matrix is generally very sparse, which results in M being much smaller than nm, especially when both n and m are large.

With a given training set, the recommendation system can predict scores of items that have not been scored by the user. Matrix factorization is one of the most popular methods for prediction because of its high accuracy and easy implementation. In the matrix factorization, each user is represented by a d-dimensional vector, also called a personal profile [1]. At the same time, each item is also represented by a d-dimensional vector, also known as the profile of the item. Then, the relevance of the item to the user can be represented by the inner product of the two vectors [11]. Thus, for users and items, the corresponding hidden factor vector forms are $U = u_{\{1:n\}}$ and $V = v_{\{1:m\}}$ [12], respectively. In this paper, the user profile is represented by u_i, $u_i \in R^d, 1 \leq i \leq n$, and the profile of the item is represented by $v_j \in R^d$, $1 \leq j \leq m$ and their values are solved by minimizing the regularized mean square error

$$arg \quad min = \frac{1}{M} \sum_{r_{ij} \in D} (r_{ij} - u_i^T v_j)^2 + \lambda_u \sum_{i-1}^{n} \|u_i\|^2 + \lambda_v \sum_{j=1}^{n} \|v_j\|^2 \qquad (5)$$

Where $\frac{1}{M} \sum_{r_{ij} \in D} (r_{ij} - u_i^T v_j)^2$ is a loss function that measures the distance between two matrices, and $\lambda_u \sum_{i-1}^{n} \|u_i\|^2 + \lambda_v \sum_{j=1}^{n} \|v_j\|^2$ is a regular factor used to constrain parameters to avoid overfitting, Where λ_u, λ_v are normal numbers. The obtained u_i and v_j can predict the relevance of the unrated item to the user by calculating their inner product $u_i^T \times v_j$.

We use the stochastic gradient descent (SGD) to minimize the formula (5). Using the SGD, U and V can be calculated by using u_i and v_j as follows:

$$v_j^t = v_j^{t-1} - \gamma_t \{\nabla_{v_j} + 2\lambda_v v_j^{t-1}\} \qquad (6)$$

$$u_j^t = u_i^{t-1} - \gamma_t (\nabla_{u_i} + 2\lambda_u u_i^{t-1}\} \qquad (7)$$

Where u_j^t and v_j^t are the value of u_i and v_j at t iterations, γ_t is a positive number, which represents the learning rate when the number of iterations is t. ∇_{u_i}, ∇_{v_j} are gradients of u_i and v_j, respectively, which can be obtained from the following equation:

$$\nabla_{u_i} = -\frac{2}{M} \sum_{r_{ij} \in R} y_{ij} v_j (r_{ij} - u_i^T v_j) \qquad (8)$$

$$\nabla_{v_j} = -\frac{2}{M} \sum_{r_{ij} \in R} y_{ij} u_i (r_{ij} - u_i^T v_j) \qquad (9)$$

Since each user does not rate all items, in reality, the number of rated items is much smaller than the total items. Therefore, in this paper, the user first filters out the possible types of graded items, and then only updates the related items' gradients locally, while ignoring the others.

3   A New Differentially Private Matrix Factorization Algorithm

3.1   System Model

The experimental environment of this paper is assumed to be that the recommendation system is untrusted, and the user does not want his private information to be obtained by the recommendation system. Our goal is to allow the system and individual users to get more accurate recommendations using smaller space, time and communication costs.

Figure 1 shows how our system works. In our system, we first perturb each user's scored items to satisfy ϵ_1-differential privacy. Then upload the disturbed data to the recommendation system. Because l is much smaller than m, the sensitivity of the gradient matrix is much less than $2m$, and the communication cost will be greatly reduced. After obtaining the relevant item, the user calculates the gradient matrix $\bigtriangledown_V$ of 1 items. Then, using the dimensionality reduction method proposed by Shin et al. [1], the object gradient matrix $\bigtriangledown_V$ is projected into the low-dimensional space to further compress the communication cost. After perturbed the data is sent to the recommendation system. Then, the server updates V by calculating the item gradient matrix of all users and sends the updated V to each user. In this way, after k iteration, the user can obtain the correlation between items and himself by calculating $u_i^T \times v_j$.

Since M cannot be obtained locally, the approximate calculation is generally performed by replacing M with the number of users n. The number of iterations k, the number of users n, the privacy budget ϵ, the regular coefficients λ_v and λ_u, as well as the learning rate γ_t are all given by the recommendation system.

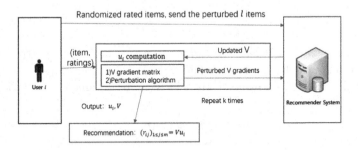

Fig. 1. Overview of our recommender system.

3.2   A New Solution for Protecting Items and Ratings

Since a user always wants to upload data about all items, and the total number of items m is generally very large [1], the sensitivity of V is very large. However, the number of items related to the user is much smaller than the total number of items. Therefore, we assume the number of rated items is l rather than m and ensure the rated items which satisfy ϵ_1-differential privacy. Then the randomized gradient of the l items is uploaded to the server. Thus, the communication cost changes from $O(m)$ to $O(l)$, noting $l \ll m$.

In the algorithm private-GD-DR, we first assume that the number of each user's related item is l. If the number of items scored by the user is greater than l, we select l items randomly from the scored items; otherwise, we select one item from the unscored items until the total number is up to l [3]. Each user u_i selected item is represented by a vector l_i of length l bits, the value of one item being scored is 1, the value of the unrated value is 0, and the item number of the corresponding position is recorded by the vector m_i. Then, each bit in the vector l_i is perturbed using the RAPPOR method to obtain l_i^*, and the corresponding item number of the element having a value of 0 in the perturbed vector is replaced with the remaining unattached item label. The resulting m_i^* after the disturbance is sent to the server. In the following paper, m_i' is a complement of m_i.

Theorem 1. *The rating item selection described above satisfies ϵ_1-differential privacy.*

Proof. It is assumed that l_{i1} and l_{i2} are two sets of binary items, and they are all equal in length l. Assume that F is the perturbation method for the item to be uploaded in the algorithm private-GD-RAPPOR, and any possible output of F is l_i. We have

$$\frac{\Pr\left[F\left(l_{i1}\right) = l_i\right]}{\Pr\left[F\left(l_{i2}\right) = l_i\right]} \le \frac{max_{l_{i1}} \Pr\left[F\left(l_{i1}\right) = l_i\right]}{max_{l_{i2}} \Pr\left[F\left(l_{i2}\right) = l_i\right]}$$

$$= \frac{\prod_{j=1}^{l} \frac{e^{\frac{\varepsilon_1}{2l}}}{e^{\frac{\varepsilon_1}{2l}}+1}}{\prod_{j=1}^{l} \frac{1}{e^{\frac{\varepsilon_1}{2l}}+1}}$$

$$\le e^{\frac{\varepsilon_1}{2l} * l}$$

$$< e^{\varepsilon_1}$$

Therefore, the theorem is proved.

3.3 Accuracy Improvement via Dimension Reduction

After one user u_i gets the m_i^*, he uses m_i^* to calculate the ∇_V. At the same time, ∇_U is calculated using all the related items. As a result, we can further reduce the dimension of user data.

Let $q \ll l$, let Φ be a $q * l$ random matrix whose element φ_{kj} is a Bernoulli distribution with mean 0 and variance $\frac{1}{q}$. Φ is shared between the user and the recommendation system, and the user i does not upload the item gradient ∇_V^i but uploads $\nabla_B^i (\nabla_B^i = \Phi \nabla_V^i)$ [4]. Before uploading the data, it is only necessary to add noise to the method proposed by Jingyu Hua et al., and finally, send $\nabla_B^{i,*}$ to the server. The server restores the sparse matrix by using a sparse recovery algorithm. The recommendation system will calculate the restored data

---

Algorithm 1. Private-GD-DR

Require: l_i, m_i, m'_i, $1 =< i <= n$, positive integer q, predefined iteration number k, and privacy parameter ϵ, rated set D.

Ensure: Item profile matrix $V \in R^{m \times d}$

1: Generate a $q \times l$ random matrix Φ whose entries are drawn from Gaussian distribution with mean 0 and standard deviation $\frac{1}{\sqrt{q}}$ and send Φ to users, $\nabla^\star_B$ is the pseudo inverse matrix of Φ

2: Initialize U, V and a counter $iter = 0$, $arraym \in R^{n \times l}$

3: **for** $i = 1; i < n; i++$ **do**

4:     **for** $j = 1; j < l; j++$ **do**

5:         Draw T $Bernoiulli$ $\left(\frac{e^{\frac{\epsilon}{2l}}}{e^{\frac{\epsilon}{2l}}+1}\right)$

6:         **if** $T = 1$ **then**

7:             $m^*_{ij} = m_{ij}$

8:         **else**

9:             select p uniformly at random from $\{1, 2, ..., m - l\}$

10:             $m^*_{ij} = m'_{ip}$

11:         **end if**

12:     **end for**

13:     $arraym_i = m^*_i$

14: **end for**

15: **while** $iter \leq k$ **do**

16:     Initialize $\nabla^\star_B \in \{0\}^{m \times d}$

17:     **for** $i = 1; i < n; i++$ **do**

18:         Initialize $x^*_i \in \{0\}^{q \times d}$

19:         Derive $\nabla^i_V = \{-2u_i(r_{ij} - u_i^T v_j)\}_{j \in arraym_i, (i,j) \in D}$

20:         Compute $x_i = \Phi \nabla^i_V$

21:         Sample s uniformly at random from $\{1, 2, ..., q\}$

22:         Sample p uniformly at random from $\{1, 2, ..., d\}$

23:         If$(x_i)_{s,l} \notin [-1, 1]$, project $(x_i)_{s,l}$ onto $[-1, 1]$

24:         Draw T $Bernoiulli$ $\left(\frac{(x_i)_{s,l}(e^{\frac{\epsilon_2}{k}}-1)+e^{\frac{\epsilon_2}{k}}+1}{2(e^{\frac{\epsilon_2}{k}}+1)}\right)$

25:         **if** $T = 1$ **then**

26:             $(x^\star_i)_{s,p} = qd\frac{e^{\frac{\epsilon_2}{k}}+1}{e^{\frac{\epsilon_2}{k}}-1}$

27:         **else**

28:             $(x^\star_i)_{s,p} = -qd\frac{e^{\frac{\epsilon_2}{k}}+1}{e^{\frac{\epsilon_2}{k}}-1}$

29:         **end if**

30:         **for** $j = 1; j < l; j++$ **do**

31:             $q = arraym_{[i][j]}$

32:             Compute $\nabla^\star_{B[q][p]} = \nabla^\star_{B[q][p]} + \nabla^\dagger_{B[:][l]}(x^\star_i)_{s,p}$

33:         **end for**

34:     **end for**

35:     Compute $\nabla^\star_B = \nabla^\star_B/n$ and send $\nabla^\star_B$ to users

36:     $iter = iter + 1$

37:     Get ∇^i_U from (8), and $u_i = u_i - \gamma_t\{\nabla^i_U + 2\lambda_u u_i\}$

38:     $V = V - \gamma_t\{(\nabla^\star_V - \eta^\star_V) + 2\lambda_u V\}$

39: **end while**

40: **return** V.

and feedback the results to each user. In this way, after k times of iteration, the recommendation system and users can obtain the final updated V [16], and the updated u_i is obtained only by user i.

Theorem 2. *The graded item gradient update method described above satisfies ϵ_2-differential privacy.*

Proof. Suppose ∇_B^i and $\nabla_B^{i'}$ are two arbitrary gradient matrices of user i, let ∇_B^i and $\nabla_B^{i'} \in [-1, 1]^{q \times l}$. Suppose M is the perturbation method for the gradient of the item in the algorithm private-GD-RAPPOR, and any possible output of M is $\nabla_B^{i',*}$. We have

$$\frac{\Pr\left[M\left(\nabla_B^{i,*}\right) = v | \nabla_B^i\right]}{\Pr\left[M\left(\nabla_B^{i,*}\right) = v | \nabla_B^{i',*}\right]} \leq \frac{max_{l_{i1}} \Pr\left[M\left(\nabla_B^{i,*}\right) = v | \nabla_B^i\right]}{max_{l_{i2}} \Pr\left[M\left(\nabla_B^{i,*}\right) = v | \nabla_B^{i',*}\right]}$$

$$= \frac{e^{\varepsilon_2/k} - 1 + e^{\varepsilon_2/k} + 1}{-e^{\frac{\varepsilon_2}{k}} + 1 + e^{\frac{\varepsilon_2}{k}} + 1}$$

$$= e^{\varepsilon_2/k}$$

Therefore, the V obtained for each iteration satisfies $\frac{\varepsilon_2}{k}$-differential privacy. So, the V obtained after k iterations satisfies ε_2 -differential privacy. Thus, the theorem is proved. It can be seen from the sequence composability that the total algorithm satisfies ε-differential privacy [3], where $\varepsilon = \varepsilon_1 + \varepsilon_2$.

Because the privacy budget $\frac{\varepsilon}{k}$ allocated for each iteration decreases linearly with the number of iterations, the deviation caused by each disturbance to increase linearly with k. To reduce the influence of the number of iterations, we add a learning correction parameter f_k of the item gradient. From the above analysis and experimental verification, when $f_k = \frac{1}{k}$, the deviation will be significantly reduced. As shown in Table 1, when the related items are reduced from m to d, the time complexity is greatly reduced.

Table 1. Time cost at each iteration.

	User	Server
Hua et al. [2]	$O(md)$	$O(nmd)$
Xiao et al. [1]	$O((md)\log(m))$	$O((mnd)\log(m))$
Ours	$O((ld)\log(l))$	$O((nld)\log(l))$

4   Experiment and Results

The database tested in this paper is two movie data sets, which are MovieLens and LibimSeTi [1]. The MovieLens dataset contains 20M rating information from

138,493 people for 26,744 movies. The scale for this data set is from 0.5 to 5. The LibimSeTi dataset contains 135,359 ratings for 135,359 people on 26,509 movies. The other parameter settings are the same as Shin et al. We compare Shin et al., Hua et al., and our algorithm on two data sets from five aspects.

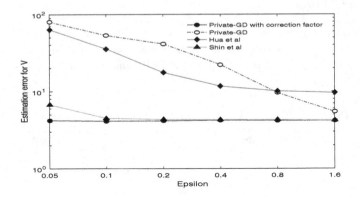

Fig. 2. On MovieLens, the estimation errors $\|V^* - V\|_{max}$ for each algorithm.

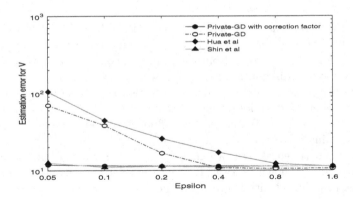

Fig. 3. On LibimSeTi, the estimation errors $\|V^* - V\|_{max}$ for each algorithm.

First, we compare the difference between the contour matrix of the items obtained by each algorithm. Figures 2 and 3 shows the estimated results of each algorithm after ten iterations on the MovieLens and the LibimSeTi data sets. The estimate of Hua et al. decreases linearly with an increase of ε but is significantly larger than other algorithm results. Experimental results obtained by Shin's algorithm also decreases with an increase of ε, but it is stable after reaching 4.19 due to the addition of the learning correction parameter $\frac{1}{k^2}$. When the modified learning parameters are not added, the estimation difference is higher than that of Shin et al. lower than the Hua et al. algorithm. However, when the learning correction parameter $\frac{1}{k}$ is added, our algorithm performs better when the privacy budget is lower.

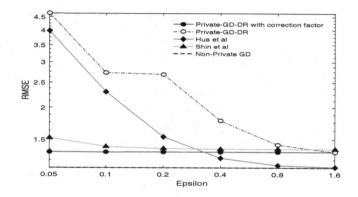

Fig. 4. On MovieLens, the prediction RMSEs for each algorithm.

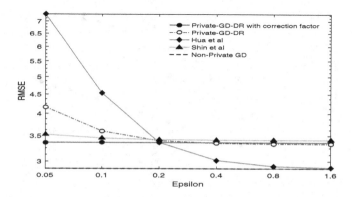

Fig. 5. On LibimSeTi, the prediction RMSEs for each algorithm.

Besides, to compare the mean square error of the results, we analyze the mean square error results for each algorithm after ten iterations, as shown in Figs. 4 and 5. For the two data sets, our algorithm is superior to the algorithms of Hua et al. and Shin et al. when ε is small. At the same time, Hua et al. satisfy $m\varepsilon$-differential privacy, and our algorithm satisfies ε differential privacy. Since our algorithm adds a correction parameter $\frac{1}{k}$ at each iteration, the mean square error does not increase significantly with k when k is large. Because the Libimseti data set has a larger scale, the resulting mean square error is larger than the MovieLens.

To test the accuracy of algorithm prediction, one data set is divided into ten parts, and their CDF (joint allocation function) is calculated separately. Nine of the ten data sets were used as training samples and the last one was used as a test sample. The prediction error $|\widehat{r_{ij}} - r_{ij}|$ of the test sample is finally calculated by 10 iterations of each training sample. $\widehat{r_{ij}}$ is the system prediction score, r_{ij} is the true score. Figures 6 and 7 show the test results of the two data sets for estimation.

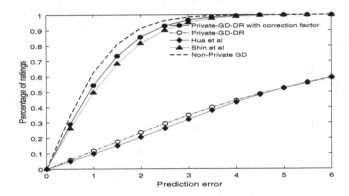

Fig. 6. On MovieLens, the prediction errors $|\widehat{r_{ij}} - r_{ij}|$ for each algorithm.

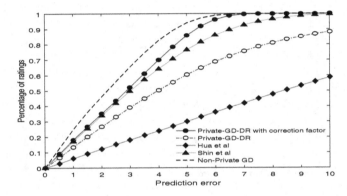

Fig. 7. On LibimSeTi, the prediction errors $|\widehat{r_{ij}} - r_{ij}|$ for each algorithm.

To evaluate the accuracy of the recommendation, we calculate the f-score of each user's recommended top-10 items, as shown in Figs. 8 and 9. In the data set MovieLens, the f-score increases with the increase of privacy budget, and when the privacy budget is small, our algorithm recommends more accuracy. In the data set LibimSeTi, when the privacy budget is small, The quality of our algorithm and Shin's algorithm recommendation are very stable, but our algorithm has a higher accuracy than Shin's algorithm. The reason can be seen in Figs. 4 and 5. The percentage of predicted errors in the MovieLens increases with the increase of the privacy budget faster than in the data set LibimSeTi, so the resulting f-score changes are more obvious.

Finally, to evaluate the influence of the iteration number, it can be analyzed by calculating the RMSE of each algorithm, as shown in Fig. 10. On the MovieLens dataset, the algorithms iteratively calculate 1, 2, 3, 4, 5, 10, 20, and 50 times, respectively, with a fixed privacy budget of 0.1. With the increase of the privacy budget, our algorithm with a suitable learning rate parameter of this algorithm can converge faster than other algorithms, thus the curve drops faster.

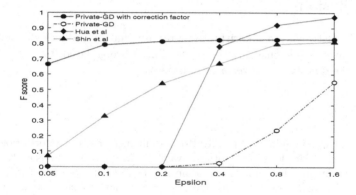

Fig. 8. On MovieLens, the F-score for each algorithm.

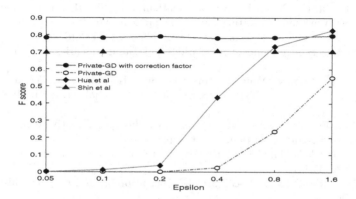

Fig. 9. On LibimSeTi, the F-score for each algorithm.

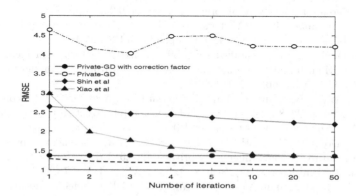

Fig. 10. On MovieLens, the prediction RMSEs of each algorithm after k iterations when $\epsilon = 0.1$.

5 Conclusion

The matrix factorization algorithm we propose sharply reduces the space and time complexity while ensuring the protection of user-related items and ratings as well as the quality of the recommendation.

References

1. Shin, H., Kim, S., Shin, J., Xiao, X.: Privacy enhanced matrix factorization for recommendation with local differential privacy. In: IEEE Transactions on Knowledge and Data Engineering, vol. 30, no. 9, pp. 1770–1782, 1 September 2018
2. Hua, J., Xia, C., Zhong, S.: Differentially private matrix factorization. In: IJCAI, pp. 1763–1770 (2015)
3. Qin, Z., Yang, Y., Yu, T., Khalil, I., Xiao, X., Ren, K.: Heavy hitter estimation over set-valued data with local differential privacy. In: CCS (2016)
4. Chen, R., Li, H., Qin, A.K., Kasiviswanathan, S.P., Jin, H.: Private spatial data aggregation in the local setting. In: ICDE, pp. 289–300 (2016)
5. Fanti, G.G., Pihur, V., Erlingsson, U.: Building a RAPPOR with the unknown: privacy-preserving learning of associations and data dictionaries. PoPETS **3**, 41–61 (2016)
6. Nguyen, T., Xiao, X., Yang, Y., Hui, S.C., Shin, H., Shin, J.: Collecting and analyzing data from smart device users with local differential privacy. In: IEEE ICDE arXiv:1907.00782 [cs.DB] (2019)
7. Shen, Y., Jin, H.: EpicRec: towards practical differentially private framework for personalized recommendation. In: CCS, pp. 180–191 (2016)
8. Xin, Y., Jaakkola, T.: Controlling privacy in recommender systems. In: NIPS, pp. 2618–2626 (2014)
9. Bassily, R., Smith, A.D.: Local, private, efficient protocols for succinct histograms. In: STOC, pp. 127–135 (2015)
10. Fanti, G., et al.: Building a rappor with the unknown: privacy-preserving learning of associations and data dictionaries. PoPETS **2016**(3), 41–61 (2016)
11. Nguyen, T., et al.: Collecting and analyzing data from smart device users with local differential privacy. arXiv preprint arXiv:1606.05053 (2016)
12. He, X., Machanavajjhala, A., Ding, B.: Blowfish privacy: tuning privacy-utility trade-offs using policies. In: SIGMOD, pp. 1447–1458 (2014)
13. Zheng, D., Xiong, Y.: A unified probabilistic matrix factorization recommendation algorithm. In: 2018 International Conference on Robots & Intelligent System (ICRIS), Changsha, pp. 246–249 (2018)
14. Liu, W., Wang, B., Wang, D.: Improved latent factor model in movie recommendation system. In: 2018 International Conference on Intelligent Autonomous Systems (ICoIAS), Singapore, pp. 101–104 (2018)
15. Sun, H., Dong, B., Wang, H.W., Yu, T., Qin, Z.: Truth inference on sparse crowdsourcing data with local differential privacy. In: 2018 IEEE International Conference on Big Data (Big Data), Seattle, WA, USA, pp. 488–497 (2018)
16. Zhao, X., Li, Y., Yuan, Y., Bi, X., Wang, G.: LDPart: effective location-record data publication via local differential privacy. IEEE Access **7**, 31435–31445 (2019)
17. Lv, L., Zhang, Z., Zhang, L.: A periodic observers synthesis approach for LDP systems based on iteration. IEEE Access **6**, 8539–8546 (2018)

18. Li, N., Qardaji, W., Su, D., Cao, J.: Privbasis: frequent itemset mining with differential privacy. PVLDB **5**(11), 1340–1351 (2012)
19. McSherry, F.D.: Privacy integrated queries: an extensible platform for privacy-preserving data analysis. In: SIGMOD, pp. 19–30 (2009)

Fully Anonymous Blockchain Constructed Based on Aggregate Signature and Ring Signature

Tianfu Chen[✉], Zhenghua Qi[✉], and Jiagen Cheng

School of Computer, Nanjing University of Posts and Telecommunications,
Nanjing, China
18852000787@163.com, qizh@njupt.edu.cn

Abstract. Aiming at the problem that transaction amount and the identity of the two parties can be analyzed and predicted to reveal the privacy of the user from the open and transparent transaction information in the traditional Bitcoin system, a fully anonymous blockchain system is constructed by combining the aggregate signature and the ring signature in this paper. The scheme combines the advantages of aggregate signature and ring signature, uses aggregate signature to protect the transaction amount privacy, uses ring signature to protect the address privacy of both parties, and at the same time compresses the transaction information size while protecting the privacy, saving a certain space overhead. Through comparing with the evaluation and analysis of various blockchain privacy protection schemes, it is concluded that the scheme takes both security and performance into account, that is, the privacy protection of transaction information is greatly improved when the reasonable overhead is increased.

Keywords: Aggregate signature · Ring signature · Full anonymous blockchain · Privacy protection

1 Introduction

In 2008, Nakamoto published a bitcoin white paper on the topic of a peer-to-peer electronic cash system [1]. As a result, blockchain technology came into being. Blockchain technology is a brand new decentralized infrastructure and distributed computing paradigm that uses encrypted chained block structures to validate and store data, utilize distributed node consensus algorithms to generate and update data, and utilize automated scripting code (smart contracts) to program and manipulate data [2]. This ensures that the blockchain has the characteristics of decentralization, timing, collective maintenance, and verifiability. Therefore, blockchain has been widely used in the design of systems such as data storage, data validation, sharing economy, dynamic key management, and supply chain financing.

With the rapid development and application of blockchain technology, its privacy issues have received extensive attention. Due to the existence of the blockchain consensus mechanism, different nodes will calculate and verify the transaction data on the blockchain, so the transaction record data on the blockchain must be made public.

© Springer Nature Switzerland AG 2019
F. Liu et al. (Eds.): SciSec 2019, LNCS 11933, pp. 250–261, 2019.
https://doi.org/10.1007/978-3-030-34637-9_19

To some extent this approach increases the transparency and credibility of the data, but from another perspective it also poses a risk of privacy breaches. Among them, the privacy protection of the identity of the two parties and the transaction amount should be paid more attention. In order to make the blockchain have a broader application prospect, data privacy protection is an important prerequisite.

This paper will combine the aggregate signature and ring signature to construct the blockchain system to realize the full anonymity which protects both two parties and the transaction content, and also ensure that the scheme has high computational efficiency. Aggregating signatures allows an efficient algorithm to aggregate n signatures on n different messages from n different users into a single signature. A ring signature is a signature generated using a single private key and a set of unrelated public keys. The advantage of compressing information by using aggregated signatures not only saves storage space but also protects privacy, and the ring signature protects the account information of the participating signature entities, further enhancing the anonymous security of the system.

2 Background

2.1 Bitcoin Blockchain System

Users and miners are two types of entities in the Bitcoin blockchain system. When the user conducts the transaction operation, the transaction information is generated and goes into transaction pool for waiting. The miners will first verify the legality of these transactions and then package them to generate blocks, and then use the proof of work to get the Nonce value. After that, they broadcast the legal block on the whole network and update the UTXO pool. The following is a case where Alice initiates a transaction to Bob as an example to show the transaction initiation and authentication process: Alice broadcasts the generated transaction information, and the nearby miners receive and verify it. The miners pack several legitimate transactions into blocks and then broadcast them to the entire network. At the same time an unspent output will be added to the Bob address. The entire transaction process is shown in Fig. 1.

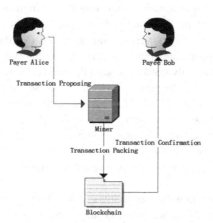

Fig. 1. Transaction process

The Bitcoin transaction structure contains transaction ID, lock time, input and output transaction, etc. The transaction ID is the hash value of the transaction entity data; the lock time locks the UTC (International Standard Time) generated by the transaction; the current transaction amount is derived from the output of the previous transaction, and the input transaction inherits the source of the amount. The input transaction needs to prove its legal ownership by the signature of the corresponding export transaction public key address. The output transaction points to different output addresses according to different transactions. The Bitcoin blockchain system generates a public key and signature based on an elliptic curve digital signature algorithm (ECDSA). The ECDSA public key performs a number of hash transformations to generate an output address. The output address can be used as a change address, which enables splitting and merging of amounts. The transaction structure is shown in Fig. 2.

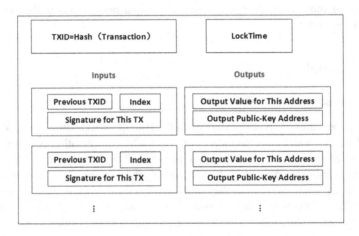

Fig. 2. Transaction structure

2.2 Aggregate Signature

An aggregate signature [3] is a variant signature that combines any number of signatures into a single signature. It contains five algorithms: key generation algorithm (Gen), signature algorithm (Sign), verification algorithm (Verify), aggregate signature algorithm (AggS) and aggregate signature verification algorithm (AggV). The aggregation signature algorithm only needs to obtain the individual signature/pair of the user participating in the signature to generate an aggregate signature. The aggregate signature verification algorithm only needs to aggregate the signature, aggregate the user public key and the message set to verify the validity of the aggregate signature. The information that the aggregated signature requires to be signed in the aggregation process is different from each other.

The unidirectional aggregation signature scheme of the reference document [4] is as follows.

The parameter conventions are as follows: p is a large prime, G and G_1 are both elliptic curve group, g is the generator of group G, $e_1 : G \times G \to G$ is a bilinear map.

I. Key generation: The private key for user i is a random number $x_i \xleftarrow{R} Z_p$. Public key is $PK_i = g^{x_i} \in G$. The total number of users is k.

II. Signature: The message to be signed is $M_i \in \{0,1\}^*$. Hash transform is $H_i = Hash(M_i) \in G$. Signature is $\delta_i = H_i^{x_i} \in G$.

III. Verification: The equation $e_1(PK = g^{x_i}, H_i) = e_1(g, \delta_i = H_i^{x_i})$ is true.

IV. Aggregate signature: The requirements for M_i are different, and the result of the aggregation is signature $\delta = \prod_{i=1}^{k} \delta_i = \prod_{i=1}^{k} H_i^{x_i} = \prod_{i=1}^{k} (Hash(M_i))^{x_i}$.

V. Aggregate signature verification: Verify that the equation $\prod_{i=1}^{k} e(v_i = g_1^{x_i}, h_i =$
$e(g_1, \delta = \prod_{i=1}^{k} \delta_i = \prod_{i=1}^{k} h_i^{x_i})$ is true.

The security of this aggregate signature scheme depends on the random prediction model, which requires a gap Diffie-Hellman (GDH) group that is difficult to assume a computational Diffie-Hellman (CDH) problem but a deterministic Diffie-Hellman (DDH) problem, and the original image of the bilinear map should be a different group (co-GDH). The difficulty of extracting independent signature individuals from the aggregate signature can be solved by solving the CDH problem [5], which explains the unidirectionality of this aggregate signature.

2.3   Ring Signature

Ring signature [6] is a new signature technology proposed in the context of anonymous disclosure of secrets, which can be regarded as a special group signature. It does not require a trusted center to exist, and the signer only needs to randomly select several other public keys, and then complete the signature by combining its own public and private keys. For a signature verifier, he can only get the signature set of the signer, not the signature that belongs to the set. In the application scenario where data needs to be protected for a long time, the unconditional anonymity of the ring signature is of great significance.

Assume that the total number of users is n, and each user u_i corresponds to a public-private key pair $\{PK_i, SK_i\}$. It mainly contains three algorithms: key generation algorithm (Gen), signature algorithm (Sign), verification algorithm (Verify).

I. Key generation: This is a Probabilistic Polynomial Time (PPT) algorithm. Each user u_i outputs a corresponding public-private key pair $\{PK_i, SK_i\}$ by inputting respective security parameters p_i, and each user's generated public-private key may be generated by different public key systems.

II. Signature: This is a PPT algorithm. When the message m, the public key set of the n ring members $\{PK_1, PK_2, ..., PK_n\}$ and the private key SK_s of one of the members are input, a signature R (a parameter in R will be ring according to certain rules) for the message m is output.

III. Verification. This is a deterministic algorithm. After inputting the message and the corresponding signature information pair (m, R), if "R" is the ring signature of m, "True" is output, otherwise "False" is output.

3   Fully Anonymous Blockchain Scheme

3.1   System Parameter Convention

PK is the signature public key; A, a are the payment public key and private key of the user respectively; r_i is a random number generated by the sender of the transaction; P_i, δ_i are the one-time public key and signature of a transaction respectively; is, os are the sum of the input amount and the sum of the output amount respectively; z represents the number of transactions; n represents the number of users participating in the ring signature; Tx is the transaction information. (For the sake of convenience, this paper uses an abbreviation to refer to this scheme, called ARFA.)

3.2   Transaction Generation and Verification

The user generates transaction information when the transaction is executed, and the miner verifies the legality of the transaction. In order to ensure that the user who initiated the transaction can only operate on the amount of the transaction he owns, and cannot freely generate or destroy the transaction amount, this requires the miner to verify the transaction.

For the transaction situation of multiple input and output, in order to hide the transaction amount of any single transaction, the scheme will adopt the elliptic curve algorithm to protect: select G as the generator of F_p to perform the encryption operation first to achieve the homomorphic characteristic. A malicious attacker can still obtain the transaction amount by controlling several inputs and outputs. To this end, the introduction of random numbers in the scheme increases the input and output delivery mode so that the verification does not pass, and the attacker cannot successfully attack. By adding an aggregate signature algorithm, ARFA compresses the signature length of a multi-input and output transaction to the signature length of a single input-output transaction while hiding the transaction amount. The aggregate signature scheme combined with the blockchain system is as follows.

I. Key generation: The aggregated user entity collection is $U_1 = \{u_1, u_2, \ldots, u_k\} \subseteq U$. $u_i \in U_1$'s signature private key is a random number $x_i \xleftarrow{R} Z_p$. The signature public key is $PK_i = g_2^{x_i} \in G_2$. The payment private key is $a_i \in E$. The payment public key is $A_i = a_i \cdot G \in E$.

II. Signature: If the user whose public key is A_i is ready to deliver an amount to the user whose public key is B_i. The sender of the transaction first generates a random number $r_i \in [1, n-1]$. Then the one-time public key $P_i = H_s(r_i B_i) \cdot G + A_i$ and the signature $\delta_i = P_i^{x_i} \in G_1$ are calculated. Also $R = r \cdot G$ will be packaged in the transaction. Then the sender of the transaction randomly selects

$d_i \in Z_p$ and calculates $iR_i = d_i \cdot G$, $ih_i = H(iR_i \| in_{a_i})$ and $is_i = d_i \cdot ih_i + in_{a_i}$. Afterwards, he continues to randomly select $t_j \in Z_p$ and calculate $oR_j = t_j \cdot G$, $oh_j = H(oR_j \| out_{a_j})$ and $os_j = t_j \cdot oh_j + out_{a_j}$. $(1 \le i \le k)$

III. Aggregate signature: Aggregate multiple signatures into one signature, that is,
$\delta \leftarrow \prod_{i=1}^{k} \delta_i \in G_1$. The input delivery mode is $\sum_{i=1}^{n} is_i$ and the input delivery mode is $\sum_{j=1}^{m} os_j$.

IV. Aggregate signature verification: Known the user collection of aggregate signature $U_1 \subseteq U$, the aggregate signature $\delta \in G_1$, the one-time public key $P_i = H_s(r_iB_i) \cdot G + A_i$ and the signature public key PK_i for each user u_i, the aggregate signature can be verified by calculation $P'_i = H_s(b_i \cdot R_i) \cdot G + A_i$. If the equation

$$e(\delta, g_2) = \prod_{i=1}^{k} e(P'_i, PK_i)$$ is true, the verification is successful, otherwise it fails.

The following is a combination of the aggregate signature and the ring signature to further improve the fully anonymous blockchain system based on the transaction amount and the transaction parties. The aggregate key is generated first, and the process refers to the above scheme. Secondly, the aggregate signature is combined with the ring signature to form an aggregate ring signature: $1 \le i \le z$, $1 \le j \le n$, the public key $PK_{i,j} \in G_2$, z transaction informations $Tx_i = \{0,1\}^*$, z private key x_i corresponding to the public key PK_{s_i} that needs to be ring signed. For all $j \ne s_i$, randomly select $a_{i,j} \xleftarrow{R} Z_p$. Calculate $tx_i = H(Tx_i) \in G_1$ and set $\delta_{s_i} = \left(tx_i / \psi \left(\prod_{j \ne s_i} PK_{i,j}^{a_{i,j}} \right) \right)^{1/x^i}$.

For all $j \ne s_i$, let $\delta_{ij} = g_1^{a_{i,j}}$, then output aggregate ring signatures $\delta = \left\langle \prod_{i=1}^{k} \delta_{i,1}, \ldots, \prod_{i=1}^{k} \delta_{i,n} \right\rangle \in G_1^n$. Finally, perform aggregate ring signature verification: Given $PK_{i,j}$, z transactions $Tx_i = \{0,1\}^*$ and aggregation ring signatures δ, calculate $tx_i = H(Tx_i) \in G_1$ and verify $\prod_{i=1}^{z} e(tx_i, g_2) = \prod_{j=1}^{n} e\left(\prod_{i=1}^{z} \delta_{ij}, \prod_{i=1}^{z} PK_{i,j} \right)$.

3.3 Transaction Packaging

In order to obtain the block reward, the miner needs to package the legal transaction into a block after the transaction is verified, and carry out the corresponding workload proof. All transactions packaged into the block are verified by the transaction. There is no reference to the unverified transaction, so these transactions can save the intermediate proof and only contain contents: $tx_i, a_{i,j}, \delta_{s_i}, PK_{i,j}$.

According to the unidirectional aggregation signature scheme [4]: this aggregation scheme requires that all signature messages participating in the aggregation are different. So the miner verifies the random number $a_{i,j}$ for each transaction to ensure that the signed messages are different. Transactions for the same random number can be put on hold for a while, waiting to be packaged into subsequent blocks for processing.

In order to solve the problem that the block storage space is limited, the number of transactions that the block can accommodate can be increased by removing the secondary information: the transaction output public key in the block can remove the encrypted public key, and only the signature of the transaction recipient is required. The key is used to prove the ownership of the transaction.

In addition, since the original transaction is an index established for the different transaction output in a single transaction, and the full anonymous blockchain system is an index established for all transaction outputs in the block that disrupts the transaction order. Thus the construction of the UTXO pool will change.

4   Evaluation of the Scheme

In this chapter, the security of the scheme is analyzed firstly to evaluate its anonymous security. Then, compared with other schemes, the efficiency of the public key ciphertext length and the transaction block size are analyzed. Finally, the rationality of the proposed scheme is summarized.

4.1   Security of the Scheme

ARFA is based on the unidirectional aggregation signature scheme [4] and the ring signature scheme [6]. The security of unidirectional aggregate signatures depends on the CDH difficulty problem on the co-GDH group [4, 5]. The aggregation selection key model [4] indicates that the security of the aggregation signature scheme is equivalent to the absence of an adversary that can falsify the aggregate signature.

Given a host A's public key to complete the existence of an aggregated signature forgery (existence forgery means that the adversary attempts to use the aggregated signature of other transaction sets to falsify the aggregated signature of the specified transaction set). The adversary A can obtain all the public keys except the challenger C public key, even the signature of the challenger C. The possibility that an attacker gains the following Game wins is called the attacker's advantage $AdvAggSig_A$ [4, 7].

- Game: Attacker A and Challenger C participate in the game.
- Initialization: Attacker A randomly generates a public key pk_1.
- Query: Attacker A signs the selected sub-transaction set with its randomly generated public key pk_1.
- Response: Attacker A obtains other $k - 1$ public keys $\{pk_2, ..., pk_k\}$ and spoofs the aggregated signature with the $k - 1$ public keys and pk_1. At the same time, attacker A can also obtain the sub-transaction set $\{Tx_1, ..., Tx_k\}$, and then output the aggregate signature δ of k users.

The condition for the attacker A to win: only if the aggregate signature generated for the sub-transaction set $\{Tx_1, ..., Tx_k\}$ corresponding to the public key $\{pk_1, ..., pk_k\}$ is valid and non-trivial.

Definition 1. If the following conditions are true, the aggregated signature attacker $A(t, q_H, q_s, N, \varepsilon)$ destroys the aggregated signature scheme of the N users in the aggregated selective key mode.

I. t is the longest execution time of A.
II. q_H is the maximum number of hash function queries executed by A. q_s is the maximum number of signature prediction queries executed by A.
III. AdvAggSig$_A$ is at least ε.
IV. Forged aggregate signatures are executed by up to N users

Theorem 1. (G_1, G_2) is a bilinear group pair of co-Diffie-Hellman, the order of each group is p, and the corresponding generator is g_1, g_2. It also contains a homogeneous mapping of G_2 to G_1, a bilinear mapping $e : G_1 \times G_2 \rightarrow G_T$. Compared to the existence of forgery in the aggregated selection key model, if all t satisfies $t \leq t' - c_{G_1}(q_H + 2q_s + N + 4) - (N - 1)$ and all ε satisfies $\varepsilon \geq e(q_s + N) \cdot \varepsilon'$ (e is the natural logarithm and c_{G_1} is the time spent on exponentiation and inversion operations on G_1), then the bilinear aggregate signature scheme on (G_1, G_2) is safe based on $(t, q_H, q_s, N, \varepsilon)$.

With the continuous development of ring signatures, their unforgeable security models can be classified into three types according to different security levels. The security model of the ring signature scheme [6] is as follows: there is a signer K, an attacker B. K obtains the ring public key set $\{pk_1, pk_2, ..., pk_n\}$ through the ring member set I (n is the total number of all members in the ring). B sends a message m_i to the K with a polynomial of no more than l for the ring signature inquiry of I_i. After obtaining the ring signature I_i, m, δ, B cannot obtain the ring signature I_i, m, δ of the message m with a non-negligible probability ($I' \subset I, B \notin I', m \notin$ {Inquired message m_i}). Then it is safe in Model1.

Through the transaction verification, the scheme can make the transaction initiator unable to falsify the encryption amount during the transaction generation process. The miner without the encryption scheme private key can only verify the legality of the transaction. In the implementation of the scheme, the encrypted public key of the transaction payee in the blockchain data may be deleted to increase the number of transactions that can be accommodated in the block. The aggregated signature guarantees the transaction amount privacy by aggregating the data. The ring signature guarantees the privacy of both parties by protecting the subject account information of the participating signature. Therefore, this blockchain scheme is fully anonymous.

4.2   Efficiency Analysis of the Scheme

Public Key and Ciphertext Length. According to the current hardware system, the selection requirements for cryptographic security parameters are as follows. The decomposition scheme based on the large integer is 2048b (256B), and the security parameter based on the elliptic curve scheme is 256b (32B). In addition, points on the elliptic curve expressed using 256b can be represented by 33B [8]. In ARFA, 32B is used to represent the elliptic curve of the aggregated signature. The ring signature scheme uses 256B to represent the large composite number.

In order to increase the number of transactions that can be accommodated in the block, the scheme removes the public key of the encrypted transaction in the block transaction output address after the miner verifies the legality of the transaction. Therefore, the length of the transaction public key on the blockchain is $|PK| = |g^x| = $ 33B. Encrypted transactions require a large number of modulo, so the ciphertext length of ARFA is $|n| = 256$B.

Regardless of P2PKH, the original bitcoin blockchain system output amount space is 8B, ECDSA public key space is 33B. The ECDH key and ECDSA public key length are both 33B, a total of 66B [9]. The ciphertext is in the form of Pedersen's promise, and the promised ciphertext is a point on the elliptic curve with a length of 33B. If the security (large integer decomposition requires a large number of 256B) is the same, then the Paillier ciphertext required by the Dumb Account system [10] requires 512B to represent the modulo n^2 group. The encrypted public key is a large composite number and a group generator. Considering the ECDSA signature public key at the same time, the total public key length is 256*2 + 33 = 545B.

Size of the Trading Block. Compared with the original Bitcoin blockchain scheme, ARFA converts the plaintext storage amount into the ciphertext on modulo n group, so the transaction size will increase accordingly. The aggregated signatures are used to aggregate the signatures of all transactions in the block into a signature, and the encryption scheme public key is removed from the transaction inclusion process, which in turn reduces the transaction size in the block.

The original Bitcoin blockchain system has an average block size of 644.2kB in recent years, and the number of transactions accommodated is 1682 [11]. Removing the block header and related information of about 100B, the size of each transaction is about 392B. Among them, the data that is not related to input and output at the beginning and end of the transaction is 8B. Regardless of the P2PKH case and the input/output counter size: the single input includes the reference previous transaction hash value 32B, the index 4B, the ECDSA signature 64B, and the sequence number 4B. The single output includes the ECDSA public key 33B and the amount 4B. Therefore, when the input and output are equal, there are about 2.65 input and output. Combine the public key and ciphertext length of each scheme in Sect. 3.2.1, and calculate the transactions number included in each scheme block when the input and output are equal, as shown in Table 1.

Table 1. Comparison of Public Key Length, Ciphertext Length and Transactions Number

Efficiency analysis indicator	Public key length(/B)	Ciphertext length(/B)	Transactions number(/PCS)
Traditional Bitcoin System	33	\	1682
Standard CT [8]	66	33	1208
Dumb Account [10]	545	512	207
This Scheme (ARFA)	33	256	687

According to the comprehensive Table 1 analysis, although ARFA has no advantage over the ciphertext length of the standard encrypted transaction, the standard encrypted transaction still needs an additional communication channel to notify the payee of the specific transaction amount when the user performs the transaction, and the payee cannot verify whether to receive the transactions amount.

5   Related Work

In view of the privacy leakage problem of blockchain, the research on privacy protection mechanism is mainly focused on three aspects: network layer, transaction layer and application layer [12]. The network layer defense mechanism is mainly to increase the difficulty of the attacker collecting network layer data, which can be completed by restricting access, malicious node detection and shielding, and network layer data confusion. The trading layer protection mechanism focuses on preventing malicious nodes from obtaining accurate transaction data. Data distortion, data encryption, and data restriction publishing technologies can be adopted. The focus of the application layer defense mechanism is from the user's point of view. Commonly used methods are blockchain applications and blockchain procedures with privacy protection mechanisms.

This paper focuses on the privacy protection of the transaction layer. At present, three measures are taken for the privacy protection of the digital currency agreement in the transaction layer:

1. Data distortion based solution: the coin mechanism: The coinage mechanism was first proposed by Chaum in a paper [13] published in 1981, initially to achieve anonymous communication between the two parties. In order to confuse the connection between the two parties, Maxwell proposed the idea of CoinJoin in 2013 [14]. Although this mechanism successfully confuses the connection between the two parties, this method only protects the user's identity privacy, and does not take privacy protection measures for the transaction amount.
2. Protection scheme based on encryption mechanism: The objects that need to be encrypted in the blockchain mainly include the parties to the transaction and the contents of the transaction. In digital currency applications, alternative currencies based on encryption mechanisms have emerged, such as Dash [15], Monroe [16], ZeroCoin [17], and ZeroCash [18]. They all solve the privacy problem of transaction data to a certain extent, and the principles are different, so the blockchain scenarios are different. The key technology of Dash is to mix multiple transactions of multiple users into a single transaction through some master nodes. In order to solve the problem that the Dash master node is controlled, Monroe proposes an encryption scheme that does not rely on the central node: the ring transaction is used to hide the real transaction address. ZeroCoin's flaw is that it only protects the privacy of the payer. The use of zero-knowledge proof for ZeroCash avoids malicious user attacks in Monroe, allowing users to hide transaction information only by interacting with the cryptocurrency itself. However, the process of generating proof by the zero-knowledge proof algorithm is very slow and the efficiency has a bottleneck.

3. Protection scheme based on restricted release: ARFA means to directly remove information related to privacy from the database. Compared with the mechanism of mixed currency and encryption, the purpose of ARFA is to fundamentally eliminate the hidden dangers of privacy. At present, the payment of lightning and the division of the alliance chain and the private chain are born based on the idea of ARFA.

6   Conclusion

This paper combines the aggregate signature and the ring signature to construct a full anonymous blockchain system, which solves the privacy protection and performance of the cryptocurrency to some extent. Compared with the separate aggregation signature scheme and the separate ring signature scheme, ARFA not only conceals the address and transaction amount of both parties, but also compresses the signature space and improves the performance of the blockchain system. Compared with the traditional bitcoin system, the capacity for introducing the stored ciphertext due to the improvement of security performance is also reasonable. The conversion of the ring signature scheme to the prime order group and the research based on the ECC field can further improve the efficiency of the scheme. The future work will continue to be improved on the basis of ARFA.

References

1. Nakamoto, S. Bitcoin: a peer-to-peer electronic cash system (2008)
2. Yong, Y., Feiyue, W.: Blockchain: the state of the art and future trend. J. Autom. **42**(4), 481–494 (2016)
3. Yang, T., Kong, L., Hu, J., et al.: A survey of polymeric signatures and their applications. Comput. Res. Dev. **2012**(s2), 192–199 (2012)
4. Boneh, D., Gentry, C., Lynn, B., Shacham, H.: Aggregate and verifiably encrypted signatures from bilinear maps. In: Biham, E. (ed.) EUROCRYPT 2003. LNCS, vol. 2656, pp. 416–432. Springer, Heidelberg (2003). https://doi.org/10.1007/3-540-39200-9_26
5. Coron, J.-S., Naccache, D.: Boneh *et al.*'s *k*-element aggregate extraction assumption is equivalent to the Diffie-Hellman assumption. In: Laih, C.-S. (ed.) ASIACRYPT 2003. LNCS, vol. 2894, pp. 392–397. Springer, Heidelberg (2003). https://doi.org/10.1007/978-3-540-40061-5_25
6. Guoyin, Z., Lingling, W., Chunguang, Ma.: Progress in ring signature research. J. Commun. **28**(5), 109–117 (2007)
7. Micali, S., Ohta, K., Reyzin, L.: Accountable-subgroup multisignatures. In: Proceedings of the 8th ACM Conference on Computer and Communications Security, pp. 245–254. ACM (2001)
8. Maxwell, G. Confidential transactions (2015). https://people.xiph.org/~greg/confidential_values.txt. Accessed 21 Nov 2016
9. Gibson, A.: An investigation into confidential transactions (2016)
10. Wang, Q., Qin, B., Hu, J., et al.: Preserving transaction privacy in Bitcoin. Future Gener. Comput. Syst. (2017)

11. Blockchain Ltd.: Blockchain Charts. https://blockchain.info/en/charts. Accessed 02 Nov 2018
12. Zhu, L.: A survey of research on blockchain privacy protection. Comput. Res. Dev. (2017)
13. Chaum, D.L.: Untraceable electronic mail, return addresses, and digital pseudonyms. Commun. ACM **24**(2), 84–90 (1981)
14. Maxwell, G. CoinJoin: Bitcoin privacy for the real world. In: Post on Bitcoin Forum (2013)
15. Cachin, C.: Architecture of the hyperledger blockchain fabric. In: Workshop on Distributed Cryptocurrencies and Consensus Ledgers, vol. 310 (2016)
16. Monero: About monero. https://getmonero.org/knowledge-base/about. Accessed 10 June 2017
17. Sasson, E.B., Chiesa, A., Garman, C., Green, M., Miers, I., Tromer, E., Virza, M.: Zerocash: decentralized anonymous payments from bitcoin. In: 2014 IEEE Symposium on Security and Privacy, pp. 459–474. IEEE (2014)
18. Miers, I., Garman, C., Green, M., Rubin, A.D.: Zerocoin: Anonymous distributed e-cash from bitcoin. In 2013 IEEE Symposium on Security and Privacy, pp. 397–411. IEEE (2013)
19. Van Saberhagen, N.C.: v2. 0, 17(10) (2013). CryptoNote.org

FDIA-Identified Overloaded Power Lines

Da-Tian Peng[1(✉)], Jianmin Dong[1], Qinke Peng[1], Bo Zeng[2],
and Zhi-Hong Mao[2]

[1] Xi'an Jiaotong University, Xi'an 710049, Shaanxi, China
{pengdatian,jianmind23}@stu.xjtu.edu.cn, qkpeng@xjtu.edu.cn
[2] University of Pittsubrgh, Pittsburgh, PA 15260, USA
{bzeng,zhm4}@pitt.edu

Abstract. Blackout events indicate that the overloaded power lines are
the chief culprit to trigger the large-scale cascading failures hidden in
the power grid. In order to protect the grid from the cascading failures,
this paper aims to design a false data injection attack for the operators
to identify the overloaded power lines. A leader-follower game-theoretic
bi-level optimization model is formulated to maximize the set of overloaded power lines. To evaluate the performance of our proposed method,
numerical simulations are performed on the IEEE 14-bus, 30-bus, 57-bus,
and 118-bus systems. The results of Monte Carlo experiments indicate
that the occurrence frequency of overloaded power lines is the most in
our method.

Keywords: Bilevel optimization · Cascading failure · False data
injection attack · Overloading

1 Introduction

Smart grid is a typical *cyber-physical system* (CPS), integrating the advanced
technologies of computer, communication, and control. Broadly, a power grid is
divided into the generators that supply the power, the transmission system that
carries the power from the generating centers to the load centers, and the distribution system that feeds the power to nearby customers. In the modern society,
power grid is a critical energy infrastructure to support nearly all industrial
and economic systems. Thus, the security assurance is vital for every electrical
component deployed to supply, transfer, and consume electricity [1].

On August 2003, an overheated power line drooped into the foliage, causing
a widespread power outage throughout parts of the Northeastern between USA
and Canada [2]. This blackout event indicates that the overloaded power lines
are the chief culprits who cause the large-scale cascading failures. Generally,
cascading failures often hide in the grid. Only when some initial triggers are
activated due to the storm, high temperature, fire, or cyber attack, cascading

Supported in part by National Key R&D Program of China under Grant
2018YFC0809001.

F. Liu et al. (Eds.): SciSec 2019, LNCS 11933, pp. 262–277, 2019.
https://doi.org/10.1007/978-3-030-34637-9_20

failures happen immediately. Indeed, the overloaded power lines play a role of trigger, like the first fallen card in the domino game. Therefore, it is significant to screen overloaded power lines for preventing cascading failures. Especially, in the electricity maintenance phase, the staff can purposefully monitor these identified sensitive lines, saving lots of human resources. Even in the holistic power planning phase, the identification result can guide the operator to amend the vulnerabilities for the precaution of line outages in advance. Nevertheless, a main challenge is how to effectively screen out the overloaded power lines from the whole grid.

Cascading failure is a process in a system of interconnected parts where the initial failure of one or few parts can break the original load equilibrium and then trigger the sequential failures of other parts one after another until a new equilibrium is established. This phenomenon is also known as butterfly, avalanche, and domino effect. In practice, most power grids have adopted N-1 secure criterion. However, multiple hidden failures may co-occur at a very short period of time beyond the N-1 secure capacity and such N-k contingencies can cause the uncontrolled successive loss of interdependent elements. To understand, predict, and prevent cascading failures, the existing studies have made great advances in modeling the cascade propagation patterns [3–10], which can be classified into two aspects. (i) Some stochastic simulations were performed to mimic as many cascade as possible by randomly isolating one or multiple lines ORNL-PSerc-Alaska (OPA) model described the DC power flow-based dynamic process and analyzed the selforganization criticality [3]. An improved OPA model interpreted the iterative load redistribution in the fast dynamic process and the evolution of power planning in the slow dynamics process [4]. A feed forward neural network model was trained in the database from simulating N-k contingency induced cascading failures to learn cascading patterns [5]. (ii) Some dynamic models were built to capture the cascade propagation characteristics. An interaction model was proposed by using the tripping probability of each component and the interactions between component failures to identify key lines [6]. A swing equation was introduced into calculating dynamical transient flows to forecast the critical lines [7]. A general interdependent models analyzed the robustness of interacting networks subject to cascading failures [8]. An unified percolation and overload failure model found that cascading failures showed spatially long-range correlated with correlations decaying slowly with distance [9]. An integrated model was built using the concepts of complex networks and electrical laws to illustrate that the decentralized generator locations might greatly increase the robustness of the grid [10]. The above studies either need a mass of simulations to enumerate all possible cascade paths or formulate a complex model to consider the specified operation conditions. Instead of these simulations with heavy computational burden and complex but non-generalized model, we introduce the generative adversarial strategy to reveal the weak portion of the whole grid. Specifically, we attempt to design a most-effectiveness attack and cause the most possible overloaded lines that are the trigger of cascading failures. When these overloaded lines are screened, the staff only monitor these lines to prevent cascading failures. That is, if the first possible fallen card is stood up all the time, the domino game never occur.

With the increasing integration of cyber and physical components, power grid is becoming vulnerable to cyber attacks. For instance, on December 2015, a synchronized and coordinated cyber attack compromised three Ukrainian regional electric power distribution companies and this blackout were caused by remote cyber intrusions, impacting approximately 225,000 customers for several hours [11]. The investigation report from an interagency team indicated that some malware such as Trojan, KillDisk and BlackEnergy had been found to erase selected files and corrupt the master boot record for rendering system inoperable [12]. A typical stealthy attack, *false data injection attack* (FDIA) can inject the well-designed false data into the meters' measurements without being detected by the bad data detection (BDD) and then mislead the controller to make erroneous decisions. An attacker was able to perform the long-term interception for the operational data and had sufficient prior-knowledge for launching a successful FDI attack [13]. Hence, a feasible solution is to identify the overloaded lines using FDIA to model the decision-making process between attacker and target grid's controller (security constrained economic dispatch (SCED)).

Indeed, some existing studies have focused on designing different game-theoretic strategies to undermine transmission lines in the physical layer. For example, a load redistribution attack strategy was proposed that may cause multiple line overloadings [14]. A game-theoretic strategy was presented to maximize the total power flows of all overloaded lines [15], a two-stage line outage model to trigger the hidden N-k contingency [16], two multi-stage screening models to maximize the joint probabilities of the line trippings [17] and the number of the tripped lines [18]. These studies indicate that the leader-follower game-theoretic framework is general to study the attack-defense interaction. Following this framework, we formulate a bi-level model to deeply study how FDIA may induce the line overloading and even tripping. However, these studies are confined in a *targeted* strategy, aiming to overload a set of prespecified power lines, e.g., Ref. [14] and [19]. Apparently, an *untargeted* strategy is significant to identify as many overloaded lines as possible for the whole grid. In this work, we study the untargeted strategy, where the attackers do not pre-select the set of transmission lines to attack but, instead, formulate the optimization problem to screen the most possible overloaded lines in the whole grid. Meanwhile, in order to evaluate the performance of our method, we perform Mente Carlo experiments to simulate the initial stage of cascading failures. Main contributions of our work include:

(i) We reveal the vulnerability of power grid under the FDIA, motivating to make some protection mechanisms for the power grid.
(ii) We formulate a leader-follower bilevel optimization problem to model the adversarial interaction between attacker and SCED, identifying the most possible overloaded lines and reformulate this bi-level model into single-level mixed integer liner program (MILP) for computational tractability.

(iii) We evaluate the proposed attack strategies on the IEEE 14-bus, 30-bus, 57-bus, and 118-bus systems. Especially, we perform Monte Carlo experiments to simulate the initial stage of the cascading failures.

The rest of this paper is organized as follows: Sect. 2 give the problem formulation; Sect. 3 describes the solution strategy to solve the bi-level optimization; Sect. 4 performs the numerical simulations; and Sect. 5 concludes this work.

2 Problem Formulation

To ease the representation of a power grid, the power grid can be modeled as an undirected graph $\mathcal{G} = (V, E)$, as shown in Fig. 1, where the node set V is the collection of buses that are connected to generators and/or loads, and the link set E the collection of transmission lines that are equipped the circuit breakers. It is worth noting that a circuit breaker is always a standard configuration to protect a line from damage caused by excess current from an overload or short circuit, which is an automatically operated electrical switch to interrupt flow after a fault is detected. Table 1 lists the notations involved in this paper.

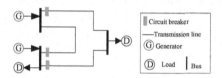

Fig. 1. An undirected graph modeling a power grid.

Recall that we always stand the operators' side to analyze the attacker's decision-making process how to cause the most overloaded lines. To this end, we first introduce the FDIA-induced line tripping and then formulate a bi-level optimization model.

2.1 FDIA-Induced Line Tripping

In the following, we describe how the FDIA may induce the line overloading and even tripping. First, suppose that the attackers are able to tamper the readings of partial load meters stealthily. The false load injection model is formulate as

$$\tilde{P}_d = P_d + \Delta P_d \tag{1}$$

where ΔP_d satisfies the following constraints

$$\begin{cases} \mathbf{1}^\mathrm{T} \Delta P_d = 0 & (2) \\ -\tau P_d \preceq \Delta P_d \preceq \tau P_d & (3) \end{cases}$$

Table 1. Notation list

Symbol	Description	Symbol	Description
V_g	Set of buses linked to generators	V_d	Set of buses linked to loads
N_g	Size of V_g	N_d	Size of V_d
N_b	Size of V	N_f	Size of E
k	Index of generators	l	Index of transmission lines
$N_a^{\max}$	Maximum number of available load	τ	Detection coefficient, $\tau \in [0,1]$
E^o	Overloading set of transmission lines	γ_m	Marginal loading ratio
γ_o	Line overloading ratio	γ	Line loading ratio
c_g	Unit generation cost	K_f	Bus-branch reactance matrix
$P_g^{\min}$	Lower bounds of generation capacity	K_s	Injection shift factor matrix
$P_g^{\max}$	Upper bounds of generation capacity	K_d	Bus-load incidence matrix
$P_f^{\max}$	Upper bounds of line's thermal limit	K_g	Bus-generator incidence matrix
P_d	Loads before attacks	K_b	System susceptance matrix
P_g	Generation power before attacks	$\tilde{P}_d$	Loads after attacks
$\tilde{\theta}$	Estimated phase angles after attacks	$\tilde{P}_g$	Generation power after attacks
$\tilde{P}_f$	Estimated power flow after attacks	$\bar{\theta}$	Actual phase angles after attacks
$\tilde{P}_g^*$	Optimal generation after attacks	$\bar{P}_f$	Actual power flow after attacks
z	Binary indicator of line overloading	ΔP_f	Incremental power flow
α	Binary indicator of load modification	ΔP_d	Injected false load
$\lambda, \underline{\nu}, \overline{\nu}$	KKT multipliers	$\xi, \underline{\delta}, \overline{\delta}$	KKT multipliers

Constraint (2) ensures the generation-load balance and (3) indicates that ΔP_d can bypass the threshold-based bad data detector, which is configured in the supervisory control and data acquisition (SCADA) of the control center to supervise whether the outliers exist in the raw measurements of the load meters through comparing the prespecified threshold with the residue between measurements and their estimations. Namely, (2) and (3) characterize the stealthiness behavior of FDIA. Note that the attackers can estimate τ by performing the long-term reconnaissance and extracting the boundary of these historical data.

Second, when these contaminated readings $\tilde{P}_d$ are sent to the control center, the SCED will be misguided to allocate a new generation order to each generator in the process of calculating optimal power flow (OPF). Consequently, the corrupted power flow is estimated in the SCED as

$$\tilde{P}_f = K_s(K_g\tilde{P}_g - K_d\tilde{P}_d) \tag{4}$$

which is constrained within the range $-P_f^{\max} \preceq \tilde{P}_f \preceq P_f^{\max}$. Meanwhile, the generators produce these corrupted generation power accordingly. Here we have the nodal power balance equations before and after attacks as

$$\mathbf{1}^{\mathrm{T}}P_d = \mathbf{1}^{\mathrm{T}}P_g \quad \text{and} \quad \mathbf{1}^{\mathrm{T}}\tilde{P}_d = \mathbf{1}^{\mathrm{T}}\tilde{P}_g,$$

respectively. Since the sum of injected false load is zero as (2), the above two equalities are consistent numerically, i.e.,

$$1^T P_d = 1^T P_g = 1^T \tilde{P}_d = 1^T \tilde{P}_g.$$

These equalities indicate that before attacks, $\tilde{P}_g$ matches $\tilde{P}_d$, However, after attacks, $\tilde{P}_g$ mismatches P_d. The mismatching will result in the load redistribution in the physical layer.

Third, according to the Kirchhoff's Law, the load redistribution calculates the actual power flow as

$$\bar{P}_f = K_s(K_g \tilde{P}_g - K_d P_d). \tag{5}$$

Comparing (4) and (5), we have

$$\Delta P_f = \bar{P}_f - \tilde{P}_f = K_s K_d \Delta P_d. \tag{6}$$

Further, we have the following forms from (3) and (6),

$$\begin{cases} |\Delta P_{f,l}| \leq \tau |[K_s K_d P_d]_l| \\ |\bar{P}_{f,l}| \leq \bar{P}_{f,l}^{\max}, \quad \forall l \in E \end{cases} \tag{7}$$

where $[K_s K_d P_d]_l$ denotes the lth element of the vector $K_s K_d P_d$ and $\bar{P}_{f,l}^{\max} = P_{f,l}^{\max} + \tau |[K_s K_d P_d]_l|$. The above inequalities indicate that the actual power flow of multiple transmission lines might exceed their thermal limits, forming a set of overloaded lines E^o, defined as

$$E^o = \{l \mid \gamma_l \geq \gamma_o, \gamma_l = |\bar{P}_{f,l}|/P_{f,l}^{\max}, l \in E\}$$

Note that E^o is not pre-specified in this study, which is different from the previous studies [14,19] where the attackers artificially preselect a set of transmission lines to be overloaded. This untargeted strategy is more effective to identify the more transmission lines that may be overloaded.

Fourth, when the transmission lines are overloaded, these lines may trip with a high probability. To characterize the stochastic process of line tripping, some studies introduce the cumulative distribution function (CDF), e.g., the exponential-based CDF model [20], normal-based CDF model [21], and uniform-based CDF model [22]. Here we adopt the uniform-based CDF model as follows

$$p(\gamma_\ell) = \begin{cases} 0 & 0 \leq \gamma_\ell < 1.00 \\ 2.50(\gamma_\ell - 1) & 1 \leq \gamma_\ell < 1.40 \quad \forall \ell \in \mathbb{E}. \\ 1 & \gamma_\ell \geq 1.40 \end{cases} \tag{8}$$

Figure 2 illustrates the mapping between the line loading ratio and line tripping probability. Any line whose loading ratio is below the overloading ratio $\gamma_o = 1.00$ will never trip under the normal operation. As the line loading ratio γ_l increases up to the marginal loading ratio $\gamma_m = 1.40$, the line tripping probability increases gradually until 1.00.

2.2   Bilevel Optimization Model

Recall that our main purpose is to identify the most possible overloaded lines, i.e., maximize $|E^o|$, the total number of overloaded lines. Figure 3 shows a leader-follower game-theoretic framework to describe the decision-making interaction between attacker and SCED. The attacker is the game leader in the upper level and launch the FDIA to inject the false load ΔP_d into the readings of load meters. The SCED in the contaminated cyber/information layer is the game follower in the lower level and can perform optimal power flow (OPF) to dispatch the corrupted generation $\tilde{P}_g$ into the physical grid after receiving the corrupted load measurements $\tilde{P}_d$. Due to the mismatching of $\tilde{P}_g$ and P_d in the physical grid, the power flow will be recalculated to redistribute $\bar{P}_f$ for all power lines. This situation provides a possible opportunity to generate the most possible overloaded transmission lines. Then we formulate a bi-level model as follows

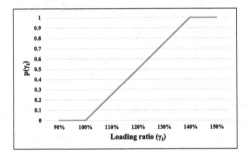

Fig. 2. Line tripping probability distribution as loading ratio increases.

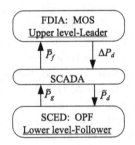

Fig. 3. A diagram of leader-follower game-theoretic framework.

$$\max_{\Delta P_d} \mathbf{1}^{\mathrm{T}} z \tag{9}$$

$$\text{s.t. } \tilde{P}_d = P_d + \Delta P_d, \ \mathbf{1}^{\mathrm{T}} \Delta P_d = 0, \ -\tau P_d \preceq \Delta P_d \preceq \tau P_d$$

$$\gamma_l \geq \gamma_o \Leftrightarrow z_l = 1, \ z_l \in \{0,1\} \qquad\qquad \forall l \in E \tag{10}$$

$$K_b \bar{\theta} = K_g \tilde{P}_g - K_d P_d \tag{11}$$

$$\bar{P}_f = K_f \bar{\theta} \tag{12}$$

$$\Delta P_{d,k} \neq 0 \Leftrightarrow \alpha_k = 1, \ \alpha_k \in \{0,1\} \qquad \forall k \in V_d \tag{13}$$

$$\mathbf{1}^{\mathrm{T}} \boldsymbol{\alpha} \leq N_a^{\max} \tag{14}$$

$$\tilde{\boldsymbol{P}}_g^* \in \arg \left\{ \min \boldsymbol{c}_g^{\mathrm{T}} \tilde{\boldsymbol{P}}_g : \text{s.t.} \right. \tag{15}$$

$$K_b \tilde{\theta} = K_g \tilde{\boldsymbol{P}}_g - K_d \tilde{\boldsymbol{P}}_d \qquad \qquad (\boldsymbol{\lambda}) \tag{16}$$

$$\tilde{\boldsymbol{P}}_f = K_f \tilde{\theta} \qquad \qquad (\boldsymbol{\xi}) \tag{17}$$

$$\boldsymbol{P}_g^{\min} \preceq \tilde{\boldsymbol{P}}_g \preceq \boldsymbol{P}_g^{\max} \qquad \qquad (\underline{\boldsymbol{\nu}}, \overline{\boldsymbol{\nu}}) \tag{18}$$

$$- \boldsymbol{P}_f^{\max} \leq \tilde{\boldsymbol{P}}_f \preceq \boldsymbol{P}_f^{\max} \qquad \qquad (\underline{\boldsymbol{\delta}}, \overline{\boldsymbol{\delta}}) \left. \right\}. \tag{19}$$

The decision-making process of SCED misled by the attack is formulated in the lower level (15)-(19). Objective (15) minimizes the total generation costs. (16) and (17) perform the Kirchhoff's Law. (18) and (19) consider the generation capacity and lines' thermal limit, respectively. The decision-making process of attacker is formulated in the upper level (9)-(14). To indicate the line overloading state, we define a binary indicator $\boldsymbol{z}$ in (10): $z_l = 1$ if and only if the lth line is overloaded, i.e, $\gamma_l \geq \gamma_0$; otherwise, $z_l = 0$. Thus, the sum of all elements of $\boldsymbol{z}$, i.e., $\mathbf{1}^{\mathrm{T}} \boldsymbol{z}$, can be used to quantify the total number of overloaded lines in E^o. Maximizing the objective function (9) is to obtain the most overloaded lines. (11) and (12) perform the Kirchhoff's Law again, due to the load redistribution. To indicate the modification state of load meters' readings, we also define a binary indicator $\boldsymbol{\alpha}$ in (13): $\alpha_k = 1$ if and only if the reading of kth load meter is modified, i.e., $\Delta P_{d,k} \neq 0$; otherwise, $\alpha_k = 0$. (14) denotes that the total number of modified meters is no more than the specified maximum number $N_a^{\max}$.

The above bi-level optimization problem cannot be solved directly, because it contains bi-level objective functions and some logical constraints. To solve them feasibly, we will present some effective solution strategies in the next section.

3 Solution Strategy

In this section, we introduce how the foregoing bi-level optimization model is reformulated into a single-level MILP problem.

3.1 Linearization Approach

To linearize $|\bar{P}_{f,l}|$, $l \in E$, we introduce a binary variable $\beta_l \in \{0,1\}$ and write $|\bar{P}_{f,l}| = \bar{P}_{f,l}\beta_l - \bar{P}_{f,l}(1 - \beta_l)$. We define an auxiliary variable $\eta_l \in \mathbb{R}$: $\eta_l = \bar{P}_{f,l}\beta_l$, which is the product of a binary variable and a continuous variable. Referred to the bounds $|\bar{P}_{f,l}| \leq \bar{P}_{f,l}^{\max}$ mentioned in (7), we linearize this product as

$$\begin{cases} -\bar{P}_{f,l}^{\max} \leq \eta_l \leq \bar{P}_{f,l}^{\max} \\ -\bar{P}_{f,l}^{\max}\beta_l \leq \eta_l \leq \bar{P}_{f,l}^{\max}\beta_l \\ \eta_l \geq \bar{P}_{f,l} - (1 - \beta_l)\bar{P}_{f,l}^{\max} \\ \eta_l \leq \bar{P}_{f,l} + (1 - \beta_l)\bar{P}_{f,l}^{\max} \end{cases} \quad \forall l \in E. \tag{20}$$

Hence, the nonlinear term $|\bar{P}_{f,l}|$ in (10) can be substituted by the linear form

$$|\bar{P}_{f,l}| = 2\eta_l - \bar{P}_{f,l}.\tag{21}$$

The logical constraint (10) can be rewritten in its linear form

$$2\eta_l - \bar{P}_{f,l} - \gamma_o P_{f,l}^{\max} \ge z_l, \quad \forall l \in E.\tag{22}$$

After introducing two new binary variables α_+^k and α_-^k, we can rewrite (13) in a mixed integer linear form

$$\begin{cases} -\tau P_{d,k}\alpha^k \le \Delta P_{d,k} \le \tau P_{d,k}\alpha^k \\ \Delta P_{d,k} \ge -\tau P_{d,k}(1-\rho_+^k) + \epsilon\alpha_+^k \\ \Delta P_{d,k} \le \tau P_{d,k}(1-\rho_-^k) - \epsilon\alpha_-^k \\ \alpha_+^k + \alpha_-^k - 2\alpha^k \le 0 \qquad \forall k \in V_d \\ \alpha_+^k + \alpha_-^k + \alpha^k \le 2 \\ \alpha_+^k + \alpha_-^k - \alpha^k \ge 0 \\ \alpha_+^k, \alpha_-^k, \alpha^k \in \{0,1\} \end{cases}\tag{23}$$

where ϵ is a small positive real number.

3.2 Karush–Kuhn–Tucker (KKT) Conditions

We use the KKT conditions to transform the bi-level optimization problem into a single-level MILP problem. We can derive the dual conditions of (15)–(19) as

$$\begin{cases} \boldsymbol{c}_g - \boldsymbol{K}_g^{\mathrm{T}}\boldsymbol{\lambda} - \underline{\boldsymbol{\nu}} + \overline{\boldsymbol{\nu}} = 0 \\ \boldsymbol{K}_b^{\mathrm{T}}\boldsymbol{\lambda} + \boldsymbol{K}_f^{\mathrm{T}}\boldsymbol{\xi} = 0 \\ -\boldsymbol{\xi} - \underline{\boldsymbol{\delta}} + \overline{\boldsymbol{\delta}} = 0 \end{cases}\tag{24}$$

and obtain the linearized complementary slackness conditions as

$$\begin{cases} 0 \le \underline{\nu}_k \le M\underline{\psi}_{g,k} \\ \tilde{P}_{g,k} - P_{g,k}^{\min} \le M(1 - \underline{\psi}_{g,k}) \\ 0 \le \overline{\nu}_k \le M\overline{\psi}_{g,k} \qquad \forall k \in V_g \\ P_{g,k}^{\max} - \tilde{P}_{g,k} \le M(1 - \overline{\psi}_{g,k}) \\ \underline{\psi}_{g,k} + \overline{\psi}_{g,k} \le 1 \\ \underline{\psi}_{g,k}, \overline{\psi}_{g,k} \in \{0,1\} \end{cases}\tag{25}$$

$$\begin{cases} 0 \le \underline{\delta}_l \le M\underline{\psi}_{f,l} \\ \tilde{P}_{f,l} + P_{f,l}^{\max} \le M(1 - \underline{\psi}_{f,l}) \\ 0 \le \overline{\delta}_l \le M\overline{\psi}_{f,l} \qquad \forall l \in E \\ P_{f,l}^{\max} - \tilde{P}_{f,l} \le M(1 - \overline{\psi}_{f,l}) \\ \underline{\psi}_{f,l} + \overline{\psi}_{f,l} \le 1 \\ \underline{\psi}_{f,l}, \overline{\psi}_{f,l} \in \{0,1\} \end{cases}\tag{26}$$

where $\underline{\psi}_{g,k}$, $\overline{\psi}_{g,k}$, $\underline{\psi}_{f,l}$, and $\overline{\psi}_{f,l}$ are the auxiliary binary variables, M a big positive real number, and we set $M = 1/\epsilon$ in this paper.

Therefore, we obtain the single-level MILP problem as follows

$$\max_{\Delta P_d} \sum_{l \in E} z_l$$

$$\text{s.t. } (1) - (3), (11), (12), (14), (16) - (19),$$
$$(20), (21), (23) - (26).$$

This MILP problem can be solved directly in a commercial solver: CVX-Gurobi, a package for solving convex programming [23].

4 Numerical Illustration

In this section, we perform numerical simulations on IEEE 14-bus, 30-bus, 57-bus, and 118-bus systems. Their configuration parameters are referred to Matpower, a popular platform of IEEE test systems [24], including P_d, K_b, K_s, K_g, K_d, K_f, c_g, $P_g^{\min}$, $P_g^{\max}$, and $P_f^{\max}$. For additional simulation parameters, we specify $N_a^{\max} = 10$, 15, 20, 90 for IEEE 14-bus, 30-bus, 57-bus, and 118-bus systems, respectively, $\tau = 0.5$, $\gamma_o = 1$, and $M = 10^6$.

4.1 Overloaded Power Lines Under Three Scenarios

To evaluate the attack effectiveness of our proposed method, we compare it with no attack and random attack. Here when the power system is normally operating without suffering any attack, this scenario is called no attack. When the attacker can modify the readings of available load meters by a perturbation ΔP_d that is generated randomly in the feasible region formed by constraints (2) and (3), this scenario is called random attack. To fairly evaluate the effectiveness of random attack, we adopt Monte Carlo experiment to set the experimental times $L = 1000$. Namely, we stochastically select 1000 feasible solution for random attack to obtain its average performance on every IEEE test system.

Table 2. Simulation Results Under Three Scenarios

Scenario	14-bus		30-bus		57-bus		118-bus	
	$|E^o|$	η	$|E^o|$	η	$|E^o|$	η	$|E^o|$	η
No attack	0	0%	0	0%	0	0%	0	0%
Random attack	2.89	28.5%	1.53	12.17%	3.27	17.65%	1.27	4.10%
Our method	5	40.56%	4	32.03%	7	30.65%	26	43.43%

To measure the performance of different strategies, we use two indices: the total number of overloaded transmission lines, denoted $|E^o|$ and the percent of power flow loaded in overloaded transmission lines and in all transmission lines, denoted η. Table 2 lists the simulation results under three scenarios: no attack, random attack, and our proposed method. Under no attack, the four IEEE test systems are normal in operation and have no overloaded transmission lines. Compared to random attack, our method can cause more overloaded transmission lines, because $|E^o|$ of our method is greater than that of random attack for all IEEE test systems. The larger-scale power grid might be more sensitive to our method than other smaller-scale grid, e.g., the total number of overloaded transmission lines is 26 in IEEE 118-test system whereas the total number is below 10 in IEEE 14-bus, 30-bus, and 57-bus systems. In addition, η of our method is more than 30% in the four test systems, indicating that the more number of overloaded transmission lines and the more percent of power flow. Moreover, η of our method is much larger than that of random attack for all test systems, illustrating that the our proposed attack strategy is more effective than random attacks for compromising the power systems.

Take IEEE 14-bus and 30-bus systems for examples in Figs. 4 and 5, respectively, where the overloaded transmission lines are marked in red and the non-overloaded lines in black. The graphical results clearly display the distributions of overloaded transmission lines before and after attacks. Obviously, our method can identify more overloaded lines and thus assist the operators to screen out more vulnerable electrical component. It is worth noting that only two lines are overloaded in the random attack, i.e., (6−11) and (7−9) (see Fig. 5(b)) while five lines are overloaded in our method (see Fig. 5(c)), but the overloaded line (6 − 11) in Fig. 5(b) is normal in Fig. 5(c). Because the random attack has no the most powerful attack effectiveness to cause the worst case and the perturbation ΔP_d is randomly generated from a sample of Monte Carlo experiment so that the line overloading events also become uncertain and random.

(a) No attack   (b) Random attack   (c) Our method

Fig. 4. Distribution of overloaded transmission lines of IEEE 14-bus system.

4.2   Line Tripping Events in Monte Carlo Experiments

As seen from the above simulations, our method can cause the overloading of multiple power lines. Once these overloaded lines trip with a high probability,

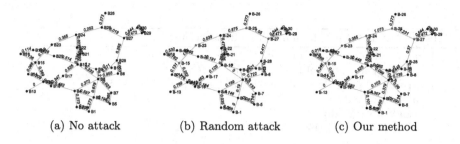

(a) No attack   (b) Random attack   (c) Our method

Fig. 5. Distribution of overloaded transmission lines of IEEE 30-bus system.

cascading failures might be triggered and more transmission lines fail successively. In the following, we simulate the initial stage of cascading failures to verify the practical effectiveness of our method. We have mentioned that the line
tripping is a stochastic process, as seen in Fig. 2. It is natural to adopt Monte
Carlo simulation for simulating this random process well. We count the occurrence frequency of line tripping events for the four test systems under no attack,
random attack, and our method. The generating draws follow the line tripping
probability $p(\gamma_l)$ as (8). We define a binary indicator $I_l \in \{0, 1\}$ for the lth line:
if the lth line trips, $I_l = 1$; otherwise, $I_l = 0$. We also define N_e, the total number
of random events, which is set 1000, and $M_j, j \in \mathbb{Z}^+$, the specified number of
line tripping events, $M_j = j$, and N_m the maximum specified number of line
tripping events, which is set 5 for IEEE 14-bus, 30-bus, and 57-bus systems and
set 14 for IEEE 118-bus system. We specify a random matrix $R \in \mathbb{R}^{N_e * N_f}$, and
$R_{l,i}$ is a random numbers uniformly distributed within $[0, 1]$. We use a counter
C_o to record the number of line tripping events, which is initialized 0. The total
number of line tripping events is stored in matrix $S \in \mathbb{R}^{N_m * N_e}$. Algorithm 1
illustrates the Monte Carlo experiment clearly.

The simulation results are shown in Fig. 6, where the total number of line
tripping events is counted in 1000 random events under the three strategies for
the four IEEE test systems. Under no attack, the total number of line tripping
events concentrates on 1000, the mode appears at $M_1 = 0$, and the numbers
of both one-line and two-line tripping events are 0. These results are consistent
with the performance of a power grid under normal operations where the line
tripping event is very rare. Under the random attack, the total number of the
no line tripping event decreases to 577, 822, 348, and 758 in IEEE 14-bus, 30-
bus, 57-bus, and 118-bus systems, respectively. The total number of one-line
tripping events increases to 241, 160, 476, and 133, respectively. Except that
the mode of IEEE 57-bus system appears at $M_2 = 1$, the modes of other three
systems still appear at $M_1 = 0$. Under our proposed attack strategies, the mode
of IEEE 30-bus system shifts to 2 whereas that of IEEE 118-bus system shifts
to 10, and the mode of IEEE 14-bus system lies between 0 and 1 whereas that
of IEEE 57-bus system lies between 1 and 2. These results indicate that our
proposed method is more effective than random attack to induce the tripping
of multiple transmission lines simultaneously and increase the occurrence risk of

---

Algorithm 1. Count the number of line tripping events.

Input: The vector of line tripping probability, $p(\gamma)$;
                The matrix of random numbers, R;
Output: The matrix of the number of line tripping events, S;
  for $i = 1 : N_e$ do
    for $l = 1 : N_f$ do
      if $R_{l,i} \le p(\gamma_l)$ then
        $I_l = 1$;
      else
        $I_l = 0$;
      end if
    end for
    for $j = 1 : N_m$ do
      $C_o \to 0$;
      if $\sum_l I_l = M_j$ then
        $C_o \leftarrow C_o + 1$;
      else
        $C_o \leftarrow C_o$;
      end if
      $S_{j,i} \leftarrow C_o$;
    end for
  end for
  return $\frac{1}{N_e} \sum_i S_{j,i}$ as the number of line tripping events.

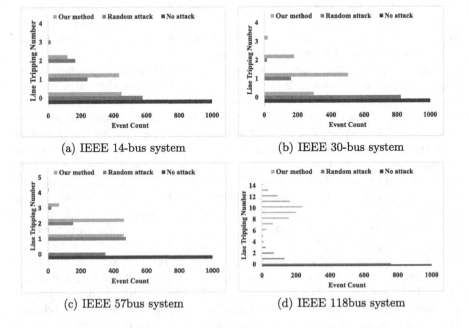

(a) IEEE 14-bus system

(b) IEEE 30-bus system

(c) IEEE 57bus system

(d) IEEE 118bus system

Fig. 6. Distribution of line tripping events in 1000 random experiments.

cascading failures. In Particular, IEEE 118-bus system is the most sensitive to our proposed method because the line tripping events always occur from five-line to fourteen-line. These results conform to that in Table 2.

5 Conclusion and Discussion

From system operators' perspective, we utilize the generative adversarial strategy to identify the most possible overloaded lines that may trigger the large-scale cascading failures. For analyzing this worst case, we propose a leader-follower game-theoretic bi-level optimization problem to model the decision-making interaction between attacker and SCED. The effectiveness of our proposed strategy is verified on IEEE test systems in numerical simulations, where Monte Carlo experiments indicate that the proposed strategy can cause the line tripping events with the most occurrence frequency.

Our study also reveals that the smart grid becomes vulnerable to the intentional FDIA, which can motivate operators to develop some mitigation schemes for protecting the grid from cascading failures. For instance, the nonzero elements of ΔP_d^* can indicate which is the sensitive load meters, which can be tampered to inject the false load data that can perturb the supply-demand balance of power flow; every element of E^o can locate the vulnerable transmission lines, which is easy to be overloaded and even tripped due to the lower thermal rating. Thus, this study can guide us to closely monitor the sensitive load meters and their readings and meanwhile update the physical configuration of the vulnerable transmission lines with the higher thermal rating for tolerating the extra power flow. We believe that our work is significant to apply at both the electricity maintenance and the power planning for the security assurance of power grid.

In addition, it is worth noting that this FDIA is an one-shot attack strategy because when ΔP_d^* is carefully designed well, the attackers can launch the FDIA by accordingly tampering the available load meters. After the attacker can successfully modify the related load meters, multiple transmission lines are overloaded and even tripped automatically as the power grid is operating. Namely, nearly all of attack time concentrates on the stealthy modification of load meters. In the future, we also focus on developing the detection countermeasures to prevent the FDIA.

References

1. Cintuglu, M.H., Mohammed, O.A., Akkaya, K., Uluagac, A.S.: A survey on smart grid cyber-physical system testbeds. IEEE Commun. Surv. Tutor. **19**(1), 446–464 (2017)
2. U.S.-Canada Power System Outage Task Force: Final Report on the August 14, 2003 Blackout in the United States and Canada: Causes and Recommendations. https://www.energy.gov/sites/prod/files/oeprod/DocumentsandMedia/BlackoutFinal-Web.pdf. Accessed Apr 2004

3. Carreras, B.A., Lynch, V.E., Dobson, I., Newman, D.E.: Critical points and transitions in an electric power transmission model for cascading failure blackouts. Chaos **12**(4), 985–994 (2002)
4. Mei, S., He, F., Zhang, X., Wu, S., Wang, G.: An improved OPA model and blackout risk assessment. IEEE Trans. Power Syst. **24**(2), 814–823 (2009)
5. Youwei, J., Ke, M., Zhao, X.: N-k induced cascading contingency screening. IEEE Trans. Power Syst. **30**(5), 2824–2825 (2015)
6. Qi, J., Sun, K., Mei, S.: An interaction model for simulation and mitigation of cascading failures. IEEE Trans. Power Syst. **30**(2), 804–819 (2014)
7. Schafer, B., Witthaut, D., Timme, M., Latora, V.: Dynamically induced cascading failures in power grids. Nat. commun. **9**(1), 1975 (2018)
8. Buldyrev, S.V., Parshani, R., Paul, G., Stanley, H.E., Havlin, S.: Catastrophic cascade of failures in interdependent networks. Nature **464**(7291), 1025 (2010)
9. Daqing, L., Yinan, J., Rui, K., Havlin, S.: Spatial correlation analysis of cascading failures: congestions and blackouts. Sci. Rep. **4**, 5381 (2014)
10. Xi, Z., Chi, K.T.: Assessment of robustness of power systems from a network perspective. IEEE J. Emerg. Sel. Top Circ. Syst. **5**(3), 456–464 (2015)
11. E-ISAC, SANS: Analysis of the cyber attack on the Ukrainian power grid: Defense use case (2016). https://ics.sans.org/duc5
12. ICS Alert: Cyber-attack against Ukrainian critical infrastructure (2018). https://www.us-cert.gov/ics/alerts/IR-ALERT-H-16-056-01
13. Liang, G., Weller, S.R., Zhao, J., Luo, F., Dong, Z.Y.: The 2015 ukraine blackout: implications for false data injection attacks. IEEE Trans. Power Syst. **32**(4), 3317–3318 (2017)
14. Tan, Y., Li, Y., Cao, Y., Shahidehpour, M.: Cyber-attack on overloading multiple lines: a bilevel mixed-integer linear programming model. IEEE Trans. Smart Grid **9**(2), 1534–1536 (2018)
15. Tan, Y., Li, Y., Cao, Y., Shahidehpour, M., Cai, Y.: Severe cyber attack for maximizing the total loadings of large-scale attacked branches. IEEE Trans. Smart Grid **9**(6), 6998–7000 (2018)
16. Che, L., Liu, X., Wen, Y., Li, Z.: A mixed integer programming model for evaluating the hidden probabilities of N-k line contingencies in smart grids. IEEE Trans. Smart Grid **10**(1), 1036–1045 (2019)
17. Che, L., Liu, X., Ding, T., Li, Z.: Revealing impacts of cyber attacks on power grids vulnerability to cascading failures. IEEE Trans. Circ. Syst. II Exp. Briefs **66**(6), 1058–1062 (2019)
18. Che, L., Liu, X., Li, Z., Wen, Y.: False data injection attacks induced sequential outages in power systems. IEEE Trans. Power Syst. **34**(2), 1513–1523 (2019)
19. Liu, X., Li, Z.: Trilevel modeling of cyber attacks on transmission lines. IEEE Trans. Smart Grid **8**(2), 720–729 (2017)
20. Henneaux, P.: Probability of failure of overloaded lines in cascading failures. Int. J. Electr. Power Energy Syst. **73**, 141–148 (2015)
21. Zima, M., Andersson, G.: On security criteria in power systems operation. In: Proceedings of the IEEE Power Engineering Society General Meeting, San Francisco, CA, USA, pp. 3089–3093 (2005). https://doi.org/10.1109/PES.2005.1489533
22. Chen, J., Thorp, J.S., Dobson, I.: Cascading dynamics and mitigation assessment in power system disturbances via a hidden failure model. Int. J. Electr. Power Energy Syst. **27**(4), 318–326 (2005)

23. Grant, M., Boyd, S.: CVX: Matlab software for disciplined convex programming, version 2.1. http://cvxr.com/cvx. Accessed Dec 2018

24. Zimmerman, R.D., Murillo-Sanchez, C.E., Thomas, R.J.: MATPOWER: steady-state operations, planning, and analysis tools for power systems research and education. IEEE Trans. Power Syst. **26**(1), 12–19 (2011)

Optimal Key-Tree for RFID Authentication Protocols with Storage Constraints

Wang Shao-Hui[1,2,3(✉)], Zhang Yan-Xuan[1,2,3], Ke Chang-Bo[1,2,3], Xiao Fu[1,2,3], and Wang Ru-Chuan[1,2,3]

[1] College of Computer, Nanjing University of Posts and Telecommunications, Nanjing 210023, China
wangshaohui@njupt.edu.cn
[2] Jiangsu High Technology Research Key Laboratory for Wireless Sensor Networks, Nanjing 210023, China
[3] Jiangsu Key Laboratory of Big Data Security and Intelligent Processing, Nanjing 210023, China

Abstract. Tree-based RFID authentication protocols provide an efficient solution for lowering authentication delay, but level of privacy provided by tree-based systems decreases considerably if some members are compromised and secret keys are probed. In the RFID system, Tags are severely limited in terms of computational power and storage. A large amount of research focused on optimizing the key-tree has been launched, yet none of them consider the Tags' storage constraints.

In this paper, we introduce a new privacy metric expression for measuring the resistance of the system to a single compromised member; we furtherly extend the research work of Buttyan et al. and Beye et al. by proposing two optimization problems respecting storage constraints. In addition, we show how to construct the optimal key-tree in order to maximize the system's resistance to single member compromise under the constraints on the Tags' number, the maximum authentication delay and the number of the keys stored in the Tag.

Keywords: RFID · Authentication protocol · Key-tree · Anonymity · Storage constraint

1 Introduction

Radio Frequency Identification (RFID) is a wireless technology for convenient automatic identification of physical objects, originally intended to replace bar codes. RFID systems are typically composed of RF Tags, RF Readers and backend Server. Most Tags consist of an antenna connected to a microchip, and the use of silicon-based microchips enables a range of functionality to be integrated into the Tags, including readable/writable storage and limited computing capability. The Readers broadcast an RF signal to access information stored on the Tags. This information can range from static identification numbers to user written data or data computed by the Tag.

© Springer Nature Switzerland AG 2019
F. Liu et al. (Eds.): SciSec 2019, LNCS 11933, pp. 278–292, 2019.
https://doi.org/10.1007/978-3-030-34637-9_21

However, the communication channel between the Tag and Reader is wireless, so RFID systems are vulnerable to various forms of passive or active attacks. RFID technology has triggered significant concerns on its security and privacy as the Tags' information can be read or traced by malicious Readers from a distance without the owner's awareness [1]. In traditional computing systems, many security and privacy problems can be solved by utilizing cryptographic techniques. Unfortunately, RFID Tags are highly resource constrained and cannot support strong cryptography, which means that supporting strong public key cryptographic primitives on low-cost Tags is not a viable option today, therefore there is a strong need for lightweight symmetric cryptographic primitives [2].

Over the past few years, many researchers have developed dozens of protocols to tackle the authentication and privacy problems of RFID systems. The protocols based on symmetric cryptosystems are divided into two categories: one based on hash functions or block ciphers, such as hash chain protocol, randomized hash locking protocol etc. [3–7], which trigger the research development of the design and analysis of lightweight block ciphers and hash functions; the other based on simple operations such as AND, XOR, Rotation [8–10] or the LPN(Learning Parity in the Presence of Noise)problem [11–15]. LPN based authentication is not only theoretically secure in terms of provable security, but also provides better efficiency than classical symmetric ciphers.

In the privacy-preserving symmetric key based protocols, the Tag and Reader share with the same secret keys, thus they are faced with the following paradox. In one hand, Tag must encrypt its identity with its secret keys so that only authorized Readers can extract the identity. On the other hand, Readers must first decide which secret keys should be used to authenticate the Tag. As a consequence, the server must perform a brute force search in its database to identify the Tag. That is, for each Tag entry in the database, the server computes a symmetric cryptographic operation with the corresponding Tag's secrets and checks whether the result matches with the received response produced by the target Tag. Such a tedious search procedure will raise scalability issues as the Tag increases.

Molnar and Wagner [16] proposed the tree-based authentication protocol in 2004 to tackle the authentication delays problem. More precisely, the complexity of the authentication procedure in the Molnar-Wagner scheme is logarithmic in the number of potential Tags, in contrast with the linear complexity of the simple key search approach. Since different Tags share their partial keys, if one Tag is compromised and its memory has been probed through invasive tampering, the adversary can learn partial keys for several other Tags as well, which will enable him to decipher some of their responses, resulting in reduced anonymity and facilitating tracking.

Buttyan, Holczer and Vajda [17] first analyzed the information leakage problem resulting from Tag corruption in the tree-based authentication protocol. They introduced the concept of trees with variable branching factors to better preserve anonymity in case of attack. They also have quantified the resulting loss of anonymity in the system, solved the optimization problem with given number of the Tag and the maximum authentication delay. Beye and Veugen [18] furtherly improved upon Buttyan et al.'s research. They found that the constraint condition on exact number of the Tag may provide inferior solutions, so they formulated a new optimization problem given the minimum number of the Tags, which led to better results.

However, low-cost RFID Tags usually have extremely limited storage and computational capabilities. The two optimization problems in [17] and [18] do not take the Tags' storage constraints into consideration. In this paper, we extend Buttyan et al.'s and Beye et al.'s results, and propose two improved key-tree optimization problems under the constraints on the Tags' number, the maximum authentication delay and the number of the keys stored in the Tag. Besides, we present the corresponding algorithms for determining the optimal parameters of the key-tree to maximize the resistance of single Tag compromise.

The rest of the paper is organized as follows: In Sect. 2, we introduce a new metric expression to measure the level of privacy provided by key-tree based authentication systems under single Tag compromise; In Sect. 3, we extend Buttyan et al.'s and Beye et al.'s work to formulate two optimization problems respecting storage constraints. In addition, we reprove the four lemmas in [17] utilizing the new privacy metric expression; In Sect. 4, we mainly brings forward two algorithms to solve the new optimization problems, and experiment results with the applicable parameters are illustrated in Sect. 5. Finally, conclusions are drawn in Sect. 6.

2   Resistance to Single Member Compromise

To overcome the high authentication delay problem in the symmetric key based RFID authentication protocols, Molnar and Wagner [16] presented the tree-based authentication infrastructure. We assume the number of the Tag is N, and the Reader will keep a full key-tree with l levels and branching factors $B = (b_1, b_2, \ldots, b_l)$, i.e., the different nodes in the same level have the same number of children nods. Each leaf represents a Tag member, which is denoted as $T_0, T_1, \ldots, T_{N-1}$. It is obvious to see that $N = \prod_{i=1}^{l} b_i$. There is a unique key assigned to each edge, and the leaf node possesses the keys assigned to the edges of the path starting from the root and ending in the given leaf. Figure 1 gives an example of a key-tree with 3 levels and branching factors $B = (3, 3, 2)$. So the Tag number is 18, and left most Tag T_0 possesses three different keys $\{k_1, k_{11}, k_{111}\}$.

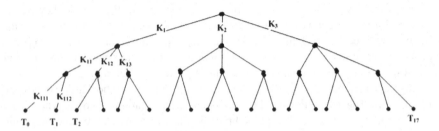

Fig. 1. Illustration of a key-tree

In Fig. 1, if the Reader wants to authenticate the Tag with the secret keys $\{k_{i_1}, k_{i_2}, k_{i_3}\}$, a classic symmetric key based RFID authentication protocol is executed as the following steps:

Step 1. Reader generates and sends a random value N_r to the Tag;

Step 2. Tag generates a random value N_t, computes and sends three values to the Reader: $H(k_{i_1}, N_r, N_t)$, $H(k_{i_2}, N_r, N_t)$ and $H(k_{i_3}, N_r, N_t)$, where H function can be some secure hash function, such as MD5.

Step 3. The Reader tries all the possible key in the first level to compute $H(k_i, N_r, N_t), (i = 1, 2, 3)$ to find which value matches the response $H(k_i, N_r, N_t)$. Once the first key is identified, the verifier continues to search through second-level keys that reside below the already identified first-level key in the tree to determine which second-level key has been used in the same way. This process continues until all keys are identified, and thus authenticating members are identified.

Buttyan et al. defined the maximum authentication delay as D_{max}, and it can be easily computed as $D_{max} = \sum_{i=1}^{l} b_i$, which is logarithmic in the number of Tags. The problem of tree-based authentication scheme is that upper-level keys in the tree are shared by many Tags. For example, in Fig. 1, the two Tags T_0 and T_1 share the same first and second level keys k_1 and k_{11}. Therefore, if some Tag is compromised and its keys has been leaked, the adversary gains partial knowledge of the keys of other members, which obviously reduces the privacy provided by the RFID system.

Accordingly, Buttyan et al. [17] quantified the resulting anonymity leakage in the tree-based authentication protocol utilizing the concept of anonymity set [19]. In addition, they presented an optimization problem to maximize RFID system's resistance to single Tag compromise under the constraints on the maximum authentication delay. Here we measure the level of anonymity leakage from the following basic probability problems.

Problem: Given a full key-tree with l levels and branching factors $B = (b_1, b_2, \ldots, b_l)$, a unique key is assigned to each edge, and the leaf node possesses the keys assigned to the edges of the path starting from the root to the given leafTag. After corrupting any leaf node and obtaining all the secret keys stored, a passive adversary chooses two different random Tags. The problem is to calculate the probability of distinguishing these two Tags through eaves dropping the communication messages of the above tree-based RFID authentication protocol.

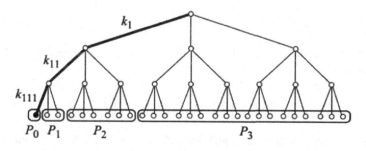

Fig. 2. Partition when T_0 is Corrupted

We know the total number of the Tag is $N = \prod_{i=1}^{l} b_i$, and we suppose the leftmost Tag T_0 is corrupted. As shown in Fig. 2, we utilize the same method in [17] to partition the Tag members into $l+1$ set $P_0, P_1, \ldots, P_l$, where:

- P_0 contains the compromised Tag only, i.e. T_0;
- P_1 contains the Tags whose parent node is the same as that of T_0, and those are not in set P_0;
- P_2 contains the Tags whose grandparent node is the same as that of T_0, and those are not in $P_0 \cup P_1$;
- P_l contains the Tags who have the same root node as that of T_0, and those are not in $P_0 \cup P_1 \cup \ldots \cup P_{l-1}$.

Choosing two different random Tag T_x and T_y among all the possible Tags(including the corrupted Tag T_0, due to the one-way nature of Hash function, if the passive adversary expects to distinguish them utilizing the tree-based RFID authentication protocol, the t the following l condition:

1. $T_x \in P_l \wedge T_y \notin P_l$
2. $(T_x \in P_{l-1}) \wedge T_y \notin (P_l \cup P_{l-1})$
3. $(T_x \in P_{l-2}) \wedge T_y \notin (P_l \cup P_{l-1} \cup P_{l-2})$

....

l. $(T_x \in P_1) \wedge T_y \notin (P_l \cup P_{l-1} \cup \ldots \cup P_1)$

We can deduce the probability that passive adversary can distinguish T_x and T_y is:

$$\text{Pr}_D^*(B) = \left((b_1 - 1)b_2^2 \cdots b_l^2 + (b_2 - 1)b_3^2 \cdots b_l^2 + \ldots + (b_l - 1)\right)/C_N^2$$

In order to facilitate the following discussion, we substitute $N^2/2$ for C_N^2, and the resistance to single member compromise is defined as follows:

Definition 2.1. Given a full key-tree with l levels and branching factors $B = (b_1, b_2, \ldots, b_l)$ in the tree based RFID authentication protocol, the total number of Tags N is $\prod_{i=1}^{l} b_i$, and the resistance to single member compromise is defined as $\text{Pr}(B) = 1 - \text{Pr}_D(B)$, where

$$\text{Pr}_D(B) = 2\left((b_1 - 1)b_2^2 \ldots b_l^2 + (b_2 - 1)b_3^2 \ldots b_l^2 + \ldots + (b_l - 1)\right)/N^2$$

In [17], the resistance to single member compromise, denoted as R(B), is quantified as

$$R(B) = \left(1 + (b_l - 1)^2 + \sum_{i=1}^{l-1} (b_i - 1)^2 \prod_{j=i+1}^{l} b_j^2\right)/N^2$$

It is easy to verify that $\text{Pr}(B)$ equals to R(B), which means these two variables are the same value but with different expression.

3 RFID Number Optimization Problem with Storage Constraints

In this section, we reconsider the optimization problem as phrased by Buttyan et al. and Beye et al. In [17], Buttyan et al. presented the following optimization problem of finding the best branching factors to maximize $\Pr(B)$:

Definition 3.1. Exact Number Optimization Problem (ENO-Problem for short) Given the Tag's number N and the upper bound D_{max} of the maximum authentication delay, ENO-Problem is to find a branching factor vector $B = (b_1, b_2, \ldots, b_l)$ such that $\Pr(B)$ is maximal subject to the following two constraints:

$$N = \prod_{i=1}^{l} b_i, \quad \sum_{i=1}^{l} b_i \leq D_{max} \tag{1}$$

In [18], Beye and Veugen found the condition $N = \prod_{i=1}^{l} b_i$ can result in inferior solutions, especially when N does not have good prime factorization. So they improved Buttyan et al.'s work and presented a new optimization problem as follows:

Definition 3.2. Minimum Number Optimization Problem (MNO-Problem) [18] Given N and D_{max} as in Definition 3.1, MNO-Problem is to find the branching factors $B = (b_1, b_2, \ldots, b_l)$ that maximize $\Pr(B)$ subject to the following constraints:

$$\prod_{i=1}^{l} b_i \geq N, \quad \sum_{i=1}^{l} b_i \leq D_{max} \tag{2}$$

RFID Tags are typically low-cost devices, so their computation and storage capabilities are severely constrained. The optimization problem in Definitions 3.1 and 3.2 do not consider the storage requirements of RFID systems. It is obvious that the leaf node in the key-tree with l levels will store l different secret keys. Here we improve the above two optimization problems through putting the storage requirement into consideration.

Definition 3.3. Exact Number Optimization Problem with Storage Constraints (sENO-Problem for short) Given N, D_{max} as in Definition 3.1, and l_{req} of the number of the secret keys stored in the Tags, sENO-Problem is to find a branching factors.
$B = (b_1, b_2, \ldots, b_{l_{req}})$ so that $\Pr(B)$ is maximal subject to the following constraints:

$$N = \prod_{i=1}^{l_{req}} b_i, \quad \sum_{i=1}^{l_{req}} b_i \leq D_{max} \tag{3}$$

Just as the improvement on the ENO-Problem, we put forward the corresponding improved optimization problem on MNO-Problem under the storage constraints.

Definition 3.4. Minimum Number Optimal Problem with Storage Constraints, (sMNO-Problem) Given the three parameters N, D_{max}, l_{req}, the sMNO-Problem is to find the vector $B = (b_1, b_2, \ldots, b_{l_{req}})$ that maximizes $\Pr(B)$ subject to the following constraints:

$$\prod_{i=1}^{l_{req}} b_i \geq N, \quad \sum_{i=1}^{l_{req}} b_i \leq D_{max} \tag{4}$$

Buttyan et al. analyzed the ENO-Problem through a series of lemmas that will lead to an algorithm to solve theproblem. In the following, we list and simplify the proof of four lemmas in [17] utilizing the new expression $\Pr(B)$. The following four lemmas are also the theoretic basis for our algorithms.

Lemma 3.1. Given N and D_{max}, and let $B = (b_1, b_2, \ldots, b_r)$ be a branching factor satisfying constraints (1) of the optimizationproblem. Supposing $B' = (b'_1, b'_2, \ldots, b'_r)$ is the branch vector consisting of the sorted elements of B in decreasing order, i.e.$b'_1 \geq b'_2 \geq \ldots \geq b'_r$, then $\Pr(B') \geq \Pr(B)$.

Proof: Let us assume B' is obtained from B with the bubble sort algorithm. The basic step of this algorithm is to change two neighboring elements if they are not in the right order.

Considering branching factors $B_1 = (b_1, \ldots, b_i, b_{i+1}, \ldots, b_r)$, let us suppose $b_i < b_{i+1}$, then the algorithm changes the order of b_i and b_{i+1} to obtain new branching factors $B_2 = (b_1, \ldots, b_{i+1}, b_i, \ldots, b_r)$. According to the definition of $\Pr(B)$, we can finally express $\Pr(B_2) - \Pr(B_1)$ as follows:

$$\Pr(B_2) - \Pr(B_1) = 2\left((b_i - 1)b_{i+1}^2 \cdots b_r^2 + (b_{i+1} - 1)b_{i+2}^2 \cdots b_r^2 - (b_{i+1} - 1)b_i^2 \cdots b_r^2 - (b_i - 1)b_{i+2}^2 \cdots b_r^2\right)/N^2$$
$$= 2(b_{i+1} - b_i)(b_{i+1} - 1)(b_i - 1)b_{i+2}^2 \cdots b_r^2/N^2$$

Considering the condition $b_i < b_{i+1}$, $b_i, b_{i+1} \geq 1$, we can get the conclusion $\Pr(B_2) \geq \Pr(B_1)$. This means, when sorting the elements of B, $\Pr(B)$ improves by every step, and thus, $\Pr(B') \geq \Pr(B)$ must hold.□

Lemma 3.2. Let $B = (b_1, b_2, \ldots, b_r)$ be a sorted branching factors (i.e., $b_1 \geq b_2 \geq \ldots \geq b_r$). The lower and upper bounds on $\Pr(B)$ can be given as follows (the bounds are different from those of [17]):

$$1 - 2\left(\frac{b_1 - 1}{b_1^2} + \frac{2}{3b_1^2}\right) \leq \Pr(B) \leq 1 - \frac{2(b_1 - 1)}{b_1^2}$$

Proof: Because $N = \prod_{i=1}^{r} b_i$, we can obtain the upper bound of the lemma:

$$\Pr_D(B) \geq \frac{2(b_1 - 1)b_2^2 \ldots b_r^2}{N^2} = \frac{2(b_1 - 1)b_2^2 \ldots b_r^2}{b_1^2 b_2^2 \ldots b_r^2} = \frac{2(b_1 - 1)}{b_1^2}$$

To achieve the lower bound, for every i in $2, 3, \ldots, r$, we replace $b_i - 1$ with b_i, and we can get:

$$\Pr_D \leq \frac{2((b_1 - 1)b_2^2 \ldots b_r^2 + b_2 b_3^2 \ldots b_r^2 + \ldots b_r)}{N^2} = 2\left(\frac{(b_1 - 1)}{b_1^2} + \frac{1}{b_1^2}\left(\frac{1}{b_2} + \frac{1}{b_2 b_3} + \ldots + \frac{1}{b_2^2 b_3^2 \ldots b_{r-1}^2 b_r}\right)\right)$$

$$\leq 2\left(\frac{(b_1 - 1)}{b_1^2} + \frac{1}{b_1^2}\left(\frac{1}{2} + \frac{1}{8} + \frac{1}{32} + \ldots\right)\right) = 2\left(\frac{b_1 - 1}{b_1^2} + \frac{2}{3 b_1^2}\right)$$

The proof is the same as that in [17]. Lemma 3.2 implies that in order to find the solution to the optimization problem, b_1 should be maximized.   □

Lemma 3.3. Given N and D_{max}, if $B = (b_1, b_2, \ldots, b_r)$ and $B' = (b_1', b_2', \ldots, b_r')$ are two sorted branching factors that satisfy the constraints (1) of the optimization problem, then $b_1 > b_1'$ implies $\Pr(B') \leq \Pr(B)$.

Proof: According to Lemma 3.2, for branching factors $B' = (b_1', b_2', \ldots, b_r')$, we know:

$$\Pr(B') \leq 1 - \frac{2(b_1' - 1)}{b_1'^2}$$

We can also calculate the compromise resistance probability of branching factors $B = (b_1, b_2, \ldots, b_r)$ according to Lemma 3.2 in the same way:

$$\Pr(B) \geq 1 - 2\left(\frac{b_1 - 1}{b_1^2} + \frac{2}{3 b_1^2}\right)$$

Because $b_1 > b_1'$, it is easy to see $\Pr(B) \geq 1 - 2\left(\frac{b_1'}{(b_1' + 1)^2} + \frac{2}{3(b_1' + 1)^2}\right)$. Now we consider the in equality:

$$1 - \frac{2(b_1' - 1)}{b_1'^2} \leq 1 - 2\left(\frac{b_1'}{(b_1' + 1)^2} + \frac{2}{3(b_1' + 1)^2}\right)$$

then we can obtain the inequality: $(b_1')^2 - 3b_1' - 3 \geq 0$, thus we get the conclusion: when $b_1' \geq 4$, $b_1 > b_1'$ implies $\Pr(B') \leq \Pr(B)$.

For the conditions of $b_1' \in \{2, 3\}$, we can also prove $\Pr(B') \leq \Pr(B)$ utilizing the same discussion in [17]. Our proof simplifies the discussion of this lemma in [17]. Buttyan et al. only proved when $b_1' \geq 5$ implies $\Pr(B') \leq \Pr(B)$, and thus, they have to discuss three cases of $b_1' \in \{2, 3, 4\}$ respectively.   □

Lemma 3.4. Given N and D_{max}, let $B = (b_1, b_2, \ldots, b_r)$ and $B' = (b_1', b_2', \ldots, b_r')$ be two sorted branching factors satisfying the constraints (1). For all $1 \leq i \leq j \leq \min(r, r')$, $b_{j+1} > b_{j+1}'$, if $b_i > b_i'$, then $\Pr(B) \geq \Pr(B')$.

Proof: The probability of distinguishing two Tags $\Pr_D(B)$ must satisfy the following equation:

$$
\begin{aligned}
\Pr_D(B) &= \frac{2(b_1 - 1)}{b_1^2} + \frac{2}{b_1^2}\left(\frac{(b_2 - 1)}{b_2^2} + \frac{(b_3 - 1)}{b_2^2 b_3^2} + \ldots + \frac{(b_r - 1)}{b_2^2 b_3^2 \ldots b_r^2}\right) \\
&= \frac{2(b_1 - 1)}{b_1^2} + \frac{1}{b_1^2}\Pr_D(B_1)
\end{aligned}
$$

where $B_1 = (b_2, b_3, \ldots, b_r)$. In the same way, we know that for $B_1' = (b_2', b_3', \ldots, b_r')$:

$$
\Pr_D(B) = \frac{2(b_1' - 1)}{b_1'^2} + \frac{1}{b_1'^2}\Pr_D\left(B_1'\right)
$$

Utilizing the relationship of $\Pr(B) = 1 - \Pr_D(B)$, and the conclusion of Lemma 3.3, we know Lemma 3.4 must hold. $\qquad\square$

4   Algorithms for Optimal Trees on SENO(SMNO)-Problem

We first present an exhaustive algorithm to find the solution to the sENO-Problem. As to the sorted branching factors $B = (b_1, b_2, \ldots, b_r)$, we let $\{B\}$ denote the set $\{b_1, b_2, \ldots, b_r\}$, $\prod B$ denote $\prod_{i=1}^{r} b_i$ and $\sum B$ denote $\sum_{i=1}^{r} b_i$.

Exhaustive Solution. Given the three parameters N, D_{max}, l_{req}, we suppose the set B is composed of all the prime factors of N. The sENO-Problem can be settled in the following intuitive algorithm:

Algorithm 1. Exhaustive Solution to sENO-Problem

Step 1. An empty list *List* with two columns is constructed;

Step 2. Partition set $\{B\}$ into l_{req} subset$\{B_1\}, \ldots, \{B_{l_{req}}\}$, if $\sum_{i=1}^{l_{req}}(\prod B_i) \leq D_{max}$, the partition set $\{\prod B_i, \ldots, \prod B_{l_{req}}\}$ is arranged in decreasing order, and filled in thefirst column of *List*, meanwhile value ofmax$\{\prod B_i, \ldots, \prod B_{l_{req}}\}$ is filled in the second column of the *List*.

Step 3. Try all the partition of$\{B\}$ and repeat step 2, andoutput the partition with the maximum first level. If more than onepartition have the same first level in the second column, then the successive level isconsidered.

From Lemma 3.4, we know the output of Algorithm 1 must be the optimal solution to sENO-Problem. However, the algorithm is less efficient especially when the number of set $\{B\}$ is large. In addition, given three parameters N, D_{max},l_{req}, we can not determine whether sENO-Problem has solution efficiently.

In the following subsections, we will present a much more efficient algorithm to settle sENO-Problem.

4.1   Minimal Sum Problem with Static Product

Considering the Definition 3.3, we know if sENO-Problem has a solution, there exists at least one l_{req} divisor $(b_1, b_2, \ldots, b_{l_{req}})$ of Tag number N satisfying the condition (3). To determine whether or not sENO-Problem has a solution, we should find out the minimum value $\sum_{i=1}^{l_{req}} b_i$ can be reached with the constraint $N = \prod_{i=1}^{l_{req}} b_i$.

Now, we consider the following problem:

Definition 4.1. Minimal Sum Problem with Static Product (MSSP-Problem) Given positive integers n and r, the problem is to find positive integers $x_i (i = 1, 2, \ldots, r)$ that minimize $\sum_{i=1}^{r} x_i$ with the constraint $n = \prod_{i=1}^{r} x_i$.

If we allow x_i to be a positive real number, it is clear that the solution to the above problem is $x_i = \sqrt[r]{n}, i = 1, 2, \ldots, r$. Regarding the constraint of integer solutions, we use the following two necessary and sufficient conditions presented by Ma [20].

Theorem 4.1. [20] Given positive integer n and $r = 2$, the necessary and sufficient condition that positive integers x_1 and x_2 satisfying $x_1 + x_2$ is minimum and $x_1 \cdot x_2 = n$ is:

$$x_1 = \min\{d : d|n \wedge d \geq \sqrt[2]{n}\}$$

namely, $|x_1 - x_2|$ also achieves the minimum value.

When considering any given integer r, Ma gave the following theorem:

Theorem 4.2. [20] Given positive integer n and r, the necessary and sufficient condition that positive integers $x_i (i = 1, 2, \ldots, r)$ satisfying $\sum_{i=1}^{r} x_i$ is minimum and $n = \prod_{i=1}^{r} x_i$ is:

$$|x_i - x_j| \leq |x - y|, \text{ for any } i \neq j$$

where x and y are arbitrary positive integers satisfying $x_i \cdot x_j = x \cdot y$.

Although Ma gave the necessary and sufficient condition of the solution to the problem, he did not show how to find the solution. Here, we propose a heuristic algorithm to output the integer solution $x_i (i = 1, 2, \ldots, r)$ fulfilling the condition of the problem.

Algorithm 2. Heuristic Solution to MSSP-Problem

Choose any set $B = (x_1, x_2, \ldots, x_r)$ satisfying $\prod B = n$, and elements in B are arranged in ascending order.

(loop) for $i = 1, 2, \ldots, r$

   for $j = i + 1, \ldots, r$

     let $x_i = \min\{d : d | (x_i \cdot x_j) \wedge d \geq \sqrt[2]{x_i \cdot x_j}\}$ and $x_j = \max\{d : d | (x_i \cdot x_j) \wedge d \leq \sqrt[2]{x_i \cdot x_j}\}$

Rearrange the elements in B in ascending order, and go to (loop).

Else output B.

Taken $n = 27000$ and $r = 4$ as an example, B is initially set as $\{3,10,30,30\}$, and the output solution is $\{10,12,15,15\}$. The intermediate states of B along with the Algorithm 2 are listed as follows:

$\{5,6,30,30\} \rightarrow \{6,10,15,30\} \rightarrow \{10,10,15,18\}$

4.2   Optimal Trees on sENO-Problem

In this subsection, we present the Algorithm 3 to settles ENO-Problem. We define our algorithm as a recursive function f, which takes three following input parameters:

1. positive integer n, its initial value is the number N of the Tags;
2. positive integer d, its initial value is the maximum authentication delay D_{max};
3. positive integer r, its initial value is l_{req}.

We also denote Algorithm 2 as function g with the input parameters including number n and r, and its output are r integers $x_1, x_2, \ldots, x_r$, which make $\sum_{i=1}^{r} x_i$ reach the minimal value on the constraint $n = \prod_{i=1}^{r} x_i$.

Algorithm 3. Solution to sENO-Problem\\

---

1. Run $g(n, r) \rightarrow \{x_1, x_2, \ldots, x_r\}$; if $\sum_{i=1}^{r} x_i > d$, Output Fail.
2. Otherwise Run $f(n, d, r)$
2.0 Define an empty set S;
2.1 Search for the integer $n' = \max\{m : m | n \wedge m \notin S\}$;
2.2 Run $g(n/n', r - 1) \rightarrow \{x_1, x_2, \ldots, x_{r-1}\}$;
    2.3 If $n' + \sum_{i=1}^{r-1} x_i > d$, then $S = S \cup \{n'\}$, and go to step 2.1;
2.4 Otherwise if $n' = n$, return n';
2.5 Otherwise if $n' \neq n$, return $n' || f(n/n', d - n', r - 1)$

Here n/n' denotes integer division operation. The operation of the above algorithm can be described as follows: the algorithm first runs function g to check whether the optimization problem has a solution or not; additionally, from the detail construction of function f, we can see the output of function f is the largest possible value that respects the upper bound on the maximum authentication delay. The algorithm successively improves the branching factor vector by maximizing its elements, starting with the first element, and then proceeding to the next element. So we can see the output of Algorithm 3 is the solution to the sENO-Problem because of Lemma 3.4.

4.3   Optimal Trees on SMNO-Problem

In [18], Beye and Veugen proved that the four lemmas in Sect. 3 still hold under the constraint condition (2). Obviously the solution to sENO-Problem may not necessarily be the solution to sMNO-Problem. Considering $N = 27000$, $D_{max} = 90$ and $l_{req} = 4$, we know the optimal branching factors for sENO-Problemis $B = (60,18,5,5)$, but $B^* = (62,18,5,5)$ certainly satisfies the constraint condition (4), and $\Pr(B^*) = 0.9682 > \Pr(B)$.

Now, we propose an enumeration Algorithm 4 to settle the sMNO-Problem, and the algorithm is presented as pseudo code in C language.

Algorithm 4. Solution to sMNO-Problem

Define l_{req} variables $b_1, b_2, ..., b_{l_{req}}$.

for $(b_1 = D_{max}; b_1 \geq \lceil D_{max}/l_{req} \rceil; b_1\texttt{--})$

   for $(b_2 = D_{max} - b_1; b_2 \geq 1; b_2\texttt{--})$

   ....

for $(b_{l_{req}} = D_{max} - \sum_{i=1}^{l_{req}-1} b_i; b_{l_{req}} \geq 1; b_{l_{req}}\texttt{--})$

Output the first variable vector$(b_1, b_2, ..., b_{l_{req}})$ satisfying$\prod_{i=1}^{l_{req}} b_i \geq N$.

To reduce the number of loop operations, we can see $D_{max} = \sum_{i=1}^{l_{req}} b_i \leq b_1 \cdot l_{req}$, so $D_{max} \geq b_1 \geq \lceil D_{max}/l_{req} \rceil$. The computational complexity of algorithm 4 is about $O((D_{max})^{l_{req}})$, which is independent of the tags' number N. We only need the first suitable vector, so the algorithm can output the vector efficiently according to applicable parameters.

If Algorithm 4 has output a vector $(b_1, b_2, ..., b_{l_{req}})$, it is clear the elements must be arranged in decreasing order, and $(b_1, b_2, ..., b_{l_{req}})$ is the first vector that satisfies the constraint condition (4). For any i, the element b_i is the possible largest number that can be reached when b_{i-1} is determined, so from Lemma 3.4, we know the output vector is the optimal solution to sMNO-Problem.

5 Experiment Comparison

We conduct the experiments with the classical parameters $N = 27000$, $D_{max} = 90$ considered in [17] and [18], and we set l_{req} to be 4. Table 1 illustrates the operations of the algorithm 3. The optimal branching factor vector for ENO-Problem in [17] is $B = \{72, 5, 5, 5, 3\}$ and $\Pr(B) = 0.9725$. The number n initially equals to 27000. We have known the output of $g(n, 4)$ is $\{10, 12, 15, 15\}$, which means the optimization problem has a solution. The first row of the table corresponds to the levels of the recursion of f function during the execution. The optimal branching factor vector can be read out from the last column of the table, while $\times$ means the chosen n' can not satisfy the requirement of the maximum authentication delay. Taken the first row as an example, now $n' = 72$, and $g(n/n', r-1) = g(375, 3) \rightarrow \{15, 5, 5\}$, the authentication delay is $72 + 5{+}5 + 15 = 97 > 90$, therefore n' can not be the first element of the optimization solution vector. The final optimal branching factor vector for $N = 27000$, $D_{max} = 90$ and $l_{req} = 4$ is $B = (60, 18, 5, 5)$, and the real maximum authentication delay is 88, and $\Pr(B) = 0.9672$.

Table 1. Illustration of Algorithm 3 with input (27000, 90, 4)

RL	n	n'	$g(n/n', r-1)$	S	r	d	Output
1	27000	72	15, 5, 5		4	90	$\times$
		60	10, 9, 5	72	4	90	60
2	450	25	6, 3		3	30	$\times$
		18	5, 5	18	3	30	18
3	25	5	5		2	12	5
4	5	5			1	7	5

As to the sMNO-Problem, the optimal branching factors for MNO-Problem in [18] with parameters $N = 27000$, $D_{max} = 90$ are $B = (73, 5, 3, 3, 3, 3)$ and $\Pr(B) = 0.9736$. When we limit $l_{req} = 4$, utilizing algorithm 4, we can obtain the optimal branching factors for sMNO-Problem are $B = (67, 10, 7, 6)$. In that case, the to al number of Tag is 28140, and $\Pr(B) = 0.9706$.

6 Conclusions

In this paper, we propose two optimization problems respecting storage limitation (sENO-Problem and sMNO-Problem) in key-tree based RFID authentication system, which aim at minimizing the loss of privacy under single member compromise. The constraint conditions of sENO-Problem are Tags' exact number, maximum authentication delay, secret keys' number; while those of sMNO-Problem are Tags' minimum number, maximum authentication delay, secret keys' number. We also present Algorithm 3 and Algorithm 4 to solve these two optimization problems respectively through finding the optimal branching factors. The principle of the algorithms that lies in the privacy of efficient tree-based RFID authentication protocols is heavily dependent on the branching factor at the top layer. In the view of applicable parameters, the executions of the algorithms are efficient. However, we do not discuss the complexity of the algorithms in detail, and the complexity analysis of the algorithm 3 will be considered in the future work.

However, in our work, we only consider passive adversary who only eaves drops the authentication messages. In practice, active adversaries can utilize side-channel information to attack thesystem. Beye and Veugen [21] first launched the research on anonymity for key-trees with adaptive adversaries. How to expand our current results by taking side-channel knowledge and adaptive adversaries into considerations will be another problem worthy of careful consideration.

Acknowledgements. This work is supported by National Natural Science Foundation of China (Grant No. 61572260, 61572261, 61672016, 61872192), and Scientific & Technological Support Project of Jiangsu Province (No. BE2015702).

References

1. Garfinkel, S., Juels, A., Pappu, R.: RFID privacy: an overview of problems and proposed solutions. IEEE Secur. Priv. Mag. **3**(3), 34–43 (2005)
2. Preneel, B.: Using cryptography well. Printed Handout (2010). http://secappdev.org/handouts/2010/Bart
3. Lee, S.M., Hwang, Y.J., Lee, D.H., Lim, J.I.: Efficient authentication for low-cost RFID systems. In: Gervasi, O., Gavrilova, M.L., Kumar, V., Laganà, A., Lee, H.P., Mun, Y., Taniar, D., Tan, C.J.K. (eds.) ICCSA 2005. LNCS, vol. 3480, pp. 619–627. Springer, Heidelberg (2005). https://doi.org/10.1007/11424758_65
4. Liu, Z., Peng, D.: True random number generator in RFID systems against traceability. In: IEEE Consumer Communications and Networking Conference - CCNS2006, Las Vegas, USA, pp. 620–624 (2005)
5. Ohkubo, M., Suzuki, K., Kinoshita, S.: Cryptographic approach to "Privacy-Friendly" tags. In: RFID Privacy Workshop, USA (2003). http://www.rfidprivacy.us/2003/agenda.php
6. Avoine, G., Oechslin, P.: A scalable and provably secure Hash based RFID protocol. In: Third IEEE International Workshop on Pervasive Computing and Communication Security, PerCom, pp. 110–114 (2005)
7. Tsudik, G.: YA-TRAP: yet another trivial RFID authentication protocol. In: International Conference on Pervasive Computing and Communications – PerCom, pp. 640–643 (2006)
8. Gope, P., Hwang, T.: A realistic lightweight authentication protocol preserving strong anonymity for securing RFID system. Comput. Secur. **55**, 271–280 (2015)
9. Luo, H., Wen, G., Su, J., Huang, Z.: SLAP: Succinct and light weight authentication protocol for low-cost RFID system. Wireless Netw. **24**, 1–10 (2016)
10. Rahman, F., Hoque, M.E., Ahamed, S.I.: Anonpri: a secure anonymous private authentication protocol for RFID systems. Inf. Sci. **379**, 195–210 (2017)
11. Hopper, N.J., Blum, M.: Secure human identification protocols. In: Boyd, C. (ed.) ASIACRYPT 2001. LNCS, vol. 2248, pp. 52–66. Springer, Heidelberg (2001). https://doi.org/10.1007/3-540-45682-1_4
12. Katz, J., Shin, J.S., Smith, A.: Parallel and concurrent security of the HB and HB + protocols. J. Cryptol. **23**(3), 402–421 (2010)

13. Gilbert, H., Robshaw, M.J.B., Seurin, Y.: Good Variants of HB $^+$ Are Hard to Find. In: Tsudik, G. (ed.) FC 2008. LNCS, vol. 5143, pp. 156–170. Springer, Heidelberg (2008). https://doi.org/10.1007/978-3-540-85230-8_12

14. Cash, D., Kiltz, E., Tessaro, S.: Two-round man-in-the-middle security from LPN. In: Theory of Cryptography, TCC 2016-A, pp. 225–248 (2016)

15. Lyubashevsky, V., Masny, D.: Man-in-the-middle secure authentication schemes from LPN and weak PRFs. In: Advances in Cryptology—CRYPTO, pp. 308–325 (2013)

16. Molnar, D., Wagner, D.: Privacy and security in library RFID: issues, practices, and architectures. In: Proceedings 11th ACM Conference Computer and Communication Security (CCS 2004), pp. 210–219 (2004)

17. Buttyán, L., Holczer, T., Vajda, I.: Optimal key-trees for tree-based private authentication. In: Danezis, G., Golle, P. (eds.) PET 2006. LNCS, vol. 4258, pp. 332–350. Springer, Heidelberg (2006). https://doi.org/10.1007/11957454_19

18. Veugen, T., Beye, M.: Improved anonymity for key-trees. In: Radio Frequency Identification: Security and Privacy Issues - 8th International Workshop, RFID Sec 2012, LNCS 7739, pp. 31–47 (2013)

19. Chaum, D.: The dining cryptographers problem: unconditional sender and recipient untraceability. J. Cryptol. 1(1), 65–75 (1988)

20. Ma, K.J.: The minimum sum constant product problem with constaints on positive integers. J. Qufu Normal Univ. (Nat. Sci.) 3, 47–49 (1983)

21. Beye, M., Veugen, T.: Anonymity for key-trees with adaptive adversaries. In: Rajarajan, M., Piper, F., Wang, H., Kesidis, G. (eds.) SecureComm 2011. LNICST, vol. 96, pp. 409–425. Springer, Heidelberg (2012). https://doi.org/10.1007/978-3-642-31909-9_23

Towards Realizing Authorized Encrypted Search with Designed Access Policy

Lin Mei, Chungen Xu$^{(\boxtimes)}$, Lei Xu, Zhongyi Liu, Xiaoling Yu, and Zhigang Yao

School of Science, Nanjing University of Science and Technology,
Nanjing 210094, China
wangmumu2244@gmail.com, xuchung@njust.edu.cn, xuleicrypto@gmail.com,
ZhongyiLiu950217@outlook.com, yuxiaoling12@gmail.com,
zhigangyao1995@gmail.com

Abstract. Searchable encryption enables users to search the encrypted data outsourced in a third party. Recently, to serve a wide scenario of data sharing application, multi-user searchable encryption (MUSE) is proposed to realize the encrypted data search for multiple users. In this paper, we concentrate on addressing the authorized keyword search problem for a team with fixed unauthorized members and propose a novel puncture public key encryption with keyword search (PPEKS) scheme with designed access policy. Compared with the existing schemes, our proposal has the following features: our scheme supports team authorized search rather than single-user authorization; the data owner only needs one encrypted copy for all authorized members which is one copy one user in traditional MUSE schemes. In addition, we also conduct a rigorous security analysis on our scheme and make a functional comparison of our scheme with other MUSE schemes. Finally, we perform comprehensive efficiency evaluations on a laptop.

Keywords: Cloud storage · Multi-user · Adaptive chosen keyword attack · Access policy · Standard model

1 Introduction

Due to the advent of information technology, one may enjoy the convenience brought by cloud storage, users can outsource their data to a third party (cloud) to save their local cost. Compared to physical storage, data on the cloud gets rid of the limitations of physical devices. When the data is needed, they can access them at any time, anywhere via a device like a laptop or mobile phone. Benefitting from these features, more and more users begin to outsource their data to enjoy the cloud services provided by third-party servers. However, data outsourcing services bring convenience to people while posing some security issues as well. The third-party server may always be untrusted, that means it may maliciously use or leak user's data. Therefore, storing data, especially private data, on the cloud without any safeguard raises confidentiality and privacy concerns. A generic approach to keep the data privacy is to encrypt them before

© Springer Nature Switzerland AG 2019
F. Liu et al. (Eds.): SciSec 2019, LNCS 11933, pp. 293–307, 2019.
https://doi.org/10.1007/978-3-030-34637-9_22

uploading them to the cloud. But doing so will bring another problem, i.e., the encrypted data loses its underlying meaning, if one wants to retrieve the documents with some expected keywords, she needs to download all her data and decrypt them for search, which is impractical and inefficient. Therefore, how to realize the secure storage and efficient retrieval of data on the cloud is an urgent problem to be solved.

Searchable encryption (SE) is a cryptographic primitive that enables users to perform search on the encrypted data stored on the cloud with a search token which can only be generated by the authorized users with their secret key. Multi-user searchable encryption (MUSE) is an extension of the traditional SE, which supports encrypted data search among multiple users for data sharing application. However, existing research on MUSE primarily focuses on authorization for a single user, not a group, which means the data owner needs to generate a unique ciphertext for each user when she wants to authorize a file to multiple users. The authorize process has tremendous communication and computation overhead. Furthermore, some existing schemes require the data owner to be online to grant search capabilities for users, which is impractical for the data owner. Many MUSE schemes can only achieve the goal of coarse-grained access control, which makes the authorization accuracy lower. In regard to the security of MUSE schemes, many of them only consider the non-adaptive chosen keyword attack but ignoring the adaptive chosen keyword attack.

Since the attribute-based encryption (ABE) can provide a flexible approach to realize access control. ABE can be exploited to construct SE schemes with such advantage, which is of great significance in the multi-user setting. Inspired by the technique of non-monotonic ABE [11] and puncturable encryption proposed by Matthew et al. [7], we construct a novel puncture public key encryption with keyword search (PPEKS) scheme with designed access policy to solve the issues outlined above. Specifically, we employ a set of tags to specify each user in our scheme, where every user can be identified by a tag. Data owner needs to set the access policy, i.e. who are not authorized, for each keyword before uploading the encrypted data. Then she just needs to execute a designed encryption algorithm with tags of unauthorized members, namely the access policy, so that only the authorized users can search the corresponding data. When the number of unauthorized users of a team (hereafter called it threshold) is preset to d, the size of keyword ciphertexts is constant even if some new members add to the team. In terms of security, our scheme is expected to resist adaptive chosen keyword attack in the standard model which ensures that neither ciphertexts nor search token can be distinguished in the adaptive security game.

1.1 Related Works

Song et al. [13] gave the first solution to encrypted search problem for data stored in an untrusted server. However, their scheme is inefficient as it needs to scan the whole file to search for a single keyword. After Song's work, many searchable symmetric encryption(SSE) schemes have been proposed based on different techniques or functionalities. In order to enhance the efficiency of encrypted data search, Goh et al. [6] proposed an SSE scheme using pseudo-random functions and bloom filters. Then, Kamara et al. [8] proposed the first dynamic SSE scheme, extended the inverted index approach, which is introduced by [4]. Since the capability of conjunctive search is needed in the SSE system, Cash et al. [2] proposed a highly scalable SSE with support for boolean queries.

In order to realize the data sharing between multiple data readers and multiple data writers, Curtmola et al. proposed the first multi-user searchable encryption (MUSE) scheme [4] to achieve this goal. In their scheme, they combined the broadcast encryption with a single-user SSE scheme to realize the key management and user access rights setting. However, since all users in their scheme share a single key, all users need to update their keys once someone's right is revoked, which causes a huge revoke cost. After Curtmola's research, more scholars paid attention to MUSE and proposed many creative schemes [1,10,14,18]. Except for the overhead of user rights revocation, key management is also a concern in the MUSE. Bao et al. introduced a trusted third party (TTP) to manage the enrolment and revocation of users [1]. In their scheme, the TTP is responsible for sending secret key to each user and the complementary key of each user to the server so that only the authorized users allowed to write and search the database. Then, to provide users with the flexible fine-grained access control, Zhao et al. proposed an MUSE scheme based on attribute-based encryption (ABE) and attribute-based signature (ABS) [18]. Recent MUSE schemes focus more on the result rank and verification [9,17] to improve efficiency and security.

In general, the research on the protection of outsourced data has become increasingly important in recent years. And MUSE has also become a hot topic in current research due to its practicality. More and more researchers are working to balance the search efficiency and security of MUSE scheme [3,16]. Since it's not easy to achieve efficiency and multi-user at the same time, how to guarantee the security under the premise of ensuring the two conditions is still to be studied.

1.2   Our Contribution

In this paper we mainly propose a fine-grained multi-user searchable encryption scheme for encrypted data retrieval in the cloud, our contributions can be summarized as follows:

1. **Multi-user.** With the multi-user setting, our scheme can support flexible data sharing of data within an organized team. Each user can generate the ciphertext based on some access policies, and only the authorized ones can search them.
2. **Non-interactive.** We deploy the access policy to encrypt the data, once the user satisfies the access policy, she can search the data on her own without interacting with the data owner.
3. **Efficient.** Our scheme also has a super feature in data storage. The size of the ciphertext is constant and will not increase with the number of the authorized users. In addition, there is no need to update the key of the current members even someone joins in.

4. **Privacy-preserving.** Comparing with prior arts, this paper prefers to deal with a stronger security model. Our system is proven to satisfy both the keyword ciphertext indistinguishability and the trapdoor indistinguishability under the adaptive chosen-keyword attacks.

1.3   Organization

We organize the rest of this paper as follows: Sect. 2 lists the background knowledge on pairing with its security assumptions and reviews the definition as well as the security game of our proposed PPEKS scheme. Section 3 overviews the proposed scheme and defines the related threat models. Section 4 gives the proposed scheme and Sect. 5 performs the formal security analysis. Experimental evaluation is given in Sect. 6. Finally, we give a brief conclusion in Sect. 7.

2   Preliminaries

We first review the knowledge of pairing and its hardness assumption, and then give the function of PPEKS. The security models of PPEKS are listed at the end of this section.

2.1   Bilinear Pairing and Hardness Assumption

Let $\mathbb{G}_1$ and $\mathbb{G}_2$ be two cyclic groups with prime order p, and g be the generator of $\mathbb{G}_1$. A map $e\colon \mathbb{G}_1 \times \mathbb{G}_1 \to \mathbb{G}_2$ is bilinear if it satisfies the following three conditions:

1. Bilinear: For all element $u, v \in \mathbb{G}_1$ and $x, y \in Z_p^*$, we have $e(u^x, v^y) = e(u, v)^{xy}$;
2. Non-degeneracy: $e(g, g) \neq 1$;
3. Computability: There exists an efficient algorithm to compute the value of $e(g^x, g^y)$ for any $x, y \in Z_p^*$.

Given a tuple $(g,\ g^a, g^b, g^c, g')$, where $g, g^a, g^b, g^c \in \mathbb{G}_1$ and $g' \in \mathbb{G}_2$. The DBDH problem in $(\mathbb{G}_1, \mathbb{G}_2)$ is to decide if $g' = e(g, g)^{abc}$. The advantage for a probabilistic polynomial-time(PPT) adversary $\mathcal{A}$ to solve the above problem is:

$$Adv_{DBDH}(\mathcal{A}) = |\Pr[\mathcal{A}(g, g^a, g^b, g^c, e(g, g)^{abc}) = 1] - \Pr[\mathcal{A}(g, g^a, g^b, g^c, g') = 1]|$$

Definition 1 (DBDH assumption). *We say that the DBDH assumption holds if $Adv_{DBDH}(\mathcal{A})$ is negligible for $\mathcal{A}$.*

Given a tuple (g, g^a), where $g, g^a \in \mathbb{G}_1$. The DL problem in $\mathbb{G}_1$ is to compute the value of a. The advantage for a PPT adversary $\mathcal{A}$ to solve the above problem is:

$$Adv_{DL}(\mathcal{A}) = |\Pr[\mathcal{A}(g, g^a) = a]|$$

Definition 2 (DL assumption). *We say that the DL assumption holds if $Adv_{DL}(\mathcal{A})$ is negligible for $\mathcal{A}$.*

2.2 Definition and Security

In this section, we will first give the framework of our proposed scheme and the correctness definition of it. Then, the security models of our scheme are presented.

- **Setup**$(1^k, d) \longrightarrow \{\text{SP, MSK}\}$: It takes as input a security parameter k, the threshold d, and outputs the system parameter SP and the master secret key MSK.
- **Derive**$(\text{SP, MSK}, \tau) \longrightarrow \{\text{SK}_\tau\}$: It takes as input the system parameter SP, the master secret key MSK and the user's tag τ, and outputs the secret key SK_τ for the user.
- **Encrypt**$(\text{SP}, w, \text{T}^\dagger) \longrightarrow \{\text{CT}_w\}$: It takes as input the system parameter SP, the keyword w and the set $\text{T}^\dagger$ consisting of the unauthorized users' tags, and outputs the keyword ciphertext CT_w.
- **TokGen**$(w^*, \text{SK}_\tau, \text{SP}) \longrightarrow \{\text{ST}_{w^*}\}$: It takes as input the keyword w^*, the secret key SK_τ and the system parameter SP, and outputs the search token ST_{w^*}.
- **Test**$(\text{ST}_{w^*}, \text{CT}_w) \longrightarrow \{0 \text{ or } 1\}$: It takes as input the search token ST_{w^*} and the keyword ciphertext CT_w, and outputs 1 if $w = w^*$ and $\tau \notin T^\dagger$, otherwise outputs 0.

A PPEKS scheme is correct if the **Test** protocol always returns the correct result when searching over the encrypted database (EDB) with the token ST, where the EDB and ST are generated by **Encrypt** and **TokGen** protocols, respectively. We define the correctness as follows.

Definition 3. *(Correctness): Let* $\Pi = ($**Setup, Derive, Encrypt, TokGen, Test**$)$ *be a PPEKS scheme.* Π *is correct if for all* $k \in \mathbb{N}$, *for all* $d \in \mathbb{N}$, *for all master secret keys* MSK *and system parameters* SP *output by* **Setup***$(1^k, d)$, *for all tags* $\tau \in \{0,1\}^*$, *for all secret keys* SK_τ *output by* **Derive***(SP, MSK, τ), *for all keywords* w, *for all* d-*size tag sets* $\text{T}^\dagger$ *and for all ciphertext* CT_w *output by* **Encrypt***(SP, w, $\text{T}^\dagger$), *if* $w = w^*$ *and the tag* $\tau \notin \text{T}^\dagger$, *then* **Test***$(\text{ST}_{w^*}, \text{CT}_w)$ *returns the correct response with all but negligible probability when* ST_{w^*} *is output by* **TokGen**$(w^*, \text{SK}_\tau, \text{SP})$.

Definition 4 (CT-IND-CKA game). *Let* k *be the security parameter and* d *be the threshold parameter,* $\mathcal{A}$ *be the adversary,* $\mathcal{B}$ *be the challenger, and* W *be the keyword space.*

- **Setup.** *The setup algorithm* **Setup**$(1^k, d)$ *and the secret key generation algorithm* **Derive***(SP, MSK, τ) are excused by* $\mathcal{B}$. *Get the system parameters* SP, *the master secret key* MSK *and the secret key* SK_τ *for the user. Then* $\mathcal{B}$ *sends the system parameters* SP *to* $\mathcal{A}$.
- **Query phase 1.** $\mathcal{A}$ *adaptively makes the queries to oracles:*
  - *Ciphertext query* $\langle w \rangle$: *Adversary* $\mathcal{A}$ *can adaptively ask* $\mathcal{B}$ *the ciphertext for any keyword* $w \in W$ *of her choice. Challenger* $\mathcal{B}$ *generates the keyword ciphertext* $\text{CT}_w = $ **Encrypt***(SP, w, $\text{T}^\dagger$) and returns it to* $\mathcal{A}$.

- *Token query $\langle w \rangle$: Adversary $\mathcal{A}$ can adaptively ask $\mathcal{B}$ the search token for any keyword $w \in W$ of her choice. Challenger $\mathcal{B}$ generates the search token of keyword $ST_w = \mathbf{TokGen}(w, SK_\tau, SP)$ and returns it to $\mathcal{A}$.*
- *Test query $\langle CT_w, ST_{w'} \rangle$: Adversary $\mathcal{A}$ can adaptively ask $\mathcal{B}$ the relation of CT_w and $ST_{w'}$. Challenger $\mathcal{B}$ runs the $\mathbf{Test}(ST_w, CT_{w_i})$ and returns 1 to $\mathcal{A}$ if ST_w and CT_{w_i} are corresponding to the same keyword and the ST_w doesn't satisfy the access policy of CT_{w_i} or 0 otherwise. The test query simulates the behavior of an adversary who verifies the keyword guess by performing the $\mathbf{Test}$ algorithm or using the server as a test oracle.*

- **Challenge.** *As long as $\mathcal{A}$ determines to end the phase 1, she will submit two different keywords w_0 and w_1 as her challenge. The only restriction is that the ciphertext of w_0 and w_1 cannot been queried in phase 1. After receiving the two keywords, $\mathcal{B}$ randomly selects a bit $b \in \{0,1\}$ and creates a challenge ciphertext CT_{w_b} which is sent to $\mathcal{A}$. It should be noted that the access policy of the challenge ciphertext CT_{w_b} should contain the tag τ.*
- **Query phase 2.** *$\mathcal{A}$ adaptively makes the queries to oracles as in phase 1. Notice that both keywords w_0 and w_1 should not be queried to get their ciphertexts.*
- **Guess.** *$\mathcal{A}$ outputs the guess $b' \in \{0,1\}$. If $b' = b$, $\mathcal{A}$ wins the game.*

We define the advantage of $\mathcal{A}$ in CT-IND-CKA game is $Adv^{CT}(\mathcal{A}) = |Pr[b' = b]\text{-}1/2|$

Definition 5. *A PPEKS scheme is assumed to be CT-IND-CKA secure if the advantage $Adv^{CT}(\mathcal{A})$ defined above is negligible.*

Definition 6 (ST-IND-CKA game). *Let k be the security parameter and d be the threshold parameter, $\mathcal{A}$ be the adversary, $\mathcal{B}$ be the challenger, and W be the keyword space.*

*The definition of ST-IND-CKA game is totally consistent with the Definition 4. Except for replacing the ciphertext CT_{w_b} with the search token ST_{w_b} during the Challenge step and the adversary must satisfy the access policy defined in the **Encrypt**.*

We define the advantage of $\mathcal{A}$ in ST-IND-CKA game is $Adv^{ST}(\mathcal{A}) = |Pr[b' = b] - 1/2|$

Definition 7. *A PPEKS scheme is assumed to be ST-IND-CKA secure if the advantage $Adv^{ST}(\mathcal{A})$ defined above is negligible.*

3   Problem Statement

In this section, we first present an overview of our scheme. Then we define our threat model.

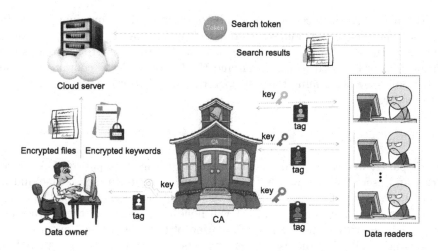

Fig. 1. Overview of the system

3.1 System Overview

The proposed (PPEKS) scheme involves a central authority (CA), the data owner, the cloud server, and the data reader. As shown in Fig. 1, our scheme considers the following three parties:

- **Central authority:** The central authority (CA) plays the role of key generator, it initializes the system with the security and threshold parameters and outputs the public key and master secret key. In addition, it is responsible for computing the secret key for the users according to their tags.
- **Users:** Each user in the team should submit a tag representing their identity to the CA. The users can be data owner or data reader. As the data owner, she encrypts the data and uploads it to the cloud, and as the data reader, she submits the search query to the cloud server with a valid token.
- **Server:** The server can be deployed by a third-party cloud service provider. It stores the encrypted keywords with unauthorized tags set $T^\dagger$ and performs a search query when receiving search token.

The architecture of our scheme is illustrated in Fig. 1. First of all, all users are required to submit a tag representing their identities to the CA in our scheme. And CA needs to know the threshold of this team in advance. Then it generates the system parameters (SP) and master secret key (MSK) for this team. In addition, CA will generate a specific key for each user based on their unique tags, which we name it secret key (SK) in this paper. When a user wants to share her data securely with some other users in this team, she first encrypts the keywords extracted from the data with SP and the access policy, i.e., a set of tags of those who are not authorized, and then sends it with the ciphertext generated by a symmetric encryption algorithm to the cloud server. We omit the ciphertext generation process in this paper, because it can be any symmetric encryption algorithm, e.g., AES. Once someone wants to search for data containing a certain keyword, she generates a valid search token of the keyword by her secret key and sends it to the cloud server. The server will check if the ciphertext contains the certain keyword related to the token and the tag of reader is contained in the access policy by performing the test operation and return the search results to data reader.

3.2 Threat Models

In this paper, we consider the threat models including three parties: CA, cloud server and users. We assume that CA is a trusted entity in our scheme and it sends the legal secret keys to registered users under a secure channel. The cloud server is "honest but curious", i.e., it will honestly perform all the operations, but be curious to get the hidden information of the search token and the corresponding results. For the user, when she acts as a data owner, she is reliable, while as a data reader she is not trusted anymore and attempts to recover the underlying information.

4   Our Construction

In this section, we will first present our fine-grained multi-user searchable encryption scheme with Fig. 2, and then explain the scheme in detail and show the correctness of our scheme at the end of this section.

4.1   Our PPEKS Scheme

Our construction is shown in Fig. 2. The scheme is described in detail as follows. By default, all users in the team have submitted an identity tag to the CA before all steps begin (write the identity tag set for all users as T).

Setup$(1^k, d)$. In this stage, the CA takes the security parameter k and the threshold value d as inputs, and outputs the system parameters and the master secret key. Specifically, it first chooses a group $\mathbb{G}$ with prime order p, a generator g and a hash function $H : \{0,1\}^* \to Z_p$. Then it samples a d-degree polynomial $q(\cdot)$ whose coefficient is denoted by the vector $(a_d, a_{d-1}, \ldots, a_0)$, where a_i is the coefficient of the i-th term. It then chooses random exponents r, $\alpha \in Z_p$ and sets $g_1 = g^\alpha$, $g_2 = g^{a_0}$. Here we define $V(x) = g^{q(x)}$, note that t_0 is a special tag that is not contained in T. Finally, it computes the system parameters SP $= (g, g_1, g_2, g^{q(1)}, \ldots, g^{q(d)})$, and the master secret key MSK $= (sk_0^{(1)}, sk_0^{(2)}, sk_0^{(3)}, sk_0^{(4)}, sk_0^{(5)})$, where $sk_0^{(1)} = g_2^{\alpha+r}$, $sk_0^{(2)} = V(H(t_0))^r$, $sk_0^{(3)} = g^r$, $sk_0^{(4)} = t_0$, $sk_0^{(5)} = V(H(t_0))$.

Derive$(\text{SP}, \text{MSK}, \tau)$. For each member in the team, CA takes the master secret key MSK and the user's tag $\tau \in \{0,1\}^* \setminus \{t_0\}$ as input, and returns her a valid secret key. As shown in Fig. 2, it first parses the MSK as $(sk_0^{(1)}, sk_0^{(2)}, sk_0^{(3)}, sk_0^{(4)}, sk_0^{(5)})$, where the values of $sk_0^{(i)}(i = 1, \ldots, 5)$ are showed in the previous

Setup($1^k, d$)
Central authority:
1: Choose a group G of prime order p, a generator g and a hash function $H:\{0,1\}^* \to Z_p$
2: $(a_d, a_{d-1}, \ldots, a_1, a_0) \xleftarrow{R} Z_q^{d+1}$
3: $q(x) \leftarrow a_d x^d + a_{d-1} x^{d-1} + \ldots + a_1 x + a_0$
4: $r, t_0 \xleftarrow{R} \{0,1\}^*, V(x) \leftarrow g^{q(x)}$
5: $g_1 \leftarrow g^\alpha, g_2 \leftarrow g^{a_0}$
6: $\mathrm{SP} \leftarrow (g, g_1, g_2, V(1), \ldots, V(d))$
7: $sk_0^{(1)} \leftarrow g_2^{\alpha+r}, sk_0^{(2)} \leftarrow V(H(t_0))^r$
8: $sk_0^{(3)} \leftarrow g^r, sk_0^{(4)} \leftarrow t_0, sk_0^{(5)} \leftarrow V(H(t_0))$
9: $\mathrm{MSK} \leftarrow (sk_0^{(1)}, sk_0^{(2)}, sk_0^{(3)}, sk_0^{(4)}, sk_0^{(5)})$

Derive(SP, MSK, τ)
Central authority:
1: $(g, g_1, g_2, g^{q(1)}, \ldots, g^{q(d)}) \leftarrow \mathrm{SP}$
2: $(sk_0^{(1)}, sk_0^{(2)}, sk_0^{(3)}, sk_0^{(4)}, sk_0^{(5)}) \leftarrow \mathrm{MSK}$
3: $r_0, r_1, \lambda' \xleftarrow{R} Z_p$
4: $sk_{n0} \leftarrow (sk_0^{(1)} \cdot g_2^{r_0 - \lambda'}, sk_0^{(2)} \cdot (sk_0^{(5)})^{r_0}, sk_0^{(3)} \cdot g^{r_0}, sk_0^{(4)}, sk_0^{(5)})$
5: $sk_{n1} \leftarrow (g_2^{\lambda' + r_1}, V(H(\tau))^{r_1}, g^{r_1}, \tau, V(H(\tau)))$
6: $\mathrm{SK}_\tau \leftarrow [sk_{n0}, sk_{n1}]$
7: Send SK_τ to the user.

Encrypt(SP, w^*, $\mathrm{T}^\dagger$)//$\mathrm{T}^\dagger$ is the set of unauthorized tags.
Data owner:
1: $(g, g_1, g_2, V(1), \ldots, V(d)) \leftarrow \mathrm{SP}$
2: $(t_1, t_2, \ldots, t_d) \leftarrow \mathrm{T}^\dagger$
3: $s \xleftarrow{R} Z_p$
4: $ct^{(1)} \leftarrow e(g_1, g_2)^{sH(w^*)}, ct^{(2)} \leftarrow g^s$
5: $ct^{(3,1)} \leftarrow V(H(t_1))^s, ct^{(3,2)} \leftarrow V(H(t_2))^s, \ldots, ct^{(3,d)} \leftarrow V(H(t_d))^s$
6: $\mathrm{CT}_{w^*} \leftarrow (ct^{(1)}, ct^{(2)}, ct^{(3,1)}, \ldots, ct^{(3,d)}, \mathrm{T}^\dagger)$
7: Send CT_{w^*} to the server.
Server:
8: Store CT_{w^*}

TokGen(w, SK_τ, SP)
Data reader:
1: $(g, g_1, g_2, V(1), \ldots, V(d)) \leftarrow \mathrm{SP}$
2: $[sk_{n0}, sk_{n1}] \leftarrow \mathrm{SK}_\tau$

3: $(sk_{n0}^{(1)}, sk_{n0}^{(2)}, sk_{n0}^{(3)}, sk_{n0}^{(4)}, sk_{n0}^{(5)}) \leftarrow sk_{n0}$
4: $(sk_{n1}^{(1)}, sk_{n1}^{(2)}, sk_{n1}^{(3)}, sk_{n1}^{(4)}, sk_{n1}^{(5)}) \leftarrow sk_{n1}$
5: $r' \xleftarrow{R} Z_p$
6: $st_{n0}^{(1)} \leftarrow (sk_{n0}^{(1)})^{H(w)} \cdot g_2^{r'}$
7: $st_{n0}^{(2)} \leftarrow (sk_{n0}^{(2)})^{H(w)} \cdot (sk_{n0}^{(5)})^{r'}$
8: $st_{n0}^{(3)} \leftarrow (sk_{n0}^{(3)})^{H(w)} \cdot g^{r'}, st_{n0}^{(4)} \leftarrow sk_{n0}^{(4)}$
9: $st_{n0} \leftarrow (st_{n0}^{(1)}, st_{n0}^{(2)}, st_{n0}^{(3)}, st_{n0}^{(4)})$
10: $st_{n1}^{(1)} \leftarrow (sk_{n1}^{(1)})^{H(w)} \cdot g_2^{r'}$
11: $st_{n1}^{(2)} \leftarrow (sk_{n1}^{(2)})^{H(w)} \cdot (sk_{n1}^{(5)})^{r'}$
12: $st_{n1}^{(3)} \leftarrow (sk_{n1}^{(3)})^{H(w)} \cdot g^{r'}, st_{n1}^{(4)} \leftarrow sk_{n1}^{(4)}$
13: $st_{n1} \leftarrow (st_{n1}^{(1)}, st_{n1}^{(2)}, st_{n1}^{(3)}, st_{n1}^{(4)})$
14: $\mathrm{ST}_w \leftarrow (st_{n0}, st_{n1})$
15: Send ST_w to the server.

Test(ST_w, CT_{w^*})
Server:
1: $(st_{n0}, st_{n1}) \leftarrow \mathrm{ST}_w$
2: $(st_{n0}^{(1)}, st_{n0}^{(2)}, st_{n0}^{(3)}, st_{n0}^{(4)}) \leftarrow st_{n0}$
3: $(st_{n1}^{(1)}, st_{n1}^{(2)}, st_{n1}^{(3)}, st_{n1}^{(4)}) \leftarrow st_{n1}$
4: $(ct^{(1)}, ct^{(2)}, ct^{(3,1)}, \ldots, ct^{(3,d)}, \mathrm{T}^\dagger) \leftarrow \mathrm{CT}_{w^*}$
5: $(t_1, t_2, \ldots, t_d) \leftarrow \mathrm{T}^\dagger$
6: **for** i=0 to 1 **do**
7: $\quad \mathrm{T}_i^\dagger \leftarrow (st_{ni}^{(4)}, t_1, t_2, \ldots, t_d)$
8: $\quad u_i^* \leftarrow \prod_{t_j \in \mathrm{T}_i^\dagger \setminus \{st_{ni}^{(4)}\}} \frac{-H(t_j)}{H(st_{ni}^{(4)}) - H(t_j)}$
9: $\quad$ **for** k=1 to d **do**
10: $\quad\quad u_{ki} \leftarrow \prod_{t_j \in \mathrm{T}_i^\dagger \setminus \{t_k\}} \frac{-H(t_j)}{H(t_k) - H(t_j)}$
11: $\quad$ **end for**
12: $\quad z_{i1} \leftarrow e(st_{ni}^{(1)}, ct^{(2)})$
13: $\quad z_{i2} \leftarrow e(st_{ni}^{(2)}, ct^{(2)})^{u_i^*}$
14: $\quad z_{i3} \leftarrow e(st_{ni}^{(3)}, \prod_{k=1}^d (ct^{(3,k)})^{u_{ki}})$
15: $\quad Z_i \leftarrow \frac{z_{i1}}{z_{i2} \cdot z_{i3}}$
16: **end for**
17: $c \leftarrow \frac{ct^{(1)}}{\prod_{i=0}^1 Z_i}$
18: **if** c = 1 **then**
19: $\quad$ return 1
20: **else**
21: $\quad$ return 0
22: **end if**

Fig. 2. Our basic encrypted data search scheme construction

step. Then, it randomly selects three numbers r_0, r_1, λ' from Z_p and computes (sk_{n0}, sk_{n1}) according to **Derive** algorithm. Finally CA sends the secret key $\mathrm{SK}_\tau = (sk_{n0}, sk_{n1})$ to the user.

Encrypt(SP, w^*, $t_1, t_2, \ldots, t_d$). When the data owner wants to share the data with some certain members in her team. She first collects the tags out of her willingness and puts them in a set which can be called access policy, we denote it as $\mathrm{T}^\dagger = \{t_1, t_2, \ldots, t_d | t_i \in \{0,1\}^* \setminus \{t_0\}\}$. Then she takes the public key PK, keyword w^*, and the $\mathrm{T}^\dagger$ as input, and outputs the ciphertext as follows: Sample a random number $s \in Z_p$, and compute the ciphertext

$CT_{w^*} = (ct^{(1)}, ct^{(2)}, ct^{(3,1)}, ct^{(3,2)}, \ldots, ct^{(3,d)}, T^\dagger)$, the computational procedure can be found in the **Encrypt** algorithm from Fig. 2.

TokGen(w, SK_τ). This algorithm describes how the data reader generates a valid search token for a certain keyword w. She takes her secret key SK_τ and the keyword w as inputs, and performs **TokGen** protocol to compute the token $ST_w = (st_{n0}, st_{n1})$, where st_{n0} and st_{n1} are described in the **TokGen** algorithm in Fig. 2. Once the token is generated, she sends the query request with the token ST_w to the server.

Test(ST_{w^*}, CT_w). Once the server received token ST_{w^*} from data reader, it tests which keyword ciphertext is related to the keyword w^* and whether the data reader is authorized to the keyword w^*. On input the search token ST_{w^*} received from data reader and the keyword ciphertext CT_w from encrypted database. First, parse ciphertext CT_w as $(ct^{(1)}, ct^{(2)}, ct^{(3,1)}, ct^{(3,2)}, \ldots, ct^{(3,d)}, T^\dagger)$, the search token ST_{w^*} as (st_{n0}, st_{n1}) and st_{ni} is parsed into ($st_{ni}^{(1)}$, $st_{ni}^{(2)}$, $st_{ni}^{(3)}$, $st_{ni}^{(4)}$) for $i = 0, 1$. Next, compute the equations $(u_i^* \cdot q(H(st_{ni}^{(4)}))) + \sum_{k=1}^d (u_{ki} \cdot q(H(t_k))) = q(0) = a_0$ to get the coefficients $u_i^*, u_{1i}, \ldots, u_{di}$. This can be solved by using the Lagrange interpolation polynomial. While the data reader is authorized to the keyword w^*, its tag will belong to the tag set $T^* = T \backslash T^\dagger$ and therefore the coefficients can be computed successfully. Finally, compute Z_i according to the **Test** algorithm. Check: $c \overset{?}{=} 1$, where $c = ct^{(1)} / \prod_{j=0}^1 Z_j$. If yes, it means that $w = w^*$. Otherwise, not.

Theorem 1. *The propose PPEKS scheme is correct.*

Proof. The correctness can be verified as follows.
  For k = 1 to d, we have

$$u_{k0} = \prod_{t_i \in T_0^\dagger \backslash \{t_k\}} \frac{-H(t_i)}{H(t_k) - H(t_i)}, u_{k1} = \prod_{t_i \in T_1^\dagger \backslash \{t_k\}} \frac{-H(t_i)}{H(t_k) - H(t_i)}$$

and

$$u_0^* = \prod_{t_i \in T_0^\dagger \backslash \{st_{n0}^{(4)}\}} \frac{-H(t_i)}{H(st_{n0}^{(4)}) - H(t_i)}, u_1^* = \prod_{t_i \in T_1^\dagger \backslash \{st_{n1}^{(4)}\}} \frac{-H(t_i)}{H(st_{n1}^{(4)}) - H(t_i)}$$

this can be done if the tag $\tau \notin T_1^\dagger$. Then if $w^* = w$, the following equations hold:

$$Z_0 = \frac{z_{01}}{z_{02} \cdot z_{03}} = \frac{e(st_{n0}^{(1)}, ct^{(2)})}{e(st_{n0}^{(2)}, ct^{(2)})^{u_0^*} \cdot e(st_{n0}^{(3)}, \prod_{k=1}^d (ct^{(3,k)})^{u_{k0}})} = e(g^{(\alpha - \lambda')H(w)}, g^{sa_0})$$

$$Z_1 = \frac{z_{11}}{z_{12} \cdot z_{13}} = \frac{e(st_{n1}^{(1)}, ct^{(2)})}{e(st_{n1}^{(2)}, ct^{(2)})^{u_1^*} \cdot e(st_{n1}^{(3)}, \prod_{k=1}^d (ct^{(3,k)})^{u_{k1}})} = e(g^{\lambda' H(w)}, g^{sa_0})$$

$$c = \frac{ct^{(1)}}{\prod_{j=0}^1 Z_j} = \frac{e(g_1, g_2)^{sH(w^*)}}{e(g^{\alpha H(w)}, g^{sa_0})} = 1$$

5   Security Analysis

In this section, we show that our PPEKS scheme is IND-CKA secure in the standard model.

Theorem 2. *Our PPEKS scheme satisfies the CT-IND-CKA security under the DBDH assumption in the standard model.*

Proof. Here we will show that if there is an adversary $\mathcal{A}_{CT}$ that can break the CT-IND-CKA security of our PPEKS scheme with a non-negligible advantage ε, then it's equivalent to the existence of an algorithm $\mathcal{A}_{DBDH}$ that can solve the DBDH problem with the same advantage.

Let $(p, \mathbb{G}_1, \mathbb{G}_2, e, g, A = g^a, B = g^b, C = g^c, X)$ be an instance of the DBDH problem. $\mathcal{A}_{DBDH}$ tries to distinguish X and $e(g, g)^{abc}$, then it interacts with the adversary $\mathcal{A}_{CT}$ as follows:

Setup. The algorithm $\mathcal{A}_{DBDH}$ randomly chooses a d-degree polynomial $q(\cdot)$ whose constant term is equal to a_0, sets $V(x) = g^{q(x)}$ and $g_2 = g^{a_0}$. Then it selects one hash function $H : \{0,1\}^* \to Z_p$, two random numbers $\alpha, r \in Z_p$, $t_0 \in \{0,1\}^*$, and sets $g_1 = g^\alpha$. Set the master key MSK, a five-tuple, which consists of the following five parts: $sk_0^{(1)} = g_2{}^{\alpha+r}, sk_0^{(2)} = V(H(t_0))^r, sk_0^{(3)} = g^r, sk_0^{(4)} = t_0, sk_0^{(5)} = V(H(t_0))$. To generate the secret key, it randomly chooses three numbers $r_0, r_1, \lambda' \in Z_p$ and sets $\mathrm{SK}_\tau = (sk_{n0}, sk_{n1})$, where

$$sk_{n0} = (g_2{}^{\alpha+r+r_0-\lambda'}, V(H(t_0)^{r+r_0}, g^{r+r_0}, t_0, V(H(t_0)))$$
$$sk_{n1} = (g_2{}^{\lambda'+r_1}, V(H(\tau))^{r_1}, g^{r_1}, \tau, V(H(\tau)))$$

Finally, it sends the SP=$(g, A^{a_0}, B^\alpha, V(1), \ldots, V(d))$ to the adversary $\mathcal{A}_{CT}$.

Query Phase 1. The adversary $\mathcal{A}_{CT}$ adaptively queries the oracles. The algorithm $\mathcal{A}_{DBDH}$ responds in the following form:

Ciphertext query $\langle w \rangle$: The algorithm $\mathcal{A}_{DBDH}$ samples a random number $s \in Z_p$ to generate the keyword ciphertext $\mathrm{CT}_w = (ct^{(1)}, ct^{(2)}, ct^{(3,1)}, ct^{(3,2)}, \ldots, ct^{(3,d)}, \mathrm{T}^\dagger)$, where $ct^{(1)} = e(A^{a_0}, B^\alpha)^{sH(w)}$, $ct^{(2)} = g^s, ct^{(3,1)} = V(H(t_1'))^s, \ldots, ct^{(3,d)} = V(H(t_d'))^s, t_i' \neq \tau(1, \ldots, d)$. Finally, $\mathcal{A}_{DBDH}$ returns CT_w to $\mathcal{A}_{CT}$.

Token query $\langle w \rangle$: The algorithm $\mathcal{A}_{DBDH}$ randomly selects a number $r' \in Z_p$, generates the search token of keyword $\mathrm{ST}_w = (st_{n0}, st_{n1})$, where

$$st_{n0} = (st_{n0}^{(1)}, st_{n0}^{(2)}, st_{n0}^{(3)}, st_{n0}^{(4)}), st_{n0}^{(1)} = g_2{}^{(\alpha+r+r_0-\lambda')H(w)+r'}$$
$$st_{n0}^{(2)} = V(H(t_0))^{(r+r_0)H(w)+r'}, st_{n0}^{(3)} = g^{(r+r_0)H(w)+r'}, st_{n0}^{(4)} = t_0$$
$$st_{n1} = (st_{n1}^{(1)}, st_{n1}^{(2)}, st_{n1}^{(3)}, st_{n1}^{(4)}), st_{n1}^{(1)} = g_2{}^{(\lambda'+r_1)H(w)+r'}$$
$$st_{n1}^{(2)} = V(H(t_\tau))^{r_1 H(w)+r'}, st_{n1}^{(3)} = g^{r_1 H(w)+r'}, st_{n1}^{(4)} = \tau$$

and returns it to $\mathcal{A}_{CT}$.

Test query $\langle CT_w, ST_{w'} \rangle$: The algorithm $\mathcal{A}_{DBDH}$ runs the **Test**(ST_w, CT_{w_i}) and returns 1 to $\mathcal{A}_{CT}$ if the keyword corresponding to ST_w and CT_{w_i} is the same and the ST_w doesn't satisfy the access policy of CT_{w_i} or 0 otherwise.

Challenge. In this step, the adversary $\mathcal{A}_{CT}$ will submit two different keywords w_0 and w_1 as her challenge. The only restriction is that both two keywords should not been queried in phase 1. The algorithm $\mathcal{A}_{DBDH}$ randomly selects a bit $\beta \in \{0,1\}$. Then it choose a random number $s^* \in Z_p$ and compute $CT_{w_\beta} = (X^{\alpha a_0 s^* H(w_\beta)}, g^{\alpha a_0 cs^*}, V(H(t_1))^{\alpha a_0 cs^*}, \ldots, V(H(t_d))^{\alpha a_0 cs^*})$. It should be noted that there is must one tag t_i equals to τ. Otherwise, the adversary can transform the ciphertext of w_β to the ciphertext of any other keyword, and distinguish w_0 and w_1 by using the **Test**. Finally, it returns the challenge ciphertext CT_{w_β} to the adversary $\mathcal{A}_{CT}$.

Query Phase 2. The adversary $\mathcal{A}_{CT}$ adaptively makes the queries to oracles as in phase 1. Notice that both keywords w_0 and w_1 should not been queried to get their ciphertexts.

Guess. The adversary $\mathcal{A}_{CT}$ outputs the guess $\beta' \in \{0,1\}$. If $\beta = \beta'$ which means that $X = e(g,g)^{abc}$, the algorithm $\mathcal{A}_{DBDH}$ outputs 1 or 0 otherwise.

Next, we analyze the advantage of the algorithm $\mathcal{A}_{DBDH}$ in solving the DBDH problem. In the challenge phase, if $X = e(g,g)^{abc}$, then let $s' = s^* \cdot \alpha a_0 c$. We will get $CT_{w_\beta} = (ct^{(1)}, ct^{(2)}, ct^{(3,1)}, \ldots, ct^{(3,d)})$, where

$$ct^{(1)} = e(g,g)^{ab\alpha a_0 cs^* H(w_\beta)} = e(A,B)^{s' H(w_\beta)}, ct^{(2)} = g^{\alpha a_0 cs^*} = g^{s'}$$

$$ct^{(3,1)} = g^{\alpha a_0 cs^* q(H(t_1))} = V(H(t_1))^{s'}, \ldots, ct^{(3,d)} = g^{\alpha a_0 cs^* q(H(t_d))} = V(H(t_d))^{s'}$$

It's clear that when $X = e(g,g)^{abc}$, CT_{w_β} is a valid ciphertext of the keyword w_β. And the adversary $\mathcal{A}_{CT}$ wins the game with the probability: $|Pr[\beta' = \beta] - 1/2| = \varepsilon$. In another case, when X is a random element in the group $\mathbb{G}_2$, the adversary $\mathcal{A}_{CT}$ can obtain no additional information from the ciphertext of the keyword w_β. Therefore, the guess β' satisfies $Pr[\beta' = \beta] = 1/2$. In summary, the advantage of the algorithm $\mathcal{A}_{DBDH}$ to solve the DBDH problem satisfies the following equation:

$$|Pr[\mathcal{A}_{DBDH}(p, \mathbb{G}_1, \mathbb{G}_2, e, g, g^a, g^b, g^c, e(g,g)^{abc}) = 1 | a,b,c \in Z_p]$$
$$- Pr[\mathcal{A}_{DBDH}(p, \mathbb{G}_1, \mathbb{G}_2, e, g, g^a, g^b, g^c, X) = 1 | a,b,c \in Z_p \wedge X \in \mathbb{G}_2]|$$
$$= |(1/2 \pm \varepsilon) - 1/2|$$
$$= \varepsilon$$

This complete the proof of Theorem 2.

Theorem 3. *Our PPEKS scheme satisfies the ST-IND-CKA security under the DL assumption in the standard model.*

The proof of this theorem can be reduced to DL assumption, we will not state it in detail due to the space limit.

6 Experimental Evaluation

This section mainly discusses the performance of our proposed scheme. As shown in Table 1, We first compare our scheme with some existing MUSE schemes from the functionality and security perspective. To make it easily understand, we explain the meaning of abbreviations as follows. TTP-free stands for no third trusted party is needed in the scheme; Autonomy means the data owner can authorize users' access rights without the help of other entities; Fine-grained indicates the scheme can achieve the fine-grained access control; KS-free means that there is no need to share keys between users to realize the multi-user setting; CKA means the scheme can be secure under the adaptive CKA; Constant represents that the scheme can achieve the constant length of ciphertext when the number of authorized users increases.

Table 1. Comparisons of our scheme with some existing schemes.

Schemes	TTP-free	Autonomy	Fine-grained	KS-free	CKA	Constant
[1]	×	×	×	×	×	✓
[5]	×	×	✓	✓	×	✓
[18]	×	×	✓	×	×	×
[15]	✓	✓	✓	×	×	✓
[12]	×	×	✓	✓	✓	✓
Ours	✓	✓	✓	✓	✓	✓

×: the scheme does not satisfy the feature;
✓: the scheme satisfies the feature.

Then we write a program for experiments, which is conducted on a laptop with Windows 10 Intel (R) Core (TM) i5-5200U CPU @ 2.20GHz and 4GB RAM. In our experiments, the tag and keyword space are consists of 100 and 1000 strings randomly selected in $\{0,1\}^*$, respectively. And we use the jpbc library to implement cryptographic operations.

First, for a given team with 100 users, we study the effect of threshold value "d" on computational efficiency. As shown in Fig. 3(a), we can find that the increase of "d" has little effect on **TokGen** efficiency. The time cost of **Setup** and **Encrypt** protocols will increase with the size of the "d", this is because both of the two protocols need to perform corresponding operations with these "d" unauthorized tags as input. Figure 3(a) shows that it takes about 1.25 s to generate the system parameters-master secret key pairs and 1.40 s to encrypt one keyword while the threshold size is 50. As the **Setup** is one-time work, so we omit its cost in our scheme.

To further explore the relationship between the threshold and encryption efficiency, we conduct more experiments to evaluate the time costs for encrypting 1000 keywords under different thresholds. Figure 3(b) indicates that, for a given threshold, the time cost of encryption increases with the number of keywords.

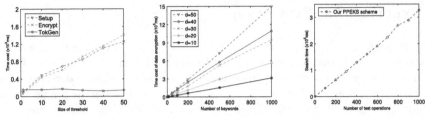

(a) The computation cost   (b) The computation cost   (c) The computation cost of
of data encryption   test operations

Fig. 3. Experimental results

In the case of $d = 50$, it takes about 1.49×10^3 s to encrypt 1000 keywords. In addition, we can obtain some interesting results from Fig. 3(b), i.e., the more members are authorized by the data owner in a team, the less time she needs to encrypt the data. As mentioned above, when the number of authorized members is 50, the time cost for encrypting 1000 keywords is 1.49×10^3 s, which will reduce to 312 s when the number of authorized members increases to 90.

Finally, we evaluate the search performance on an encrypted dataset of 1000 keyword ciphertexts with a given token. Figure 3(c) records the time it takes for each test for $d = 10$, it needs 326 ms to fulfill one test. When the size of dataset increases, the matching time increases linearly.

7   Conclusion

This paper deals with the problem of multi-user encrypted search for the data outsourced in a third party. We design a novel PPEKS scheme in this paper, it enables users to search the data following some certain access policy. The scheme has been proven to be CKA-secure against PPT adversary through a series of security games and difficult assumptions under the standard model. We also analyze the computational overhead of our scheme in detail after proving the security, the results show that our scheme is greatly balanced with efficiency and security. In future work, we will focus on constructing an MUSE system that does not require a specific threshold and to be secure under the keyword guessing attack.

Acknowledgment. This work is partially supported by the Fundamental Research Funds for the Central Universities (No. 30918012204) and Postgraduate Research & Practice Innovation Program of Jiangsu Province (KYCX18_0378).

References

1. Bao, F., Deng, R.H., Ding, X., Yang, Y.: Private query on encrypted data in multi-user settings. In: Chen, L., Mu, Y., Susilo, W. (eds.) ISPEC 2008. LNCS, vol. 4991, pp. 71–85. Springer, Heidelberg (2008). https://doi.org/10.1007/978-3-540-79104-1_6

2. Cash, D., Jarecki, S., Jutla, C., Krawczyk, H., Roşu, M.-C., Steiner, M.: Highly-scalable searchable symmetric encryption with support for boolean queries. In: Canetti, R., Garay, J.A. (eds.) CRYPTO 2013. LNCS, vol. 8042, pp. 353–373. Springer, Heidelberg (2013). https://doi.org/10.1007/978-3-642-40041-4_20

3. Cui, J., Zhou, H., Zhong, H., Xu, Y.: Attribute-based keyword search with efficient revocation in cloud computing. Inf. Sci. **423**, 343–352 (2018)

4. Curtmola, R., Garay, J.A., Kamara, S., Ostrovsky, R.: Searchable symmetric encryption: improved definitions and efficient constructions. In: Proceedings of CCS 2006, pp. 79–88. ACM (2006)

5. Dong, C., Russello, G., Dulay, N.: Shared and searchable encrypted data for untrusted servers. J. Comput. Secur. **19**(3), 367–397 (2011)

6. Goh, E.: Secure indexes. Cryptology ePrint Archieve, Report 2003/216 (2003). http://eprint.iacr.org/2003/216

7. Green, M.D., Miers, I.: Forward secure asynchronous messaging from puncturable encryption. In: Proceedings of Symposium on Security and Privacy 2015, pp. 305–320. IEEE Computer Society (2015)

8. Kamara, S., Papamanthou, C., Roeder, T.: Dynamic searchable symmetric encryption. In: Proceedings of CCS 2012, pp. 965–976. ACM (2012)

9. Liu, X., Yang, G., Mu, Y., Deng, R.: Multi-user verifiable searchable symmetric encryption for cloud storage. IEEE TDSC (2018)

10. Liu, Z., Wang, Z., Cheng, X., Jia, C., Yuan, K.: Multi-user searchable encryption with coarser-grained access control in hybrid cloud. In: Fourth International Conference on Emerging Intelligent Data and Web Technologies, pp. 249–255. IEEE Computer Society (2013)

11. Ostrovsky, R., Sahai, A., Waters, B.: Attribute-based encryption with non-monotonic access structures. In: Proceedings of CCS 2007, pp. 195–203. ACM (2007)

12. Sharma, D., Jinwala, D.C.: Multiuser searchable encryption with token freshness verification. Secur. Commun. Netw. **2017**, 6435138:1–6435138:16 (2017)

13. Song, D.X., Wagner, D.A., Perrig, A.: Practical techniques for searches on encrypted data. In: Proceedings of SSP 2000, pp. 44–55. IEEE Computer Society (2000)

14. Sun, W., Yu, S., Lou, W., Hou, Y.T., Li, H.: Protecting your right: Verifiable attribute-based keyword search with fine-grained owner-enforced search authorization in the cloud. IEEE Trans. Parallel Distrib. Syst. **27**(4), 1187–1198 (2016)

15. Tang, Q.: Nothing is for free: Security in searching shared and encrypted data. IEEE Trans. Inf. Forensics Secur. **9**(11), 1943–1952 (2014)

16. Xu, X., Weng, C.Y., Yuan, L.P., Wu, M.E., Tso, R., Sun, H.M.: A shareable keyword search over encrypted data in cloud computing. J. Supercomput. **74**(3), 1001–1023 (2018)

17. Zhang, W., Lin, Y., Xiao, S., Wu, J., Zhou, S.: Privacy preserving ranked multi-keyword search for multiple data owners in cloud computing. IEEE Trans. Comput. **65**(5), 1566–1577 (2016)

18. Zhao, F., Nishide, T., Sakurai, K.: Multi-user keyword search scheme for secure data sharing with fine-grained access control. In: Kim, H. (ed.) ICISC 2011. LNCS, vol. 7259, pp. 406–418. Springer, Heidelberg (2012). https://doi.org/10.1007/978-3-642-31912-9_27

Forward Private Searchable Encryption with Conjunctive Keywords Query

Zhigang Yao, Chungen Xu$^{(\boxtimes)}$, Lei Xu, and Lin Mei

School of Science, Nanjing University of Science and Technology, Nanjing, China
zhigangyaocrypto@outlook.com, xuchung@njust.edu.cn,
xuleicrypto@gmail.com, wangmumu2244@gmail.com

Abstract. Dynamic searchable symmetric encryption (DSSE) allows addition and deletion operation on an encrypted database. Recently, several attack works (such as IKK) show that existing SSE definition which leaks access pattern and search pattern cannot capture the adversary in the real world. These works underline the necessity for forward privacy. To achieve forward privacy, updating search token is considered as a simple yet efficient method. In this paper, we concentrate on scenario of updating a batch of files containing the same keyword and propose an efficient forward private searchable encryption (EFSE) scheme with a novel batch update. In this scenario, by batch update method, the search token corresponding to the keyword only needs to be updated once. Then for each file in the batch, we use updated search token combining number of this file in the batch to transform the pair (file, keyword) into encrypted index. In the scenario mentioned above, the number of updating search token operation in our EFSE is 1, while the one in existing forward private searchable encryption scheme based on updating search token is the size of batch. In addition, by integrating Cash's OXT scheme, we extend our EFSE scheme to support conjunctive keywords query. Finally, we give the rigorous security analysis for our proposed two schemes and give performance evaluation for the basic one.

Keywords: Forward private · Searchable encryption · Conjunctive keywords query · Dynamic

1 Introduction

Searchable symmetric encryption (SSE) is a cryptographic system which enables keyword search over encrypted data while protecting the privacy of both the data and query. Generally, each SSE scheme contains three parties of functionality including encryption, generating search token and search. Encryption transforms a pair (file, keyword) into a ciphertext called encrypted index. Search token is a ciphertext of query keywords, and it will be used for search. Search operation is performed by cloud server to output all files matching the given search token. Dynamic searchable symmetric encryption (DSSE) is a class of SSE supporting

© Springer Nature Switzerland AG 2019
F. Liu et al. (Eds.): SciSec 2019, LNCS 11933, pp. 308–322, 2019.
https://doi.org/10.1007/978-3-030-34637-9_23

dynamic database. DSSE allows a user to dynamically add and delete data over an encrypted database without rebuilding the encrypted index. Nowadays, DSSE is demanded in cloud storage.

For the leakage of SSE, Curtmola [7] firstly gave the formal definition about the leakage of access pattern and search pattern. IKK [13] attack is the first one which utilizes the leakage of access pattern to fully recover the user's query by the statistical method. By further study of leakage, Cash [4] proposed an efficient attack called leakage abuse attack. Based on their work, Zhang [22] proposed a generic attack for DSSE schemes called file-injection attack. This attack shows that cloud server could recover the keyword in past search query by injecting as few as 10 files. This attack also dangers the security of most DSSE schemes, since in these schemes, the newly injecting files could match the previous search query. These attack works underline the need for a new security definition called *forward privacy*.

In previous work, ORAM based schemes like [6,12] protect forward privacy. But they expend a large bandwidth overhead on communication between server and user. Aiming at the problem of deficiency of ORAM based schemes, Bost [2] proposed a practical SSE scheme utilizing trapdoor permutation. In Bost's scheme, data owner keeps the search token for each keyword, which is used to generate encrypted index or decrypt encrypted index stored on cloud server. When updating a file f containing keyword w, data owner needs to use trapdoor permutation to update the search token corresponding to this keyword, and stores new search token. Then data owner uses this updated search token to generate encrypted index for the pair (f, w). In this setting, the new add file cannot be matched by previous search token, and before the next query, new search token is kept secret against cloud server. Thus, forward privacy is protected. Later, Song [18] improved Bost's work by replacing the trapdoor permutation with pseudorandom permutation. In their schemes, each search token is corresponding to a pair (file, keyword). When updating a batch of files containing the same keyword, the number of updating search token operation is linear with the size of the batch. This batch update is not efficient.

1.1 Our Contribution

In this paper, we focus on forward private searchable encryption with efficient batch update. Our contribution is summarized as follows:

- We propose an efficient forward private searchable encryption (EFSE) scheme with a novel batch update. Inspired by Song's FAST scheme [18], we use pseudorandom permutation to update search token. By our batch update method, when updating a batch of files containing the same keyword, search token corresponding to this keyword only needs to be updated once. Then for each file in the batch, we use this updated search token combining number of this file in the batch to transform the pair (file, keyword) into encrypted index (In fact, we identify files with their indexes). In this setting, the updated search token could match this batch of files. In this scenario of batch update, number of updating search token operation in our EFSE scheme is 1, while the one in Song's FAST [18] or Bost's scheme [2] is the size of batch.

- The proposed EFSE scheme achieves a high level of update performance and search performance. In particular, EFSE scheme supports parallel search operation. When given current search token, cloud server first calculates all previous search tokens. Because each search token matches a batch of files, cloud server can use these search tokens to do the search operation at the same time. We conduct the performance evaluation by implementing EFSE scheme as well as other schemes [2,18]. The experiment result confirms that our EFSE scheme has good update performance and search performance. In addition, we present a rigorous security analysis for EFSE scheme.
- We extend our EFSE scheme to support conjunctive keywords query by integrating Cash's OXT scheme [5]. Our extending scheme achieves the tradeoff between efficiency and query functionality. We conduct a rigorous security analysis for the extending scheme.

2   Related Work

Song [17] was the first to propose the practical searchable encryption (SE) scheme, whose search time is linear with the database size. To improve the search efficiency, Goh [9] introduced secure index to searchable encryption and proposed the Z-IDX scheme based on bloom filter and pseudorandom function. Curtmola [7] utilized inverted index to generate the secure index, and achieved sublinear search time. These schemes mentioned above all support dynamic update, but they must rebuild the encrypted index when updating. It is not efficient for dynamic update. Kamara [14] was the first to propose the dynamic searchable symmetric encryption (DSSE) scheme. His scheme could support dynamic addition or deletion operation, and achieve the sublinear search time.

In 2004, Golle [10] proposed a searchable encryption scheme with conjunctive keywords query whose search complexity is linear with the size of the database. Some other schemes [1,3] share the same problem. In 2012, Cash [5] proposed the OXT scheme which achieves the sublinear search complexity. In 2013, Moataz [16] proposed an efficient construction which is only based on vector operation.

In 2012, Islam [13] introduced the IKK attack which is a statistical attack utilizing the leakage of access pattern. Considering a range of threats including the IKK attack, Cash [4] was the first to introduce the "leakage abuse attack". Zhang [22] improved their work, and proposed the "file injecting attack" which can recover the keywords of a query in a high probability. Some other work [11,15] also focused on the "leakage abuse attack". To mitigate the "leakage abuse attack", Xu [20] proposed a database padding method which achieves optimal padding overhead.

Stefanov [19] was the first to state the conception of forward privacy. In addition, he proposed a forward private DSSE scheme based on non-trivial ORAM technology. But this scheme brings a large bandwidth overhead when updating. As early as 2005, Chang [6] put forward a scheme which ensures forward privacy.

Unfortunately, this scheme includes large bandwidth overhead and large cloud server storage. Some ORAM [8,12] based schemes share the same problem, i.e. large bandwidth overhead. In 2016, Bost [2] proposed an efficient forward private SSE scheme utilizing the trapdoor permutation. Based on Bost's work, Song [18] used the pseudorandom permutation to construct a more efficient forward private SE scheme. Yoneyama [21] proposed the verifiable forward private SSE scheme. Zuo [23] proposed the forward private SSE scheme supporting range query.

3   Preliminaries

3.1   Dynamic Searchable Symmetric Encryption

A dynamic searchable symmetric encryption scheme $\Pi = (Setup, Update, Search)$ can be described as follows:

- $Setup(\lambda, DB) \longrightarrow (EDB, (K, \sigma))$ is run by data owner, it inputs a security parameter λ and a database $DB = (ind_i, W_i)_{i=1}^{D}$, where ind_i is the file index, D is total number of files, W_i is the set of keywords. It outputs the encrypted database EDB, secret key K and state σ.
- $Update(K, \sigma, ind, w, op; EDB) = (Update_C(K, \sigma, ind, w, op), Update_S(EDB))$ is a protocol between data owner and cloud server. Data owner inputs the secret key K, the state σ, a file index ind, a keyword w, and an operation $op \in \{add, del\}$. Data owner outputs the encrypted index $Update_C(K, \sigma, ind, w, op)$ for (ind, w) pair. The cloud server's input is the encrypted database EDB. When receiving the encrypted index, according to the operation op, the cloud server inserts the (ind, w) pair into EDB, or deletes this pair from EDB.
- $Search(K, \sigma, w; EDB) = (Search_C(K, \sigma, w), Search_S(EDB))$ is a protocol between data owner and cloud server. Data owner inputs the secret key K, the state σ, a keyword w to generate the search query. The cloud server's input is the encrypted database EDB. When receiving the search query, the cloud server searches over EDB, and returns the corresponding file indexes.

3.2   Security Definition

Let $\Pi = (Setup, Update, Search)$ be a dynamic searchable symmetric encryption scheme, $\mathcal{A}$ be an adversary, S be a simulator with the leakage function $\mathcal{L} = (\mathcal{L}_{Setup}, \mathcal{L}_{Update}, \mathcal{L}_{Search})$, λ be the security parameter. Two probabilistic experiments $\mathbf{Real}_{\mathcal{A}}^{\Pi}(\lambda)$, $\mathbf{Ideal}_{\mathcal{A},S}^{\Pi}(\lambda)$ are shown as follows:

- $\mathbf{Real}_{\mathcal{A}}^{\Pi}(\lambda)$: At the beginning, an adversary chooses a database DB. The experiment runs $Setup(\lambda, DB)$, and returns EDB to the adversary. Then the adversary adaptively chooses query q_i. If q_i is update query (it can be described as $q_i = (op_i, w_i, ind_i)$), the experiment answers the query by running $Update (K, \sigma, ind_i, w_i, op_i; EDB)$. If q_i is search query (it can be described as $q_i = (i, w_i)$), the experiment answers the query by running $Search(K, \sigma, w_i; EDB)$. Finally, the adversary outputs a bit $b \in \{0, 1\}$.

- **Ideal**$_{\mathcal{A},\mathcal{S}}^{\Pi}(\lambda)$: At the beginning, an adversary chooses a database DB. Then the simulator runs $Setup(\mathcal{L}_{Setup}(DB))$ and returns the result to adversary. Then the adversary adaptively chooses query q_i. If q_i is update query, the simulator runs the $Update(\mathcal{L}_{Update}(q_i))$ and returns the result to adversary. If q_i is search query, the simulator runs the $Search(\mathcal{L}_{Search}(q_i))$ and returns the result to adversary. Finally, the adversary outputs a bit $b \in \{0,1\}$.

Definition 1. *Π is called $\mathcal{L}$-adaptively-secure SSE, if for any probabilistic polynomial time (PPT) adversary $\mathcal{A}$, there exists a PPT simulator $\mathcal{S}$ such that:*

$$|Pr(\mathbf{Real}_{\mathcal{A}}^{\Pi}(\lambda) = 1) - Pr(\mathbf{Ideal}_{\mathcal{A},\mathcal{S}}^{\Pi}(\lambda) = 1)| \leq negl(\lambda)$$

Definition 2. *(Forward Privacy) An $\mathcal{L}$-adaptively-secure searchable encryption scheme is called forward private, if given an update query $q_i = (op_i, w_i, ind_i)$, its update leakage is (i, op_i, ind_i).*

4   System Overview

In this section, we propose an overview on the system of EFSE. The major notation is introduced in Table 1.

Table 1. Notations

Notation	Meaning
$\oplus$	The XOR operation
$\xleftarrow{\$}$	Choose uniformly
$\perp$	Non-existent
ST	Search token
ind	The index of a file
$DB(w)$	The index set of files containing keyword w
$|DB(w)|$	The size of set $DB(w)$

4.1   System Architecture

The architecture of our EFSE system is shown in Fig. 1. In EFSE, data owner outsources encrypted index and his encrypted data to cloud server; cloud server provides cloud storage and keywords search service.

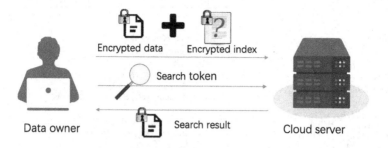

Fig. 1. System structure of EFSE on the two-party model

4.2 System Model

In this paper, file is identified with its index. So we concentrate on how to use file index to generate the encrypted index, how to use search token to search over encrypted index and get the corresponding file indexes. In addition, we concentrate on addition operation, rather than deletion operation.

The EFSE scheme is a collection of three protocols described as follows:

- $Setup(\lambda) \longrightarrow \{k_s, T, W, K\}$ is run by data owner. It takes as input a security parameter λ, and outputs a random string k_s. It also initializes three maps T, W, K, where W is kept by data owner, T, K are kept by cloud server.
- $Update(add, w, DB(w), k_s, W; T, K)$ is a protocol between data owner and cloud server. The protocol can be divided into $Update_C(add, w, DB(w), k_s, W)$ and $Update_S(T, K)$. The former one is performed by data owner, and the latter one is performed by cloud server. Data owner's input is keyword w, database $DB(w)$, secret key k_s and map W. By the former protocol, for each $ind \in DB(w)$, data owner transforms (ind, w) into encrypted index. Then data owner sends these encrypted indexes to cloud server. Cloud server's input is maps T and K. When receiving encrypted indexes, cloud server inserts them into maps T and K.
- $Search(w, k_s, W; T, K) = (Search_C(w, k_s, W), Search_S(T, K))$ is a protocol between data owner and cloud server. Data owner inputs keyword w, secret key k_s, and map W to generate the search query. Cloud server's input is maps T, K. When receiving the search query, cloud server performs search operation over T, K, and outputs file indexes corresponding to the search query.

5 Construction

In this section, we give the concrete construction for EFSE scheme and the extension scheme: forward private searchable encryption with conjunctive keywords query (FSECQ). Some tools that our schemes use are introduced as follows:

Let H, H_1, H_2, H_3 be four different keyed hash functions, where $H : \{0,1\}^\lambda \times \{0,1\}^* \longrightarrow \{0,1\}^\lambda$, $H_1 : \{0,1\}^\lambda \times \{0,1\}^* \longrightarrow \{0,1\}^\lambda$, $H_2 : \{0,1\}^\lambda \times \{0,1\}^* \longrightarrow$

```
Setup(λ)                                    17:  K[Ukey] ⟵ Ckey
Data owner:                                 Search(w, ks, W; T, K)
 1:  ks ←$ {0,1}^λ                          Data owner:
 2:  T, W, K ⟵ empty map                     1:  tw ⟵ H(ks, w)
Update(add, w, DB(w), ks, W; T, K)           2:  (STc, c) ⟵ W[w]
Data owner:                                  3:  send (tw, STc, c) to server
 1:  tw ⟵ H(ks, w)                          Server:
 2:  (STc, c) ⟵ W[w]                         4:  for g = c to 2 do
 3:  if (STc, c) = ⊥ then                    5:     Ukey ⟵ H1(tw, STg)
 4:      ST0 ←$ {0,1}^λ, c ⟵ 0              6:     Ckey ⟵ K[Ukey]
 5:  end if                                  7:     kg||rg ⟵ Ckey ⊕ H2(tw, STg)
 6:  kc+1, rc+1 ←$ {0,1}^λ                   8:     STg-1 ⟵ F^-1(kg, STg)
 7:  STc+1 ⟵ F(kc+1, STc)                    9:  end for
 8:  Ukey ⟵ H1(tw, STc+1)                   10:  Using STi(i ∈ {1, 2, ⋯, c}):
 9:  Ckey ⟵ kc+1||rc+1 ⊕ H2(tw, STc+1)      11:  IND ⟵ {}
10:  W[w] ⟵ (STc+1, c + 1)                  12:  j ⟵ 1
11:  for j = 1 to |DB(w)| do                13:  UT ⟵ H1(tw, STi||j)
12:      UTj ⟵ H1(tw, STc+1||j)             14:  while T[UT] ≠ ⊥ do
13:      ej ⟵ indj ⊕ H2(tw, STc+1||j)       15:     e ⟵ T[UT]
14:  end for                                16:     ind ⟵ e ⊕ H2(tw, STi||j)
15:  send (Ukey, Ckey); {UTj, ej}j=1,⋯,|DB(w)| 17:  IND ⟵ IND ∪ {ind}
     to the server.                         18:     j ⟵ j + 1
Server:                                     19:     UT ⟵ H1(tw, STi||j)
16:  T[UTj] ⟵ ej, j = 1, 2, ⋯, |DB(w)|      20:  end while
                                            21:  Return IND
```

Fig. 2. Efficient forward private searchable encryption

$\{0,1\}^{2\lambda}$, $H_3 : \{0,1\}^\lambda \times \{0,1\}^* \longrightarrow Z_p^*$. Besides, $F : \{0,1\}^\lambda \times \{0,1\}^\lambda \longrightarrow \{0,1\}^\lambda$ is a pseudorandom permutation (F^{-1} is inverse permutation).

5.1 EFSE Construction

Shown in Fig. 2, our basic scheme mainly consists of three protocols: setup, update and search. Then, three protocols are described as follows:

Setup. Data owner inputs security parameter λ. Then he chooses a random string $k_s \in \{0,1\}^\lambda$ as the secret key, and outputs three empty maps T, W, K. Specifically, T, K will be kept by cloud server. T is used to record the encrypted index. K is used to record the ciphtertext of the secret key k which is used to update the search token. W is used to record current search token ST for each updated keyword, and it is stored locally.

Update. The update protocol shown in Fig. 2 is to generate the encrypted index for $DB(w)$. The data owner generates the encrypted index and sends it to cloud server, cloud server stores it. The detail description is shown as follows:

Firstly, data owner inputs secret key k_s and the keyword w, outputs t_w by $t_w \longleftarrow H(k_s, w)$. Then, he looks up $W[w]$ to get (search token, counter) pair (ST_c, c). If $W[w] = \bot$, then data owner initializes the search token by $ST_0 \xleftarrow{\$} \{0,1\}^\lambda$, c is set to 0.

In order to update the search token, data owner chooses two random strings k_{c+1}, r_{c+1} with length λ. Then, he updates the search token by $ST_{c+1} \longleftarrow F(k_{c+1}, ST_c)$. Besides, k_{c+1} is encrypted by $Ckey \longleftarrow k_{c+1} || r_{c+1} \oplus H_2(t_w, ST_{c+1})$, while $Ukey$ is generated by $H_1(t_w, ST_{c+1})$. Last but not the least, $(ST_{c+1}, c + 1)$ is recorded in $W[w]$.

Specifically, $DB(w) = \{ind_j\}_{j=1,\cdots,|DB(w)|}$. For each $ind_j \in DB(w)$, data owner calculates UT_j by $UT_j \longleftarrow H_1(t_w, ST_{c+1}||j)$. Then he generates the encrypted index by $e_j \longleftarrow ind_j \oplus H_2(t_w, ST_{c+1}||j)$. Finally, $(Ukey, Ckey)$ and $\{UT_j, e_j\}_{j=1,\cdots,|DB(w)|}$ are sent to cloud server.

Upon receiving these message, cloud server records $(Ukey, Ckey)$ pair in map K by $K[Ukey] \longleftarrow Ckey$, and records each (UT_j, e_j) pair in T by $T[UT_j] \longleftarrow e_j$.

Search. The search protocol shown in Fig. 2 is to query for keyword w. Data owner generates the search query, while the cloud server performs the search operation and returns the search result to data owner. Detail description of search protocol is shown as follows:

Firstly, data owner generates long term session key by $t_w \longleftarrow H(k_s, w)$. Then, he looks up $W[w]$ to get the (search token, counter) pair (ST_c, c). Finally, he sends the search query (t_w, ST_c, c) to the cloud server.

After receiving the search query (t_w, ST_c, c), cloud server obtains $Ukey$ by $Ukey \longleftarrow H_1(t_w, ST_c)$. Then cloud server gets $Ckey$ from $K[Ukey]$. Next, $k_c || r_c$ is generated by $Ckey \oplus H_2(t_w, ST_c)$. Finally, cloud server gets the previous search token ST_{c-1} by $ST_{c-1} \longleftarrow F^{-1}(k_c, ST_c)$. Similarly, if given ST_g, cloud server could obtain its previous search token ST_{g-1}. Finally, cloud server obtains $ST_1, ST_2, \cdots, ST_c$

We recall that each ST_i is corresponding to a batch of files, and cloud server could use this search token combining the file number to decrypt the encrypted index. In Fig. 2, when given search token $ST_i(i \in \{1, 2, \cdots, c\})$, cloud server firstly initializes $j = 1$ and an empty list **IND**. Then cloud server initializes UT by $UT \longleftarrow H_1(t_w, ST_i||j)$. In the "while loop" of the search protocol (line 14–20 in Fig. 2), the cloud server decrypts the encrypted index to get the indexes of the batch of files which is corresponding to ST_i. In this way, cloud server obtains the indexes of files corresponding to ST_1, the indexes of files corresponding to ST_2, ..., and the indexes of files corresponding to ST_c. Finally, cloud server returns these indexes to data owner.

5.2   FSECQ Construction

Our FSECQ scheme is the extension scheme for EFSE scheme, and supports conjunctive keywords query. It mainly consists of three protocols: setup, update and search.

Setup. The setup protocol is identical with the one in our EFSE scheme except that in FSECQ scheme, an additional set Xet is set up, and three extra random strings $k_X, k_I, k_Z \in \{0,1\}^\lambda$ are chosen by data owner.

Update. The update protocol is same with the one in EFSE scheme except some changes. For each keyword, the corresponding pair (ST_c, c) is changed to

```
Search                                      14:        (e, y) ←─── T[UT]
Server:                                     15:        for k = 2 to n do
 1: for g = c to 2 do                       16:            if Tag[k, l]ʸ ∈ Xset then
 2:     Ukey ←─── H₁(t_{w₁}, ST_g)          17:                counter ←─── counter + 1
 3:     Ckey ←─── K[Ukey]                    18:            end if
 4:     k_g||r_g ←─── Ckey ⊕ H₂(t_{w₁}, ST_g) 19:        end for
 5:     ST_{g-1} ←─── F⁻¹(k_g, ST_g)        20:        if counter = n − 1 then
 6: end for                                  21:            ind ←─── e ⊕ H₂(t_{w₁}, ST_i||j)
 7: IND ←─── {}                              22:            IND ←─── IND ⋃{ind}
 8: l ←─── 1                                 23:        end if
 9: for i = 1 to c do                        24:        j ←─── j + 1
10:     j ←─── 1                              25:        l ←─── l + 1
11:     UT ←─── H₁(t_{w₁}, ST_i||j)          26:        UT ←─── H₁(t_{w₁}, ST_i||j)
12:     while T[UT] ≠ ⊥ do                    27:    end while
13:         counter ←─── 0                    28: end for
                                             29: Return IND
```

Fig. 3. The search operation on cloud server in FSECQ scheme

pair (ST_c, c, v), where the new added counter v initializes to 0, and is used to record the number of updated files containing this keyword. Except generating $(Ukey, Ckey)$ and $(UT_j, e_j)_{j=1,\cdots,|DB(w)|}$, for each ind_j in $DB(w)$, data owner additionally calculates $y_j \longleftarrow (H_3(k_Z, w||v+j))^{-1} \cdot H_3(k_I, ind_j)$, and generate extra $xtag_j$ by $xtag_j \longleftarrow g^{H_3(k_X, w) \cdot H_3(k_I, ind_j)}$. At the end of update, the new pair is $(ST_{c+1}, c+1, v+|DB(w)|)$ which will be recorded in $W[w]$. $(Ukey, Ckey)$, $\{xtag_j\}_{j=1,\cdots,|DB(w)|}$, and $\{UT_j, (e_j, y_j)\}_{j=1,\cdots,|DB(w)|}$ are sent to cloud server.

Upon receiving these message, cloud server records $Ckey$ in $K[Ukey]$, and stores each (e_j, y_j) in $T[UT_j]$. Then each $xtag_j$ is appended to $Xset$.

Search. To query the conjunctive keywords $w_1 \wedge \cdots \wedge w_n$, data owner first looks up $W[w_1]$ to obtain (ST_c, c, v). Then, for the keyword w_1, data owner generates the search query (t_{w_1}, ST_c, c) whose operation is similar to the one in EFSE scheme. Next, for other keyword $w_k(k = 2, \cdots, n)$, data owner generates each $Tag[k, l]$ by $g^{H_3(k_Z, w_1||l) \cdot H_3(k_X, w_k)}$, where $l = 1, \cdots, v$. Finally, the search query for conjunctive keywords $w_1 \wedge \cdots \wedge w_n$ is $(t_{w_1}, ST_c, c, \{Tag[k, l]\}_{k=2,\cdots,n;l=1,\cdots,v})$. The search query is sent to cloud server.

Upon receiving the search query, cloud server performs the decryption operation to obtain all previous search tokens (line 1–6 in Fig. 3). This decryption operation is same with that in EFSE. Then, the operation in line 7–29 shows that cloud server decrypts the encrypted index and returns all indexes of files which contains all keywords $w_1, \cdots, w_n$.

6   Security Analysis

In this section, we introduce the threat model and conduct the security proof for our two schemes briefly.

6.1   Threat Model

Our EFSE system and its extension both consist of two parties: *data owner, cloud server*. In this paper, the cloud server is considered to be honest but curious, which means that (1) cloud server intends to obtain some private information from the encrypted data or search queries, (2) cloud server obeys the prescribed protocols.

Let $Hist = \{DB_i, q_i\}_{i=1}^{n}$ be a history, where DB_i is a database (In this paper, DB_i can be viewed as the index set of files), and q_i is a query. Let $Q = \{q_1, q_2, \cdots, q_n\}$ is the query list for $Hist$. If q_i is an update query, then q_i can be described as (op_i, w_i, DB_i); If q_i is a search query, then it can be described as (i, w_i). Then access pattern is $ap(w) = \{i|q_i \in Q, q_i \text{ contains } w\}$. Search pattern is $sp(w) = \{i|q_i \in Q, q_i \text{ is a search query for keyword } w\}$.

In our system, search pattern and access pattern are revealed to cloud server. Besides, we also assume that the search token is upload to server through secure channel.

6.2   Security Proof

Theorem 1. *Let F be the pseudorandom permutation, H, H_1, H_2 be three hash functions modeled as random oracles. Define leakage $\mathcal{L} = (\mathcal{L}_{Setup}, \mathcal{L}_{Update}, \mathcal{L}_{Search})$ as*

$$\mathcal{L}_{Setup} = \bot$$
$$\mathcal{L}_{Update}(add, w, DB_i) = (i, add, DB_i)$$
$$\mathcal{L}_{Search}(w) = (sp(w), ap(w))$$

Then, EFSE is $\mathcal{L}$-adaptively-secure SSE scheme with forward privacy.

Proof. Obviously, the update leakage satisfies the Definition 2. So we conclude that our basic scheme is forward private. Then we construct some games **Real**, G_1, G_2, G_3, G_4, **Ideal** to prove that our EFSE scheme satisfies the Definition 1, where H, H_1, H_2 are modeled as random oracle.

Firstly, **Real** is the real world game. In G_1, instead of generating t_w by H, the experiment stores a map T_w which is used to store tuple (w, t_w). When t_w is needed, the experiment looks up the table H. If $T_w[w]$ exists, returns $T_w[w]$ as t_w; Otherwise, the experiment randomly chooses a string $s \in \{0,1\}^{\lambda}$ as t_w, and stores (w, t_w) in T_w. Because H is modeled as random oracle and k_s is kept secret against the adversary, G_0 and G_1 are indistinguishable.

In G_2, we replace all strings generated by the random oracle H_1 in the update protocol by random strings. In the search protocol, the experiment utilizes these random strings to program the random oracle H_1. In addition, in G_2, the experiment maintains a map K'. In the update protocol, after generating k_{c+1}, $(w\|c+1, k_{c+1})$ is stored in K'. After the update and before the next query, the adversary could not obtain the query result $H_1(t_w, ST_{c+1})$, since ST_{c+1} is kept secret against the adversary. The probability that the adversary guesses

ST_{c+1} correctly by chance is $poly(\lambda) \cdot (\frac{1}{2^\lambda} + negl(\lambda))$. Then we conclude that G_2 and G_1 are indistinguishable.

In G_3, we replace all strings generated by the random oracle H_2 in the update protocol by random strings. In the search protocol, the experiment utilizes these random strings to program the random oracle H_2. Similarly, we conclude that G_2 and G_3 are indistinguishable.

In G_4, ST and k are generated only when performing the search protocol. In the update protocol, the experiment sends same number of random strings to the cloud server. Then we conclude that G_3 and G_4 are indistinguishable, since search token and the one in G_3 are at the same distribution.

In **Ideal**, instead of inputting the actual data, the simulator inputs the leakage which is defined by leakage function. Then we conclude that G_4 and **Ideal** are indistinguishable.

Finally, to sum up, the **Real** and **Ideal** are indistinguishable.

To analyze the security of our extension scheme, without loss of generality, we focus on 2-conjunctive keywords search, and introduce the lemma and theorem as follows:

Lemma 1. *(DDH assumption)Let G be a cyclic group whose order is λ, g is its generator. We say that DDH assumption holds if for any probabilistic polynomial time adversary $\mathcal{A}$, these exists a negligible function negl satisfies that*

$$|Pr[\mathcal{A}(g, g^a, g^b, g^{ab}) = 1] - Pr[\mathcal{A}(g, g^a, g^b, g^c) = 1]| < negl(\lambda)$$

where a, b, c are chosen uniformly from Z_p^*.

Theorem 2. *Let F be the pseudorandom permutation, H, H_1, H_2, H_3 be four hash functions modeled as random oracles. Define leakage $\mathcal{L} = (\mathcal{L}_{Setup}, \mathcal{L}_{Update}, \mathcal{L}_{Search})$ as*

$$\mathcal{L}_{setup} = \perp$$
$$\mathcal{L}_{update}(add, w, DB_i) = (i, add, DB_i)$$
$$\mathcal{L}_{search}(w_1 \wedge w_2) = (\{sp(w_i), ap(w_i)\}_{i=1,2})$$

Then, FSECQ is $\mathcal{L}$-adaptively-secure SSE scheme with forward privacy.

Proof. Similarly, the update protocol does not leak any information about the keyword. So our extension scheme is forward private. Then we construct several games (**Real**, $G_1, \cdots, G_7$, **Ideal**) to prove that our extension scheme is $\mathcal{L}$-adaptively-secure SSE scheme.

Real is the real world game. G_1, G_2, G_3 are same with the one in proof of Theorem 1.

Compared with G_3, in G_4, the first change is that y_j is recorded in $Y[w, ind_j]$, where Y is a map indexed by a keyword and a file index. The second change is that $xtag_j$ is recorded in $X[w, ind_j]$, where X is also a map indexed by a keyword and a file index. Two maps are maintained by the experiment. Obviously, we conclude that G_3 and G_4 are indistinguishable.

In G_5, y_j is replaced by a random element in Z_p^* and it will be stored in $Y[w, ind_j]$. For convenience, we replace $Tag[2, l]$ by $\tilde{T}ag[w_2, l]$. If $X[w_2, ind_l] \neq \perp$, $Tag[w_2, l]$ is evaluated by $X[w_2, ind_l]^{(Y[w_1, ind_l])^{-1}}$; Otherwise, $Tag[w_2, l]$ is evaluated by $A[w_1, w_2, l] = g^{H_3(k_Z, w_1 \| l) \cdot H_3(k_X, w_2)}$, where map A is maintained by the experiment. The change can be observed by adversary only if adversary could query the random oracle H_3. But k_I and k_Z are random strings which are kept secret against the adversary. Thus, G_4 and G_5 are indistinguishable.

In G_6, $xtag_j$ is chosen randomly, and is recorded in $X[w, ind_j]$. In the search protocol, if $X[w_2, ind_l] = \perp$, and $A[w_1, w_2, l] = \perp$, then $Tag[w_2, l]$ is evaluated by random string which will be recorded in $A[w_1, w_2, l]$. In addition, if $X[w_2, ind_l] = \perp$, and $A[w_1, w_2, l] \neq \perp$, $Tag[w_2, l]$ is evaluated by $A[w_1, w_2, l]$. Finally, by Lemma 1, we conclude that G_6 and G_5 are indistinguishable.

In G_7, ST and k are generated only when performing the search protocol. This change is similar with the one in G_4 in proof of Theorem 1. Similarly, we conclude that G_6 and G_7 are indistinguishable.

In **Ideal**, instead of inputting actual data, the simulator inputs the leakage which is defined by leakage function. Then we conclude that G_7 and **Ideal** are indistinguishable.

Finally, to sum up, **Real** and **Ideal** are indistinguishable.

7   Performance Evaluation

In this section, we evaluate the performance of our EFSE scheme by comparison with Song's FAST scheme [18] and Bost's scheme [2].

7.1   Experiment Setup

In this paper, we implement our EFSE scheme in java (JDK 1.8). The security parameter λ is set to 128bits. For the pseudorandom permutation, we use AES. For hash functions H, H_1, we use HMAC-MD5. For hash function H_2, we use HmacSHA256. The index of file ind is set to 256 bits.

To ensure fair, the security parameters in the rest schemes are set to 128bits. When implementing Song's scheme, we use MD5 for hash function h, and SHA-256 for hash function H_1, H_2. In addition, for pseudorandom function F, and pseudorandom permutation P, we use AES. File index $ind\|op$ is set to 128 bits. When implementing Bost's scheme, we use HMAC-MD5 for the PRF, and the keyed hash function H_1, H_2. In addition, for trapdoor permutation π, we use RSA, where the key size is set to 512 bits. File index is also set to 128 bits.

The server and the data owner are deployed on the same laptop. The laptop is x64 instance running Windows 10 containing Intel core i7-7500U 2.7 GHz cpu, 4 GB RAM, and 250 GB SSD.

7.2   Experiment Results

Update. Figure 4(a) shows the update performance of our EFSE scheme, FAST and Bost's scheme. In our experiment, the IO cost and communication overhead are excluded from the update cost. When testing updating, each time we update a batch of files containing same keyword (its index set is $DB(w)$), the size of batch is ranging from 2E5 to 1E6 (step length is 2E5). Shown in Fig. 4(a), vertical axis represents the update time, and horizontal axis represents the number of files (i.e. the size of batch). The experiment result shows that our EFSE scheme has a better performance. Because of our novel batch update, each file in this batch shares the same search token. Thus, for a batch, the search token only needs to be updated once. But in Song's FAST or Bost's batch update, the search token needs to be updated n times, where n is the size of $DB(w)$.

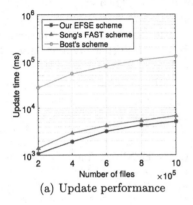   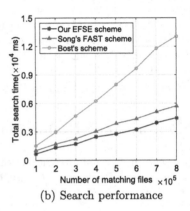

(a) Update performance   (b) Search performance

Fig. 4. Experimental results

Search. Figure 4(b) shows the search performance of our EFSE scheme, FAST and Bost's scheme. In our experiment, IO cost and communication overhead are excluded from the search cost. The search cost includes the cost about generating search token and the one about the search operation. We first conduct batch update, and then we conduct the search test. In the Fig. 4(4), vertical axis represents search time, while the horizontal axis represents the number of files which match the query. The experiment result shows that our EFSE scheme has a better performance. The cost for generating search token in our EFSE scheme is similar to others. That cost is nearly 0.002 ms. The search time per file in our EFSE scheme is about 0.0056 ms while the one in FAST is 0.0071 ms, and the one in Bost's scheme is 0.016 ms.

8   Conclusion

In this paper, we propose the efficient forward private searchable encryption scheme (EFSE). This scheme utilizes a novel batch update method, and achieves a high level of update performance and search performance. Then, in order to extend EFSE to support conjunctive keywords query, we propose the forward private searchable encryption with conjunctive keywords query (FSECQ) scheme. This scheme achieves optimal computational overhead while supporting conjunctive keywords query. Meanwhile, we give the rigorous security proof for our two schemes. Finally, we implement our EFSE scheme as well as other works [2,18]. The experiment result shows that our EFSE achieves better update performance and search performance.

Acknowledgement. This work is supported by the Fundamental Research Funds for the Central Universities (No. 30918012204).

References

1. Ballard, L., Kamara, S., Monrose, F.: Achieving efficient conjunctive keyword searches over encrypted data. In: Qing, S., Mao, W., López, J., Wang, G. (eds.) ICICS 2005. LNCS, vol. 3783, pp. 414–426. Springer, Heidelberg (2005). https://doi.org/10.1007/11602897_35
2. Bost, R.: $\sum o\varphi o\varsigma$: Forward secure searchable encryption. In: Proceedings of CCS 2016, pp. 1143–1154. ACM (2016)
3. Byun, J.W., Lee, D.H., Lim, J.: Efficient conjunctive keyword search on encrypted data storage system. In: Atzeni, A.S., Lioy, A. (eds.) EuroPKI 2006. LNCS, vol. 4043, pp. 184–196. Springer, Heidelberg (2006). https://doi.org/10.1007/11774716_15
4. Cash, D., Grubbs, P., Perry, J., Ristenpart, T.: Leakage-abuse attacks against searchable encryption. IACR Cryptology ePrint Archive 2016/718 (2016)
5. Cash, D., Jarecki, S., Jutla, C., Krawczyk, H., Roşu, M.-C., Steiner, M.: Highly-scalable searchable symmetric encryption with support for boolean queries. In: Canetti, R., Garay, J.A. (eds.) CRYPTO 2013. LNCS, vol. 8042, pp. 353–373. Springer, Heidelberg (2013). https://doi.org/10.1007/978-3-642-40041-4_20
6. Chang, Y.-C., Mitzenmacher, M.: Privacy preserving keyword searches on remote encrypted data. In: Ioannidis, J., Keromytis, A., Yung, M. (eds.) ACNS 2005. LNCS, vol. 3531, pp. 442–455. Springer, Heidelberg (2005). https://doi.org/10.1007/11496137_30
7. Curtmola, R., Garay, J.A., Kamara, S., Ostrovsky, R.: Searchable symmetric encryption: improved definitions and efficient constructions. In: Proceedings of CCS 2006, pp. 79–88. ACM (2006)
8. Garg, S., Mohassel, P., Papamanthou, C.: TWORAM: round-optimal oblivious RAM with applications to searchable encryption. IACR Cryptology ePrint Archive 2015/1010 (2015)
9. Goh, E.: Secure indexes. IACR Cryptology ePrint Archive 2003/216 (2003)
10. Golle, P., Staddon, J., Waters, B.: Secure conjunctive keyword search over encrypted data. In: Jakobsson, M., Yung, M., Zhou, J. (eds.) ACNS 2004. LNCS, vol. 3089, pp. 31–45. Springer, Heidelberg (2004). https://doi.org/10.1007/978-3-540-24852-1_3
11. Grubbs, P., Sekniqi, K., Bindschaedler, V., Naveed, M., Ristenpart, T.: Leakage-abuse attacks against order-revealing encryption. In: Proceedings of SP 2017, pp. 655–672. IEEE Computer Society (2017)

12. Hoang, T., Yavuz, A.A., Guajardo, J.: Practical and secure dynamic searchable encryption via oblivious access on distributed data structure. In: Proceedings of ACSAC 2016, pp. 302–313. ACM (2016)
13. Islam, M.S., Kuzu, M., Kantarcioglu, M.: Access pattern disclosure on searchable encryption: Ramification, attack and mitigation. In: Proceedings of NDSS 2012. The Internet Society (2012)
14. Kamara, S., Papamanthou, C., Roeder, T.: Dynamic searchable symmetric encryption. In: Proceedings of CCS 2012, pp. 965–976. ACM (2012)
15. Kellaris, G., Kollios, G., Nissim, K., O'Neill, A.: Generic attacks on secure outsourced databases. In: Proceedings of CCS 2016, pp. 1329–1340. ACM (2016)
16. Moataz, T., Shikfa, A.: Boolean symmetric searchable encryption. In: Proceedings of ASIA CCS 2013, pp. 265–276. ACM (2013)
17. Song, D.X., Wagner, D.A., Perrig, A.: Practical techniques for searches on encrypted data. In: Proc. of S&P 2000, pp. 44–55. IEEE Computer Society (2000)
18. Song, X., Dong, C., Yuan, D., Xu, Q., Zhao, M.: Forward private searchable symmetric encryption with optimized I/O efficiency. CoRR abs/1710.00183 (2017)
19. Stefanov, E., Papamanthou, C., Shi, E.: Practical dynamic searchable encryption with small leakage. In: Proceedings of NDSS 2014. The Internet Society (2014)
20. Xu, L., Yuan, X., Wang, C., Wang, Q., Xu, C.: Hardening database padding for searchable encryption. In: Proceedings of INFOCOM 2019, pp. 2503–2511. IEEE (2019)
21. Yoneyama, K., Kimura, S.: Verifiable and forward secure dynamic searchable symmetric encryption with storage efficiency. In: Qing, S., Mitchell, C., Chen, L., Liu, D. (eds.) ICICS 2017. LNCS, vol. 10631, pp. 489–501. Springer, Cham (2018). https://doi.org/10.1007/978-3-319-89500-0_42
22. Zhang, Y., Katz, J., Papamanthou, C.: All your queries are belong to us: the power of file-injection attacks on searchable encryption. In: Proceedings of of USENIX Security 2016, pp. 707–720. USENIX Association (2016)
23. Zuo, C., Sun, S.-F., Liu, J.K., Shao, J., Pieprzyk, J.: Dynamic searchable symmetric encryption schemes supporting range queries with forward (and backward) security. In: Lopez, J., Zhou, J., Soriano, M. (eds.) ESORICS 2018. LNCS, vol. 11099, pp. 228–246. Springer, Cham (2018). https://doi.org/10.1007/978-3-319-98989-1_12

PAFR: Privacy-Aware Friends Retrieval over Online Social Networks

Yuxi Li, Fucai Zhou$^{(\boxtimes)}$, and Zifeng Xu

Software College, Northeastern University, No. 195 Chuangxin Road,
Hunnan Distinct, Shenyang 110000, China
eliyuxi@gmail.com, fczhou@mail.neu.edu.cn, dk@tnimdk.com

Abstract. Online Social Networks (OSNs) are online services that people use to build social relations with other people. Friends retrieval over OSNs is an important activity among users. However, in existing friends retrieval solutions, user may leak private and sensitive information, such as personal data and friends relation. Traditional end-to-end encryption methods can protect users' information, while it is not available for them to share contents with others. In this paper, aiming at preventing attack launched by the service provider, we propose PAFR, a Privacy-Aware Friends Retrieval scheme over OSNs. Inspired by private set interaction protocols, our scheme allows user to upload his encrypted contents to server, obliviously connect with others as friends, and retrieve friends with specific content. In addition, we design a dual-server model where two non-collude servers $\mathcal{S}_1$ and $\mathcal{S}_2$ perform secure sorting protocol to retrieve the ranked relevant friends without learning the underlying query and friends relationship. Compared with the approach with single server holding the whole knowledge of the OSN, each of them only has a part of the information make our scheme achieve a high level of privacy. Both security and performance analysis demonstrate that our scheme has both a very light user workload and a moderate server workload while being secure against user-server collusion.

Keywords: Online social networks · Private set interaction · Dual-server model · Friends retrieval

1 Motivation

Online social networks (OSNs) such as Facebook, Twitter, and Google+, are online services that allow users to connect with others. It is becoming the center of users due to they can offer many services closely related to their everyday life.

This work was supported in part by the Natural Science Foundation of China under Grant Nos. 61772127and 61472184, the National Science and Technology Major Project under Grant No. 2013ZX03002006, the Liaoning Province Science and Technology Projects under Grant No. 2013217004, the Fundamental Research Funds for the Central Universities under Grant N151704002.

F. Liu et al. (Eds.): SciSec 2019, LNCS 11933, pp. 323–338, 2019.
https://doi.org/10.1007/978-3-030-34637-9_24

Consider a scenario that in a social network, there is a server that has a database that contains all users' contents and their relationships. If a user Alice wants to retrieve her nearest friend, she can directly send her location to the server, the server searches all her friends' locations and get the result. Such kind of friend retrieve service is a general application of content-based search over OSNs. However, in such process, user leaks her personal profiles and search pattern. It is getting increasingly important that the information exchanged among users should take privacy into consideration. It is crucial and very related to critical life threatening situations. For instance, in 2018, a second Cambridge Analytica whistleblower had harvested the personal data of users' profiles in Facebook without their consent and used it for political purposes, which affects way more than 87 million users [1,2].

Therefore, in order to protect the social community, privacy-aware schemes in OSNs should be provided. It should satisfies with the following security characters: identity privacy, content privacy and closeness privacy. Specifically, identity privacy is essential, since some malicious adversary may gather users' identities in OSNs that resulting in users suffering from blackmails and kidnappers [3]. It can be achieved by using a pseudonym to hide user's real identity. Content privacy is also important as contents are the most related information and is very existence relates to critical life-threatening situations. The use of the profiles by others can be just for gaining more information, such as financial, location, confidential data, etc. If such data are used illegally, it can be even dangerous to the user's safety [4]. In privacy-aware setting, user's contents can only be shared with his friends who are treated as trust parties in user's view [5]. Whats more, the closeness value of each friend pair is also useful for adversary to perform different kinds of data mining for different purposes [6]. Therefore it should be preserved and should not be available in the server side.

Traditional end-to-end encryption methods [7,8] can protect users' contents, while it is not available for users to share contents with other. To protect users' privacy while remain their contents retrievable, the straightforward way is searchable encryption [9,10]. The most widely known architecture in searchable encryption is user encrypts his database and builds search structure at local, and upload them to the server. He can send search token to the server to perform search in the database encrypted by his own key. However, in social network setting, there are multiple users with different keys, how to search the multi-key based encrypted social network is a problem that needs to be solved.

To solve such problem, a naive way is to share keys among friends [11]. Suppose a user has q friends, when he wants to search contents among his friends, he should generate q search tokens and send them to the server. Multi-key searchable encryption [23] allows users to share files with each other selectively. However, it seems very difficult with this approach to prevent the server from learning a large amount of information, as such scheme has a significant leakage profile since tokens from different users can applied on the same encrypted value, thus the search keyword can be known to the server if the server colluded with some users. As a result, in OSNs scenario, the corruption of one user impacts the privacy of other users, even if they are far from the corrupted user in the OSN graph. The problem comes from that a token can be applied to any encrypted contents after transformation. A single user colluding with the server can then have access to the whole OSNs. To the best of our knowledge, there are very few studies on privacy-aware social network under multiple keys.

Besides, there are many schemes are proposed focusing on privacy-aware peer-to-peer OSNs. Most of them base on the private set intersection (PSI) protocols [14–16]. However, these solutions are involved in a large number of high computational cost, or rely on third-party certification for input information, where user needs to bear the additional computational overhead. Vaidya et al. [14] established a friend-of-friend prediction model in mobile social networks based on n-party secret sharing protocol, while the model cannot resist brute force attack. Zhang et al. [15] proposed the concept of fine-grained privacy information matching protocol, by giving preference to each profile, and using similarity function to measure the matching degree. Based on that, Niu et al. [16] designed the privacy information matching protocol based on the weight or level of the profile itself and the social strength of the participant.

To reduce computational cost, some privacy profile matching protocols based on non-encryption methods are proposed recently. Fu et al. [17] proposed the privacy profile matching scheme based on Bloom Filter. Sun et al. [18] proposed lightweight privacy profile matching scheme with less computing cost, which doesn't using encryption algorithm, only involves the hash SHA-256 operation, but Bloom Filter and its dispersion column function is public. The above two schemes cannot resist brute force attack, resulting in privacy information leakage.

Our Contribution. Based on the aforementioned observations, we propose PAFR, a Privacy-Aware Friend Retrieval scheme over OSNs. Our contributions are described as follows:

- In our construction, we allow user to encrypt profiles by his secure key at local and upload them to the OSNs service provider. We design a oblivious connect protocol for adding friends where user's profiles can be obliviously shared with others. Inspired by the idea of private set intersection, we propose a secure profile-based search method among friends.
- We build a dual-server model where two non-collude servers S_1 and S_2 implementing the OSNs service provider. S_1 plays the roll to store the social network structure, and S_2 is responsible to store user's encrypted contents. Compared with single server holding the whole knowledge, each of them only has a part of the information make our scheme achieve a high level of privacy. To achieve friends retrieving and ranking by closeness order, we design a secure sorting protocol between S_1 and S_2 to get the sorted friends without learning the underlying searching words and the friends list.
- Our scheme offers high level of privacy while having a minimal cost for the users. We define the leakage functions $\mathcal{L}_1$ to $\mathcal{L}_4$ to formally abstract the information that are leaked to the servers in different phases, and give the formal security analysis under ideal/real world paradigm to claim that our scheme is adaptively $\mathcal{L}$-semantically secure. The performance analysis shows the scheme we present have both a very light user workload and a moderate server workload while being secure against user-server collusion.

2   Cryptographic Tools

Paillier Encryption. Paillier encryption [20] is a probabilistic asymmetric algorithm for public key cryptography. The message space M for the encryption is Z_N, where N is a product of two large prime numbers p and q. For a message $m \in Z_N$, we denote $[m] \in Z_N^2$ to be the encryption of m with the public key PK. It has the addition homomorphic properties:: $\forall m_1, m_2 \in Z_N, E(m_1)E(m_1) = E(m_1 + m_2)$. Our construction relies on a generalization of Paillier encryption [21]. The message space expands to Z_{N^s} for $s > 1$, and the ciphertext space is under the group $Z_{N^{s+1}}$. This generalization allows one to doubly encrypt messages and use the additive homomorphism of the inner encryption layer under the same secret key. We denote $[\![m]\!]$ as ciphertext of m using the second layer. This nested encryption preserves the structure over inner ciphertexts and allows one to manipulate it as follow: $[\![m_1]\!]^{[m_2]} = [\![[m_1][m_2]]\!] = [\![[m_1 + m_2]]\!]$.

PSI-DH. Our scheme is partly inspired by the idea of Private Set Intersection based on DiffieHellman problem (PSI-DH) [24]. It involves a sender with set Y and a receiver with set X. The receiver picks a random value $\alpha \in Z_k$ and sends $H(x)^\alpha, x \in X$ to the sender. The sender picks a random value $\beta \in Z_k$ and sends both $(H(x)^{\alpha\beta}, x \in X$ and $(H(y)^\beta, y \in Y$. Finally the receiver computes $(H(y)^{\beta\alpha}, y \in Y$ and is able to see which elements of X are in Y without learning anything about the elements in $Y - X$.

EncSort. We use the state-of-art efficient and secure sort protocol *EncSort* as building block to get the encrypted sorted results [22]. It is executed between two parties P_1 and P_2 and takes as input a public/secret key pair (PK, SK) of a semantically secure cryptosystem $\{\mathcal{KeyGen}, \mathcal{Enc}, \mathcal{Dec}\}$, where SK is known to P_2 but not P_1. P_1 has an array $A = [\mathcal{Enc}(v_i)], i \in (1, N)$ of N elements where each element is encrypted individually using PK. The goal is for P_1 to obtain an array $B = [\mathcal{Enc}(v_j)], j \in (1, N)$, where $v_j = v_\pi(i)$ and $i \in (1, N)$, a re-encryption of a sorted array A. Neither P_1 nor P_1 learn anything about the plaintext values of A (e.g., their initial order, frequency of the values) while running the protocol.

3   Problem Statement

Consider a social network contains many users, every user has his own profiles, such as age, location, job and so on. A social network provider creates a social network structure database that contains all the users information. A closeness value in the structure represents the closeness of every friends pair. In our privacy-aware social network, user's profiles and the closeness between friends are considered as private, so they are encrypted at local. The service provider collects all the encrypted values and constructs a the encrypted social network structure which should maintain searchable. Users can search his friends who have specific profiles. Server should be able to perform searching over his friends in the encrypted social network structure. Searchable encryption can achieve this goal. However, if a user wants search over his friends' encrypted values, he has to ask for different keys from his friends, and separately search over each of his friends' profiles using different tokens, which is troublesome and inefficient for social networks. What's more, anther challenge is how to get his sorted closeness friends that each friend's profiles satisfied user query token.

One solution would be that when user connect with others, the server transforms his encrypted profiles into a copy that is specific to his friend. With transformation, users don't need to ask for different keys every time when he wants to search. In the security aspect, queries from different users are not applied on the same encrypted profiles. It provided security against user-server collision. However, the server is able to link a transformed profile to the original encrypted profile it originates from. A question that arises is then: Who will perform this transformation step? The answer cannot be the users, as this does not seem practical. Having the server perform it is also problematic: the entity performing translation is able to link a transformed profile to the original encrypted profile it originates from. Finding a profile transformation process that hides such kind of information seems hard.

To solve this problem, we build a dual-server model: one server performs the profile transformation and sends the transformed one to the other server, named the proxy server The idea is that, when proceeding query and match, the proxy server sees the matching transformed profile but does not see which users they correspond to, while the server sees the relations between transformed and encrypted contents but does not see the queries and matches. To protect against user-server collusion, we assumed that two servers not colluding with each other.

3.1 Architecture

PAFR allows users to connect with other as friend privately and retrieve friends based on profiles through OSN server. As shown in Fig. 1, PAFR consists in three types of entities: Users $\mathcal{U}$, a server $\mathcal{S}_1$, a proxy server $\mathcal{S}_2$.

- $\mathcal{U}$ contains n users $(u_1, ..., u_n)$. Each user $u_i \in \mathcal{U}$ creates his own profile set $P_i = (p_1, ..., p_d)$, encrypts P_i to C_i and upload C_i to $\mathcal{S}_1$. Every user can connect with others as his friends dynamically and later search for friends whose encrypted profiles contains some keyword p. After uploading the C_i to $\mathcal{S}_1$, user only needs to store constant size data (key) in local client.
- $\mathcal{S}_1$ acts as the service provider that provides the social network service to $\mathcal{U}$. $\mathcal{S}_1$ has a graph $\mathcal{G} = (\mathcal{V}, \mathcal{E})$ that contains the whole social network. The vertex $v_i \in \mathcal{V}$ represents the information that the server knows about a user $u_i \in \mathcal{U}$. If two users $u_i \in \mathcal{U}$ and $u_j \in \mathcal{U}$ are friends with each other, there will exist an edge $e_{ij} \in \mathcal{E}$ between vertexes v_i and v_j in the graph $\mathcal{G}$.
- $\mathcal{S}_2$ acts as an collaborator of $\mathcal{S}_1$. For every user $u_i \in \mathcal{U}$, $\mathcal{S}_2$ hass a graph $\mathcal{G}_i = (\mathcal{V}_i, \mathcal{E}_i)$. The vertexes in $\mathcal{G}_i$ represent user u_i and his friends. An edge $e_{ij} \in \mathcal{E}_i$ between vertices v_i and v_j in the graph $\mathcal{G}_i$ stores encrypted closeness information about the friendship between u_i and u_j, which is dynamically updated by the friendship getting closer. $\mathcal{S}_2$ can interact with $\mathcal{S}_1$ to perform secure sorting protocol get the sorted search result.

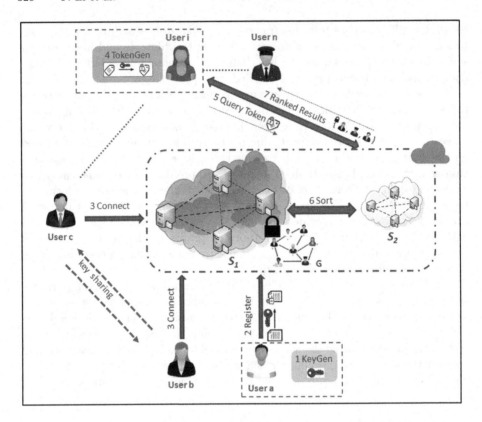

Fig. 1. The architecture

Security Model. We consider the non-collude servers S_1 and S_2 as honest-but-curious adversaries, which is similar to most of prior works in the dual-server model (e.g., [12,13]). Particularly, they will follow protocols honestly, yet they are curious about inferring the private information and will do so independently. Such an security assumption makes sense because in practice cloud service providers are well-established and business-driven parties who do not want to harm their reputation and thus avoid behaving maliciously and collusion. Meanwhile, on the practical service deployment side, protocols under honest-but-curious model would present much more efficient implementation than protocols under the malicious adversary model. What's more, since there are multiple users in our dual-server architecture, the servers cannot tell when two queries from different users that query for the same profile or not.

3.2 Formal Definitions

Definition 1. *PAFR consists 6 polynomial time algorithms and protocols:*

1. $(\mathcal{G}, params) \leftarrow Setup(1^k)$: *is a probabilistic algorithm run by $\mathcal{S}_1$ that takes a security parameter 1^k as input, outputs public parameter params and an undirect graph structure $\mathcal{G}$.*
2. $(k_i, (PK_i, SK_i)) \leftarrow KeyGen(params)$: *is a probabilistic algorithm run by the user u_i that takes params as input, generates his key k_i and his homomorphic key pair (PK_i, SK_i).*
3. $(\bot, \mathcal{G}_i, \mathcal{G}') \leftarrow Register(u_i(P_i, k_i), S_2(\bot), S_1(\mathcal{G}))$: *is an interactive protocol run by user u_i , S_2 and S_1. User u_i takes his key k_i and his profile P_i as input, S_1 takes $\mathcal{G}$ as input, after the protocol, S_2 outputs a graph $\mathcal{G}_i$ for u_i, S_1 outputs an updated $\mathcal{G}'$.*
4. $(k_{i,j}, k_{j,i}, (\mathcal{G}'_i, \mathcal{G}'_j), \mathcal{G}') \leftarrow Connect(u_i(k_i), u_j(k_j), S_2(\mathcal{G}_i), S_1(\mathcal{G}))$: *is an interactive protocol among server S_1, S_2, u_i and u_j. u_i and u_j take their keys k_i and k_j as input, S_2 takes $\mathcal{G}_i$ and $\mathcal{G}_j$ as input, and S_1 takes $\mathcal{G}$ as input, the output of S_2 is the updated $\mathcal{G}'_i$ and $\mathcal{G}'_j$, the other three party have no output.*
5. $(\bot, \bot, I) \leftarrow Query(u_q(k_q, p), S_1(\mathcal{G}), S_2(\mathcal{G}_i, k))$: *is an interactive protocol run by user u_q, S_1 and S_2 that user u_q takes his key k_q and the query profile $p \in \{0, 1\}^*$ as input, S_2 takes $\mathcal{G}_i$ as input, and S_1 takes $\mathcal{G}$ as input, the output of S_2 is a unsorted query results I.*
6. $(\bot, I_R) \leftarrow Sort(S_1(SK_q), S_2(I))$: *is an interactive protocol run by S_1 and S_2 that S_2 takes unsorted query results I_R as input, and S_1 takes SK_q as input, the output of S_2 is a sorted query results I_R.*

3.3 Security Definition

The security definition will be formalized by the four leakage functions $\mathcal{L}_1$, $\mathcal{L}_2$, $\mathcal{L}_3$ and $\mathcal{L}_4$, which denote the information leaked to $\mathcal{S}_1$ and $\mathcal{S}_2$ in different phases of the scheme. We formalize the ideal/real world paradigm for PAFR. In the real world $Real(1^k)$, the protocol between the adversarial servers and user executes just like the real scheme. In the ideal world $ideal(1^k)$, there exists two simulators Sim_1 and Sim_2 who get the leakage information from leakage functions $\mathcal{L}_1$ to $\mathcal{L}_4$ and try to simulate the execution of $\mathcal{S}_1$ and $\mathcal{S}_2$ in the real world. We give the formal definition as follow.

Definition 2. *Adaptive $\mathcal{L}$-Semantically Secure. Given the scheme described in Definition 1 and consider the following probabilistic paradigms where, $\mathcal{U} = (u_1, \ldots, u_n)$ are users, $\mathcal{A}_1$ and $\mathcal{A}_2$ are two non-colluding honest-but-curious adversaries, Sim_1 and Sim_2 are two polynomial times simulators, and $\mathcal{L}_1$ to $\mathcal{L}_4$ as leakage functions.*

    $Real(1^k)$: It is run among the two adversaries $\mathcal{A}_1$, $\mathcal{A}_2$ and the users $\mathcal{U}$ using the real scheme. $\mathcal{A}_1$ initializes a empty graph structure $\mathcal{G}$, every user $u_i \in \mathcal{U}$ computes his keys $k \leftarrow KeyGen(params)$ and send $\mathcal{A}_1$ his encrypted profiles C_i and his friends list $L(u_i)$, sends $\mathcal{A}_2$ $L(u_i)$, $C_{i,j}$ and the encrypted closeness value $x_{i,j}$ for all his friends. After that, by Register and Connect, $\mathcal{A}_1$ updates $\mathcal{G}$

that contains the received values. $\mathcal{A}_2$ constructs n graph $(\mathcal{G}_1, \ldots, \mathcal{G}_n)$, each graph contains the information about user and his friends information and the edges in each graph is encrypted closeness value $x_{i,j}$. After that, polynomial times queries $(q_1, \ldots, q_t)$ are made by different users to $\mathcal{A}_2$. For each query q_i, the query user u_q, $\mathcal{A}_1$ and $\mathcal{A}_2$ run the protocol $Query(u_q(k_q, p), \mathcal{A}_1(\mathcal{G}), \mathcal{A}_2(\mathcal{G}_i, k))$. After the execution of the protocol, $\mathcal{A}_2$ sends the encrypted result I_R to user u. Finally, $\mathcal{A}_1$ outputs $Output_{\mathcal{A}_1}^{Real(1^k)}$, and $\mathcal{A}_2$ outputs $Output_{\mathcal{A}_2}^{Real(1^k)}$.

$\mathbf{Ideal(1^k)}$: It is run by the two simulators Sim_1 and Sim_2. Sim_1 and Sim_2 do not interact with users, it responds to queries using randomly generated data, with these leakage functions as the only input. By the information leaked from $\mathcal{L}_1$ and $\mathcal{L}_2$, Sim_1 builds simulated structure $\widetilde{\mathcal{G}}$ and Sim_2 builds simulated structures $(\widetilde{\mathcal{G}}_1, \ldots, \widetilde{\mathcal{G}}_n)$. After that, there are q polynomial times queries $(q_1, \ldots, q_t)$ send to Sim_2. Sim_2 uses $\mathcal{L}_3$ to simulate $Query(Sim_1^{\mathcal{L}_3()}(\widetilde{\mathcal{G}}), Sim_2^{\mathcal{L}_3()}(\widetilde{\mathcal{G}}_i))$. After the execution of the protocol, Sim_2 uses $\mathcal{L}_4()$ to get the simulated result $\widetilde{I}_R$. Finally, Sim_1 outputs $Output_{Sim_1}^{Ideal(1^k)}$, and Sim_2 outputs $Output_{Sim_2}^{Ideal(1^k)}$.

We say that our scheme is adaptive $\mathcal{L}$-semantically secure if for all polynomial time $\mathcal{A}_1$ and $\mathcal{A}_2$, there exists polynomial time simulators Sim_1 and Sim_2 such that the following two distribution ensembles are computationally indistinguishable: $Output_{\mathcal{A}_{1/2}}^{Real(1^k)} \approx Output_{Sim_{1/2}}^{Ideal(1^k)}$

4   Construction

Let $\mathcal{H} : (0,1)^* \rightarrow \mathbb{G}$ be a collision-resistant hash function, it can hash any bit string into a DDH-hard group $\mathbb{G}$ of order ζ. Let $\mathcal{PE} = \{KeyGen, Enc, Dec\}$ be the Pallier encryption scheme [24]. The construction works as follows:

- **Setup.** In Setup phase, on input the security parameter 1^k, the server $\mathcal{S}_1$ initialize a graph structure $\mathcal{G} = (\mathcal{V}, \mathcal{E})$. We denote $\mathcal{G}$ as the global graph. It contains n vertexes $|\mathcal{V}| = n$, each vertex $v_i \in \mathcal{V}$ represents the information that the server collects about a user $u_i \in \mathcal{U}$. An edge $e_{ij} \in \mathcal{E}$ between vertices v_i and v_j stores information about the friendship between u_i and u_j. If u_i and u_j are not friends, then e_{ij} does not exist. Both of $\mathcal{V}$ and $\mathcal{E}$ are empty at initialization.

- **KeyGen.** To join in the system, u_i should first generate his own keys: u_i randomly select a value $sk_i \in \mathbb{Z}_k$, acting as secret key to encrypt her profiles. Moreover, he initializes her public/secret key pairs $(PK_i, SK_i) \leftarrow \mathcal{PE}.KeyGen(1^k)$ by Paillier encryption: PK_i is used to encrypt the closeness value between him and his friend, and SK_i is used for decrypt the closeness and identities of the query results.

- **Register.** To register, user u_i should first generate his identity id_i and create his profile vector $P_i = (p_i^1, \ldots, p_i^m)$. To hide P_i, for every $p_i^j \in P_i$, he first computes the hash value by using the hash function $\mathcal{H}$: $\mathcal{H}(p_i^j)$, and encrypts it into c_i^j: $c_i^j \leftarrow \mathcal{H}(p_i^j)^{sk_i}$. Then he forms encrypted profiles $C_i = (c_i^1, \ldots, c_i^m)$ and send (C_i, id_i, SK_i) to $\mathcal{S}_1$. $\mathcal{S}_1$ adds a vertex v_i to graph $\mathcal{G}$, which is initialized with $id_i||C_i||SK_i$. Moreover, u_i also sends sk_i to S_2, S_2 initializes a new graph G_i for u_i: $G_i = (V_i, E_i)$. In G_i, the vertexes V_i represent user u_i and all of his friends. An edge $e_{ij} \in E_i$ between v_i and v_j in G_i stores the closeness value between u_i and u_j. After that, u_i only needs to store constant size data (key) in local client.

- **Connect.** Every user can connect other as his friend dynamically. When u_i wants to connect with u_j, he sends request to S_2. S_2 adds a vertex v_j in u_i's social graph G_i, and store id_j in vertex v_j in G_i. To authorize u_j to retrieve his encrypted profiles C_i, u_i and u_j generate a random search key $k_{j,i} \in Z_k^*$ by secure key exchange protocol and send it to the server S_1. S_1 adds $k_{j,i}$ into the edge e_{ij} between v_i and v_j in G.

  To achieve secure query, S_1 and S_2 conduct the profile transfer protocols for u_i and u_j: for u_i, S_1 first retrieves the vertex $v_j \in G$ and gets u_j's encrypted profiles C_j in v_j, and transfers C_j into u_i-specific profiles vector $C_{j,i}$: $C_{j,i} = (c_{j,i}^1, \ldots, c_{j,i}^d)$, in which $c_{j,i}^i \in C_{j,i}$ is a "double encryption" value of c_j^i: $c_{j,i}^i \leftarrow (c_j^i)^{k_{j,i}}$. Then S_1 sends $C_{j,i}$ to S_2. S_2 adds a vertex v_j in G_i, and updates the vertex v_j into $id_j||C_{j,i}$. S_2 also generates a closeness value x_j with initial value 0. The value x_j represents closeness between u_i and u_j. S_2 encrypts x_j with PK_i into $[x_j]$: $[x_j] \leftarrow PE.Enc_{PK_i}(x_j)$, and adds it to the edge x_j between v_i and v_j. It can be dynamically updated due to the addition homomorphic property of Paillier encryption(it is another scope of work which we shall not discuss here).

- **Query.** Users can send query to S_2 for retrieving friends with some specific profiles. If the query user u_q wants to query for whether he has friends who has the profile p, he should first generate his token τ_q: $\tau_q = (t_1, \ldots, t_d)$, in which $t_i = H(p)^{k_{q,i}}$, where $k_{q,i}$ is u_q's search key for his friend u_i. Then u_q submits τ_q to S_2. Upon receiving τ_q, S_2 computes the transformed token t_i' for each $v_i \in G_q$: $t_i' = t_i^{sk_q}$. Then S_2 traverses each $v_i \in G_q$ to look up for value t_i'. If the value t_i' does exist in vertex v_i, we say that user with id_i is matched. For every matched id_i, S_2 also retrieves $[x_q]$ from the edge between v_i and v_q in G_q. S_2 traverses each t_i' in the graph G_q to get all the matched ids and the correspond closeness values. The search result contains the set $I = \{(id_1, [x_1]), \ldots, (id_d, [x_d])\}$.

- **Sort.** Since the set $I = \{(id_1, [x_1]), \ldots, (id_d, [x_d])\}$ is encrypted by Paillier encryption. The randomness property of Paillier encryption prohibits S_2 from sorting them and returning the friends identifiers ranked by their closeness values to the user u_q. To achieve ranking, we build a secure key-value sort protocol between S_1 and S_2 to privately sort the closeness of the matched friends based on EncSort. First of all, to prevent S_1 from learning the order, S_2 encrypts each $id_i \in I$ for $1 \leq i \leq d$ to $[id_i]$ with PK_q: $[id_i] \leftarrow PE.Enc_{PK_q}(id_i)$, and generates $I' = \{([id_1], [x_1]), \ldots, ([id_d], [x_d])\}$. Then S_1 and S_2 perform $EncSort$: S_2 inputs $I' = \{([id_1], [x_1]), \ldots, ([id_d], [x_d])\}$ that it wants to sort and S_1 inputs Paillier encryption secret key SK_q. By Batcher's sorting networks [22], they sort the elements of each pair at every level of the network. For each level i, for every pair $([id_x], [x_x]), ([id_y], [x_y])$: S_2 computes $\{z\} := [2^l][x_i][x_y]^{-1} \mod n^2 (l > k)$. It blinds $[z]$: randomly chooses $r \in (0, 1)^{l+k}$, computes $[d] := [z][r] \bmod n^2$. and sends $[d]$ to $\mathcal{S}_1$. $\mathcal{S}_1$ and $\mathcal{S}_2$ both compute $d' \leftarrow \mathcal{PE}.Dec_{SK_q}([d])$ and $r' := r \bmod 2^l$. $\mathcal{S}_1$ and $\mathcal{S}_2$ engage in a private input comparison protocol (e.g. the DGK protocol [25]) to compare d' and r'. Then $\mathcal{S}_2$ receives the ciphertext of the comparison result $||\lambda||$, which satisfies $\lambda = 1 \rightarrow d' < r'$. Then $\mathcal{S}_1$ retrieves the l−th bit of d', denotes it as d_l and sends it to $\mathcal{S}_2$. At the same time, $\mathcal{S}_1$ retrieves $||r_l||$: the l−th bit of r', and computes $||v|| = ||d_l|| * ||r_l|| * ||\lambda||$. They performs the bit re-encryption and the encrypted chosen protocol [26] to get the ranked $||\lambda||$. After $O((log d)^2)$ times Batchers protocol, $\mathcal{S}_2$ obtains the final ranked results I_R: $I_R = \{([id'_1], [x'_1]), \ldots, ([id'_d], [x'_d])\}$ encrypted using the first layer of Paillier encryption. I_R is a re-encryption of array I', which includes the encrypted ranked closeness values with the corresponding encrypted identities which is satisfied $\mathcal{PE}.Dec_{SK_q}([x'_1]) <, \ldots, < \mathcal{PE}.Dec_{SK_q}([x'_d])$. Finally, $\mathcal{S}_2$ sends the final result I_R to user u_q. u_q can decrypt each $[id_i]$ with his secret key SK_q: $id_i \leftarrow \mathcal{PE}.Dec_{SK_q}[id_i]$ and get the sorted friends identities $R = (id_1, \ldots, id_d)$ that matches the search profile p.

5   Analysis

5.1   Security Analysis

In the following, we analyze the security of our scheme. We need to capture the leakage functions of our PAFR construction:

- $\mathcal{L}_1$: In the register protocol, given user u_i's encrypted profile vector $C_i = (c_i^1, \ldots, c_i^m)$, $\mathcal{S}_1$ can learn the size of C_i: $|C_i|$, the number of c_i: m, and the length of each items $|c_i^j|_{c_i^j \in C_i}$. We denote these by $\mathcal{L}_1$, i.e., $\mathcal{L}_1 = (|C_i|, m, |c_i^j|_{c_i^j \in C_i})$.

- $\mathcal{L}_2$: The connect phase reveals $\mathcal{S}_2$ the length of the transformed encrypted profiles $|C_{j,i}|_{e_{j,i} \in \mathcal{G}_i}$ for every user u_i and the length of the corresponding closeness values $|x_j|_{e_{j,i} \in \mathcal{G}_i}$. We denote these by $\mathcal{L}_2$, i.e., $\mathcal{L}_2 = (|C_{j,i}|_{e_{j,i} \in \mathcal{G}_i}, |x_j|_{e_{j,i} \in \mathcal{G}_i})$.

- $\mathcal{L}_3$: In the query protocol, we assume that t times queries are send to $\mathcal{S}_2$. The queries are from different users. For each query q_i, $\mathcal{S}_2$ gets the query token τ_i, it can only see the size of τ_i: $|\tau_i|$, query user id id_q and the number of matched $\#[id_i]_{1<i<d}$ the relationship between them. We denote these by $\mathcal{L}_3$, i.e., $\mathcal{L}_3 = ((|\tau_1|, \#[id_i]_{1<i<d}), \ldots, (|\tau_t|, \#[id_j]_{1<j<d}), t)$.

- $\mathcal{L}_4$: In the sorting protocol $\mathcal{S}_1$ and $\mathcal{S}_2$ perform sort by pairs $\{([id_x], [x_x]), ([id_y], [x_y])\}$ in $(log d)^2$ times. For each pairs, $\mathcal{S}_2$ gets $([x_x], [x_y], l)$, $\mathcal{S}_1$ gets $\{([z], [\lambda])\}$. We denote these by $\mathcal{L}_4$, i.e., $\mathcal{L}_4^{\mathcal{S}_1} = \{([z]_i, [\lambda]_i)_{1<i<(log m)^2}\}$, $\mathcal{L}_4^{\mathcal{S}_2} = \{([x_x]_i, [x_y]_i, l)_{1<i<(log m)^2}\}$.

Theorem 1. *If Paillier encryption is CPA-secure, $\mathcal{H}$ is a collision-resistant hash function, the DDH problem in G cannot be solved in polynomial time, and the DGK protocol is proved semantic secure, in random oracle model, then our scheme is Adaptive $\mathcal{L}$-Semantically Secure.*

Proof. The primary goal of providing this proof is to construct two simulators Sim_1, Sim_2 that can generate the simulated values in Ideal(1^k) using the information given in these leakage functions described above. We show that the outputs of the simulator Sim_1 and Sim_2 is indistinguishable from the view of $\mathcal{A}_1$ and $\mathcal{A}_2$ in Real(1^k) using a sequence of hybrid games, where each of them simulates one or more non-revealed encrypted values than the previous game. As a consequence the first hybrid game corresponds to Real(1^k) and the last one corresponds to Ideal(1^k).

Game$_1$: Given the information received from $\mathcal{L}_1$, the simulator Sim_1 can randomly choose m random strings to construct a simulated $\widetilde{C}_i = (\widetilde{c}_i^1, \ldots, \widetilde{c}_i^m)$, the length of every $\widetilde{c}_i^j$ is $|c_i^j|$. Sim_1 uses these structures to build a simulated graph structure $\widetilde{\mathcal{G}}$. In Real(1^k), the vertex in graph $\mathcal{G}$ is initialized with $id_i||C_i||SK_i$, in which id_i, SK_i are random values chosen by u_i, and $C_i = (c_i^1, \ldots, c_i^m)$, where $c_i^j = \mathcal{H}(p_i^j)^{sk_i}$. If the hash function $\mathcal{H}$ is pseudo-random and the Decision Diffie-Hellman problem exists in PPT time, then $\widetilde{\mathcal{G}} \approx \mathcal{G}$. For all polynomial time $\mathcal{A}_1$, he cannot distinguish the simulated $\widetilde{\mathcal{G}}$ with the real graph structure $\mathcal{G}$. Therefore, the two distribution ensembles are computationally indistinguishable: $\text{Output}_{\mathcal{A}_1}^{\text{Real}(1^k)} \approx \text{Output}_{Sim_1}^{\text{Game}_1}$.

Game$_2$: It is the same as $Game_1$ except the following differences: in $Game_1$, if u_j is a friend of u_i, then $\mathcal{A}_2$ can get $C_{j,i} = (c_{j,i}^1, \ldots, c_{j,i}^d)$, in which $c_{j,i}^i$ is a "re-encryption" value of c_j^i : $c_{j,i}^i \leftarrow (c_j^i)^{k_{j,i}}$ and get $[x_{ij}]$: $[x_{ij}] \leftarrow \mathcal{PE}.\mathcal{E}nc_{PK_i}(x_{ij})$. In this game, given the information received from $\mathcal{L}_2$, the simulator Sim_2 could learn the number of every user's friends: $\#L(u_i)$. Moreover, for every user u_i, Sim_2 could also learn m: the number of $c_{j,i}^i$ in $C_{j,i}$, the length of every $c_{j,i}^i$: $|c_{j,i}^i|$ and the corresponding closeness values $|x_{ij}|$. Then it can construct $\widetilde{C}_{j,i}$, which contains $\#L(u_i)$ random strings with the length of $|c_i^j|$. Sim_2 uses these structures to build simulated graph structures $(\widetilde{\mathcal{G}}_1, \ldots, \widetilde{\mathcal{G}}_n)$. For every $\widetilde{\mathcal{G}}_i$, the vertexes and edges contains randomly chosen strings $|\widetilde{id}_j||\widetilde{C}_{j,i}|$ and $\widetilde{x}_{ij}$ with the length of $|id_j||C_{j,i}|$ and $|x_{ij}|$. If the Paillier encryption is CPA-secure, then $\widetilde{x}_{ij} \approx x_{ij}$, and the Decision Diffie-Hellman problem exists in PPT time, then $\widetilde{C}_{j,i} \approx C_{j,i}$, so $\widetilde{\mathcal{G}}_i \approx \mathcal{G}_i$. For all polynomial time Sim_1, he cannot distinguish the simulated $(\widetilde{\mathcal{G}}_1, \ldots, \widetilde{\mathcal{G}}_n)$ from the real $(\mathcal{G}_1, \ldots, \mathcal{G}_n)$. Therefore, the two distribution ensembles are computationally indistinguishable: $\text{Output}_{Sim_2}^{\text{Game}_2} \approx \text{Output}_{Sim_2}^{\text{Game}_1}$.

Game$_3$: It is the same as $Game_2$ except the following difference: in $Game_2$, for each query q_i, Sim_2 runs Query protocol with the query user u_q. The query user u_q sends query token to Sim_2 in the form of τ_q: $\tau_q = (t_1, \ldots, t_d)$, which $t_i = H(p)^{k_{q,i}}$. Sim_2 generates query result $I = \{(id_1, [x_1]), \ldots, (id_d, [x_d])\}$. In $Game_3$, by access the leakage function $\mathcal{L}_3$, Sim_2 can learn $|t_i|$ and d: the length of each item and the number of items in τ_q. For a number of queries $(q_1, \ldots, q_t)$, Sim_2 checks if either of the query q_i appeared in any previous query. It needs to consider the following two cases:

- If q_i doesn't appear in any previous query, Sim_2 runs the simulation of Query protocol to generate the simulated $\widetilde{I}_i$ with the simulated $\widetilde{x}_{ij}$ and $\widetilde{id}_{ij}$.
- If q_i appears in any previous query q_j, Sim_2 returns the previous results $\widetilde{I}_j$.

If the Paillier encryption is CPA-secure, then $\tilde{x}_{ij} \approx x_{ij}$, therefore $\tilde{I} \approx I$. For all polynomial time Sim_2, he can not distinguish the simulated $\tilde{I}$ from the real I. Therefore, the two distribution ensembles are computationally indistinguishable: $\text{Output}_{Sim_2}^{Game_3} \approx \text{Output}_{Sim_2}^{Game_2}$.

Game₄: It is Ideal(1^k) which is the same with $Game_3$ except the following difference: Since $\mathcal{A}_1$ and $\mathcal{A}_2$ interact with each other for comparing values by $(\log d)^2$ times in $Game_3$, the simulators Sim_1 and Sim_2 should simulate $\mathbb{A}_1$ and $\mathbb{A}_2$ with the leakage functions $\mathcal{L}_4$ by each pairs $(\log d)^2$ times in Batcher's protocol to get the final simulation value. At every pairs i, $\mathcal{A}_1$'s view can be denoted as $view_{\mathcal{A}_1} = (SK_P, [\![z]\!], \|\lambda\|)$, in which SK_P is the secret key of Paillie Encryption. Given $(SK_P, [\![z]\!], [\lambda])$, we can build a simulated Sim_1:

- Randomly choose $\tilde{\lambda}$, compute $\|\tilde{\lambda}\|$ to denote $x_x \leq x_y$
- Randomly choose $\tilde{z} \leftarrow (0, 2^{\lambda+l}) \bigcap Z$
- Encrypt $\tilde{z}$ by Paillier encryption to get $[\tilde{z}] \leftarrow \mathcal{PE}.\mathcal{Enc}_{PK_P}(z)$
- Output $view_{Sim_2} = (SK_P, l, [\tilde{z}], \|\tilde{\lambda}\|)$

In Game₃, z is equal to $x + r$, in which x is a l-bits integer and r is a $l+\lambda$-bits integer, so the distribution of $\tilde{z}$ is indistinguishable from z. We can get $(SK_P, [\tilde{z}]) \approx (SK_P, [z])$. Moreover, since the distribution of $\tilde{z}$ and z are independent of t, so $(SK_P, l, [\tilde{z}] \| \|\tilde{\lambda}\|) \approx (SK_P, l, [z], \|\tilde{\lambda}\|)$. In a similar way, at every pairs i, $\mathcal{A}_2$'s view can be denoted as $view_{\mathcal{A}_2} = (([x_x]_i, [x_y]_i, l, PK_P, r, \|\lambda\|, [z_l])$. We can build a Sim_2 to simulate $\mathcal{A}_2$:

- Choose $\tilde{r} \leftarrow (0, 2^{\lambda+l}) \bigcap Z$
- Choose two random values $\tilde{\lambda}, \tilde{z}_l$, generate two ciphertexts $\|\tilde{\lambda}\|, \|\tilde{z}\|$
- Output $view_{Sim_2} = ([x_x], [y_y], l, PK_P, \tilde{r}, [\tilde{z}_l])$.

In both $view_{\mathcal{A}_2}$ and $view_{Sim_2}$, r is extracted from uniform distribution $(0, 2^{\lambda+l}) \bigcap Z$, $[\tilde{z}_l]$ is the ciphertext of Paillier encryption which is randomness, so $([x_x], [y_y], l, PK_P) \approx ([x_x], [y_y], l, PK_P, r, [\tilde{z}_l])$. Besides, r and $\tilde{r}$ are extracted from the same uniform distribution, based on the CPA-secure Paillier encryption, we can get: $view_{\mathcal{A}_2}$ and $view_{Sim_2}$ are computational indistinguishable.

What's more, since $\|\tilde{\lambda}\| \approx \|[x_x] \leq [x_y]\|$, then $(SK_P, l, [z], \|\tilde{\lambda}\|) \approx (SK_P, l, [z], \|[x_x] \leq [y_y]\|)$. Due to the semantic security in random oracle model of DGK, Sim_1 and Sim_2 can get d ciphertexts that unsorted from the leakage function $\mathcal{L}_4$. Then, Sim_1 and Sim_2 can simulate $(\log m)^2$ times Bathcer's protocols. At the end of the sort protocol, $\text{Output}_{Sim_1}^{Ideal(1^k)}$ looks indistinguishable from the the output $\text{Output}_{Sim_1}^{Game_3}$. Also, since Sim_2 has no additional output by this game, so $\text{Output}_{Sim_2}^{Ideal(1^k)}$ looks indistinguishable from the the output $\text{Output}_{Sim_2}^{Game_3}$: $\text{Output}^{Ideal}(1^k)_{Sim_1} \approx \text{Output}_{Sim_1}^{Game_3}$.

For all polynomial time $\mathcal{A}_1$ and $\mathcal{A}_2$, there exists polynomial times simulators Sim_1 and Sim_2 such that: $\text{Output}_{\mathcal{A}_{1/2}}^{Real(1^k)} \approx \text{Output}_{Sim_{1/2}}^{Ideal(1^k)}$. Therefore, we can meet the security definition defined in Definition 2, that is, our scheme is adaptively $\mathcal{L}$-semantically secure.

5.2   Performance Analysis

In this section, we measure the performance of PAFR by evaluating the complexity in terms of computation complexity and communication overhead. We also compare the properties with other recent related schemes that supporting result ranking.

Formally, let m be the number of profiles, q be the number of query keywords in a single token, and d be the average friends number. In PAFR, the register cost for user is linear in the size of the profile collection. Hence, user need to perform $O(m)$ work before uploading the encrypted profiles to $\mathcal{S}_1$. In addition, $(\mathcal{G}_1, \ldots, \mathcal{G}_n)$ are stored in S_2. $\mathcal{G}_i$ includes the shared profiles, which has a linear size in the number of profiles and friends number $O(m*d)$. However, this will not affect the scheme's practicality, since the original encrypted profiles can be safely stored in S_1, such that there is no need to submit them to S_2 when performing query. During the query phase, user sends a token for q profiles to S_2 and as a result obtains I_R of size d as a result of ordered friends identifiers. Hence, token generation time for user is $O(q)$ and overall communication cost between the user and S_2 in the worst case is $O(q*d)$. S_2 queries in $O(q)$ time and sums the corresponding closeness vectors in $O(q*d)$ time, i.e., to obtain identifiers for all the matched friends. Sort phase takes $O(d(logd)^2)$ rounds of communication between S_1 and S_2 since Bathcer's sorting network gives the dominating cost. Hence, our construction gives only a $O(logd)$ multiplicative overhead over a non-secure construction. If S_1 and S_2 operate in parallel the run time overhead can be dropped to $O((logd)^2)$.

Therefore, the performance guarantees: Register takes user $O(m)$ time and space; Query takes user $O(q)$ time to generate a token, the communication complexity between user and S_2 is $O(q+d)$; the space complexity for S_1 and S_2 are $O(q*d)$ and $O(1)$; and the Sort phase takes $O((logd)^2)$ for both S_1 and S_2.

Table 1. Comparison

	Accuracy	Updatable	Server Model	Homomorphic Tools	$Comp_u$	$Comp_S$
[26]	No	No	Single	–	$O(m)$	$O(m^2)$
[27]	Yes	No	Single	LWE-Brakerski	$O(q*d)$	$O(q*d+m^2)$
[28]	No	No	Two	Paillier	$O(d(logd))$	$O(d(logd))$
Ours	Yes	Yes	Two	Paillier/GM	$O(d)$	$O((logd)^2)$

m: keywords space; q: the number of query keywords; d: the items number.

We compare PAFR with the related secure search schemes [26–28] in Table 1. For accuracy, [26] calculates the number of matched keywords in each item based on Inner Scalar Product and ranks items by computing weights, [27] clusters similar items by LSH functions. However, the false positives rate in above schemes cannot be negligible since the keyword-to-item significance leaves out of consideration, so they cannot provide exact ranking. In PAFR, the servers compare the encrypted closeness weights to obtain the precise ranking for matched friends.

For security, [26] hides the search and access pattern based on heuristic method, so the security is out of comparison. [27] builds the search index based on fully homomorphic encryption, which reaches high security but leads to high computation cost. [28] introduces non-collusion servers models, one of which can access the plaintext of result. PAFR encrypts the closeness weight based on Paillier homomorphic encryption, so servers can rank the search results without obtaining any information of related plaintext. For efficiency, in [26], the server can only perform search without ranking, it sends back all the matched items to user and user performs ranking at local, which still occurs high computation and communication workload at user-side. The search computation cost is $O(m^2)$, and the query size is $O(m)$ which is linear with the size of keywords space. To achieving ranking, the server computes all the matched items weights, the ranking computation cost is $O(d * m^2)$, where d is the items number. In [27], the frequency of keywords is encrypted by fully homomorphic encryption, that occurs $O(q * d + m^2)$ computation cost for ranking. In [28], the storage cost of collaborative server is linear with the items number $O(d)$. In PAFR, the query computation cost of server and user are both related with query keywords number and friends number $O(q * d)$. And the computation cost for ranking is $O((logd)^2)$. From Table 1, we can demonstrate that PAFR has both a very light user workload and a moderate server workload while being secure against user-server collusion.

6   Conclusion

In this paper, we propose PAFR, a privacy-aware friends retrieval scheme over OSNs, aiming at preventing attack launched by the service provider. PAFR allows user to upload his encrypted contents to server, connect with others in an oblivious method, and query for retrieving his friends with specific keyword. In addition, we adopt the dual-server model where two non-collude servers $\mathcal{S}_1$ and $\mathcal{S}_2$ implementing the role of the service provider. Based on that, we design closeness-based secure sorting protocol to let the servers perform friends sorting and return the ranked relevant result to user without learning the underlying query words and the friends relationship. Both security and performance analysis demonstrate that PAFR has both a very light user workload and a moderate server workload while being secure against user-server collusions. As future work, our aim is to extend PAFR to be secure against fully malicious adversaries, and to efficiently support more functions in OSNs. We also plan to improve its efficiency to reduce the computation cost associated with query and sort phase.

References

1. https://www.cnn.com/2018/04/08/politics/cambridge-analytica-data-millions/index.html
2. https://www.washingtonpost.com/business/economy/how-cambridge-analyticas-whistleblower-became-facebooks-unlikely-foil/2018/03/21

3. Raso Mattos, L.R., Varadharajan, V., Nallusamy, R.: Data protection and privacy preservation using searchable encryption on outsourced databases. In: Thampi, S.M., Zomaya, A.Y., Strufe, T., Alcaraz Calero, J.M., Thomas, T. (eds.) SNDS 2012. CCIS, vol. 335, pp. 178–184. Springer, Heidelberg (2012). https://doi.org/10.1007/978-3-642-34135-9_18
4. https://www.nytimes.com/2017/09/07/business/equifax-cyberattack.html
5. Waldman, A.E.: Privacy, sharing, and trust: the Facebook study. Case W. Res. L. Rev. **67**, 193 (2016)
6. Ferrag, M.A., Maglaras, L., Ahmim, A.: privacy-preserving schemes for ad hoc social networks: a survey. IEEE Commun. Surv. Tutor. **19**(4), 3015–3045 (2017)
7. Standard, Data Encryption. Data encryption standard. Federal Information Processing Standards Publication (1999)
8. Rijmen, V., Daemen, J.: Advanced encryption standard. Proceedings of Federal Information Processing Standards Publications, National Institute of Standards and Technology, pp. 19–22 (2001)
9. Curtmola, R., Garay, J., Kamara, S., Ostrovsky, R.: Searchable symmetric encryption: improved definitions and efficient constructions. J. Comput. Secur. **19**(5), 895–934 (2011)
10. Cash, D., et al.: Dynamic searchable encryption in very-large databases: data structures and implementation. In: NDSS, vol. 14, pp. 23–26, February 2014
11. https://patents.google.com/patent/US9602605B2/en
12. Parit, S.C., Rachh, R.: Ciphertext Policy Attribute Based Encryption (2017)
13. Baden, R., Bender, A., Spring, N., Bhattacharjee, B., Starin, D.: Persona: an online social network with user-defined privacy. In: Proceedings of the ACM SIGCOMM (2009)
14. Vaidya, J., Clifton, C.: Secure set intersection cardinality with application to association rule mining. J. Comput. Secur. **13**(4), 593–622 (2005)
15. Zhang, R., Zhang, Y., Sun, J., Yan, G.: Fine-grained private matching for proximity-based mobile social networking. In: INFOCOM, 2012 Proceedings IEEE, pp. 1969–1977. IEEE, March, 2012
16. Niu, B., Li, X., Zhu, X., Li, X., Li, H.: Are you really my friend? Exactly spatiotemporal matching scheme in privacy-aware mobile social networks. In: Tian, J., Jing, J., Srivatsa, M. (eds.) SecureComm 2014. LNICST, vol. 153, pp. 33–40. Springer, Cham (2015). https://doi.org/10.1007/978-3-319-23802-9_5
17. Fu, Y., Wang, Y.: BCE: A privacy-preserving common-friend estimation method for distributed online social networks without cryptography. In: 2012 7th International ICST Conference on Communications and Networking in China (CHINA-COM), pp. 212–217. IEEE, August 2012
18. Sun, J., Zhang, R., Zhang, Y.: Privacy-preserving spatiotemporal matching. In: INFOCOM, 2013 Proceedings IEEE, pp. 800–808. IEEE, April 2013
19. Popa, R.A., Zeldovich, N.: Multi-key searchable encryption. IACR Cryptology ePrint Archive 2013, p. 508 (2013)
20. Paillier, P.: Public-key cryptosystems based on composite degree residuosity classes. In: Stern, J. (ed.) EUROCRYPT 1999. LNCS, vol. 1592, pp. 223–238. Springer, Heidelberg (1999). https://doi.org/10.1007/3-540-48910-X_16
21. Damgrd, I., Jurik, M., Nielsen, J.B.: A generalization of Pailliers public-key system with applications to electronic voting. Int. J. Inf. Secur. **9**(6), 371–385 (2010)
22. Baldimtsi, F., Ohrimenko, O.: Sorting and searching behind the curtain. In: Böhme, R., Okamoto, T. (eds.) FC 2015. LNCS, vol. 8975, pp. 127–146. Springer, Heidelberg (2015). https://doi.org/10.1007/978-3-662-47854-7_8

23. Batcher, K.E.: Sorting networks and their applications. In: AFIPS Spring Joint Computing Conference (1968)
24. Sun, H., Jafar, S.A.: The capacity of private information retrieval. IEEE Trans. Inf. Theory **63**(7), 4075–4088 (2017)
25. Damgrd, I., Geisler, M., Krigaard, M.: Homomorphic encryption and secure comparison. J. Appl. Cryptol. **1**(1), 22–31 (2008)
26. Cao, N., Wang, C., Li, M., et al.: Privacy-preserving multi-keyword ranked search over encrypted cloud data. IEEE Trans. Parallel Distrib. Syst. **25**(1), 222–233 (2014)
27. Strizhov, M., Ray, I.: Multi-keyword similarity search over encrypted cloud data. In: Cuppens-Boulahia, N., Cuppens, F., Jajodia, S., Abou El Kalam, A., Sans, T. (eds.) SEC 2014. IAICT, vol. 428, pp. 52–65. Springer, Heidelberg (2014). https://doi.org/10.1007/978-3-642-55415-5_5
28. Xia, Z., Wang, X., Sun, X., et al.: A secure and dynamic multi-keyword ranked search scheme over encrypted cloud data. IEEE Trans. Parallel Distrib. Syst. **27**(2), 340–352 (2016)

An ID-Based Linear Homomorphic Cryptosystem and Its Applications for the Isolated Smart Grid Devices

Zhiwei Wang[1,2,3,4(✉)], Zhiyuan Cheng[1], and Nianhua Yang[3,4]

[1] School of Computer, Nanjing University of Posts and Telecommunications,
Nanjing, China
zhwwang@njupt.edu.cn
[2] Guangxi Key Laboratory of Cryptography and Information Security,
Guilin, China
[3] Jiangsu Key Laboratory of Big Data Security & Intelligence Processing,
Nanjing, China
[4] School of Statistics and Information, Shanghai University of International Business
and Economics, Shanghai, China

Abstract. In this paper, we propose an ID-based linear homomorphic cryptosystem, which consisted of an ID-based encryption scheme with homomorphic property and a linearly homomorphic signature scheme, where the linearly homomorphic signature scheme is compatible with the privacy-protection data aggregation. Then, we propose a secure and efficient ID-based meter report protocol for the isolated smart grid devices, which can not only protect against unauthorized reading, unintentional errors and maliciously altering messages, but also achieve privacy-preserving for the customers. We provide security analysis of our protocol in context of five typical attacks. The implementation of our protocol on the Intel Edison Platform shows that our protocol is efficient enough for the physical constrained devices, like smart grid devices.

Keywords: Isolated smart grid device · ID-based linear homomorphic cryptosystem · ID-based meter report protocol · Edison platform

1 Introduction

In order to avoid the management cost of public-key certificates, Shamir introduced the concept of identity-based cryptography in 1984 [9]. The idea is to derive public keys directly from the user's unique identifiers, such as telephone numbers, social insurance number and email address etc. The corresponding private key is generated from the user's public key by using the secret key of a central authority that is named as Private Key Generator or PKG for short. Up to now, most of identity based schemes are constructed from bilinear pairing, such as Boneh and Franklin's identity based encryption scheme [10]. Günther [11] designed an additive homomorphic identity based encryption scheme based

© Springer Nature Switzerland AG 2019
F. Liu et al. (Eds.): SciSec 2019, LNCS 11933, pp. 339–353, 2019.
https://doi.org/10.1007/978-3-030-34637-9_25

on Boneh and Franklin's scheme. The conception of homomorphic cryptosystem was proposed by Johnson et al. [1]. The notion of homomorphic cryptosystem is an important primitive and allows to validate computation over encrypted and authenticated data. Homomorphic cryptosystem can be employed in many applications, such as electronic business, cloud computing and smart grid. Nowadays, there are many types of homomorphic cryptosystems have been proposed [12,13], but there are few homomorphic cryptosystems, designed in ID-based cryptography. Since the management of public-key certificates is cumbersome in the public key-based cryptosystems, it is meaningful to design homomorphic cryptosystems in ID-based cryptosystems.

The smart grid network is considered as the next generation electricity supply network, which is widely different from the traditional grid [2–4]. However, not all smart grid devices are connected to the smart grid data communication network. For example, some customers' homes are located sparsely and far away from the cloud center of ESP, and thus, it would be a heavy cost to extend the smart grid network for covering their isolated smart grid devices.

The meter report protocol is used to calculate the total power consumption data for each individual customers in a long term, for example one month, which provides energy forecast for the ESP [5]. For the isolated smart grid device, a smart reader device acts as a bridge between the ESP and it as Fig. 1. Usually, the smart reader device needs to read the isolated smart meter more frequently for monitoring the energy supply, but the fine-grained metering data may leak the personal information of customers. Actually, the smart reader device only need to send the long-term data to the ESP. Moreover, the reader device is usually a mobile and portable device, and it is apt to be lost or broken, then will be used by the attacker. Thus, a secure and efficient data aggregation mechanism is required in the meter report protocol for isolated smart grid devices.

Recently, several privacy-protection aggregation schemes have been proposed. Li et al. [6] constructed an incremental aggregation scheme based on a virtual aggregation tree relies on the topology of network. Garcia et al. [5] proposed an aggregation scheme combined with additive secret sharing. Lu et al. [7] proposed an efficient privacy-preserving scheme for multidimensional data structure. The three schemes are all based on Pallier's homomorphic encryption technology. Fan et al. [8] proposed an data aggregations scheme based on the subgroup indistinguishability assumption. All the above aggregation schemes are designed for aggregating individual usage date from different customers, and they are all based on the public-key based cryptography. Recently, Wang and Xie proposed a privacy-protection metering data protocol for the isolated smart devices [19], which is still based on the public-key based cryptography.

This paper aims to propose an ID-based linear homomorphic cryptosystem based metering report protocol for the isolate smart grid devices. The metering data should be encrypted and aggregated securely for protecting against attacks and privacy preserving. The reader device should be considered as an un-trusted device. Furthermore, both the smart grid devices and the reader devices have only restricted resources, and thus all the cryptographic schemes in the protocol should provide the high performance in terms of efficiency.

The contributions of this paper can be listed as follows: (1) We propose an ID-based linear homomorphic cryptosystem which consists of an ID-based encryption scheme [11] with homomorphic property and a linearly homomorphic signature scheme. (2) We present an ID-based linear homomorphic cryptosystem based metering report protocol for the isolate smart grid devices. In our design, the only work of reader device is to aggregate the metering data and submit the long-term data. It has no private keys, and thus it cannot be used to forge or decrypt the metering data, even it has been controlled by an attacker. (3) We provide security analysis to our protocol in context of five typical attacks. (4) To evaluate the appropriacy of our protocol for the resource constrained devices, we implement our protocol on the Intel Edison Platform which is a development system for Internet of Things devices.

Organization. Some related mathematical concepts to our construction and proof are reviewed in Sect. 2. An ID-based linear homomorphic cryptosystem is proposed in Sect. 3. The secure and privacy-protection identity based meter report protocol for isolated smart grid devices is proposed in Sect. 4. We analyze our protocol against five typical attacks in Sect. 5. Section 6 discusses the performance of our protocol on the platform of MacBook Pro and Edison. Finally, we conclude our paper in Sect. 7.

2 Review of Mathematical Concepts

In this section, we will review some related mathematical concepts for our construction and proof.

We assume that G and G_T are two cyclic groups with the prime order p. We define $e : G \times G \to G_T$ be the bilinear map as it has the following properties:

1. Bilinear: $\forall g_1, g_2 \in G, a_1, a_2 \in Z_p, e(g_1^{a_1}, g_2^{a_2}) = e(g_1, g_2)^{a_1 a_2}$.
2. Non-degenerate: $\exists g \in G, e(g, g) \neq 1$.
3. Efficient Computability: There exists an efficient algorithm to compute $e(g_1, g_2)$ for all $g_1, g_2 \in G$.

We define the Decisional Bilinear Diffie-Hellman (DBDH) assumption [11] over G as follows.

Definition 1 (DBDH Assumption). *Let $Gen(1^\iota)$ be a group generation algorithm that, takes as input a security parameter ι, outputs a description of a prime order group $\Theta = \{p, G, G_T, e\}$. The DBDH Assumption over group G states that for any probability polynomial-time (PPT) attackers $\mathbf{A}$, given a tuple $(g, p, e, g^{x_1}, g^{x_2}, g^{x_3})$ for randomly chosen $x_1, x_2, x_3 \xrightarrow{R} Z_p$ and g is a generator of G, the advantage for $|Pr[\mathbf{A}(g, p, e, g^{x_1}, g^{x_2}, g^{x_3}, h_b) = b] - 1/2|$ is negligible in ι, where $h_0 = e(g, g)^{x_1 x_2 x_3}, h_1 = e(g, g)^{\omega}, \omega \xrightarrow{R} Z_p$ and $b \in_R \{0, 1\}$.*

Then, we define the q-strong Diffie-Hellman (q-SDH) assumption over G as follows.

Definition 2 (q-SDH Assumption). *Let $Gen(1^\iota)$ be a group generation algorithm that, takes as input a security parameter ι, outputs a description of a prime order group $\Theta = \{p, G, G_T, e\}$. The q-SDH Assumption over group G states that for any probability polynomial-time (PPT) attackers, given a tuple $(g, g^\beta, g^{\beta^2}, \cdots, g^{\beta^q})$ for randomly chosen $\beta \xrightarrow{R} Z_p$ and $g \xrightarrow{R} G$, the advantage for obtaining a solution $(\gamma, g^{1/(\beta+\gamma)})$ is negligible in ι, where $\gamma \in Z_p$.*

3   Design of ID-Based Linear Homomorphic Cryptosystem

3.1   An ID-Based Linear Homomorphic Cryptosystem

In this section, an ID-based linear homomorphic cryptosystem is presented, which consists of an ID-based encryption scheme with homomorphic property [11] and a linearly homomorphic signature scheme, where the linearly homomorphic signature scheme is compatible with the privacy-protection data aggregation. There are three roles in this cryptosystem: sender, receiver, and collector. The sender is responsible for encrypting and signing his data, while the collector is responsible for computing the sum of the data only with the ciphertexts and the aggregation of sender's signature. The receiver accepts the outputs of collector only if the aggregated signature is true.

Some notations in the cyrptosystem can be defined here.

- $H : \{0,1\}^* \to G$ is a cryptographic hash function.
- $H_2 : \{0,1\}^* \to Z_p^*$ is a one-way hash function.
- x is the master secret key for the generation of ID-based private key.
- ID_R is the identity information of receiver.
- ID_S is the identity information of sender.
- r is the random number chosen by sender for encryption.
- s is the random number chosen by sender for generating the signature.

The ID-based linear homomorphic cryptosystem consists of five algorithms: *Setup, KeyGen, Enc&Sign, Aggr, Decrypt&Verif.*

- **Setup:** The private key generator (PKG) generates two bilinear groups parameters $(G, G_T, e : G \times G \to G_T)$ and $(G_T, G_\omega, e_T : G_T \times G_T \to G_\omega)$ with a security parameter λ, where G, G_T and G_ω are all prime order groups with order $p > 2^\lambda$. Let g and g_t be the generators of G and G_T respectively. Then, PKG selects a random $x \in Z_p$, and computes $y = g^x$. It chooses a cryptographic hash function $H : \{0,1\}^* \to G$ and a one-way hash function $H_2\{0,1\}^* \to Z_p^*$. Finally, PKG publishes the master public parameters as $mpk = (p, g, g_t, G, G_T, e, e_T, y, H, H_2)$, and keeps the master private key $msk = x$.
- **KeyGen:** PKG generates the private key of receiver as $d_{ID_R} = H(ID_R)^x$, and the private key of sender as $d_{ID_S} = H(ID_S)^x$, and then distributes these private key securely. The security channel between PKG and sender only need to be constructed once, and PKG goes offline after the registration phase.

It does not need to cost too much to maintain the security channels. The receiver computes $W = e(H(ID_R), y)^1$, and sends it to the sender.

- **Enc&Sign:** The sender selects $s \in_R Z_p$, and publishes $S = g^s$ and $S_t = g_t^s$. When the sender wants to encrypt the data m for the receiver, the sender chooses $r \in Z_p$ randomly and computes a ciphertext $CT = (c_1, c_2, c_3) = (g^r, g_t^r, g_t^m W^r)$. Then, the sender computes the signature as

$$\sigma_1 = d_{ID_S}^{1/(s+H_2(ID_R))} \tag{1}$$

$$\sigma_2 = (c_3)^{1/(s+H_2(ID_R))}. \tag{2}$$

Finally, it sends $\{CT, (\sigma_1, \sigma_2)\}$ to the collector.

- **Aggr:** After receiving $\{CT, (\sigma_1, \sigma_2)\}$ from the sender, the collector can verify the identity of sender by checking

$$e(\sigma_1, S \cdot g^{H_2(ID_R)}) = e(H(ID_S), Y) \tag{3}$$

If the signature σ_1 is true, then the ciphertext/signature pair $\{CT_i, (\sigma_1, \sigma_2)\}$ can be stored. Suppose that there are n ciphertext/signature pairs $\{CT_i, (\sigma_1, \sigma_{2i})\}_{i \in [1,n]}$ have been stored in the collector. Then, the collector can compute the encrypted sum of the data as $CT = \prod_{i=1}^n CT_i = (\prod_{i=1}^n c_{1i}, \prod_{i=1}^n c_{2i}, \prod_{i=1}^n c_{3i}) = (C_1, C_2, C_3)$ and the aggregated signature as $\sigma_2 = \prod_{i=1}^n \sigma_{2i}$. Finally, it sends them to the receiver.

- **Decrypt&Verif:** When the receiver receives $\{CT, (\sigma_1, \sigma_2)\}$, it decrypts the sum data as

$$\bar{M} = C_3 / e(d_{ID_R}, C_1). \tag{4}$$

Then, the sender can compute the discrete log of $\bar{M}$ on the base of g_t to get M. Finally, the receiver verifies σ_2 by checking

$$e_T(\sigma_2, S_t \cdot g_t^{H_2(ID_R)}) = e_T(g_t, g_t)^M \cdot e_T(W, C_2). \tag{5}$$

The correctness of the above formulas will be depicted as follows:

Equation (3):

$$
\begin{aligned}
& e(\sigma_1, S \cdot g^{H_2(ID_R)}) \\
&= e(d_{ID_S}^{1/(s+H_2(ID_R))}, g^s \cdot g^{H_2(ID_R)}) \\
&= e(d_{ID_S}, g) \\
&= e(H(ID_S), Y)
\end{aligned}
$$

---

[1] W is pre-computed by reciever, and will be stored in the sender, since the pairing operation is considered as a very time-consuming cryptographic operation. Then, there is no pairing operations in the encryption and signing phase of the sender.

Equation (4):

$$\bar{M} = C_3/e(d_{ID_R}, C_1)$$

$$= \prod_{i=1}^{n} g_t^{m_i} W^r / e(H(ID_R)^x, \prod_{i=1}^{n} g^{r_i})$$

$$= \prod_{i=1}^{n} g_t^{m_i} \cdot \prod_{i=1}^{n} W^{r_i} / \prod_{i=1}^{n} e(H(ID_R)^x, g)^{r_i}$$

$$= \prod_{i=1}^{n} g_t^{m_i} = g_t^{\sum_{i=1}^{n} m_i}$$

Equation (5):

$$e_T(\sigma_2, S_t \cdot g_t^{H_2(ID_R)})$$

$$= e_T(\prod_{i=1}^{n}(c_{3i})^{1/(s+H(ID_R))}, S_t \cdot g_t^{H_2(ID_R)})$$

$$= e_T(\prod_{i=1}^{n}(g_t^{m_i} W^{r_i}), g_t)$$

$$= e_T(g_t, g_t)^{\sum_{i=1}^{n} m_i} \cdot e_T(W, \prod_{i=1}^{n} g_t^{r_i})$$

$$= e_T(g_t, g_t)^M \cdot e_T(W, C_2)$$

The ID-based encryption scheme used in the cryptosystem can be proved IND-ID-CPA secure under the DBDH assumption and CDH assumption, and the proofs are omitted. The linearly homomorphic signature scheme is based on Boneh and Boyen signature [14], which has been proved strongly unforgeability against a weak attacker under the q-SDH assumption.

4   Design of the Identity-Based Meter Report Protocol for Isolated Smart Grid Devices

4.1   Identity-Based Meter Report System Model

There are four roles in the system model, including private key generator (PKG), electricity service provider (ESP), reader, and isolated smart grid device, where the PKG is located in the ESP, as shown in Fig. 1. In the identity-based meter report protocol, the PKG generates the identity-based private keys for the ESP and the isolated smart grid device, and it goes offline after the registration phase. Subsequently, the reader attempts to collect fine-grained metering data from the isolated smart grid device at short intervals. After a long period, such as one month, the reader sends the total electricity consumption data to the ESP. Several types of attacks may be possible for such a collection procedure.

Firstly, an attacker may listen in on the communications between the reader and the isolated smart grid device to obtain the metering data or alter the messages. Secondly, a corrupted reader may be used to obtain the power usage data of the isolated smart grid device. Thirdly, a corrupted reader may provide incorrect total power usage data to the ESP. Fourthly, a fake ESP worker may analyze the fine-grained power usage data to identify the daily activities of the customer. Finally, a customer may provide payment to an incorrect ESP because of communication errors.

The identity-based meter report model is graphically summarized in Fig. 1. To monitor the energy supply, the reader needs to read from the isolated smart grid device much more frequently than it reports to the ESP. At regular intervals, the ESP obtains only the long-term electricity usage data of the customer from the reader.

Fig. 1. Identity-based meter report model for isolated smart grid devices

4.2   Protocol Construction

The proposed protocol consists of five phases. For convenience, some notation is defined here.

- $H : \{0,1\}^* \rightarrow G$ is a cryptographic hash function.
- $H_2 : \{0,1\}^* \rightarrow Z_p^*$ is a one-way hash function.
- x is the master secret key for the generation of identity-based private keys.
- ID_{esp} is the identity information of the electricity service provider.
- ID_{is} is the identity information of the isolated smart grid device.
- r_i is the ith random number chosen by the isolated smart grid device for encryption.
- s is the random number chosen by the isolated smart grid device for the generation of signatures during a given period.

(1) Initialization Phase:

- **PKG:** The PKG generates two bilinear group parameters $(G, G_T, e : G \times G \rightarrow G_T)$ and $(G_T, G_\omega, e_T : G_T \times G_T \rightarrow G_\omega)$ with a security parameter λ, where G, G_T and G_ω are all prime order groups of order $p > 2^\lambda$. Let g and g_t be the generators of G and G_T, respectively. Then, the PKG selects a random $x \in Z_p$ and computes $y = g^x$. It chooses a cryptographic hash function $H : \{0,1\}^* \rightarrow G$ and a one-way hash function $H_2\{0,1\}^* \rightarrow Z_p^*$. Finally, the PKG publishes the master public parameters as $mpk = (p, g, g_t, G, G_T, e, e_T, y, H, H_2)$ and stores the master private key as $msk = x$.

(2) Registration Phase:

- **PKG:** Let ID_{esp} denote the identity of the ESP, and let ID_{is} denote the identity of the isolated smart device. The PKG generates the private key of the ESP as $d_{ID_{esp}} = H(ID_{esp})^x$ and the private key of the isolated smart device as $d_{ID_{is}} = H(ID_{is})^x$, and it then securely distributes these private keys. A secure channel between the PKG and the isolated smart device needs to be constructed only once (e.g., through issuing a tamper-proof smart card), and the PKG goes offline after the registration phase. Therefore, a high cost is not required to maintain secure channels.
- **ESP:** The ESP computes $W = e(H(ID_{esp}), y)^2$ and sends it to the isolated smart grid device.

(3) Reading Phase:

- **Isolated smart grid device:** At the beginning of a given long-term aggregation period, the isolated smart grid device selects $s \in_R Z_p$ and publishes $S = g^s$ and $S_t = g_t^s$. When the reader needs to collect the metering data m_i for the ith time instance during this period, the device randomly chooses $r_i \in Z_p$ and computes a ciphertext $CT_i = (c_{1i}, c_{2i}, c_{3i}) = (g^{r_i}, g_t^{r_i}, g_t^{m_i} W^{r_i})$. We assume that the reader reads the metering data n times during a single period. There is a limitation that $\sum_{i=1}^{n} m_i$ should not be an excessively large number. The device computes the signature as

$$\sigma_1 = d_{ID_{is}}^{1/(s+H_2(ID_{esp}))} \tag{6}$$

$$\sigma_{2i} = (c_{3i})^{1/(s+H_2(ID_{esp}))}. \tag{7}$$

Finally, it sends $\{CT_i, (\sigma_1, \sigma_{2i})\}$ to the reader.
- **Reader:** After receiving $\{CT_i, (\sigma_1, \sigma_{2i})\}$, the reader verifies the identity of the isolated smart grid device by checking that[3]

$$e(\sigma_1, S \cdot g^{H_2(ID_{esp})}) = e(H(ID_{is}), Y). \tag{8}$$

If the signature σ_1 is valid, then the reader stores $\{CT_i, (\sigma_1, \sigma_{2i})\}$.

(4) Aggregation Phase:

- **Reader:** At the end of a long period, such as one month, the reader must aggregate the total power usage data of the isolated smart grid device. We assume that the reader has read the smart grid device n times during this period, and thus, n ciphertext/signature pairs $\{CT_i, (\sigma_1, \sigma_{2i})\}_{i \in [1,n]}$ have been stored in the reader. The reader computes $CT = \prod_{i=1}^{n} CT_i = (\prod_{i=1}^{n} c_{1i}, \prod_{i=1}^{n} c_{2i}, \prod_{i=1}^{n} c_{3i}) = (C_1, C_2, C_3)$ and $\sigma_2 = \prod_{i=1}^{n} \sigma_{2i}$ and then reports $\{CT, (\sigma_1, \sigma_2)\}$ to the ESP.

---

[2] W is pre-computed by the ESP and will be stored in the isolated smart grid device, since the pairing operation is considered to be a very time-consuming cryptographic operation. Thus, no pairing operations are performed during the reading phase of the isolated smart grid device.

[3] This signature also involves the identity of ESP, which prevent the customer from paying for an improper ESP.

(5) Decryption and Verification Phase:

- **ESP:** When the ESP receives $\{CT, (\sigma_1, \sigma_2)\}$, it first verifies the identity of the isolated smart grid device by checking Eq. (3). Then, the ESP computes

$$\bar{M} = C_3 / e(d_{ID_{esp}}, C_1). \tag{9}$$

Since the long-term power usage data $M = \sum_{i=1}^{n} m_i$ is guaranteed not to be an excessively large number, the ESP can compute the discrete logarithm of $\bar{M}$ with base g_t to obtain M. Finally, the ESP verifies σ_2 by checking that

$$e_T(\sigma_2, S_t \cdot g_t^{H_2(ID_{esp})}) = e_T(g_t, g_t)^M \cdot e_T(W, C_2). \tag{10}$$

5 Security Analysis

Our identity-based meter report protocol is designed to prevent unauthorized parties from reading or maliciously altering data and to protect the private information of customers. In this section, we analyze the security properties of our protocol in the context of five typical attacks in a smart grid system, and use the Proverif tool to verify the formal security of our protocol.

5.1 Against Attacks from External Parties

To obtain unauthorized information, external attackers may eavesdrop on the communication channels between the reader and the isolated smart grid device or between the ESP and the reader. In our protocol, all metering data are encrypted by the identity of the ESP and can only be decrypted using its private key. The identity-based encryption scheme used in our protocol satisfies IND-ID-CPA security under the DBDH assumption. External attackers also cannot maliciously alter metering data from the isolated smart grid device because they cannot forge the appropriate signature. Our linearly homomorphic signature scheme is unforgeable under the q-SDH assumption and Boneh-Boyen signatures [14].

5.2 Against Attacks from the Isolated Smart Grid Device

If an isolated smart grid device is controlled by an attacker, it may be used to mimic other legitimate smart grid devices. In our protocol, we use linearly homomorphic signature technology to prevent a falsified smart grid device from performing reader-device and ESP-device authentication. The first component of the linearly homomorphic signature is used to authenticate the identity of the isolated smart grid device, and it is unforgeably secure under Boneh-Boyen signatures.

5.3   Against Compromise Attacks from the Reader

An attacker may use a lost legitimate reader to obtain unauthorized information or maliciously alter the long-term power usage data of a smart grid device; such an attack is called an internal attack from the reader. During the reading phase, such a legitimate reader can verify the signature of the device. However, the power usage data m_i cannot be recovered from the ciphertext $CT_i = g_t^{m_i} W^{r_i}$ because the reader cannot obtain the ESP's private key, $d_{ID_{esp}}$. During the aggregation phase, the reader also cannot decrypt CT to determine $\bar{M}$ and obtain the long-term power usage data because it does not require the private key for aggregating the linearly homomorphic signatures. Moreover, the linearly homomorphic signature (σ_1, σ_2) prevents the reader from altering the long-term power usage data. The unforgeability of our linearly homomorphic signature scheme is proven by Theorems 2 and 3. The properties of linearly homomorphic signatures also protect the correctness and integrity of the long-term power usage data.

5.4   Against Internal Attacks from the ESP

Suppose that some legitimate workers from the ESP make malicious attacks to analyze the private information of customers, such as their daily activity. After receiving the ciphertext/signature pair $\{CT, (\sigma_1, \sigma_2)\}$ from the reader, the ESP can compute $\bar{M} = C_3/e(d_{ID_{esp}}, C_1)$ to recover the long-term power usage data. However, the ESP cannot decrypt the individual metering data m_i from CT because it does not know each corresponding random number r_i.

5.5   Against Man-in-the-Middle Attacks

In reader-device and ESP-device authentication, the linearly homomorphic signature scheme is used to authenticate the device's identity and the ciphertexts. Thus, any man-in-the-middle attacker cannot mimic a legitimate device to fool the reader or the ESP. The first component of the linearly homomorphic signature scheme provides strong defense against man-in-the-middle attacks because an attacker cannot convince the reader or ESP to accept its identity.

5.6   Formal Security of Protocol

It is very difficult by trial to find vulnerabilities from the complex security protocol. Thus, we use the Proverif tool [16,17] to formally verify the security of our protocol. Obviously, the secrecy value mentioned for our protocol is the metering power usage data m. Furthermore, there are also authentication properties, and we declare the events as follows:

event acceptsISG(m,identity), which is used to record a fact that the isolated smart grid device considers it has accepted to run the protocol with the reader and ESP, with the metering data as the first argument and the ESP's identity as the second.

event termESP(m,identity), which means that the ESP believes it has terminate a protocol run.

event termReader(identity), which means that the reader believes it has terminate a protocol run.

Executing our protocol with Proverif produces the output as Fig. 2, which informs us that authentications of isolated smart grid device to reader and ESP holds, and the secrecy of meter data also holds. Both acknowledge the correctness and safety of our protocol.

```
promote:proverif1.96 wangzw$ ./proverif ID_meter_report_protocol_for_ISG.pv | gr
ep "RES"
RESULT event(termReader(y_55)) ==> event(acceptsISG(x_54,y_55)) is true.
RESULT event(termESP(x_370,y_371)) ==> event(acceptsISG(x_370,y_371)) is true.
RESULT not attacker(m[]) is true.
```

Fig. 2. Output of Proverif

6 Implementation and Performance Analysis

6.1 Communication Overhead

The communication cost of meter report protocol for isolated smart grid devices can be divided into two parts: (1) communications between isolated smart grid devices and readers; (2) communications between readers and ESPs. In our simulation, we choose MNT elliptic curve with order of 160 bits and embedded degree $k = 6$. Then, the elements in Z_p, G, and G_T are represented by 160, 161, and 960 bits under this curve. In our protocol, in reading phase, the isolated smart grid device sends the encrypted meter data and signature to the reader. The form of ciphertext and signature involves 3 elements in G and 2 elements in G_T. In aggregation phase, the reader sends encrypted total power usage data and signature to the ESP, which also includes 3 elements in G and 2 elements in G_T. Thus, the total communication cost of our protocol is 600 bytes. Table 1 presents a comparison of communication overheads between Jo et al.'s protocol [18] and our protocol, and Jo et al.'s protocol is also the only existing privacy-preserving protocol against collector(reader) compromise attacks. Table 1 shows that the communication overhead of Jo et al.'s protocol is much more heavy than our protocol, since they use Paillier homomorphic encryption algorithm (The module $N = 1024$ bits) for privacy-preserving. Unlike Jo et al.'s protocol [18], our protocol is designed for the isolated smart grid devices, and the communication overhead between readers and ESPs should be low. For most isolated smart grid devices, readers are usually installed temporarily, and the connections between ESPs and readers are often wireless connections.

We use ns 2 (version 2.34) to simulate end-end wireless communication delays. For isolated smart grid devices, there are usually both wireless connections that connects isolated smart grid devices and readers, and connects readers and ESPs.

Table 1. Comparison of communication loads

	Jo et al.	Our protocol
Isolated Smart Grid Device-Reader	1080 bytes	300 bytes
Reader-ESP	1344 bytes	300 bytes
Total	2424 bytes	600 bytes

Table 2 shows the simulation parameters. In our simulation, the link distance from the isolated smart grid device to the reader is assumed to 25 m, and the distance from the reader and the ESP is assumed to 50 to 100 miles. The result shows that the communication delay on link of the isolated smart grid device to the reader is negligible, and the average communication delay between the reader and ESP is 6.23 to 7.79 s. We cannot ignore the communication delay of between the reader and the ESP. As previously analyzed, the communication overhead is low in our protocol, and the reader only need to send the total power usage data once at the end of the billing period. Thus, our protocol is more feasible for isolated smart grid devices than the protocol of [18].

Table 2. Parameters for the communication simulation

Simulation parameter	Value
Number of nodes	3
Message size (bytes)	300, 300
Mac protocol	802.11p
Route protocol	DSDV
Simulation Time(s)	150

6.2 Computational Cost

We implemented our protocol on two different platforms. The first one is a MacBook Pro with an Intel Core i5 CPU (2.5 GHz) with 4 GB of RAM running OS X 10.9.3. The second one is an Intel Edison development platform with a dual-core, dual-threaded Intel Atom CPU (500 MHz) with 1 GB of RAM running Yocto Linux v1.6. The Intel Edison development platform is considered a good choice for rapidly prototyping and producing Internet of Things (IoT) devices. In a smart grid network, many devices are resource-constrained, and the Intel Edison development platform can ideally simulate such smart grid devices. We implemented our protocol in C using the Pairing-Based Cryptography (PBC) library [15], which provides implementations of the basic arithmetic and pairing operations.

Table 3 shows the time costs during the reading phase for the isolated smart grid device and the reader device. The time cost for the isolated smart grid device is only approximately 0.42 s when our protocol is run on the Edison platform. The reader device requires 0.39 s for signature verification on the Edison platform. The values in Table 3 are the average values over 100 randomized runs. Figure 3 shows the time costs of the reader device (on the two different platforms) during the aggregation phase, where the time consumption increases with an increasing number of ciphertext/signature pairs to be aggregated. From Table 3 and Fig. 3, we can see that the reading phase and aggregation phase of our protocol are very efficient for resource-constrained smart grid devices. Table 4 shows the time cost of decryption for the ESP, which is approximately 0.42 s on the MacBook.

Table 3. Time costs during the reading phase

Platform	MacBook	Intel Edison
Isolated Smart Grid Device	0.0196 s	0.42 s
Reader Device	0.015 s	0.39 s

Table 4. Time cost during the decryption and verification phase

Platform	MacBook	Intel Edison
Decryption and Verification	0.42 s	9 s

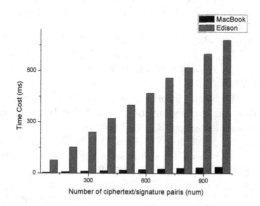

Fig. 3. Time cost of the reader during the aggregation phase

7   Conclusion

Privacy preservation and un-trusted reader are two important issues in the metering report of isolated smart grid device. Thus, in order to protect users' privacy information and against the un-trusted reader, we design an ID-based linear homomorphic cryptosystem based metering data protocol for the isolated smart grid devices. We give security analysis to our protocol in context of five typical attacks in smart grid. Finally, the implementation of our protocol on the Edison platform shows that our protocol is efficient enough for the resource-constrained devices.

Acknowledgment. This research is partially supported by the National Natural Science Foundation of China under Grant No. 61672016, the Jiangsu Qing Lan Project, the Humanities and Social Science Research Planning Fund of the Education Ministry of China under grant No. 15YJCZH201, Guangxi Key Laboratory of Cryptography and Information Security (No. GCIS201815).

References

1. Johnson, R., Molnar, D., Song, D., Wagner, D.: Homomorphic signature schemes. In: Preneel, B. (ed.) CT-RSA 2002. LNCS, vol. 2271, pp. 244–262. Springer, Heidelberg (2002). https://doi.org/10.1007/3-540-45760-7_17
2. Niyato, D., Xiao, L., Wang, P.: Machine-to-machine communications for home energy management system in smart grid. IEEE Comm. Mag. **49**(4), 53–59 (2011)
3. Fadlullah, Z.M., Fouda, M.M., Kato, N., Takeuchi, A., Iwasaki, N., Nozaki, Y.: Toward intelligent machine-to-machine communications in smart grid. IEEE Comm. Mag. **49**(4), 60–65 (2011)
4. Liang, H., Choi, B., Zhuang, W., Shen, X.: Towards optimal energy store-carry-and-deliver for PHEVs via V2G system. In: Proceedings of IEEE INFOCOM 2012, pp. 25–30, March 2012
5. Garcia, F.D., Jacobs, B.: Privacy-friendly energy-metering via homomorphic encryption. In: Cuellar, J., Lopez, J., Barthe, G., Pretschner, A. (eds.) STM 2010. LNCS, vol. 6710, pp. 226–238. Springer, Heidelberg (2011). https://doi.org/10.1007/978-3-642-22444-7_15
6. Li, F., Luo, B., Liu, P.: Secure information aggregation for smart grids using homomorphic encryption. In: Proceedings of the 1st IEEE International Conference on Smart Grid Communication, pp. 327–332 (2010)
7. Lu, R., Liang, X., Li, X., Lin, X., Shen, X.: EPPA: an efficient and privacy-preserving aggregation scheme for secure smart grid communications. IEEE Trans. Parallel Distrib. Syst. **23**(9), 1621–1631 (2012)
8. Fan, C.-I., Huang, S.-Y., Lai, Y.-L.: Privacy-enhanced data aggregation scheme against internal attackers in smart grid. IEEE Trans. Ind. Inform. **10**(1), 666–675 (2014)
9. Shamir, A.: Identity-based cryptosystems and signature schemes. In: Blakley, G.R., Chaum, D. (eds.) CRYPTO 1984. LNCS, vol. 196, pp. 47–53. Springer, Heidelberg (1985). https://doi.org/10.1007/3-540-39568-7_5
10. Boneh, D., Franklin, M.: Identity-based encryption from the Weil pairing. In: Kilian, J. (ed.) CRYPTO 2001. LNCS, vol. 2139, pp. 213–229. Springer, Heidelberg (2001). https://doi.org/10.1007/3-540-44647-8_13

11. Günther, F., Manulis, M., Peter, A.: Privacy-enhanced participatory sensing with collusion resistance and data aggregation. In: Gritzalis, D., Kiayias, A., Askoxylakis, I. (eds.) CANS 2014. LNCS, vol. 8813, pp. 321–336. Springer, Cham (2014). https://doi.org/10.1007/978-3-319-12280-9_21

12. Freeman, D.M.: Improved security for linearly homomorphic signatures: a generic framework. In: Fischlin, M., Buchmann, J., Manulis, M. (eds.) PKC 2012. LNCS, vol. 7293, pp. 697–714. Springer, Heidelberg (2012). https://doi.org/10.1007/978-3-642-30057-8_41

13. Wang, Z., Sun, G., Chen, D.: A new definition of homomorphic signature for identity management in mobile cloud computing. J. Comput. Syst. Sci. **80**(3), 546–553 (2014)

14. Boneh, D., Boyen, X.: Short signatures without random oracles and the SDH assumption in bilinear groups. J. Cryptol. **21**, 149–177 (2008). Extended abstract in Advances in Cryptology EUROCRYPT 2004

15. Lynn, B.: The pairing-based cryptography (PBC) library. http://crypto.stanford.edu/pbc

16. Blanchet, B.: Automatic verification of security protocols in the symbolic model: the verifier ProVerif. In: Aldini, A., Lopez, J., Martinelli, F. (eds.) FOSAD VII. LNCS, vol. 8604, pp. 54–87. Springer, Cham (2014). https://doi.org/10.1007/978-3-319-10082-1_3

17. Cheval, V., Blanchet, B.: Proving more observational equivalences with ProVerif. In: Basin, D., Mitchell, J.C. (eds.) POST 2013. LNCS, vol. 7796, pp. 226–246. Springer, Heidelberg (2013). https://doi.org/10.1007/978-3-642-36830-1_12

18. Jo, H.J., Kim, S., Lee, D.H.: Efficient and privacy-preserving metering protocols for smart grid systems. IEEE Trans. Smart Grid **7**(3), 1732–1742 (2016)

19. Wang, Z., Xie, H.: Privacy-preserving meter report protocol of isolated smart grid devices. Wirel. Commun. Mob. Comput. **2017**, 8 (2017)

Implicit-Key Attack on the RSA Cryptosystem

Mengce Zheng$^{(\boxtimes)}$ and Honggang Hu

Key Laboratory of Electromagnetic Space Information, CAS,
University of Science and Technology of China, Hefei, China
{mczheng,hghu2005}@ustc.edu.cn

Abstract. In this paper, we address the security evaluation issue of the RSA cryptosystem with implicitly related private keys. We formulate the attack scenario and propose a novel implicit-key attack using the lattice-based method. When given public information (N_1, e_1), (N_2, e_2) and the amount of shared bits of the private keys d_1 and d_2, one can conduct the implicit-key attack to factor N_1, N_2 in polynomial time under a certain condition. We show that the RSA cryptosystem is more insecure when taking the implicitly related keys into consideration. The experimental results are provided to verify the validity of our proposed attack.

Keywords: RSA cryptosystem · Cryptanalysis · Implicit-key attack · Lattice · Coppersmith's techniques

1 Introduction

The RSA cryptosystem [14] is the most attractive one in public key cryptography and plays an important role in the field of cybersecurity. The main mathematical equation is $ed \equiv 1 \bmod \varphi(N)$, where e, d, N and $\varphi(N)$ are described as follows. $N = pq$ is the product of two large primes of the same bit-size. The respective public and private keys e, d are also called public/encryption and private/decryption exponents. $\varphi(N) = (p-1)(q-1)$ is Euler's totient function of N. To encrypt an integer m, one computes $c = m^e \bmod N$. To decrypt a ciphertext c, one needs to compute $c^d \bmod N$.

The security of the RSA cryptosystem has been investigated in [1,12]. Since Coppersmith [4] introduced the lattice-based method, its variations have been widely used for attacking the RSA cryptosystem such as [2,5–7,10,16]. Among the various attacks, the partial key exposure attack and the implicit factoring problem are two attractive ones.

In 2005, Ernst et al. [7] presented several concrete attacks that work up to full size exponents. This attack type was first studied by Boneh, Durfee, and Frankel in [3]. In other words, partial key exposure attack can be seemed as the problem of attacking RSA with an oracle providing explicit information about d. In 2009, May and Ritzenhofen [13] proposed a new approach to factor RSA modulus with an oracle providing implicit information about p. To be specific,

© Springer Nature Switzerland AG 2019
F. Liu et al. (Eds.): SciSec 2019, LNCS 11933, pp. 354–362, 2019.
https://doi.org/10.1007/978-3-030-34637-9_26

for RSA moduli $N_1 = p_1 q_1$ and $N_2 = p_2 q_2$ with α-bit q_i and p_1, p_2 share at least t many least significant bits (LSBs), it has been proved that if $t > 2(\alpha + 2)$, one can find q_1 and q_2. Thus, N_1 and N_2 can be factored easily. Other cases such as shared most significant bits (MSBs), shared middle bits [8] and some improved methods [15] were proposed afterwards.

Inspired by the partial key exposure attack and the implicit factoring problem with existing drawbacks, we concentrate on a weaker setting, where some implicit information about the private keys is given. We informally formulate the following scenario related to the implicit-key attack. Let (N_1, e_1, d_1) and (N_2, e_2, d_2) be two different RSA key pairs with N_1, N_2 of the same bit-size. Suppose we know some implicit information about the private keys, i.e. the amount of shared MSBs and LSBs of d_1 and d_2. The goal is to factor N_1 and N_2 in polynomial time from the knowledge of the implicitly related private keys.

It is opposed to the previous cryptanalyses dealing with only one RSA key pair. Our work can cover other similar works and make further improvements. Once RSA instances are generated with imperfect randomness or backdoored keys, one may encounter such attack scenario. Though such implicit-key attack may not directly influence the security of the RSA cryptosystem. We consider the following issues for which our theoretical study may be interesting. One is to deeply disclose the vulnerability of RSA with weaker conditions. Moreover, we want to investigate how one can further extend previous attacks, where partial key exposure and implicit hint are combined.

We adapt the Jochemsz-May strategy [10] as a main mathematical tool to solve the common root of multivariate equations. To achieve theoretical effects, the lattice-based method relies on the following heuristic assumption. One can obtain algebraically independent polynomials by the lattice-based method, and then efficiently solve the common root by the Gröbner basis computation. This heuristic assumption always holds in the simulated experiments like previous works in the literature. We want to point out that the theoretical results stated below are asymptotic since we require the dimension of the corresponding lattice to be preferably large.

The rest of the paper is organized as follows. We provide the basic knowledge of lattice reduction theory and the condition for finding the common root in Sect. 2. In Sect. 3, we formulate the concrete attack scenario and present the implicit-key attack. In Sect. 4, we provide the experimental results with more details. Finally, concluding remarks are given in Sect. 5.

2   Preliminaries

In this section, we briefly introduce the LLL algorithm [11] and Coppersmith's techniques (also stated as Howgrave-Graham's lemma [9]). Then, we provide the condition for finding the common root and simply mention the running time. One can refer to [12] for more details about the lattice-based method.

A lattice $\mathcal{L}$ spanned by linearly independent vectors $\boldsymbol{b}_1, \ldots, \boldsymbol{b}_m \in \mathbb{R}^n$ is the set of all their integer linear combinations. Thus, the lattice $\mathcal{L}$ can be written as $\mathcal{L}(\boldsymbol{b}_1, \ldots, \boldsymbol{b}_m) = \{\sum_{i=1}^{m} z_i \boldsymbol{b}_i | z_i \in \mathbb{Z}\}$. For $i = 1, \ldots, m$, we regard each basis vector $\boldsymbol{b}_i$ as a row vector, which generates so-called $m \times n$ basis matrix B. The determinant of $\mathcal{L}$ is calculated as $\det(\mathcal{L}) = \sqrt{\det(BB^T)}$. We usually consider a full-rank lattice for $m = n$ and hence $\det(\mathcal{L}) = |\det(B)|$.

The LLL algorithm proposed by Lenstra, Lenstra, and Lovász [11] is practically used for finding approximately non-zero short lattice vectors due to its efficient running results. We provide the following substratal lemma about its outputs.

Lemma 1. *Let $\mathcal{L}$ be a lattice spanned by a basis $(\boldsymbol{b}_1, \boldsymbol{b}_2, \ldots, \boldsymbol{b}_m)$. The LLL algorithm outputs a reduced basis $(\boldsymbol{v}_1, \boldsymbol{v}_2, \ldots, \boldsymbol{v}_m)$ in polynomial time. For $1 \leq i \leq m$, the first i many reduced basis vectors satisfy*

$$\|\boldsymbol{v}_1\|, \|\boldsymbol{v}_2\|, \ldots, \|\boldsymbol{v}_i\| \leq 2^{\frac{m(m-1)}{4(m+1-i)}} \det(\mathcal{L})^{\frac{1}{m+1-i}}.$$

The following lemma presented by Howgrave-Graham [9] gives a criterion for judging whether the desired small root of a modular equation is also a root over $\mathbb{Z}$. To a given polynomial $g(x_1, \ldots, x_n) = \sum a_{i_1, \ldots, i_n} x_1^{i_1} \cdots x_n^{i_n}$, its norm is defined as $\|g(x_1, \ldots, x_n)\|^2 := \sum |a_{i_1, \ldots, i_n}|^2$.

Lemma 2. *Let $g(x_1, \ldots, x_n) \in \mathbb{Z}[x_1, \ldots, x_n]$ be an n-variate integer polynomial, which is a sum of at most m monomials. Suppose that (1) $g(\tilde{x}_1, \ldots, \tilde{x}_n) \equiv 0 \bmod R$, where $|\tilde{x}_1| < X_1, \ldots, |\tilde{x}_n| < X_n$, and (2) $\|g(x_1 X_1, \ldots, x_n X_n)\| < R/\sqrt{m}$. Then $g(\tilde{x}_1, \ldots, \tilde{x}_n) = 0$ holds over the integers.*

Applying the lattice-based method, we can combine Lemma 1 with Lemma 2 to solve modular/integer polynomials. Once having the first l reduced vectors, one can solve the unknown variables for $2^{\frac{m(m-1)}{4(m+1-l)}} \det(\mathcal{L})^{\frac{1}{m+1-l}} < R/\sqrt{m}$, which can be further reduced to $\det(\mathcal{L}) \leq R^{m-\epsilon}$ with an error term ϵ, or a simplified condition $\det(\mathcal{L}) < R^m$. We can construct an upper/lower triangular basis matrix by the lattice-based method. The lattice determinant can be calculated as $\det(\mathcal{L}) = R^{u_R} \prod_{i=1}^{n} X_i^{u_i}$, where u_i denotes the exponent sum of each X_i or R that appear on the diagonal in the corresponding basis matrix. Hence, the condition $\det(\mathcal{L}) < R^m$ can be rewritten as $R^{u_R} \prod_{i=1}^{n} X_i^{u_i} < R^m$.

We sketch the lattice-based method and derive the crucial condition for finding small roots of integer polynomials. Lattice-based attacks using Coppersmith's techniques start with an integer/modular equation in some unknown parameters of given RSA instances. To carry out the proposed implicit-key attack, we aim to find a suitable root of a five-variate integer polynomial $f(x_1, x_2, x_3, x_4, x_5)$.

First, we need to estimate the upper bounds X_i as mentioned in Lemma 2. Moreover, we define the largest size of an individual term in $f(x_1, x_2, x_3, x_4, x_5)$ as $X_\infty = \|f(x_1 X_1, x_2 X_2, x_3 X_3, x_4 X_4, x_5 X_5)\|_\infty$ that is related to the definition of a sufficient large modulus R. Then, a lattice basis matrix is constructed using the shift polynomials defined in two monomial sets S and T. Based on the Jochemsz-May strategy, the solvable condition reduces to $X_1^{s_1} X_2^{s_2} X_3^{s_3} X_4^{s_4} X_5^{s_5} < X_\infty^{s_g}$ for $s_j = \sum_{T \setminus S} i_j$ and $s_g = |S|$ in our proposed implicit-key attack. More details about the concrete lattice construction for a given specific polynomial will be described in Sect. 3.

Under the above condition, we can compute the first l reduced basis vectors using the LLL algorithm and then obtain the equations $f_1, \ldots, f_l$ that all share the same root over the integers. Next, we use the Gröbner basis computation to extract the common root. The running time depends on the time of reducing the basis matrix and extracting the common root. For conducting the implicit-key attack on concrete RSA instances, both of them can be done in polynomial time.

3 Implicit-Key Attack

We describe the implicit-key attack by providing the concrete construction for two RSA instances (N_1, e_1, d_1) and (N_2, e_2, d_2). Consider a general case when e_1, e_2 are of arbitrary bit-size and d_1, d_2 share some MSBs and LSBs leaving one different block in the middle. Unless otherwise noted, N in this paper denotes the greater one of N_1, N_2 and $\log_2 N$ denotes their bit-size (suppose two RSA moduli are of the same bit-size). Our main result is stated as follows.

Theorem 1. *Let $N_1 = p_1 q_1, N_2 = p_2 q_2$ be two different RSA moduli of the same bit-size, and p_1, q_1, p_2, q_2 be primes of the same bit-size. Let e_1, d_1, e_2, d_2 satisfy $e_1 d_1 \equiv 1 \bmod \varphi(N_1)$ and $e_2 d_2 \equiv 1 \bmod \varphi(N_2)$, such that $e_1 = N^{\alpha_1}, e_2 = N^{\alpha_2}$ and $d_1, d_2 \approx N^\delta$. Suppose that d_1 and d_2 share $\beta_1 \log_2 N$ MSBs and $\beta_2 \log_2 N$ LSBs. Then N_1, N_2 can be factored in polynomial time if*

$$\delta < \frac{(\alpha + \beta - 1)(1 + 10\tau + 20\tau^2) - 10\tau^2 - 30\tau^3}{4 + 30\tau + 40\tau^2} - \frac{\alpha}{2} + 1,$$

where $\alpha = \alpha_1 + \alpha_2$, $\beta = \beta_1 + \beta_2$ and τ is the only positive root of

$$120x^4 + 180x^3 + (86 - 20\alpha - 20\beta)x^2 + (16 - 8\alpha - 8\beta)x - \alpha - \beta + 1 = 0.$$

Proof. From the main equation of the RSA cryptosystem, namely $ed \equiv 1 \bmod \varphi(N)$, we have $e_1 d_1 = k_1(N_1 + 1 - p_1 - q_1) + 1$ and $e_2 d_2 = k_2(N_2 + 1 - p_2 - q_2) + 1$ for two unknown positive integers k_1 and k_2. Multiplying the above equations by e_2 and e_1 respectively and then subtracting, we have

$$e_1 e_2(d_1 - d_2) = e_2 k_1(N_1 + 1 - p_1 - q_1) + e_2 - e_1 k_2(N_2 + 1 - p_2 - q_2) - e_1. \quad (1)$$

Consider we know $d_1, d_2 \approx N^\delta$ sharing $\beta_1 \log_2 N$ MSBs and $\beta_2 \log_2 N$ LSBs. Hence, it implies that $d_1 = d_{\mathrm{MSB}} 2^{(\delta - \beta_1) \log_2 N} + \bar{d}_1 2^{\beta_2 \log_2 N} + d_{\mathrm{LSB}}$ and $d_2 = d_{\mathrm{MSB}} 2^{(\delta - \beta_1) \log_2 N} + \bar{d}_2 2^{\beta_2 \log_2 N} + d_{\mathrm{LSB}}$, where d_{MSB} and d_{LSB} are shared MSBs and LSBs, $\bar{d}_1$ and $\bar{d}_2$ are different values in the middle block. Substituting d_1 and d_2 into (1), it can be rewritten as

$$e_1 e_2(\bar{d}_2 - \bar{d}_1) N^{\beta_2} + e_2 k_1(N_1 + 1 - p_1 - q_1) - e_1 k_2(N_2 + 1 - p_2 - q_2) + e_2 - e_1 = 0.$$

The known values are $a_1 = e_1 e_2 N^{\beta_2}$, $a_2 = e_2(N_1 + 1)$, $a_3 = -e_1(N_2 + 1)$, $a_4 = -e_2$, $a_5 = e_1$, and $a_6 = e_2 - e_1$. The unknown variables are $x_1 = \bar{d}_2 - \bar{d}_1$, $x_2 = k_1$, $x_3 = k_2$, $x_4 = p_1 + q_1$, and $x_5 = p_2 + q_2$. We aim to find a suitable root of $f(x_1, x_2, x_3, x_4, x_5) := a_1 x_1 + a_2 x_2 + a_3 x_3 + a_4 x_2 x_4 + a_5 x_3 x_5 + a_6$.

If e_1 and e_2 have a nontrivial great common divisor, one can do the division to make the polynomial irreducible. Suppose we know $e_1 = N^{\alpha_1}$ and $e_2 = N^{\alpha_2}$. The upper bounds X_i are estimated as follows. $X_1 = N^{\delta-\beta}$ for $\beta = \beta_1 + \beta_2$, $X_2 = N^{\alpha_1+\delta-1}$, $X_3 = N^{\alpha_2+\delta-1}$, and $X_4 = X_5 = N^{1/2}$. The maximal coefficient X_∞ can be easily calculated as $X_\infty \approx N^{\alpha+\delta}$ for $\alpha = \alpha_1 + \alpha_2$.

We follow the Jochemsz-May strategy [10] and use extra shifts of x_4 and x_5 for solving $f(x_1, x_2, x_3, x_4, x_5)$. Define two monomial sets S and T for two integers $s \geq 1$ and $t \geq 0$.

$$S = \bigcup_{0 \leq j_4, j_5 \leq t} \left\{ x_1^{i_1} x_2^{i_2} x_3^{i_3} x_4^{i_4+j_4} x_5^{i_5+j_5} \,\middle|\, x_1^{i_1} x_2^{i_2} x_3^{i_3} x_4^{i_4} x_5^{i_5} \text{ is a monomial of } f^{s-1} \right\},$$

$$T = \bigcup_{0 \leq j_4, j_5 \leq t} \left\{ x_1^{i_1} x_2^{i_2} x_3^{i_3} x_4^{i_4+j_4} x_5^{i_5+j_5} \,\middle|\, x_1^{i_1} x_2^{i_2} x_3^{i_3} x_4^{i_4} x_5^{i_5} \text{ is a monomial of } f^s \right\}.$$

Through the expansion of f^{s-1} and f^s, we know the relation of $x_1^{i_1} x_2^{i_2} x_3^{i_3} x_4^{i_4} x_5^{i_5}$ in S and T to their exponents i_1, i_2, i_3, i_4, i_5, respectively.

Let $R = X_\infty X_1^{s-1} X_2^{s-1} X_3^{s-1} X_4^{s-1+t} X_5^{s-1+t}$, we define $f' = a_6^{-1} f \bmod R$ and the shift polynomials below,

$$g_{i_1,i_2,i_3,i_4,i_5} : x_1^{i_1} x_2^{i_2} x_3^{i_3} x_4^{i_4} x_5^{i_5} f' X_1^{s-1-i_1} X_2^{s-1-i_2} X_3^{s-1-i_3} X_4^{s-1+t-i_4} X_5^{s-1+t-i_5},$$
$$\text{for } x_1^{i_1} x_2^{i_2} x_3^{i_3} x_4^{i_4} x_5^{i_5} \in S,$$

$$g'_{i_1,i_2,i_3,i_4,i_5} : x_1^{i_1} x_2^{i_2} x_3^{i_3} x_4^{i_4} x_5^{i_5} R,$$
$$\text{for } x_1^{i_1} x_2^{i_2} x_3^{i_3} x_4^{i_4} x_5^{i_5} \in T \backslash S.$$

The lattice $\mathcal{L}$ is constructed by the coefficient vectors of g_{i_1,i_2,i_3,i_4,i_5} and g'_{i_1,i_2,i_3,i_4,i_5} with $x_i X_i$ substituting for each x_i. We have $u_R = |T \backslash S|$, $u_j = \sum_T i_j$ and $m = |T|$. More precisely, the diagonal elements of g_{i_1,i_2,i_3,i_4,i_5} is equal to R/X_∞ and $u_j = \sum_S i_j + \sum_{T \backslash S} i_j$. So $R^{u_R} \prod_{i=1}^5 X_i^{u_i} < R^m$ implies $R^{u_R}(R/X_\infty)^{s_g} \prod_{i=1}^5 X_i^{s_i} < R^{u_R+s_g}$ for $s_j = \sum_{T \backslash S} i_j$ and $s_g = |S|$, which can be reduced to

$$X_1^{s_1} X_2^{s_2} X_3^{s_3} X_4^{s_4} X_5^{s_5} < X_\infty^{s_g}. \tag{2}$$

We now calculate s_j for $j = 1, \ldots, 5$ and s_g by above definitions. Taking $t = \tau s$ for $\tau \geq 0$ and omitting the lower term for simplicity, we obtain

$$s_g = s_1 = \frac{1}{120}(1 + 10\tau + 20\tau^2)s^5, \quad s_2 = s_3 = \frac{1}{120}(2 + 15\tau + 20\tau^2)s^5,$$

$$s_4 = s_5 = \frac{1}{120}(1 + 10\tau + 30\tau^2 + 30\tau^3)s^5.$$

We substitute the values of X_j, s_j and X_∞, s_g into the condition (2) and obtain $1 + 10\tau + 30\tau^2 + 30\tau^3 + (1 + 10\tau + 20\tau^2)(\delta - \beta) + (2 + 15\tau + 20\tau^2)(\alpha + 2\delta - 2) < (1 + 10\tau + 20\tau^2)(\alpha + \delta)$. It leads to

$$\delta < \frac{(\alpha + \beta - 1)(1 + 10\tau + 20\tau^2) - 10\tau^2 - 30\tau^3}{4 + 30\tau + 40\tau^2} - \frac{\alpha}{2} + 1.$$

As α and β are already given, the value of the right side can be maximized by an optimal value of τ. It is easy to see that τ is the only positive root of

$$120x^4 + 180x^3 + (86 - 20\alpha - 20\beta)x^2 + (16 - 8\alpha - 8\beta)x - \alpha - \beta + 1 = 0.$$

We can obtain four integer polynomials f_1, f_2, f_3 and f_4 apart from f by the proposed implicit-key attack. Moreover, f, f_1, f_2, f_3 and f_4 share the common root $(\bar{d}_2 - \bar{d}_1, k_1, k_2, p_1 + q_1, p_2 + q_2)$ over the integers. Thus, we can extract $p_1 + q_1$ and $p_2 + q_2$ that directly lead to the factorization of N_1 and N_2. $\square$

If e_1 and e_2 are of full bit-size, i.e. $\alpha = 2$, we immediately know τ is the only positive root of $120x^4 + 180x^3 + (46 - 20\beta)x^2 - 8\beta x - \beta - 1 = 0$. Therefore, we show that N_1, N_2 can be factored in polynomial time for $\beta = \beta_1 + \beta_2$ if

$$\delta < \frac{(\beta + 1)(1 + 10\tau + 20\tau^2) - 10\tau^2 - 30\tau^3}{4 + 30\tau + 40\tau^2}. \tag{3}$$

We illustrate the above condition (3) with respect to various β's in Fig. 1. It is oblivious that we achieve higher insecure bound on δ as β increases, which means that the RSA cryptosystem with implicitly related keys is more vulnerable.

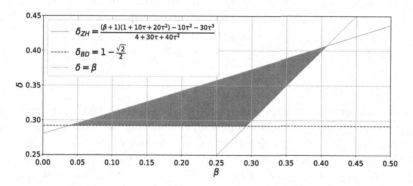

Fig. 1. The comparison of previous result (i.e. $\delta < \delta_{BD}$) and ours (i.e. $\delta < \delta_{ZH}$). The gray region shows our asymptotic improvement using the proposed implicit-key attack.

4   Experimental Results

To achieve the asymptotic bound on δ, the parameter $\tau = t/s$ should be less than 0.2 from our theoretical observation. For the smallest positive integer $t = 1$, s should be at least 6. Therefore, the dimension of the corresponding lattice will be $m = 966$, which seems impossible for our simulated experimental environment. Thus, we always choose $t = 0$ (i.e. $\tau = 0$) in the simulated numerical experiments.

The experiments were carried out by `SageMath` under Windows 10 running on a laptop with Intel Core i7-8550U CPU 1.80 GHz. The numbers for generating the parameters of two RSA instances were chosen at random. During the experiments, we collected much more polynomials satisfying our requirement and extracted the common root by the Gröbner basis computation.

We would generate 1024-bit moduli in the experiments and all the public exponents appeared are near full bit-size for simplicity. The δ_t-column provides the theoretical bound on δ for fixed β_1 and β_2 (with $\tau = 0$). The δ_e-column provides the experimental bound on δ for the same β_1, β_2 and $\log_2 N = 1024$ in distinct lattice settings. We denote the dimension of the corresponding lattice by m and the running time of the proposed attack is denoted by Time in seconds.

For given two distinct 1024-bit moduli and d_1, d_2 sharing some MSBs and LSBs, we choose $s = 1, 2, 3$ and $t = 0$ to construct the lattices. Hence, we need to reduce 6-dimensional, 21-dimensional and 56-dimensional lattices using the LLL algorithm. The results of the comparison of the theoretical and experimental insecure bounds are showed in Table 1.

Table 1. The theoretical and experimental results of the proposed implicit-key attack

$\log_2 N = 1024$			$s = 1,\ m = 6$		$s = 2,\ m = 21$		$s = 3,\ m = 56$	
β_1	β_2	δ_t	δ_e	Time	δ_e	Time	δ_e	Time
0.043	0.043	0.271	0.259	0.004	0.264	0.623	0.270	47.59
0.064	0.101	0.291	0.280	0.004	0.286	0.621	0.291	47.17
0.107	0.142	0.312	0.300	0.004	0.307	0.682	0.311	37.23
0.150	0.150	0.325	0.315	0.005	0.321	0.522	0.325	32.02

In each experiment, we collected sufficient polynomials sharing the common root over the integers. Then we put several equations into the Gröbner basis computation and finally obtained the correct values of $p_1 + q_1$ and $p_2 + q_2$, which lead to the factorization of N_1 and N_2, respectively. If the Gröbner basis computation did not directly output the desired root, we would first calculate the value of x_3 and then extract the solution of the remaining variables. As the lattice dimension gets larger, the experimental insecure bound becomes higher and the running time gets longer. From Table 1, we observe that $s = 3$ is already enough for performing the implicit-key attack since the experimental result is very close to the theoretical bound.

5   Concluding Remarks

In this paper, we focus on a new attack scenario concerning implicitly related private keys. Our goal is to factor RSA moduli using the implicit information about the related keys. We propose the implicit-key attack based on Coppersmith's techniques, which is applied for solving modular/integer polynomials as a powerful tool.

The proposed implicit-key attack can reveal the vulnerability of the RSA cryptosystem with implicitly related keys. We further verify the validity of the proposed attack by several numerical experiments. We would like to extend the implicit-key attack for an arbitrary number n of unknown variables. However, it seems less efficient as n gets greater since the running time is exponential in n.

Acknowledgments. The authors would like to thank the anonymous reviewers for their valuable comments and suggestions. This work was partially supported by the National Natural Science Foundation of China (Grant No. 61632013) and Anhui Initiative in Quantum Information Technologies under Grant AHY150400.

References

1. Boneh, D.: Twenty years of attacks on the RSA cryptosystem. Not. AMS **46**(2), 203–213 (1999)
2. Boneh, D., Durfee, G.: Cryptanalysis of RSA with private key d less than $N^{0.292}$. IEEE Trans. Inf. Theory **46**(4), 1339–1349 (2000)
3. Boneh, D., Durfee, G., Frankel, Y.: An attack on RSA given a small fraction of the private key bits. In: Ohta, K., Pei, D. (eds.) ASIACRYPT 1998. LNCS, vol. 1514, pp. 25–34. Springer, Heidelberg (1998). https://doi.org/10.1007/3-540-49649-1_3
4. Coppersmith, D.: Small solutions to polynomial equations, and low exponent RSA vulnerabilities. J. Cryptol. **10**(4), 233–260 (1997)
5. Coron, J.-S.: Finding small roots of bivariate integer polynomial equations revisited. In: Cachin, C., Camenisch, J.L. (eds.) EUROCRYPT 2004. LNCS, vol. 3027, pp. 492–505. Springer, Heidelberg (2004). https://doi.org/10.1007/978-3-540-24676-3_29
6. Coron, J.-S.: Finding small roots of bivariate integer polynomial equations: a direct approach. In: Menezes, A. (ed.) CRYPTO 2007. LNCS, vol. 4622, pp. 379–394. Springer, Heidelberg (2007). https://doi.org/10.1007/978-3-540-74143-5_21
7. Ernst, M., Jochemsz, E., May, A., de Weger, B.: Partial key exposure attacks on RSA up to full size exponents. In: Cramer, R. (ed.) EUROCRYPT 2005. LNCS, vol. 3494, pp. 371–386. Springer, Heidelberg (2005). https://doi.org/10.1007/11426639_22
8. Faugère, J.-C., Marinier, R., Renault, G.: Implicit factoring with shared most significant and middle bits. In: Nguyen, P.Q., Pointcheval, D. (eds.) PKC 2010. LNCS, vol. 6056, pp. 70–87. Springer, Heidelberg (2010). https://doi.org/10.1007/978-3-642-13013-7_5
9. Howgrave-Graham, N.: Finding small roots of univariate modular equations revisited. In: Darnell, M. (ed.) Cryptography and Coding 1997. LNCS, vol. 1355, pp. 131–142. Springer, Heidelberg (1997). https://doi.org/10.1007/BFb0024458
10. Jochemsz, E., May, A.: A strategy for finding roots of multivariate polynomials with new applications in attacking RSA variants. In: Lai, X., Chen, K. (eds.) ASIACRYPT 2006. LNCS, vol. 4284, pp. 267–282. Springer, Heidelberg (2006). https://doi.org/10.1007/11935230_18
11. Lenstra, A.K., Lenstra, H.W., Lovász, L.: Factoring polynomials with rational coefficients. Math. Ann. **261**(4), 515–534 (1982)
12. May, A.: Using LLL-reduction for solving RSA and factorization problems. In: Nguyen, P.Q., Vallée, B. (eds.) The LLL Algorithm, pp. 315–348. Springer, Heidelberg (2010). https://doi.org/10.1007/978-3-642-02295-1_10

13. May, A., Ritzenhofen, M.: Implicit factoring: on polynomial time factoring given only an implicit hint. In: Jarecki, S., Tsudik, G. (eds.) PKC 2009. LNCS, vol. 5443, pp. 1–14. Springer, Heidelberg (2009). https://doi.org/10.1007/978-3-642-00468-1_1

14. Rivest, R.L., Shamir, A., Adleman, L.: A method for obtaining digital signatures and public-key cryptosystems. Commun. ACM **21**(2), 120–126 (1978)

15. Sarkar, S., Maitra, S.: Approximate integer common divisor problem relates to implicit factorization. IEEE Trans. Inf. Theory **57**(6), 4002–4013 (2011)

16. Zheng, M., Hu, H., Wang, Z.: Generalized cryptanalysis of RSA with small public exponent. Sci. China Inf. Sci. **59**, 032108:1–032108:10 (2016)

High-Efficiency Triangle Counting
on the GPU

Yang Wu[1], Shikang Yu[1], Yurong Song[2,3(✉)], Guoping Jiang[2,3], and Xiao Tu[1]

[1] School of Computer Science, Nanjing University of Posts and Telecommunications,
Nanjing 210003, China
[2] School of Automation, Nanjing University of Posts and Telecommunications,
Nanjing 210003, China
songyr@njupt.edu.cn
[3] Jiangsu Engineering Lab for IOT Intelligent Robots (IOTRobot),
Nanjing 210023, China

Abstract. Triangle counting is an important step in calculating the network clustering conffient and transitivity, and is widely used in important role recognition, spam detection, community discovery, and biological detection. In this paper, we introduced a GPU-based load balancing triangle counting scheme (GBTCS), which contains three techniques. First, we designed an algorithm for preprocessing the graph to obtain the CSR (Compressed Sparse Row Format) representation of the graph, which not only can reduce half of the memory usage of GPU, but also distribute the computational overhead to the core of the GPU. Second, we designed a SIMD (Single Instruction Multiple Data)-based set intersection algorithm that improves the thread parallel performance on the GPU. Third, we designed a load balancing algorithm to dynamically schedule the GPU workload. Performance evaluations demonstrate that our proposed scheme is 5x to 120x faster than the serial CPU algorithm.

Keywords: Triangle counting · CSR representation · Set intersection · Workload balance

1 Introduction

With the prosperity of big data, triangle counting has been widely used in important role recognition, spam detection, community discovery, and biological detection. Triangle counting algorithm mainly used in counting the number of intersections of the neighbor lists to identify the triangles in the graph, which plays an important step in calculating the network clustering coefficient and transitivity.

The traditional triangle counting algorithm traverses each vertex or edge of the graph, finds the intersection of the two lists, and once it finds a common adjoining vertex, it finds a triangle. Considering the rise of big data and complex networks, the traditional triangle counting algorithm cannot find the exact number of triangles in an acceptable time [10,13,15].

© Springer Nature Switzerland AG 2019
F. Liu et al. (Eds.): SciSec 2019, LNCS 11933, pp. 363–370, 2019.
https://doi.org/10.1007/978-3-030-34637-9_27

The current GPU, which has many times more computational core than the CPU, is an ideal platform for accelerating the triangle counting algorithm. We have observed that there is already some work to explore this direction [4,10,14]. However, these tasks do not make good use of the computing resources of the GPU. For example, [4] a merge-based triangle counting method is used on the GPU, which is a migration of serial CPU algorithms. If the degree distribution of the graph is not an average distribution, serious branch divergence problems may occur due to tasks cannot be evenly distributed to the GPU core. Also, these algorithms need to reserve a large amount of GPU memory space for the intermediate data structure, which limits the size of the processed graphics [10]. In this case, it is important to make full use of GPU memory and to utilize the computational features of the GPU to design a triangle counting scheme.

In this paper, aiming at above challenging problems, we propose a GPU-based load balancing triangle counting scheme. The main contributions of this paper are summarized as follows.

1. We designed an algorithm for preprocessing graphs. After conversion to the CSR representation, the data structure size is reduced by approximately two times. In the process of preprocessing the graph, the transform of the undirected graph to the directed graph will make the degree distribution more even, and the computing tasks assigned by the cores of the GPU are relatively uniform.
2. We designed a SIMD-based set intersection algorithm. Our method uses one neighbor list as the query list and the other as the comparison list. Then multiple GPU cores check the value of the comparison list based on the query list. The algorithm solves the problem of branch divergence and low memory access efficiency of traditional algorithms.
3. The traditional triangle count will evenly distribute the nodes to the core of the GPU during the parallelization process. Due to the different degrees of nodes, the workloads of different threads are different, which will reduce the performance of parallel computing. To this end, we designed a load balancing algorithm to dynamically schedule the GPU workload and improve parallel efficiency.

2   Related Work

The applications of triangle counting are widely used. With the introduction of clustering coefficient, it has become an important metric for data scientists. It is also used in detecting web spam [1], evaluating the quality of different community discovery algorithms [6,16], finding close communities [9].

Given a undirected graph $G = (V, E)$, there are several computational approaches for triangle counting: enumerating all node triples $O(|V|^3)$, or adjacency set intersection. Schank et al. [11] were the first to distinguish and bind these methods. Adjacency set intersection can be completed in many ways: sort set intersection, binary search and hash table.

In order to reduce the time complexity of triangle counting, many algorithm optimization techniques have been developed. For example, Green and Bader [2] propose a combinatorial optimization that reduces the number of necessary intersections and provide a better complexity bound. Green et al. [3] shows a scalable technique for workload-balancing triangle counting on a shared-memory system. Shun and Tangwongsan [12], Polak [8], and Pearce [7] show approaches to reduce the computational requirements by looking for triangles in the directed graph rather than the undirected graph, and the directed graph is obtained by the pretreatment of the undirected graph.

Leist et al. [5] presents the triangle counting of the first GPU algorithm using each thread to perform a different intersection. This proved inefficient due to the workload balancing problem caused by unbalanced nodes degree distribution. Green et al. [4] demonstrates the way parallelize set intersections by splitting them into subsets of finer granularity. This work takes the number of threads per intersection as a parameter to be configured. And the GPU cannot effectively leverage workload balancing and introduce overhead (in some cases, overhead control execution). Wang et al. [14] demonstrates several additional different strategies for implementing triangle counting on the GPU, including matrix multiplication.

3   Algorithms in GBTCS

In this section we show how to manipulate the data in the graph format to facilitate triangle counting, which involves preprocessing and representation of the graph format. We also calculate the number of triangles more efficiently by improving the set intersections on the GPU. In addition, we gain further efficiency gains by distributing the vertices of the triangles to the core of the GPU.

3.1   Representation of the Graph

An undirected graph is usually represented by a number of edges, each of which consists of a source vertex and a destination vertex, as shown in Fig. 1(a). We show the undirected graph as a directed graph. When the degree of vertex a is less than the degree of b or the degree of a is equal to the degree of b but the number of a is more than the number of b, define $a \prec b$, and the undirected edge $\{a, b\}$ after directionalization, a points to b. The undirected triangle $\triangle_{u,v,w}$ becomes a directed triangle $\triangle_{u,v,w}$, where the vertex u is called the cone vertex, and the edge $\{v, w\}$ is called the pivot edge, as shown in 1(b). According to the above rules, a new edge list is obtained, as shown in Fig. 1(c).

Large-scale graphs are generally sparse graphs. The use of adjacency matrices can result in a large amount of memory waste and even memory overflow. In addition, using traditional adjacency matrices to allocate a separate memory for each node for storage of adjacent nodes, memory allocation and release operations, result in memory fragmentation, seriously affecting the efficiency of the algorithm. To avoid the above problem, we use the CSR (Compressed Sparse Row) format to construct the adjacency list. The CSR structure is represented by two large arrays: adjList and nodeIndex, adjList is used to store adjacent nodes of all nodes, and nodeIndex is used to save each node of the starting subscript in adjList, as shown in Fig. 1(d).

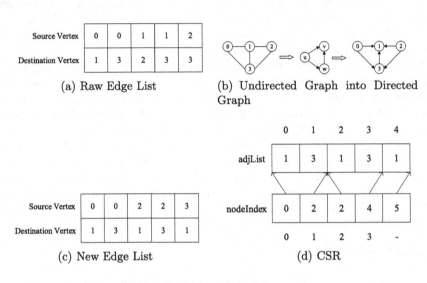

(a) Raw Edge List

(b) Undirected Graph into Directed Graph

(c) New Edge List

(d) CSR

Fig. 1. Representation of the graph

3.2 Set Intersection

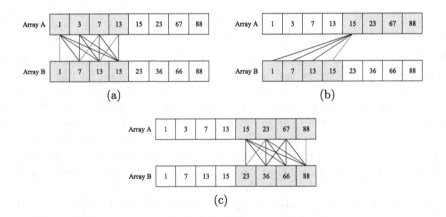

Fig. 2. Set Intersection on GPU Using 4 as the Block Size

The most basic operation in triangle counting is the set intersection. If set intersection is executed in parallel in each block of the GPU, the degree of the endpoints of the different edges may vary greatly, resulting in severe branch divergence. So we design a SIMD-based set intersection algorithm. Figure 2 shows an example of our algorithm with a block size of 4.

Algorithm first read in two ordered arrays A and B, and take the value of array B as the base value of the GPU's four kernels. Each kernel compares its own base value with the four values of the current block of array A. When compared to greater than the base value, the comparison can be stopped, as shown in Fig. 2(a). If an equal value is encountered, the number of intersecting sets is increased by one. After comparing the block, compare the last element of the current block, perform the block shift, and repeat the above steps until all the block traversal is completed, as shown in Figs. 2(b) and (c).

3.3 Workload Balance on the GPU

The GPU triangle count assigns nodes to different blocks in a node-by-node manner. In each block, the contiguous list of two endpoints of each edge is parallelized by GPU threads, and parallel merging and summing each thread in the block. The number, between blocks, is accumulated using atomic operations.

Traditional GPU triangle counting distributes nodes evenly to each thread of the GPU during the parallelism of nodes. Because the degree of each node is different, the thread workload of different blocks is different, which will reduce the performance of GPU parallel computing.

The solution is to adopt dynamic scheduling. Each idle block acquires new nodes according to the latest node recorded and offset, thus ensuring balanced thread workload and improving parallel efficiency.

4 Results

The experiments presented in this paper were carried out on a NVIDIA 1080Ti GPU and Intel(R) Xeon(R) Gold 5122 CPU 3.60 GHz and 64 GB RAM. Our CUDA code is compiled with the NVIDIA Compiler (nvcc) using CUDA version 9.0. The host compiler is gcc, version 5.4.0 and compile flag set to $O3$.

The algorithms are tested using real world graphs and networks taken from the HPEC Graph Challenge [10]. By default, all graphs are treated as undirected, and duplicate edges removed.

4.1 GPU vs. CPU Comparison

This section shows the performance comparison of the triangle counting on the GPU and CPU. As shown in Table 1, the GPU can accelerate the time overhead of 5x to 120x. The results show that although the advantages on the smaller graph are smaller, on the larger graph and the graph with partial distribution, the GPU program of the paper can bring quite fast speed.

4.2   Comparisons with Graph Challenge Champions

We compared our GPU triangle counting results with some projects focused on triangle counts. Briefly, TCKK [15] uses a linear algebraic kernel to count triangles on a single computer. The computer is equipped with an E5-2698 v3 intel CPU processor with 512 g of memory, 32 cores and 64 threads. Nv [10] uses an Nvidia Titan X pascal GPU. Note that since these projects are not open source, we compare their data directly to GBTCS from their papers. Figure 3 shows the performance of GBTCS, Nv, and TCKK on three Graph 500 data sets (from 23 to 25) and on Twitter.

Table 1. Triangle counting performance comparison between CPU and GPU

DataSet	NodeNum	EdgeNum	TriangleCount	CpuCost(s)	GpuCost(s)
roadNet-PA_adj	1088092	1541898	67150	0.06415	0.00316
roadNet-TX_adj	1379917	1921660	82869	0.05306	0.00405
roadNet-CA_adj	1965206	2766607	120676	0.09891	0.0051
ca-CondMat_adj	23133	93439	173361	0.00885	0.00122
email-Enron_adj	36692	183831	727044	0.027	0.00524
email-EuAll_adj	265214	364481	267313	0.03784	0.00184
soc-Epinions1_adj	75879	405740	1624481	0.08139	0.00735
soc-Slashdot0811_adj	77360	469180	551724	0.11307	0.0066
soc-Slashdot0902_adj	82168	504230	602592	0.13759	0.00665
amazon0302_adj	262111	899792	717719	0.07176	0.00221
loc-gowalla_edges_adj	196591	950327	2273138	0.10603	0.00661
amazon0312_adj	400727	2349869	3686467	0.2408	0.00398
amazon0505_adj	410236	2439437	3951063	0.25744	0.00416
amazon0601_adj	403394	2443408	3986507	0.25098	0.00414
cit-Patents_adj	3774768	16518947	7515023	3.50662	0.0275
ca-AstroPh_adj	18772	198050	1351441	0.02334	0.00342
cit-HepTh_adj	27770	352285	1478735	0.04278	0.00472
cit-HepPh_adj	34546	420877	1276868	0.09278	0.00403
flickrEdges_adj	105938	2316948	107987357	1.78855	0.09799
graph500-scale18-ef16_adj	174147	3800348	82287285	3.63493	0.2118
graph500-scale19-ef16_adj	335318	7729675	186288972	9.07368	0.41732
graph500-scale20-ef16_adj	645820	15680861	419349784	22.9305	0.68375
graph500-scale21-ef16_adj	1243072	31731650	935100883	56.5171	1.38296
graph500-scale22-ef16_adj	2393285	64097004	2067392370	141.604	3.1076
graph500-scale23-ef16_adj	4606314	129250705	4549133002	361.082	5.74552
graph500-scale24-ef16_adj	8860450	260261843	9936161560	891.446	12.8818
graph500-scale25-ef16_adj	17043780	523467448	21575375802	2293.09	30.1524
twitter_rv.net	61578415	1468365182	34824916864	2396.93	22.4301

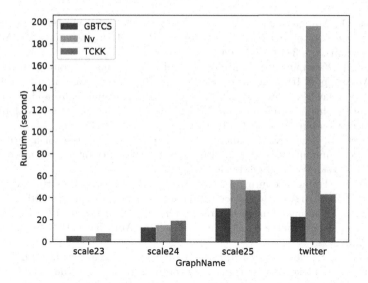

Fig. 3. GBTCS vs Graph Challenge champions

5   Conclusion

The rise of graphical analysis systems has created a way to measure and compare the capabilities of these systems. Graphical analysis has unique scalability difficulties. The community of machine learning, high-performance computing, and visual analytics has struggled with these difficulties for decades and has developed ways to create challenges that drive these communities forward.

This paper proposes an improved GPU-based set intersection method to make triangle calculations more efficient. In addition, the problem of branch divergence caused by the uneven distribution of node degrees in the graph is solved by load balancing in the GPU.

Acknowledgment. This research has been supported by the National Natural Science Foundation of China (Grant Nos. 61672298, 61873326, 61373136, 61802155), the Philosophy Social Science Research Key Project Fund of Jiangsu University (Grant No. 2018SJZDI142) and the Research Foundation for Humanities and Social Sciences of Ministry of Education of China (Grant Nos. 17YJAZH071).

References

1. Becchetti, L., Boldi, P., Castillo, C., Gionis, A.: Efficient semi-streaming algorithms for local triangle counting in massive graphs. In: Proceedings of the 14th ACM SIGKDD International Conference on Knowledge Discovery and Data Mining, pp. 16–24. ACM (2008)
2. Green, O., Bader, D.A.: Faster clustering coefficient using vertex covers. In: 2013 International Conference on Social Computing, pp. 321–330. IEEE (2013)

3. Green, O., Munguía, L.M., Bader, D.A.: Load balanced clustering coefficients. In: Proceedings of the First Workshop on Parallel Programming for Analytics Applications, pp. 3–10. ACM (2014)
4. Green, O., Yalamanchili, P., Munguia, L.M.: Fast triangle counting on the GPU. In: Workshop on Irregular Applications: Architectures & Algorithms (2014)
5. Leist, A., Hawick, K.A., Playne, D.P.: GP-GPU and multi-core architectures for computing clustering coefficients. In: Proceedings of International Conference on Scientific Computing (CSC 2011). CSREA, pp. 3–9 (2011)
6. Leskovec, J., Lang, K.J., Mahoney, M.: Empirical comparison of algorithms for network community detection. In: Proceedings of the 19th International Conference on World Wide Web, pp. 631–640. ACM (2010)
7. Pearce, R.: Triangle counting for scale-free graphs at scale in distributed memory. In: 2017 IEEE High Performance Extreme Computing Conference (HPEC) (2017)
8. Polak, A.: Counting triangles in large graphs on GPU. In: 2016 IEEE International Parallel and Distributed Processing Symposium Workshops (IPDPSW), pp. 740–746, May 2016
9. Prat-Pérez, A., Dominguez-Sal, D., Brunat, J.M., Larriba-Pey, J.L.: Shaping communities out of triangles. In: Proceedings of the 21st ACM International Conference on Information and Knowledge Management, pp. 1677–1681. ACM (2012)
10. Samsi, S., et al.: Static graph challenge: subgraph isomorphism. In: High PERFORMANCE Extreme Computing Conference, pp. 1–6 (2017)
11. Schank, T., Wagner, D.: Finding, counting and listing all triangles in large graphs, an experimental study. In: Nikoletseas, S.E. (ed.) WEA 2005. LNCS, vol. 3503, pp. 606–609. Springer, Heidelberg (2005). https://doi.org/10.1007/11427186_54
12. Shun, J., Tangwongsan, K.: Multicore triangle computations without tuning. In: IEEE International Conference on Data Engineering (2015)
13. Voegele, C., Lu, Y.S., Pai, S., Pingali, K.: Parallel triangle counting and k-Truss identification using graph-centric methods. In: 2017 IEEE High Performance Extreme Computing Conference (HPEC) (2017)
14. Wang, L., Wang, Y., Yang, C., Owens, J.D.: A Comparative Study on Exact Triangle Counting Algorithms on the GPU (2016)
15. Wolf, M.M., Deveci, M., Berry, J.W., Hammond, S.D., Rajamanickam, S.: Fast linear algebra-based triangle counting with KokkosKernels. In: High Performance Extreme Computing Conference (HPEC), 2017 IEEE, pp. 1–7. IEEE (2017)
16. Yang, J., Leskovec, J.: Defining and evaluating network communities based on ground-truth. Knowl. Inf. Syst. 42(1), 181–213 (2015)

A New Pairing-Free Certificateless Signature Scheme for Internet of Things

Zhenchao Zhang[1], Yali Liu[1,2(✉)], Xinchun Yin[1,3], and Xincheng Li[1]

[1] College of Information Engineering, Yangzhou University,
Yangzhou, Jiangsu, China
[2] College of Computer Science and Technology,
Jiangsu Normal University, Xuzhou, Jiangsu, China
liuyali@jsnu.edu.cn
[3] Guangling College, Yangzhou University,
Yangzhou, Jiangsu, China

Abstract. The Internet of Things (IoT) has been more and more popular in people's lives because it can bring convenience to our lives. Communication between IoT smart devices is vulnerable to various attacks. Therefore, designing a lightweight and secure cryptographic protocol for IoT applications is an important task. In this paper, we find that Jia *et al.*'s certificateless signature scheme cannot resist public key replacement attacks. Then, we propose a new certificateless signature scheme (PK-CLS) to resist super type I and type II adversaries. Finally, we prove the security of our PK-CLS scheme in the random oracle model.

Keywords: Internet of Things (IoT) · Certificateless signature · Public key replacement attack

1 Introduction

With the popularity of Internet of Things (IoT) information and communication technologies, IoT is becoming more and more popular in people's lives. According to Gartner [1], the influence of IoT in our daily activities is increasing with a projected 26 billion connected devices by 2020.

In IoT applications, smart objects are usually used to collect data, transfer the data to the server and the data to other smart objects through the public networks. However, due to the nature of some IoT services, security and privacy protection of the data become important. Moreover, some smart objects have low computing power and storage capacity. Generally, traditional encryption and signature schemes are difficult to be implemented on these resource-limited devices. Due to the limited resources of IoT devices, many researchers pay more attention to construct lightweight authentication protocols [2].

In order to solve the key escrow problem, Al-Riyami and Paterson [3] first proposed the certificateless signature (CLS) scheme. Al-Riyami *et al.* defined two different types of adversaries in the security model. A type I adversary could

© Springer Nature Switzerland AG 2019
F. Liu et al. (Eds.): SciSec 2019, LNCS 11933, pp. 371–379, 2019.
https://doi.org/10.1007/978-3-030-34637-9_28

implement public key replacement attacks even if it does not have knowledge of the master secret key. Moreover, a type II adversary stands for a malicious key generation center (KGC). It means a type II adversary is a malicious KGC who knows the master secret key, but cannot replace users' public keys. In 2007, Huang et al. [4] also defined three security levels in the security models of CLS, which are referred to as normal, strong and super adversaries, respectively. A normal adversary can only obtain signatures from legal users. And further, if the public key of a legal user has been replaced, a strong adversary can get a legal signature as long as the secret value is known. While a super type adversary can still get a legal signature although the public key has been replaced with an unknown secret value.

Huang et al. [5] showed that the scheme in [3] is attackable under the public key replacement attack. Shim [6] pointed out that the scheme in [4] is vulnerable to public key replacement attacks launched by the type I adversary. In 2005, Gorantla and Saxena [7] designed lightweight CLS. But unfortunately, Cao et al. [8] demonstrated that scheme [7] cannot resist super type I adversaries. In 2006, Yap et al. [9] designed a pairing-based CLS scheme under the computational Diffie-Hellman assumption.

Because the cost of the bilinear pairing is very high, He et al. [10] proposed a CLS scheme without bilinear pairings. Many other schemes without bilinear pairings can be found in the literature [11–18]. However, the schemes [12,15,16, 18] are vulnerable to the type I adversary [16,17,19,20]. The schemes [10,13] cannot resist the type II adversary [21]. In 2018, Jia et al. [17] proposed a CLS scheme for IoT deployment. However, we will show the scheme still suffers from severe security flaws.

The remaining of the article is structured in the following 5 parts. In Sect. 2, we discuss the security problem in Jia et al.'s [17] scheme. In Sect. 3, we present an improved PK-CLS scheme. The security analysis of our PK-CLS scheme are discussed in Sect. 4. Finally, Sect. 5 concludes the paper.

2   Vulnerability of Jia Et Al.'s Scheme

Jia et al. [17] claimed that their CLS scheme is unforgetable against super type I and type II adversaries. However, we find Jia et al.'s scheme cannot resist public key replacement attack. Let $\mathcal{A}_\mathcal{I}$ and $\mathcal{C}_\mathcal{I}$ represent a super type I adversary and a challenger, respectively.

(1) $\mathcal{A}_\mathcal{I}$ asks CreateUser query on the input ID^* and receives ID^*'s public key $PK_i = (R_i, Q_i)$ as output.

(2) $\mathcal{A}_\mathcal{I}$ chooses $z \in Z_q^*$, calculates $h_i = (ID^*, R_i)$, sets $R_i^{'} = R_i$, and computes $Q_i^{'} = zP - h_i P_{pub}$. Then $\mathcal{A}_\mathcal{I}$ asks ReplacePublicKey query to change the public key of ID^* to $PK_i^{'} = (R_i^{'}, Q_i^{'})$.

(3) $\mathcal{A}_\mathcal{I}$ randomly picks $t^{'} \in Z_q^*$ and calculates $T^{'} = t^{'} P = (T_x, T_y)$, and sets $r^{'} = T_x \bmod q$. And $\mathcal{A}_\mathcal{I}$ chooses a forged message m^* and calculates $v^{'} = H_3(ID^*, m^*, h_i, PK_i^{'}, T^{'})$ and $\tau^{'} = ((zr^{'} + v^{'})/t^{'}) \bmod q$.

(4) $\mathcal{A}_I$ can forge a valid signature $\sigma' = (T', \tau')$ on the chosen message m'. Noting that ExtractSecretValue query, ExtractPartialPrivateKey query and Sign query have never been asked, and the forged signature $\sigma' = (T', \tau')$ on message m^* will be verified to be VALID since $\tau'T' = ((zr' + v')/t')t'P = (zr' + v')P = v'P + r'(Q_i' + h_iP_{pub})$. That means $\mathcal{A}_I$ could successfully forge a signature. Therefore, this scheme is not secure against super type I adversaries.

3 Our Improved Scheme

In Jia *et al.*'s [17] scheme, we observe that $Q_i + h_iP_{pub}$ in the verifier's equation is the sum of two points on the elliptic curve. Once the replaced public key Q_i contains $-h_iP_{pub}$, h_iP_{pub} will be eliminated when the equation is calculated. Therefore setting P_{pub} becomes meaningless when the scheme faces the type I adversary. We slightly modify Jia et al.'s scheme to make it a secure scheme. Then, PK-CLS is described in detail.

(1) Setup: The KGC generates a master key s and public parameters *Params* based on the input security parameter λ. The *Params* = $(G, P, P_{pub}, H_1, H_2)$ are published, where P is a generator on an elliptic additive group G of order q over finite field F_p and $P_{pub} = sP$. The master key s is kept secret. Besides, H_1 and H_2 denotes two one-way hash functions: $H_1 : \{0,1\}^* \times G \to Z_q^*$; $H_2 : \{0,1\}^* \times Z_q^* \times G \times G \to Z_q^*$.

(2) Partial-Private-Key-Extract: The KGC randomly chooses $r_i \in Z_q^*$ for the user with identity ID, and computes $R_i = r_iP$, $h_i = H_1(ID, R_i)$, $s_i = (r_i + h_is) \mod q$. The value (s_i, R_i) is sent to the user as his partial private key. This partial private key can be verified by the equation $s_iP = R_i + h_iP_{pub}$, because $s_iP = (r_i + h_is)P = R_i + h_iP_{pub}$.

(3) Set-Secret-Value: The user randomly chooses $x_i \in Z_q^*$ as the secret value.

(4) Set-Private-Key: The private key SK_i represents (s_i, x_i).

(5) Set-Public-Key: The public key PK_i represents (R_i, P_i) where $P_i = x_iP$.

(6) Sign: Given *Params*, m, ID and SK_i as input, the signer randomly chooses $t \in Z_q^*$ and calculates $T = tP$, $h_i = H_1(ID, R_i)$. Then signer computes $v = H_2(ID, m, h_i, PK_i, T)$ and $\tau = (t/(s_i + vx_i)) \mod q$. Finally, the signer generates the signature $\sigma = (T, \tau)$.

(7) Verify: On receiving *Params*, ID, PK_i and $\sigma = (T, \tau)$ with message m, the verifier calculates $h_i = H_1(ID, R_i)$, $v = H_2(ID, m, h_i, PK_i, T)$ and then checks if the equation $\tau(R_i + h_iP_{pub} + vP_i) = T$ is satisfied. If it's true, σ is treated as genuine and thus it returns VALID. Otherwise, it returns INVALID. The correctness of the scheme is guaranteed by the following equation.

$$\tau(R_i + h_iP_{pub} + vP_i)$$
$$= (t/(s_i + vx_i))(R_i + h_iP_{pub} + vP_i)$$
$$= (t/(r_i + h_is + vx_i))(r_i + h_is + vx_i)P$$
$$= tP$$
$$= T.$$

4   Security Analysis

Our PK-CLS scheme is analyzed formally to be provably secure against both super type I and type II adversaries based on the difficulty of elliptic curve discrete logarithm problem (ECDLP) under the random oracle model.

Lemma 1. According to the security model, if a super type I adversary $\mathcal{A}_\mathcal{I}$ could succeed in Game 1 with non-negligible probability β in a polynomial time, $\mathcal{C}_\mathcal{I}$ could get the solution to the ECDLP problem with the possibility:

$$\beta' \geq (1 - q_{H_1}/q)^{q_{cu}}(1 - 1/q_{cu})^{q_{ep}}(1/q_{cu})(1 - q_{H_2}/q)\beta.$$

In the equation above, q_{H_1}, q_{H_2} ,q_{cu} and q_{ep} represent the number of H_1 queries, H_2 queries, CreateUser queries and ExtratPrivateKey queries, respectively.

Proof. Assuming $\mathcal{A}_\mathcal{I}$ could succeed in Game 1 with possibility β, the challenger $\mathcal{C}_\mathcal{I}$ is required to solve the problem in which $Q = sP$ where P is a generator of group G over an elliptic curve with an order q. $\mathcal{C}_\mathcal{I}$ sets $P_{pub} = Q$ and needs to compute s according to the attacker's forged signature. In the following processes, $\mathcal{C}_\mathcal{I}$ maintains three lists (L_1, L_2 and L_u) which are initially empty to record the information about H_1, H_2 and CreateUser queries.

- **Phase 1.** $\mathcal{C}_\mathcal{I}$ randomly chooses an ID^* as the target identity, and sets public parameters $Params = (G, P, P_{pub} = Q)$ and sends $Params$ to $\mathcal{A}_\mathcal{I}$.
- **Phase 2.** $\mathcal{A}_\mathcal{I}$ can request the following oracles in polynomial times.
  - H_1 query. When $\mathcal{A}_\mathcal{I}$ asks H_1 oracle with (ID, R_i) as input, $\mathcal{C}_\mathcal{I}$ searches the list L_1 and returns the record if the information of (ID, R_i) already exists. Otherwise, $\mathcal{C}_\mathcal{I}$ queries CreateUser(ID) and extracts h_i from the returned parameters and sends it to $\mathcal{A}_\mathcal{I}$.
  - H_2 query. When $\mathcal{A}_\mathcal{I}$ asks the H_2 oracle with (ID, m, h_i, PK_i, T) as input, $\mathcal{C}_\mathcal{I}$ searches the list L_2 and returns the record if (ID, m, h_i, PK_i, T) already exists. Otherwise, $\mathcal{C}_\mathcal{I}$ randomly picks $v \in Z_q^*$, calculates $V = vP$, which sets $H_2(ID, m, h_i, PK_i, T) = v$. $\mathcal{C}_\mathcal{I}$ sends v to $\mathcal{A}_\mathcal{I}$ at last.
  - CreateUser(ID). When $\mathcal{A}_\mathcal{I}$ asks the CreateUser oracle with ID as input, $\mathcal{C}_\mathcal{I}$ searches the list L_u and returns the PK_i if there exists a record of ID. Otherwise, $\mathcal{C}_\mathcal{I}$ will complete the following steps to create a record and add it to L_u. If $ID \neq ID^*$, $\mathcal{C}_\mathcal{I}$ randomly chooses s_i, h_i, x_i, and computes $R_i = s_iP - h_iP_{pub}$, $P_i = x_iP$. If $ID = ID^*$, $\mathcal{C}_\mathcal{I}$ randomly chooses r_i, h_i, x_i and sets $R_i = r_iP$, $P_i = x_iP$, $s_i = null$. In addition, if $\mathcal{C}_\mathcal{I}$ checks and finds there exists a record ($ID, R_i, H_1(ID, R_i)$) but $H_1(ID, R_i) \neq h_i$, $\mathcal{C}_\mathcal{I}$ aborts Game 1. Otherwise, $\mathcal{C}_\mathcal{I}$ returns PK_i to $\mathcal{A}_\mathcal{I}$ and adds the record (ID, s_i, x_i, R_i, P_i) and (ID, R_i, h_i) to the lists L_u and L_1.
  - ReplacePublicKey(ID, x_i', PK_i'). $\mathcal{C}_\mathcal{I}$ will replace the user's public key with (x_i', PK_i'). We assume that the CreateUser query has been executed with the identity of ID. And given the ability of a super type I adversary, $\mathcal{A}_\mathcal{I}$ doesn't need to provide the value of x_i, which means x_i can be null.

- ExtractSecretValue(ID). $\mathcal{C}_\mathcal{I}$ searches the list L_u and returns x_i to $\mathcal{A}_\mathcal{I}$ if there exists a record (ID, s_i, x_i, R_i, P_i) on ID. Otherwise, $\mathcal{C}_\mathcal{I}$ calls CreateUser query on ID and returns x_i to $\mathcal{A}_\mathcal{I}$. In addition , $\mathcal{C}_\mathcal{I}$ may do nothing if ReplacePublicKey has been queried where x_i is null.
- ExtractPartialPrivateKey(ID). If $ID \neq ID^*$, $\mathcal{C}_\mathcal{I}$ searches the list L_u and returns s_i if the record (ID, s_i, x_i, R_i, P_i) exists. If $ID = ID^*$, $\mathcal{C}_\mathcal{I}$ aborts the game. Here we assume that CreateUser on ID has been executed.
- SuperSign(ID, m). $\mathcal{C}_\mathcal{I}$ searches for the record (ID, s_i, x_i, R_i, P_i), (ID, R_i, h_i) and $(ID, m, h_i, PK_i, T, v, V)$ in the lists L_u, L_1 and L_2 respectively. If $ID = ID^*$ or $x_i = null$ (that is ReplacePublicKey has been queried with x_i not provided), $\mathcal{C}_\mathcal{I}$ randomly chooses $T \in G$, $\tau \in Z_q^*$ and sends (T, τ) to $\mathcal{A}_\mathcal{I}$. Otherwise, $\mathcal{C}_\mathcal{I}$ randomly chooses t, $v \in Z_q^*$, and calculates $T = tP, \tau = (t/(s_i + vx_i) \bmod q$. Then, $\mathcal{C}_\mathcal{I}$ adds $(ID, m, h_i, PK_i, T, v, V)$ to L_2 and returns (T, τ) to $\mathcal{A}_\mathcal{I}$. In that case, the signature will be verified because the equation $\tau(R_i + h_i P_{pub} + vP_i) = T$ holds.

- **Phase 3.** $\mathcal{A}_\mathcal{I}$ submits a forged signature (T^*, τ^*). Then $\mathcal{C}_\mathcal{I}$ checks if the ID of this signature is ID^*. If not, $\mathcal{C}_\mathcal{I}$ ends the game. Otherwise, $\mathcal{C}_\mathcal{I}$ searches the lists L_u, L_1 and L_2 for the records (ID, s_i, x_i, R_i, P_i), (ID, R_i, h_i), $(ID, m, h_i, PK_i, T, v, V)$. If there is no records of h_i^* and v^* in the list, $\mathcal{C}_\mathcal{I}$ aborts the game. Next, if the signature can be authenticated, the equation $\tau^*(r_i^* + h_i^* s + v^* x_i^*) = t^* \bmod q$ holds. In this equation, there are only three unknown values i.e. x_i, s, and t^*. In addition, x_i is not necessarily needed according to the ReplacePublicKey query and s is the value $\mathcal{C}_\mathcal{I}$ needs to solve the ECDLP problem. According to the principle of forking lemma [4], $\mathcal{C}_\mathcal{I}$ replays the above game with the same random tape, but different responses to h_i and v hash queries. $\mathcal{A}_\mathcal{I}$ compute to generate three different signatures as follows.
  (1) $\tau^*(r_i^* + h_i^* s + v^* x_i^*) = t^*$;
  (2) $\tau^{*'}(r_i^* + h_i^{*'} s + v^{*'} x_i^*) = t^*$;
  (3) $\tau^{*''}(r_i^* + h_i^{*''} s + v^{*''} x_i^*) = t^*$.

Let the probability of $\mathcal{C}_\mathcal{I}$ solving the ECDLP problem be Pr[succ]. The equation denotes the probability that $pr[succ] = pr[E_1 \wedge E_2]$ where E_1 means the Game 1 successfully completed all the steps without being terminated and E_2 means the signature forged by $\mathcal{A}_\mathcal{I}$ with identity ID^* is verified. Suppose that $\mathcal{A}_\mathcal{I}$ can forge a valid signature with probability β, we can compute:
$pr[succ] = pr[E_1 \wedge E_2] = pr[E_1]pr[E_2 \mid E_1] = pr[E_1]\beta$.

E_1 requires these conditions corresponding to the respective probabilities:

The probability of $(1 - q_{H_1}/q)^{q_{cu}}$ represents that there exists no collisions in the CreateUser query.

The probability of $(1 - 1/q_{cu})^{q_{ep}}$ represents that $\mathcal{A}_\mathcal{I}$ doesn't query the partial private key of ID^*.

The probability of $(1/q_{cu})$ means $\mathcal{A}_\mathcal{I}$ sends the signature where $ID = ID^*$.

The probability of $(1 - q_{H_2}/q)$ denotes that the values of v about the forged signature sent by $\mathcal{A}_\mathcal{I}$ can be found in the list L_2 in Phase 3. Therefore,

$$\beta' \geq (1 - q_{H_1}/q)^{q_{cu}}(1 - 1/q_{cu})^{q_{ep}}(1/q_{cu})(1 - q_{H_2}/q)\beta.$$

Lemma 2. If there exists a super type II adversary who could win Game 2 in a polynomial time with non-negligible probability β , $\mathcal{C}_{II}$ could solve the ECDLP problem with probability β'':

$$\beta'' \geq (1 - q_{H_1}/q)^{q_{cu}}(1 - 1/q_{cu})^{q_{rp}}(1 - 1/q_{cu})^{q_{es}}(1/q_{cu})(1 - q_{H_2}/q)\beta.$$

Here q_{H_1}, q_{H_2}, q_{cu}, q_{es} and q_{rp} represent the number of H_1 queries, H_2 queries, CreateUser queries, ExtratSecretValue queries and ReplacePublicKey queries.

Proof. Assuming that $\mathcal{A}_{II}$ can win in Game 2 between $\mathcal{A}_{II}$ and $\mathcal{C}_{II}$ in polynomial time, for a given G where $Q = sP$ and s is unknown, $\mathcal{C}_{II}$ could get the value of s based on the signature given by $\mathcal{A}_{II}$. $\mathcal{C}_{II}$ maintains L_u, L_1 and L_2 initially empty for CreateUser, H_1, H_2 queries as in Game 1.

- **Phase 1.** $\mathcal{C}_{II}$ randomly picks an ID^* and a number $s \in Z_q^*$, calculates $P_{pub} = sP$, sets $Params = (G, P, P_{pub})$, C_{II} sends $Params$ and s to $\mathcal{A}_{II}$.
- **Phase 2.** $\mathcal{A}_{II}$ can ask any of the following queries in polynomial times.
  - H_1 query and H_2 query are as same as in Game 1.
  - CreateUser(ID). If there exists a record of ID, $\mathcal{C}_{II}$ returns the public key PK_i. Otherwise, if $ID \neq ID^*$, $\mathcal{C}_{II}$ randomly chooses r_i, x_i and $h_i \in Z_q^*$, and calculates $R_i = r_iP$, $s_i = (r_i + h_is)$, $P_i = x_iP$. If $ID = ID^*$, $\mathcal{C}_{II}$ randomly chooses r_i, h_i, and calculates $R_i = r_iP$, $s_i = (r_i + h_is)$, $P_i = Q$, $x_i = null$. Finally, $\mathcal{C}_{II}$ returns $PK_i = (R_i, P_i)$ to $\mathcal{A}_{II}$ and adds $(ID, r_i, s_i, x_i, R_i, P_i)$ and (ID, R_i, h_i) to the lists L_u and L_1 respectively.
  - ReplacePublicKey(ID, x_i', PK_i'): If $ID = ID^*$, $\mathcal{C}_{II}$ aborts the game. Otherwise, $\mathcal{C}_{II}$ replaces ID's public key with given PK_i' even if x_i' is null, and updates the list L_u.
  - ExtractSecretValue(ID). Note that $\mathcal{A}_{II}$ is not allowed to access the secret value of ID^*, $\mathcal{C}_{II}$ will abort the game if $ID = ID^*$. Otherwise, $\mathcal{C}_{II}$ searches the record of ID and returns x_i to $\mathcal{A}_{II}$. However $\mathcal{C}_{II}$ may outputs a null if the PK_i has been replaced with a null x_i.
  - ExtractPartialPrivateKey(ID). $\mathcal{C}_{II}$ returns s_i from the list L_u if there exists a record of ID.
  - SuperSign(ID, m). $\mathcal{C}_{II}$ searches for the records of ID in the list L_u, L_1 and L_2. If $x_i = null$, which means $ID = ID^*$ or the PK_i has been replaced with $x_i' = null$, $\mathcal{C}_{II}$ randomly chooses $T \in G$, $\tau \in Z_q^*$ and sends (T, τ) to $\mathcal{A}_{II}$. Otherwise, $\mathcal{C}_{II}$ randomly picks t and $v \in Z_q^*$, calculates $T = tP$, $\tau = (t/(s_i + vx_i)) \bmod q$. Eventually, the signature (T, τ) generated by SuperSign query, will be sent to $\mathcal{A}_{II}$ and the record $(ID, m, h_i, PK_i, T, v, V)$ will be added to L_2.
- **Phase 3.** $\mathcal{C}_{II}$ submits the forged signature (T^*, τ^*) to $\mathcal{C}_{II}$ at this stage. If the ID of this signature is not ID^*, the game will be terminated. Otherwise, $\mathcal{C}_{II}$ will check the records of ID^* in the lists L_u, L_1 and L_2, and search if v^* exists. If not, $\mathcal{C}_{II}$ aborts the game.

From the signature given by $\mathcal{A}_{II}$, we know $\tau^*(r_i^* + h_i^* s + v^* x_i^*) = t^* \bmod q$. According to the forking lemma [4], $\mathcal{C}_{II}$ can obtain another signature submitted by $\mathcal{A}_{II}$, which satisfies the equation: $\tau'^*(r_i'^* + h_i'^* s + v'^* x_i'^*) = t^* \bmod q$.

From these two equations extracted from the forged signatures where different values of h_i and v are used, we can calculate the values of x_i and t^*. $\mathcal{C}_{II}$ could get the value of x_i, which means $\mathcal{C}_{II}$ solves the ECDLP problem.

$\mathcal{A}_{II}$ successfully generates the right signature with the following conditions: There are no collisions of hash functions in the CreateUser query. The probability is $(1 - q_{H_1}/q)^{q_{cu}}$.

$\mathcal{A}_{II}$ has not queried ReplacePublicKey with ID^* as input. The probability is $(1 - q_{H_1}/q)^{q_{cu}}$.

$\mathcal{A}_{II}$ has not queried ExtractSecretValue with ID^* as input. The probability is $(1 - 1/q_{cu})^{q_{rp}}$.

The submitted signature must satisfies $ID = ID^*$. The probability is $(1/q_{cu})$.

The probability that v^* will be found in phase 3 is $(1 - q_{H_2}/q)$.

In conclusion, if $\mathcal{A}_{II}$ can complete Game 2 with a nonnegligible probability β, the probability that $\mathcal{C}_{II}$ can solve the ECDLP problem is:

$$\beta'' \geq (1 - q_{H_1}/q)^{q_{cu}}(1 - 1/q_{cu})^{q_{rp}}(1 - 1/q_{cu})^{q_{es}}(1/q_{cu})(1 - q_{H_2}/q)\beta.$$

Theorem 1. If the complexity of ECDLP holds, our PK-CLS scheme is provably adaptively chosen message and identity attacks secure against super type I and type II adversaries.

5   Conclusion

In this paper, we analyzed in detail that Jia *et al.*'s scheme [17] cannot resist public key replacement attacks. In other words, a super type I adversary can easily forge a valid signature on any message and cheat the verifier. Then we proposed an improved PK-CLS scheme to resist super type I and type II adversaries. The proposed solution is very useful in practical applications, such as identity authentication in the IoT. Finally, we conducted security analysis in the random oracle model.

Acknowledgements. This work is supported by the National Natural Science Foundation of China under Grant No. 61702237, No. 61472343, the Natural Science Foundation of Jiangsu Province, China under Grant No. BK20150241, the Special Foundation of Promoting Science and Technology Innovation of Xuzhou City, China under Grant No. KC18005, the Natural Science Foundation of the Higher Education Institutions of Jiangsu Province, China under Grant No. 14KJB520010, the Scientific Research Support Project for Teachers with Doctor's Degree of Jiangsu Normal University under Grant No. 14XLR035, and Jiangsu Provincial Government Scholarship for Overseas Studies, under which the present work was possible.

References

1. Rivera, J., der Meulen, V.R.: Gartner says 4.9 billion connected things will be in use in 2015. 11 Nov 2014 [cited 2016 Feb 20]. http://www.gartner.com/newsroom/id/2905717

2. Liu, Y.N., Wang, Y.P., Wang, X.F., et al.: Privacy-preserving raw data collection without a trusted authority for IoT. Comput. Netw. **148**, 340–348 (2019)
3. Al-Riyami, S.S., Paterson, K.G.: Certificateless public key cryptography. In: Laih, C.-S. (ed.) ASIACRYPT 2003. LNCS, vol. 2894, pp. 452–473. Springer, Heidelberg (2003). https://doi.org/10.1007/978-3-540-40061-5_29
4. Huang, X., Mu, Y., Susilo, W., Wong, D.S., Wu, W.: Certificateless signature revisited. In: Pieprzyk, J., Ghodosi, H., Dawson, E. (eds.) ACISP 2007. LNCS, vol. 4586, pp. 308–322. Springer, Heidelberg (2007). https://doi.org/10.1007/978-3-540-73458-1_23
5. Huang, X., Susilo, W., Mu, Y., Zhang, F.: On the security of certificateless signature schemes from asiacrypt 2003. In: Desmedt, Y.G., Wang, H., Mu, Y., Li, Y. (eds.) CANS 2005. LNCS, vol. 3810, pp. 13–25. Springer, Heidelberg (2005). https://doi.org/10.1007/11599371_2
6. Shim, K.A.: Breaking the short certificateless signature scheme. Inf. Sci. **179**(3), 303–306 (2009)
7. Gorantla, M.C., Saxena, A.: An efficient certificateless signature scheme. In: Hao, Y., Liu, J., Wang, Y.-P., Cheung, Y., Yin, H., Jiao, L., Ma, J., Jiao, Y.-C. (eds.) CIS 2005. LNCS (LNAI), vol. 3802, pp. 110–116. Springer, Heidelberg (2005). https://doi.org/10.1007/11596981_16
8. Cao, X., Paterson, K.G., Kou, W.: An attack on a certificateless signature scheme. IACR Cryptol. ePrint Archive **2006**, 367 (2006)
9. Yap, W.-S., Heng, S.-H., Goi, B.-M.: An efficient certificateless signature scheme. In: Zhou, X., Sokolsky, O., Yan, L., Jung, E.-S., Shao, Z., Mu, Y., Lee, D.C., Kim, D.Y., Jeong, Y.-S., Xu, C.-Z. (eds.) EUC 2006. LNCS, vol. 4097, pp. 322–331. Springer, Heidelberg (2006). https://doi.org/10.1007/11807964_33
10. He, D., Chen, J., Zhang, R.: An efficient and provably-secure certificateless signature scheme without bilinear pairings. Int. J. Commun. Syst. **25**(11), 1432–1442 (2012)
11. Tsai, J.L., Lo, N.W., Wu, T.C.: Weaknesses and improvements of an efficient certificateless signature scheme without using bilinear pairings. Int. J. Commun. Syst. **27**(7), 1083–1090 (2014)
12. Gong, P., Li, P.: Further improvement of a certificateless signature scheme without pairing. Int. J. Commun. Syst. **27**(10), 2083–2091 (2014)
13. Islam, S.K.H., Biswas, G.P.: Provably secure and pairing-free certificateless digital signature scheme using elliptic curve cryptography. Int. J. Comput. Math. **90**(11), 2244–2258 (2013)
14. Yeh, K.H., Tsai, K.Y., Fan, C.Y.: An efficient certificateless signature scheme without bilinear pairings. Multimedia Tools Appl. **74**(16), 6519–6530 (2015)
15. Wang, L., Chen, K., Long, Y., et al.: A modified efficient certificateless signature scheme without bilinear pairings. In: 2015 International Conference on Intelligent Networking and Collaborative Systems (INCOS), IEEE, pp. 82–85 (2015)
16. Yeh, K.H., Su, C., Choo, K.K.R., et al.: A novel certificateless signature scheme for smart objects in the Internet-of-Things. Sensors **17**(5), 1001 (2017)
17. Jia, X., He, D., Liu, Q., et al.: An efficient provably-secure certificateless signature scheme for Internet-of-Things deployment. Ad Hoc Netw. **71**, 78–87 (2018)
18. Karati, A., Islam, S.K.H., Biswas, G.P.: A pairing-free and provably secure certificateless signature scheme. Inf. Sci. **450**, 378–391 (2018)
19. Yeh, K.H., Tsai, K.Y., Kuo, R.Z., et al.: Robust certificateless signature scheme without bilinear pairings. In: 2013 International Conference on IT Convergence and Security (ICITCS), pp. 1–4. IEEE (2013)

20. Pakniat, N., Vanda, B.A.: Cryptanalysis and improvement of a pairing-free certificateless signature scheme. In: 2018 15th International ISC (Iranian Society of Cryptology) Conference on Information Security and Cryptology (ISCISC), pp. 1–5. IEEE (2018)
21. Tian, M., Huang, L.: Cryptanalysis of a certificateless signature scheme without pairings. Int. J. Commun. Syst. **26**(11), 1375–1381 (2013)

Author Index

Printed in the United States
By Bookmasters